INSIDE AutoLISP

Using AutoLISP to Customize AutoCAD

Joseph Smith and Rusty Gesner

With Technical Assistance from Patrick Haessly

 New Riders Publishing, Thousand Oaks, California

INSIDE AutoLISP ®

Using AutoLISP to Customize AutoCAD

By Joseph Smith and Rusty Gesner

Published by:

New Riders Publishing
Post Office Box 4846
Thousand Oaks, CA 91360 USA

First Edition, 1989

Printed in the United States of America

Library of Congress Cataloging-in-Publication Data

```
Smith, Joseph (Joseph J.)
   Inside AutoLISP.

   Includes index.
   1. AutoCAD (Computer program)  2. AutoLISP
(Computer program language)  I. Gesner, Rusty.
II. Haessly, Patrick.  III. Title.
T385.S626  1989   620'.00425'02855369      89-12090
ISBN 0-934035-47-4
```

Warning and Disclaimer

This book is designed to provide information about AutoCAD and AutoLISP. Every effort has been made to make this book complete and as accurate as possible. But no warranty or fitness is implied.

The information is provided on an "as is" basis. The authors and New Riders Publishing shall have neither liability nor responsibility to any person or entity with respect to any loss or damages arising from the information contained in this book.

Trademarks

About the Authors

Joseph Smith

Joseph J. Smith is president of ACUWARE, Inc., in Portland, Oregon. His company provides an AutoCAD-based product line called AutoPE for structural engineering drafting. He has used AutoCAD since Version 1.4 and writes about AutoCAD customization from the standpoint of a user and a developer producing commercial application packages.

Before moving to the west coast, Mr. Smith was a product manager with MiCAD Systems, Inc., in New York. He was in charge of AutoCAD systems development and provided corporate training for customized AutoCAD systems. Mr. Smith is trained as a civil engineer with a B.S. degree from Villanova University, Villanova, Pa. Prior to joining MiCAD Systems, he worked as an engineer with James T. Smith & Co., Philadelphia, Pa., and Piasecki Aircraft Corp., Philadelphia, Pa.

Rusty Gesner

B. Rustin Gesner is Director of Technical Applications for New Riders Publishing and heads New Rider's office in Portland, Oregon. He is responsible for New Rider's technical applications books and software products. He has used AutoCAD since Version 1.1 and writes about AutoCAD from the standpoint of a long-time user and from customizing AutoCAD for architectural applications.

Prior to joining New Riders, Mr. Gesner was president of CAD Northwest, Inc., Portland, Oregon. He was responsible for the sale, installation, and support of AutoCAD systems. Mr. Gesner is a registered architect. Before forming CAD Northwest, he was a practicing architect in Portland. He attended the College of Design, Art and Architecture at the University of Cincinnati, and Antioch College.

Patrick Haessly

Patrick Haessly is Product Manager at ACUWARE, Inc., in Portland, Oregon. He designs AutoCAD-based structural steel detailing programs. Mr. Haessly provided valuable support and assistance to the authors in developing the book's exercises, menus, and AutoLISP routines.

Mr. Haessly has used AutoCAD since Version 1.3. Prior to joining ACUWARE, he was a Senior Technical Developer for New Riders Publishing and the AutoCAD Systems Manager for A to Z Steel Systems, Inc., in Wilsonville, Oregon.

Table of Contents

INTRODUCTION

INSIDE AutoLISP's Origin	I-1
How INSIDE AutoLISP Is Organized	I-2
Learn By Doing	I-4
Read This — It's Important	I-4
How Exercises Are Shown	I-4
Things to Watch For	I-5
Saving Time With the INSIDE AutoLISP Disk	I-6
New Riders AutoLISP Utilities Disk 1	I-6
How to Jump Around in the Book	I-6
How Program Listings Are Shown	I-7
Prerequisites for INSIDE AutoLISP	I-8
DOS Experience and Version	I-8
UNIX, Mac, and Other Operating Systems	I-8
AutoCAD Experience, Version, and Equipment	I-8
Moving On	I-9

PART I. YOU AND AutoLISP

CHAPTER 1   Getting Started

Files for Your AutoCAD System	1-2
DOS Files	1-2
AutoCAD Files	1-2
Necessary Directories	1-2
Using UNIX Directories	1-4
Text Editors	1-5
The DOS Bootup Environment	1-5
CONFIG.SYS	1-5
AUTOEXEC.BAT	1-6
AutoCAD Program and Support Files	1-7
Setting Up AutoCAD's Configuration Files	1-7
ADI Drivers	1-8

Installing the INSIDE AutoLISP Disk   1-8
Setting Up AutoCAD   1-9
   The PGP SHELL   1-9
   Your PGP File   1-10
   How to Use SHELL PGP Commands   1-10
Starting AutoCAD With a DOS Batch File   1-12
   The IL.BAT File Settings   1-13
   Extended AutoLISP   1-14
   IL.BAT DOS Commands   1-14
Starting AutoCAD With a UNIX Script   1-15
Prototype Drawings   1-15
Configuring and Testing IL-ACAD   1-17
Our Layering Convention   1-18
Summary   1-19

CHAPTER 2   *AutoLISP*

The Benefits of AutoLISP   2-1
A Non-LISP Macro   2-1
Writing a Simple AutoLISP Expression   2-3
   Functions and Arguments   2-3
   How AutoCAD and AutoLISP Communicate   2-4
Setting a Variable   2-5
   AutoLISP's Backtalk   2-6
   Nesting AutoLISP Expressions   2-6
Getting From Macros to AutoLISP   2-7
Writing a Complete LISP Routine   2-8
   Sending Input to AutoCAD   2-9
Getting Input From the User   2-10
   Getting Points With GETPOINT   2-11
   Getting Character Input With GETSTRING   2-12
Storing and Loading LISP Programs   2-14
Evolution of a Simple Program   2-15
Combining Functions   2-18
   Eliminating Variables From Programs   2-20
   Setting and Using Variables In-Line   2-21
   Calculations Within the COMMAND Function   2-22
   In-Line Versus Setting Variables   2-23

Reading a LISP Program   2-23
ACAD.LSP: An Automatic Loading LISP File   2-25
Summary   2-26

CHAPTER 3   *Basic Elements of AutoLISP*

AutoLISP Variables and Expressions   3-1
   Variables   3-2
   AutoCAD's System Variables   3-2
   Variable Data Types   3-3
Using AutoLISP to Get and Set System Variables   3-4
Making Your Own Variables and Expressions   3-4
   The ATOMLIST   3-5
   How to Assign Values to Variables   3-6
Using GET Functions for Input   3-7
   When to Use Base Point Arguments for Rubber-Banding   3-10
   Pausing GET Functions in Menu Macros   3-10
Using Math Functions in AutoLISP   3-11
   How to Count in AutoLISP   3-12
   How to Find Minimums and Maximums   3-13
   Functions for Fractions   3-14
   How to Use Roots, Logs, Exponents, and Absolutes   3-14
   A Word About Accuracy   3-16
The String Functions   3-17
   Using STRCAT to Merge Strings   3-17
   Controlling Case With STRCASE   3-18
   How to Get Portions of Strings   3-19
Character Functions   3-20
How AutoLISP Lists Work   3-21
   How to Use List Functions   3-21
   Extracting Elements From Lists   3-22
   Using the QUOTE Function to Build Lists   3-23
   Indexed Elements: the NTH and LAST Functions   3-24
   Ordering, Adding To, and Reversing Lists   3-25
Defining Your Own Functions in AutoLISP   3-27
   Loading a LISP Function File   3-29
Documenting LISP Functions   3-30
Summary   3-31

CHAPTER 4   *Understanding Program Flow*

AutoLISP Tools and Programs   4-2
   AutoLISP Tools   4-2
   AutoLISP Programs   4-2
Conditional Testing   4-2
   Logical Functions   4-3
   Relational Functions   4-5
   When to Use EQ, =, and EQUAL   4-7
   Round-Off Error   4-7
Branching Functions   4-8
   The IF Function   4-8
   The COND Structure: A Multiple IF   4-10
Program Looping   4-12
   The REPEAT Function   4-12
   The WHILE Function   4-13
   Controlling Input With WHILE   4-15
   Accumulating Data With WHILE   4-16
   Processing Lists With the FOREACH Function   4-16
The PROGN Function   4-18
Your Programming Environment   4-19
   Local and Global Variables   4-19
   Management of Local and Global Variables   4-19
Efficient Use of Variable Names   4-23
Subroutines   4-24
   Why Use Subroutines?   4-24
Recursive Programming   4-26
Summary   4-27

CHAPTER 5   *Communicating With AutoLISP*

AutoLISP Tools and Programs   5-2
   AutoLISP Tools   5-2
   AutoLISP Programs   5-3
Determining Data Types   5-3
   Predicate Tests   5-3
Working With Strings   5-7

Prompt and String Formatting   5-7
How to Format Prompts With Expanded Codes   5-9
How to Format Strings in Menus   5-9
Selecting Text and Graphics Screen Modes   5-10
Displaying and Printing Strings and Data   5-11
Clean Displays With PRINC and PROGN   5-13
Converting Data Types   5-14
Formatting for Linear Distances   5-15
How to Control Zeros With DIMZIN   5-17
How to Round Off Numbers   5-17
How to Convert Reals To and From Integers   5-18
AutoCAD Angle Formatting and Conversion   5-19
How to Format Angles for Commands   5-21
How to Round Off Angles   5-22
Creating an ANGTOC Function   5-22
Converting Strings to Symbols   5-23
Using SET vs. SETQ   5-24
Applying Conversions and Prompt Formatting in ATEXT   5-24
Developing User Interface Functions   5-29
Formatting Default Prompts With UDIST   5-29
Adding a Base Point Argument to UDIST   5-30
Controlling Input With INITGET   5-32
How to Set Key Words With INITGET   5-33
Adding INITGET to UDIST   5-34
GETKWORD for Controlled Strings   5-36
Controlling Strings With USTR   5-38
Finishing Your User Interface Tool Kit   5-39
Summary   5-42

PART II. AutoLISP AND AutoCAD

CHAPTER 6   *Accessing the Drawing Database*

AutoLISP Tools and Programs   6-2
AutoLISP Tools   6-2
Command Programs   6-3
AutoCAD Entities   6-4
How to Get Entity Names   6-4
Error Free Entity Selection With ENTSEL   6-6

How to Step Through Entities With ENTNEXT   6-7
Controlling Visibility by Entity Name   6-7
Deleting and Restoring Entities by Name   6-8
Applying Entity Selection to Programs   6-9
Entity Selection Sets   6-11
Manipulating Selection Sets   6-13
Applying Selection Set Tools to APLATE   6-15
Optional Selection Set Modes   6-17
Filtering Selections With SSGET "X"   6-18
Using Key Words With "ENTSEL"   6-19
Developing a Selection Set Toolkit   6-21
Entity Data   6-25
Entity Association Lists and Dotted Pairs   6-27
The CONS and CDRs of Dotted Pairs   6-28
DXF Group Codes and AutoLISP   6-29
Default Entity Properties   6-35
Applying Entity Access to CSCALE   6-36
Modifying and Updating Entity Data   6-40
How to SUBSTitute Data in a List   6-41
Applying Entity Modification With BSCALE   6-42
Complex Entities: Polylines and Inserts   6-45
Applying Entity Access to Modifying Polylines   6-47
Entity Handles — Permanent Entity Names   6-51
Summary   6-54

CHAPTER 7   *AutoCAD Table Data*

AutoLISP Tools and Programs   7-2
AutoLISP Tools   7-2
Programs   7-2
Symbol Tables   7-3
Named Layers, Styles, and Views   7-6
How to Apply Layer Table Access   7-7
Exploring the Block Section   7-10
How to Find Block Data With TBLSEARCH and ENTNEXT   7-14
Applying Block Table Access to LEGEND   7-15
How to Swap Entities With LEDSWAP   7-20
Named Properties: Linetypes and More   7-22

How to Apply Linetypes to Material Takeoffs   7-25
Using PVAR to Store Variables as Linetypes   7-30
UCS and VPORT Tables   7-31
Applying VPORTS to Changing Viewports   7-35
Getting Blocks Without Loading Drawings   7-37
Summary   7-37

CHAPTER 8	*AutoLISP Input/Output*

AutoLISP Tools and Programs   8-2
  AutoLISP Tools   8-2
  Programs   8-2
Reading and Writing Data   8-3
  Reading Lines and Characters   8-3
  How to Read and Write to the Console   8-4
General File Handling   8-6
  File Handles   8-7
  Files Are Devices   8-7
  How to Open, Close, and Access Files   8-8
Writing to the Printer and Other Devices   8-11
  Applying File Access to String Conversion   8-12
Programs for Testing Files and Paths   8-14
  Extending the AutoCAD Library Path With FINDFILE 8-16
  How to Detect and Control the Current Directory   8-16
  Converting Slashes and Backslashes   8-19
  How to Format File Extensions   8-21
  Verifying File and Path Existence   8-23
  How to Back Up and Merge Files   8-26
  MERGEV and SHELL   8-28
Applying File Handling to a Hatch Pattern Generator   8-29
The ANSI Formatting Codes   8-36
  How to Use ANSI Format Codes in AutoCAD   8-37
  Making a Library of ANSI Screen Functions   8-40
Formatting Files for External Data Handling   8-42
Applying Data File Access to REFDWG   8-46
  The REFDWG Program   8-47
Summary   8-54

CHAPTER 9   *Working With AutoLISP Devices*

AutoLISP Tools and Programs   9-2
    AutoLISP Tools   9-2
    Programs   9-2
Dynamic Screen Labeling With GRTEXT   9-2
    How to Use GRTEXT   9-3
    How to Test GRTEXT's Stability   9-5
    How to Highlight and Clear GRTEXT   9-5
Drawing Vectors With GRDRAW   9-7
    How to Draw and Highlight Vectors   9-7
    How to Blank Vectors and Clear the Screen   9-9
Making a Dynamic Preview Command   9-9
    Alternatives for Displaying Screen Information   9-13
Getting Device Input With GRREAD   9-14
    How to Extract GRREAD Data   9-16
Applying GRREAD to ETEXT — An AutoCAD Text Editor   9-16
Continuous Coordinate Tracking With GRREAD   9-20
Applying GRREAD Tracking to DDRAW   9-21
Summary   9-26

PART III. USING AutoLISP TO CUSTOMIZE AutoCAD

CHAPTER 10   *AutoLISP and MENUS*

Menus, AutoLISP Tools, and Programs   10-2
    Menus   10-2
    AutoLISP Tools   10-2
    Programs   10-3
Reviewing Macros and Menus   10-3
    How to Define Pages of Macros   10-4
Designing Clean Menu Macros   10-5
    How to Prompt in Menus   10-5
    How to Clean Up Menu Output   10-6
    How to Make Clean Macros With AutoLISP   10-8
Making Menu Toggles   10-9
    How to Build Sets of Dynamic Menu Toggles   10-10

Applying AutoLISP-Menu Integration to Iso Dimensioning   10-14
   How to Make Iso Dim Text Styles and Symbols   10-14
Creating the Iso Dim Functions   10-17
Making an Iso Screen Menu   10-20
   How to Use the ISODIM Menu   10-26
   Cleaning Up the ISODIM Menu   10-28
Putting Iso Dims on Your Tablet   10-29
Using Associative Dimensioning With Iso Dimensioning   10-30
Summary   10-31

CHAPTER 11   *Automating With Attributes*

Macros, AutoLISP Tools, and Programs   11-2
   Macros   11-2
   AutoLISP Tools   11-2
   Programs   11-3
AutoCAD's Attribute Data Treatment   11-3
   How Attribute Data is Stored   11-5
   How Attribute Definitions Are Stored   11-7
Controlling Text With Attributes   11-9
   The Title Block System   11-9
Controlling Attribute Data Entry With Macros   11-13
Updating Attributes   11-17
Automating Attribute Editing   11-17
AutoLISP Timekeeping   11-20
Creating a Drawing Revision System   11-22
   Automating REVBLOCK Insertion With UPDATE.LSP   11-24
Using Attributes to Store Parametric Data   11-31
   AutoBreaking Blocks   11-31
A Word about Block Redefinition and Lost Attributes   11-40
Summary   11-41

CHAPTER 12   *Using AutoLISP to Create Parts*

Macros, AutoLISP Tools, and Programs   12-1
   Macros   12-1
   AutoLISP Tools   12-2
   Programs   12-2

What Can Parametrics Do?	12-2
The Elements of a Parametric System	12-3
Designing the Parametric System and Screen Menu	12-3
Planning External File Formats for Parametrics	12-7
How to Do Data Files	12-7
Providing Help Support	12-9
Retrieving External Parametric Data	12-11
Generating Parametric Images	12-15
Drawing a Side View of a 90-Degree Elbow	12-18
Creating Multiple Parts — the Beauty of Parametrics	12-22
How to Do Front and Back Views in One	12-22
Drawing Linear Parts — DBLINE	12-26
Adding Material Tags	12-29
How to Tag Parametric Parts	12-29
How to Tag Parts	12-31
Grouping Entities for One-Pick Selection	12-34
Summary	12-35

CHAPTER 13   *Lotus and dBASE*

Macros and Programs	13-2
Macros	13-2
AutoLISP Programs	13-3
External Programs	13-3
Making an Attribute Extract Template File	13-3
How to Format the Template File	13-3
How to Extract Attributes With ATTEXT	13-5
Importing Data Into Lotus	13-7
How to Run Lotus From a Shell	13-7
How to Automate the Link to Lotus	13-15
How to Import Data Using Lotus Macros	13-17
Bringing Data Back to AutoCAD	13-21
Using dBASE With AutoCAD	13-23
Preparing the Input Record	13-25
Tracking CAD Drawings	13-28
The PRO_TRAK Database Structure	13-30
Importing Project Data	13-31
Reporting Project Data	13-33

Time Log Reports   13-35
Running PRO_TRAK   13-36
Summary   13-37

CHAPTER 14   *AutoLISP and 3D Space*

Macros, AutoLISP Tools, and Programs   14-2
  AutoLISP Tools   14-2
2D Versus 3D Points   14-3
  How FLATLAND Works   14-3
What Makes AutoCAD Full 3D   14-5
  3D versus 2D Entities   14-5
  What Is a UCS?   14-6
  How to Work in the UCS   14-6
  Entity Extrusion Vectors   14-7
Examining Entity Data in 3D   14-8
  How Extrusion Vectors Are Stored   14-8
  ECS — the Entity Coordinate System   14-9
Translating 3D Points   14-13
  DCS — the Display Coordinate System   14-15
  How to Prompt With GRDRAW, TRANS, and the DCS   14-15
  How to Visualize Orientation With TRANS   14-16
Programming Tools for 3D   14-19
  How to Specify Polar Locations in Space   14-22
Other Helpful Polar and Curve Formulas   14-23
Drawing Tools for 3D   14-26
  How to Generate Multiple Views Via the UCS   14-27
Working With Viewports and the UCS   14-29
Alternatives to Changing UCS Planes   14-31
  How to Calculate Extrusion Vectors   14-31
  How to Update Entity 210 Codes   14-32
  Applying ECS Redefinition to Piping   14-33
Creating Flat Patterns of Pipes   14-35
Summary   14-36

CHAPTER 15   *Batch Programming*

AutoLISP Tools and Programs   15-2

AutoLISP Tools   15-2
Programs   15-2
Comparing Batch Processing Methods   15-3
AutoCAD Scripts   15-3
Menus versus Scripts   15-5
How to Import DXF Files   15-6
How to Read Data With AutoLISP   15-7
What, When, and Where for Scripts, AutoLISP, and DXF   15-11
How to Pause Scripts for Input   15-12
Creating a Script Batch Builder   15-12
How to Create a File List   15-13
How to Create a Script Command List   15-16
How to Create a Script With AutoLISP   15-17
MSCRIPT, the BATCHSCR User Interface   15-20
Making Specialized Script Builders   15-23
Creating Slides With Scripts   15-23
Scripts That Replay Slides   15-25
How to Do Unattended Plotting   15-26
Coordinating Scripts and AutoLISP   15-26
How to Create a Block Update Program   15-27
Summary   15-33

CHAPTER 16   *DXF Files and External Processing*

Macros, AutoLISP Tools, and Programs   16-2
Macros   16-2
Programs   16-2
The Drawing eXchange Format   16-2
Understanding DXF Group Codes and Data Elements   16-4
How DXF File Sections Are Organized   16-5
How to Read the DXF Header   16-6
How to Read the Tables Section   16-7
How to Read the Blocks Section   16-9
How to Read the Entities Section   16-11
Importing DXF Files   16-13
How to Work Within DXFIN's Limitations   16-14
How to Make a DXF Drawing Spell-Checker   16-15
Writing BASIC Utilities for DXF   16-17

The BASIC Language	16-17
How to Use BASIC With DXF	16-18
Translating Between Versions and Other CAD Programs	16-25
Summary	16-27

CHAPTER 17   *Controlling Your System*

System Tools and Programs	17-2
External Tools and Programs	17-2
AutoLISP Tools and Programs	17-3
Managing Your System	17-4
Directory and File Control	17-4
How to Use Set Environment Variables	17-5
How to Control Paths	17-5
DOS SUBST Directory Path Control	17-8
Controlling the Initial Drawing Setup	17-9
Setup Menus Versus ACAD.LSP	17-9
The ACAD.LSP File	17-10
How to Set Up With ACAD.LSP	17-11
How to Control Layers	17-13
New or Existing Drawing?	17-15
S::STARTUP — the Automatic Start-Up Function	17-15
Controlling Command Access	17-16
How to Undefine and Redefine Commands	17-16
Controlled Landings With a Redefined END	17-17
Controlling the Keyboard	17-19
ANSI.SYS Key Redefinition	17-20
Creating Macros On-The-Fly	17-23
Controlling Errors	17-25
How to Use the *ERROR* Function	17-25
Creating an Error-Trapping System	17-26
Reset Controls	17-31
Integrating Error Control in Programs	17-32
Controlling Function Loading	17-36
How to Control Program Loads With ILLOAD	17-36
How to Load Subroutines Automatically	17-38
How to Write Self-Loading Commands	17-39
How to Juggle Functions in Limited Memory	17-40

Managing Memory   17-41
   How to Write Efficient Programs   17-41
   How to Control AutoLISP Memory   17-42
   Understanding AutoLISP Memory   17-43
Using Extended AutoLISP   17-45
The CLEAN Alternative   17-46
Encryption and Security   17-47
   Encrypting LISP and Menus   17-47
Compacting LISP Files With LSPSTRIP   17-48
Documenting and Presenting an Application   17-50
   Commenting LISP Programs   17-50
   How to Comment Menu Files   17-51
   How to Write "How-To" Documents   17-51
   Program Presentation   17-52
   Help Text Screens and Slides   17-52
Summary   17-54
   Authors' Farewell   17-54

APPENDIX A   *Menus, AutoLISP and Programs*

An Index of INSIDE AutoLISP's Menus and Programs   A-1

APPENDIX B   *Configuration and Errors*

Selecting Text Editors   B-1
The DOS Bootup Environment   B-2
CONFIG.SYS   B-3
   Setup Problems With CONFIG.SYS   B-4
AUTOEXEC.BAT   B-4
   Problems With AUTOEXEC.BAT   B-5
Problems With DOS Environment Space   B-6
   Using DOS 2   B-7
Memory Settings and Problems   B-8
   SET Environment Memory Settings   B-9
Using INSIDE AutoLISP With a RAM Disk   B-10
Current Directory and Wrong Support File Errors   B-11
SHELL Errors   B-12
Common AutoLISP Errors   B-12

Miscellaneous Problems   B-13
Insufficient File Errors   B-13
Tracing and Curing Errors   B-14

APPENDIX C   *Reference Tables*

AutoCAD System Variables   C-1
Table and Entity DXF Group Codes   C-5
AutoLISP Function Reference Table   C-9

APPENDIX D   *The Authors' Appendix*

How INSIDE AutoLISP Was Produced   D-1
Our AUTOEXEC.BAT Files   D-1
Our Multi-Tasking Interactive Environment   D-2
Tools, Sources, and Support   D-3
    Advanced AutoCAD Classes   D-3
    The CompuServe Autodesk Forum   D-4
    Bulletin Boards   D-4
    User Groups   D-4
    Magazines   D-5
    Books   D-5
Commercial Utilities   D-5
    Hard Disk Management and Backup   D-6
    User Interface Shells   D-6
    General Utility Packages   D-6
    Freeware and Shareware   D-7
Authors' Last Word and Mail Box   D-7

INDEX

Index   X-1

Acknowledgments

Rusty would like to thank Kathy, Alicia, and Roo for their patience, encouragement, and good cheer when the going was rough, and to thank his parents for support in the endeavors which led to this book.

Joe wishes to thank his parents, Jim and Rita for giving him an abundance of love, support, and a chance at every passing opportunity, most recently this book.

Joe, Rusty, and Pat wish to thank Harbert Rice for making this project possible, and Jon DeKeles for developing the dBASE and Clipper-compiled drawing revision program, PRO_TRAK. Thanks to Todd Meisler and Kevin Coleman for graphics layout and production.

Special thanks to Christine Steel for punctilious editing, intuitive rewriting, and painstaking page layout.

The authors wish to thank Tom Mahood, Mauri Laitinen, Duff Kurland, Eric Lyons, John Sergneri, Keith Marcelius, Dave Kalish, Robert Wenig, John Forbes, and many others from Autodesk, Inc., for their help and support over the years.

Special thanks to Robert Palioca and all the staff at KETIV Technologies, Inc., for invaluable help, advice, review, and computing equipment used in developing the book.

Thanks also to Dan Stone, Ken Eichler, Dan Belmont, Eugene Jones, Bill Work, and the rest of the people at MiCAD Systems, Inc., for their many ideas and techniques that contributed to material in the book. Thanks to the people at Smith Engineering for serving as the testbed of application experiments.

Autodesk, Inc., supplied AutoCAD, Xerox Corp. supplied Xerox Ventura Publisher. Microsoft Corp. supplied Microsoft Word. Michael Cuthbertson of Symsoft provided copies of Hotshot and Hotshot Plus. Thanks to Barry Simon and Richard Wilson, the developers of CTRLALT.

Special thanks to SUN Microsystems, Inc., for providing a SUN 386i computer system, which runs both DOS and UNIX applications. Verticom, Inc., provided a 2page Display System for Ventura Publisher displays.

INTRODUCTION

Welcome to AutoLISP. We think it's one of the most interesting facets of AutoCAD. INSIDE AutoLISP's goal is to give you the power to make AutoCAD do some of the thinking, as well as most of the work, for you. From simply adding a few custom commands to developing a sophisticated AutoLISP-controlled application, INSIDE AutoLISP will give you the knowledge you need to make your AutoCAD programs work better, harder, and faster.

AutoLISP is a programming language, but it's not hard to master. We'll start with basic concepts in easy-to-follow exercises. From there, we'll gradually work up to invoking the full-blown power of AutoLISP. Although we progress in easy-to-swallow doses, the comprehensiveness and depth of this book should whet the appetite of even the most seasoned AutoLISP programmers.

This is several books in one. It is arranged so you can pick and choose among whatever information and skills you wish to gain, including:

- Tutorial how-to-use exercises for the AutoLISP functions

- Quick reference to all AutoLISP functions and techniques

- Reference tables of system variables and DXF data group codes

- Listings of our own AutoLISP utilities and applications

- How-to exercises for using our utilities and programs

- Setup and memory management techniques

The table of contents and index are extensive, to help you find the topics you want. There is also a descriptive appendix of all menus and programs contained in the book.

INSIDE AutoLISP's Origin

This is the first edition of INSIDE AutoLISP, but it's a second generation book. Our first edition of CUSTOMIZING AutoCAD was one big book!

With Release 10, AutoCAD's capabilities increased, and so did our task of showing you how to customize AutoCAD. To cover it all, we had to expand to a second book. INSIDE AutoLISP complements and extends the latest edition of CUSTOMIZING AutoCAD.

INSIDE AutoLISP's sister book, the second edition of CUSTOMIZING AutoCAD, now includes menu, macro, support library, some introductory AutoLISP material from the original edition, and new chapters on dimensioning and 3D tools.

INSIDE AutoLISP picks up where CUSTOMIZING AutoCAD leaves off. The AutoLISP and applications portions of the original CUSTOMIZING AutoCAD have been rewritten and expanded. The format has been reorganized and revised for easy access, and new introductory AutoLISP material has been added. INSIDE AutoLISP now covers the full scope of AutoLISP, and shows you how to integrate it with DOS, UNIX, dBASE, Lotus 123, and other languages such as BASIC. INSIDE AutoLISP provides the tools and techniques that you need to develop an intelligent, well-integrated, and well-controlled system.

How INSIDE AutoLISP Is Organized

INSIDE AutoLISP is organized into three major parts. These three parts guide you from setup all the way through the development of powerful applications. In addition to the topics listed below, each chapter includes example applications of its functions and techniques.

PART I., YOU AND AutoLISP, covers the basic concepts of programming with AutoLISP and explains most of the AutoLISP functions. Chapter 1 details the setup you will need to participate in our exercise sequences. Chapter 2 proves that programming with AutoLISP is easy. It focuses on AutoLISP concepts, how AutoLISP works, and AutoLISP programming style. Chapter 3 introduces the basic AutoLISP functions and programming elements common to almost all programs. Chapter 4 explains program logic, flow, and structure, and covers the functions and techniques involved. Chapter 5 focuses on communication. It discusses messages and status prompts, tools for formatting defaults and controlling input errors while working with different data types, and creating an improved user interface.

PART II., AutoLISP AND AutoCAD, covers the interaction between AutoLISP and AutoCAD. Chapter 6 explains the data format of drawing entities, and the AutoLISP functions and techniques used to access and modify them. Chapter 7 shows you the functions and format for accessing all named and defined things in the AutoCAD database, such as linetypes, text styles, and block definitions. Chapter 8 covers AutoLISP's communication with the system, such as writing data to and reading from disk files, the screen, and the keyboard. We also develop a set of file handling utilities. Chapter 9 shows you how AutoLISP can directly access the screen, digitizer (or mouse), and keyboard. This lets your programs control input, put text on the screen menu and status lines, and draw temporary lines on the screen.

PART III., USING AutoLISP TO CUSTOMIZE AutoCAD, shifts our focus from AutoLISP functions and techniques to developing applications tools and programs. However, more AutoLISP functions and techniques are covered throughout Part III. Chapter 10 reviews menus, explains how to use AutoLISP in menus, and applies it to developing an isometric dimensioning system. Chapter 11 reviews attributes, their data formats, and how AutoLISP can use attributes as drawing tools, not just as data storage slots. Chapter 12 develops the techniques of parametric drawing. With parametrics, you can create programs that draw any set of objects which share common geometric relationships, where the variations from object to object are too great to make using blocks practical. Chapter 13 applies Lotus 123 and dBASE to extracting attribute data from AutoCAD, importing it into Lotus and dBASE, creating a database for formatting reports, and bringing text back into AutoCAD. Chapter 14 explores AutoLISP and 3D, and explains how to deal with 3D data and points in various UCSs. We'll develop tools and techniques for writing programs that work in 3D. Chapter 15 covers batch programming techniques, including AutoCAD scripts and AutoLISP/DOS batch file integration. Chapter 16 explores the AutoCAD DXF file format and shows how to use it with external programs. Chapter 17 wraps up with a discussion of system management and control topics, including AutoLISP memory management.

APPENDICES. There are four appendices. Appendix A describes each of the menus, macros, and AutoLISP programs and subroutines used in the book. Appendix B covers common problems and solutions encountered in setting up and using AutoCAD and AutoLISP. Appendix C provides four valuable reference tables: a complete AutoCAD system variables table, a table of DXF entity data group codes, a table of DXF symbol table group codes, and a quick reference table of all AutoLISP functions and their syntax. Appendix D discusses the system setups and software used to produce this book, along with the authors' comments on useful software and information sources.

Learn By Doing

Learning to use AutoLISP may look like a formidable task. It isn't. We learned AutoLISP by using AutoLISP. You may also harbor the suspicion that you have to be a programmer to use AutoLISP. You don't. We wrote INSIDE AutoLISP for typical AutoCAD users like you (and us).

Read This — It's Important

We've tried hard to make this rather comprehensive AutoLISP book as easy to use and follow as possible. To avoid errors and misunderstandings, we recommend that you read the following sections before jumping into the book.

How Exercises Are Shown

The following example exercise shows our format for AutoCAD commands. Exercises use the full width of the page, with commands and instructions at the left margin. In the sequence below, "Continue in the previous drawing . . ." is an instruction step. All prompts, including operating system and AutoLISP prompts, are shown like the Command: prompt below. Prompts are shown as they will appear on your screen, although for simple commands and in repetitive sequences, we abbreviate the command dialogue. Boldface type indicates the input that you need to enter.

Example Exercise

Continue in the previous drawing, or begin a NEW drawing named IL-INTRO.

```
Command: ZOOM
All/Center/Dynamic/Extents/Left/Previous/Window/<Scale(X)>: L
Lower left corner point: <RETURN>
Magnification or Height <9.0000>: 8.5
```

Command: <Coords on>	Toggle coordinates on with <^D> or <F6>.
Select [DRAW] [LINE]	Draw from 1,1 to point ①.

```
Command: (+ 2 3)
Lisp returns: 5
```

The exercise's right-hand section provides *in-line* comments and instructions about the command sequence. Menu picks are shown in boldface with brackets, like "Select [DRAW] [LINE]." All you need to do in an exercise is follow the command sequence, refer to any in-line instructions that are provided, and input any text shown in bold. The <RETURN> is shown only where there is no other input, but we assume you will use returns as needed to enter your input. Keys are presented like <^D> for the Control-D combination, or <F6> for function key six.

Lisp returns: is used to call your attention to AutoLISP's backtalk. A *Lisp returns:* prompt won't show on your screen, but what follows it, like the 5 in the sample exercise above, will.

Pure, uninterrupted lines of command sequences can become mesmerizing. To help you with the hands-on exercises, we provide illustrations and screen shots of what you should see on your screen at key points. Remember, we had to do the exercises too! We captured our screens as we tested the prompt sequences and AutoLISP routines for the book. Bubbles, like the ① shown in the sample exercise above, key exercise instructions to a point or object in an illustration, as in the typical screen shot below.

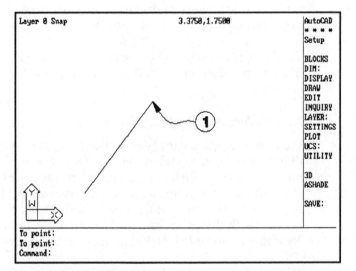

Sample Screen Shot

Things to Watch For

The printing font used in the exercises and program listings doesn't distinguish clearly between zero and the letter O, or the number one and lower case letter L. You need to watch these closely:

```
0   This is a zero.
O   This is an upper case letter O.
1   This is the number one.
l   This is a lower case letter L.
```

Saving Time With the INSIDE AutoLISP Disk

An optional disk, called the INSIDE AutoLISP Disk (or IL DISK for short), is available for use with the book. It includes all the AutoLISP (.LSP), menu (.MNU), and batch (.BAT) files used here. It also contains symbol and example (.DWG) files, and other support files used in INSIDE AutoLISP.

While not absolutely essential, the IL DISK will save you time and energy, and ensure that your customization menus, macros, and AutoLISP routines are accurate. The IL DISK releases you from tedious typing so you can focus your attention on the primary task of learning AutoLISP. The ACAD.MSG and README.DOC files on the IL DISK provide the latest updated information and corrections.

If you have the IL DISK, the menu and AutoLISP files may include completed functions and macros not yet needed in the corresponding exercises. Just ignore them until they are mentioned.

The back of the book includes an order form for the INSIDE AutoLISP disk. Instructions on installing and using the disks are given in the first chapter.

New Riders AutoLISP Utilities Disk 1

We've developed a variety of utility programs and subroutines that we didn't have room to include in this book. Some of the specific programs and subroutines will be mentioned when they relate to the topic at hand. If you think these programs and subroutines would be useful in your own application, the New Riders AutoLISP Utilities Disk 1 may also be ordered with the order form in the back of the book. Watch for additional New Riders AutoLISP Utilities Disks in the future.

How to Jump Around in the Book

To help you with the exercises, the book provides some simple icons showing you when to use files from the IL DISK, and when to create files if you don't have the disk.

 Do "this" if you have the IL DISK. This is the *disk* icon.

Do "this" if you don't have the IL DISK. This is the *no-disk* icon.

Where possible, we've made the material in the book independent, so you *can* jump in nearly anywhere. But there are a few things that need to be done in earlier chapters so material and programs in later chapters will work. These are identified with a pointing finger icon, like this.

☞   Do this; you need the material for later chapters.

These important items are flagged, by the pointing finger icon, for easy reference. There are several of them in Chapter 1. If you don't have the IL DISK, they also point you toward creating the ACAD.LSP file in Chapter 2, adding the user GET functions to ACAD.LSP in Chapter 5, and adding the DXF function to ACAD.LSP in Chapter 6.

In addition, many of the exercises and AutoLISP programs require that you load AutoLISP subroutines developed in earlier chapters. These routines will be identified in the program listings or exercises.

How Program Listings Are Shown

All AutoLISP programs, menus, and other text files used in the book are listed in the following format. If you don't have the IL DISK, the points at which you need to create the files are identified in the exercises with a no-disk icon.

```
;SHADOW BOX ROUTINE - USE AND SET VARIABLES IN-LINE
(setq ll (getpoint "\nPick LL corner: ")          ;this is a comment
      ur (getcorner "\nPick UR corner: " ll)   ;this is another comment
      ul (list (car ll) (cadr ur))
      lr (list (car ur) (cadr ll))
      pt (list (+ (car ll) (/ (- (car ur)  (car ll)) 2.0))
              (+ (cadr ll) (/ (- (cadr ur) (cadr ll)) 2.0)))
);setq
❶
(command "PLINE" ll "W" (/ (setq tx (getvar "TEXTSIZE")) 3.0) ""
        lr ur "W" "0" "" ul "C"
        "TEXT" "S" "STANDARD" "C"  pt tx "0" "INSIDE" "TEXT" "" "AutoLISP"
        "FILLET" "R" tx "FILLET" "P" ll
);command
```

The SHADOW BOX ROUTINE in SHBOX4.LSP File

❶ Listings often have black bubbles identifying key points. If so, they are followed by numbered paragraphs like this one. The right-hand comments like those shown above are in the IL DISK files. However, they are optional if you don't have the disk and create the files yourself.

➥ *NOTE: If you create the listings, remember to reload them each time you make changes when debugging (correcting errors). When testing, use an UNDO command after program errors to clean up the drawing and restore system variables.*

Prerequisites for INSIDE AutoLISP

The hardest part of INSIDE AutoLISP is typing accurately. That's why we recommend that you get the companion disk. It simplifies the typing by eliminating most of it.

You should be familiar with the major file handling commands of your operating system.

DOS Experience and Version

We recommend PC- or MS-DOS 3.0, or a later DOS version. You probably keep your AutoCAD software up to date, but it's easy to forget to update PC-DOS or MS-DOS. DOS versions 3.1 and later offer valuable features for a customizing environment, and can easily deal with environment space limitations. DOS 4 is not yet supported by AutoCAD.

UNIX, Mac, and Other Operating Systems

Although the exercises are shown in DOS example format, we have generally made them compatible with UNIX-based AutoCAD systems, and point out differences between DOS-based and UNIX-based systems.

AutoCAD's and AutoLISP's file formats are independent of the operating system. However, a few of our programs and exercises access the operating system, and may need modification for non-DOS systems. These are generally the ones that use SHELL. Most of the book is compatible with any system that runs AutoCAD, if you create the files yourself or transfer the IL DISK files by disk or network.

AutoCAD Experience, Version, and Equipment

To use this book, you should have enough experience to feel comfortable using AutoCAD. If you have worked through any of New Riders' AutoCAD books like INSIDE AutoCAD or STEPPING INTO AutoCAD, you should have no problem using this book. You should be familiar with most of AutoCAD's commands, but you don't need to be an expert. You should have general familiarity with writing menus. If you don't, we recommend that you supplement this book with CUSTOMIZING AutoCAD. You should know how to configure your AutoCAD system. Beyond that, you just need a desire to make your AutoCAD system more effective and productive.

You don't need a fast or fancy AutoCAD system. However, if your system is not running at IBM-AT speed or faster, you may find programs a little slower than you'd like. You'll need 640K of RAM to utilize AutoLISP. Extended or expanded RAM and extended AutoLISP are nice, but not required. A mouse or digitizer tablet is nearly essential.

The following sequence in AutoCAD will check your version and verify that AutoLISP is enabled.

Checking Your Version

Command: **(ver)**   Type (ver) and hit <RETURN>.
Lisp returns: "AutoLISP Release 10.0"   Or your version number.

If you got "AutoLISP Release 10.0" or higher, you're in great shape. If you got "AutoLISP Release 9" you'll have to make some adjustments. Although the IL DISK was developed on and supports AutoCAD Release 10, most of the material will work in Release 9. You'll need to edit some menus and LISP files to remove or revise commands and functions that didn't exist in Release 9. See the ACAD.MSG file on the IL DISK for more information.

If you got a bad command message, check to see that AutoLISP is not disabled by insufficient memory or the AutoLISP option on the configuration menu under "Configure operating parameters."

Moving On

Let's turn to Chapter 1 to set up and organize the DOS system environment for INSIDE AutoLISP. Then, in Chapter 2 and beyond, we'll begin to tap that AutoLISP power.

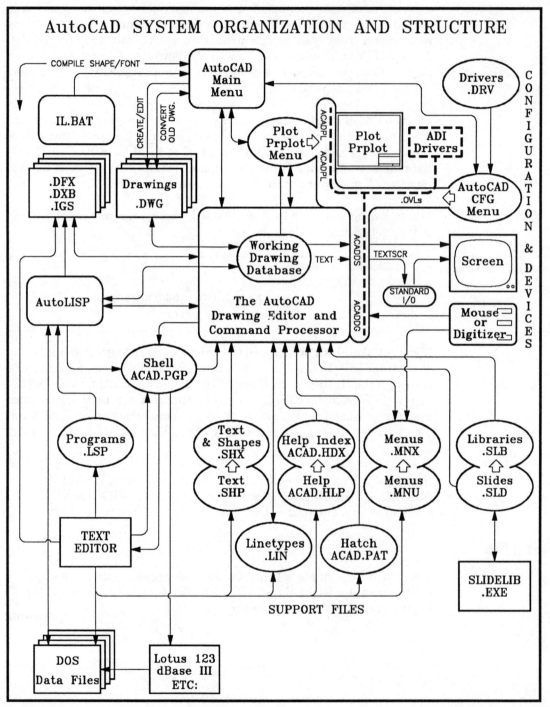

AutoCAD System Organization and Structure

CHAPTER 1

Getting Started

ORGANIZING YOUR AutoCAD SYSTEM

Few people are able to work efficiently if the tools and information they need are scattered haphazardly around their work area. AutoCAD doesn't work efficiently in a cluttered environment either. This chapter will show you how to quickly and easily set up your AutoCAD system to match our setup for this book.

Getting the right system environment is half the battle in customizing your AutoCAD program. Automating your AutoCAD system setup with a DOS batch file or UNIX script and using a text editor to create files without leaving AutoCAD are key elements. This chapter describes what you need in a text editor, shows you how to configure your operating system with the DOS CONFIG.SYS and AUTOEXEC.BAT (or UNIX) setup files, and shows you how to structure subdirectory paths. We will tell you how to install the IL DISK and how to use AutoCAD's SHELL command to suspend AutoCAD in the background while you run external programs. You will also create two prototype drawings.

There are three main benefits to organizing your AutoCAD setup. First, controlling AutoCAD's operating system environment lets you, AutoCAD, and other programs find your application files more efficiently and lets you run multiple applications and development configurations. Second, with the help of AutoCAD's SHELL command, you can flip back and forth between developing your custom routines with your text editor and testing them in AutoCAD. Finally, using a customized prototype drawing eliminates the need for inputting most AutoCAD drawing settings and allows you to standardize your drawings.

➧ *NOTE: Be sure to read the introduction before you start. It contains important information about our exercise sequences and program instructions.*

Files for Your AutoCAD System

You need to create or verify your operating support files and your IL.BAT and ACAD.PGP files to use this book. You also need to configure AutoCAD with the IL-PROTO.DWG file. We will show you how in this chapter.

DOS Files

CONFIG.SYS is a DOS root directory file that sets the general DOS environment and installs hardware devices.

AUTOEXEC.BAT is a DOS batch program that initializes DOS environment settings and installs support programs and utilities when you boot the system.

IL.BAT sets AutoCAD's DOS environment variables and starts up AutoCAD for use with INSIDE AutoLISP.

AutoCAD Files

ACAD.PGP defines the link between AutoCAD commands and DOS programs.

IL-ACAD.DWG is our default prototype drawing set up in decimal units.

IL-PROTO.DWG is our default prototype drawing set up in architectural units.

Necessary Directories

A good directory structure provides flexibility in organizing files. It increases efficiency if you limit the number of files in each directory to a reasonable number, say 100 to 200. AutoCAD provides good support for directory use by allowing you to set search paths for program and support files. Our directory structure also ensures that our exercises will not interfere with your current AutoCAD setup.

INSIDE AutoLISP assumes that your hard disk is C:, and that you have a directory structure like that shown in the Directory Structure illustration below. The exercises show a DOS style prompt that includes the current directory path. A *path* is a set order of directories. You can set a path search order in DOS. DOS searches this path for programs or batch files when you execute them. This allows you to run programs in a directory that is different from the one you're currently in. AutoCAD can also be set to search additional paths for support files.

You may be using another type of operating system or your drive letter or subdirectory names may vary from those shown. If so, you need to substitute your prompt, drive letter, and directory names wherever you encounter the C:\PATH prompts (such as C:\ACAD), C: drive, or various directory names in the book.

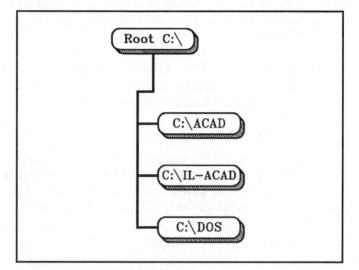

INSIDE AutoLISP Directory Structure

The IL-ACAD, ACAD, and operating system directories are necessary for this book and for its companion disk's application environment to work. Use the following exercise to make an IL-ACAD directory and set it current. Then take a look at your directory names and at the book's directory names. We will assume your DOS operating files are in a directory named DOS and that drive C: is the current drive.

Subdirectory Setup

C:\> **MD \IL-ACAD**   Makes a directory named IL-ACAD.

C:\> **DIR *.**   This lists directories and little else.
                              The directories you will need for this book are:

```
Volume in drive C is DRIVE-C
Directory of C:\

ACAD    <DIR>  12-01-88   11:27a        AutoCAD program, config. and standard files.
DOS     <DIR>  12-01-88   11:27a        All of the operating system files.
IL-ACAD <DIR>  12-01-88   11:27a        INSIDE AutoLISP support files.
3 File(s)  8753472 bytes free           Your list will be different.
```

The IL-ACAD directory will be our working and support directory. For the DOS operating system, the DOS, ACAD, and IL-ACAD directories are the minimum directories needed for the exercises in this book.

If your operating system files are not in a directory named DOS, they need to be in some other directory in your system's path. Paths are generally set in your AUTOEXEC.BAT file, as shown later in this chapter.

➥ *TIP: It helps to keep the programs and data file groups that you use in their own subdirectories. Access is faster, files don't get mixed up, and future program upgrades are easier to install.*

Using UNIX Directories

On a UNIX system, create the IL-ACAD directory in your *home directory*. Throughout the book, you will have to substitute appropriate UNIX commands and paths for the DOS commands and paths shown. The following table shows UNIX and DOS equivalents.

DOS	UNIX	Purpose
CD \	cd ~	Change to root (DOS) or home (UNIX) directory.
MD \IL-ACAD	mkdir ~/il-acad	Make book's directory.
DIR filename	ls -l filename	List directory for filename.
DIR *.	ls -d */	List directories.

Some UNIX systems may vary from these examples. Also, you will have to do a search and replace to substitute the path ~/il-acad/ for the path /IL-ACAD/ for all menu files later in the book. Depending on your system, AutoCAD may be installed in /usr/acad, /files/acad, or ~acad directories. Check with your UNIX system administrator if you aren't sure how AutoCAD is set up.

DOS doesn't care whether file names are upper or lower case, but UNIX file names are case-sensitive. Most UNIX file names are lower case, so we use lower case in our macro and LISP codes. However, in text and comments, we use upper case letters, like TEXT.TXT instead of text.txt, to set the file name apart from the text. If you use UNIX, input your file names in lower case letters.

Text Editors

You must have a text editor to write the AutoLISP programs in this book. Most word processors can create appropriate ASCII text files if they are set to use non-document, programmer's, unformatted, or whatever they call their ASCII mode. We used Norton's Editor, but any good text editor will work. Norton's Editor, Sidekick, PC Write (a "shareware" editor), Wordstar in non-document mode, the Word Perfect Library Program Editor, and the DOS program EDLIN all produce the standard ASCII file format that you will need. EDLIN is awkward and we recommend its use only as a last resort, or for temporary use until you settle on an editor. Make sure that your text editor will produce ASCII files for menu and AutoLISP development.

A good text editor is invaluable. It helps if your editor is comfortable, compact, quick, and easy to use, but there are three essential features your editor must have. It must create pure ASCII files, including the ASCII <ESCAPE> character. It must be able to merge files. And it must not automatically word wrap. AutoCAD can handle either DOS or UNIX ASCII formats. The IL DISK files are in DOS format. If you have doubts about a DOS editor's ability to produce ASCII files, see Appendix B.

➡ *NOTE: If you are using a UNIX text editor, you will find that our companion disk's text files end each line with a <^M> (a <RETURN>) and each file with a <^Z> due to their DOS text format. You may need to strip these <^M> and <^Z> characters to modify them in your editor. See your system administrator for help.*

The DOS Bootup Environment

When the computer starts up, it reads COMMAND.COM and two hidden files named IBMBIO.COM and IBMDOS.COM. Then, it looks around for some more information. It gets this environment information from two important files: CONFIG.SYS and AUTOEXEC.BAT.

You need a CONFIG.SYS file and an AUTOEXEC.BAT file, like those shown below, as a minimum base for using the book. (These files are not used in UNIX systems.)

CONFIG.SYS

The CONFIG.SYS file is the place to install *device drivers* that tell the computer how to talk to devices like disk drives, RAM disks, and unusual video cards. It is also the place to put instructions that will improve your system performance and increase your environment space for customization.

The CONFIG.SYS file must be located in the root directory. It is read automatically when your computer boots up. You may never even know it is there. We recommend that your file include the following lines.

```
BUFFERS=32
FILES=24
BREAK=ON
SHELL=C:\COMMAND.COM /P /E:512
DEVICE=C:\DOS\ANSI.SYS
```

CONFIG.SYS

The BUFFERS line allocates more RAM to hold your recently used data. Use a number from 20 to 48. The FILES line allocates more RAM to keep recently used files open. This reduces directory searching and increases data access speed. The SHELL line ensures adequate space for DOS environment variables. The ANSI.SYS line is necessary for some of the routines that you will develop in the book. It provides the full 256 ANSI character set.

 The SHELL and FILES lines are essential for ensuring sufficient environment and file space for this book's setup. Check to see if your file contains lines like those shown above. If not, see Appendix B for more information on modifying your file.

AUTOEXEC.BAT

AUTOEXEC.BAT is a batch file like any other, with one important exception: it is automatically executed every time the system is turned on. Like CONFIG.SYS, it must be in the root directory.

The AUTOEXEC.BAT file is the place to install your TSR (Terminate and Stay Resident) programs like Prokey, Sidekick, and Superkey. It also is the place to install the other setup commands and DOS environment settings that you need to complete your application environment. Examine your AUTOEXEC.BAT file. We recommend that it include the following lines.

```
PROMPT $P$G
PATH C:\;C:\DOS;
```

AUTOEXEC.BAT

PROMPT PG is extremely valuable. It causes the DOS prompt to display your current directory path so you don't get lost.

PATH is essential for automatic directory access to programs and DOS commands. The C:\ root and C:\DOS paths are necessary for this book's setup. Each path is separated by a semicolon. If your DOS files are in a different directory, substitute your directory name. You should use whatever is relevant to your setup. Your path will probably contain additional directories.

➡ *NOTE: If your AUTOEXEC.BAT doesn't contain prompt and path lines, edit it or create one in your root directory using your ASCII text editor.*

If you have problems setting up your environment, or if you want information about setting up more complex environments, see Appendix B. If you wish to install a more advanced AUTOEXEC.BAT file, a more extensive example file is given in Appendix D, the Authors' Appendix.

➡ *NOTE: The CONFIG.SYS and AUTOEXEC.BAT changes will not take effect until you reboot your computer. If you changed or created these files, reboot now with <CTRL-ALT-DEL>.*

This completes the initial setup for our operating system environment. Next, we move on to setting up AutoCAD.

AutoCAD Program and Support Files

AutoCAD is a big program, one of the biggest running on microcomputers. The ACAD.EXE file executes AutoCAD and loads core functions, but most of AutoCAD's program code is contained in several overlay files (ACADPP.OVL, ACADPL.OVL, ACADDS.OVL, and ACADDG.OVL). In addition, AutoCAD uses several support files, such as text fonts, linetypes, and hatch patterns. If you are unfamiliar with AutoCAD's file structure, take a look at the program files list in the AutoCAD Installation and Performance Guide that accompanied your software. Understanding these files will help you understand why and how things happen in AutoCAD.

Setting Up AutoCAD's Configuration Files

We assume that AutoCAD's support files are in your \ACAD subdirectory. Besides support files, AutoCAD also requires device driver, *.DRV, files during configuration. These drivers are used by the device configuration overlay files. Configuration also creates a configuration file (ACAD.CFG) that stores the settings and configuration-related system variables used by AutoCAD. After configuration, the drivers are no longer needed.

Use the following exercise to establish a separate INSIDE AutoLISP configuration to run our AutoCAD environment. This will protect your existing AutoCAD setup from being changed or disturbed as you work through this book. Copy the AutoCAD configuration overlay and the ACAD.CFG files to the \IL-ACAD directory as shown below. If your configuration files are not in the \ACAD directory, substitute your directory name for \ACAD below. For example, if your directory is \ACAD10, use CD \ACAD10.

Copying AutoCAD Files to the IL-ACAD Directory

```
C:\> CD \ACAD
C:\ACAD> COPY ACADP?.OVL \IL-ACAD\*.*
ACADPL.OVL                              Plotter overlay file.
ACADPP.OVL                              Printer/plotter overlay file.
2 File(s) copied

C:\ACAD> COPY ACADD?.OVL \IL-ACAD\*.*
ACADDS.OVL                              Display (video) overlay file.
ACADDG.OVL                              Digitizer (or mouse) overlay file.
2 File(s) copied

C:\ACAD> COPY ACAD.CFG \IL-ACAD\*.*
1 File(s) copied                        General AutoCAD configuration file.
```

ADI Drivers

ADI drivers are memory-resident TSR programs or DOS device drivers for plotters, printers, digitizers, and video cards. If you are using an ADI (Autodesk Device Interface) driver, you must install it prior to starting AutoCAD. You can install an ADI driver in your AUTOEXEC.BAT file or in your AutoCAD startup batch file unless it is designed to be installed by the CONFIG.SYS file. See Appendix B for more information on ADI drivers.

Installing the INSIDE AutoLISP Disk

It's time to install the optional INSIDE AutoLISP disk. If you don't have it yet, see the order form in the back of the book. We recommend getting the disk. It will save you a lot of typing and debugging time.

You need to copy the IL DISK files into the \IL-ACAD directory. To conserve disk space, the disk files are merged into a single file called

IL-LOAD.EXE which automatically copies all files into the current directory.

Installing the INSIDE AutoLISP DISKS

Put the IL DISK in your disk drive A:

```
C:\> CD \IL-ACAD          Change to the IL-ACAD directory.
C:\IL-ACAD> A:IL-LOAD     Copies disk files to the directory.
```

➥ *NOTE: To install the IL DISK on a UNIX system, you can install it on a DOS system first. Then copy the files by disk or across your network (if any) into your ~il-acad directory.*

Now that you've copied the disk, the ACAD.LSP file from the IL DISK will display the message, "Loading INSIDE AutoLISP Tools . . ." each time you start a new drawing in the IL-ACAD directory.

Setting Up AutoCAD

You have already created part of your system environment with the AUTOEXEC.BAT and CONFIG.SYS files. Now you need to crack AutoCAD's SHELL.

The PGP SHELL

A *shell* is an operating environment under which operating system commands and programs can be run. Many programs, such as AutoCAD, allow you to *shell out,* suspending a current operation and freeing memory to execute other commands or programs. This makes it possible for you to run programs, utilities, or DOS (or UNIX) commands without having to end AutoCAD or reload your drawing.

A few predefined *external commands* are included with AutoCAD to allow you to shell out. They are set in the ACAD.PGP file. The PGP stands for ProGram Parameter file. To see how SHELL fits into AutoCAD, look at the AutoCAD System Organization and Structure illustration at the beginning of the chapter.

SHELL's DOS access can be a general purpose access or a predefined jump to a specific DOS command or program. AutoCAD lets you customize and automate this access. If you want to customize your PGP file, see your AutoCAD Reference Manual or the book CUSTOMIZING AutoCAD (New Riders Publishing). For example, CUSTOMIZING AutoCAD shows you how to set up AutoCAD's PGP file to jump directly into editing a menu or AutoLISP file.

➥ *TIP: Customize your ACAD.PGP file by adding additional commands, utilities, or programs that you would like to access from AutoCAD.*

Your PGP File

We assume you have the standard ACAD.PGP file in your ACAD directory. If you have modified it, make sure it still includes these lines.

```
CATALOG,DIR /W,30000,*Files: ,0
DEL,DEL,30000,File to delete: ,0
DIR,DIR,30000,File specification: ,0
EDIT,EDLIN,42000,File to edit: ,0
SH,,30000,*DOS Command: ,0
SHELL,,127000,*DOS Command: ,0
TYPE,TYPE,30000,File to list: ,0
```

The Standard ACAD.PGP File

If your ACAD.PGP file is missing, copy the ACAD.PGP file from your original AutoCAD disks into your IL-ACAD directory. If your ACAD.PGP listing does not include these lines, copy it to your \IL-ACAD directory and add these lines with your text editor.

How to Use SHELL PGP Commands

We assume you know how to use standard PGP commands such as SHELL and DIR. To access a text editor, we use AutoCAD's SHELL because it is clean, simple, reasonably quick, and available to everyone. If you need a review, try this example, assuming you are in AutoCAD with the IL-ACAD directory current:

PGP Going Outside AutoCAD

```
Command: DIR                        The PGP DIR command.
File specification: ACAD*.*
Volume in drive C is DRIVE-C
Directory of C:\IL-ACAD             The files you copied earlier.


ACADPP   OVL    1314   7-06-88  11:53a
ACADPL   OVL    9555   7-16-88   8:22p
ACADDG   OVL    2461   9-04-88   4:07p
```

```
ACADDS    OVL    13842    9-14-88    5:21p
ACAD      CFG     1516    9-14-88    5:28p
```
And possibly other files. Your file sizes and dates will vary.

```
5 File(s)    2838528 bytes free
```

```
Command: SHELL
DOS Command: <RETURN>
```
Remember, SHELL sends DOS only what you enter on this prompt line. If you enter nothing with a <RETURN>, it simply dumps you into DOS:

```
Type EXIT to return to AutoCAD

The IBM Personal Computer DOS

Version 3.30 (C)Copyright International Business Machines Corp 1981, 1987
(C)Copyright Microsoft Corp 1981, 1986

C:\IL-ACAD>>
```
Enter any DOS command.

Most PGP commands jump into DOS and straight back to AutoCAD without ever showing you a DOS C:\> prompt. If you use the SHELL command and hit a <RETURN>, you simply get a DOS C:\>> with a subdirectory. The double >> indicates that AutoCAD still lurks in the background. You can run as many DOS commands and programs as you want before going back to AutoCAD with EXIT.

```
C:\IL-ACAD>> EXIT
```
Takes you back to AutoCAD.

We use SHELL to edit text files throughout the book. Here, for example, we use Norton's Editor to edit TEST.MNU in the current directory:

```
Command: SHELL
DOS Command: NE +TEST.MNU
```

➡ *NOTE: Whenever we ask you to edit or create a file, use the SHELL command and your text editor as shown above.*

You enter your editor, including any command line parameters your editor needs, at the DOS command prompt. If your editor requires additional memory, increase the 127000 value in the SHELL line of the ACAD.PGP file until it works, or create a custom PGP command. See your AutoCAD Reference Manual or CUSTOMIZING AutoCAD.

➡ *TIP: If you are a UNIX user, be careful when you exit your text editor. If you are running AutoCAD in the background, EXIT can terminate your parent process and leave AutoCAD stranded. UNIX users can use their text editors concurrently with AutoCAD, and do not need to use SHELL. Throughout this book, wherever we use the SHELL command, UNIX users should execute their programs, utilities or editors directly, then reload any modified files as needed.*

➡ *NOTE: The \ACAD\ACAD.PGP is the factory standard file. AutoCAD only recognizes the name ACAD.PGP, so any modified file needs to have the same name. Be careful not to mix your files. Keep backup copies of PGP files under unique, unusable names like ACAD-10.PGP for the Release 10 standard file, or MY-ACAD.PGP for the one you create.*

AutoCAD loads the PGP file when it starts a drawing. If you modify the PGP file, you'll have to force AutoCAD to reload the new PGP file in order to test it. Quit your drawing, then come back in and test the file.

You are nearly finished setting up. All that's left is to make an IL.BAT startup batch file and the two prototype drawings.

Starting AutoCAD With a DOS Batch File

AutoCAD lets you preset several of its startup settings. These control its memory usage and support files search order. The book's IL.BAT startup batch file sets memory allocations, file search order, and loads AutoCAD automatically.

Creating an IL.BAT File

 Use or modify the IL.BAT file from the IL-ACAD directory.

⊘ Create the new IL.BAT file shown below.

Use your text editor to create or modify the IL.BAT file to contain these lines:

```
SET ACAD=\ACAD
SET ACADCFG=\IL-ACAD
SET ACADFREERAM=20
SET LISPHEAP=25000
SET LISPSTACK=10000
C:
CD \IL-ACAD
\ACAD\ACAD %1 %2
```

```
CD\
SET ACADCFG=
SET ACAD=
```

Save and exit to DOS.

Copy IL.BAT to your root directory, or elsewhere on your PATH.
```
C:\IL-ACAD>COPY IL.BAT \*.*
```

➥ *NOTE: The IL.BAT file assumes your AutoCAD path is \ACAD. If not, substitute your path, like SET ACAD=\YOURPATH and \YOURPATH\ACAD %1 %2. If your drive for IL-ACAD is not C:, substitute your drive letter.*

➥ *NOTE: Type IL, for the IL.BAT file, when you want to start AutoCAD. If you do not use the IL.BAT file, you may get incorrect DOS environment settings. UNIX users can create an equivalent IL script described later in this chapter.*

The IL.BAT File Settings

SET ACAD= tells AutoCAD where to look if it doesn't find a needed support file in the current directory. AutoCAD searches the current directory first, then this specified support directory, then the program directory. The program directory is the directory where ACAD.EXE was started.

SET ACADCFG= tells AutoCAD where to look for configuration files. Creating several configuration directories and startup batch files is useful if you need to support more than one environment or more than one device, like different plotters.

SET ACADFREERAM= reserves RAM for AutoCAD's working storage. The default is 24K; the maximum depends on the system, usually about 24-26K. If you get "Out of RAM" or other errors, see Appendix B for more information on setting memory use.

SET LISPHEAP= allocates memory for AutoLISP functions and variables (nodes). If you use many AutoLISP programs, or if you use large AutoLISP programs, you may need to increase this value. More heap space increases AutoLISP speed by reducing the swapping (paging) of functions. If you have extended memory, using Extended AutoLISP gives you practically unlimited heap space.

SET LISPSTACK= defines AutoLISP's temporary working data area during execution. Complex AutoLISP programs using many arguments, recursive or nested routines, or large amounts of data may require more stack space.

➡ *TIP: Heap and stack space combined cannot exceed 45000 bytes. They reduce memory that otherwise is available to AutoCAD for free RAM and I/O page space. If you encounter problems running large programs, you have to adjust these settings to achieve a working balance. Don't be alarmed. It's not hard. If it works, use it. If it doesn't, change your settings until it works.*

Spaces cause errors in DOS variable names and their assigned values:

```
SET ACADCFG=\IL-ACAD        is acceptable, however
SET ACADCFG = \IL-ACAD      won't work.
```

These set environment settings do not affect memory outside AutoCAD.

Extended AutoLISP

If you have Extended AutoLISP, you can install it in the startup batch file. The startup file can also control extended memory (SET ACADXMEM=), expanded memory (SET ACADLIMEM=), and extended AutoLISP memory allocation (SET LISPXMEM=). See Chapter 10 for a more detailed explanation of extended AutoLISP memory management. If your system has more than 2 Mb of extended or expanded memory, you may find that limiting its use may improve performance. AutoCAD must use normal memory to implement extended or expanded memory. Too much extended or expanded memory starves the system for normal I/O page space and free RAM, and can actually reduce performance. See your Installation and Performance Guide for more information.

That's all there is to the settings. See our Appendix B, your AutoCAD Reference Manual, and the AutoCAD Installation and Performance Guide for more details. The rest of the IL.BAT batch file is made up of the following startup DOS commands.

IL.BAT DOS Commands

C: ensures that you are on the right drive.

CD \IL-ACAD changes the current directory to \IL-ACAD.

\ACAD\ACAD %1 %2 executes ACAD. If \ACAD is on your path, you could use ACAD alone here, but specifying the directory avoids having DOS search the path. It also avoids conflict with an ACAD.BAT file, if any exists. The %1 and %2 are replaceable parameters that you will use later in the book when you run IL.BAT. For example, to run a script with the name, NAME, you would enter IL X NAME and IL.BAT would execute this line as \ACAD\ACAD X NAME to run the script.

CD returns you to the root directory.

➡ *TIP: Use SET ACAD= and SET ACADCFG= to clear any SET ACAD=name and SET ACADCFG=name settings that you make in a startup batch file like IL.BAT. It is always good practice to have batch files clear their settings so your other AutoCAD applications will not be directed to the wrong configuration and support files. If you use EXTLISP, you may also clear its memory for other programs at the end of the IL.BAT file with REMLISP.*

Starting AutoCAD With a UNIX Script

The syntax and process of creating the UNIX equivalent of the IL.BAT file depends on your particular system environment. Consult your system administrator and refer to your AutoCAD Installation and Performance Guide for syntax. UNIX users can omit all memory settings, such as ACADFREERAM and LISPHEAP; however ACAD and ACADCFG need to be set. You also need to add the appropriate entries to change directories and to start up AutoCAD.

Prototype Drawings

AutoCAD uses a default prototype drawing named ACAD.DWG to establish its drawing environment defaults for new drawings. You can modify ACAD.DWG to create your own default setup. You can also configure AutoCAD to use any other drawing as its prototype.

To follow the book, you need a drawing setup that is consistent with ours. The easiest way to achieve this is to create new standard prototype drawings. We use two. IL-ACAD.DWG is in decimal units for an 11" x 8.5" sheet of paper and is similar to ACAD.DWG. IL-PROTO.DWG is in architectural units for a 36" x 24" sheet. Both are set up for full scale drawing and plotting. When you create different size drawings in the customization exercises, you can adjust these limits and scale settings.

First, start with fresh defaults. Then set your units and limits, along with some dimension settings. Finally, set the layer and style conventions. If you have the IL DISK, you already have the IL-ACAD.DWG and IL-PROTO.DWG files, and you can just read the following exercise.

Making the Prototypes

 You already have the prototype drawings. Just read the exercise.

Create IL-ACAD and IL-PROTO.

```
C:\IL-ACAD> IL              Use IL.BAT to start up.
Enter selection: 1          Begin a NEW drawing named IL-ACAD=.
                            The equal sign ensures default settings.
```

Make the following settings:

```
Command: SNAP               Set to 0.1.
Command: GRID               Set to 1.
Command: LIMITS             Set to 0,0 and 11,8.5.
Command: ZOOM               Zoom All.
Command: LTSCALE            Set to 0.375.

Command: UCSICON            Set to off.

Command: MENU               Enter a period for none! You will load a menu when needed.
Command: <Coords on>

Command: DIM1               Set DIMTXT to 0.125.

Command: STYLE              Create style STD with font ROMANS.
                            Set a fixed height of 0.125.
                            Default all settings except height.

Command: END                END to save IL-ACAD.

Enter selection: 1          Begin a NEW drawing named IL-PROTO=IL-ACAD.
```

Make the following settings:

```
Command: UNITS              Set Arch. (4), Denom. 64, Angular frac. 2. Default the rest.
Command: SNAP               Set to 0.25.
Command: GRID               Set to 2.
Command: LIMITS             Set to 0,0 and 36,24.
Command: ZOOM               Zoom All.

Command: DIM                Reset the following dimension variables.
```

Type these in regardless of the defaults shown:

```
        DIMASZ   3/16        DIMCEN   1/16        DIMEXO   3/32
        DIMDLI   3/8         DIMEXE   3/16
```

```
Dim: EXIT

Command: END                    END to save IL-PROTO.
```

➡ *NOTE: Most of our macros and AutoLISP routines assume a fixed height text style. AutoCAD does not prompt for height in TEXT, CHANGE and related commands if you use a fixed height. Some macros and AutoLISP programs will require modification if you need to use them on variable height styles. The prototype drawings initially fix text height for a 1:1 plot scale.*

DIMSCALE is used to control plot:drawing scale (full scale for now). You needed to type in the dimension variable settings regardless of the apparent defaults because the defaults are rounded off. For example, DIMASZ's default is 0.1800, but architectural units misleadingly round off the display to 3/16 inch.

➡ *TIP: You can create a menu and an AutoLISP-based setup routine to automatically handle all these drawing setups. See CUSTOMIZING AutoCAD for such a system.*

Configuring and Testing IL-ACAD

Your AutoCAD setup probably uses the default name ACAD.DWG as its automatic prototype drawing. New drawings will start up using this default prototype drawing unless you instruct AutoCAD to use a different prototype. Because you set up a separate configuration for INSIDE AutoLISP in the IL-ACAD directory, you can change the default without affecting your normal AutoCAD setup.

 Configure IL-ACAD as the default drawing whether you have the IL DISK or not. You should be in the Main Menu.

Configuring IL-PROTO as the Default Drawing

```
Enter selection: 5                      Configure AutoCAD.
Press RETURN to continue: <RETURN>

Enter selection <0>: 8                  Configure operating parameters.
Enter selection <0>: 2                  Initial drawing setup.

Enter name of default prototype file for new drawings
or . for none <ACAD>: IL-ACAD
```

```
Enter selection <0>: <RETURN> <RETURN> <RETURN>        Three times to save and exit
                                                       to the Main Menu.

Enter selection: 1          Begin a NEW drawing named TEST.
                            It should start up identically to the IL-ACAD you saved.

Command: QUIT               And if OK, exit to DOS.
```

Our Layering Convention

Customization requires a common layering scheme to automate drawing setups with menu macros. To do this, you need to establish your conventions in advance so that macros can be written for them. DOS uses wildcard characters to filter file names. AutoCAD uses them to filter layer names, using the same "?" and "*" syntax as DOS. Our layer names are designed for filtering. The names distinguish text from material components, and dimensions from annotations, using names like TXT01 or DIM01 and CEN02. Here is our naming convention:

Objects on Layer	Layer Names
Text	TXT01 thru TXT03
Components, assemblies, and materials	OBJ01 thru OBJ93
Dimensions	DIM01 thru DIM03
Symbols and annotations	ANN01 thru ANN93
Title sheets or forms	REF01 thru REF93
Linetypes - dashed, center, hidden...	DSH01, CEN01, HID01
thru	DSH93, CEN93, HID93
DON'T PLOT reference layers	REF00

Layer Naming Conventions

The first three characters tell you *what* you are dealing with. The two digit code describes the *appearance*. The first appearance code keys to layer linetype. The second keys to plotting 1, 2, or 3 line weight, using the color assigned to the layer. The book groups the standard seven colors and assigns them to three pens. Following are two more tables, showing the codes for linetype and pen weight:

LTYPE Code	AutoCAD Linetype	LTYPE Code	AutoCAD Linetype
0	Continuous	5	Dot
1	Dashed	6	Dashdot
2	Hidden	7	Divide
3	Center	8	Border
4	Phantom		

Weight Code	AutoCAD Color	Pen Weight	Pen Size
0	7 (white)	NA-used for ref. layers	
1	2 (yellow)	Fine	0.25mm
1	3 (green)	Fine	0.25mm
1	5 (blue)	Fine	0.25mm
2	1 (red)	Medium	0.35mm
2	4 (cyan)	Medium	0.35mm
3	6 (magenta)	Bold	0.60mm

Linetype and Pen Weight Codes

There are many alternative layering conventions, but we like ours because it's simple, yet informative. For example, OBJ12 is an objects layer using a dashed linetype with a weight code of 2 (color red or cyan) which plots with a medium pen. This is a flexible layering scheme. Feel free to adopt and modify it.

Now we should be on common ground with our starting environments. We share common bootup environments, common DOS environments for AutoCAD, and two AutoCAD prototype drawings.

Summary

Take the time to familiarize yourself with the AutoCAD files and their use. It will take much of the mystery out of how AutoCAD works. Organize your files and system by setting up a directory path search order that enables AutoCAD to find your application files efficiently. You'll find that keeping some directories (like our IL-ACAD) separate will save you from interference woes with other projects. Automate your setup procedure with your CONFIG.SYS and AUTOEXEC.BAT files. Adapt our setup to all your applications.

Make friends with your text editor — it will become one of your most prized tools. We'll begin using it right away as we move on to AutoLISP.

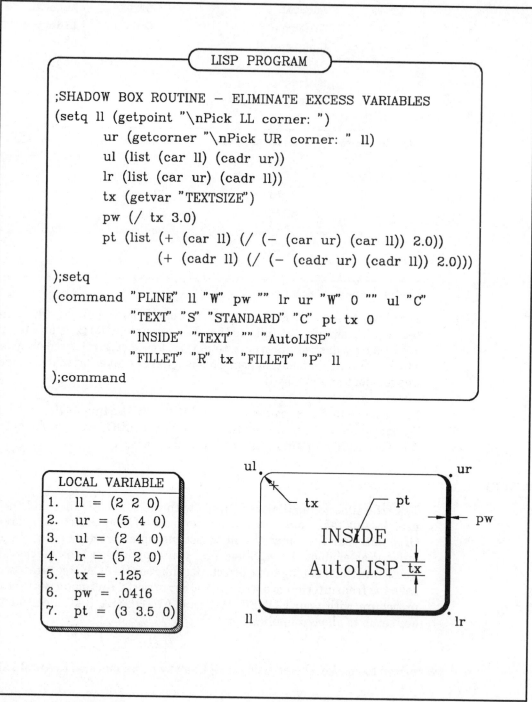

LISP PROGRAM

```
;SHADOW BOX ROUTINE - ELIMINATE EXCESS VARIABLES
(setq ll (getpoint "\nPick LL corner: ")
      ur (getcorner "\nPick UR corner: " ll)
      ul (list (car ll) (cadr ur))
      lr (list (car ur) (cadr ll))
      tx (getvar "TEXTSIZE")
      pw (/ tx 3.0)
      pt (list (+ (car ll) (/ (- (car ur) (car ll)) 2.0))
               (+ (cadr ll) (/ (- (cadr ur) (cadr ll)) 2.0)))
);setq
(command "PLINE" ll "W" pw "" lr ur "W" 0 "" ul "C"
         "TEXT" "S" "STANDARD" "C" pt tx 0
         "INSIDE" "TEXT" "" "AutoLISP"
         "FILLET" "R" tx "FILLET" "P" ll
);command
```

LOCAL VARIABLE

1. ll = (2 2 0)
2. ur = (5 4 0)
3. ul = (2 4 0)
4. lr = (5 2 0)
5. tx = .125
6. pw = .0416
7. pt = (3 3.5 0)

ul   ur

tx   pt   pw

INSIDE

AutoLISP tx

ll   lr

Diagram of SHBOX3.LSP

CHAPTER 2

AutoLISP

BASIC CONCEPTS OF PROGRAMS

Programming with AutoLISP is easier than you might think. You don't have to be a programmer to learn AutoLISP. In fact, most people have never written a program before. With just a few basic techniques, you can create powerful tools to help you automate your AutoCAD system.

The emphasis of this chapter is on learning AutoLISP programming style, not specific functions of the AutoLISP language. Therefore, we postpone explaining many of the AutoLISP functions we introduce here until later chapters. This chapter focuses on how AutoLISP works. Before you learn the details of programming in AutoLISP, you need to know what a program is, what the major elements of a program are, and the difference between second-rate and professional programming styles.

The Benefits of AutoLISP

If you have created macros before, you probably found them to be powerful tools, but somewhat limited in brainpower. A macro is like a *robot typist* entering sequences of standard AutoCAD commands. AutoLISP turns your macros into a *thinking typist,* capable of making calculations and logical decisions. AutoLISP macros can act like custom commands which prompt, instruct, and provide choices and defaults. AutoLISP programs carry this several steps further, providing even greater power, flexibility, and control.

In this chapter, you'll learn how to form AutoLISP expressions and nest expressions to make programs, use AutoLISP in menu macros, and store your programs in disk files. We will also show you how to use and define variables and how to develop an efficient programming style.

A Non-LISP Macro

We'll begin on familiar ground with menu macros. If you want to learn more about menus and macros, read CUSTOMIZING AutoCAD from New Riders Publishing. We assume you already know how to enter a simple macro in an ASCII text menu file. Make the following macro using your text editor. If you have trouble with your text editor, consult Appendix B.

If you have the IL DISK, you already have the [BUBBLE] macro in your IL02.MNU file.

```
[BUBBLE]^C^C^CCIRCLE \0.25 TEXT S STANDARD M @ .25 0 \LINE QUA \\;
```

[BUBBLE] in IL02.MNU

The [BUBBLE] macro draws a circle and line for a column grid marker on a plan. It pauses for text from the user. Test the macro with the exercise below before you continue.

A Simple Macro

Enter selection: **1**   Begin a NEW drawing named IL02.
                                 It should match the IL-ACAD prototype from Chapter 1.

You have the [BUBBLE] macro in your IL02.MNU file.

Use your text editor to create the [BUBBLE] macro above in a new menu file named IL02.MNU.

Command: **MENU**   Load IL02.
Command: **ZOOM**   Left corner 0,0 and height 4.
Select **[BUBBLE]**   Test the macro.

Command: CIRCLE 3P/2P/TTR/<Center point>: **Pick a point.**
Diameter/<Radius>: .25
Command: TEXT Start point or Align/Center/Fit/Middle/Right/Style: S
Style name (or ?) <STD>: STANDARD
Start point or Align/Center/Fit/Middle/Right/Style: M
Middle point: @
Height <0.2000>: .25
Rotation angle <0>: 0
Text: **G**   Enter the bubble text.
Command: LINE From point: QUA of
To point: Pick a quadrant of the circle.
To point: Pick any point.

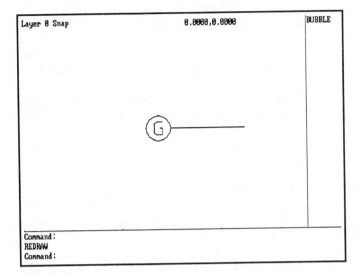

```
Layer 0 Snap                    0.0000,0.0000           BUBBLE




                              (G)————————————




Command:
REDRAW
Command:
```

The Bubble

Let's look at how an AutoLISP expression can improve the [BUBBLE] macro.

Writing a Simple AutoLISP Expression

An AutoLISP expression is the most fundamental part of writing programs. Once mastered, you will quickly learn to develop powerful programs for your own use. An expression is very easy to learn.

It begins with an opening parenthesis and ends with a closing parenthesis. A typical AutoLISP expression has this syntax: `(function argument)`.

Here are some of the rules for the expression game:

■ Every expression has opening and closing parentheses.

■ Every expression has a function name. The name must immediately follow the opening parenthesis.

■ Every expression gets evaluated (executed) and returns a result. The result is the last evaluated value, which may be nil (nothing).

Functions and Arguments

A *function* is a subroutine that tells AutoLISP what task to perform. Tasks include addition, subtraction, multiplication, division, and many others. An *argument* provides data to the function. A function may have any number of arguments or no arguments. Arguments may be variables, constants, or other functions. Some arguments are flags or optional parameters that alter the action of the function. If a function is defined to accept an argument, you must provide the function with a value for the argument. You'll find a brief description of all the AutoLISP functions in Appendix C. Refer to Appendix C to check your syntax and argument type. We will explain most of the AutoLISP functions as we encounter them throughout the book.

How AutoCAD and AutoLISP Communicate

AutoCAD needs to have a way to distinguish between AutoCAD commands and AutoLISP expressions. AutoCAD identifies an AutoLISP expression by its opening parenthesis. Each time AutoCAD detects an opening parenthesis, it passes the entire expression which follows to AutoLISP. AutoLISP evaluates the expression and returns the result to AutoCAD. AutoCAD uses the result and continues. Let's enter an expression in AutoCAD. The PROMPT function prints the words to the command line of the screen.

```
Command: (prompt "Hello world.")
Hello world.
Lisp returns: nil
```

AutoLISP evaluates the PROMPT function and prints to the screen, then returns nil. The result of PROMPT is always nil. The "Hello world." is a string. Strings are characters between quotation marks.

If you make a mistake on an expression, <^C> to cancel and re-enter it. If you keep getting a 1> and <^C> doesn't clear it, type a closing parenthesis and a <RETURN>.

In AutoLISP expressions, opening parentheses must have matching closing parentheses. Failure to close a parenthesis will give you a prompt like 1> or 2>. The AutoLISP error prompt form is n> where *n* indicates how many closing parentheses are missing.

If you get an n> error prompt and <^C>s or additional parentheses don't help, then you left out a quotation mark. Type a " and then type as many parentheses as you need. The hardest part of AutoLISP is getting matching pairs of parentheses and quotation marks!

Setting a Variable

Perhaps one of the most common programming tasks in any language is storing a value to a variable name (called a *symbol*) that can later be used by a program. AutoLISP uses the SETQ function to set variables.

setq
Sets symbol to the value of the matching expression. **(setq *symbol expression* symbol1 expression1 ...)**

AutoLISP uses variables to store information. A *variable* represents something that is not constant, something that changes its value. You use variables all the time. You multiply your tax *rate* by your *income* and (if it were only that simple) send the result to the IRS. Rate and income are variables.

In algebra class, you learned that the expression Y=3 sets the variable Y to the value of 3. In AutoLISP, the SETQ function takes the place of the equal sign and the expression is rearranged in the LISP syntax. Try the same expression using LISP format. At the AutoCAD command line, type the following expression and observe the value that is returned.

Setting Your First Variable In AutoLISP

Command: **(setq y 3)**
Lisp returns: 3

AutoCAD determines that an AutoLISP expression has been entered at the command line by the presence of the opening parenthesis. AutoCAD waits to pass the expression along to AutoLISP until you enter the closing parenthesis. Then the expression is evaluated by AutoLISP, which in turn sends the value **3** back to AutoCAD. AutoCAD would have used this value as input if a command had been active.

The value is safely stored in the variable Y. You can test this by asking AutoCAD to look up the value with an exclamation mark followed by the variable name. An exclamation mark at the command line or in a menu macro tells AutoCAD to interpret the characters which follow as AutoLISP, not AutoCAD, input. Try this at the keyboard.

Command: **!y**
Lisp returns: 3

AutoLISP's Backtalk

AutoLISP is one of the few programming languages that actually talks back to you. Every expression returns a value whether it is nil, True or data. In this case, AutoLISP printed a 3 to the screen after you typed in the expression.

Languages such as BASIC and FORTRAN do not return values after each expression. If you've ever programmed in other languages, you probably developed the habit of setting each value to a variable, then using the variable. It's a common practice, but not efficient in LISP programming. You can use AutoLISP's backtalk to your advantage when writing your programs. As a matter of fact, you have to use the returned values to form a meaningful program, which leads us to another of the key concepts of programming in AutoLISP — *nesting*.

Nesting AutoLISP Expressions

Nesting means putting one expression inside another expression. It allows the result of the inner expression to be used by the outer expression. Without nesting, your program would be a group of non-related expressions.

Say you wanted to store the name of the current AutoCAD layer in a LISP variable. The AutoLISP GETVAR function can look up the value of an AutoCAD system variable, such as the current layer, but it doesn't save the value as a LISP variable. Instead of setting a value, GETVAR returns the current value of the system variable.

getvar	*Returns the value specified by sysvar, the system variable name. Sysvar is a string value.* **(getvar** *sysvar***)**

setvar	*Sets an AutoCAD system variable specified by sysvar to the value supplied.* **(setvar** *sysvar value***)**

➥ *NOTE: You may be familiar with the SETVAR command in AutoCAD. With SETVAR, you can set system variables such as turning construction markers off and on with BLIPMODE or adjusting entity highlighting during selection with HIGHLIGHT. System variables are independent of AutoLISP variables, so you need the GETVAR and SETVAR functions to get and set their values.*

Try the GETVAR function at the keyboard. CLAYER is the AutoCAD system variable for the current layer name. It is currently set to 0.

Using GETVARs

```
Command: (getvar "CLAYER")
Lisp returns: "0"
```

Since the layer name is a string and not a number, AutoLISP puts quotation marks around it.

Without nesting, the returned value is relatively useless. However, with nesting we can store the layer name to a variable by nesting the GETVAR expression in a SETQ expression. Try this at the keyboard.

```
Command: (setq y (getvar "CLAYER"))
Lisp returns: "0"
```

```
Command: !y                     Test the value of Y again.
Lisp returns: "0"               Y is now equal to 0, not 3.
```

Believe it or not, that is the basic AutoLISP language in a nutshell. Everything you need to know about AutoLISP comes down to the idea of nesting.

As you develop your AutoLISP knowledge, you'll learn how to nest more expressions and use AutoLISP's backtalk to your advantage in programming. The process of learning AutoLISP is no harder than learning the numerous function names, what they do, and how to put them together to form programs. Let's start by converting the [BUBBLE] macro to an AutoLISP program.

Getting From Macros to AutoLISP

AutoLISP expressions can be used in menu macros. When AutoCAD reads a macro, it tests each item to see if it is an AutoLISP expression. The LISP expressions it finds are treated just as if they were entered individually from the keyboard.

Introducing AutoLISP in macros can provide powerful control over your system. It can simplify the amount of input required for a macro. It can access data, do calculations, and enter input without user interaction. If you can think of any series of steps you routinely do in AutoCAD, you can combine them in an AutoLISP macro and never have to input the same information twice.

Our [BUBBLE] needs substantial improvement. As many AutoCAD users have learned, good layer management is essential for efficient drafting. Here we will use AutoLISP to add a little layer management to our macro. Our macro will use the GETVAR function to store the current layer so that the macro can reset it after completion. If you have the IL DISK, [BUBBLE2] is in your IL02.MNU file.

```
[BUBBLE2]^C^C^C(setq y (getvar "CLAYER")) LAYER M OBJ01;;+
CIRCLE \0.25 LAYER M TXT01 ;TEXT S STANDARD M @ .25 0 \LAYER S OBJ01;;+
LINE QUA \\ LAYER S !y;;
```

[BUBBLE2] in IL02.MNU.

The macro now performs four layer changes during the command. First, it saves the current layer name and then makes the layer OBJ01, which is left current. It draws the circle for the bubble image and makes a current layer TXT01 to place the text. It resets the OBJ01 layer, then it draws the line. At the end, it resets the layer that was current at the start of the macro, using the Y variable. Try it now.

[BUBBLE2] With AutoLISP

 You have [BUBBLE2] in your IL02.MNU file.

Use your text editor to copy and edit the first macro in IL02.MNU to create [BUBBLE2].

```
Command: MENU                                      Reload IL02.MNU
Select: [BUBBLE2]                                  Test it.

Command: (setq y (getvar "CLAYER")) "0"            It first saves the current layer
Command: LAYER ?/Make/Set/New/ON/OFF/Color/Ltype/Freeze/Thaw: M
New current layer <0>: OBJ01                       and creates the OBJ01 layer.
                                                   Then it draws the circle, text,
                                                   and line as it controls layers.

Command: LAYER ?/Make/Set/New/ON/OFF/Color/Ltype/Freeze/Thaw: S
New current layer <OBJ01>: !y            Ends by restoring the layer saved as Y.
?/Make/Set/New/ON/OFF/Color/Ltype/Freeze/Thaw:
```

Writing a Complete LISP Routine

It's not a big step from adding a little AutoLISP to a macro to making a complete AutoLISP routine to replace the macro. It just takes a few more tools. The most important of these tools is the COMMAND function of AutoLISP.AutoLISP;Sending commands to AutoCAD

Sending Input to AutoCAD

The COMMAND function allows AutoLISP to communicate with AutoCAD's command processor. It takes instructions from AutoLISP and delivers them to AutoCAD as if they were entered at the keyboard or from a macro.

command

> *Sends its arguments as input to AutoCAD. Strings and numbers are taken as literal input; other arguments send the returned value of their expressions to AutoCAD as input. The COMMAND function alone executes a return, (COMMAND nil) executes a <^C>. The symbol, PAUSE (a variable set to "\"), used as a COMMAND function argument, pauses the COMMAND function for user input.*
> (command argument . . .)

The two basic rules for using the COMMAND function are:

- Put AutoCAD commands, options, and text in quotes.

- Do not precede your variable names with exclamation points.

AutoLISP takes each item of the COMMAND's argument list, evaluates any AutoLISP variables or expressions it finds, and then sends the argument list to AutoCAD. Variables can be used anywhere in the statement to supply AutoCAD with data. Strings in quotation marks are taken as literal input by AutoCAD. Expressions which evaluate to nil or the symbol T will cancel the command like a <^C>. Unquoted words are taken as AutoLISP variables. You can nest other expressions and built-in AutoLISP functions within the COMMAND function. They will be evaluated and their returned value passed to AutoCAD.

Of course, AutoCAD will reject the command input if there are any syntax or data type errors. AutoCAD doesn't care where input comes from, but it must be correct input for the command.

Each item of the command list must be one complete instruction to AutoCAD. You cannot enter half an AutoCAD command word, like ERA and later add the SE to get ERASE. You also must treat each instruction separately. AutoCAD treats (command "CIRCLE 5,5 0.25") as one erroneous instruction, not three instructions. Here is an example of the correct format for the COMMAND function.

```
COMMAND FUNCTION          EXAMPLE
(command item1 item2...)  (command "CIRCLE" "5,5" 0.25)
```

You can put numbers in quotation marks, like "0.25," but it is clearer to leave them in unquoted form, like 0.25. Don't use unquoted leading or trailing decimal points, like .25 or 25., or you will get an "invalid dotted pair" error. Points can be lists like ' (5 5) or strings like "5,5". Any value can be passed as a variable.

Because AutoCAD is independent of AutoLISP, you can interrupt a command sequence. You can let AutoCAD do half of a job, then have AutoLISP intervene and finish the job or pass control back to AutoCAD. Try an example with the CIRCLE command.

Using the COMMAND Function

```
Command: (command "CIRCLE")
CIRCLE 3P/2P/TTR/<Center point>: nil
3P/2P/TTR/<Center point>: 5,5                    Pick a point.
Diameter/<Radius>: (command 0.25)                Supply the radius.
Lisp returns: 0.250000000000000

Command: (command "CIRCLE" pause 0.25)           Try it with a PAUSE.
CIRCLE 3P/2P/TTR/<Center point>:                 The PAUSE pauses. Pick a point.
Diameter/<Radius>: 0.250000000000000
```

The AutoLISP COMMAND sends the CIRCLE command to the AutoCAD command interpreter. AutoCAD issues the prompt for the command. Since the COMMAND function always returns a nil after evaluation, AutoCAD sees the nil, does not understand it, and reissues the "3P/2P/TTR/<Center point>:" prompt. Although a nil *within* the COMMAND function cancels like a <^C>, a *returned* nil is generally ignored.

With this in mind, let's look at another of the very important tools in writing macros.

Getting Input From the User

Most programs involve the user in one form or another. To get input from the user, AutoLISP has a set of functions called the GET functions. With them, it asks users to select points and input distances, strings, numbers, and more. The [BUBBLE] macro needs to get some points from the user. It uses the GETPOINT function for this.

Getting Points With GETPOINT

The GETPOINT function can prompt the user for a point and get the point input.

getpoint

> *Returns a point. The optional point value specifies the base point of a rubber-banding line. The optional prompt string can provide specific instructions for desired point selection.*
> **(getpoint** *point prompt*)

The GETPOINT function accepts a prompt string to show the user when asking for the point. It also allows a base point to enable a rubber-band line. Try some examples at the keyboard, using SETQ to save the points.

Using GETPOINT

```
Command: (setq pt1 (getpoint "Centerpoint: "))
Centerpoint: 1,2,3

Lisp returns: (1.0 2.0 3.0)
```

Enter the expression.
LISP prints the prompt, you pick or enter the point.
The point is returned as a list of X,Y,Z values.

When we first started with AutoLISP, we entered the expression (setq y 3) and it returned 3. Now we see the point returned in the above expression as (1 2 3). AutoLISP can group information, such as the X, Y, and Z coordinates of a point in a list. A *list* is just a collection of information surrounded by parentheses. Notice that a list does not have commas between its elements. The elements of a list are separated by spaces.

➡ *NOTE: Throughout this book, you will see points shown as either 2D, containing just an X,Y coordinate, or as 3D, like the above example, with X,Y,Z coordinates.*

Let's use the rubber-band feature of the GETPOINT function. You do this by supplying a point as an argument to the function. Use the PT1 you just saved.

```
Command: (setq pt2 (getpoint "Endpoint: " pt1))
Endpoint:

Lisp returns: (1.0 4.0 3.0)
```

Enter the expression.
Move the cursor and see the rubber-band line.
Then enter the points **1,4,3**.

Let's introduce one more function to our AutoLISP tool kit, the GETSTRING function.

Getting Character Input With GETSTRING

GETSTRING asks the user for a string type of input, such as ABC or JOHN.

getstring

> *Returns a string of up to 132 characters from the user. If the optional flag argument is nil or is omitted, spaces are not allowed in the string and they act like a <RETURN> and end input. The optional prompt string can provide specific instructions for input.*
> (**getstring** *flag prompt*)

➥ *NOTE: You cannot provide another LISP expression or variable as input to a GET function. You cannot use a GET function inside a COMMAND function. Get the input first and use a variable to feed it to COMMAND.*

The GETSTRING function accepts any string of characters typed at the keyboard (or input by a non-LISP macro). It returns the string in quotation marks to let you and AutoLISP know it's a string value.

Using GETSTRING

```
Command: (setq txt (getstring "Text: "))
Text: ABC                                    LISP prints the prompt, you enter ABC.
Lisp returns: "ABC"
```

There is one important thing to remember about pausing a menu macro. You still need to use a backslash to pause for input even if you are using the COMMAND function PAUSE or one of the GET functions. The following routine finishes the conversion of the macro to a full LISP routine. If you have the IL DISK, [BUBBLE3] is already in your IL02.MNU file.

```
[BUBBLE3]^C^C^C(setq la (getvar "CLAYER"));+
(command "LAYER" "M" "OBJ01" "");+
(setq pt1 (getpoint "Centerpoint: "));\+
(setq pt2 (getpoint "Endpoint: " pt1));\+
(command "CIRCLE" pt1 0.25);+
(command "SELECT" "L" "");+
(command "LINE" pt1 pt2 "");+
```

Listing continued.

Continued listing.

```
(command "TRIM" "P" "" pt1 "");+
(command "LAYER" "M" "TXT01" "");+
(setq txt (getstring "Text: "));\+
(command "TEXT" "S" "STANDARD" "M" pt1 0.25 0 txt);+
(command "LAYER" "S" la "");
```

[BUBBLE3] in IL02.MNU

The [BUBBLE] macro first stores the current layer name in a variable and then requests only two points from the user. A rubber-band line is activated during the second point selection by including a base point in the GET expression.

Now the macro has enough information to draw the line and circle of the bubble. It uses the COMMAND function to send AutoCAD commands to the command interpreter. A layer called OBJ01 is created for the line and circle. The text height and radius of the circle is set to 0.25. Later, you'll learn how to make macros work at different scales.

Because the line is drawn to the center of the circle, we use the TRIM command to remove the extra line segment.

The macro defines a layer for the text and uses GETSTRING to ask the user for the text string. Then the entry is put in the drawing with the COMMAND function. The last step is to reset the original layer. Test the macro.

Testing the [BUBBLE] Macro

You already have the [BUBBLE3] macro in your IL02.MNU.

Create the [BUBBLE3] macro in your IL02.MNU.

Reload the IL02 menu file.

```
Select: [BUBBLE3]                          LISP expressions scroll by and GETPOINT prompts:
Command: (setq pt1 (getpoint "Centerpoint: "))
Centerpoint:                               Pick bubble center point.
Lisp returns: (1.0 1.0 0.0)                Returns your value.

Command: (setq pt2 (getpoint "Endpoint: " pt1))
Endpoint:                                  Pick second point of line.
Lisp returns: (1.0 3.0 0.0)
```

It scrolls through the CIRCLE and LINE commands using the two points as input, sets layers, and then prompts:

Text: **A**   Enter some text.

And ends by restoring the original layer.

Besides using AutoLISP expressions in menu macros, AutoLISP expressions can be used in script files, entered at the command line, or stored in LISP program files.

Storing and Loading LISP Programs

There's really nothing special about AutoLISP program files. You'll find LISP files even easier to work with than the menu we've been using. AutoLISP programs are stored in a LISP file much like menu macros are stored in a menu file. LISP files are ASCII files just like menus. But there are several minor differences:

■ LISP files must be loaded with the LOAD function prior to use.

■ Format is not important. Unlike menu files, AutoLISP ignores extra white space caused by spaces, tabs, or returns.

■ LISP files generally have an .LSP file extension.

■ Function files don't need the backslash (\) to make GET functions pause.

■ LISP programs don't need a continuation character (+) at the end of each line.

■ Menu control characters like ^O, ^C, and ^B are not used in LISP files.

■ Prompt strings can include *escape codes* to issue non-printing and control characters, like \n for <RETURN>.

■ Semicolons do not execute <RETURN>s, but mark the rest of the line as a comment. A comment can be placed anywhere in the file by preceding it with a semicolon.

■ You can indent nested expressions with spaces to make file reading easier.

Let's make an AutoLISP program file. The prompt line prints a message. The first line is a comment. Create a new ASCII file called TEST.LSP.

Making an AutoLISP File

Command: **SHELL**   Make TEST.LSP containing these two lines:

```
;MY TEST FILE
(prompt "Hello world.")
```

Save the file and return to AutoCAD.

As we've said, LISP files must be loaded into AutoLISP's memory before you can use them. The simple process of loading a file causes AutoLISP to evaluate the contents of the file.

load | *Loads the AutoLISP file specified by the filename. The optional expression will be returned if the load function fails. The optional expression is evaluated whether or not the load fails.*
(**load** *filename* expression)

Try loading the TEST file.

Loading Your First LISP File

```
Command: (load "test")
Hello world.                   It prompts you.
Lisp returns: nil
```

Evolution of a Simple Program

"Hello world" is too simple to call a real program. Real programs are rarely written in final form. They undergo an evolutionary process that continually makes them more refined and efficient. Take AutoCAD for instance. Over the past five years, we've seen a tremendous array of new features, most of which were made possible through refinement to the original program.

Let's look at how to develop an AutoLISP program. There are always steps you can take to make a program even more efficient. When we wrote the example programs and routines presented in this book, each started out clear, simple — and inefficient. After we got the basic programs working, they went through several iterations. As we added input and settings controls, error trapping, and reorganized for efficiency, they matured to the final programs shown in this text. Examine these programs and you'll pick up some of our techniques and standards.

To get started, let's follow this process of refinement through a sample sequence, the shadow box program. Unlike the bubble menu macros, the shadow box routine is entered in a LISP file. The program draws a rectangular box and prints two lines of text at the center of the box. Then the program fillets the box corners to a radius.

The first version of our program is rather wasteful of AutoLISP's variable space. It uses far more functions and variable names than are really necessary, but it's typical of the type of program the novice first writes. Take a look at the shadow box routine. If you have the IL DISK, it's the SHBOX.LSP file. Otherwise, create the file.

```
;SHADOW BOX ROUTINE
(setq ll (getpoint "\nPick LL corner: "))
(setq ur (getcorner "\nPick UR corner: " ll))
(setq x1 (car ll))
(setq y1 (cadr ll))
(setq x2 (car ur))
(setq y2 (cadr ur))
(setq ul (list x1 y2))
(setq lr (list x2 y1))
(setq tx (getvar "TEXTSIZE"))
(setq pw (/ tx 3.0))
(setq deltax (- x2 x1))
(setq hdeltax (/ deltax 2.0))
(setq deltay (- y2 y1))
(setq hdeltay (/ deltay 1.75))
(setq pt (list (+ x1 hdeltax) (+ y1 hdeltay)))
(command "PLINE" ll "W" pw "" lr ur "W" 0 "" ul "C")
(command "TEXT" "S" "STANDARD" "C" pt tx 0 "INSIDE" "TEXT" "" "AutoLISP")
(command "FILLET" "R" tx "FILLET" "P" ll)
```

Shadow Box Routine in the SHBOX.LSP File

The GETCORNER function works with a base argument like GETPOINT, except that GETCORNER graphically prompts with a rubber-band box, like an object selection window. SHBOX uses the lower left corner point of a desired rectangle as a base point and it prompts for and returns the opposite upper right corner point.

`getcorner`	*Returns a point selected as the second corner of an AutoCAD window cursor. The optional prompt string can provide specific instructions for desired point selection.* **(getcorner** *point* prompt**)**

Test the routine, then we'll introduce the other new functions presented in the program as we refine it.

Testing the SHBOX Routine

 You already have the SHBOX.LSP file.

Create the SHBOX.LSP file.

Command: **ERASE**	Clean up the screen.
Command: **(load "shbox")**	
Pick LL corner:	Pick lower left point, try 1,1.
Pick UR corner:	Upper right, try 3.5,2.5.

Commands scroll by as it draws, ending with:

```
Command: FILLET Polyline/Radius/<Select two objects>: P Select 2D polyline:
4 lines were filleted
Lisp returns: nil
```

If you entered the routine correctly, you should see the words INSIDE AutoLISP framed in the box.

You'll probably notice that none of the LISP code appears on the command line; only the COMMAND function output sent to AutoCAD appears. A menu echoes all its code to the command line, but a LISP file reads its code transparently.

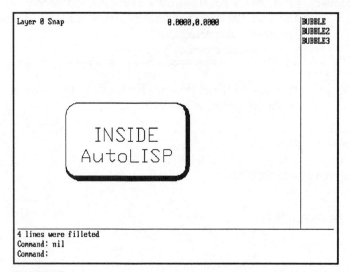

Shadow Box

One of the simplest ways to shorten the program is to group the SETQ and COMMAND function calls.

Combining Functions

The shadow box routine above contains many SETQ and COMMAND functions, repeated one after the other. There is no reason these can't be combined. Some functions, like SETQ and COMMAND, accept multiple arguments which can be grouped in a single function call. Grouping all the SETQ calls in just one call creates one long expression. The COMMAND functions can be similarly combined. The indentations in the following listing show which arguments belong to which group. The ;setq and ;command comments help identify which opening and closing parentheses match up.

```
;SHADOW BOX ROUTINE - GROUPED FUNCTION CALLS
(setq ll (getpoint "\nPick LL corner: ")
      ur (getcorner "\nPick UR corner: " ll)
      x1 (car ll)
      y1 (cadr ll)
      x2 (car ur)
      y2 (cadr ur)
      ul (list x1 y2)
```

Listing continued.

Continued listing.

```
      lr (list x2 y1)
      tx (getvar "TEXTSIZE")
      pw (/ tx 3.0)
      deltax (- x2 x1)
      hdeltax (/ deltax 2.0)
      deltay (- y2 y1)
      hdeltay (/ deltay 2.0)
      pt (list (+ x1 hdeltax) (+ y1 hdeltay))
);setq
(command "PLINE" ll "W" pw "" lr ur "W" 0 "" ul "C"
         "TEXT" "S" "STANDARD" "C" pt tx 0 "INSIDE" "TEXT" "" "AutoLISP"
         "FILLET" "R" tx "FILLET" "P" ll
);command
```

Grouped Functions in SHBOX2.LSP File

Before we test it, let's briefly explain some of the AutoLISP functions we've used.

As we mentioned before, the LIST function creates a list. A list is an expression containing one or more elements enclosed in parentheses, such as (1.0 3.0). The list (1.0 3.0) would be interpreted by AutoCAD as the point 1.0,3.0. LIST is used above to create points by combining individual X and Y values.

CAR and CADR are two functions that extract elements of lists. CAR extracts the first element of a list, so the CAR of (1.0 3.0) returns 1.0. CADR (pronounced cadder) extracts the second element of a list, so the CADR of (1.0 3.0) returns 3.0. They are used above to extract the individual X and Y coordinates for calculating the other corner and text start points.

The basic math functions are the simplest. The *division* (/) function divides its first argument by its second (and any additional) argument(s). The *subtraction* function (-) subtracts its second (and any additional) argument(s) from its first. The *addition* (+) and *multiplication* (*) functions add and multiply all of their arguments. They are used above to calculate the X and Y values of new points.

All of these functions will be more extensively explained and used in later chapters.

Testing the SHBOX2 Routine

 You already have the SHBOX2.LSP file.

Copy and edit SHBOX.LSP to create the SHBOX2.LSP file.

Command: **ERASE**	Clean up the screen.

Command: **(load "shbox2")**	And test it.
Pick LL corner:	Pick lower left point.
Pick UR corner:	Upper right.

Commands scroll by, and it draws as before.

The routine uses 15 different variable names, most of which are used only once in the program. It isn't the best example of programming but if it gets the job done, why shorten your programs?

Eliminating Variables From Programs

Shortening your programs by reducing the number of variables saves crucial space in the AutoLISP programming environment. Your programs run faster and load faster. Let's revise the program again. This time, we'll eliminate storing individual coordinates in the X1, Y1, X2, Y2 variables. Instead, we'll use the CAR and CADR functions when needed to retrieve each coordinate. If you have the IL DISK, you have the SHBOX3.LSP file.

```
;SHADOW BOX ROUTINE - ELIMINATE EXCESS VARIABLES
(setq ll (getpoint "\nPick LL corner: ")
      ur (getcorner "\nPick UR corner: " ll)
      ul (list (car ll) (cadr ur))
      lr (list (car ur) (cadr ll))
      tx (getvar "TEXTSIZE")
      pw (/ tx 3.0)
      pt (list (+ (car ll)  (/ (- (car ur)  (car ll)) 2.0))
               (+ (cadr ll) (/ (- (cadr ur) (cadr ll)) 2.0))))
);setq
(command "PLINE" ll "W" pw "" lr ur "W" 0 "" ul "C"
        "TEXT" "S" "STANDARD" "C"  pt tx 0 "INSIDE" "TEXT" "" "AutoLISP"
        "FILLET" "R" tx "FILLET" "P" ll
);command
```

Shortened Version of SHBOX3.LSP File

Now the routine is considerably smaller and uses only seven variable names. The program is more efficient, but it's a bit harder to see exactly what is happening. Generally, there is a trade-off between program clarity and program length. As an AutoLISP programmer, you'll eventually reach a balance between program complexity and reading clarity.

Testing the SHBOX3 Routine

You already have the SHBOX3.LSP file.

Copy and edit SHBOX2.LSP to create the SHBOX3.LSP file.

Command: **ERASE**   Clean up the screen.

Command: **(load "shbox3")**   And test it.

Commands scroll by, and it draws as before.

By now you should be able to notice an improvement in speed over the original shadow box program.

Setting and Using Variables In-Line

We said before that AutoLISP always returns a value. Think about how to most efficiently use the values returned by AutoLISP. In the next shadow box version, the current text height returned by the TEXTSIZE system variable is used within the COMMAND function. It replaces the TX (text height) variable with a statement that both sets and returns the TX value. The PW (polyline width) variable has been eliminated and replaced by an in-line expression using the divide function. If you have the IL DISK, you have the SHBOX4.LSP file.

```
;SHADOW BOX ROUTINE - USE AND SET VARIABLES IN-LINE
(setq ll (getpoint "\nPick LL corner: ")
      ur (getcorner "\nPick UR corner: " ll)
      ul (list (car ll) (cadr ur))
      lr (list (car ur) (cadr ll))
      pt (list (+ (car ll)  (/ (- (car ur)  (car ll)) 2.0))
               (+ (cadr ll) (/ (- (cadr ur) (cadr ll)) 2.0)))
);setq
```

Listing continued.

Continued listing.

```
(command "PLINE" ll "W" (/ (setq tx (getvar "TEXTSIZE")) 3.0) ""
        lr ur "W" "0" "" ul "C"
        "TEXT" "S" "STANDARD" "C"  pt tx "0" "INSIDE" "TEXT" "" "AutoLISP"
        "FILLET" "R" tx "FILLET" "P" ll
);command
```

Variables Set in the COMMAND in SHBOX4

At this point, you may have decided that the routine code is too obscure and hard to follow. With experience, you will be able to follow even the most complicated, deeply nested program. It just takes practice.

Testing the SHBOX4 Routine

 You already have the SHBOX4.LSP file.

Copy and edit SHBOX3.LSP to create the SHBOX4.LSP file.

Command: **ERASE**   Clean up the screen.

Command: **(load "shbox4")**   And test it.

Commands scroll by, and it draws as before.

Calculations Within the COMMAND Function

Our routine can be made even shorter. Take a look at the next version of the routine. It eliminates virtually all variables in the routine. If you have the IL DISK, you have the SHBOX5.LSP file.

```
;SHADOW BOX ROUTINE - EXTREME USE OF IN-LINE CALCULATIONS
(setq ll (getpoint "\nPick LL corner: ")
      ur (getcorner "\nPick UR corner: " ll)
);setq
(command "PLINE" ll "W" (/ (getvar "TEXTSIZE") 3.0) ""
        (list (car ur) (cadr ll)) ur "W" "0" ""
        (list (car ll) (cadr ur)) "C"
        "TEXT" "S" "STANDARD" "C"
        (list (+ (car ll)  (/ (- (car ur)  (car ll)) 2.0))
              (+ (cadr ll) (/ (- (cadr ur) (cadr ll)) 2.0)))
        (getvar "TEXTSIZE") "0" "INSIDE" "TEXT" "" "AutoLISP"
        "FILLET" "R" (getvar "TEXTSIZE") "FILLET" "P" ll
);command
```

Extreme Use of In-Line Calculations in SHBOX5.LSP

In SHBOX5, all calculations are done directly in the COMMAND function. Even the TX (text height) variable has been eliminated. Instead, repeated calls to the GETVAR function returns the TEXTSIZE system setting. Also observe that individual commands passed to the COMMAND function are not complete. We send bits of the entire command sequence as they are calculated.

Testing the SHBOX5 Routine

You already have the SHBOX5.LSP file.

Copy and edit SHBOX4.LSP to create the SHBOX5.LSP file.

Command: **ERASE**   Clean up the screen.

Command: **(load "shbox5")**   And test it.

Commands scroll by, and it draws as before.

➥ *TIP: To use the shadow box program in a menu, make a macro like [SHBOX] (load "shbox5").*

In-Line Versus Setting Variables

When should you use in-line GETVARs and calculations, and when should you set, save, and call variables? It's partly a matter of personal preference as to how compact you want your programs to be. But a few rules of thumb can help guide your efficiency. If you are going to repeatedly use a value, it's more efficient to set and call a variable than to repeatedly calculate it. Repeated GETVARs of the same system variable are less efficient than using a variable, because when AutoLISP has to access AutoCAD data, it slows down.

Reading a LISP Program

Since most of the programs given in this book have already been optimized and streamlined, you need to learn how to read others' LISP programs. It's important to remember how AutoLISP evaluates expressions.

AutoLISP evaluates from left to right within the same nesting level. To determine how AutoLISP will work its way through an expression, you must find the innermost level of nesting. This may take a little practice but soon will become second nature.

The final version of the shadow box routine used the following expression to calculate the X coordinate for the text alignment point. Set the lower left and upper right coordinates to 1,2 and 4,5 and try the expression by itself.

Evaluating Nested Expressions

```
Command: (setq ll (getpoint "Centerpoint: "))
Centerpoint: 1,2
Lisp returns: (1.0 2.0 0.0)                          0.0 is the default Z coordinate.

Command: (setq ur (getpoint "Endpoint: "))
Centerpoint: 4,5
Lisp returns: (4.0 5.0 0.0)

Command: (+ (car ll) (/ (- (car ur) (car ll)) 2.0))      Try it.
Lisp returns: 2.5
```

The following table breaks down the expression into the six steps it takes AutoLISP to process it. The boldface type on each line indicates the expression that is being evaluated in that step. The italics show the value(s) returned by the previous step.

```
                    AutoLISP Evaluation Order
1.  (+ (car ll) (/ (- (car ur) (car ll)) 2.0))    Level 4
    (+ (car ll) (/ (-    4.0    (car ll)) 2.0))
2.  (+ (car ll) (/ (-    4.0    (car ll)) 2.0))
    (+ (car ll) (/ (-    4.0      1.0  ) 2.0))
3.  (+ (car ll) (/ (-    4.0      1.0  ) 2.0))    Level 3
    (+ (car ll) (/           3.0         2.0))
4.  (+ (car ll) (/          3.0          2.0))    Level 2
    (+ (car ll)             1.5            )
5.  (+ (car ll)             1.5            )       Level 1
    (+    1.0               1.5            )
6.  (+    1.0               1.5            )
                    2.5           Final answer.
```

The first thing AutoLISP finds is the innermost expression of the nested bunch. That is the (car ur) in Line 1. Although the (car ur) and (car ll) expressions are at the same level of nesting, the (car ur) is to the left of (car ll), so it gets evaluated first.

Line 2 shows the evaluation of (car ll). After both expressions are evaluated, Line 3 uses the (– 4.0 1.0) expression to perform a minus operation. That returns a value of 3.0, which is used in Line 4 during the division function.

Line 5 gets the X coordinate of the lower left point and adds it to the 1.5. The final answer is 2.5, which is halfway between the X coordinates of 1 and 4.

Now that you can think in LISP and write a program, what's next? How about loading a program just once, then executing it repeatedly like a command? Or how about automatically loading programs when you load your drawing? The ACAD.LSP file makes it possible.

ACAD.LSP: An Automatic Loading LISP File

Almost every customized AutoCAD system using AutoLISP can benefit from a well-developed set of core AutoLISP routines. Since this group of routines is usually used by other routines (as we'll learn later in the book) it's safest to have them automatically loaded each time a drawing is entered. The ACAD.LSP file provides the method for doing this.

At the start of each drawing session, AutoCAD looks for the ACAD.LSP file, and if found, loads it. The contents of an ACAD.LSP file are created just like any other LISP file. The significance of this file is that AutoCAD loads it automatically.

If you have the IL DISK, you already have an ACAD.LSP file that contains several functions. For now, all we are interested in is the initial prompt and the DIMSCALE lines in the file.

 If you don't have the disk, you need to create the first part of the ACAD.LSP file.

```
(prompt "\nLoading INSIDE AutoLISP Tools...")
(setq #dwgsc (getvar "DIMSCALE"))
```

An ACAD.LSP File

As we develop routines that are central to the system presented in this book, we will ask you to add them to the ACAD.LSP file in your working INSIDE AutoLISP directory, unless you already have them from the IL DISK.

In order to have AutoCAD automatically load the file, you need to quit the current drawing. Upon re-entering the drawing, you should see the prompt.

Starting an ACAD.LSP File

 You already have the ACAD.LSP file.

 Create ACAD.LSP and enter the two lines shown in the table above.

Save the file and return to AutoCAD.

```
Command: QUIT          To start a new drawing and load ACAD.LSP.
Enter selection: 1     Begin a NEW drawing again named IL02.
```

After the drawing is loaded you should see:
```
Loading INSIDE AutoLISP Tools...
```

```
Command: !#dwgsc       Check to make sure this is set.
Lisp returns: 1.0      It's important for the rest of the book.
```

The DIMSCALE line sets a variable named #DWGSC each time a drawing is loaded. This is our global scale variable, and it is used to control all scale-dependent programs. We assume that DIMSCALE is the intended drawing plot scale.

➡ *NOTE: The ACAD.LSP file is searched for in the same order as any other AutoCAD support file. The first directory AutoCAD looks in is the current directory, so our ACAD.LSP file won't interfere with any other on your system.*

Summary

AutoLISP is not a difficult programming language. The crucial point to remember about AutoLISP is this: AutoLISP is groups of simple expressions, some nested within others. It is easy to write poor quality programs, but learning how to write high quality programs is just a matter of learning the functions, creating your own subroutine functions, refinement, and practice.

As you move through this book, many more AutoLISP functions are presented. Be reassured, they are no harder to learn than the simple SETQ function you learned at the start of this chapter.

Next, let's look more formally at the basic elements of AutoLISP.

CHAPTER 3

Basic Elements of AutoLISP

GETTING TO KNOW THE TOOLS

Every toolbox has a few old hammers and screwdrivers that you reach for on just about every project. AutoLISP has general tools, too, which work anywhere — even outside your AutoCAD applications. Like every programming language, AutoLISP is capable of performing math operations, getting user input, parsing strings, and defining functions.

Most of AutoLISP's tools, however, are AutoCAD-specific. Through AutoLISP, you have a direct pipeline to AutoCAD's drawing entities, reference tables, and to passing data in and out of AutoCAD. By using AutoLISP in your menu macros or alone in programs, you can save data in variables, process that data, and return it to AutoCAD. Points, distances, and other values can be stored, calculated, compared, and used in drawings and programs. You can control your drawing environment through AutoCAD system variables by storing the system variables, prompting with drawing status, and changing and restoring the settings. You can change system settings transparently during commands for more responsiveness. You can access and extract entity data, use the data in programs, and even modify entities transparently.

In this chapter, you will master the basics of data manipulation through AutoLISP by learning how to use AutoCAD and AutoLISP system variables, AutoLISP math functions, and more GET functions to obtain user input. You will also learn how to build AutoLISP lists and how to define your own AutoLISP functions. You'll get a chance to experiment with **BUBBLE,** a spin-off of the [BUBBLE] macro from Chapter 2. Here, we use it to show you how to write C:BUBBLE as an AutoLISP-defined custom command.

You can freely jump into any section of this chapter. All of the exercise sequences are independent. Just start a new drawing when starting a sequence, and QUIT when through.

AutoLISP Variables and Expressions

When AutoLISP was first introduced into the AutoCAD program, it wasn't called AutoLISP. It was just called "variables and expressions" for building macros. Don't let AutoLISP intimidate you. To start, just think of AutoLISP as it was originally introduced — variables and expressions.

Variables

In the previous chapter, you used AutoLISP variables to store information. You attached a value to a variable name with SETQ. This lets you substitute variables in place of constant values. You can use the variable names at the command prompt, in macros, or within AutoLISP expressions to perform calculations and make logical decisions. To take a closer look at variables, let's look at system variables.

AutoCAD's System Variables

When you change the settings or values of snap, osnap, or ortho, or when you just pick a point, AutoCAD saves the newly set condition, value, or point as a system variable. You use the SETVAR command to set system variables such as the 3D mesh variables SURFU and SURFTAB1. You can see all the current system variable settings by using the SETVAR command and a question mark.

Using SETVAR to See System Variables

Enter selection: **1**   Begin a NEW drawing named IL03.

Command: **SETVAR**
Variable name or ?: **?**   Gives a listing.

```
ACADPREFIX    "C:\ACAD\"            (read only)
ACADVER       "10"                  (read only)
AFLAGS        0
ANGBASE       0.00
ANGDIR        0
APERTURE      3
AREA          0.0000               (read only)
ATTDIA        0
ATTMODE       1
ATTREQ        1
AUNITS        0
AUPREC        2
AXISMODE      0
AXISUNIT      0.0000,0.0000
BACKZ         0.0000               (read only)
BLIPMODE      1
CDATE         19880216.102637209   (read only)
CECOLOR       "BYLAYER"            (read only)
CELTYPE       "BYLAYER"            (read only)
CHAMFERA      0.0000
CHAMFERB      0.0000
-- Press RETURN for more --
```

The SETVAR Display

The system variables table in Appendix C has a complete listing, along with descriptive comments, on all system variables.

Variable Data Types

Whether you have modified a system variable or created an AutoLISP variable, it belongs to one of several data classes. If you look closely at the list of system variables in Appendix C, you will see the three main data types: *string, integer,* and *real. (Points* are lists of reals.) System variables and most AutoLISP variables that you create are one of these types.

- *String* variables have text values placed in quotes to identify the value as a string. For example, the system variable ACADPREFIX is currently "C:\ACAD\." The values "3.1," "SHEET-D," "pline," "-1234," and "the quick brown fox . . . " are all strings.

- *Integers* are positive or negative whole numbers without fractions, decimal places, or decimal points. AutoCAD often uses the integers 0 and 1 to indicate whether a system variable toggle, like SNAPMODE or ORTHOMODE, is turned off (0) or on (1). Integers must be between -32768 and +32767. Larger and smaller values cause errors without warning. The values 1, 3234, and -12134 are valid integers.

- *Reals* are positive or negative numbers with decimal points. In AutoLISP, you cannot begin or end a real with a decimal. If the value is less than 1.0, you must put a 0 before the decimal point (0.123) or you will get "error: invalid dotted pair." Examples of real system variables are FILLETRAD, TEXTSIZE, and AREA. Unlike integers, real values are not limited to certain numbers. However, AutoLISP formats reals in scientific notation when the values are very large or very small. Valid reals look like 1.0, 3.75218437615, -71213.7358 and 1.234568E+17.

- *Lists* consist of one or more values of any variable type grouped within parentheses. Points are considered AutoLISP lists. The GETPOINT and GETCORNER expressions return point lists. The LASTPOINT system variable is a 3D point list with values such as: (6.5 1.5 0.0). A 2D point is a list containing only two values.

The other data types that you will encounter in this book include *symbols* (AutoLISP variable and function names), *file descriptors* (the handles AutoLISP uses to read and write files), AutoCAD *entity names* (used by AutoLISP to access entity data), *selection sets* (used by AutoLISP to handle groups of entities), and *subrs* (the AutoLISP built-in functions called subroutines).

You can control many AutoCAD drawing editor settings with system variables. Most, but not all, of the settings can be changed with the SETVAR command. Certain system variables are indicated as *read only,* meaning you can extract, but not update, their values.

You need to keep data types in mind when you're working with AutoLISP because many functions will return a bad argument type error if they receive the wrong data type. For example, (+ 1.0 var) will cause an error unless VAR is an integer or a real number.

Using AutoLISP to Get and Set System Variables

As you've seen, you can get AutoCAD system variable values with AutoLISP's GETVAR function. The similar SETVAR function sets AutoCAD system variables from AutoLISP. GETVAR is a function, not a command, but SETVAR is the name of both an AutoLISP function and an AutoCAD command. Try some SETVAR functions to see read-write and read-only system variables in the following exercise.

Using GETVAR and SETVAR to Get and Set System Variables

```
Command: (setvar "ORTHOMODE" 1)          Reset the ortho value to on.
Lisp returns: 1

Command: (setvar "CLAYER" "0")           Try to reset layer.
error: AutoCAD rejected function         You can't. It's read-only.
Lisp returns: (SETVAR "CLAYER" "0")      The offending AutoLISP function.

Command: (getvar "CLAYER")               But GETVAR can read it.
Lisp returns: "0"                        The value, the layer name.
```

AutoCAD system variables have rigidly predefined names. Most are stored in the current drawing file. You can set many of them, but you can't create, name, or eliminate them. AutoLISP variables aren't permanently stored, but you can make, name, and delete them to your heart's content.

➥ *NOTE: All string system variables are read-only.*

Making Your Own Variables and Expressions

You create a variable when you give a value to a symbol. In the shadow box exercises, you assigned a point to the symbol LL by entering the expression:

```
(setq ll (getpoint "\nPick LL corner: "))
```

AutoLISP automatically assigns a data type when you create a variable. AutoLISP variables are completely independent of AutoCAD system variables, and their names may duplicate AutoCAD system variable names. Each time you use the variable name or refer to the variable name in a macro, program, or expression, the program replaces the variable name with the value most recently assigned to that name. Don't, however, use AutoLISP function names as variable names.

Variables can be any printable combination of letters and numbers except those reserved because of their special meanings in AutoLISP. There also are some ill-advised characters that may confuse or interfere with AutoLISP when you use them in menu macros. Avoid using the following characters:

```
RESERVED AND ILLEGAL CHARACTERS: . ' " ; ( ) or <SPACE>
AutoLISP FUNCTIONS: ~ * = > < + - /
ILL-ADVISED CHARACTERS: ? ` ! \ ^ or any control character.
```

The ATOMLIST

The ATOMLIST is an AutoLISP variable that stores the symbol names of all functions and user-defined variables.

```
Command: !atomlist
(#DWGSC INTERS GRREAD GRTEXT GRDRAW GRCLEAR UPORTS TRANS HANDENT TBLSEARCH TBLNE
XT ENTUPD ENTMOD ENTSEL ENTLAST ENTNEXT ENTDEL ENTGET SSMEMB SSDEL SSADD SSLENGT
H SSNAME SSGET ANGTOS RTOS COMMAND OSNAP REDRAW GRAPHSCR TEXTSCR POLAR DISTANCE
ANGLE INITGET GETKWORD GETCORNER GETINT GETSTRING GETORIENT GETANGLE GETREAL GET
DIST GETPOINT MENUCMD PROMPT FINDFILE GETENV SETVAR GETVAR  TERPRI PRINC PRIN1 P
RINT WRITE-LINE READ-LINE WRITE-CHAR READ-CHAR CLOSE OPEN STRCASE ITOA ATOF ATOI
 CHR ASCII SUBSTR STRCAT STRLEN PAUSE PI MINUSP ZEROP NUMBERP FLOAT FIX SQRT SIN
 LOG EXPT EXP COS ATAN 1- 1+ ABS MAX MIN NOT OR AND > >= /= = <= < ~ GCD BOOLE L
SH LOGIOR LOGAND REM * - + ASSOC MEMBER SUBST LENGTH REVERSE LAST APPEND CDDDDR
CDDDAR CDDADR CDDAAR CDADDR CDADAR CDAADR CDAAAR CADDDR CADDAR CADADR CADAAR CAA
DDR CAADAR CAAADR CAAAAR CDDDR CDDAR CDADR CDAAR CADDR CADAR CAADR CAAAR CDDR CD
AR CADR CAAR CDR CAR CONS COND LISTP TYPE NULL EQUAL EQ BOUNDP ATOM NTH PAGETB P
ICKSET ENAME REAL FILE STR INT SYM LIST SUBR T MAPCAR APPLY LAMBDA EVAL *ERROR*
/ QUIT EXIT _VER VER IF UNTRACE TRACE DEFUN FOREACH REPEAT WHILE PROGN FUNCTION
QUOTE READ LOAD SETQ SET MEM VMON ALLOC EXPAND GC ATOMLIST)

Command:
```

The ATOMLIST

You can see the ATOMLIST by typing **!ATOMLIST**. The exclamation point tells AutoCAD to return the value of the AutoLISP variable that follows it.

Looking at the ATOMLIST

Command: **<F1>**   Flip to the text screen.
Command: **!ATOMLIST**   You will see the ATOMLIST display.

Your ACAD.LSP file defines the #DWGSC variable. If you have the IL DISK, your ACAD.LSP also defines other functions and variables now shown in the illustration. Any symbols at the top of the ATOMLIST, preceding #DWGSC, are user-defined symbols from your ACAD.LSP file. The symbols following #DWGSC are native to AutoLISP.

A few functions, like PAGETB, PICKSET and ENAME, are used exclusively by the AutoLISP evaluator and are not intended for users. The rest of the functions are documented here and in the AutoLISP Programmer's Reference. We have tried to use most as examples in this book.

When you assign your variable names, upper or lower case makes no difference. Try to keep your names under six characters because names over six characters require more memory. Don't begin a variable name with a number.

```
INVALID VARIABLE NAMES:                              VALID NAMES:
123 (represents an integer number)                   PT1
10.5 (represents a constant real value of 10.5)      txt
ANGLE (redefines the AutoLISP function ANGLE)        ANGL
A(1) (contains invalid characters)                   A-1
OLD SUM (contains space)                             OLD_SUM
```

How to Assign Values to Variables

You have seen that SETQ binds a stored value to a variable name. After this binding, you can use an exclamation point to supply that value to AutoCAD. The exclamation point identifies the word that follows as an AutoLISP symbol. When AutoCAD sees the ! character, it passes the variable name to AutoLISP. AutoLISP interprets it and passes its value back to the AutoCAD command processor. You can also use the variable in other AutoLISP expressions.

How do you use these simple variables and expressions to improve and enhance your macros and to write programs? So far, you have learned to create variables, assign values to them, and use the values in functions or as command input to macros. But where do you get your data values?

Using GET Functions for Input

The most common way to provide data to AutoLISP is to request it through one of the GET functions. There is a GET function for each major data type or form of drawing input. Use these functions to get (and control) drawing input for macros and programs. You used GETPOINT and GETCORNER in the previous chapter. Here are several more of the GET functions:

getdist

> *Returns a user-entered distance or the calculated distance between two user-provided points. Value may be entered by a user or determined by two user-provided points. The optional point value specifies the base point for a rubber-banding line. An optional prompt can provide specific instructions for desired point selection.*
> **(getdist** *point prompt***)**

getangle

> *Returns an angle in radians. Value may be entered by a user or determined by two user-provided points. The angle is measured counterclockwise from the X axis, unless reversed by the UNITS command. An optional point value specifies the base point for a rubber-banding line. The optional prompt string can provide specific instructions for desired point values. Use GETANGLE for rotation (relative angles).*
> **(getangle** *point prompt***)**

getorient

> *Returns a radian angle as input by a user or as calculated by two user-provided points. The angle is measured in the direction, and from the 0 degree base, set by UNITS. The optional point value specifies the base point to show a rubber-banding line. An optional prompt string can provide specific instructions for desired point values. Use GETORIENT for orientation (absolute angles).*
> **(getorient** *point prompt***)**

getreal

> *Returns a real number provided by the user. The optional prompt string can provide specific instructions for input.*
> **(getreal** *prompt***)**

getint

> *Returns an integer provided by the user. (On DOS systems, input must be between -32768 and +32767.) The optional prompt string can provide specific instructions for input.*
> **(getint** *prompt***)**

All the GET function arguments are optional. You can compose your GET functions to include prompt arguments which can ask questions or give instructions. The prompt can be any text string. All the GET functions require a backslash to pause for input if used in a menu macro.

In the shadow box routine, you saw GETPOINT and GETCORNER in action:

```
(setq ll (getpoint "Pick LL corner: ")
      ur (getcorner ll "Pick UR corner: ")
```

The `Pick LL corner:` is the GETPOINT prompt string. The LL value it gets is then used by GETCORNER as its base point for its rubber-band box. Try a couple of other input functions to get the hang of it. Type the input at the command line.

Using GET Functions for Input

Command: **(getangle "Enter angle: ")**
Enter angle: **30**　　　　　　　Or pick two points to show an angle.
Lisp returns: 0.523599　　　　AutoLISP uses and returns angles in radians, not degrees. There are 2 x pi radians in 360 degrees. One degree = 180/pi.

Command: **(* (getangle "Enter angle: ") (/ 180 pi))**　　　PI is predefined.
Enter angle: **30**
Lisp returns: 30.0

Command: **(setq pt1 (getpoint "Enter point: "))**　　　Save a point.
Enter point:　　　　　　　　　Pick a point.
Lisp returns: (2.0 2.0 0.0)

Command: **(getangle pt1 "Enter angle: ")**　　　Use pt1 as base point for rubber-banding.
Enter angle:　　　　　　　　　Pick a point.
Lisp returns: 0.96007

Command: **(getangle pt1 "Enter angle: ")**
Enter angle: **30**　　　　　　　Or you can type it.
Lisp returns: 0.523599

Command: **(getstring "Enter word: ")**
Enter word: **This**　　　　　　　The first <SPACE> enters it.
Lisp returns: "This"

Command: **(getstring T "Enter sentence: ")**   T is predefined.
Enter sentence: **This is a sentence.**   It allows <SPACES>.
Lisp returns: "This is a sentence."

Command: **(getcorner pt1 "Enter other corner: ")**   Use the base point, pt1.
Enter other corner: (5.4375 4.875 0.0)   It rubber-bands a rectangle.

For the default angular units settings, GETANGLE and GETORIENT are equivalent, but if the zero base angle or direction of increasing angles has been changed by UNITS, it's important to use the right function. Use GETORIENT for commands needing orientation (absolute angles), like TEXT. Use GETANGLE for commands needing rotation (relative angles), like INSERT.

If you followed the sequences above, you noticed that the input automatically becomes the data type requested. Invalid responses that are not the requested data type are rejected, as the GETDIST example below shows. GETSTRING will accept numbers as string data, and GETREAL will accept integers, but it converts the integers to floating-point reals. We usually use GETDIST instead of GETREAL because you can enter distance either by picking points, with optional rubber-banding, or by typing values. GETDIST treats distance as a real data type. You can input either decimal or current units, but the input is automatically converted to decimals.

Command: **(getdist "How big? ")**
How big? **HUGE**   Invalid input causes a reprompt.
Requires numeric distance or two points.
How big? **3**   Or you can pick two points.
Lisp returns: 3.0   A real.

If you use an integer, like 96, within an AutoLISP expression where it expects a real, like 96.0, AutoLISP converts it to 96.0. If you give an AutoLISP GETREAL or GETDIST function input like 96.0, 96. or 96, AutoLISP accepts and converts these values to 96.0. However, if you use a real within an AutoLISP expression that expects an integer, like the ITOA (Integer TO Ascii) function, it will cause an error.

GETPOINT always accepts 2D (X,Y) point input. However, it will return 3D (X,Y,Z) points if either of two conditions are met. If the FLATLAND system variable is set to 0 (meaning AutoCAD is in full 3D mode) or if the INITGET function initialized GETPOINT for 3D, it both accepts and returns 3D points. Recall that a point in AutoLISP is simply a list of two or three reals, like (1.5 2.0) or (1.5 2.0 6.75).

When to Use Base Point Arguments for Rubber-Banding

Base point arguments for GETDIST, GETANGLE, GETORIENT, and GETPOINT are optional. GETCORNER must have a base point. AutoCAD uses rubber-band lines on screen when you show a distance or angle by selecting points. Rubber-banding also lets you display a distance dynamically in the coordinates box on the screen. Remember that the distance<angle is displayed in the relative distance coords mode. The GETDIST, GETANGLE, GETORIENT, and GETPOINT functions all rubber band input when two points are input or a base point is set.

Placing a GET function without a base point in the middle of an ordinary AutoCAD command interferes with the normal command's rubber-banding because AutoLISP is in control, not AutoCAD. Try this:

Testing Rubber-Banding in Commands

```
Command: LINE
From point:                                 Pick a point.
To point: (setq pt (getpoint "Pick it: "))
Pick it:                                     Your rubber-banding is gone.
To point: (getpoint pt "Pick it: ")         Now it rubber-bands.
```

Use an optional base point when you need to tie the point down or when you need a rubber-banded GET function in the middle of an AutoCAD command. This will often be the case in your menu macros and programs.

Pausing GET Functions in Menu Macros

When you use the keyboard or a LISP file, the GET functions automatically pause for input. However in menu macros, you need to use the backslash character (\) for input pauses. Two AutoLISP GET functions pose problems when you use the backslash method of pause control because they can take either one or two pieces of data as input. The GETDIST and GETANGLE functions offer you a choice between picking two points or just typing the distance<angle. Typing the input requires one backslash. Picking two points requires two backslashes. If you use these functions, you need to plan ahead to prompt for the input format expected. This is not a problem for functions requiring base points because they need only typed input or one pick point.

Once you have some input, what do you do with it? It depends on what program you're writing, but you'll most probably do some math calculations.

Using Math Functions in AutoLISP

AutoLISP has several built-in math functions. In calculating the polyline width for the shadow box exercise, you added, subtracted, and divided. For example, remember the divide function in the expression:

```
(/ (setq tx (getvar "textsize")) 3)
```

This expression divided the text height by three to give you the polyline width value.

When you talk about AutoLISP functions, you say (+ 1 2) evaluates to 3. In algebra, the same function is expressed as 1 + 2 equals 3. This addition example has two arguments, both constants. But some AutoLISP math functions, like **+ - *** and **/**, can have any number of arguments. Other functions require a specific number or type of argument, and some take optional parameters or flags. Here is a list of AutoLISP math functions that you can use in your programs:

`math functions`

> **+** *returns the sum of all numbers, as integers or real numbers depending on the values.*
> **(+ number number . . .)**
>
> **-** *returns the difference of the first number subtracted from the sum of the remaining numbers. An integer or real number is returned, depending on the value.*
> **(– number number . . .)**
>
> ***** *returns the product of all numbers.*
> **(* number number . . .)**
>
> **/** *returns the quotient of the first number divided by the product of the remaining numbers.*
> **(/ number number . . .)**

Math functions accept either real or integer data types, but the data type returned depends on the rules of promotion. If all the arguments are integers, the results will be an integer and any fractional part will be dropped. However, if any argument is a real, integers will be promoted to reals and the result will be a real. Be careful to consider this or you may get bad argument errors in other functions.

You often need to do multiple calculations, which usually means nesting math functions. When nesting, remember that the evaluation order is innermost to outermost, left to right. If you have a variable used in two expressions at the same level, its value set in the left-hand expression is used in the right-hand expression.

Try some math functions at the command line and look at nesting.

Using AutoLISP Math Functions

Command: **(– 6 3 1)**   6 minus 3 minus 1.
Lisp returns: 2   All integers return an integer.

Command: **(+ 1 2.0)**   Returns a real.
Lisp returns: 3.0

Command: **(/ 3 2)**   Drops the .5 remainder.
Lisp returns: 1

Command: **(* 5 (– 7 2))**   The (- 7 2) expression is nested and evaluated first.
Lisp returns: 25

Command: **(setq a 1)**   Assigns the value 1 to a variable.
Lisp returns: 1

Command: **(+ (setq a (* a 3)) (+ a 2))**   Assigns the variable before the second expression.
Lisp returns: 8

Command: **(+ (+ a 2) (setq a (* a 3)))**   Uses the variable, then reassigns it.
Lisp returns: 14

So much for the basic math functions. Next is counting — the AutoLISP way.

How to Count in AutoLISP

Adding and subtracting by ones is called incrementing and decrementing. AutoLISP has special functions to increment or decrement a number more efficiently than by using the + and - functions. They are the **1+** and **1-** functions. These are often used to count iterations of a loop, say to step through the elements of a list one by one.

1+	*Returns number incremented by 1.* **(1+ *number*)**

1-	Returns number decremented by 1. (1- number)

Try the functions:

Incrementing and Decrementing Functions

Command: **(setq a (1+ 2))**   Increases 2 by one.
Lisp returns: 3

Command: **(setq a (1+ a))**   Increases variable A by one.
Lisp returns: 4

Command: **(setq a (1- a))**   Decreases variable A by one.
Lisp returns: 3

When counting in AutoLISP, some items are counted 0,1,2,3..., and some are counted 1,2,3,4..., so mind your zeros and ones.

How to Find Minimums and Maximums

In programs, you often need the minimum or maximum of a set of values. The functions which find them are:

min	Returns the lowest value in a series of numbers. (min number number ...)

max	Returns the highest value in a series of numbers. (max number number ...)

These are used to compare input or to find ranges of numbers. Try them:

Finding Ranges of Numbers With MIN and MAX

Command: **(min 17.0 23 93.3 -10 10.5)**   Returns minimum number of the set.
Lisp returns: -10

Command: **(max 17.0 23 93.3 -10 10.5)**   Returns maximum number of the set.
Lisp returns: 93.3

The range of our test list is -10 to 93.3.

Functions for Fractions

You'll need to work with fractional values. Say you need to format 179 inches as feet and inches. You can use integer division to get the feet, but you need a new function, REM, to get the inches. AutoLISP has two functions to work with remainders and denominators. They are:

gcd | *Returns the greatest common denominator of two integers.*
(gcd integer integer)

rem | *Returns the remainder of the first number divided by the product of the rest of the numbers.*
(rem number number . . .)

Try these at the keyboard:

Handling Fractions

Command: **(rem 12 3)**   3 goes into 12 evenly.
Lisp returns: 0.0

Command: **(/ 179 12)**   Determines the feet.
Lisp returns: 14
Command: **(rem 179 12)**   The remainder is the inches.
Lisp returns: 11

Command: **(gcd 12 20)**
Lisp returns: 4   The largest number you can divide 12 and 20 by.

How to Use Roots, Logs, Exponents, and Absolutes

The remaining AutoLISP math functions deal with exponential factors, logs, and square roots. Although used less frequently than the simple math functions, these are indispensable when the need arises. First, look at the square root, exponent, and the necessary absolute value functions.

sqrt | *Returns the square root of a number as a real.*
(sqrt number)

expt | *Returns the base number raised to the power number. The value returned is an integer or real number depending on the base and power values.*
(expt *base power***)**

abs | *Returns the absolute value of an integer or real number.*
(abs *number***)**

SQRT is straightforward except when it encounters a negative number. Then you need to convert it with ABS to avoid an error. Let's try these:

Finding Square Root, Exponent, and Absolute

Command: **(sqrt 4)**   Takes the square root of a 4.
Lisp returns: 2.0   Always returns a real.

Command: **(abs -4)**   Returns positive number.
Lisp returns: 4

Command: **(sqrt -120)**   Negatives cause errors.
Lisp returns: error: function undefined for argument
(SQRT -120)

Command: **(sqrt (abs -120))**   First convert it with ABS.
Lisp returns: 10.9545

Command: **(expt 2 3)**   Raises 2 to the third power.
Lisp returns: 8   Returns integer if both ARGs are integers.

Use ABS whenever you can't control or predict whether an argument to the SQRT function will be positive or negative.

But what do you do if you need the cubic (3rd), quadratic (4th), or any other root? And what do you use the last two math functions, the natural log and natural e exponent, for? Well, these two questions answered each other one day when we needed a cubic root to calculate a motor shaft. First, look at the functions, then we'll give you a general root expression.

exp | *Returns e raised to the power of number as a real.*
       | (exp *number*)

log | *Returns the natural log of the supplied number as a real.*
       | (log *number*)

How to Find Any Root

Command: **(log 64)**   Takes log of 64.
Lisp returns: 4.15888

Command: **(exp 4.15888)**   Raises *e* to power of 4.15888.
Lisp returns: 63.9998   That's 64 except for rounding off the argument 4.15888.

Command: **(exp (/ (log 64) 3))**   The cubic root of 64.
Lisp returns: 4.0

So you can use the expression (exp (/ (log number) root)) to find any root.

What about the inaccuracy we just observed in the EXP example?

A Word About Accuracy

The inaccuracy was because we typed the argument 4.15888, which was not the complete number. The good news is that although AutoLISP only shows six significant digits on the command line, it internally calculates to at least 14 significant digits. In a program, you would set and use the full accuracy in your variables, for example:

Command: **(setq a (log 64))**
Lisp returns: 4.15888

Command: **(exp a)**
Lisp returns: 64.0   The full accuracy.

The bad news is that there is still round-off error out at the 14th digit. If you ask if 64 and (exp (log 64)) are equal, AutoLISP will say no. When we get into the equality functions, we will show you how to deal with this.

That's about all there is to the math functions. Character strings are the next major data type.

The String Functions

In AutoLISP, a *string* can include any of the 256 ASCII characters. (You need ANSI.SYS in your CONFIG.SYS file for the characters from 128 to 255.) Most of the time you will just use the main alphanumeric and punctuation keys. Strings are commonly used to provide informational prompts, to create attribute data, and to write data to an external file. AutoCAD has one annoying limitation in strings. You can't directly set a variable to a string which exceeds 100 characters. The STRCAT function provides a solution.

Using STRCAT to Merge Strings

The STRCAT function takes any number of string arguments and combines them into a single string.

strcat

> *Returns a single string by combining all the supplied strings.*
> (strcat *string string* ...)

Try merging two strings:

Merging With STRCAT

Command: **(setq a "This is a long string that AutoLISP can't handle in a single bite because it exceeds 100 characters in length")**
Lisp returns: error: exceeded maximum string length.

Command: **(setq a "This is a longer string, but AutoLISP can handle it by building it in two bites, ")**
"This is a longer string, but AutoLISP can handle it by building it in two bites, "

Command: **(setq b "by using STRCAT to combine them into a single string.")**
Lisp returns: "by using STRCAT to combine them into a single string."

Command: **(setq a (strcat a b))**
"This is a longer string, but AutoLISP can handle it by building it in two bites, by using STRCAT to combine them into a single string."

Because string length is so variable, AutoLISP cannot anticipate the exact amount of memory required to store the string. This is why AutoLISP established the 100 character limit on string constants. Input to a GETSTRING function cannot exceed this limit and you can't have a literal "quoted string" longer than 100 characters in your programs.

A common reason for combining strings of text is to form prompts which provide defaults. For example, here is a way to provide the current layer name as a default in a prompt. Try building the prompt string using GETVAR with the STRCAT function.

How to Build Prompts

```
Command: (strcat "Enter layer name <" (getvar "clayer") ">: ")
Lisp returns: Enter layer name <0>:          The formatted string.
```

This example uses GETVAR to obtain the current layer and sandwich it between two strings to form the prompt string. The prompt, Enter layer name <0>:, shows the user the current layer name as a default.

Say we use this prompt in a GETSTRING and want to limit the input to certain layers. We need to control case.

Controlling Case With STRCASE

The STRCASE function has a simple role; it converts string case. Later, we will learn to test and compare data, but in dealing with strings, it helps to know whether you have upper, lower, or mixed case.

strcase | *Returns string converted to upper case unless the optional flag evaluates to T, which converts to lower case.*
(strcase *string* flag**)**

In most applications, you deal with strings as upper case, like this:

String Functions

```
Command: (setq il (getstring "Enter text: " T))
Enter text: Inside AutoLISP
Lisp returns: "Inside AutoLISP"


Command: (strcase il)          Force to upper case, the STRCASE default.
Lisp returns: "INSIDE AUTOLISP"


Command: (strcase il T)        Make it lower case by using a T flag.
Lisp returns: "inside autolisp"
```

In formatting prompts and file names, you sometimes need to break a string apart.

How to Get Portions of Strings

To extract a part of a string, you may need to know its length, which is returned by the STRLEN function. Then you can use the SUBSTR function to return a portion of a string.

strlen

> *Returns the number of characters in the string.*
> **(strlen** *string*)

substr

> *Returns the portion of a string from the start position number of the supplied string to either the end of the string or to the end of the number of characters specified by the optional length value.*
> **(substr** *string start* length)

SUBSTR takes three arguments: the string to dissect, the starting position of the first character you want, and the length of string to return. The length to return is an optional argument. If you do not specify a length, or if the length exceeds the string length, the remainder of the string is returned. If the start position exceeds the length, it returns nil. An example is in the exercise below.

Say you want to strip the file extension from a list of drawing files. They all end with ".DWG" but their lengths vary. The following exercise shows you how to go about it:

Command: **(substr "Inside AutoLISP" 8 4)**   Start at 8, 4 characters long.
Lisp returns: "Auto"

Command: **(setq fn "IL-PROTO.DWG")**
Lisp returns: "IL-PROTO.DWG"   A typical drawing file name.

Command: **(setq num (strlen fn))**   Get the length.
Lisp returns: 12

Command: **(substr fn 1 (- num 4))**   All but the last 4 characters.
Lisp returns: "IL-PROTO"

With SUBSTR, you can extract single characters. Now, how do you manipulate them?

Character Functions

Several AutoLISP functions operate on individual characters. These functions are useful for working with ASCII character codes. The character functions are:

chr | *Returns a single character string converted from its ASCII integer character code.*
(chr *integer*)

ascii | *Returns the first character of the string as an ASCII integer character code.*
(ascii *string*)

The character functions are case-sensitive because upper and lower cases have different ASCII codes. You can use CHR to put non-printing ASCII characters (such as control characters) into strings. You can also use it, along with STRCAT, to put a backslash in a menu string where it would otherwise make the menu pause. Give CHR and ASCII a try:

Using the CHR and ASCII Functions

Command: **(ascii "A")**
Lisp returns: 65   The ASCII integer code for capital A.

Command: **(ascii "a")**
Lisp returns: 97   The ASCII value for lower case a.

Command: **(chr 65)**
Lisp returns: "A"   A string.

Command: **(chr 2)**
Lisp returns: "\002"   The <^B> character.

Command: **(chr 47)**
Lisp returns: "/"   A slash character.

There are also several number-character conversion functions that will be covered in the chapter on communicating with AutoLISP.

➡ *NOTE: When AutoLISP returns an escape-coded character like \002, the number is the octal (base 8) ASCII value.*

The last of the major data types is the list, a key to AutoLISP.

How AutoLISP Lists Work

Although you will hear the common joke that says LISP is an acronym for "Lost-In-Stupid-Parentheses," it really stands for LISt Processing. All LISP languages, including AutoLISP, are based on the concept of a list of information. This is the important key to understanding AutoLISP.

A *list* is a group of elements of any data type, treated as one expression and stored as a single variable. An AutoLISP list may contain any number of reals, integers, strings, variables, or even other lists. Anything between an opening parenthesis and its corresponding closing parenthesis is a list. If this sounds hauntingly familiar, it is. Any expression is a list! Lists organize and process groups of information. Several system variables are lists. The LIMMAX (upper right limits) system variable, for example, is a list of reals — a point. You've already seen an LL point list, like (2.0 1.0 0.0), in the previous chapter's shadow box program. Points are among the most common elements of lists. You will also use lists to organize, access, and manipulate data.

Points Are AutoLISP Lists

Command: **(getvar "LIMMAX")**
Lisp returns: (11.0 8.5)   The upper right point of the limits.

Other examples of AutoLISP lists are ("A" "B") and ("NAME" "10.0" "DESK" "WS291A"), a list of strings, and ((1 2) (3 4) (5 6)), a list of lists.

➡ *NOTE: Curiously, nil is a list. Nil is both an atom and an empty list, ( ). Although many expressions evaluate to nil, ( ) is nil.*

How to Use List Functions

AutoLISP has many list manipulation functions. The shadow box uses the functions LIST, CAR, and CADR. LIST is simple. It just makes a list from the data you give.

`list`	Returns a list constructed from the supplied expression(s). **(list** *expression*)

Let's make some lists in AutoLISP.

Making Lists

```
Command: (list 1.0 "ABC" 3)
Lisp returns: (1.0 "ABC" 3)                    The list has real, string, and integer members.

Command: (list 1.0 "ABC" 3 (list "DEF" 4 2.0))        Put a list inside a list.
Lisp returns: (1.0 "ABC" 3 ("DEF" 4 2.0))  Lists can contain elements of other lists.
```

Since a list is a group of elements, you need a way to extract the element that you want.

Extracting Elements From Lists

You may want the first element of a list, the second, or the last. Or you may want all the elements but the first. AutoLISP provides the CAR family of functions to do this.

car
> *Returns the first element in the list. Use CAR to extract the X coordinate of a point list.*
> **(car *list*)**

cdr
> *Returns a list minus the first element in the list.*
> **(cdr *list*)**

cadr
> *Returns the second element in the list. Use CADR to extract the Y coordinate of a point list.*
> **(cadr *list*)**

caddr
> *Returns the third element in the list. Use CADDR to extract the Z coordinate of a point list.*
> **(cadr *list*)**

Once you have a point variable, or data stored in a list, these are the functions you use to manipulate it. You used CAR and CADR in the shadow box exercises. The similar CDR returns a list of all elements of the list except the first. Let's try them again, and translate a point list from the X,Y plane to the X,Z plane.

Using the CAR, CADR, CADDR and LIST Functions

```
Command: (setq pt1 (getpoint "Pick point: "))
Pick point: 2,3                    Enter the point.
Lisp returns: (2.0 3.0 0.0)  The Z component is 0.0 by default.

Command: (car pt1)                 Get the first element.
Lisp returns: 2.0                  The X component, a real is returned.

Command: (cdr pt1)                 Get all but the first element.
Lisp returns: (3.0 0.0)            A list is returned. The X component is omitted.

Command: (cadr pt1)                Get the second element.
Lisp returns: 3.0                  The Y component, another real is returned.

Command: (caddr pt1)               Get the third element.
Lisp returns: 0.0                  The Z component.

Command: (setq pt2 (list (car pt1) (caddr pt1) (cadr pt1)))   Reorder the original as X,Z,Y.
Lisp returns: (2.0 0,0 3.0)  It's a list, putting the original Y in the Z slot.

Command: LINE                      Try using the points.
From point: !pt1                   From 2,3,0.
To point: !pt2                     To 2,0,3.
To point: <RETURN>
```

Remember that the CDR function returns a list of all elements *except* the first element. There are other variations of the CAR family of functions such as CAAR, CDAR, and CADAR. In fact, combinations of up to four A's and D's can be used between the C and R to get elements of lists or lists within lists as shorthand for nesting CAR's and CDR's. For example, (cdar list) is equivalent to (cdr (car list)). Just as nested functions are processed from inner to outer, the A's and D's are "processed" from *right* to *left*, the same order that they are processed when nested. For instance, in CDAR, the A, representing CAR, returns its result to the D, representing CDR. Let's look at another way to build lists.

Using the QUOTE Function to Build Lists

The QUOTE function, which can be abbreviated as a single quotation mark, is also important. Unlike the LIST function which evaluates its contents before forming a list, QUOTE suppresses the evaluation of its expression(s). When it forms a list, it includes its contents literally.

quote	*Returns the expression without evaluation; a ' does the same function.* (quote *expression*)

Let's look again at LIST, CAR, CADR, the similar CDR, and at the QUOTE functions. Type the following input at the command line to see how these functions work.

Quoted Lists

Command: **(setq q 3.0)**
Lisp returns: 3.0

Command: **(list q r s)**   Evaluates Q and R and S as it creates the list.
Lisp returns: (3.0 nil nil)   Q is 3.0, R and S are unassigned symbols (variables) with value nil.

Command: **(quote (q r s))**   Returns the symbols unevaluated.
Lisp returns: (Q R S)

Command: **(setq test '(q r s))**   QUOTE abbreviated.
Lisp returns: (Q R S)

You can't begin input at the AutoCAD command prompt with ', spell it out as (quote ... instead. You can use the single quotation mark anywhere in an AutoLISP file.

Use LIST to build a list when all arguments are numbers, strings, or variables whose *contents* you want in the list. Use QUOTE when you want the *symbol* (variable name) instead of its contents, or when you want a function name in the list. You use QUOTE to create lists for later evaluation. QUOTE can also be applied to a single element, like (quote item) or 'Q.

Once you have created a list with LIST or QUOTE, you may need to extract one or more elements that are beyond the reach of the CAR family.

Indexed Elements: the NTH and LAST Functions

The CAR family cannot reach deep into a list unless you nest several of its functions. Nesting the CAR family is confusing. Instead, you can use the NTH function to access any element of a list, and the LAST function to return the last element of any list.

last
Returns the last element in a list.
(last *list*)

nth | *Returns the item specified by the integer position in a list. It returns nil if the integer position exceeds the list length.*
(nth *integer list*)

The NTH begins counting at zero, not one. It counts 0,1,2,3..., *not* 1,2,3.... Starting with zero is typical computer counting. Watch your zeros and ones carefully with AutoLISP functions. All AutoLISP functions do not count the same way. Take a closer look at the NTH and LAST functions.

Looking at NTH and LAST

Command: **(setq test '("ABC" 1.0 "DEF" 2 3 4 "END"))**   Make a list.
Lisp returns: ("ABC" 1.0 "DEF" 2 3 4 "END")   Returns the list.

Command: **(nth 2 test)**   Gets the third element.
Lisp returns: "DEF"   The element.

Command: **(last test)**   Gets the last element.
Lisp returns: "END"   It's an element.

Sometimes, to access a list efficiently, you need to know its length or reverse its order. Other times, you need to add to existing lists as you build data.

Ordering, Adding To, and Reversing Lists

You can change the order, add to a list and find out how many elements are in a list with AutoLISP. REVERSE flips the order of the list. LENGTH returns its length. APPEND takes any number of arguments, each a list, and merges them into a single list. MEMBER returns a sublist starting with the specified item. CONS adds a new first element to a list.

reverse | *Returns a list of items reversed from the order of the supplied list.*
(reverse *list*)

length | *Returns the number of elements in a list.*
(length *list*)

append | *Returns a single list made up of any number of lists.*
(append *list ...*)

member | *Returns the remainder of the list starting at the item if it is found. Otherwise returns nil.*
(member *item list*)

cons | *Returns a new list with the first item as the new first element of a list, if the second item is supplied as the list. If the second item is not a list, it returns a dotted pair, in the form (item . item).*
(cons *item item*)

Try each of these functions at the keyboard.

Restructuring Lists

Command: **(setq test '("ABC" 1.0 "DEF" (2 3 4) "GHI"))**   Make your list again.
Lisp returns: ("ABC" 1.0 "DEF" (2 3 4) "GHI")   Returns the list.

Command: **(length test)**   Get its length.
Lisp returns: 5   There are 7 members in the list.

Command: **(member "DEF" test)**   Returns "DEF" and the rest
Lisp returns: ("DEF" (2 3 4) "GHI")   of the list.

Command: **(reverse test)**   Reverse the order.
Lisp returns: ("GHI" (2 3 4) "DEF" 1.0 "ABC")   Only the elements are reversed, not their contents.

Command: **(setq test (append test '("JKL" 5 6)))**   Add a list to the list.
Lisp returns: ("ABC" 1.0 "DEF" (2 3 4) "GHI" "JKL" 5 6)   Returns the new list.

Command: **(cons "START" test)**   Add a new first element.
Lisp returns: ("START" "ABC" 1.0 "DEF" (2 3 4) "GHI" "JKL" 5 6)   Returns the new list.

Command: **(cons 1 2)**   Creates a valid dotted pair.
Lisp returns: (1 . 2)

A dotted pair is a special kind of list that you will need to use to access drawing database entities. Some list functions, such as LENGTH, do not accept dotted pairs.

Now that you have worked with the basic AutoLISP functions, you may want to know how to create your own. As you will see, defining your own functions is creating a special form of list.

Defining Your Own Functions in AutoLISP

AutoLISP functions are created and defined with the DEFUN (DEFine-FUNction) function. You can pass data into the function, manipulate and use the data with your function's program statements, and then pass the data back to AutoLISP and AutoCAD.

defun | *Creates a function with a given name. The argument list can supply variables to be passed to the function. Argument list variables following an optional slash are variables that are local to the function. The function will evaluate the program statement(s) and return the result of the last expression evaluated. Prefixing a C: to the function name will create a lisp command that acts like a standard AutoCAD command. Defining an S::STARTUP function in the ACAD.LSP file will create an automatic executing function.*
(defun *name* **(***argument* ... **/** *local* ...**)** *expression* ...**)**

DEFUN defines a function by constructing a structured list of the program statements. Here is the general format and an example of a DEFUN statement.

```
GENERAL FORMAT                EXAMPLE
(defun NAME (ARGUMENTS)       (defun greeting (name age)
    PROGRAM STATEMENTS...          (prompt "Hello ")
                                   (prompt name)
                                   (prompt " today you are ")
                                   (prompt age)
)                             )
```

The *name* of a function can be any name you wish, using upper, lower, or mixed case characters. Like variable names, avoid using reserved names from the ATOMLIST. If you use a reserved name, you will redefine the original AutoLISP function. If you do redefine an AutoLISP function, the original meaning will be unavailable until you start a new drawing. Like variable names, certain characters should not be used as or within function names. To review, these illegal and ill-advised characters are:

```
RESERVED AND ILLEGAL CHARACTERS:   .  '  "  ;  ( )  or  <SPACE>
AutoLISP FUNCTIONS:   ~ * = > < + - /
ILL-ADVISED CHARACTERS: ?  `  !  \  ^  or any control character.
```

If you put the reserved characters '"; ( ) immediately after a function or variable name without an intervening space, they will not be recognized correctly. To avoid confusion, don't use any reserved characters as part of a function name, and don't input them directly after a name without an intervening space.

Arguments are variables used to refer to the data passed into the function. The number of arguments must match the number of pieces of data passed to the function. The arguments are assigned in order, left to right, to the values supplied. Functions defined with the C: prefix do not accept arguments. They generally use GET functions to acquire data.

Program *statements* are the core of your function. Program statements follow the general rules of AutoLISP evaluation. The results of the last-evaluated statement are returned from the function.

In the previous chapter, you created several [BUBBLE] macros, which had the limitation of being accessible only from the menu. Using DEFUN to create a function gives it the advantage of being accessible from the keyboard. DEFUNs can also be put in macros. The shadow box program you made required loading each time you wished to execute it. While loading per execution is memory-efficient for infrequently used routines, it adds load time to each use of frequently used programs. DEFUNs, once loaded, are available until the drawing is ended.

Write a function with DEFUN. Go into your text editor and create a new file named BUBBLE.LSP, typing in the statements exactly as shown below. Check your parentheses carefully. Although indenting the statements has no effect on the program, it makes them easier to read. Use spaces to indent instead of tabs. The BUBBLE function is a remake of the original [BUBBLE] macro from the previous chapter. If you have the IL DISK, you already have the BUBBLE.LSP file.

This program saves the current layer with GETVAR, then gets the point input. A rubber-band line is activated during the second point selection by including a base point in the GET expression. It draws a circle and line on the OBJ01 layer, then puts the bubble text on layer TXT01. The last step resets the layer to the original layer.

```
;C:BUBBLE command
(prompt "Please wait. Loading BUBBLE command...")
(defun C:BUBBLE ()
  (setq la (getvar "CLAYER")
        pt1 (getpoint "Centerpoint: ")
        pt2 (getpoint "Endpoint: " pt1)
  );setq
  (command "LAYER" "M" "OBJ01" ""
           "LINE" pt1 pt2 ""
           "CIRCLE" pt1 0.25
           "TRIM" "L" "" pt1 ""
           "LAYER" "M" "TXT01" ""
  );command
  (setq txt (getstring "Text: "))
  (command "TEXT" "S" "STANDARD" "M" pt1 0.25 0 txt "LAYER" "S" la "")
);defun
```

BUBBLE Command Function in BUBBLE.LSP File

In this format, the value of indenting expressions becomes obvious. It's easy to see the beginning and end of each expression.

To test the program, you need to load it into AutoCAD.

Loading a LISP Function File

When loading a function file, AutoLISP reads the function definitions and stores them in memory, but doesn't execute them. AutoLISP won't execute the user-defined functions within the file until it is explicitly instructed to execute them. However, expressions in the file, like the prompt (prompt "Please wait. Loading BUBBLE command..."), are executed while loading.

Use AutoLISP's LOAD function to load function files. (AutoCAD's LOAD command loads shape definitions.) AutoLISP's LOAD automatically assumes the file extension .LSP unless you give it another extension.

Now let's load the new BUBBLE command.

Using the BUBBLE Command

 You have the BUBBLE command in your BUBBLE.LSP file.

Create the BUBBLE command as shown above in a file named BUBBLE.LSP.

`Command: ZOOM`	Left corner 0,0 with height 4.
`Command: (load "bubble")`	Loads the file BUBBLE.LSP.
`Please wait. Loading BUBBLE command...`	You'll get this message.
`Command: BUBBLE`	Start the command.
`Centerpoint:`	Pick first point at **2,2**.
`Endpoint:`	Next point at **2,6**.
	Commands scroll, it draws a circle, a line and trims, then:
`Text: A`	Enter some text.
	And it restores the original layer.
`Command: QUIT`	

Documenting LISP Functions

The BUBBLE function is a simple example of a LISP function. As you become more efficient with AutoLISP, you will quickly collect a library of LISP functions and files. A large number of your programs will have many lines of expressions. Adding informative comments and using indentation to show function structure can make managing your LISP functions an easier task.

Examine the BUBBLE function below. It is identical to the previous function except for added comments. The beginning comment has been expanded to provide more information about what the function does. The comments following each expression explain its purpose.

```
;* C:BUBBLE draws a grid bubble and line on layer OBJ01,
;* the bubble text is provided by the user and drawn on layer TXT01.
(prompt "Please wait. Loading BUBBLE command...")
(defun C:BUBBLE ()
  (setq la (getvar "CLAYER")              ;Save current layer
        pt1 (getpoint "Centerpoint: ")    ;Get centerpoint of bubble
        pt2 (getpoint "Endpoint: " pt1)   ;Get endpoint of line
  );setq
  (command "LAYER" "M" "OBJ01" ""         ;Make layer OBJ01
           "LINE" pt1 pt2 ""              ;Draw grid line
           "CIRCLE" pt1 0.25             ;Draw grid circle
```

Listing continued.

Continued listing.

```
         "TRIM" "L" "" ptl ""                    ;Trim line inside circle
         "LAYER" "M" "TXT01" ""                  ;Make layer OBJ02
  );command
  (setq txt (getstring "Text: "))               ;Get bubble text
  (command "TEXT" "S" "STANDARD" "M" ptl 0.25 0 txt "LAYER" "S" la "")  ;Draw bubble text
);defun
;*
```

Documented BUBBLE Command Function

Adding a comment to a function gives you a clear picture of its purpose and how it is accomplished. An additional feature we have adopted is to use the asterisk (*) at the beginining of major comments. The DOS FIND command can be used to print every comment that begins with ;* without opening the file. This provides us with an easy way to examine our LISP files. For example, type the following at the DOS prompt:

```
FIND ";*" BUBBLE.LSP
```

If you have several functions defined in a file, the extra ;* at the end of each function provides a space between comments displayed by the FIND command. Later, we will introduce a custom utility that expands this feature.

This form of documentation is used throughout the rest of the book. We have kept it simple to save space. In your own program listings, you may want to include more information such as date; programmer's name; revision description; and support files, LISP subroutines, and global variables required by the function.

Annotating your functions may seem like a lot of effort now, but if you ever have to analyze a year-old, 300-line program, you'll be glad you did.

Summary

At this point, you've seen all the basic AutoLISP functions. You know the different variable types, how to use AutoLISP to get and set system variables, how to create your own variables, and how to define your own functions. You've met the GET family and learned quite a bit about using AutoLISP to make mathematic manipulations. Above all, you've mastered the important concept of lists, and you've learned to make them do your bidding through the CAR functions. You have the tools — now it's time to work on technique. The next chapter concentrates on adding a little body and structure to your programs.

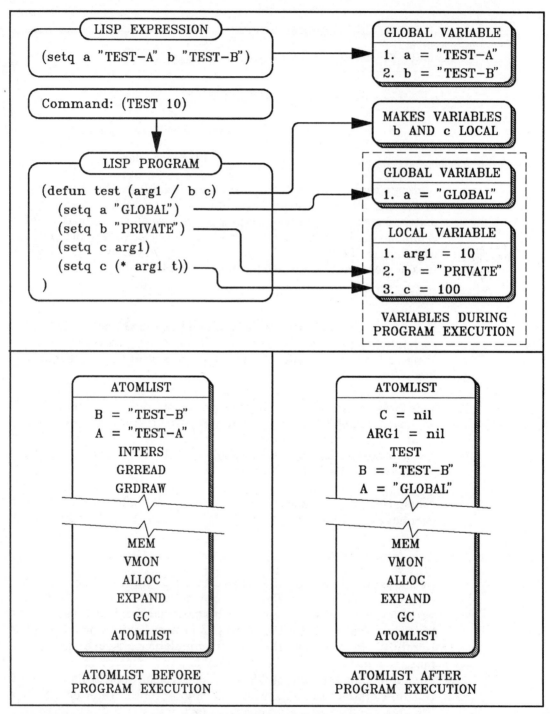

AutoLISP LOCALS, GLOBALS, and the ATOMLIST

CHAPTER 4

Understanding Program Flow

STRUCTURING AUTOLISP PROGRAMS

AutoLISP is a dialect of the LISP language, derived from XLISP. AutoLISP is actually a separate program that coexists with the AutoCAD program under the operating system. AutoLISP passes data and instructions to and from AutoCAD. An AutoLISP program is actually a list of *data*. How you structure and process the list is the topic of this chapter. By making a list containing functions, strings, integers, and real numbers, you make a simple program.

To go beyond simple programs, you need ways to make decisions and control the flow of information and commands in your programs. In this chapter, you will see the basic functions that create test conditions, make logical decisions, and make loops and repeats in program flow. This flow, or direction, is set by the way you organize your program statements using AutoLISP's logical functions and relational operators.

You will also learn to organize and control your variables and defined functions. AutoLISP manages variables and functions with the ATOMLIST. It's important to distinguish between global and local variables in AutoLISP programs to prevent one program from unintentionally confusing another. We will delve deeper into function definitions and discuss when and why to use them as subroutines to form large programs.

There are a number of ways to control program flow. You can use nil and non-nil to test values, and you can use logical functions like AND and OR or relational functions like LESS THAN and EQUAL TO. You can make looping programs to construct data lists using AutoLISP's REPEAT function. AutoLISP's FOREACH function enables you to batch process data lists. You can also use subroutines and recursive routines to control program flow.

AutoLISP Tools and Programs

AutoLISP Tools

GETPTS is a subroutine that builds a list of points.

DIAM is a GET diameter function that presents the previous diameter as a default.

AutoLISP Programs

SLOT draws solid slotted holes. It asks for the center of the slot, the slot diameter and the slot length, and uses a polyline to fill in the slotted area.

DRAW constructs a list of points, processes the list, and places circles at each point.

The SLOT program illustrates how to manage local and global variables. DRAW is used to demonstrate subroutines and recursive programming.

Conditional Testing

Every program follows a direction or flow. The programs in the previous chapters had linear flows — from one step to the next with no options. Most programs are more complex, with options, choices, and forks in their streams. Program flow is determined by testing conditions within the program. After a condition is tested, the program branches or flows to a specific portion of the program. Branching directs the flow of your AutoLISP program.

Conditional statements are your tools for controlling the branching of your AutoLISP programs. A simple conditional branch might be *if* **test** is true, **then** do this, **else** do that.

The test values in AutoLISP always evaluate to *nil* and *T* (true, non-nil). If something has no value, it's *nil*. If it has a value, it's *T*. AutoLISP's logical functions work on a nil and non-nil basis. In testing, true means that as long as there is some value, the test is *passed*. Since everything in AutoLISP is either nil or has a value, any expression can act as a test.

Logical and relational functions compare values and return the results that branching functions use as their tests.

Logical Functions

A *logical* function determines how one or more items are compared. The basis for comparison is whether something is true or nil. Logical functions return either *T* for non-nil or *nil* for false. The basic logical functions are AND, OR, and NOT.

and

> Returns T if all expressions are true, otherwise returns nil and ceases evaluation at the first nil expression encountered.
> `(and expression ...)`

or

> Returns T if one of the expressions is true. Otherwise returns nil or ceases evaluation at the first true expression encountered.
> `(or expression ...)`

not

> NOT is simple. It takes a single argument and returns the opposite. NOT returns T if its argument is nil; and returns nil if its argument is non-nil.
> `(not item)`

The table below gives examples for the logical functions. As you look at the table, A and B are T (non-nil) and C is nil.

LOGICAL FUNCTIONS	WILL RETURN
(and a b c)	nil
(and a b)	T
(and b (getpoint "Pick: "))	Depends on input
(or c a b)	T
(or c)	nil
(not (or a b))	nil
(not c)	T

AutoLISP Logical Functions

Both the AND and the OR functions can take any number of arguments. The AND function returns T if all its arguments have values (non-nil), otherwise, it returns nil. The OR function returns T if any of its arguments has a value, otherwise it returns nil. OR stops evaluating and returns T as soon as it sees the first non-nil atom. In the same way, AND quits evaluating and returns nil as soon as it encounters a nil argument.

Reading this carefully explains why, with no arguments, (and) is T, but (or) is nil!

Be careful when you put other functions inside AND or OR. Whether an argument is evaluated depends on the values of preceding arguments. In the GETPOINT example below, AND will return T if any point is input, or nil if a <RETURN> is entered. However, if B was nil, the GETPOINT would never even be evaluated.

Try a few hands-on examples. First set some variables, then try the logical functions.

Looking At Logical Functions

Command: **(setq a "MARY" b 36)**	Returns 36.
Command: **!stuff** *Lisp returns:* nil	This should be nil.
Command: **(and b (getpoint "Pick: "))** Pick: *Lisp returns:* nil	All must be non-nil to return T. Hit a <RETURN>. GETPOINT returned nil and so must AND.
Command: **(and b (getpoint "Pick: "))** Pick: *Lisp returns:* T	Pick a point. GETPOINT returned T and so must AND.
Command: **(and stuff (getpoint "Pick: "))** *Lisp returns:* nil	Only asks for a point if STUFF is non-nil. Getpoint is not evaluated.
Command: **(or 1 a stuff)** *Lisp returns:* T	Only one needs to be non-nil.
Command: **(or stuff (getpoint "Pick: "))** Pick: *Lisp returns:* T	STUFF is nil, but OR keeps looking for a non-nil item. Pick a point. Getpoint made OR return T.
Command: **(not stuff)** *Lisp returns:* T	Reverses sense of value.

As we've said, whether a function that is nested inside an AND or OR argument gets evaluated depends on the values of preceding arguments. However, you can use this to your advantage.

AND and OR are often used to prevent errors. For example, math functions given nil input fail with bad arguments. If you put the calculation inside a logical function, you can first verify its arguments.

NOT simply reverses the sense of nil and true. It always returns the opposite of its argument. Some functions, such as PROMPT, always return nil. Nesting such functions in a NOT allows you to place them harmlessly in the path of an AND.

Error and Input Control With AND, OR, and NOT

```
Command: (setq c (+ stuff 3))              STUFF is not a number, it's nil.
Lisp returns: error: bad argument type
(+ STUFF 3)
(SETQ C (+ STUFF 3))


Command: (and stuff (setq c (+ stuff 3)))  Check it first.
Lisp returns: nil                          No error.
Command: !c
Lisp returns: nil                          But C doesn't get set.


Command: (and (or stuff (setq stuff (getint "Gimme stuff: ")))
1> (setq c (+ stuff 3)))
Gimme stuff: 6                             Enter an integer.
Lisp returns: T
Command: !c                               Check C.
Lisp returns: 9


Command: (and c (prompt "Setting STUFF to C... ") (setq stuff c))
Lisp prompts and returns: Setting STUFF to C... nil
Command: !stuff            Check STUFF. It wasn't reset to C because
Lisp returns: 6            the SETQ wasn't reached since PROMPT returned nil.


Command: (and c (not (prompt "Setting STUFF to C... ")) (setq stuff c)) Try a NOT.
Lisp prompts and returns: Setting STUFF to C... T
Command: !stuff           Check STUFF.
Lisp returns: 9
```

As you see, you can put GET functions inside a logical function, but to use the input values, you have to add SETQs to the expressions.

Logical functions test only for a T (non-nil) value. They do not allow a comparison of values. Use relational functions to perform this type of test.

Relational Functions

A *relational* function evaluates the relationship between two or more items. Like logical functions, relational operators return either a T if the expression is true (non-nil), or nil if the expression is false. Relational operations include: *less than, greater than, equal to,* and *not equal to.*

Relationals

eq returns T if the first variable expression is identically bound to the second variable. Otherwise returns nil.
`(eq variable variable)`

equal returns T if the first expression is equal to the second expression. Otherwise returns nil. The optional accuracy (fuzz) value determines how accurate two numbers must be to be considered equal.
`(equal expression expression accuracy)`

= returns T if atoms are numerically equal, otherwise returns nil. Only numbers and strings are valid.
`(= atom atom ...)`

/= returns T if atoms are numerically not equal, otherwise returns nil. Only numbers and strings are valid.
`(/= atom atom)`

< returns T if each atom is numerically less than the following atom, otherwise returns nil. Only numbers and strings are valid.
`(< atom atom ...)`

<= returns T if each atom is numerically less than or equal to the following atom, otherwise returns nil. Only numbers and strings are valid.
`(<= atom atom ...)`

> returns T if each atom is numerically greater than the following atom, otherwise returns nil. Only numbers and strings are valid.
`(> atom atom ...)`

>= returns T if each atom is numerically greater than or equal to the following atom, otherwise returns nil. Only numbers and strings are valid.
`(>= atom atom ...)`

Generally, the arguments given to relational functions may be any data type.

Except for EQ, EQUAL, = and /=, these relational operators may have multiple arguments, comparing the first argument to all other arguments.

When to Use EQ, =, and EQUAL

The equal functions have different applications. Use the = character for numbers (unless round-off error causes inequality) and strings. Use EQ to test items that are identical (bound to the same object with SET or SETQ). EQUAL can test the equivalency of items that evaluate to the same value, and also works well for round-off filtering. In the following examples, X is '(A B C), Y is 1.5 and Z also is '(A B C).

EXAMPLE	READ AS	RETURNS
(< 2 y)	2 is less than Y — false	nil
(> 2 y 3)	2 is greater than Y or 3 — false	nil
(<= 1.5 y)	1.5 is less than or equal to Y	T
(>= 2 y)	2 is greater than or equal to Y	T
(= 1.5 y)	1.5 is equal to Y	T
(equal 1.5 y)	1.5 evaluates to same as Y	T
(eq z x)	Z is identical to X — false	nil
(equal z x)	Z evaluates to same as X	T
(/= 2 y)	2 is not equal to y	T

AutoLISP Relational Functions

Try a couple of the relational functions at the keyboard.

Using Relational Functions

Command: **(setq a 65 b 66)**
Lisp returns: 66   The last atom SETQed.

Command: **(< a b)**   Is A less than B?
Lisp returns: T   Yes.

Command: **(= a (ascii "A"))**   Is variable A equivalent to character A?
Lisp returns: T   Yes, the ASCII number for A is 65.

Command: **(= nil ' ())**
Lisp returns: T   Remember nil is the empty list.

Round-Off Error

The EQUAL function has a *fuzz factor* that can be used to deal with round-off in math calculations. Although AutoLISP internally calculates to at least fourteen significant digits, the round-off of the least significant digit often prevents = and EQ from seeing equals as equal. EQUAL's fuzz factor solves this. Try a comparison.

How to Filter Round-Off

Command: **(setq a (sqrt 10))**   Test square root of 10.
Lisp returns: 3.16228   Internally, AutoLISP uses 3.162277660168379523.

Command: **(setq b (expt a 2))**   A squared.
Lisp returns: 10.0

Command: **(= b 10)**   Are they equal?
Lisp returns: nil   No. Even 3.162277660168379523 was rounded off.

Command: **(equal b 10 0.00000000001)**   Test it with 10 decimals accuracy.
Lisp returns: T   They're *equal*.

When you debug your programs, watch for round-off causing unexpected results. See the next chapter for another way of handling round-off, using RTOS. The RTOS method is better for deliberate rounding off during calculations.

Testing conditions in a program is only useful if you can make the program react to the conditions. Relationals are most commonly used to control the branching functions of your programs.

Branching Functions

AutoLISP has two branching functions, IF and COND. All branching conditions need a conditional test to perform a branch. These conditional test expressions usually use *logical* and *relational* functions, but a conditional test may use any AutoLISP expression, even a single variable.

The IF Function

The simplest and most frequently used program branching function is the IF function, sometimes called *if-then-else*. In plain English, AutoLISP thinks, "If the condition is T, then execute the first expression, else (if it is nil) execute the second expression."

if | *If the test is not nil, the first expression is evaluated. If the test is nil, the optional second expression is evaluated. The function returns the value of the evaluated expression.*
(if ***test expression*** *expression***)**

For example, here is a simple IF expression:

```
(if test "YES" "NO")
```

```
EXAMPLE            IF TEST IS
(if test
  "YES"            true, then returns:   "YES"
  "NO"             nil, else returns:    "NO"
)
```

IF has two possible paths in the example above. Assume the variable TEST has a value. The IF condition test is true and the *then* statement is executed, which returns the value of "YES." The *else* statement, an optional statement of the IF structure, is executed only when the condition is not true.

Try a hands-on function which prompts for Yes or No and executes the correct response.

Trying IF

```
Command: (defun C:TEST ()
1> (setq ans (getstring "Are you ready to go yet? Y/N? "))
1> (if (or (= ans "y")(= ans "Y")) (prompt "Good - THEN come on.")
2> (prompt  "ELSE stay home!")))
Lisp returns: C:TEST

Command: TEST
Are you ready to go yet? (Y/N) Y        Enter Y.
Good - THEN come on.nil
Command: TEST
Are you ready to go yet? (Y/N) N        Enter N.
ELSE stay home!nil
```

Notice how OR dealt with upper and lower case. As an alternative, you could have used (= (strcase ans) "Y").

IF is restricted to simple either-or situations with a single *then* and a single *else* expression. Later in this chapter, we'll use a function called PROGN to program around this.

You can nest IFs and combine them with ANDs and ORs to deal with more complex options. Nested IFs, ANDs, and ORs may be efficient, but they can make programming complicated. The COND function provides an easy-to-understand alternative.

The COND Structure: A Multiple IF

COND works much like IF, except COND can evaluate any number of test conditions. Think of COND as a multiple IF routine. The general format is shown below.

```
(cond
  (first test-condition  first statements ... )
  (second test-condition second statements ... )
  ... more tests and statements ...
  (T last-statements ... )
)
```

The COND function evaluates each test condition until it evaluates a test condition that is non-nil. COND then processes the statement(s) associated with that condition. COND only processes the statements of the first non-nil condition.

cond
> *Evaluates expression(s) of the first non-nil test. Any number of (test expression...) lists are scanned for the test case. The value of the last-evaluated expression is returned. COND ceases further evaluation after finding a non-nil condition or after completing the list of tests.*
> **(cond (test expression ...) ...)**

COND takes any number of lists as its arguments. Each argument must contain a test followed by the expressions to be evaluated. COND interprets the first item of each list as that list's test condition. It evaluates all expressions within the first non-nil list.

Since COND looks for the first non-nil condition, you want to make sure you test the most likely conditions before you test the least likely conditions. Putting your most likely non-nil conditions first increases your program's speed. The COND function is a good way to make programs branch based on a series of conditions. You can make the last test a test that is always non-nil, like the symbol T. Then its expression will be evaluated if none of the others is non-nil. This is a good place for an error prompt or a statement that lets you know that the conditions weren't evaluated.

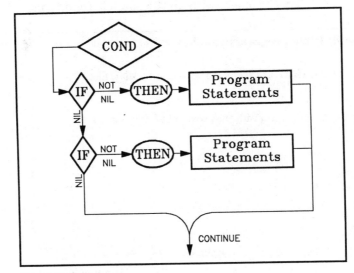

The COND Structure

```
[FITTING]^C^C^C+
(setq ans (strcase (getstring "Fitting type (E90/E45/RED/TEE): ")));\+
(cond ((not ans) (prompt "Error: No fitting type entered.^M"));+
((= ans "E90") (prompt "Ninety deg elbow.^M"));+
((= ans "E45") (prompt "Forty-five deg elbow.^M"));+
((= ans "RED") (prompt "Reducer.^M"));+
((= ans "TEE") (prompt "Tee, non-reducing.^M"));+
(ans (prompt "Error: Unknown fitting type.^M"));+
);
```

The [FITTING] COND Macro in IL04.MNU

The COND structure above has six branches or directions in which the program may go. The first condition tests to see if you have entered a value. Notice that it uses NOT to reverse the sense of the atom. Then a series of equality tests are made to determine which fitting type is entered. Finally, if no matching type is found, yet the variable ANS has a value, the unknown fitting error is returned.

The [FITTING] macro uses the STRCASE function to force its test argument to upper case. This eliminates your need to check upper and lower case entries.

Try the macro with all the possible conditions.

Using COND for Multiple Program Branches

  You have the [FITTING] COND macro in your IL04.MNU file.

  Create an IL04.MNU menu with the above [FITTING] macro.

```
Command: MENU                                Load IL04.

Select [FITTING]
Fitting type (E90/E45/RED/TEE): RED          It all scrolls by, then:
Reducer.
Lisp returns: nil

Select [FITTING]
Fitting type (E90/E45/RED/TEE): <RETURN>     Try other variations.
Error: Unknown fitting type.                 The ANS variable is nil.
Lisp returns: nil
```

COND allows you to test input for a variety of choices and act upon the choices. But how can you control the program if invalid input is entered and none of the conditions are true? You can loop and retry. Next we'll learn about making a program loop.

Program Looping

Like many other programming languages, AutoLISP has several methods to cause a series of program steps to loop, or execute repeatedly. You can use these looping structures to reduce the number of statements in the program, continue a routine until a user action terminates it, converge on a mathematical solution, verify input, or batch process a list of data. These tools are the REPEAT, WHILE, and FOREACH functions.

The REPEAT Function

AutoLISP's REPEAT function is a simple looping structure. Consider using REPEAT if your macros need to repeat some task a specific number of times. The REPEAT function executes any number of statements the specified number of times. All expressions get evaluated once each loop. REPEAT returns the value of the last expression on the last loop.

repeat
> *Evaluates each expression by the number of times specified. Number must be an integer.*
> (repeat *number expression* ...)

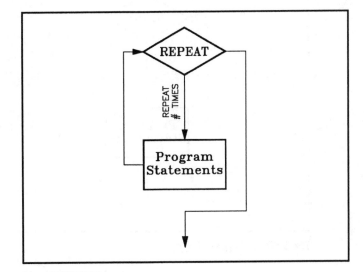

The REPEAT Structure

Let's type a simple repeating statement at the AutoCAD command line, draw a small circle, and animate it.

REPEAT Animation With AutoCAD

```
Command: CIRCLE                    Draw a circle near the right side of the screen.
Command: (setq pt (getpoint "Center of rotation: "))
Center of rotation:                Pick a point in the center of the screen.

Command: (repeat (getint "Enter steps: ")
1> (command "ROTATE" "L" "" pt "3"))
Enter steps: 20                    And it moves on around.
```

REPEAT works fine if you can predetermine the number of loops. Otherwise, a more flexible type of looping function is the WHILE function.

The WHILE Function

The WHILE function loops like REPEAT, except WHILE has a conditional test. WHILE continues to loop through its series of statements until the condition is nil.

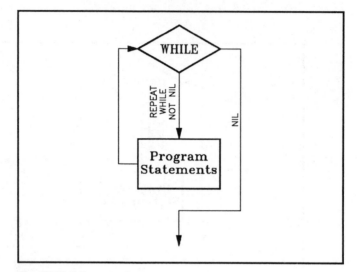

The WHILE Program Loop

while	*Evaluates the expressions as long as the test returns T or is non-nil. Each loop of a WHILE function tests the condition and, if non-nil, evaluates each of the statements included within the closing parenthesis. WHILE returns the last evaluation of the last completed loop. If no loops are completed, it returns nil.* **(while *test expression* ...)**

Unlike the IF function, WHILE does not have an alternate *else* set of statements to execute if the condition fails the test. However, like COND and REPEAT, WHILE lets you include an unlimited number of statements in the loop. WHILE allows an indefinite but controllable number of loops.

Using a WHILE Loop Function

```
Command: (setq count 4  data '(A B C D E F G H I J))      Start count at 4.
Lisp returns: (A B C D E F G H I J)

Command: (while (< count 10) (print (nth count data))      WHILE count is 4 to 9.
1> (setq count (1+ count)))
E
F
G
H
I
J 10
```
AutoLISP returns 10, the value of COUNT at the end of the WHILE loop.

The 1+ function is often used in WHILE loops to increment a counter to process a list. In this case, COUNT started with 4 (the fifth element because NTH counts 0,1,2 …).

Controlling Input With WHILE

WHILE is good for validating input, looping until the input meets the test. Here's the [FITTING] macro renamed to [FITTING2] with a WHILE added.

```
[FITTING2]^C^C^C(while (not (and ;+
(setq ans (strcase (getstring "Fitting type (E90/E45/RED/TEE): ")));+
(cond ((not ans) (prompt "Error: No fitting type entered.^M"));+
((= ans "E90") (prompt "Ninety deg elbow.^M"));+
((= ans "E45") (prompt "Forty-five deg elbow.^M"));+
((= ans "RED") (prompt "Reducer.^M"));+
((= ans "TEE") (prompt "Tee, non-reducing.^M"));+
(ans (prompt "Error: Unknown fitting type.^M"));+
))));
```

The [FITTING2] WHILE Macro in IL04.MNU

[FITTING2] differs from [FITTING] by adding a *while-not-and* to the first line and three closing parentheses to the last line. The AND lets WHILE test both GETSTRING and COND. WHILE needs non-nil to continue. Our COND returns nil for invalid input. The NOT reverses the test so it returns T to make WHILE loop until it gets valid input. We added an ANS variable to each of the good conditions to make them return non-nil, which NOT reverses to nil, causing WHILE to exit. We also removed the backslash from the third line. It could have been moved to the end. But WHILE makes the entire macro a single expression. It completes evaluation, then stops anyway, so the backslash isn't needed.

Using WHILE for Input Control

 You have the [FITTING2] COND macro in your IL04.MNU file.

Copy and edit [FITTING] to make the [FITTING2] COND macro in IL04.MNU.

```
Command: MENU
Select [FITTING2]
Fitting type (E90/E45/RED/TEE): <RETURN>
Error: Unknown fitting type.
Fitting type (E90/E45/RED/TEE): RED
Reducer.
Lisp returns: nil
```

Reload IL04.

It all scrolls by, then prompts:

But now it reprompts:

This is a form of program iteration. Iteration means that a loop is continued until the results of one or more expressions calculated or determined within the loop terminate the loop. The conditional test for an iteration usually contains some variable whose value gets changed during the course of the loop, such as a counter or input value.

Accumulating Data With WHILE

WHILE is also good for creating lists to hold variable quantities of input data. Any number of points can be entered and combined as a single list variable, as shown below. This example continues to add points until it gets nil input from GETPOINT. Try it at the keyboard.

Using WHILE to Build a Point List

```
Command: (defun getpts ( / pt ptlist)
1> (while (setq pt (getpoint "\nEnter point or RETURN when done: "))
2> (setq ptlist (append ptlist (list pt)))))
Lisp returns: GETPTS

Command: (getpts)
Enter point, or RETURN when done:        Enter as many as you like.
Enter point, or RETURN when done:        Then <RETURN> to exit.
Lisp returns: ((4.3 5.6 0.0) (4.3 6.2 0.0)  (5.0 6.2 0.0) (5.3 5.6 0.0) (6.1 6.0 0.0)
(6.5 5.6 0.0) (6.5 5.0 0.0) (7.2 5.0 0.0))
```

The GETPTS function keeps asking for a point and adding the point to a list of points (the PTLIST). It uses the APPEND function to merge the new point into the PTLIST. As soon you press <RETURN>, the loop stops and the list is returned.

➡ *TIP: GET functions are often put in a WHILE loop to test input; one example would be to see if the input is a member of a list.*

You can use WHILE and increment a counter to step through and process all or part of a list. However, if you need to process all of a list and the counter value is not needed by other expressions during each loop, the FOREACH function is more efficient.

Processing Lists With the FOREACH Function

The FOREACH function pops each item out of a list and uses it in a temporary variable in subsequent statements. FOREACH is used in many programs to perform a function on each member of a list.

foreach

> *Evaluates the expression, substituting each element in the list for a symbol for one loop of the expression(s). The symbol is an alias variable that is temporarily set to each item from the list for one loop. The expression(s) in the loop must refer to the current item of the list by its alias. The value of the symbol is local to the FOREACH.*
>
> (foreach *symbol list expression* ...)

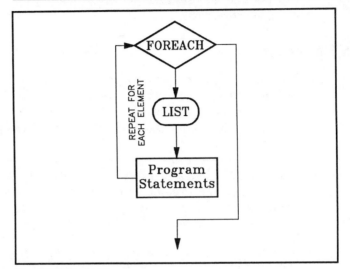

The FOREACH Structure

In the following exercise, use the GETPTS function from the previous WHILE exercise to create a list of points. Then, start a LINE command and see how the FOREACH function works.

Using the FOREACH Function

```
Command: (setq ptlist (getpts))
Enter point, or RETURN when done:          Enter 6 to 8 points, then <RETURN>.
Lisp returns: ((4.3 5.6 0.0) (4.3 6.2 0.0) (5.0 6.2 0.0) (5.3 5.6 0.0) (6.1 6.0 0.0)
(6.5 5.6 0.0) (6.5 5.0 0.0) (7.2 5.0 0.0))

Command: LINE
From point: (foreach pt ptlist (command pt))
To point:                                   Prompts scroll as the lines are drawn.
To point: nil
To point: <RETURN>
```

In this simplified example, the LINE command alone would have accomplished as much. After all, you just picked the points. However, if the point list is calculated or supplied from some other source, you'll need FOREACH.

The COND, WHILE, and FOREACH functions all take multiple expressions. Another function, PROGN, groups multiple expressions into a single expression.

The PROGN Function

The PROGN function makes a group of expressions act as one, returning the last value. Remember, IF is limited to only a single *then* and a single *else* expression. This restricts your programming. If you want to execute several IF statements, the PROGN function is indispensable.

progn
Evaluates a series of expressions, returning the value of the last expression. The arguments can be any number of valid AutoLISP expressions.
(progn *expression* **...)**

Use PROGN to execute multiple arguments as the *then* or *else* of an IF function, for example:

```
EXAMPLE                        IF TEST IS
(if test
  (progn                       True, then sets ortho on and
    (setvar "ORTHOMODE" 1)
    "YES"                      returns:   "YES"
  )
  (progn                       nil, else sets ortho off and
    (setvar "ORTHOMODE" 0)
    "NO"                       returns:   "NO"
  )
)
```

Now that we've examined the structure and flow of a program, let's look at the environment in which your programs live.

Your Programming Environment

The ATOMLIST contains AutoLISP's environment. When you looked at the ATOMLIST earlier, you saw the names of the AutoLISP built-in functions. The ATOMLIST also holds all your defined function names and variables. You need to control your variables to keep the programming environment clean and efficient. Otherwise, a variable set in one program can affect another program that uses the same variable name.

Local and Global Variables

A variable is *global* unless you make it local. A global variable has its value stored in the ATOMLIST. This global value is available to any function, any menu item, and at the command line.

You can make a variable *local* by declaring it in the DEFUN argument list when you define a function. Variables declared with DEFUN are defined exclusively within the function. Their symbol names are listed in the ATOMLIST. However, AutoLISP makes a small localized environment in which it temporarily stores values of local variables, so they don't affect values on the ATOMLIST. Think of it as a local "atomlist" that works much the same way as the general ATOMLIST. Recall the DEFUN format:

```
(defun name (argument ... / local ...) expression ...)
```

Arguments and *locals* are the declared variables. Arguments are always local, and locals may also be added after the slash without being arguments. This localization also applies to nested function definitions. If you nest a DEFUN in another DEFUN, and declare its name local in the outer DEFUN's argument list, the inner DEFUN is local to the outer.

When and why declare locals? You usually don't need your function's variables to stay around after the function is executed. Declaring them local saves memory. Further, you seldom want your function's variables changing the values of any global variables. In most cases, you'll want to make all your function's variables local. If you want an argument available outside the function, you have to set its value to a different name, or return its value, because the DEFUN's arguments are automatically local.

Management of Local and Global Variables

The SLOT program listing shows the use of localized variables. To localize a variable, you place the variable after any arguments for the function. You need to separate the arguments from locals with a slash (/).

```
;* SLOT.LSP draws solid slotted polyline holes from prompted input.

(prompt "Loading SLOT command...")
(if #diam nil (setq #diam 0.25))                       ;initial default #diam
(defun C:SLOT ( / tmpdia lngth pt1 pt2 pt3 pt4 pt5 pt6)
  (while (setq pt1 (getpoint "\nInsertion point: "))   ;center of slot
    (prompt "\nSlot diameter <")                       ;start prompt
    (princ #diam)                                      ;print default
    (setq tmpdia (getdist ">: ")                       ;finish prompt and getdist
          lngth (getdist "\nSlot length: ")
    );setq input
    (if tmpdia (setq #diam tmpdia))                    ;Resets #diam if entered by user.
                                                       ;Calculations
    (setq pt2 (polar pt1 0.0 (/ (- lngth #diam) 2.0)) ;Center of end radius
          pt3 (polar pt2 (/ pi 2.0) (/ #diam 4.0))    ;Endpt of straight segment
          pt4 (polar pt3 pi (- lngth #diam))          ;Endpt of straight segment
          pt5 (polar pt4 (* pi 1.5) (/ #diam 2.0))    ;Endpt of straight segment
          pt6 (polar pt5 0.0 (- lngth #diam))         ;Endpt of straight segment
    );setq calculations

                                                       ;Output commands to AutoCAD

    (command "PLINE" pt3 "W" (/ #diam 2.0) ""
             pt4 "ARC" pt5 "LINE" pt6 "ARC" "CLOSE"
    );command
  );while loop
);defun
;*
```

The SLOT Function in SLOT.LSP

The C:SLOT command function draws solid slotted holes. It uses WHILE to repeat as long as it gets an insertion point. It tests its diameter input with an IF. It takes no arguments but localizes several variables. We intentionally did not localize the #DIAM variable so we could show how it has global value. The #DIAM variable is used as a default for diameter. The function asks for the center of the slot, the slot diameter and slot length, and uses a polyline entity to fill in the slotted area. The points for the function are shown in the Solid Slot Hole illustration.

The calculations are done by using AutoLISP's basic divide, subtract, and multiply functions. SLOT also uses PI and POLAR. PI is a predefined real that saves you the trouble of defining it.

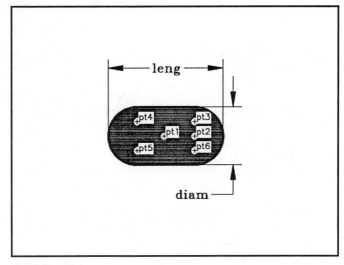

Solid Slot Hole

polar	Returns a point calculated at an angle and distance from a supplied base point. **(polar *point angle dist*)**

Let's see the global and local variables by testing the SLOT command function.

Testing the Slot Command

 You have C:SLOT in your SLOT.LSP file.

 Create the SLOT.LSP file as shown in the listing above.

```
Command: !#diam            Test the value.
Lisp returns: nil          Initially it should be nil.
Command: !lngth
Lisp returns: nil
Command: (setq tmpdia 0.3) Set a global value ATOMLIST.
Lisp returns: 0.3

Command: (load "SLOT")
Loading SLOT command...     The prompt in the SLOT.LSP file.
Lisp returns: C:SLOT
```

```
Command: !#diam                          Retest the value.
Lisp returns: 0.25                       It was set in the SETQ at the top of the SLOT.LSP file.

Command: SLOT
Insertion point:                         Pick a point.
Slot diameter <0.25>: 0.5                Enter a new diameter.
Slot length: 2                           And a length.
PLINE                                    The PLINE command draws the slot, and WHILE loops.
Insertion point: <RETURN>                Exits the WHILE loop and ends.

Command: SLOT                            Try it again.
Insertion point:                         Pick a point.
Slot diameter <0.5>: <RETURN>            Accept the default.
Slot length: 1.5
PLINE
Insertion point: <RETURN>                Exits the WHILE loop and ends.

Command: !lngth                          It was localized.
Lisp returns: nil                        It still has no value.

Command: !#diam                          It was not localized.
Lisp returns: 0.5                        Its last value in the function is its global value.
Command: !tmpdia                         Check another local variable.
Lisp returns: 0.3                        Locals never change globals of the same name.
```

The #DIAM variable was not localized, so its global value changed. This allowed the SLOT command to use its previous value as a default the second time we tried the command. We like to indicate our global variables with a leading # character.

The LNGTH value was localized. If we wanted to use it as a default, we could have left it global and added code to the program similar to the #DIAM setting code. Prior to running SLOT, LNGTH was nil. Afterwards, it still was nil. Any possible use of LNGTH made by other programs was protected from interference by its localization.

The danger in omitting internal function variables from the local list is that if they are used for other purposes, their global values get overwritten. This includes all function names, which are actually special global variables. If we had defined a function named LNGTH, and failed to declare the C:SLOT LNGTH variable local, SLOT would have redefined our LNGTH function as the number 1.5. A common oversight is to use a variable name that is also the name of either an AutoLISP function or your own function. It's especially hard to find program bugs caused by this.

➠ *NOTE: Be careful to choose variables names that are not already built-in ATOMLIST function names.*

SLOT was a C: command function, so it couldn't have arguments. Since arguments are automatically local, their values outside of the function always remain unchanged.

Efficient Use of Variable Names

Even a local variable has a spot on the ATOMLIST. Let's take a closer look at the ATOMLIST, and see how it stores variables and functions. We'll use the NTH and EVAL functions to look at individual items.

Looking Into the ATOMLIST

Load and run the previous SLOT program, if you aren't still in the same drawing.

```
Command: !ATOMLIST                              Our first line is:
(PT6 PT5 PT4 PT3 PT2 PT1 LNGTH TMPDIA C:SLOT #DIAM ...   And so on . . .

Command: (nth 9 atomlist)       Look at #DIAM. NTH starts with 0. See the note below.
Lisp returns: #DIAM             The symbol name.
Command: (eval (nth 9 atomlist))
Lisp returns: 0.5                            The value of #DIAM.

Command: (nth 8 atomlist)                    See the note below.
Lisp returns: C:SLOT
Command: (eval (nth 8 atomlist))            Returns the function definition:
Lisp returns: ((/ TMPDIA LNGTH PT1 PT2 PT3 PT4 PT5 PT6) (WHILE (SETQ PT1 (GETPOINT
"\nInsertion point: ")) (PROMPT "\nSlot diameter ") and so on . . .
```

➠ *NOTE: In the exercise, count to the positions of #DIAM and C:SLOT, and subtract 1 to determine the numbers to use with NTH. The order and contents of the ATOMLIST vary and the ATOMLIST may not always be available, so a program that depends on accessing it can be precarious.*

eval	*Returns the results of evaluating the expression.* `(eval expression)`

If you have a lot of programs with a lot of variables, you will likely experience the dreaded errors, "insufficient node space" or "insufficient string space," and run out of AutoLISP memory. (A *node* is 10 or 12 bytes, depending on your system.)

While localizing a variable, or setting a global variable or function definition to nil, eliminates the node space needed to store its value, its place on the ATOMLIST still uses at least two nodes. There are several easy habits you can develop to reduce wasted node space.

First, make the length of variable and function names six characters or less. Seven or more characters demand string space to store the symbol name. String and node space both come from the same memory pool: the *heap*.

Second, reuse the same variable and function names over and over in all your programs. Use unique names like our #DIAM for globals, but use common names for locals. Use PT for a point, NUM for a number, VAR for a junk variable and so on. Don't make up new descriptive variable names for every program. Use tired old standard names from program to program. Keep a dictionary of standard variables, use them repeatedly, and you will conserve nodes. (We sometimes have to violate our own advice and use overly descriptive names to make our programs easier to follow.)

Lastly, set global variables and functions to nil when they are no longer needed. Make infrequently used programs as one-shot LISP files that are executed as they are loaded, instead of defined functions that need ATOMLIST space for their values (definitions).

Another memory-saving technique is to avoid repeating identical code in different programs. You can use subroutines to do this.

Subroutines

A *subroutine* is a function that is used, or called, by other functions. For tasks common to several programs, this is more efficient than repeating the code in each program. Usually, each subroutine is responsible for one task. Any function can call any other function as a subroutine (assuming it's the correct argument type). You've already been using a lot of subroutines, and it's good programming style. Each built-in AutoLISP function is a subroutine that performs a single task. You use built-in subroutines by nesting them in other built-in functions or by calling them from your user-defined functions.

Why Use Subroutines?

Besides making more efficient use of memory by not duplicating code, subroutines make writing and debugging programs easier. It's far simpler to find errors in small one-task chunks of code than in deeply nested complex listings.

Creating large programs is easier when you break up the program tasks into several subroutines, even if they may never be used in other programs. The main program function calls each of the other functions.

To see how subroutines work, let's define a couple. You already have two likely candidates for subroutines. The previous GETPTS function is a subroutine that builds a list of points. The #DIAM portion of the SLOT command can easily be extracted as a subroutine. Both are called by the DRAW function to mimic a repeating CIRCLE command.

```
;* DRAW is an example program to show the use of subroutines.
;* It just draws multiple circles.

(defun draw ()                        ;The main program calls the subroutines
  (diam)                              ;sets #DIAM with the DIAM subroutine
  (foreach pt (getpts)                ;call GETPTS subroutine and do each point
    (command "CIRCLE" pt "D" #diam)   ;uses the global #DIAM
  );foreach
);defun

;* GETPTS builds a list of points
(defun getpts ( / pt ptlist)
  (while (setq pt (getpoint "\nEnter point or RETURN when done: "))
    (setq ptlist (append ptlist (list pt)))
  );while
);defun

(if #diam nil (setq #diam 0.25))      ;initial default #diam

;* DIAM gets a new diameter, or uses the default set as #DIAM
(defun diam ( / tmpdia)
  (prompt "\nDiameter <")             ;start prompt
  (princ #diam)                       ;print default
  (setq tmpdia (getdist ">: "))       ;finish prompt and getdist
  (if tmpdia (setq #diam tmpdia))     ;Resets #diam if entered by user
);defun
```

DRAW.LSP File

The file contains two subroutines, GETPTS and DIAM. DRAW calls each of the subroutines to build the necessary data it draws from. Notice how the GETPTS function returns a list which is set to the PTS variable. However, no variable needs to be set from the results of the DIAM function because it sets the #DIAM value globally. There are many ways to structure and pass data between functions. Notice that the PT variable is local to the FOREACH, so it does not need to be localized in DRAW.

Let's test the program. Run the subroutines individually, then test them as a complete program.

Testing Subroutine Action

   You have the DRAW functions in your SLOT.LSP file.

   Create the DRAW.LSP file as shown in the listing above.

```
Command: (load "draw")            Load the file.
Lisp returns: DIAM                The last evaluated value.

Command: (getpts)                 Get a list of points.
Enter point or RETURN when done:  Select several points, then <RETURN>.
Lisp returns: ((1.0 2.0 0.0) (2.0 3.0 0.0) (5.0 6.0 0.0) (8.0 2.0 0.0)) The list of
                                                                         points.

Command: (diam)                   Call the diameter function.
Diameter <0.25>: .5               Enter a value.
Lisp returns: 0.5

Command: (draw)                   Try the complete program.
Diameter <0.5>: <RETURN>          Take the default.
Enter point or RETURN when done:  Select several points, then <RETURN>.
                                  It runs through several CIRCLE commands.
CIRCLE 3P/2P/TTR/<Center point>: Diameter/<Radius>: D Diameter:
Command: nil
```

So far, we have been looping programs within themselves using WHILE, REPEAT, and FOREACH. It's also possible to make programs loop by calling themselves as subroutines. This is sometimes called recursive looping.

Recursive Programming

Typically, recursive programs are those which make an internal call to run themselves. Recursive programming is not a common technique. It's sometimes used in resolving mathematical problems by converging on a solution. Our simple example just makes DRAW repeat in a continuous loop. To demonstrate the technique, we'll change the DRAW function in the DRAW.LSP file to call itself after drawing the circles.

```
(defun draw ()                          ;The main program calls the subroutines
  (diam)                                ;sets #DIAM with the DIAM subroutine
  (foreach pt (getpts)                  ;call GETPTS subroutine and do each point
    (command "CIRCLE" pt "D" #diam)     ;uses the global #DIAM
  );foreach
  (draw)
);defun
```

Recursive DRAW Function in DRAW.LSP

Test the recursive action of the program.

Recursive Program Testing

Whether you have the IL DISK or not, edit your DRAW.LSP file and add (draw) to the end of the DRAW function.

Command: **(load "draw")**	Reload the file.
Lisp returns: DRAW	The last evaluated value.
Command: **(draw)**	Start the program.
Diameter <0.5>: **2**	
Enter point or RETURN when done:	Select several points, then <RETURN>.
	It draws the circles, then:
Diameter <2.0>:	DRAW calls itself again.
Enter point or RETURN when done:	Select several points, then <RETURN>.
	It draws the circles, then:
Diameter <2.0>: **<^C>**	DRAW calls itself until cancelled.
Cancel	
Lisp returns: error: Function cancelled	And displays the code.

Summary

These are the basics of program structures, program control, and variable and subroutine management. Structuring a program involves using logical functions to direct the flow, conditional functions to make the program branch, and looping functions to cause iterations in the program. Managing variables and subroutines is mainly consistent use of a few good programming habits.

In the next chapter, we move on to communicating with AutoLISP, with more string functions, data conversion functions, and program-user interaction. We'll develop a user interface with input checking tools and default displays to make programs friendly and error-free.

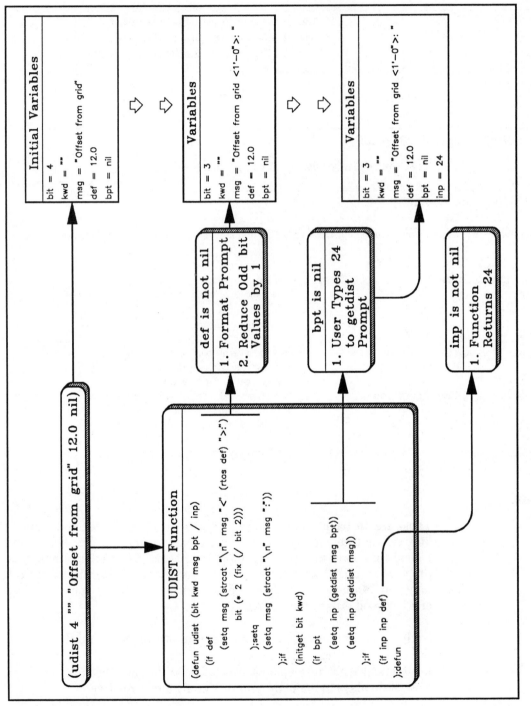

A Custom UDIST Function

CHAPTER 5

Communicating With AutoLISP

CREATING USER INTERFACE TOOLS

The user interface is that part of a program which communicates with the user. This communication includes prompting for and getting data, and keeping the user informed through messages and status prompts. A good interface not only keeps the user aware of what the program is doing, but does so with easy-to-use, forgiving programs.

To develop easy-to-use programs with AutoLISP, you need to master the user interface. You've seen how easy it is to get data input with the GET functions, but they offer little in the way of error-trapping features. Dependable, error-trapping programs offer guidance through defaults and don't choke or crash your system when they receive erroneous input. Understanding the types of data your programs require and using your AutoLISP tools to handle different data types will help you format defaults and anticipate control input errors to make your programs friendly.

The first half of this chapter provides the nitty gritty functions that you need to deal with data types and informational prompting. It shows you how to test and convert data types, how to process, format, display, and print strings, how to convert and merge numbers into strings, and how to convert strings to numbers or symbols. These are core functions you will use throughout this book and in your own programs. These functions will help you correctly process and organize data, pass data to and from external programs, pass data to AutoCAD commands, and program user interfaces.

You can use these core functions, for example, to provide the special handling in AutoLISP that linear and angular distances require to pass data to AutoCAD commands. This will allow your programs to display numbers in familiar formats.

The second half of this chapter concentrates on the user interface. It combines the core data type and conversion functions with the get, conditional, and string functions from previous chapters. These create an improved family of GET functions that we call our *user GET functions*. The user GET functions format defaults and control input to provide a consistent way to communicate and check user input.

The chief benefit of the user GET functions is dependable, efficient programs. You can guide and control user input by displaying formatted default values that show the type of input your program is requesting.

In this chapter, you will learn how to:

- Use the BOUNDP, LISP, MINUSP, and ZEROP functions to test and determine data type.

- Format prompts and strings, then display and print them using PROMPT, PRINT, PRIN1, and PRINC.

- Make AutoCAD write text along a curve.

- Convert numbers to strings and format them in linear or angular dimensions using ATOF, ATOI, and ANGTOS.

- Make your own set of GET functions that automatically present default values, check for proper input, and accept key response-type words.

You can freely jump into any section in the first half of this chapter, although the ATEXT program requires you to know the ANGTOC function. In the chapter's second half, the UDIST function is built in several steps.

☞   If you don't have the IL DISK, you need to add the ANGTOC and all user GET functions to your ACAD.LSP file for use in the rest of the book. If you have the disk, you already have them in your ACAD.LSP file.

AutoLISP Tools and Programs

AutoLISP Tools

ANGTOC is a subroutine used to format AutoLISP angles for use in AutoCAD commands.

The following seven user GET functions show defaults, and filter and format user input. You will find they make friendly user input easier to program:

UDIST is a function that improves on the AutoLISP GETDIST function.

UANGLE is similar to UDIST for the GETANGLE function.

UPOINT improves on the GETPOINT function.

UINT formats defaults, prompts, and filters input for the GETINT function.

UREAL uses the GETREAL function, but filters input and formats prompts and defaults.

USTR formats a string prompt and uses the GETSTRING function.

UKWORD implements the GETKWORD function of AutoLISP, but formats prompts and filters input.

AutoLISP Programs

ATEXT.LSP is a program that draws text along a curve or arc segment. Many readers have found it invaluable.

Determining Data Types

Sometimes AutoLISP programs fail, leaving you stumped as to the cause of the failure. User-defined functions, the AutoLISP built-in functions, and AutoCAD commands expect to receive and process specific types of data. Understanding the types of data will help you to eliminate data-type errors in your programs. If you give an AutoLISP built-in function the wrong type of data, it generates an error message. The AutoLISP TYPE function will help you determine the data type of any variable or expression. Here is a recap of the simple data types supported by AutoLISP:

DATA TYPE:	TYPE FUNCTION RETURNS:
STRings	"STR"
REALs	"REAL"
INTegers	"INT"
LISTs	"LIST"
SYMbols (variable names)	"SYM"

type

> *Returns the type of the item such as real, integer, string, list, and so on.*
> (**type** *item*)

TYPE returns the data type as a string, or it returns nil if the type is undefined. AutoLISP also provides a set of predicates to test data type.

Predicate Tests

A PREDICATE is a simple test function that returns T or nil. You are familiar with several predicate tests. The logical, equality, and relational functions, such as AND, OR, NOT, <, <=, EQ, and /= are all predicates. The data type predicates are:

```
BOUNDP   Determines if a SYMbol variable is bound to a value.
LISTP    Determines if an item is a LIST.
MINUSP   Determines if a REAL or INTeger number is negative.
NUMBERP  Determines if an item is a number (REAL or INTeger).
ZEROP    Determines if a REAL or INTeger number is zero.
```

Using a predicate is a more efficient way to determine data type than using a comparison statement. For example (listp a) is more efficient than (= (type a) "LIST")). By comparing the returned string from the TYPE function to the word "LIST," you get a T or nil, like the LISTP predicate. The predicates are more efficient in program speed and size, since the predicate test requires only one AutoLISP evaluation.

➥ *NOTE: Remember, nil is an empty list, so (listp nil) returns T, but (type nil) returns nil.*

If you just need to determine whether a variable has any value other than nil, use the BOUNDP predicate to perform the test.

boundp
> *Returns T if the atom is bound to a value, otherwise returns nil.*
> (boundp *atom*)

When testing with BOUNDP, you need to quote the variable name. AutoLISP typically evaluates each item it sees. The QUOTE function tells AutoLISP not to evaluate the contents of the item, but to take it verbatim.

If you do not quote the variable A, then the contents of A, not A, get tested. Using 'A is AutoLISP shorthand for (quote A). Since BOUNDP is the only predicate that directly tests a symbol, it is the only predicate that needs a quoted argument.

Predicates are not frequently used because your GET functions or other sources of input generally control the data type. One application for predicates is to check data read into AutoLISP from a file. The wrong data type can crash a program with a hard-to-find error. Checking the data with predicates won't prevent the error from stopping the program, but will allow you to pinpoint the error and exit the program gracefully. You might also use predicates in programs that use global default variables. Checking to see if a variable is the correct data type is safer than just checking for any non-nil value. If the data is the wrong type, your program can then prompt with a preset default instead of crashing.

Let's see how TYPE and BOUNDP work.

Testing Data Types

`Enter selection:`	Begin a NEW drawing named IL05 and try these tests.
`Command:` **(type a)**	Returns nil. A is not defined.
`Command:` **(type 'a)**	Returns SYM. It's an undefined symbol.
`Command:` **(boundp 'a)**	Returns nil, still undefined.
`Command:` **(setq a "TEST")**	Returns "TEST," the value A is set to.
`Command:` **(type a)**	Returns STR, now A is a string.
`Command:` **(setq aa a)**	Returns "TEST," the value of A passes through to AA.
`Command:` **(setq aa 'a)**	Returns A. Reset AA to symbol A, not its value.
`Command:` **(boundp aa)**	Returns T, the value of AA is A, which is bound to "TEST."
`Command:` **(type aa)**	Returns SYM. Tests the contents of AA, the symbol A.
`Command:` **!AA**	Returns A. The content of AA is a symbol.
`Command:` **(boundp a)**	Still returns nil. You have to quote it.
`Command:` **(boundp 'a)**	Returns T. Now it's bound to "TEST."
`Command:` **(if (boundp 'a) "TRUE" "NIL")**	Returns "TRUE."
`Command:` **(if a "TRUE" "NIL")**	Returns "TRUE." Everything's T or nil. A is "TEST" so it's T.

As the last example shows, you do not need to use BOUNDP in a conditional test. The variable alone acts as a test. Let's look more closely at the rest of the predicates.

atom	*Returns T if item is not a list, otherwise returns nil.* `(atom item)`

listp	*Returns T if item is a list. Otherwise returns nil.* `(listp item)`

minusp	*Returns T if number is negative. Otherwise returns nil.* `(minusp number)`

null	*Returns T if item is bound to nil. Otherwise returns nil. Typically used for lists.* (null *item*)

numberp	*Returns T if item is a number. Otherwise returns nil.* (numberp *item*)

zerop	*Returns T if number equals 0 (zero). Otherwise returns nil.* (zerop *number*)

The other predicates also test the contents of a symbol, but some caution is advised. LISTP works on any list, but you need to be careful if the variable is undefined. Remember, nil is an empty list, so LISTP returns T for any symbol that evaluates to nil. Don't let this test trip you up. An alternative is shown below. NUMBERP and MINUSP work on either real or integer data types, but they do not distinguish between the two types. Use a TYPE test to see if a number is a real or an integer. MINUSP and ZEROP will return an error if the item tested is not a number. The predicate tests shown below provide safe alternatives for LISTP, MINUSP, and ZEROP if you can't be sure the tested value is a number. ZEROP is a safe, efficient test if the value being tested is sure to be a number, for example:

```
(setvar "HIGHLIGHT" (if (zerop (getvar "HIGHLIGHT")) 1 0)))
```

This toggles the HIGHLIGHT system variable to 1 (on) if it's zero (off), and toggles it off if it's on.

In these tests, you do not put the symbol argument in quotations. Try these predicate tests.

More Predicate Tests

Command: **(setq a ' (0.0 0.0))**	Sets A to a list.
Command: **(listp a)**	Returns T. The contents of A are a list.
Command: **!b**	Returns nil. It's undefined.
Command: **(listp b)**	Returns T. Although B is undefined!
Command: **(and b (listp b))**	Returns nil. A safer list test.
Command: **(numberp 1.0)**	Returns T. It's a number.
Command: **(zerop 0)**	Returns T. It's a zero value.
Command: **(zerop b)**	A dangerous test.

```
error: bad argument type
Lisp returns: (ZEROP B)
Command: (= 0 b)                              Returns nil. A safer zero test.

Command: (minusp -1)                          Returns T. It's negative.
Command: (minusp b)
error: bad argument type
Lisp returns: (MINUSP B)
Command: (< b 0)                              Returns T. Not safe. B isn't negative. It's nil!
Command: (and (numberp b) (minusp b))        Returns nil. A safer minus test.

Command: (= (type 1.0) 'REAL)                Returns T. Identifies what type of number it is.
```

The last example determines whether the number is a real or an integer by using the TYPE function and comparing the returned string. You can use all of these predicates in IF, WHILE, and COND tests. You might also use MINUSP (and NUMBERP) for such things as preventing a negative value from causing an AutoCAD command error when finding a circle's diameter.

Working With Strings

In most programs, the main application for strings is to provide prompts. You work faster and make fewer errors if a command guides you with clear prompts, useful defaults, and informative status messages. These are essential for learning a customized system quickly. Many of the string functions presented in the earlier chapters will enable you to provide intelligent prompts, defaults, and messages. These functions assist in parsing and combining strings to form your prompts. You also use the AutoLISP print functions, flipscreen functions, and data to string conversion functions. Let's look at the AutoLISP representations of the ASCII formatting characters such as line feed, tab, and backspace.

Prompt and String Formatting

Programming languages allow you to control the format of your strings. Formatting includes positioning prompts and setting the columns in which strings start, as well as setting character color and underscoring. In the next few examples, we will look at simple cases of string formatting in AutoLISP, but we'll leave the more stylized color and underscoring formatting features to the chapter on AutoLISP Input/Output.

The ASCII control characters cause the screen or printer to format a string. These control codes are generally invisible to the user and cannot be directly entered. AutoLISP provides two ways to include these characters within a string. You have already seen the CHR function. For example, (chr 9) is a tab. You can use CHR along with STRCAT to put control codes in strings.

A more efficient way is to use *expanded* ASCII codes. You expand an AutoLISP string code by representing it as a backslash and an alphabetical or numeric code, like **\n** for new line. Expansion means representing a single ASCII character as a two-character AutoLISP code. When the string is sent to an output device like the screen or printer, the AutoLISP codes are converted back to ASCII control characters to give the desired formatting effect.

Formatting codes all begin with the backslash character (\) and are followed by a key letter or number. The AutoLISP-defined control codes for expanded code formatting are:

EXPANDED CODE	ASCII CODE	MENU CODE	FUNCTIONAL MEANING
\n	010	^J	Causes a new line (line feed). The cursor moves to the far left and down one line.
\t	009		Moves cursor one tab to the right.
\10	008	^H	Moves cursor back one space (10 is the octal value for ASCII 8).
\r	013	^M	A true return. Moves the cursor to the far left, but doesn't start a new line.
\e	027		The <ESC> escape character. See the AutoLISP: Input/Output chapter.
\\	092		Use this when you need an actual "\" backslash to appear in a string.
\nnn			The nnn is octal code for an ASCII character. Converts ASCII decimal to base 8 octal for nnn.

➥ *NOTE: The keyboard <RETURN> actually issues the ASCII 13 (return) plus ASCII 10 (line feed). However, when AutoLISP receives keyboard input, it sees <TAB>, <RETURN>, and <SPACE> only as ASCII 10 codes.*

An important application of these formatting codes is in formatting data written to files by AutoLISP. The most frequent formatting task that you will encounter is to make a prompt start on a new line. You do this by including a \n in the string. We used this in some of the earlier prompt examples. The format code key characters, like the n in \n, must be lower case. Typically, you place the \n at the beginning of the string.

How to Format Prompts With Expanded Codes

The following example shows you how to set a string with the new line expanded code, then display it with PROMPT. The example also shows a tab formatting code that gives you a convenient way to align text in columns. The "\t" character will advance to invisible stops on the screen. A typical screen has ten such stops, one at column one and nine tab stops. Try making a string of nine tabs with numbers following each tab.

Using Expanded ASCII Codes

Command: **(setq il "\nInside AutoLISP\nis fun!\n")**   String with expanded codes.
Lisp returns: "\nInside AutoLISP\nis fun!\n"

Command: **(prompt il)**   Sends string to the screen:
Inside AutoLISP   The \n gives you a new line.
is fun!   The \n returns again.
Lisp returns: nil

Command: **(setq b "1 \t2 \t3 \t4 \t5 \t6 \t7 \t8 \t9 \t10\n")**   Sets the tab codes.
Lisp returns: "1 \t2 \t3 \t4 \t5 \t6 \t7 \t8 \t9 \t10\n"

Command: **(prompt b)**   Sends string to the screen.
1   2   3   4   5   6   7   8   9   10
Lisp returns: nil

You cannot use these expanded formatting codes in menu macros because the backslash causes AutoCAD to pause the menu.

How to Format Strings in Menus

In a menu macro, even in an AutoLISP string, the AutoCAD menu interpreter reads and interprets the characters first, then feeds them to the AutoLISP string. If the characters are control character codes, they can affect the menu macro's command line output.

When you need to force a return in a menu macro string, use a ^M. Type a caret, then M. The ^J acts the same as ^M. Create a test menu and try a few of these codes. The ^I for tab does not space correctly, so avoid it.

Using Menu Control Codes

Start a test IL05.MNU menu file and enter this macro.
[^M TEST](textscr) (prompt "^MInside AutoLISP^Mis fun!^M");

Save and exit to AutoCAD.

```
Command: MENU
Select [^M TEST]
```
Load the IL05 menu.
It displays:

```
Inside AutoLISP
is fun!
Lisp returns: nil
```

In some cases, your prompts may include more lines than the normal three lines the AutoCAD command prompt area can display. When this happens, you need to flip to the text screen. AutoLISP provides two functions for setting the current screen.

Selecting Text and Graphics Screen Modes

If you have a single screen system, you may have to flip screens to display your prompts. The TEXTSCR and GRAPHSCR functions accomplish this.

graphscr

> *Switches from the text screen to the graphics screen on single screen systems.*
> **(graphscr)**

textscr

> *Switches from the graphics screen to the text screen on single screen systems.*
> **(textscr)**

Another useful screen function is TERPRI, whose sole purpose is to start a new line. You can use it with REPEAT to clear the text screen. These three functions take no arguments.

terpri

> *Prints a new line on the screen.*
> **(terpri)**

Try these three functions. Flip to the text screen, clear it by printing 25 line feeds, and then return to the graphics screen.

Using TEXTSCR, GRAPHSCR, and TERPRI

```
Command: (textscr)
```
Returns nil and flips to the text screen.

```
Command: (repeat 25 (terpri))
```
Returns nil, but does 25 new lines first.

```
Command: (graphscr)
```
Returns nil and flips back to graphics.

If your screen displays more that 25 text lines, use a larger number in the REPEAT with TERPRI.

Use GRAPHSCR and TEXTSCR whenever AutoLISP or AutoCAD puts your program on the wrong screen. Use TERPRI to clear part or all of the text screen before displaying lists of data or important prompts. For example, you might have a program that inserts a block and automatically puts in an attribute string selected from a list. You would use TEXTSCR to flip to the text screen and TERPRI to clear it. Then you would use PROMPT or one of the print functions to display the choices and a GETKWORD to make the selection.

So far, we've only used the PROMPT function to display strings. AutoLISP has other print functions which display or print any type of data.

Displaying and Printing Strings and Data

AutoLISP has a total of four built-in functions that can print a string. These are PROMPT, PRINT, PRIN1, and PRINC.

prompt

> *Displays a string statement in the screen's prompt area.*
> (prompt *string*)

The difference between PROMPT and the PRINT, PRIN1, and PRINC functions, is that PROMPT can only accept a string-type argument. The other three functions can print any expression. You can only direct PROMPT to the screen. You can use the other three functions to print data to external files or to any device.

princ

> *Prints and returns the expression, except control characters are not evaluated. If the optional file-desc is supplied and the file is open for writing, output is redirected to file-desc. If the optional file-desc is missing or the file is closed, the expression is printed to the screen.*
> (princ *expression* file-desc)

PRINT and PRIN1 print any control codes in their data arguments as expanded codes, like \n instead of an actual new line. PRINC uses control codes instead of expanded codes in its output, so \n or (chr 10) will cause an actual new line. PRINT also adds a new line before the data and adds a space after the data. PRIN1 and PRINC do not add extra lines or spaces.

print	*Prints a new line and the expression to the screen and returns a new line and expression. PRINT adds a new line before and a space after the data. If the optional file-desc is supplied and the file is open for writing, output is redirected to file-desc. If the optional file-desc is missing or the file is closed, the expression is printed to the screen.* **(print *expression* file-desc)**

prin1	*Prints the expression to the screen and returns the expression. If the optional file-desc is supplied and the file is open for writing, output is redirected to file-desc. If the optional file-desc is missing or the file is closed, the expression is printed to the screen.* **(prin1 *expression* file-desc)**

Use the PROMPT function for simple screen printing of prompts and status messages. PROMPT is the only function that always displays its message on both screens of dual-screen systems.

Use PRINC, PRINT, or PRIN1 if you need to print non-string data, unless the data can be easily converted to a string for PROMPT. We cover conversion functions in the next section. These three print functions also return their original argument data.

You also use PRINC, PRINT, or PRIN1 with a file argument to print data to a file or device. If the data is a string, PRINC prints it unquoted. PRINT and PRIN1 print quoted strings. For example (princ "string") prints *string* without quotes, but (print "string") and (prin1 "string") print "string" with quotes. Printing to files and devices is a topic of the chapter on AutoLISP Input/Output.

Try a few print functions on the screen, the default device.

Using PROMPT, PRINT, PRIN1, and PRINC

Command: **(prompt "\tInside AutoLISP")**   Tabs before "Inside AutoLISP," then returns nil.
Lisp prompts and returns: Inside AutoLISPnil

Command: **(prin1 "\tInside AutoLISP")**   What goes in is printed and returned verbatim.
Lisp prints and returns: "\tInside AutoLISP""\tInside AutoLISP"   Expands tab as ^t.

Command: **(print "\tInside AutoLISP")**   The same as PRIN1 except it prints an extra
Lisp prints: (a blank line)   line before and space after.
Lisp prints and returns: "\tInside AutoLISP" "\tInside AutoLISP"

Command: **(print (strcat (chr 9) "Inside AutoLISP"))**   The (chr 9) is expanded as a \t.

Lisp prints and returns: "\tInside AutoLISP" "\tInside AutoLISP"

Command: **(princ "\tInside AutoLISP")**   Tabs over, prints, but always returns \t expanded.
Lisp prints and returns: Inside AutoLISP"\tInside AutoLISP"

These print functions also have a use not envisioned by the developers of AutoLISP; they suppress returned values and clean up the display. This became a stated feature by popular demand.

Clean Displays With PRINC and PROGN

If called without arguments, PRINT, PRIN1, and PRINC return no visible characters. Unlike anything else in AutoLISP, they seem to return nothing. Actually, they return an ASCII 00, the null character, as a symbol data type instead of a string. You can take advantage of their clean finish to enhance your user interface.

Prompts in menus return an annoying nil, as you have seen. Try the following exercise to control them.

How to Suppress Nil and Returned Values

Command: **(princ)**   Finished cleanly. Prints and returns null, ASCII 00.
Command: **SHELL**   Edit your IL05.MNU to test PRINC and PROGN.
                 Copy and add the following two [PRINC] and [PROGN] macros:

```
[^M TEST ](textscr) (prompt "^MInside AutoLISP^Mis fun!^M");
[PRINC   ](textscr)(prompt "^MInside AutoLISP^Mis fun!^M") (princ);
[PROGN   ](progn (textscr) (prompt "^MInside AutoLISP^Mis fun!^M") (princ));
```

Save and exit to AutoCAD.

Command: **MENU**   Reload IL05.

Select: **[^M TEST]**   It prints the prompt, but TEXTSCR and PROMPT each return nil.
Inside AutoLISP
is fun!
Lisp returns: nil

Select: **[PRINC]**   It cleanly prompts, without returned nils:
Inside AutoLISP
is fun!
Lisp returns: Nothing is returned.

Select: **[PROGN]**   The same as [PRINC].

In the [PRINC] example, all the expressions in the menu were run together without intervening spaces. That caused AutoLISP to read and evaluate them as if they were a single expression. TEXTSCR's and PROMPT's returned values were suppressed. Only PRINC's value was returned, and it was invisible. If you have complex or multi-line menu items, it is safest to use PROGN to ensure that it is evaluated as a single expression, as in the [PROGN] example. Recall that PROGN simply groups multiple expressions as one. Using PRINC as the last expression in the PROGN ensures that its null will be the last value returned. When you do this, remember to remove intervening backslashes as you did in the [FITTING2] macro, which was similarly nested in a *while-not-and* expression in Chapter 4.

Programs and AutoLISP files also return their often-distracting last-evaluated value. We use PRINC at the end of AutoLISP functions and function files to suppress these returned values. For example, recall the BUBBLE command function in Chapter 3:

```
;* C:BUBBLE command
(prompt "Please wait. Loading BUBBLE command...")
(defun C:BUBBLE ()

   ...and the rest of the program, then...

  (command "TEXT" "S" "STANDARD" "M" pt1 0.25 0 txt "LAYER" "S" la "")
  (princ)
);defun
```

BUBBLE With Nil Suppressed

Adding (princ) as the last expression before the closing parenthesis of the defun makes BUBBLE return nothing instead of nil. Add a similar (princ) as the last line of any AutoLISP file and it will return nothing when loading.

For flexibility in combining different data types in prompts, and to include defaults, you need to be able to convert other data types to strings. AutoLISP obliges with tools to convert most data types.

Converting Data Types

In many cases, you need to convert a number to a string. In Chapter 4's SLOT command, we created a crude default with (princ #diam). To create a proper default prompt, you need to convert it to a string. AutoLISP has several easy-to-use functions to convert numbers to strings and strings to numbers. The ITOA (Integer TO Ascii) function takes only one argument, an integer number.

itoa | *Returns a string conversion of an integer.*
(itoa integer)

To convert strings into real numbers, AutoLISP gives you the ATOF (Ascii TO Floating point) function, and for integers, it gives you the ATOI (Ascii TO Integer) function.

atof | *Returns a real number converted from a string.*
(atof string)

atoi | *Returns an integer converted from a string.*
(atoi string)

These two functions take string-type arguments and return the desired data type. Try them.

String and Number Conversions

Command: **(itoa 24)**   Returns "24." It's a string.

Command: **(atof "24.5")**   Returns 24.5. A floating point real number with decimals.

Command: **(atof "24")**   Returns 24.0, adding the decimal.

Command: **(atoi "24.5")**   Returns 24, an integer with fractional values discarded.

These number formats are simple. But converting real numbers to strings and formatting linear distances and angular rotations are more involved.

Formatting for Linear Distances

AutoCAD's UNITS command controls how distances are formatted on-screen. By controlling the formatting of real numbers, you can write data to external files for post-processing by other programs, create custom dimensioning commands or place distances as text in the drawing, or issue prompts with defaults. The RTOS function extends AutoCAD's numeric formatting into AutoLISP.

rtos

> *Returns a string conversion of the supplied number in the current UNITS setting format, unless the optional mode and accuracy override it.*
>
> (**rtos** *number* mode accuracy)

RTOS (Real TO String) performs a data-type conversion. RTOS represents the string as an AutoCAD linear distance. When called without its optional arguments, RTOS uses the current linear format (the LUNITS system variable) and precision (the LUPREC system variable) set in AutoCAD. For instance, when the drawing units are set to architectural, the default arguments of RTOS display the number in feet and inches. Remember that the precision affects only the units displayed, not the accuracy drawn.

RTOS accepts two optional arguments to control the string format based on the AutoCAD units and precision settings. The linear unit *mode* settings are:

MODE	SYSTEMS OF UNITS	EXAMPLE
1	1. Scientific	1.55E+01
2	2. Decimal	15.50
3	3. Engineering	1'–3.50"
4	4. Architectural	1'–3 1/2"
5	5. Fractional	15 1/2

The linear units *accuracy* argument is simply the number of decimal places to format. For fractional units, the accuracy value is applied to the decimal value, then the resulting value is converted to a fraction. The fractional default is 64ths; the accuracy argument 5 rounds off to 32nds, 4 to 16ths, 3 to 8ths, 2 to 4ths, 1 to halves and 0 rounds to a whole number.

Using RTOS

Command: **(rtos 8.5)**
Lisp returns: "8.5000"

Called with no arguments, it uses default settings.

Command: **(rtos 12.625 4)**
Lisp returns: "1'–0 5/8""

Mode argument 4 converts to architectural units.

Command: **(rtos 12.625 4 2)**   Now a precision of 2 places
Lisp returns: "1'-0 3/4""   gives this result.

➡ *NOTE: RTOS is intended for formatting strings for visual display, not for input to AutoCAD commands. RTOS formats like the AutoCAD status line. The decimal form works fine when passed along to any AutoCAD command requesting a distance, but AutoCAD balks at other formats such as architectural. When passing data to an AutoCAD command, just use a real number instead.*

The AutoCAD DIMZIN dimension variable also affects the formatted string returned by RTOS.

How to Control Zeros With DIMZIN

DIMZIN controls how zeros are formatted. DIMZIN 0 is the default and suppresses all zeros except the zero between a foot and a fractional inch value. Such zero values, as in 2'-0 1/4", are never suppressed. DIMZIN 1 includes all zeros. DIMZIN 2 includes feet and suppresses zero inches, while DIMZIN 3 suppresses feet and includes inches. DIMZIN values 0 through 3 control architectural units. The added values of 4 and 8 control decimal zeros. Adding 4 suppresses leading zeros and adding 8 suppresses trailing zeros in decimal dimensions. The 4, 8, or both are added to the desired architectural 0, 1, 2, or 3 value to control both. So, for instance, to include all zeros in fractions but suppress all zeros in decimals, add 1+4+8 to get a DIMZIN of 13. Try these RTOS and DIMZIN examples:

Controlling Zeros With DIMZIN

Command: **SETVAR**   Set DIMZIN to 9 (1+8).
Command: **(rtos 8.5 4)**   Architectural.
Lisp returns: "0'-8 1/2""   DIMZIN 1 includes 0 feet.
Command: **(rtos 8.5)**   Decimal.
Lisp returns: "8.5"   DIMZIN 8 strips trailing zeros.

Command: **SETVAR**   Reset DIMZIN to 0.

The RTOS function can also be used to round off real and integer data types.

How to Round Off Numbers

You can nest RTOS in an ATOF or ATOI to return rounded-off numbers, like this:

Rounding Off Numbers

Command: **(atof (rtos 12.625 2 2))**   Rounds off to two places.
Lisp returns: 12.63

Command: **(* 100 (atoi (rtos (/ 12345 100) 2 0)))**   Rounds off to hundreds.
Lisp returns: 12300

Two AutoLISP functions convert directly between real numbers and integers.

How to Convert Reals To and From Integers

If you need to express a real value as an integer string, you can't use ITOA or you'll get a bad argument error. Use the FIX function to first convert it to an integer, then use ITOA. AutoLISP also provides the FLOAT function to convert integers to reals.

fix	*Returns an integer value of the number and drops the remainder.* **(fix number)**

float	*Returns a real value of the number.* **(float number)**

FIX always truncates (rounds down) the decimal component. If you want to round it to the nearest integer, see the technique in the following exercise. Try a few integer-to-real conversions.

Converting Between Integer and Real Numbers

Command: **(itoa 3.5)**
error: bad argument type
Lisp returns: (ITOA 3.5)

Command: **(fix 3.5)**   Returns 3 as integer.

Command: **(itoa (fix 3.5))**   Returns "3" as string.

Command: **(itoa (fix (atoi (rtos 3.5 2 0))))**   Rounds to nearest integer.
Lisp returns: "4"

Command: **(float 4)**   Returns 4.0 as real.

That completes the linear distance and number conversions. ANGTOS (ANGle TO STRing) handles angle-to-string formatting and conversion.

AutoCAD Angle Formatting and Conversion

You need to control angle format for the same types of reasons you need to control real numbers: to write external files, create custom dimensions, place angles as drawing text, or to prompt with defaults. You also use angle conversion to format angles passed to AutoCAD commands because AutoLISP angular calculations use only radians. The ANGLE function returns the angle between two points.

angle

> *Returns an angle in radians from the X axis in a counterclockwise direction to a line between the two points.*
> **(angle** *point point***)**

The angle is returned in radians. One radian is pi degrees. One degree is 1/pi radians, or 1/3.141593. Internally, AutoCAD also keeps track of angles in radian units. All angles are stored in radians but displayed in the current angular settings set by the UNITS command.

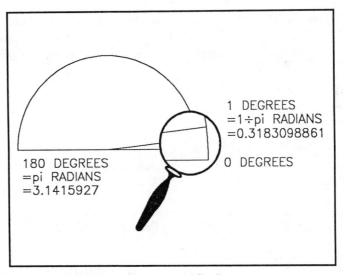

Relationship Between Degrees and Radians

Looking at Radians

```
Command: (angle '(0 0) '(-1 0))
Lisp returns: 3.141593                    Which is pi, or 180 degrees.
```

angtos	Returns a string conversion of an angle from radians to the units specified by mode. The conversion defaults to the current angular units mode and precision unless otherwise specified with the optional mode and precision arguments. (**angtos** *angle* mode precision)

The ANGTOS optional *mode* argument defaults to the system variable AUNITS, and optional precision arguments default to the AUPREC system variable. Remember that the precision affects only the units displayed, not the accuracy drawn. The AutoCAD UNITS angular formats and their AutoLISP *mode* format codes are:

CODE	SYSTEM OF ANGLE MEASUREMENT	EXAMPLE
0	1. Decimal degrees	45.0000
1	2. Degrees/minutes/seconds	45d0'0"
2	3. Grads	50.0000g
3	4. Radians	0.7854r
4	5. Surveyor's units	N 45d0'0" E

➡ *NOTE: The angular format code numbers are not the same numbers used in the AutoCAD UNITS command. The angle system variable settings begin with 0, and are one less then the angular UNITS choices.*

Using ANGTOS

Command: **(angtos pi 0 3)**
Lisp returns: "180.000"

Command: **(angtos pi 3 3)**   Radian format.
Lisp returns: "3.142r"   The "r" is a problem.

Command: **(angtos pi 2 3)**   Grads format.
Lisp returns: "200.000g"   Problem is with the "g."

Command: **(angtos (* pi 0.25) 4 3)**
Lisp returns: "N 45d0'0" E"   Oh no — spaces!

In the above exercise, the **r** in the radians "3.142r," the **g** in the grads "200.000g," and the spaces in the surveyor's "N 45d0'0" E" all cause problems if you try to use them as AutoCAD command input.

➥ *NOTE: ANGTOS is intended for formatting a string for visual display, not for AutoCAD command input. ANGTOS formats like angles on the AutoCAD status line. While the decimal form works fine when passed along to any AutoCAD command requesting "Rotation angle," AutoCAD balks at the radian, grads, and surveyor's units formats returned by ANGTOS.*

How to Format Angles for Commands

AutoCAD does not treat all forms of angles equally. Because a number in radians is not the same number in grads or degrees, AutoCAD angles are dependent on the user's current settings. So 3.14 radians is not equal to 3.14 grads or 3.14 degrees.

However, AutoCAD provides a way around this. If you precede a decimal angle passed to AutoCAD with a double angle bracket (<<), AutoCAD considers it as decimal degree input regardless of the current angular units setting.

When you want to convert angles for display only, use ANGTOS. If you intend to pass the string to an AutoCAD command, say for the text rotation angle, use your own function. We will call this function ANGTOC (ANGgle TO Command). Try ANGTOS at the AutoCAD command prompt:

Using ANGTOS

```
Command: UNITS
```
Set the system of angle measurement to:
5. Surveyor's units   N 45d0'0" E

```
Command: (setq ang (getangle "Angle: "))
Angle: 45
Lisp returns: 0.785398
```
Set an angle.
1/4 of pi in radians.

```
Command: (angtos ang)
Command: (strcat "<<" (angtos ang 0 8))
```
Returns "N 45d0'0" E."
Returns "<<45.00000000" as universal decimal.

```
Command: LINE
```
Draw line from 1,1 to 6,1 to test angles.

```
Command: ROTATE
Select objects: L
Base point: 1,1
<Rotation angle>/Reference: (angtos ang)
Requires numeric angle, second point, or option key word.
<Rotation angle>/Reference: (strcat "<<" (angtos ang 0 8))
```
Select Last and <RETURN>.

"N 45d0'0" E" fails for input.

Rotates OK.

```
Command: UNITS
```
Set back to decimal angles.

ANGTOS can result in round-off error when converting from radians.

How to Round Off Angles

Round-off error is a common problem with AutoCAD and AutoLISP calculations. You can use RTOS and ATOF to round off the ANGTOS results, as shown below.

Rounding Angles

Command: **(angtos 3.14159265 0 8)**   Try pi.
Lisp returns: "179.99999979"   Rounded off.

Command: **(rtos (atof (angtos 3.14159265 0 8)) 2 6)**   This is a way to round off.
Lisp returns: "180.000000"

Let's put it together in a function called ANGTOC.

Creating an ANGTOC Function

If you have the IL DISK, the ANGTOC function is already in your ACAD.LSP file. If you don't have the disk, create the ANGTOC function and put it in your ACAD.LSP file now.

```
;* ANGTOC is an angle formatting function that takes an angle
;* argument in radians and returns it with 6 decimal places
;* in a form universally acceptable to AutoCAD command input.

(defun angtoc (ang)
  (setq ang
    (rtos (atof (angtos ang 0 8)) 2 6)
  )
  (strcat "<<" ang)
);defun
;*
```

The ANGTOC Angle to Command Function in ACAD.LSP

ANGTOC is a good tool that you will use with the ATEXT command in the following section. It's also used by other functions as a subroutine, so test it before we move on.

Testing the ANGTOC Function

You have the ANGTOC function in your ACAD.LSP file.

Add the above ANGTOC function to your ACAD.LSP file.

Command: **(load "acad")**   Reload the ACAD.LSP file.

Command: **(angtoc 3.14159265)**   Try it.
Lisp returns: "<<180.000000"

One uncommon but vitally important data conversion is from strings to AutoLISP symbols or expressions.

Converting Strings to Symbols

The READ function converts the first element (list or atom) of a string to an AutoLISP expression. If the string contains blanks, READ will only use the first word, unless the blanks are within a list. READ is most often used to build a variable name by creating it as a string and converting it to a symbol. This is used if you need to create a series of variables, perhaps using STRCAT to append an incremented number to a base name. READ can also be used to convert data, read in the form of a list from an external data file, into a list.

read | *Returns a symbol of the first atom or list in a string.*
(read *string*)

Try converting a string created with STRCAT to a variable.

Making Variables From Strings

Command: **(read "b")**   Returns B, a symbol.
Command: **(type (read "b"))**   Returns SYM.

Command: **(setq inc (itoa 2))**   Returns "2," setting up for:

Command: **(set (read (strcat "b" inc)) 123)**   STRCAT "b" to "2" and set B2 to the value 123.
Lisp returns: 123   The value of the new symbol B2.

Command: **!b2**   Returns 123, the value set to b2.

Command: **QUIT**

The STRCAT of "b" and "2" creates "b2," which READ returns as B2, a symbol.

Using SET vs. SETQ

There is a difference between the use of SET in the exercise above and the usual SETQ. Because the SETQ function does not evaluate its symbol argument(s), the READ in (setq (read ...) would never get evaluated. Instead, we use SET, which evaluates its first argument and sets its contents to the value of its second argument.

set
> *Sets a quoted symbol with the value of the expression. An unquoted symbol can set values indirectly.*
> (set *symbol expression*)

In the case above, SET evaluated its first argument, the READ expression in the example, and set its value, B2, to the value of the second argument, 123. SETQ (which stands for SET Quote) treats its first argument as if the argument were in quotation marks. The expressions (set 'b 321) and (setq b 321) are equivalent.

Applying Conversions and Prompt Formatting in ATEXT

It's time for an example which puts these data type conversions, angle handling, and default prompt formatting controls together in the ATEXT (Arc TEXT) command function. ATEXT places text in an arc, treating each character as a separate text entity. ATEXT gets the user text string, midpoint, radius, and orientation, and uses the style defaults. It then calculates each character's placement and executes a TEXT command in a REPEAT loop. ATEXT uses the DISTANCE function to determine the radius of the text arc.

distance
> *Returns a distance between two 3D or 2D points.*
> (distance *point point*)

The ATEXT.LSP function is shown in the diagram below. The function definition follows. The numbered bubbles identify the major parts of the function, which are explained following the program listing.

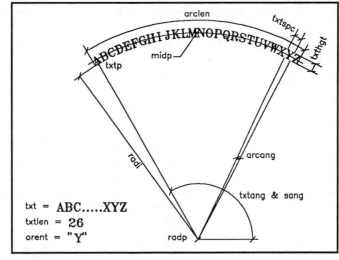

ATEXT.LSP Diagram

```
;* ATEXT types text in an arc. The function requires the midpoint of
;* the text, the radius point, and the orientation. It uses the current
;* style, no fixed height styles allowed. It uses the ANGTOC function.

(defun C:ATEXT ( / midp radp txt radi txtlen txtspc txthgt arclen arcang sang orent
txtang txtp char)
  (setq cmdech (getvar "CMDECHO"))              ;save command echo
  (setvar "CMDECHO" 0)                          ;turn command echo off
  (graphscr)
❶
  (setq                                         ;assign variables
    radp (getpoint "\nPick radius center point: " )     ;get radius point
    midp (getpoint "\nPick middle point of text: " radp) ;get midpoint of text
    txthgt (getdist (strcat "\nText height <"          ;get text height
                    (rtos (setq txt (getvar "TEXTSIZE")))) ;offer default
                    ">: "
            )           )
    txthgt (if txthgt txthgt txt)               ;set to default if nil
    txt (getstring "\nText: " T)                ;get text string
    radi (distance radp midp)                   ;determine radius
    txtlen (strlen txt)                         ;determine string length
    orent (strcase (getstring "\nIs base of text towards radius point <Y>: ")) ;orientation
  );setq
```

Listing continued.

Continued listing.

❷
```
(if (or (= orent "") (= orent "Y"))       ;calculate new radius length based on orientation
  (setq radi (- radi (/ txthgt 2)))
  (setq radi (+ radi (/ txthgt 2)))
);end if
```
❸
```
(setq
  arclen (* txtlen txthgt)              ;calculate arc length
  txtspc (/ arclen txtlen)              ;calculate arc length of one character
  arcang (/ arclen radi)                ;calculate arc angle of one character
  sang (- (+ (angle radp midp) (/ arcang 2)) (/ txtspc radi 2))   ;calc start angle
  count 1                               ;initialize counter
);setq
```
❹
```
(repeat txtlen                          ;insert character loop
  (if (or (= orent "") (= orent "Y"))   ;test text angle
    (setq   ;calc angle for character towards radius and character position in string
      txtang (angtoc (- sang (/ pi 2))) ;format angle with << for universal units
      txtpos count
    )
    (setq   ;calc angle for character away from radius and character position in string
      txtang (angtos (- sang (* pi 1.5)) 0)
      txtpos (- (1+ txtlen) count)
    )
  )
  (setq
    txtp (polar radp sang radi)                   ;calculate character point
    char (substr txt txtpos 1)                    ;get text character
  );setq
  (command "TEXT" "C" txtp txthgt txtang char)    ;execute text command
  (setq
    count (1+ count)                              ;increment counter
    sang (- sang (/ txtspc radi))                 ;calculate new start angle
  );setq
);repeat
```
❺
```
(setvar "CMDECHO" cmdech)                         ;restore command echo
(princ)                                           ;ends program cleanly
);end defun
;*
```

The C:ATEXT Function in the ATEXT.LSP File

As you examine ATEXT, notice the use of the GRAPHSCR, RTOS, ANGTOC, ANGTOS, and PRINC functions. The main sections of ATEXT are:

❶ Uses the GET functions to get input from the user. You need the center of the arc text, a point on the radius, the text height, and the string of text to be used. RTOS formats the current TEXTSIZE system variable as the height default. If you <RETURN> for the default, TXTHGT is nil and is reset to TEXTSIZE by the (if txthgt... expression. The GETSTRING for base text orientation is similarly set to nil if <RETURN> accepts its <Y> default.

❷ The orientation (whether the text faces toward or away from the center of the arc) is used to recalculate the RADI radius.

❸ Computes the arc length required for the text. Calculates the space between characters and the start angle for the first character.

❹ Uses a REPEAT to loop the program. Each loop calculates the placement of a character along the arc, uses ANGTOC and ANGTOS to format angles, and executes the text command.

❺ Restores the system variables to the values saved at the beginning, and then ends the function. The CMDECHO system variable is used to suppress the AutoCAD TEXT command prompts during execution of the ATEXT command.

Try the ATEXT command in AutoCAD:

Testing the ATEXT Function

Enter selection: **1**   Begin a NEW drawing again named IL05.

 You have the ATEXT.LSP file.

 Create the C:ATEXT function in a file named ATEXT.LSP.

Command: **(load "atext")**   Load the file.
Lisp returns: C:ATEXT

Command: *(angtoc pi)*   Make sure ANGTOC was loaded by ACAD.LSP.
Lisp returns: "<<180.000000"

Command: **STYLE**   Set STANDARD current, default all settings.
                      STD, our prototype style, was fixed height.

```
Command: ATEXT                              Start the command.
Pick radius center point:                   Pick the radius point.
Pick middle point of text:                  Pick the middle point.
Text height <0.2000>: .25
Text: THIS IS CURVED TOWARD THE CENTER      Enter the text.
Is base of text towards radius point <Y>:   <RETURN> for the default.
```

Try other options as well. It works in any orientation.

Your screen should look like the Arc Text Routine illustration.

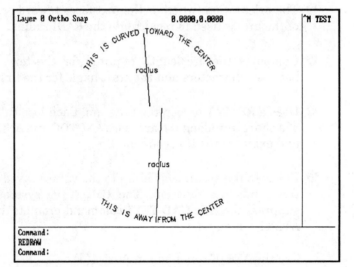

The Arc Text Routine

This version of ATEXT requires a non-fixed height text style. TEXT and related commands do not prompt for height if the style has a fixed height. This causes problems in programs like this, so we restricted this program to work only with non-fixed height styles. You can program around this by using AutoLISP's AutoCAD table access functions, but that is a topic for a later chapter. There is a version of ATEXT on the IL DISK file named ATEXT2.LSP that works with any style.

In ATEXT, we formatted a default prompt in the TXTHGT, GETDIST, and ORENT GETSTRING inputs. This took a bit of programming. It would be more effective if we could standardize default handling in a set of modified GET functions.

Developing User Interface Functions

Many program problems arise from poor user interface. Two of the most common problems are confusing prompts and lack of input error-checking. This section contains several exercises that show you how to format user prompt strings and check for errors. To control and restrict input, AutoLISP's INITGET function filters the GET functions. This section culminates in a customized set of user interface functions that format defaults, control input with INITGET, and incorporate the GET family of functions. These functions will be used by many other programs in this book, so you will need to add them to your ACAD.LSP file before moving on to the next chapter. If you have the IL DISK, the functions are already in your ACAD.LSP file.

Let's start with the UDIST function.

Formatting Default Prompts With UDIST

UDIST concatenates several strings and issues the built-in AutoLISP GETDIST function. We'll first create a simple version of UDIST and then add features as we go.

If you have the IL DISK, the final UDIST function is already in your ACAD.LSP file, but you will learn more if you follow the steps and add the features to the first simple UDIST function. The basic UDIST is in the IL DISK's UDIST.LSP file. You need to load it to replace the completed ACAD.LSP version for testing in your current drawing.

```
;* UDIST User interface distance function

(defun udist (msg def / inp)
  (if def                                           ;test for a default
    (setq msg (strcat "\n" msg " <" (rtos def) ">: ")    ;string'em with default
    );setq
    (setq msg (strcat "\n" msg ": "))                ;without default
  );if
  (setq inp (getdist msg))     ;the GET command
  (if inp inp def)             ;compare the results, return appropriate value
);defun
;*
```

UDIST Function in UDIST.LSP

The UDIST function takes two arguments: MSG, the prompt string message, and DEF, the value which shows in the prompt's default angle brackets. First, UDIST tests to ensure that the default has a value. If the default is non-nil, it uses STRCAT to set the message string to include the converted default. The function uses RTOS to format the raw value and display it in the user's current units. The closing parenthesis of the first SETQ is placed down one line to make adding more code to the function easier. If DEF is nil, a colon and a space are appended to MSG by the second SETQ, but no <default> is prompted for.

Then GETDIST is issued with the constructed MSG prompt. The value returned is tested by (if inp inp def) to see if the user actually entered a value, or if <RETURN> was hit to accept the default. If a value was entered for INP, IF returns it, else it returns the default value. Since the IF statement is the last statement in the function, its results are passed out of the function. Test the function.

Using Defaults With UDIST

You have UDIST in the UDIST.LSP file. Load it to replace the ACAD.LSP version.

Create UDIST in a new file named UDIST.LSP.

```
Command: (load "udist")                 Load the UDIST.LSP file.
Command: (udist "Enter size" 24.0)      Try it.
Enter size <24.0000>:                   Hit <RETURN> to accept the default.
Lisp returns: 24.0

Command: (udist "Enter size" nil)       Give a nil default.
Enter size: 124                         No default is shown.
Lisp returns: 124.0                     Returns the entered value.

Command: (udist "Enter size" nil)       Try it again with nil.
Enter size:                             Just hit <RETURN> this time.
Lisp returns: nil                       The same as the normal GETDIST returns.
```

Adding a Base Point Argument to UDIST

We frequently use UDIST within other functions to prompt for a distance. To make it do everything that GETDIST can, we need to add another argument to pass along a base point. The new parts of the function are shown in boldface type in the program listing below.

```
;* UDIST User interface distance function

(defun udist (msg def bpt / inp)
  (if def                                        ;test for a default
    (setq msg (strcat "\n" msg " <" (rtos def) ">: ")   ;string'em with default
    );setq
    (setq msg (strcat "\n" msg ": "))            ;without default
  );if
  (setq inp
    (if bpt                    ;check for a base point
      (getdist msg bpt)        ;and use it in the GET commands
      (getdist msg)
  ) );setq&if
  (if inp inp def)             ;compare the results, return appropriate value
);defun
;*
```

UDIST Function With Base Point Feature Added

If the base point argument, BPT, is supplied, UDIST uses the new first GETDIST. If BPT is nil, it uses the second GETDIST without a base point. The IF returns one of the GETDISTs to set INP. First set the base point, then try the function with and without a base point.

Testing UDIST With a Base Point

Even if you have the IL DISK, edit UDIST.LSP as shown above.

Command: **(load "udist")**   Reload the lisp file.

Command: **(setq bpt (getpoint "Base point: "))**
Base point: Pick a base point.
Lisp returns: (4.0 2.0 0.0)   Yours may be different.

Command: **(udist "Enter width" nil bpt)**   Rerun without a default distance.
Enter width: It rubber-bands. Pick a distance.

Repeat UDIST with another nil for no base point.

Normally, GETDIST returns nil if you enter a <RETURN> as input. We use this in handling a default. But if there is no default, nil will also be returned by our UDIST. In most programs where you get a distance, a nil will either cause a math function to fail or cancel a COMMAND function. We've already used a WHILE to loop and reprompt for input, but the INITGET function provides a better way.

Controlling Input With INITGET

INITGET is a built-in AutoLISP function that initializes the types of input allowed or disallowed for a GET function call. For instance, you can disallow negative values, zeros, or a null response, and the GET function automatically repeats until a suitable answer is given.

Program failure may be caused by errors in the programmer's logic or by failing to consider all possibilities, but the major cause of errors is unexpected input. The INITGET function allows you to filter and prevent bad input. When should you use INITGET? You should use it in virtually all programs that take GET input.

The INITGET function also adds the capability of accepting a key word and returning a string instead of a number or distance value to the GET functions.

initget

> *Establishes options for GETxxx functions. The bits set input filtering options, and the string sets key words.*
> (**initget** *bits string*)

This INITGET-type of control is established by passing integer bits (numbers) to the function. The bits and their resulting controls are shown in the following table:

INITGET CONTROL BIT	RESULTING CONTROL OVER INPUT
1	A value must be given. Null values are unacceptable input.
2	Requires input other than zero.
4	Input must be greater than zero. Disallows negative input.
8	No limit checking of points, regardless of LIMCHECK system variable.
16	Returns full 3D (XYZ) instead of 2D (XY) points.
32	Shows a dashed rubber-band line only if pop-up menus are available.

You can use any combination of integer bits to gain the level of input control that you need. Adding all the control bits together (+ 1 2 4 8 16 32), you get 63. This is your full arsenal of input control.

➥ *NOTE: If the FLATLAND system variable is on, AutoLISP returns 2D points. You must use the 16 bit code to force the return of 3D points or else turn FLATLAND off. If FLATLAND is off, the 16 code has no effect, and 3D points are always returned.*

You must use INITGET once before each GET function that you wish to control. INITGET's settings are not saved after the GET function is evaluated. INITGET takes two arguments, an integer value with a combination between 1 and 63 and an optional string. The integer value establishes the type of input or point controls for the GET call.

When given unacceptable input, INITGET makes AutoCAD reissue the original prompt without causing an error. AutoLISP will accept the input only when it is the proper type. The following exercise shows how to use the INITGET call.

Using INITGET

Command: **(initget 1)**   Filters out null input.
Lisp returns: nil

Command: **(getdist "Offset: ")**   Try a distance.
Offset: Just hit <RETURN>.

Requires numeric distance or two points.   It refuses to accept the null input.
Offset: **12**   Give a numeric value.
Lisp returns: 12.0

Now that you can control input error, you might want the input flexibility that key words offer.

How to Set Key Words With INITGET

Many AutoCAD commands allow key words in their input. For example, the familiar ARC command prompts with Center/<Start point>: to which you can enter a C or pick a point. Whether you enter a C, a CEN or a Cen, AutoCAD sees it as selecting the key word, "Center." INITGET makes it possible for you to add key words that act like real AutoCAD commands to your custom AutoLISP command prompts.

The optional string argument of INITGET passes a string of key words to any of the GET functions, with the exception of GETSTRING and GETVAR. Key words in an INITGET string argument permit the user to enter these words instead of the natural data type of the particular GET function.

There are two formats for specifying the key word string in INITGET. In the first format, "Key WOrd LIST," the upper case letters are the required portion. Entering K, KE, or KEY returns KEY; entering WO, WOR, or WORD all return WORD but W alone is not enough; and LIST must be entered in its entirety. This is the usual and easiest format.

In the second format, the required portion follows a comma. For example, "KEY,K WORD,WO LIST" is equivalent to "Key WOrd LIST" above.

Key words are always returned in the same case they're shown in the INITGET argument list. Try an example of GETPOINT with INITGET.

How to Work With Key Words

```
Command: (initget "Working Reference Origin")          Try it.
Lisp returns: nil

Command: (getpoint "Working/Reference/Origin or pick point: ")
```
                                                       Use the GETPOINT function.
```
Working/Reference/Origin or pick point: W  Enter either a lower or upper case W.
Lisp returns: "Working"
```

Notice how AutoLISP returns the key word, not what you entered. Your input case has no effect. As long as the characters you enter match all or part of the key word, AutoLISP returns the entire key word. Experiment a little and verify that AutoLISP does return a consistent value.

You only need to enter the capitalized portions of the key words for the match to succeed. In cases containing key words with similar spellings, like ON and OFF, you have to tell INITGET to distinguish between the two by capitalizing up to the second character. Some users prefer to use the full key word spelling because it aids in the readability of their programs, others prefer to keep it short. Follow your own preference.

Adding INITGET to UDIST

You can extend the UDIST function to control your input by adding bit and key word arguments and an INITGET function.

If you have the IL DISK, the ACAD.LSP file contains the UDIST function as shown below. If you don't have the disk, modify UDIST.LSP and add it to your ACAD.LSP file. This will finalize UDIST, so while you're at it, add a bit more documentation.

```
;* UDIST User interface distance function
;* BIT (0 for none) and KWD key word ("" for none) are same as for INITGET.
;* MSG is the prompt string, to which a default real is added as <DEF> (nil
;* for none), and a : is added. BPT is base point (nil for none).
;*
(defun udist (bit kwd msg def bpt / inp)
  (if def                                        ;test for a default
    (setq msg (strcat "\n" msg " <" (rtos def) ">: ")  ;string'em with default
          bit (* 2 (fix (/ bit 2)))) ;a default and no null bit code conflict so
    ) ;setq                                  ;this reduces bit by 1 if odd, to allow null
    (setq msg (strcat "\n" msg ": "))                  ;without default
  ) ;if
  (initget bit kwd)
  (setq inp
    (if bpt                        ;check for a base point
      (getdist msg bpt)            ;and use it in the GET commands
      (getdist msg)
  ) ) ;setq&if
  (if inp inp def)                 ;compare the results, return appropriate value
) ;defun
;*
```

UDIST Function With INITGET Support

We use a <RETURN> value of nil to accept our default in UDIST. An INITGET 1 bit disallows null input. This works fine if we have no default, but conflicts when we want a default. An INITGET bit code of 1 is *no null*. Using a bit code of 1 will always make BIT an odd value. To control this, if a DEF default exists and the bit is odd, the (* 2 (fix (/ bit 2))) expression reduces BIT by one. This expression rounds down to the next even integer. This handles a UDIST call that tries to disallow null input, yet has a default value to show. Both the default and control bit then work together. This effect is shown in the following exercise.

Testing **UDIST** for **INITGET** Control

 This final UDIST is in your ACAD.LSP file.

 Add UDIST to your ACAD.LSP file and modify it to match the listing above.

Command: **(load "acad")**   Reload the ACAD.LSP file.
                                        It will automatically load when you load a drawing.

```
Command: (udist 0 "" "Offset from grid" 12.0 nil)        0 is the no-bit code and
                                                          "" is the no-key word code.

Offset from grid <12.0000>: <RETURN>        Accept the default.
Lisp returns: 12.0                          Works as it did before.


Command: (udist 4 "" "Offset from grid" 12.0 nil)        A 4 control bit (no negatives).
Offset from grid <12.0000>: -24             Enter a negative value.
Value must be positive.
Offset from grid <12.0000>: 24
Lisp returns: 24.0


Command: (udist 4 "Working Reference Origin"             A key word string.
1> "Working/Reference/Origin or enter offset" 12.0 nil)
Working/Reference/Origin or enter offset <12.0000>: w    Enter w.
"Working"                                                Same as before.


Command: (udist 1 "" "Offset from grid" 12.0 nil)        Default, but null input OK.
Offset from grid <12.0000>: <RETURN>                     Accept the default.
Lisp returns: 12.0                                       The default.
```

That is the fully developed UDIST function. Next, we'll develop similar functions to augment the rest of the GET functions. The first of these is for a GET function we haven't yet looked at, GETKWORD.

GETKWORD for Controlled Strings

GETKWORD is a special GET function that accepts only the key words defined with INITGET as input. It works exactly like the INITGET-initiated key word input in the other GET functions, except it accepts no other strings, points, distances, angles, or numbers. Using it for selecting choices from a list is better than using GETSTRING because GETKWORD rejects all irrelevant input and reprompts.

getkword

> *Returns a string matching the key word input by the user. Key words are specified in the (initget) function. The optional prompt string can provide specific instructions for input.*
> (getkword *prompt*)

GETKWORD should be a part of your user interface library. Shown below is the UKWORD function which we will use throughout the remainder of the book.

```
;* UKWORD User key word. DEF, if any, must match one of the KWD strings
;* BIT (1 for no null, 0 for none) and KWD key word ("" for none) are same as
;* for INITGET. MSG is the prompt string, to which a default string is added as
;* <DEF> (nil or "" for none), and a : is added.
;*
(defun ukword (bit kwd msg def / inp)
  (if (and def (/= def ""))                      ;test for both nil and null string
    (setq msg (strcat "\n" msg " <" def ">: ")   ;string'em with default
          bit (* 2 (fix (/ bit 2))))             ;a default and no null bit code conflict so
    );setq                                       ;this reduces bit by 1 if odd, to allow null
    (setq msg (strcat "\n" msg ": "))            ;without default
  );if
  (initget bit kwd)                              ;initialize the key words
  (setq inp (getkword msg))                      ;and use the GET command
  (if inp inp def)                               ;compare the results, return appropriate value
);defun
```

UKWORD Function in ACAD.LSP File

The function works just like the UDIST function except there is no base point option to the function. GETKWORD is strictly a character string input type of function. Try it out.

Testing the UKWORD Function

UKWORD is in your ACAD.LSP file. Reload it to replace the previous UDIST definition.

Copy and edit the UDIST function to create UKWORD in your ACAD.LSP file.

Command: **(load "acad")**   Reload the file.

Command: **(ukword 1 "LAyer LType Color" "Change what?" "Color")**
                                                No null, give "Color" as a default.
Change what? <Color>: **<RETURN>**   Hit return for the default.
"Color"   The full key word.

Command: **(ukword 1 "LAyer LType Color" "Change what?" "Color")**   Enter it again.
Change what? <Color>: **L**   Give an ambiguous response.
Ambiguous response, please clarify...   AutoCAD detects the trouble.
LAyer or LType? **LA**   It shows the key word options.
"LAyer"   The full key word.

You can't use INITGET key words or bit controls with the GETSTRING function. But you can program a way to set a no-null bit in a user string function.

Controlling Strings With USTR

Using key words makes no sense with GETSTRING because strings can have any value anyway. If you need key words, use GETKWORD or UKWORD. But to get general string input, with or without a default, use the following USTR (User STRing) function. The USTR function formats a prompt, shows defaults, and disallows a null input (an empty string of ""). It does this without the benefit of the INITGET function. When set to disallow null input, USTR uses a WHILE loop to reprompt if the user enters a <RETURN> or a space. If a default is set, the no-null input control is ignored.

```
;* USTR User interface string
;* If BIT=1 no null "" input allowed, 0 for none, BIT ignored if DEF present.
;* MSG is the prompt string, to which a default string is added as <DEF> (nil
;* or "" for none), and a : is added. If SPFLAG T, spaces are allowed in string.
;*
(defun ustr (bit msg def spflag / inp nval)
  (if (and def (/= def ""))                  ;test for both nil and null string
    (setq msg (strcat "\n" msg " <" def ">: ") ;then include the default string
          inp (getstring msg spflag)         ;get input, ignore no null bit
          inp (if (= inp "") def inp)         ;if null input, return default
    );setq
    (progn
      (setq msg (strcat "\n" msg ": "))       ;make string without the default
      (if (= bit 1)                           ;if no null bit set to 1
          (while (= "" (setq inp (getstring msg spflag)))) ;then get input, no ""
          (setq inp (getstring msg spflag))   ;else get input, "" ok
    ) );progn&if
  );if
  inp
);defun
;*
```

USTR Function for String Input

The USTR function can handle strings with or without spaces. Set this control by the fourth argument. The first argument sets whether a null input is allowed. Let's test the function.

How to Control String Input With USTR

You have USTR in your ACAD.LSP file. You need not reload it.

Copy and edit the UKWORD function to create USTR in your ACAD.LSP file.

```
Command: (load "acad")      Reload the file.

Command: (ustr 0 "Enter a string" "A String" nil)      Set for null input ok, a default,
                                                         and no spaces.
Enter a string <A String>: <RETURN>      <RETURN> for the default.
Lisp returns: "A String"

Command: (ustr 1 "Enter a string" nil nil)      Set no null input allowed,
                                                 no default.
Enter a string: <RETURN>      Hit <RETURN>. It reprompts for input.
Enter a string: ROO
Lisp returns: ROO

Command: (ustr 0 "Enter a string" nil nil)      Null input ok, no default,
                                                 no spaces.
Enter a string: Crystal time      Try to type it.
Lisp returns: "Crystal"      Spaces are disallowed. A space terminates.

Command: (ustr 1 "Enter a string" nil T)      No null, but allow spaces.
Enter a string: Crystal time      Type it.
Lisp returns: "Crystal time"      The whole string is accepted.
```

We'll use several other user interface functions as subroutines in AutoLISP programs throughout the book. Unless you have the IL DISK, you need to make them now.

Finishing Your User Interface Tool Kit

Create these functions to augment the rest of the AutoLISP GET family of input. Use your text editor to copy duplicates of the UDIST function. Then edit them to appear as shown below. The functions are: UINT, UANGLE, UPOINT, and UREAL. UANGLE and UPOINT are most similar to the UDIST function and its base point argument. UINT and UREAL are also similar to UDIST, but they don't use a base point.

```
;* UINT User interface integer function
;* BIT (0 for none) and KWD key word ("" for none) are same as for INITGET.
;* MSG is the prompt string, to which a default integer is added as <DEF> (nil
;* for none), and a : is added.
;*
(defun uint (bit kwd msg def / inp)
  (if def                                             ;test for a default
    (setq msg (strcat "\n" msg " <" (itoa def) ">: ")     ;string'em with default
          bit (* 2 (fix (/ bit 2)))   ;a default and no null bit code conflict so
    )                                          ;this reduces bit by 1 if odd, to allow null
    (setq msg (strcat "\n" msg ": "))                    ;without default
  );if
  (initget bit kwd)
  (setq inp (getint msg))         ;use the GETINT function
  (if inp inp def)                ;compare the results, return appropriate value
);defun
;*


;* UREAL User interface real function
;* BIT (0 for none) and KWD key word ("" for none) are same as for INITGET.
;* MSG is the prompt string, to which a default real is added as <DEF> (nil
;* for none), and a : is added.
;*
(defun ureal (bit kwd msg def / inp)
  (if def                                             ;test for a default
    (setq msg (strcat "\n" msg " <" (rtos def 2) ">: ")    ;string'em with default
          bit (* 2 (fix (/ bit 2)))   ;a default & no null bit code conflict so
    )                                          ;this reduces bit by 1 if odd, to allow null
    (setq msg (strcat "\n" msg ": "))                    ;without default
  );if
  (initget bit kwd)
  (setq inp (getreal msg))        ;the GETREAL function
  (if inp inp def)                ;compare the results, return appropriate value
);defun
;*


;* UPOINT User interface point function
;* BIT (1 for no null, 0 for none) and KWD key word ("" for none) are same as
;* for INITGET. MSG is the prompt string, to which a default point variable is
;* added as <DEF> (nil for none), and a : is added. BPT is base point (nil for none).
```

Listing continued.

Continued listing.

```
;*
(defun upoint (bit kwd msg def bpt / inp)
  (if def                                           ;check for a default
    (setq pts (strcat
                 (rtos (car def)) "," (rtos (cadr def)) ;formats X,Y 2D pt as string
                 (if                                ;formats 3D ,Z if supplied and FLATLAND off
                   (and (caddr def) (= 0 (getvar "FLATLAND")))
                   (strcat "," (rtos (caddr def)))
                   ""
                 ) );if&strcat
          msg (strcat "\n" msg " <" pts ">: ")      ;string them with default
          bit (* 2 (fix (/ bit 2)))    ;a default and no null bit code conflict so
    )                                  ;this reduces bit by 1 if odd, to allow null
    (setq msg (strcat "\n" msg ": "))               ;or without
  );if a default was specified
  (initget bit kwd)
  (setq inp
    (if bpt                           ;check for base point
      (getpoint msg bpt)              ;and use it
      (getpoint msg)                  ;but not if nil
  ) );setq&if
  (if inp inp def)                    ;evaluate results and return proper value
);defun
;*

;* UANGLE User interface angle function
;* BIT (1 for no null, 0 for none) and KWD key word ("" for none) are same as
;* for INITGET. MSG is the prompt string, to which a default real in rads is
;* added as <DEF> (nil for none), and a : is added. BPT is base point (nil for none).
;*
(defun uangle (bit kwd msg def bpt / inp)
  (if def
    (setq msg (strcat "\n" msg " <" (angtos def) ">: ")
          bit (* 2 (fix (/ bit 2)))
    )
    (setq msg (strcat "\n" msg ": "))
  )
  (initget bit kwd)
  (setq inp
```

Listing continued.

Continued listing.

```
   (if bpt
     (getangle msg bpt)
     (getangle msg)
 ) )
  (if inp inp def)
);defun
;*
```

Additional User Get Functions in ACAD.LSP File

Use these in lieu of the standard GET functions whenever you want input to offer key words, to offer defaults, or to be controlled by INITGET bit code restrictions.

Finishing Your User Interface Tools

 You have the above functions in your ACAD.LSP file. You need not reload it.

Copy and edit the UDIST function to create the four functions shown above in your ACAD.LSP file.

Command: **(load "acad")**   Reload the file.

Test these in the same manner as the previous functions with various bit codes, key words, defaults, prompts, and base points.

Command: **QUIT**

Test these functions well if you don't have the IL DISK. Make sure your ACAD.LSP includes UDIST, UKWORD, USTR, UINT, UREAL, UPOINT, and UANGLE. They'll be used by other functions throughout the rest of the book.

Summary

Think about your own requirements. You'll find yourself using functions from this chapter in all your programs.

While the predicates are not frequently used, they can be invaluable in finding errors resulting from uncontrolled input. They can also trap output errors, like AutoCAD commands that can only accept certain data types. Think about making your own predicate (T nil) tests to trap errors and branch conditionals, such as a predicate to test if a distance falls within an acceptable range.

Use TEXTSCR and GRAPHSCR to control where you look, TERPRI to clean up the text screen, and PROMPT and the print functions to present what you see. PROMPT and the prompt strings built into the GET functions are the core to the user interface of your programs. To make prompts intelligent and responsive, you need to format and combine distances, angles, and other data types in them. For this, program with the data type conversion functions and use STRCAT to create formatted prompts.

But why reinvent all that programming for every input sequence or prompt? Use our user GET functions for input. Create specialized input functions if you have another standard input need, say to restrict input to a certain range or group of values, or to limit input string lengths to format notes that will fit in a given space.

Create custom input functions to feed attributes. Attribute data often must match exact formats or even exact words to be usable in later processing. Using key words to let users select strings from a list, or filtering and testing string input can protect data integrity.

Use key words to make command programs that look and feel like AutoCAD commands. Use key words to present lists of choices, like selecting pipe sizes from a table.

Use SET instead of SETQ when you create or get the variable name from an indirect source. SET evaluates the variable name argument and sets its contents. SETQ doesn't evaluate it; it means SET Quote. For example, if VLIST is a whole list of variable names, you could use SET to efficiently set each to nil with: `(foreach var vlist (set var nil))`.

Use PRINC to suppress returned values so programs load and run cleanly. Combine it in a PROGN in macros for clean programs and prompts.

When dealing with angles, make yourself a degrees-to-radians function for general use. Use AutoLISP's ANGTOS for angle prompts and status. Use our ANGTOC for command input.

Above all, use our customized user GET functions in your programs. The bottom line will be simplified programming, informative prompts, and error-free user input.

Next we'll take a look at the AutoCAD drawing database to see what AutoLISP can do with it. Hint: a whole lot!

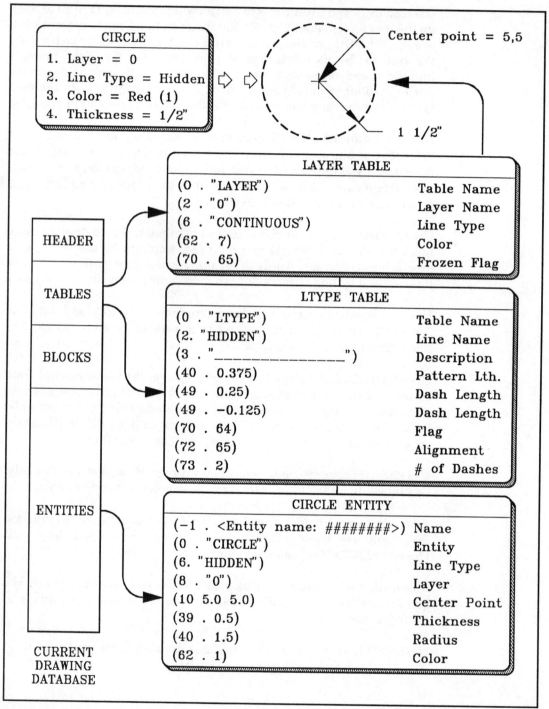

Accessing the Drawing Database

CHAPTER 6

Accessing the Drawing Database

POWER TO THE PROGRAMS

We all think of AutoCAD as a *drawing* tool, but AutoCAD is also a behind-the-scenes database manager. Each drawing entity exists as a data record in AutoCAD's *drawing database*. Like most databases you might think of, AutoCAD's drawing database stores records containing names and numbers. But it also describes the geometric entities, text strings, attributes, reference tables, and environment settings of your AutoCAD drawings. Like any good database manager, AutoCAD stores and sorts, adds and deletes, and lists and reports its records of drawing information. This chapter will show how you can use AutoLISP to access and manipulate the drawing database directly, bypassing AutoCAD commands. The functions, techniques, and tools in this chapter give you the power to let AutoLISP and AutoCAD catch up to your imagination.

The nearly complete control AutoLISP gives you over the AutoCAD drawing data gives you important customizing benefits. You can modify, tally, or delete drawing objects using your own custom editing commands — commands that AutoCAD doesn't provide. You can make your custom programs more intelligent, able to search the drawing to automatically select entities. This automatic search makes it easy to select groups or types of drawing entities. You also can use entity access to make material counts for processing by programs outside AutoCAD. You can individually highlight or control the visibility or color of entities in your programs to provide visual information. Finally, direct modification of entities is sometimes faster or more versatile than using AutoCAD editing commands.

In this chapter, you will learn how to:

- Get entity names from AutoCAD, and step through entities in the drawing database using ENTGET, ENTSEL, ENTLAST, and ENTNEXT.

- Use ENTGET to retrieve an entity data list, DXF codes to identify types of entity data, and ASSOC to extract specific data for AutoLISP manipulation and calculation.

- Work with selection sets, using SSGET, SSLENGTH, SSNAME, SSDEL, SSADD, and SSMEMB to select, group, and process sets of drawing entities.

- Delete, undelete, and modify entities using ENTDEL, ENTMOD, ENTUPD, and SUBST to develop commands that are not available in AutoCAD.

- Select and identify entities by their handles, the permanent names which can be assigned to AutoCAD entities.

- Process complex entities, like polylines and blocks with attributes, using ENTGET and ENTNEXT.

These are all-important functions that you will use in many of your programs. The entity access functions often make the difference between basic, functional programs and intelligent, powerful programs that require minimal user interaction. The useful tools and example programs we develop in this chapter are listed below:

AutoLISP Tools and Programs

AutoLISP Tools

DXF is a simple subroutine that retrieves the data element of an association list. You will need to add this to your ACAD.LSP file.

UENTSL is another user interface GET function. It adds INITGET features and a default key word to ENTSEL, which lacks that versatility.

SSTOOLS.LSP is a set of subroutines that add, subtract, and cross-check selection sets of entities.

SSINTER builds a selection set common to two selection sets.
SSUNION adds two selection sets together.
SSDIFF creates a selection set of the difference between two sets.

CATCH.LSP is on the New Riders AutoLISP Utilities Disk 1. It contains two functions. C:MARK marks the drawing database. Then CATCH selects the newly created entities which follow the mark.

HEX-INT.LSP is also on the New Riders AutoLISP Utilities Disk 1. It is a set of hexadecimal arithmetic tools that make dealing with entity handles easier.

Command Programs

C:MOFFSET is a command that creates equally spaced multiple offsets of a single selected object. It eliminates the need to repeatedly select the entity during the AutoCAD OFFSET command.

C:APLATE is an area calculator that subtracts the area of holes and cutouts on any plate-like surface.

C:CSCALE automatically adjusts the existing drawing scale of selected annotations and symbols (text and block entities) relative to intended plot scale. It maintains existing insertion points.

C:BSCALE is a program that specifies block insertion scale factors. It allows independent rescaling of X, Y, and Z factors of an existing block without reinserting the block in the drawing.

C:RCLOUD is a program that lets you sketch a crude revision cloud that is reprocessed into a neatly reformatted cloud.

We use the DXF function in almost all programs which access entity data. It's easier than spelling out the separate functions that are otherwise required to get the values. SSTOOLS allows automatic selections like "Give me all the text in the drawing *except* text on LAYER DIM02." APLATE is great for any material-estimating application that works with flat patterns. You will find CSCALE easier to use than SCALE because it does the scale calculations for you based on your drawing-to-plot scale, maintaining existing insertion points for multiple entities. Many readers find the BSCALE command particularly useful because it performs scaling not directly possible with an AutoCAD command. It's great for 3D blocks. Drawing revision clouds manually is easy but tedious until you try our RCLOUD. CATCH is invaluable for selecting the new entities created by exploding blocks, polylines, 3D meshes, and dimensions.

The techniques in these programs apply to many other applications. For example, RCLOUD's methods could be applied to other polyline processing, such as in a program to generate parametric gears.

The plate and holes drawn in the first exercise are also used in several following exercises, so SAVE the IL06 drawing after you draw the plate. The IL06A drawing is similarly used throughout the second half of the chapter, so SAVE it in its initial form also. Then QUIT your IL06 and IL06A drawings when you take breaks, so you can edit them as existing drawings in later exercises.

AutoCAD Entities

Every entity in an AutoCAD drawing has a unique identification number like <Entity name: 60000030>. This *entity name* (or *ename*, for short) is the only means you have to retrieve entity data through AutoLISP. The entity name points to the data defining the entity in the drawing database and helps your programs access the entity information they need.

How to Get Entity Names

AutoLISP has three functions to get entity names directly from the AutoCAD database. They are:

entlast
> *Returns the last nondeleted entity name in the database.*
> **(entlast)**

entnext
> *Returns the first nondeleted entity name in the database. If the optional ename is provided, the next nondeleted entity name immediately following the ename is returned.*
> **(entnext** *ename***)**

entsel
> *Returns a list containing the entity name and the point coordinates used to pick the entity. The optional prompt string can provide specific instructions for entity selection.*
> **(entsel** *prompt***)**

ENTSEL insists on picking a single entity with a point pick, like the BREAK and OFFSET commands do. You can't use other object selection devices, such as windows. ENTSEL can take an optional prompt like the GET functions, but if you do not supply one, ENTSEL defaults to the familiar "Select object:" prompt.

AutoCAD keeps its database in the same order in which you create entities. Entity names and orders are maintained throughout the entire editing session. Erased or deleted entities remain in the database and are just *turned off*. The entity names change when you reload a drawing because deleted entities are purged from the database when a drawing is called up for editing.

➡ *NOTE: While you can currently depend on entities to remain in the order of their creation throughout the life of a drawing, be warned that Autodesk has said that this may change in future versions.*

AutoLISP can easily tell you the first or last entity in the current database with ENTNEXT and ENTLAST.

Let's create a plate with cutout holes to allow us to observe entity order. The illustration shows how the plate should look. You can make it any size you wish. It will be used in several following exercises, so SAVE it, and QUIT if you need to take a break.

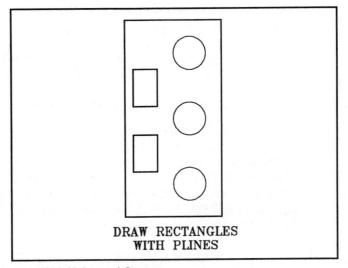

Plate With Holes and Cutouts

Selecting an Entity With ENTSEL, ENTNEXT, and ENTLAST

Edit an EXISTING drawing named IL06 and skip the PLINE, CIRCLE, BASE, and SAVE below.

Begin a NEW drawing named IL06 and do the PLINE, CIRCLE, BASE, and SAVE below.

```
Command: PLINE          Draw the plate with rectangular cutouts
Command: CIRCLE         and round holes.
Command: BASE           Put at lower left corner of plate, to use as a block later.
Command: SAVE           Save the plate for later exercises in this chapter.

Command: (setq frst (entnext))                  Gets the first entity.
Lisp returns: <Entity name: 60000018>           Your name may differ.
```

```
Command: (setq lent (entlast))                          Gets the last entity.
Lisp returns: <Entity name: 600002B8>

Command: (setq plate (entsel "Select the plate outline: "))    With optional prompt.

Select the plate outline:                               Pick the outline.
Lisp returns: (<Entity name: 60000018> (3.6 1.0 0.0))   Your data differs.
```

You can pass entity names to any AutoCAD command requesting object selection where Last is allowed as an option. AutoCAD commands accept entity names regardless of which function is used to retrieve them. But you can't *create* entity names like you can create other variables. An entity name isn't a string or a symbol that you can SETQ to a variable, it's an ename data type.

You can't pass entity names to AutoCAD commands that *require* selection by point picking, but you can use an ENTSEL type list.

Error Free Entity Selection With ENTSEL

You can supply the list returned by ENTSEL to any AutoCAD command selection prompt that allows point picking, except for the FILLET and CHAMFER commands. Using an ENTSEL style list in an AutoCAD object selection command to select a specific entity is a powerful technique. We've all been frustrated by having AutoCAD find the wrong entity. Issuing an ENTSEL list with the COMMAND function ensures selection of the right entity, even in heavy traffic.

The ENTSEL function returns a list containing both the entity name and the point used to pick it. Use OSNAP if you need to be sure that the point you picked actually lies on the selected object, because the AutoCAD pick box permits selection of entities *near* the pick point. CAR returns the entity name of an ENTSEL list, and CADR returns its point value.

You can also create an ENTSEL style list. For instance, if your program has just drawn a line from PT to PT1, you can get its name and save it as an ENTSEL list with (setq ents1 (list (entlast) pt). Then, even after many other entities have been drawn, (command ents1) will always select it at a normal AutoCAD command object selection prompt.

You can't use INITGET key words with ENTSEL, but you can get around this restriction with the GETPOINT and SSGET functions by building an ENTSEL style list. This technique and the SSGET function are shown later in the chapter.

How to Step Through Entities With ENTNEXT

ENTNEXT enables you to step through the AutoCAD database entity by entity. ENTNEXT, called without an argument, returns the first entity of the database. Pass an optional entity name argument to ENTNEXT and AutoLISP returns the next entity that follows it.

We'll use the REDRAW function to highlight the entities as we step through them.

Controlling Visibility by Entity Name

The REDRAW function with an ename argument redraws a specific entity. If you give it a mode argument as well as an entity name, you can temporarily highlight the entity. A REDRAW *function* without arguments redraws the entire drawing (in the current viewport), just like the REDRAW *command*.

redraw	*Redraws the current viewport unless ename is provided, in which case the entity represented by ename is redrawn. The mode option redraws the entity in four possible ways: 1 = standard redraw, 2 = reverse redraw (blank), 3 = highlight redraw, and 4 = de-highlight.* (**redraw** *ename mode*)

REDRAW *mode* 1, which simply redraws the entity, is the default. Mode 2 blanks the entity, but doesn't really erase it. Mode 3 highlights, and mode 4 de-highlights. Not all video displays support highlighting.

Try redrawing the entities in order, displaying them with ENTNEXT. We use a half second DELAY command to slow the function down enough to see the entity order. Watch the polyline vertexes carefully as they redraw.

Stepping Through With ENTNEXT and REDRAW

Continue in the previous drawing, or edit an EXISTING drawing named IL06.

```
Command: (setq ent (entnext))             Get the first entity.
Command: (while (setq ent (entnext ent)) (command "DELAY" 500) (redraw ent 3))
                                          Highlight each.

Command: (redraw)                         Redraws them all.
```

Notice that the first polyline was highlighted segment by segment, and that the other polylines were highlighted as a whole, then each of their vertexes blinked. A polyline is a complex entity, consisting of a head entity and multiple vertex entities. ENTNEXT steps through the head and each vertex entity in order. The (setq ent (entnext)) did not highlight the first polyline head entity, the first entity in the drawing. The first loop of the WHILE highlighted the next entity, a vertex. The other polyline heads were highlighted before their vertexes, so you didn't see their individual segments highlight, only their vertexes blink.

Use this to highlight individual polyline segments, or attributes in blocks (which are handled similarly). The direction of a polyline is very important to 3D surfacing commands like RULESURF. Use this technique to highlight the polyline's first segment as a visual prompt to show direction.

REDRAW only controls the visibility of entities, and doesn't redraw deleted entities. The ENTDEL function offers control over entity deletion.

Deleting and Restoring Entities by Name

ENTDEL is an entity data function that deletes entities. It erases one entity at a time, and is quicker than the ERASE command. It can also unerase a previously deleted entity.

entdel

> *Deletes or restores the ename depending on its status in the current editing session.*
> (entdel *ename*)

Try erasing the second entity of the database by entity name, then use ENTDEL to delete the first entity.

Using ENTDEL to Delete and Restore Entities

Continue in the previous drawing, or edit an EXISTING drawing named IL06.

```
Command: ERASE
Select objects: (setq frst (entnext))                    Get the first entity.
Select objects: <RETURN>                                 and <RETURN> to erase.

Command: OOPS                                             Bring it back.

Command: (entdel frst)                                   Deletes the FRST entity.
```

Command: **OOPS** *Invalid*	Try to bring it back. OOPS can't... because AutoCAD didn't erase it.
Command: **(entdel frst)**	And it's back.

You can toggle entities between being erased and being visible. To bring a deleted entity back, you can ENTDEL it again even if the AutoCAD ERASE command deleted the entity.

Applying Entity Selection to Programs

Let's explore entity names a bit more by making a program called MOFFSET. MOFFSET creates equally spaced multiple offsets of a selected entity without having to reselect the entity. It's kind of like a concentric array command.

```
;* C:MOFFSET is a multiple offset command. It requires the user to show the
;* offset direction, select one object, tell how many times to offset it
;* and give a direction for the offset. It requires the User GET functions.
;*
(defun C:MOFFSET( / ent spt dist)
  (setq #mdist (udist 1 "" "Offset distance" #mdist nil) ;the distance to offset
        ent (entsel "\nSelect object to offset: ")        ;get the object
        spt (upoint 1 "" "Select side" nil (cadr ent))    ;get which side
        #mnum (uint 5 "" "How many times" #mnum)          ;# times
  );setq
  (setq dist #mdist)                      ;set a variable to the distance interval
  (repeat #mnum                           ;program loop
    (command "offset" dist ent spt "")    ;run the offset command
    (setq dist (+ dist #mdist))           ;increment the offset distance
  );repeat
  (princ)                                 ;clean ending
);defun
(princ)                                   ;clean loading
;*
```

The C:MOFFSET Function in MOFFSET.LSP File

When requesting input, MOFFSET uses the user interface functions that you developed in the previous chapter. These functions supply default values and check for valid input. Note that the #MNUM and #MDIST variables are global defaults. They are not on the local variable list, so their defaults carry over to repeated uses of the MOFFSET command. MOFFSET uses the DIST variable for the incremented offset distance value with each REPEAT loop. With each loop, DIST is incremented by the original offset distance #DIST until the program has looped #MNUM times.

Notice the use of ENT, an ENTSEL style entity list. It is fed to the OFFSET command by the COMMAND function, and (cadr ent) returns the pick point as a base point for the UPOINT function.

The user GET functions should have loaded with the ACAD.LSP file. Without them, MOFFSET will fail.

Using the MOFFSET Function

Continue in the previous drawing, or edit an EXISTING drawing named IL06.

You already have the C:MOFFSET function in your MOFFSET.LSP file.

Create the C:MOFFSET function as shown above, in a file named MOFFSET.LSP.

Command: **ERASE**	Get rid of all but one cutout polyline and a circle.
Command: **(load "moffset")**	Load the function.
Command: **MOFFSET**	Try the function.
Offset distance: **0.25**	Distance first, like the OFFSET command prompt.
Select object to offset:	Select the polyline.
Select side:	Pick a side.
How many times: **5**	
Command: **MOFFSET**	Try it again and see the defaults.
Offset distance <0.25>: **<RETURN>**	Accept the default.
Select object to offset:	Select the circle.
Select side:	Pick a side.
How many times <5>: **<RETURN>**	Accept the default.
Command: **QUIT**	

Your screen should look similar to the Multiple Offsets illustration.

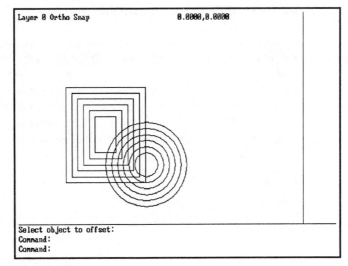

Multiple Offsets

If you want MOFFSET to further mimic the OFFSET command's syntax, you can add a key word option and test to allow a "Through point" option. In some versions of AutoCAD, OFFSET does not allow suppression of highlighting, which would otherwise speed it up.

You will use these entity access functions in many programs. For example, in this chapter's BSCALE command function, we use ENTSEL and ENTGET to select an entity and ensure that it is indeed a block. The RCLOUD program, also in this chapter, uses ENTGET, ENTNEXT, and ENTLAST. And GROUP.LSP, on the New Riders AutoLISP Utilities Disk 1, uses every one of these functions: ENTSEL, ENTGET, ENTNEXT, ENTLAST, ENTDEL, and REDRAW. GROUP.LSP lets you create *groups* of entities that can be selected with a single pick. You can manipulate them like a block without creating a block. This technique is used for parts created by parametric programs.

So far, we've worked with just one entity at a time. Next, we'll look at AutoCAD selection sets and how AutoLISP uses them.

Entity Selection Sets

AutoCAD's *selection sets* are nothing more than groups of entities. Most of AutoCAD's edit commands operate on selection sets. At the start of each edit command, AutoCAD asks for the set of objects to edit. You can use selection modes like Window or Crossing, or you can just pick by point, whatever is most convenient for you. AutoLISP's SSGET function mimics the AutoCAD object selection process, so you can select groups of entities to work with in AutoLISP.

ssget

> *Returns a selection set of entities. If SSGET fails, it returns nil. With no arguments (or a nil), SSGET uses AutoCAD's standard object selection to get a user selection. The optional mode argument specifies options to automate selection without user input. Modes are "P" for Previous, "L" for Last, "W" for Window, and "C" for Crossing. One optional point argument alone selects a single point, or two points following a mode select Window or Crossing boxes. An "X" mode returns entities matching a filtering list based on any combination in the DXF group codes table which follows.*
>
> **(ssget** *mode* **point point)**

DXF GROUP CODES

DXF	FIELD	DXF	FIELD
0	Entity type	38	Elevation (Rel. 11 will drop)
2	Block name	39	Thickness
6	Linetype name	62	Color number
7	Text style name	66	Attributes
8	Layer name	210	3D extrusion direction

You can use the SSGET function with or without arguments. If called with no arguments, SSGET issues AutoCAD's standard "Select objects:" prompt. SSGET returns the name of a selection set. This name must be set to a variable to process the set. Let's create a couple of selection sets.

Creating Selection Sets With SSGET

Edit an EXISTING drawing named IL06.

```
Command: (setq ss1 (ssget))          Window everything, including the plate.
Select objects: W
First corner:
Other corner: 6 found.
Select objects: <RETURN>
Lisp returns: <Selection set: 1>    And "ss1" says it is selection set number 1.
```

The selection set number has no real significance to your program. AutoLISP simply receives a handle from AutoCAD which references that set of objects. The returned value <selection set *n*> is a reference to the selection set *n* created during the current drawing session. The variable set to the selection set manipulates the set.

➥ *NOTE: AutoLISP can't keep more than six AutoLISP selection sets "open" at one time. Open means the selection set is still set to a variable. If you don't reset your variables to nil, declare them local, or reuse the names, you may run out of sets. We use SS, SS1, SS2, SS3, and SS4 over and over again to help limit the number of sets open. If you run out, SSGET returns nil and programs will fail.*

Manipulating Selection Sets

Selection sets are like lists, but they are PICKSET, not LIST data types. The list handling functions don't work for them. But AutoLISP has several other functions that operate on selection sets.

sslength

> *Returns the number of entities in a selection set.*
> **(sslength** *selection-set***)**

ssmemb

> *Returns the entity name if it is in the selection set. Otherwise returns nil.*
> **(ssmemb** *ename selection-set***)**

ssname

> *Returns the entity name of the number position of the selection set. The first entity is number 0.*
> **(ssname** *selection-set number***)**

ssadd

> *Creates an empty selection set when no arguments are provided. If the optional entity name is provided, a selection set is created with just that entity name. If an entity name is provided with an existing selection set, it is added to the selection set.*
> **(ssadd** *ename selection-set***)**

ssdel

> *Deletes the entity name from the selection set and returns the entity name.*
> **(ssdel** *ename selection-set***)**

The SSLENGTH function returns the number of entities in a set, like LENGTH does for lists. An individual entity can be returned from the selection set with the SSNAME function, like NTH for lists. SSMEMB tells if an entity is included in a set, like MEMBER for lists. Entities can be added or removed from selection sets with the functions SSADD and SSDEL. If you use no arguments, SSADD creates a null (empty) set.

A Look at Selection Set Functions

```
Command: (sslength ss1)      How many did you select in the previous exercise?
Lisp returns: 6
```

```
Command: (ssdel (setq plate (car (entsel))) ss1)    Select the plate to remove from the set.
Lisp returns: <Selection set: 1>            It's still the same selection set name.
```

```
Command: SELECT                              Check which one is not included.
Select objects: !SS1
5 found.                                     The plate outline doesn't highlight.
```

```
Command: !PLATE                              Returns <Entity name: 60000018>.
Command: (ssmemb plate ss1)                  See if PLATE is a member.
Lisp returns: nil                            No, because you just subtracted it.
```

```
Command: (ssadd plate ss1)                   Add it back to the set.
Lisp returns: <Selection set: 1>
```

```
Command: SELECT                              Which ones are included.
Select objects: !SS1
6 found.                                     Back to the full set.
```

```
Command: (ssmemb plate ss1)                  See if entity is a member.
Lisp returns: <Entity name: 60000018>       AutoLISP tells us it's back in.
```

```
Command: (ssname ss1 0)                      Gets first entity from the set.
Lisp returns: <Entity name: 600001f8>
```

The SSADD and SSDEL functions have one important difference from other AutoLISP functions. They directly modify the variable set to the selection set. When you add or remove entities from an existing selection set using SSADD or SSDEL, you do not need to again SETQ the variable bound to that set. When you CONS or APPEND a list, you must reset your variable to the modified list that is returned, like (setq lst (append new lst)). However you can just (ssadd new ss) or (ssdel ent ss1) and the entity names NEW and ENT will be added and removed directly from the selection sets stored as the variables SS and SS1.

SSNAME is sort of an "NTH" function of selection sets, to get the names of individual entities. You give SSNAME the name of the selection set and the index number of the entity you want, and it returns the name of the entity. When you use SSNAME, remember to start counting with 0! The first entity is really the 0th element from the beginning. For example, count 0 to 5 for six elements.

Applying Selection Set Tools to APLATE

Selections sets are powerful tools. Let's make a command, called APLATE, to calculate the area of a plate with cutouts and holes removed from it. To help you get started, the first part of the example reviews the addition and subtraction features of AutoCAD's AREA command.

To review, try adding the area of the plate polyline in the AREA command and then subtracting a circle. Your areas may vary from ours.

Reviewing the Accumulative AREA Command

Continue in the previous drawing, or edit an EXISTING drawing named IL06.

```
Command: AREA
<First point>/Entity/Add/Subtract: A
<First point>/Entity/Subtract: E
(ADD mode) Select circle or polyline:              Select the plate polyline.
Area = 28.0000, Perimeter = 22.0000
Total area = 28.0000
(ADD mode) Select circle or polyline: <RETURN>    Back to the original prompt.
<First point>/Entity/Subtract: S
<First point>/Entity/Add: E
(SUBTRACT mode) Select circle or polyline:         Select a circle.
Area = 0.7854, Circumference = 3.1416
Total area = 27.2146                                The accumulated area.
(SUBTRACT mode) Select circle or polyline: <RETURN> <RETURN>   Return twice.
```

Our C:APLATE command prompts for and gets the name of an entity using the ENTSEL function. If you have the IL DISK, the APLATE function is in the file APLATE.LSP. Otherwise, you can make the file now.

```
;* APLATE calculates the area of a plate, automatically subtracting
;* the area of any included holes or openings.
;*
(defun C:APLATE ( / plate ss1 count emax)
  (setq plate (entsel "\nPick the plate outline: "))   ;get the plate outline
  (prompt "\nSelect all holes and cutouts...")         ;tell them what to select
  (setq ss1 (ssget))                                   ;get the selection set
  (ssdel (car plate) ss1)                              ;exclude the plate from ss1
```

Listing continued.

Continued listing.

```
❶
  (command "area" "a" "e" plate "" "s" "e")          ;start the command
  (setq count 0                                      ;set initial count value
        emax (sslength ss1)                          ;find the max count value
  );setq
❷
  (while (< count emax)                              ;start the program loop
    (command (ssname ss1 count))                     ;pass entity name to command
    (setq count (1+ count))                          ;increment the counter
  );while
  (command "" "")                                    ;exit the command
❸
  (prompt (strcat "\nFinal area is " (rtos (getvar "AREA"))"sq.")) ;last area
  (princ)                                            ;clean ending
)defun
(princ)                                              ;clean loading
;*
```

APLATE Command in APLATE.LSP File

❶ The APLATE command gets the necessary input from the user. Then it starts the AREA command, adds the first entity, and begins to subtract entities. It leaves the AREA command that was sent to AutoCAD via the COMMAND function unfinished at the point where AutoCAD expects an entity name. Then, it starts a counter to loop through the selection set so that each entity in the set may be sent to the AREA command and subtracted from the running total. SSLENGTH is used to obtain the number of entities in the selection set so that an index counter of the set can be maintained.

❷ The program loops through the selection set one at a time and passes the extracted name to the command processor. The counter is incremented at the end of each loop cycle.

❸ When the loop is finished, the AREA command is finished with two <RETURN>s. The last area total is reported. AutoCAD keeps the final area total in the AREA system variable.

Using the APLATE Command

Continue in the previous drawing, or edit an EXISTING drawing named IL06.

 You have the APLATE command in your APLATE.LSP file.

 Create the APLATE command in a file named APLATE.LSP.

Command: **(load "aplate")**	Load the file.
Command: **APLATE**	It prompts:
Pick the plate outline:	Pick it.
Select all holes and cutouts...	
Select objects:	Select them.
Select objects: **<RETURN>**	It scrolls by and you get:
Final area is 22.9438	Your area may vary.

The secret of the APLATE command is its ability to loop through each entity of a selection set, feeding each entity in turn to a command. This can be applied to many automated entity editing problems. You can extend the specific techniques used in C:APLATE to other area calculation programs, like making patterns or doing floor plan calculations.

So far, we've used the general form of the SSGET function, a call without optional arguments. Next, we'll take a look at the selection set modes of the SSGET function.

Optional Selection Set Modes

Until now, you determined your selection sets by manually picking entities. AutoLISP provides the SSGET function's optional *modes* to automate getting selection sets. Most of the normal object selection methods are available to the SSGET function. These modes, with examples, are shown in the following table.

SSGET FORM	PURPOSE
(ssget '(0 5))	selects entity passing thru 0,5
(ssget "L")	selects last entity
(ssget "P)	selects previous selection set
(ssget "W" '(0 0) '(5 5))	objects within window 0,0 to 5,5
(ssget "C" '(0 0) '(5 5))	objects crossing box 0,0 to 5,5
(ssget "X" *entity-data*)	retrieves entities matching data

You can assign the returned set to any AutoLISP variable with the SETQ function.

When you use SSGET with the "W" or "C" options, you need to supply two corner points. You can't pick the corner points.

The following example shows how you can select all objects crossing the limits of the drawing using SSGET "W" and the limits system variables as window arguments.

Using SSGET Modes

Continue in the previous drawing, or edit an EXISTING drawing named IL06.

```
Command: (ssget "C" (getvar "LIMMIN") (getvar "LIMMAX"))    Crossing limits.
Lisp returns: <Selection set 1>

Command: (ssget "P")                                        Get the previous set.
Lisp returns: <Selection set 2>

Command: (setq pt (getpoint "Pick: "))                      Save a point.
Pick:                                                       Pick a circle.
Lisp returns: (5.5 4.0 0.0)

Command: (ssget pt)                                         Select an entity by a point.
Lisp returns: <Selection set: 3>
```

Next, we'll look at a special form for filtering specific classes of entities from the entire drawing database into a selection set.

Filtering Selections With SSGET "X"

With the X mode, SSGET searches through the drawing entities. If you use (ssget "X") alone, without any entity property list, it returns a selection set of all non-deleted entities in the drawing. With an optional entity property list, it compares entities to a list of properties. You can't do that with normal AutoCAD object selection. Entities that match all the properties in the list are returned in the selection set.

A property list can contain any number of requirements in any order. However, each property type can only appear once in each list. The entity properties are restricted to those shown in the following table and must be in the form of DXF codes. You'll learn more about DXF codes later in this chapter.

CODE	DESCRIPTION	EXAMPLE
0	Name of the entity	(0 . "LINE")
2	Insert block name	(2 . "ARROW")
6	Name of linetype	(6 . "CENTER")
7	Text style name	(7 . "STANDARD")
8	Name of the layer	(8 . "OBJ02")
38	Elevation	(38 . 144.0)
39	Thickness	(39 . 6.0)
62	Color number	(62 . 1)
66	Attributes for block insert	(66 . 1)
210	3D extrusion direction	(210 1.0 0.0 -0.5)

SSGET X Property Codes

Property lists consist of one or more dotted pairs. Each pair has a DXF code preceding the data, just like an entity data list. You can create the list by beginning it with a single quotation mark '. For example:

```
(ssget "x" '((0 . "CIRCLE") (8 . "OBJ01")))
```

In this example, SSGET would create a selection set of every circle that is on Layer OBJ01.

Using SSGET X

Command: **LAYER**   Make a new layer OBJ01. Leave it current.
Command: **CIRCLE**   Draw two circles on Layer OBJ01.

Command: **(ssget "X")**   Gets all entities in database.
Lisp returns: <Selection set 4>

Command: **(ssget "X" '((0 . "CIRCLE") (8 . "OBJ01")))**   Gets all circles on Layer OBJ01.
Lisp returns: <Selection set 5>   But ignores circles on Layer 0.

Getting selection sets with SSGET has two great advantages. First, it works without user intervention, reducing errors. Second, it works fast. Let's apply what we've done so far to improve upon the ENTSEL function.

Using Key Words With "ENTSEL"

Now we have the tools to create an ENTSEL-like function that offers the key word, default, and no null features of last chapter's user GET functions. The format (ssname (ssget point) 0) will return an entity name if one is found at point POINT. This can be used to get around ENTSEL's inability to use INITGET key words. Just set your key words with INITGET, then prompt for a point with GETPOINT. If you get a key word, use it. But if a point was selected, use the point to get an entity and create an ENTSEL style list. Here's the function:

```
;* UENTSL User interface ENTSEL function adds no null and key words to "ENTSEL"
;* BIT (0 for none, 1 to disallow null input) and KWD key word ("" for none)
;* are fed to INITGET. MSG is the prompt string, to which a default key word
;* string is added as <DEF> ("" or nil for none), and a : is added.
;*
(defun uentsl (bit kwd msg def / inp ss)
  (if (and msg (/= msg "")) nil (setq msg "Select object")) ;default prompt
  (if (and def (/= def ""))                              ;test for a default word
    (setq msg (strcat "\n"  msg  " <"  def  ">: ")        ;then string'em with default
          bit 0  ;if a default, then null input accepts it, so turn off no null
    );setq
    (setq msg (strcat "\n" msg ": "))                    ;else without default
  );if
  (initget bit kwd)
  (setq inp (getpoint msg))                              ;and use it in GETPOINT
  (cond                                                  ;and return a value
    ( (= (type (setq kwd (if inp inp def))) 'STR)        ;if key word or default
      kwd                                                ;string, return it
    )
    ( (not inp) nil )                                    ;if null, return nil
    ( (setq ss (ssget inp))                              ;else get ename with point
      (if ss (list (ssname ss 0) inp) nil)              ;return ENTSEL list or nil
  ) );cond&T
);defun
;*
```

The UENTSL "ENTSEL" Function in UENTSL.LSP

By now, these user GET functions should be old hat, so we'll skip showing them in exercises. UENTSL is similar to UPOINT, with a few differences. It only supports INITGET BIT values 0 and 1. The first IF in UENTSL is needed to mimic ENTSEL's default prompt if none is supplied. The value returned by the GETPOINT must be carefully analyzed by the COND to return the proper value. The first condition returns any key word or default string value. The second returns nil if null input was allowed and received. The last condition builds and returns the ENTSEL style string, or returns nil if no object is found.

Unfortunately, there is no way to mimic the AutoCAD pickbox cursor in UENTSL, so it just uses the usual crosshairs.

You have UENTSL.LSP if you have the IL DISK. If you don't have the disk and the function looks useful to you, create it and test it. If you use UENTSL often in your programs, add it to your ACAD.LSP file.

Besides its ENTSEL limitations, AutoLISP is missing other tools you need to work with entity selection sets. Some of your more advanced programs will require the ability to merge two selection sets, find common entities in selection sets (a union), or subtract selection sets.

Developing a Selection Set Toolkit

In this section, we will develop a set of tools called SSTOOLS to manipulate selection sets. When AutoLISP lacks the tools to do something, see if AutoCAD can help solve your problem. Here is a classic case. Since AutoCAD can add and subtract selection sets with the Add and Remove options, use AutoCAD's SELECT command to make the selection set, then use the Previous option of the SSGET function to define the set in AutoLISP.

SSUNION uses the SELECT command to merge (form a union of) all entities in two selection sets. SSDIFF subtracts one set from another using the object selection's Remove mode. SSDIFF is similar to SSUNION in its code. SSINTER finds the intersection of entities common to two sets. With these, you can make automatic selections like "give me all the text in the drawing *except* text on Layer DIM02."

The SSTOOLS are shown in the following diagrams.

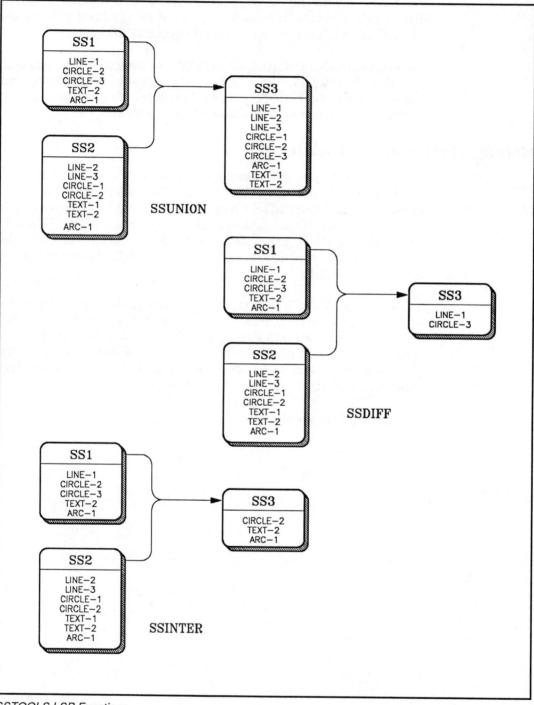

SSTOOLS.LSP Functions

Here is the program listing for the SSTOOLS.LSP file.

➡️ *TIP: To create SSDIFF, copy SSUNION, change its name and description, and add an "R" to the* (command... *line.*

```
;* SSTOOLS.LSP is a kit of selection set tools. They all return ss3, a global.
;* SSUNION adds two selection sets using the SELECT command & creates new ss3.
;* It must be used prior to the command which is to receive its selection.
;*
(defun ssunion (ss1 ss2 / hilite ss3)
  (setq hilite (getvar "HIGHLIGHT"))      ;speeds up selection
  (setvar "HIGHLIGHT" 0)
  (command "SELECT" ss1 ss2 "")           ;uses the select command to combine set
  (setq ss3 (ssget "P"))                  ;combined set is the previous
  (setvar "HIGHLIGHT" hilite)
  ss3                                     ;returns ss3
);defun
;*


;* SSDIFF subtracts ss2 from ss1 using the Select command & creates new ss3
(defun ssdiff (ss1 ss2 / hilite ss3)
  (setq hilite (getvar "HIGHLIGHT"))      ;speeds up selection
  (setvar "HIGHLIGHT" 0)
  (command "SELECT" ss1 "R" ss2 "")       ;uses the select command Remove mode
  (setq ss3 (ssget "P"))                  ;combined set is the previous
  (setvar "HIGHLIGHT" hilite)
  ss3                                     ;returns ss3
);defun
;*


;* SSINTER takes the common entities (intersection) of ss1 and ss2
;* and returns new ss
(defun ssinter (ss1 ss2 / count count1 count2 smax smax1
                smax2 more less name / hilite ss3
               )
  (setq count 0                           ;set counters
        count1 0
        count2 0
        smax1 (sslength ss1)              ;get number of entities in sets
        smax2 (sslength ss2)
        ss3 (ssadd)                       ;start a new empty set
  );setq
```

Listing continued.

Continued listing.

```
(if (>= count1 count2)                    ;find out which has more entities
   (setq more ss1 less ss2 smax smax1)    ;flip names around
   (setq more ss2 less ss1 smax smax2)
);if
(while (< count smax)                      ;start a program loop
   (setq name (ssname more count))         ;get the entity name
   (if (ssmemb name less)                  ;see if it's in the other set
       (ssadd name ss3)                    ;if it is, add it to the output set
   );if
   (setq count (1+ count))                 ;increment counter
);while
ss3                                        ;pass out new set
);defun
;*
;*end of SSTOOLS.LSP
```

The SSTOOLS.LSP File

➤ *NOTE: Although the COMMAND technique used in SSUNION and SSDIFF is efficient, it's limited. It can't be used transparently in AutoCAD because it uses the SELECT command. In contrast, SSINTER finds the intersection of entities common to both sets by stepping through the entities. The function uses SSNAME to get entity names from one selection set and check them with the membership of another set using SSMEMB. You could write versions of SSUNION and SSDIFF with the same techniques to determine membership.*

Comparing Selection Sets With SSTOOLS

Continue in the previous drawing, or edit an EXISTING drawing named IL06.

 You have these functions in SSTOOLS.LSP.

Create the SSTOOLS.LSP file shown above.

```
Command: (load "sstools")              Load the functions.
Command: (setq ss1 (ssget))            Select the plate, including holes and circles.
Lisp returns: <Selection set: 5>

Command: (setq ss2 (ssget))            Select the rectangular holes.
Lisp returns: <Selection set: 6>

Command: (setq ss4 (ssget))            Yes, SS4. Select the circles.
Lisp returns: <Selection set: 7>
```

```
Command: (setq ss3 (ssunion ss2 ss4))       Test SSUNION.
Select objects:   2 found.
Select objects:   3 found.
Select objects:
Lisp returns: <Selection set: 8>

Command: SELECT                             Check it.
Select objects: !SS3                        The new set. All the holes and circles.
5 found.                                    Strike <RETURN> to finish.

Command: (setq ss3 (ssdiff ss1 ss2))        Test SSDIFF. It scrolls by.
Command:  SELECT                            Enter !SS3 to check it.
                                            All but the rectangular holes.

Command:  SELECT                            You can use SSINTER in a command.
Select objects: (ssinter ss1 ss2)           Only the rectangles.
2 found.
Command: QUIT                               You don't need the drawing.
```

➡ *NOTE: Be careful when stepping through selection sets and using SSDEL. For example, if you SSDEL the fifth entity before you have processed the sixth, the sixth entity becomes the fifth and will be missed because you have already processed the fifth. To deal with this, always decrement your counter and max values whenever you do an SSDEL while stepping through a set. Alternatively, you might try adding the good entities to a different selection set, instead of deleting the bad ones from the original set, as you step through.*

You've now conquered selection sets. You can easily select all the polylines on Layer PIPING with color 5 (blue for water), except those that are linetype DASHED (for demolition). You can step through each one in your selection set, but can you add their lengths? Now that you can build sets of entities, you need to know how to retrieve usable data for each entity.

Entity Data

Your use of selection sets would be limited if you were not able to access individual entity data. You need to get information like coordinates, scales, text strings, and properties, so that you can use AutoLISP to make calculations and modifications to your data. AutoLISP's ENTGET function enables you to retrieve entity data.

entget	*Returns a list of data describing the entity specified by the entity name.*
	`(entget ename)`

ENTGET peeks into the AutoCAD database and returns data for the entity you request. The only argument ENTGET takes is an entity name. The data is returned in an association list, like:

```
((-1 . <Entity name: 60000018>) (0 . "LINE") (8 . "0")
(10 1.0 1.0 0.0) (11 2.0 3.0 4.0) (210 0.0 0.0 1.0))
```

Let's create a few entities to work with. You'll need a line, 3D face, text, and a block insert (remember a block's entity is called an *insert*). If you have the IL DISK, you have this in the IL06A.DWG. If not, create it now and SAVE it. Use the IL06 drawing from the beginning of this chapter to insert as a block. After saving IL06A, you should QUIT when you take breaks. You will use the saved version in later exercises.

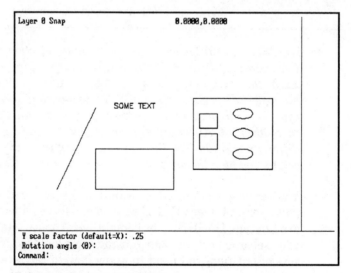

Entities to Test in IL06A.DWG

Setting Up Entities for the ENTGET Exercises

Edit an EXISTING drawing named IL06A and skip the rest of this sequence.

Begin a NEW drawing named IL06A and do the following.

```
Command: LINE       Draw from 1,1,0 to 2,3,4.
Command: TEXT       Center justified at 3,3,0, enter "SOME TEXT"
Command: 3DFACE     From 2,1,0 to 4,1,0 to 4,2,2 to 2,2,2.
```

Command: **INSERT**   Insert IL06 as a block at 4.5,1.5,
                               with an X scale of 0.5, Y of 0.25, and 0 rotation.
Command: **SAVE**   You'll use IL06A in several following exercises.

Let's examine the entity data list format. Select the text with the ENTSEL function, then use CAR and ENTGET to retrieve its data list.

Looking at Entity Data

Command: **(setq en (entsel))**
Select object: Pick the text.

Lisp returns: (<Entity name: 60000030> (2.8 3.0 0.0))   Your pick point may differ.

Command: **(setq ed (entget (car en)))**
Lisp returns: ((–1 . <Entity name: 60000030>) (0 . "TEXT") (8 . "0") (10 2.46726 3.0
0.0) (40 . 0.125) (1 . "SOME TEXT") (50 . 0.0) (41 . 1.0) (51 . 0.0) (7 . "STD") (71
. 0) (72 . 1) (11 3.0 3.0 0.0) (210 0.0 0.0 1.0))

ENTSEL listed the entity name and point, saved as EN. So you used CAR to extract the first atom, the entity name. Your entity names may vary from the book's examples. ENTGET took the entity name and returned the entity data as an association list, a particularly efficient type of list that makes data retrieval easier.

Entity Association Lists and Dotted Pairs

An association list is a list of nested lists. We'll call them sublists. The association list format makes retrieving its sublists easy. The first element of each sublist acts as a *key,* a word or code used in retrieving the sublist. AutoLISP's ASSOC function returns the sublist that starts with the specified key from an association list.

assoc | *Returns a list containing the item from a list of lists.*
          | **(assoc item list)**

Any list can be treated as an association list as long as its *first* element is a sublist. For example, if X is ((1 data) (2 more) 3 4 5), then (assoc 1 x) will return (1 data). The atoms 3 4 5 are not lists and are ignored by ASSOC.

You generally use the LIST function to create an association list. Most of the sublists in entity data association lists are in a special format called a *dotted pair*. A dotted pair is a two-element list with a *dot* (a period) separating the elements, like (item . item).

The CONS and CDRs of Dotted Pairs

You can make your own dotted pair list using CONS, AutoLISP's basic list CONStruction function. By definition, the dotted pair can have only two elements. A dotted pair is more efficient in memory usage than an ordinary two-element list. When working with entity data, AutoLISP uses the dotted pair form of lists.

cons

> *Adds item as a new first element of list and returns the new list, if supplied, as its second argument.*
> (cons *item list*)
>
> *Returns a dotted pair in the form (item . item), if the second argument is not a list.*
> (cons *item1 item2*)

Having dotted pairs in your entity data lists lets you use the CDR function to retrieve the data, regardless of the number of items. CDR returns all but the first element of a list. The CDR of a point sublist from an entity data list like (cdr ' (11 3.0 3.0 0.0)) returns (3.0 3.0 0.0) as a normal point list.

However, the CDR of a dotted pair is different. It returns the rest of the list as an item, an atom, not a list. For instance, (cdr ' (1 . "SOME TEXT")) returns "SOME TEXT" not ("SOME TEXT"). Why? Well, recall that (cons item *list*) creates a normal list, adding a new first element to a list. Conversely, (cdr list) returns that list without its first element. But (cons item1 *item2*) returns a *dotted pair*, so to be consistent, (cdr dotted-pair) returns only *item2*, not a list. A complete explanation of LISP theory in general, along with a description of the internal storage structure of data, can be found in any textbook on LISP language. Try David Touretsky's LISP, A Gentle Introduction to Symbolic Computation.

To see CONS, CDR, and ASSOC work together, try creating a dotted pair and getting data from an association list using the key "8," the code for layer.

Looking at Association Lists

Continue in the previous drawing, or edit an EXISTING drawing named IL06A.

```
Command: (setq ed (entget (car (entsel))))          Get the text data again.
Select object:                                       Pick the text.
Lisp returns: ((-1 . <Entity name: 60000030>) (0 . "TEXT") (8 . "0") (10 2.46726 3.0
0.0) (40 . 0.125) (1 . "SOME TEXT") (50 . 0.0) (41 . 1.0) (51 . 0.0) (7 . "STD") (71
. 0) (72 . 1) (11 3.0 3.0 0.0) (210 0.0 0.0 1.0))

Command: (assoc 8 ed)                                Give the code and entity list.
Lisp returns: (8 . "0")                              It returns the association sublist.

Command: (cdr (assoc 8 ed))                          And the data itself with CDR of the group.
Lisp returns: "0"                                    Returns "0," the layer name.

Command: (cons 8 "0")                                Make a dotted pair.
Lisp returns: (8 . "0")                              Just like the sublist above.
```

There are fourteen keys in the simple text association list above, and many more in complex entities. Obviously, we need to find out what these key codes mean.

DXF Group Codes and AutoLISP

AutoCAD uses the DXF (Drawing eXchange Format) codes to report entity data. A DXF code precedes each type of data, like a point, layer name, elevation, and so on. The DXF code lets programs manage AutoCAD's entity data without relying on the data's order. In fact, the order you get in your examples may vary from the order we show.

The complete DXF codes are shown in two tables: the Entity DXF Groups (in this chapter); and the Table DXF Groups (in the next chapter). These tables are reproduced again in Appendix C for easy reference. As the following chart shows, the DXF codes break down into several major groups.

Code Values	Data Type	Major Uses
0-9, 999	Strings	Entity type, named objects, text values, handles.
10-37	Reals	Coordinates.
38, 39	Reals	Elevation, thickness.
40-59	Reals	Scale factors, angles.
60-79	Integers	Colors, flags, counts, modes.
80-209	Unused	
210, 220, 230	Reals	X, Y, Z extrusion direction.

Major DXF Code Groups

The following exercise shows the listings and DXF codes for some common entities. Examine the entities shown. Then draw other entity types and look at their data on your own.

Using DXF Codes

Continue in the previous drawing, or edit an EXISTING drawing named IL06A.

```
Command: (entget (car (entsel)))
Select object:
Lisp returns:
((-1 . <Entity name: 60000018>)
(0 . "LINE")
(8 . "0")
(10 1.0 1.0 0.0)
(11 2.0 3.0 4.0)
(210 0.0 0.0 1.0))
```
Select the line entity.

The entity name.
The entity type.
Its layer name.
First endpoint.
Second endpoint.
Extrusion direction.

```
Command: (entget (car (entsel)))
Select object:
Lisp returns:
((-1 . <Entity name: 60000060>)
(0 . "INSERT")
(8 . "0")
(2 . "IL06")
(10 4.5 1.5 0.0)
(41 . 0.5) (42 . 0.25) (43 . 0.5)
(44 . 0.0) (45 . 0.0)
(50 . 0.0)
(70 . 0) (71 . 0)
(210 0.0 0.0 1.0))
```

Try the IL06 block insert.

The entity name.
The entity type.
Its layer.
The block name.
Insertion point.
X, Y, and Z scale factors.
Minserted column and row distance are none.
Block rotation angle.
Minserted column and row counts are none.
Extrusion direction.

```
Command: (entget (car (entsel)))        Pick the text.
Select object:
Lisp returns:
((-1 . <Entity name: 60000030>)         Entity name.
(0 . "TEXT")                            Entity type.
(8 . "0")                               Layer name.
(10 2.46726 3.0 0.0)                    AutoCAD's text alignment point.
(40 . 0.125)                            Text height, preset style or not.
(1 . "SOME TEXT")                       Text string.
(41 . 1.0)                              Width factor.
(50 . 0.0)                              Rotation angle.
(51 . 0.0)                              Obliquing angle.
(7 . "STD")                             Style name.
(71 . 0)                                Generation flag, if mirrored, upside down.
(72 . 1)                                Justification flag. 1 means centered.
(11 3.0 3.0 0.0)                        Optional alignment point, like centered.
(210 0.0 0.0 1.0))                      Extrusion direction.

Command: (entget (car (entsel)))
Select object:                          Pick the face.
Lisp returns:
((-1 . <Entity name: 600002BC>)         Entity's name.
(0 . "3DFACE")                          Entity type.
(8 . "0")                               Layer name.
(10 2.0 1.0 0.0)                        1st point.
(11 4.0 1.0 0.0)                        2nd point.
(12 4.0 2.0 2.0)                        3rd point.
(13 2.0 2.0 2.0))                       4th point.
(70 . 0)                                Invisible edges flag.
```

It may take some practice to recognize all the DXF codes above. We believe it's more important to know where to find information than to try to know it all. Refer to the following Entity DXF Group Codes table for assistance. In reading the table, note that it lists the codes as they are formatted in the name.DXF file created by the DXFOUT command. There are minor differences in the format returned by ENTGET. One important difference is in the formatting of point values. The point codes are the 10, 20, 30, 210, 220, and 230 series. The DXF file and table break points down into individual coordinates, like 11 for an insert X coordinate, 21 for the Y coordinate, and 31 for the Z. For convenience in AutoLISP, ENTGET returns all three coordinates in an association list with the code for the appropriate X code. For instance, ENTGET would return an insert point as an 11 code with X, Y, and Z values, like (11 . 1.0 2.0 3.0).

ENTITY DXF GROUP CODES

LN = LINE	PT = POINT	CI = CIRCLE
AR = ARC	TR = TRACE	TX = TEXT
3F = 3DFACE	SH = SHAPE	SQ = SEQEND
IN = INSERT	AD = ATTDEF	AT = ATTRIB
VT = VERTEX	DM = DIMENSION	SD = SOLID
PL = POLYLINE		

ENTITIES

CODE	DESCRIPTION	LN	PT	CI	AR	TR	SD	TX	SH	IN	AD	AT	PL	VT	DM	3F	SQ
0	Entity Type	-1	-1	-1	-1	-1	-1	-1	-1	-1	-1	-1	-1	-1	-1	-1	-1
-1	Entity Name (Primary)	-1	-1	-1	-1	-1	-1	-1	-1	-1	-1	-1	-1	-1	-1	-1	-1
-2	Entity Name (Secondary)									-2			-2				
1	Primary Text Value							1			1	1			1		
2	Name: Shape, Block, Tag								2	2	2	2			2		
3	Prompt String										3						
5	Handle (Hexadecimal String)	5	5	5	5	5	5	5	5	5	5	5	5	5	5	5	5
6	Linetype Name	6	6	6	6	6	6	6	6	6	6	6	6	6	6	6	6
7	Text Style Name							7			7	7					
8	Layer Name	8	8	8	8	8	8	8	8	8	8	8	8	8	8	8	8
10	X of Start or Insert Point	10						10	10	10	10	10		10	10		
	X of Center Point		10	10	10												
	X of Corner Point					10	10									10	
11	X of Definition Point																
	X of Elev. Point (2D Poly)												11				
	X of End or Insert Point	11															
	X of Corner Point					11	11									11	
	X of Alignment Point							11			11	11					
	X of Middle Point of Dim.														11		
12	X of Corner Point					12	12									12	
	X of Insert Point														12		
13	X of Corner Point					13	13								13	13	
14	X of Definition Point														14		
15	X of Definition Point														15		
16	X of Definition Point														16		
20	Y of Start or Insert Point	20						20	20	20	20	20		20	20		
	Y of Center Point		20	20	20												
	Y of Corner Point					20	20									20	
21	Y of Definition Point																
	Y of Elev. Point (2D Poly)												21				
	Y of End or Insert Point	21															
	Y of Corner Point					21	21									21	
	Y of Alignment Point							21			21	21					
	Y of Middle Point of Dim.														21		
22	Y of Corner Point					22	22									22	
	Y of Insert Point														22		
23	Y of Corner Point					23	23								23	23	
24	Y of Definition Point														24		
25	Y of Definition Point														25		
26	Y of Definition Point														26		
30	Z of Start or Insert Point	30				30	30	30	30	30	30	30	30	30	30	30	
	Z of Center Point		30	30	30												

Group Code	Description	1	2	3	4	5	6	7	8	9	10	11	12	13
	Z of Corner Point										30		30	
	Z of Definition Point											30		30
	Z of Elev. Point (2D Poly)	31												
31	Z of End Point							31		31	31		31	
	Z of Corner Point											31		
	Z of Alignment Point			31										
	Z of Middle Point of Dim.													32
32	Z of Corner Point			32								32		
	Z of Insert Point					32								
33	Z of Corner Point			33								33		33
	Z of Definition Point											34		
34	Z of Definition Point											35		
35	Z of Definition Point											36		
36	Z of Definition Point											38		38
38	Z of Definition Point	38	38	38	38	38	38	38	38			39		39
	Entity Elevation	39	39	39	39	39	39	39	39					
39	Entity Thickness	40	40		40	40	40	40	40	40				
40	Radius, Height, Size or Width													
41	Leader Length, X Scale Factor or Width		41		41	41	41	41	41	41				
42	Y Scale Factor or Bulge						42	42						
43	Z Scale Factor						43							
44	Column Spacing						44							
45	Row Spacing						45							
50	Rotation Angle, Start Angle	50		50	50	50	50	50			50			
51	Curve Fit Tangent, End Angle, Obliquing Angle, Angle From Horizontal	51		51	51	51	51	51						
62	Color	62	62	62	62	62	62	62	62	62	62	62	62	62
66	Entities Follow Flag						66	66						
70	Dimension Type, Vertex or Polyline Flag, Attribute Flag, Column Count, Invisible Edges Flag					70	70	70	70	70	70			
71	Text Generation Flag, Row Count, Mesh M Vertex Count					71	71	71	71	71		71		
72	Text Justification, Mesh N Vertex Count					72	72	72	72	73		72		
73	Field Length, Smooth Surface M Density, Smooth Surface N Density					73	73	73	73	74				
74	Smooth Surface Type						75							
210	X of Extrusion Point	210	210	210	210	210	210	210	210	210	210	210	210	210
220	Y of Extrusion Point	220	220	220	220	220	220	220	220	220	220	220	220	220
230	Z of Extrusion Point	230	230	230	230	230	230	230	230	230	230	230	230	230

➡ *NOTE: The Release 10 FLATLAND system variable affects the data returned. FLATLAND provides 2D vs. 3D control over entity data. FLATLAND is a temporary setting to allow Release 10 to be compatible with programs written for AutoCAD Release 9. With FLATLAND on (set to 1), Release 10 AutoCAD acts as much as possible like Release 9. While FLATLAND is on, AutoLISP returns entity data in a 2D form consistent with pre-3D AutoCAD. We strongly recommend keeping FLATLAND set to 0 (off) and building your programs with 3D compatibility in mind. The FLATLAND variable will be dropped in future versions of AutoCAD.*

➡ *NOTE: For byblock linetypes, the DXF group stores "BYBLOCK" like any other linetype name. But for byblock colors, it stores the integer 0 as a color code instead of "BYBLOCK." This is because all linetypes are stored as strings, but all colors are stored as integers.*

Not all key elements of an entity's association data list are DXF codes. The -1 and -2 key element codes represent primary and secondary entity names. These minus key codes are not true DXF codes because the information associated with them is not stored as part of the drawing file. These key codes are used to return the temporary entity names created during a drawing session.

To simplify the retrieval of entity data, let's make a simple subroutine called DXF.LSP. DXF's purpose is to accept a DXF group code and an entity list. It returns the data item as the CDR of the group codes association list. You can use the DXF function to simplify entity data retrieval. DXF is used by other functions throughout the rest of the book.

Put the following function in your ACAD.LSP file.

```
;* DXF takes an integer dxf code and an entity data list.
;* It returns the data element of the association pair.
(defun dxf (code elist)
  (cdr (assoc code elist))        ;finds the association pair, strips 1st element
);defun
;*
```

DXF Function in ACAD.LSP File

Now let's try getting some data from the entities.

Using the DXF Function

Continue in the previous drawing, or edit an EXISTING drawing named IL06A.

 DXF is in your ACAD.LSP file. You need not reload it.

Add the DXF function shown above to your ACAD.LSP file and reload it.

Command: **(load "acad")**   Reload your ACAD.LSP file.

Command: **(setq ed (entget (car (entsel))))**   First set the entity data list to ED.
Select object: Pick the text, then enter:

Command: **(dxf 7 ed)**   Gets the text style name.
Lisp returns: "STD"   It works.

Command: **(dxf 11 ed)**   Try another.
Lisp returns: (3.0 3.0 0.0)   Returns a point list.

Some default entity properties are not stored, so they can't be returned by AutoLISP.

Default Entity Properties

Every entity resides on a layer and therefore has a DXF code 8. However, there are four kinds of entity properties that are reported only if the value is *not* the default setting. They are:

DEFAULT ENTITY PROPERTIES		
PROPERTY	DEFAULT	DXF CODE
ELEVATION	0.0	38
THICKNESS	0.0	39
LINETYPE	BYLAYER	6
COLOR	BYLAYER	62

These four, plus the layer property, are the same properties presented as options by AutoCAD's CHANGE command. All but elevation (which will be dropped in Release 11) are also CHPROP command options. If set to their default values, an association sublist for the property is not returned. For example, if an entity has a thickness other than zero, the thickness sublist is returned as part of the entity's data list. Otherwise, the sublist is not reported. Similarly, entities with color and linetype BYLAYER will not return a sublist of that data.

Applying Entity Access to CSCALE

It's time for an example that pulls things together. The CSCALE program below shows you how to process sets of entities, retrieve their data, modify the data, and update the entities in the AutoCAD drawing. It rescales text and inserted block entities using the SSGET, SSLENGTH, SSNAME, and ENTGET functions, and our DXF and UDIST subroutines.

So why do you need CSCALE when you can just use the SCALE command? The SCALE command rescales all selected entities indiscriminately, relative to a single base point. That's fine for drawing objects, but annotation text and symbols like bubbles complicate things. If you change the intended plot scale of a drawing or rescale a detail, you may want annotations to remain unchanged in size or to be scaled to an intermediate size. Yet you need each annotation to remain at its own insert point. Using one SCALE command and selecting only annotation text and symbols would offset each relative to SCALE's single base point. Using repeated SCALE commands is too tedious. CSCALE solves this by automatically stepping through each annotation entity and scaling it relative to its individual base point.

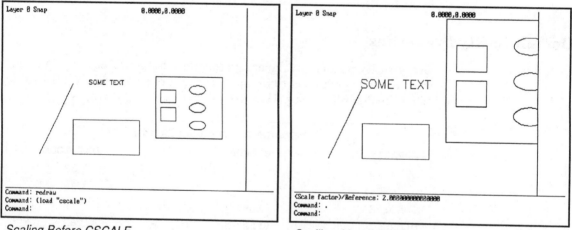

Scaling Before CSCALE   *Scalling After CSCALE*

```
;* C:CSCALE changes the scale of selected text and blocks based on a new scale
;* factor and the current drawing scale factor. It uses the global #DWGSC scale
;* as a default. It requires the UDIST user GET function and the DXF function.

(defun C:CSCALE ( / ss1 oldsc fact count emax en ed et dxf72)
```

Listing continued.

Continued listing.

❶
```
(prompt "\nSelect text and blocks to rescale...")        ;tell what to pick
(if (setq ss1 (ssget))                                    ;get the selections
  (progn
    (setq fact                                            ;ratio new/old scale
          (/ (udist 1 "" "New scale factor" #dwgsc nil)   ;get new scale factor
             (udist 1 "" "Old scale factor" #dwgsc nil)   ;get old scale factor
          )
          count 0                                         ;initialize counter
          emax (sslength ss1)                             ;find max no. of entities in set
    );setq
    (prompt "\nSearching...")                             ;keep user informed
```
❷
```
    (while (< count emax)                                 ;start program loop
      (setq en (ssname ss1 count)                         ;get an entity name
            ed (entget en)                                ;entity data
            et (dxf 0 ed)                                 ;entity type
      );setq
      (prompt ".")                                        ;give a dot each loop
      (cond                                               ;filter entity type
```
❸
```
        ( (= et "TEXT" )                                  ;check for text
          (setq dxf72 (dxf 72 ed))                        ;store the alignment flag
          (cond                                           ;filter on text alignment
            ( (= dxf72 0)                                 ;starting point
              (command "scale" en "" (dxf 10 ed) fact)    ;rescale it
            )
            ( (< dxf72 3)                                 ;1 & 2 are center and right
              (command "scale" en "" (dxf 11 ed) fact)    ;use 2nd point
            )
            ( (= dxf72 3)                                 ;skip it, prompt
              (prompt "\nIgnoring ALIGNED text string")
            )
            ( (= dxf72 4)                                 ;middle text
              (command "scale" en "" (dxf 11 ed) fact)    ;use 2nd point
            )
            ( (= dxf72 5)                                 ;fit text, skip it, prompt
              (prompt "\nIgnoring FIT text string")
            )
```

Listing continued.

Continued listing.

```
        );cond alignment
      );text

❹
      ( (= et "INSERT")                              ;check for block inserts
        (command "scale" en "" (dxf 10 ed) fact)    ;use dxf 10 insertion point
      );insert
    );cond
    (setq count (1+ count))
  );while
  );progn
  );if
  (princ)                                           ;finish cleanly
);defun
(princ)                                             ;load cleanly
;*
```

The CSCALE Function in CSCALE.LSP File

❶ The CSCALE command function starts with a prompt and an SSGET to select the objects. The rest of the program is nested in an IF and PROGN, so if object selection fails, the program will abort gracefully. If object selection succeeds, it prompts for the scaling factors and computes the ratio for SCALE. The scale factors are usually entered relative to intended plot scale.

❷ In the next part of the function, WHILE loops through the selection set. First, it checks each entity type and extracts appropriate information from the data. Entities other than text and block inserts are skipped. The function uses a COND statement instead of an IF statement. It's easier to do multiple tests and add support for future entity types with COND.

The text alignment group code is 72. The function extracts the value of the DXF group code 72. Each supported alignment of the TEXT command has a different value coded in the 72 group data. Use this alignment code to determine which point of the entity data should serve as the base point of the SCALE command. Text entities have two points, a 10 and 11 group code. The 10 code is always the lower left point of the text string, but it is not always the point by which the text was aligned. Middle, right, and centered text use the second point (11 code) to place text in the drawing. AutoCAD always begins text at the lower left starting point. The alignment flag tells you which point is significant to the alignment of the text entity. The points are shown in the Text Alignment Points illustration.

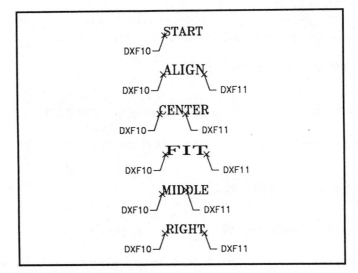

Text Alignment Points

❸ When the alignment code matches the test number (0 thru 5), the entity name EN is passed to the SCALE command. Depending on the alignment code, either the starting point (10 code) or the optional alignment point (11 code) is passed to the command. Notice how the function does this by nesting it right in the middle of a COMMAND function. The scale ratio is supplied by the FACT variable.

The function tests for each of the alignment codes, but skips over the aligned and fit types of text and prompts you that it skipped. The function assumes that if the text is aligned or fitted text, it was made that way for a purpose. If your application requires a different treatment, substitute code for the prompts.

After testing, the function updates the entity using the SCALE command. It is easier to let AutoCAD do the calculations with SCALE than to calculate the alignment points for all possible cases.

❹ Last, CSCALE looks at the INSERT entities. An INSERT entity has one point value, its insertion point. The function extracts the value and uses it as the base point for the SCALE command. CSCALE loops until all entities are done, then cleanly ends with PRINC.

The CSCALE function relies on the DXF and UDIST user interface functions in the ACAD.LSP file. They should load automatically. Try it now.

Changing Scales With CSCALE

Continue in the previous drawing, or edit an EXISTING drawing named IL06A.

 You have CSCALE in your CSCALE.LSP file.

 Create the CSCALE function shown above in a file named CSCALE.LSP.

```
Command: (load "cscale")                         Load the file.

Command: CSCALE                                  Test it.
Select text and blocks to rescale...
Select objects:                                  Window everything.
New scale factor <1.0000>: 2
Old scale factor <1.0000>: <RETURN>              It was full scale.

Searching....SCALE          Commands scroll by, and it rescales only the text and block.
```

CSCALE ignored the line and 3D face. If it had found fit or aligned text, it would have ignored them also, while prompting with "Ignoring FIT text string..." and "Ignoring ALIGNED text string..." phrases. Refer to the Scaling Without CSCALE and the Scaling With CSCALE illustrations shown previously.

➥ *TIP: You normally want CSCALE to distinguish between annotation symbol blocks and drawing object blocks. If you keep annotation symbol blocks on a unique layer(s), modify CSCALE to check layer and skip blocks on other layers.*

The CSCALE program is lazy; it uses the AutoCAD SCALE command to do the work. Next let's take a look at how AutoLISP can modify an entity's data directly.

Modifying and Updating Entity Data

You can modify and update existing entities using two AutoLISP built-in functions, ENTMOD and ENTUPD. They accomplish things that are impossible with AutoCAD commands, like differentially rescaling the X, Y, and Z scales of blocks.

List handling functions like CDR, ASSOC (or our DXF), and SUBST modify an entity data list. Then ENTMOD passes the modified list of entity data back to AutoCAD for handling.

entmod	*Updates an entity in the database with a new entity data description list. Except for complex entities (polyline vertexes and block attributes), the entities are immediately regenerated on the screen with the new data.* **(entmod list)**

ENTMOD updates the entity name contained in the -1 group of the entity data list. Let's look at how ENTMOD works by changing our text string from "SOME TEXT" to "That's silly." First, get the entity data name with ENTSEL and its data with ENTGET. Then, use ASSOC to extract the old data sublist that you want to change, and CONS to replace the sublist.

Extracting Old and Making New Data for ENTMOD

Continue in the previous drawing, or edit an EXISTING drawing named IL06A.

```
Command: (setq ed (entget (car (entsel))))    Set ED to the text data.
Select object:                                Select the text, it sets ED to:
Lisp returns: ((-1 . <Entity name: 60000030>) (0 . "TEXT") (8 . "0") (10 2.4726 3.0
0.0) (40 . 0.125) (1 . "SOME TEXT") (50 . 0.0) (41 . 1.0) (51 . 0.0) (7 . "STD") (71
. 0) (72 . 1) (11 3.0 3.0 0.0) (210 0.0 0.0 1.0))

Command: (setq old (assoc 1 ed))
Lisp returns: (1 . "SOME TEXT")                Grab a group using the ASSOC function.

Command: (setq new (cons 1 "That's silly!"))
Lisp returns: (1 . "That's silly!")            Make a new sublist group to swap.
```

You can modify the entity data list using the SUBST function.

How to SUBSTitute Data in a List

To modify an entity, you must first get new data into the entity data list. SUBST substitutes a new element for an old element in a list. It avoids the need to dismantle a list with CARs, CDRs, and their cousins, and then reassemble the list to change data within it.

subst	*Returns a list with the new item replacing every occurrence of the old item in the supplied list.* **(subst new old list)**

For   example,   (subst 'newroo 'oldfoo ' (glu you to oldfoo)) returns (glu you to newroo). SUBST is most often used to update data lists, so let's try an exercise. We named the variables OLD and NEW to help show how the function works.

Modifying Entities With SUBST and ENTMOD

Continue in the previous drawing, with the ED, OLD, and NEW variables previously set.

Command: **(setq ed (subst new old ed))**   Substitute and it returns the new list:

Command: **(entmod ed)**   AutoLISP tells AutoCAD to update the entity. Look at the screen.
Lisp returns: ((-1 . <Entity name: 60000030>) (0 . "TEXT") (8 . "0") (10 2.4726 3.0 0.0) (40 . 0.125) (1 . "That's silly!") (50 . 0.0) (41 . 1.0) (51 . 0.0) (7 . "STD") (71 . 0) (72 . 1) (11 3.0 3.0 0.0) (210 0.0 0.0 1.0))

Because SUBST replaces *all* old elements of a list with the matching new element, there is no way to discriminate between duplicated data in a list. This is not a problem in entity data association lists, because each key code is unique. If you accidently create an entity data list with two sublists having the same key code, ENTMOD will ignore the first.

If ENTMOD succeeds, it returns the data list. If it fails, it returns nil. ENTMOD cannot create a new entity name, or modify the entity type or handle. If you need to change these, create a new entity and modify it. AutoCAD is very strict in applying a modified entity list to the drawing database. ENTMOD will not create new linetypes, text styles, or blocks. You must define these items prior to their use by ENTMOD. ENTMOD will, however, create new layers if needed.

➡ *TIP: Using AutoLISP's entity modification functions to manipulate entities is usually faster and more certain than using AutoCAD's editing commands. However, note that UNDO cannot undo an ENTMOD.*

Applying Entity Modification With BSCALE

The next exercise shows you how to do variable XYZ scaling of blocks after they have been inserted. This program is called BSCALE (Block SCALE). Why do you need it? The AutoCAD CHANGE and SCALE commands can only rescale X, Y, and Z equally. Differential scaling, say to scale Z without affecting X or Y, is difficult in AutoCAD. You have to LIST the entity, note its insertion point, scale and rotation factors, layer, and other settings. Then erase it and reinsert it with a new scale. And if the block has attributes, it gets worse.

BSCALE makes this a snap. It directly updates the insert entity without affecting attributes or any properties. The BSCALE command is particularly useful for attribute-laden and 3D blocks.

```
;* C:BSCALE changes the X, Y, and/or Z values of existing blocks without
;* affecting properties or attributes. It uses the DXF and UREAL functions,
;* which must be loaded.
(defun C:BSCALE ( / en ed old41 old42 old43 new41 new42 new43)
❶
  (if (and (setq en (entsel "\nSelect block to rescale: "))   ;get the block
           (= (dxf 0 (setq ed (entget (car en)))) "INSERT")   ;test if an insert
       );and
❷
      (entmod                                                 ;update entity
        (setq old41 (dxf 41 ed)                               ;extract old X
              old42 (dxf 42 ed)                               ;old Y
              old43 (dxf 43 ed)                               ;old Z
              new41 (ureal 1 "" "X scale factor" old41)       ;prompt for new X
              new42 (ureal 1 "" "Y scale factor" old42)       ;new Y
              new43 (ureal 1 "" "Z scale factor" old43)       ;new Z
❸                                                             ;change data in entity list
              ed (subst (cons 41 new41) (cons 41 old41) ed)   ;change X
              ed (subst (cons 42 new42) (cons 42 old42) ed)   ;change Y
              ed (subst (cons 43 new43) (cons 43 old43) ed)   ;change Z
        )                                                     ;setq returns ed
      );entmod
  );if
  (princ)                                                     ;end cleanly
);defun
(princ)
;*
```

BSCALE Function in BSCALE.LSP File

❶ BSCALE starts by prompting for a block with ENTSEL. It uses an IF-AND to make sure the user has selected an entity and that the entity is an insert (block), storing the entity data list as ED. If the AND fails, the function aborts cleanly, skipping the ENTMOD section.

❷ If the test passes, the function executes ENTMOD, which is applied to the final value returned by SETQ. SETQ first extracts the old X, Y, and Z scale factors with our DXF routine, saving them as old41, old42, and old43 (group codes 41, 42, and 43). Then it uses UREAL to get the new scales, NEW41, NEW42, and NEW43. UREAL uses the old scales as defaults.

❸ Finally, SETQ resets ED to the new values. It uses SUBST to substitute the new scales for the old data on the entity list, using the CONS structure to build each data group. It does this three times, one for each scale factor, returning the last value to the ENTMOD which updates the entity.

Try BSCALE on the IL06 block in your IL06A drawing.

Variable XYZ Rescaling of Blocks With BSCALE

Continue in the previous drawing, or edit an EXISTING drawing named IL06A.

 You have the BSCALE command in your BSCALE.LSP file.

Create the above C:BSCALE command in a file named BSCALE.LSP.

```
Command: (load "bscale")            Load the new file.

Command: BSCALE                     Test it:
Select block to rescale:            Select the IL06 block insert.
X scale factor <0.5000>: 0.25
Y scale factor <0.2500>: <RETURN>
Z scale factor <0.5000>: 0          And it rescales!
```

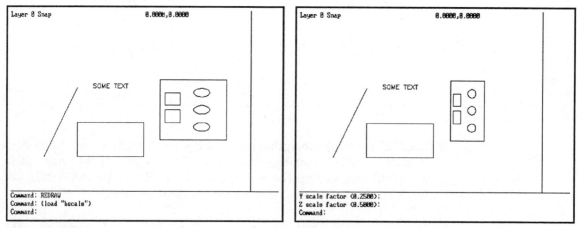

Before BSCALE   After BSCALE

Modifying lines, arcs, circles, and blocks without attributes is relatively simple. These are all single entity records in the database. Other entities encompass multiple entity data records. These are known as complex entities.

Complex Entities: Polylines and Inserts

Complex entities like polylines, block inserts with attributes, and 3D meshes all have what we call *subentities*. A complex entity consists of both a main *head* entity, and a tail sequence of an unlimited number of subentities terminated by a *seqend* (sequence end) entity. Subentities are always treated as part of the main entity. The following diagram helps explain one of these long-tailed, single-headed creatures.

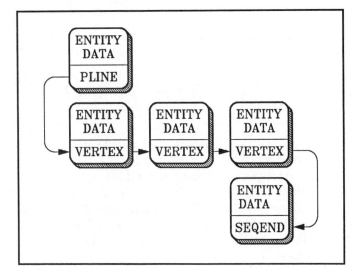

Complex Entities

SSGET and ENTSEL return only the names of main entities. They skip subentities. You retrieve subentities by stepping through the entity database from the head entity name with the ENTNEXT function. ENTNEXT with an entity name argument returns the name of the next entity following the entity's name. ENTNEXT does not discriminate between main and subentities. The ENTNEXT function is your main method for accessing the subentities. You start with a head entity name and ENTNEXT to the first subentity, then use the subentity name to get the next subentity, and so on until you reach the seqend entity.

Let's look at some complex entities, starting with the head entity of a polyline. As usual, you retrieve entity data using ENTGET, but you only get the head entity. It gives you some useful information about the entire entity. First, the 70 code of 1 tells you the polyline is closed. The 40 and 41 codes retain the starting and ending width of the polyline segment.

You get subentities by using the entity name, which is the -1 DXF group. Get the name of the first subentity using ENTNEXT and DXF.

Looking at Complex Entities

Continue in the previous drawing, or edit an EXISTING drawing named IL06A.

```
Command: PLINE                                    Draw from 1,4 to 4,3 to 5,4 and close it.
Command: (setq ed (entget (car (entsel))))        Set the ED and EN variables.
Select object:                                    Select the PLINE.
Lisp returns: ((-1 . <Entity name: 60000078>) (0 . "POLYLINE") (8 . "0") (66 . 1) (10
0.0 0.0 0.0) (70 . 1) (40 . 0.0) (41 . 0.0) (210 0.0 0.0 1.0) (71 . 0) (72 . 0) (73 .
0) (74 . 0) (75 . 0))

Command: (setq en (entnext (dxf -1 ed)))          Next entity after head.
Lisp returns: <Entity name: 60000090>            It's a new name.

Command: (setq ed (entget en))                    Get its data.
Lisp returns: ((-1 . <Entity name: 60000090>) (0 . "VERTEX") (8 . "0") (10 1.0 4.0
0.0) (40 . 0.0) (41 . 0.0) (42 . 0.0) (70 . 0) (50 . 0.0))
```

Subentities of a polyline are called vertexes. A vertex data list contains a point location, starting and ending width, curve fit, curve bulge radius, and tangent information. In addition, there is always the typical property data. The data list also includes the name of the next subentity of the polyline via the -1 DXF code. Let's continue stepping through the polyline until we find its seqend. Use a WHILE-AND to check to see if you've found the seqend. If not, PRINT the data. When you find the seqend, the WHILE stops.

How to Stop at the SEQEND

Continue in the previous drawing, with EN set to <Entity name: 60000090> as above.

```
Command: (progn (while (and (setq en (entnext en)) (setq ed (entget en))
3> (/= "SEQEND" (dxf 0 ed))) (print ed)) (princ))
Lisp returns:                                     The remaining two vertexes.
((-1 . <Entity name: 600000a8>) (0 . "VERTEX") (8 . "0") (10 4.0 3.0 0.0) (40 . 0.0)
(41 . 0.0) (42 . 0.0) (70 . 0) (50 . 0.0))
((-1 . <Entity name: 600000c0>) (0 . "VERTEX") (8 . "0") (10 5.0 4.0 0.0) (40 . 0.0)
(41 . 0.0) (42 . 0.0) (70 . 0) (50 . 0.0))

Command: !ed                                      And ED was last set to the seqend.
((-1 . <Entity name: 600000d8>) (0 . "SEQEND") (8 . "0") (-2 . <Entity name:
60000078>))

Command: QUIT
```

You step through block inserts with attributes in the same way. We examine attributes in detail in Chapter 11.

You can't step backwards through a polyline or block. So if you have the entity name or data for a vertex or attribute, how can you find its head entity? That's what the second entity name group, the -2 group, in the seqend is for. It contains the name of the head entity.

Now that we can step though polylines and stop at the seqend, let's develop a command that applies this to automating drawing revision clouds.

Applying Entity Access to Modifying Polylines

Putting a revision cloud on a manual drawing is an easy task, to which you can add a creative flair. In CAD it's normally tedious, creativity aside. So, we wrote RCLOUD. It's a command that draws revision clouds and shows you how to modify subentities. You can build loops, change polyline widths or data flags, erase, edit, and update polyline vertexes with the techniques given in RCLOUD. RCLOUD is surprisingly simple. The program uses ENTSEL and ENTGET to get the polyline head, ENTNEXT and ENTGET to process each vertex, and APPEND and ENTMOD to add a bulge to each vertex.

If you have a polyline with many vertexes, won't doing an ENTMOD of each vertex cause a lot of tedious polyline regenerations? Not really. ENTMOD only updates the data list for complex entities, not the screen. AutoLISP provides the ENTUPD function so you can update the screen when you want to.

entupd

> *Allows selective updating of polyline vertexes and block attribute entity names after ENTMODs have been performed.*
> (entupd *ename*)

ENTUPD is primarily for polylines and attribute-laden blocks, but it will regenerate any entity. It can take the head or a subentity data list as an argument, and it will regenerate the entire complex entity. Let's see how it's used in RCLOUD.

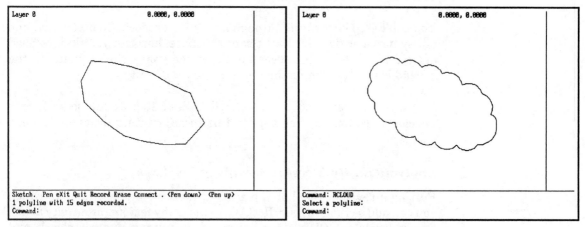

Pollyline Before Revision Cloud   **Polyline After Revision Cloud**

```
;* C:RCLOUD draws a revision cloud using sketch. We recommend creating the
;* polyline counterclockwise with SKETCH, with SKPOLY set to 1.
;* Requires DXF subroutine.
;*
(defun C:RCLOUD ( / head hdata bulge en ed)
❶
  (if (and                                             ;get head data list
       (setq en (entsel "\nSelect a polyline: "))      ;get entity
       (= (dxf 0 (setq hdata (entget (car en))))) "POLYLINE") ;is it polyline
      );and
      (progn                                           ;OK, proceed
❷
       (entmod (subst '(70 . 1) '(70 . 0) hdata))      ;if open pline, close it
       (setq bulge (list (cons 42 0.5)))               ;make the bulge association list
       (setq en (dxf -1 hdata))                        ;get first subentity - vertex
❸
       (while (and (setq en (entnext en))              ;loop through each vertex
                   (setq ed (entget en))               ;get vertex data
                   (/= "SEQEND" (dxf 0 ed))            ;if seqend, we're done
              );and
              (setq ed (append ed bulge))              ;tack on the bulge association list
              (entmod ed)                              ;modify the subentity
       );while
```

Listing continued.

Continued listing.

```
        (entupd en)                                    ;update the entire polyline
  ) );if&progn
  (princ)
);defun
(princ)
;*
```

RCLOUD Program in RCLOUD.LSP File

❶ First RCLOUD uses the same IF-AND test as the previous BSCALE to ensure that a polyline entity has been selected. If OK, the PROGN containing the rest of the function is evaluated.

❷ We ENTMOD the 70 (open or closed flag) code to make sure the polyline is closed. It is not necessary to check or test the existing 70 group. If it is (70 . 0), SUBST will replace it with (70 . 1). If it is (70 . 1) already, SUBST ignores it.

❸ The WHILE-AND steps through each vertex until it ends at the seqend, just as it did in the previous exercise. Each vertex gets a 42 bulge group added by APPEND, not SUBST. When AutoCAD fits a curve to a polyline, it stores the segments between the vertexes as bulges. Bulges are represented in the vertex entity data as a 42 group. A typical bulge group looks like (42 . 0.5).

The magnitude of the bulge is a numerical factor that takes into account the included angle between the two vertex points. A bulge value of 1 will draw semicircles between the vertexes, and 0 is a straight line. After some testing, we found a half-unit bulge was pleasing for clouds. See the Bulge illustration below.

The function passes the new list back to AutoCAD via the ENTMOD function.

❹ Finally, (entupd en) regenerates the entire polyline.

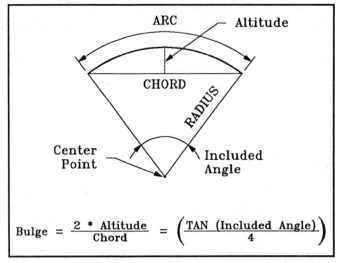

Bulge Formula

Let's try the program. Use the SKETCH command to create your initial polyline before using the RCLOUD command. Use the AutoCAD system variable SKPOLY to generate polyline sketches instead of lines.

It's hard to start and stop sketching at the same point, so RCLOUD lets you be a little sloppy around the end of the sketch. Just draw the last segment near the beginning of the polyline, but don't try to join them. This way, RCLOUD can force the polyline to close, giving a pleasant cloud.

Testing the RCLOUD Command

Enter selection: **1**   Begin a NEW drawing named CLOUD.

You have C:RCLOUD in your RCLOUD.LSP file.

Create the above C:RCLOUD function in a file named RCLOUD.LSP.

Command: **(load "rcloud")**   Load the file.

Command: **SETVAR**   Turn SKPOLY to 1 (draw polylines).
<Ortho off> <Snap off>   Toggle these off.
Command: **SKETCH**   Set record length to 1.
                                        Draw a counterclockwise oval shape.
Command: **RCLOUD**   Run the command.
Command: **QUIT**

As you draw clouds and test your function, you may see that RCLOUD draws the bulges to the inside when drawn clockwise, and to the outside when drawn counterclockwise. Use this quirk to your advantage.

➡ *TIP: To put this in a menu macro, we suggest the following:*

```
[RCLOUD  ]^C^C^CSETVAR SKPOLY 1 SNAP OFF ORTHO OFF SKETCH;+
(* (getvar "DIMSCALE") 0.5)(if C:RCLOUD nil+
(load "rcloud"));RCLOUD SNAP ON ORTHO ON
```

Unlike most AutoCAD commands, SKETCH in a macro doesn't need a backslash character to pause the command. After setting the sketch increment, the command automatically pauses for a return. Make the increment 1/2-inch in final plot size, or 0.5 of the DIMSCALE variable (our drawing scale setting).

While RCLOUD is simple, it demonstrates some key points. It shows you how to add new entity groups to an existing entity, how to individually update the head and subentities with ENTMOD, and how to regenerate the entire complex entity with ENTUPD. Most importantly, it may lead you to think of other ways to apply these functions. How can you improve them? What else can you do?

You can modify C:RCLOUD to create a program that smooths polyline contours generated when tracing contours with SKETCH. Or, with a little more work, you can make it draw mechanical gears and parts. Because AutoCAD gives you control over the curvature of each drawing segment, there is no limit on what you can generate.

Entity Handles — Permanent Entity Names

Now that you've seen entity names like <Entity name: 60000050>, you may be trying to write programs that use the names to keep track of data. This won't work from one drawing session to another because entity names change each time a drawing is loaded. Entity *handles* eliminate the problem of shifty entity names. A handle is an optional, permanent identification tag assigned to every entity in a drawing. Each entity is guaranteed to have a unique handle ID throughout its life in the drawing. When an entity is deleted, the handle is retired forever from the drawing. Copies of entities and exploded entities get new handles. No handle name is ever repeated in the same drawing.

Entity handles are activated by the HANDLES command in AutoCAD. Handles can be turned off in a drawing, but only by a user because the operation requires a response to a random question. This means that

AutoLISP can activate, but not disable, entity handles. If handles are on, the read-only HANDLES system variable is 1. Handles show up in the LIST command output, and in the entity data list as a hexadecimal (base 16) string value in a 5 group.

Handles are useful for a variety of applications such as linking to external databases, grouping entities within a drawing, or as an easy way to remember the name of an important entity in your drawing. In Chapter 12, we'll use handles in a program that groups parametric parts for easy handling. This is how to turn entity handles on.

Turning on Entity Handles

Edit an EXISTING drawing named IL06A.

```
Command: LIST                          List the block. It has no handle.
Command: (entget (car (entsel)))       The data list includes no 5 group.
Command: HANDLES                       Turn them on.
Handles are disabled.
ON/DESTROY: ON
Command: (entget (car (entsel)))       Now the data list includes (5 . "4").
Lisp returns: ((-1 . <Entity name: 60000060>) (0 . "INSERT") (8 . "0") (5 . "4") (2 .
"IL06") (10 4.5 1.5 0.0) (41 . 0.5) (42 . 0.25) (50 . 0.0) (43 . 0.5) (70 . 0) (71 .
0) (44 . 0.0) (45 . 0.0) (210 0.0 0.0 1.0))

Command: CIRCLE                        Draw a 0.8 radius circle at 1,4.
Command: LIST                          List the circle. It has handle number 5.
```

➡ *NOTE: If you don't have the IL DISK, and you made a mistake and erased an entity when you originally created the IL06A drawing, your handle numbers may vary from what we show. Use your numbers in the following exercise.*

When entity handles are turned on, AutoCAD assigns a handle to each main entity in the drawing, even deleted entities. But subentities do not get handles. The handles are stored in the data for each entity under the DXF 5 code. A handle is a read-only string data type. Your programs cannot create or update a handle. You have no control over the handle names generated by AutoCAD.

If entities already have names, why do we need handles? As we said, entity names are reassigned in each drawing session. Entity names deleted in the previous session are dropped. This transient nature makes entity names useless for tying entities to external databases, or for any session-to-session function.

Handles are permanent, sequentially assigned for the life of the drawing. Handles of deleted entities simply become harmless gaps in the sequence. Once a handle is assigned, an external database can depend upon it forever.

You can use the handle to get to the entity without searching the drawing database entity by entity. AutoLISP's HANDENT function returns the *entity* name associated with an entity *handle*.

handent

> *Returns the entity name corresponding to the permanent handle name if handles have been enabled.*
> (handent *handle*)

Let's try grabbing the circle entity by its handle.

Using Entity Handles

Continue in the previous drawing.

Command: **(handent "4")**   Get entity name for handle "4"
Lisp returns: <Entity name: 60000060>   The first entity.

Command: **(handent "5")**   Get entity name for handle "5"
Lisp returns: <Entity name: 60000078>   The last circle entity.

We only have a few handles in our drawing, so our handle numbers are small. If you have lots of entities, the numbers will be hex strings like "1A67EB0". These become too large to convert to integer, or even real, values for AutoLISP. Yet a program may know the handle number of an entity and need to calculate the handle number of another, or even the next, entity. So the HEX-INT.LSP file on the New Riders AutoLISP Utilities Disk 1 gives you a few tools for dealing with hex math. They are HTOI (Hex TO Integer), ITOH (Integer TO Hex), HX+1 (HeX plus 1), HX+HX (HeX plus HeX), and HX+INT (HeX plus INTeger).

Entity handles provide a quick way to uniquely identify and retrieve the current session's entity name. Entity handles are a new feature with many possible applications. Their most powerful uses are in complex database applications; however you will find other uses. Here are a few suggestions:

You can *link* entities to a block without having to include them in the block definition. Just define the block with an attribute to hold the names of associated entity handles. And write a program to process the handle's entities accordingly when the mother block is edited. In fact, the GROUP.LSP program on the New Riders AutoLISP Utilities Disk 1 uses handles to create *groups* — sets of entities that can be selected by picking a single member entity. This allows parametric parts to be manipulated as easily as blocks, yet remain editable.

Handles can be used to put permanent marks in your drawing database to chronologically log who, what, or when an entity was added to the drawing. You could include a starting and ending marker entity placed each time a user logs on or off. The times and key entity handles can be maintained in a key attribute block or in an external ASCII file created and maintained by AutoLISP. You can add commands to highlight entities added by a user.

As a further example of the power of these functions, we put two other tools on the New Riders AutoLISP Utilities Disk 1. CATCH.LSP contains two functions. C:MARK marks the drawing database before you do an operation that creates any set of hard-to-select entities. Then after you create the new entities, (catch) will transparently select everything following the mark. CATCH is great for selecting the new entities created by exploding blocks, polylines, 3D meshes, and dimensions.

CATCH.LSP also includes LAST-N, a function that works like the Last object selection option, but lets you specify how many entities to grab.

Summary

Accessing AutoCAD's database through AutoLISP dramatically increases your control over your drawings. AutoLISP helps you modify, delete, or search for specific entities. The power of AutoCAD selection sets lets you process groups of entities in your own custom way.

With ENTLAST, ENTNEXT, and ENTSEL, you can select entities and get their entity names. ENTSEL returns the pick point, so it can be fed to AutoCAD commands that demand picking by point. With ENTDEL, ENTUPD, and REDRAW, you can delete, update (regenerate), and redraw entities. SSGET, SSLENGTH, SSMEMB, SSNAME, SSADD, and SSDEL allow you to select, sort, and manipulate groups of entities.

SSGET "X" provides you with a way to select all entities instantly, or to select filtered groups of entities. Our SSTOOLS.LSP provides further ways to combine and cross-filter groups.

With ENTGET, ASSOC, and CONS, you can access the entity data for use in your programs. SUBST, ENTMOD, and ENTUPD give you the tools to directly modify entities, faster and more efficiently than with AutoCAD commands. And handles and HANDENT allow you to keep track of entities.

Before moving on to table access in the next chapter, we offer a passing idea for using entity access. Does it ever annoy you when an AutoCAD command like FILLET fails because it finds the wrong entity? Try writing a filtered command that rejects invalid entities and automatically reselects to find the proper entity.

Let's move on to accessing and using the data in AutoCAD's table definitions, like the definitions of blocks, styles, linetypes, layers, views, viewports, and UCSs.

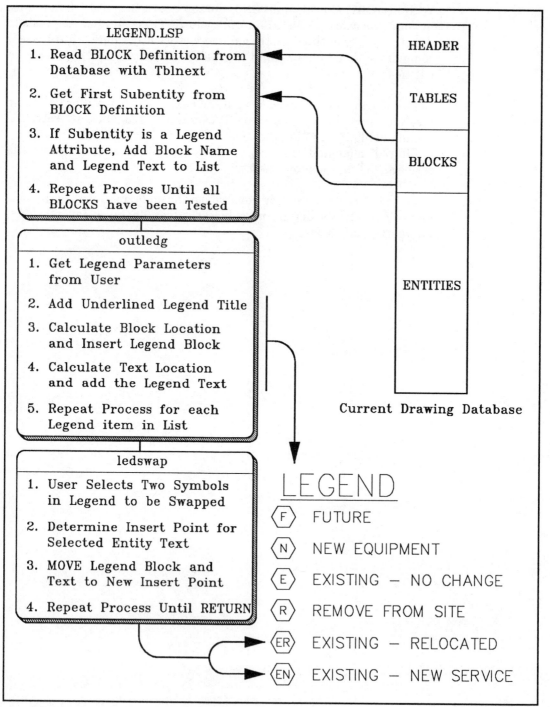

LEGEND.LSP

1. Read BLOCK Definition from Database with Tblnext

2. Get First Subentity from BLOCK Definition

3. If Subentity is a Legend Attribute, Add Block Name and Legend Text to List

4. Repeat Process Until all BLOCKS have been Tested

outledg

1. Get Legend Parameters from User

2. Add Underlined Legend Title

3. Calculate Block Location and Insert Legend Block

4. Calculate Text Location and add the Legend Text

5. Repeat Process for each Legend item in List

ledswap

1. User Selects Two Symbols in Legend to be Swapped

2. Determine Insert Point for Selected Entity Text

3. MOVE Legend Block and Text to New Insert Point

4. Repeat Process Until RETURN

HEADER

TABLES

BLOCKS

ENTITIES

Current Drawing Database

LEGEND

⟨F⟩   FUTURE

⟨N⟩   NEW EQUIPMENT

⟨E⟩   EXISTING – NO CHANGE

⟨R⟩   REMOVE FROM SITE

⟨ER⟩ EXISTING – RELOCATED

⟨EN⟩ EXISTING – NEW SERVICE

The LEGEND Program

CHAPTER 7

AutoCAD Table Data

DEALING IN DEFINITIONS

You need full access to the drawing database to give your applications complete control over AutoCAD. The entity data access techniques you learned in Chapter 6 are powerful, but your tool box is still not complete. Manipulating AutoCAD's definitions of layers, linetypes, views, styles, blocks, UCSs, and viewports will complete your control and flexibility. These are all the named things, places, and properties in the drawing database. AutoCAD calls the tables that store these definitions the *symbol tables*. Here, symbol doesn't merely mean blocks, inserts or shapes; it means a *word that represents something*, like "DASHED" represents a particular type of patterned line.

The information defined in AutoCAD's LAYER, LTYPE, VIEW, STYLE, BLOCK, UCS, and VPORT symbol tables can be accessed through AutoLISP. Although you can access the definitions stored in any table, you can't directly change definitions like you change entity data. This is because many entities are generally dependent upon the definitions, so direct modification could wreak wholesale havoc to your drawing. To change table data, use the commands that affect the table. For instance, the LINETYPE command modifies the LTYPE table and the BLOCK command modifies the BLOCK table.

You can, however, use table data in your programs to control drawing choices and prevent user errors. For example, without access to the STYLE table, the ATEXT program in Chapter 5 was able to deal only with variable height text. Accessing the STYLE table would have enabled it to determine whether a text height style was fixed or variable, and then prompt and initiate command options appropriately. In fact, the ATEXT2.LSP file on the IL DISK does exactly that.

In this chapter, you will learn how to scan AutoCAD's drawing reference tables with AutoLISP's TBLSEARCH and TBLNEXT functions. You can use these functions to make intelligent block definitions that contain unique attribute data. By accessing block definitions in the BLOCK table, you can determine a block's characteristics, then apply that information to your own application, such as processing attributes to generate a legend of symbol blocks in a drawing. You can use the LTYPE table and linetypes to store drawing data — not just to draw simple graphic line patterns. Use your linetype data access in developing your own applications, such as storing material definitions in your drawing linetypes so you can extract data to do material takeoffs. You can detect and automatically change active viewports through the VPORTS table and VPORTS function. Learn the UCS data format so you can make your programs verify and set needed UCSs.

AutoLISP Tools and Programs

AutoLISP Tools

SETVP changes AutoCAD's active viewport from within AutoLISP.

TAKOFF outputs a DXF file for lineal material take-offs. It reports all entity data drawn in specially named linetypes, accessing the LTYPE table to get the linetype name list for processing.

Programs

WLAYER.LSP defines the WLAYER command, which scans the drawing's LAYER table. It prompts the user with each layer, asking if it should be erased, skipped, or wblocked to a drawing file named for the first eight characters of the layer's name.

LEGEND.LSP is a program that creates a legend by scanning the BLOCK table and extracting all specially defined legend blocks. It builds a legend and places the legend in the drawing at a user-specified location. The program has three functions. LEGEND collects legend blocks and formats them. OUTLEDG draws the legend, taking a paired list of data (block and description) and putting it in the AutoCAD drawing as a list of symbols and text. LEDSWAP lets the user easily swap or rearrange the paired items in the legend.

PVAR.LSP is a program on the New Riders AutoLISP Utilities Disk 1. It provides functions for creating a personal variable system which can retain up to 254 variable values in a drawing's LTYPE table. Unlike normal AutoLISP variables, these variables are retained when you end a drawing. You can use numeric or string variables. The system has several functions. PVAR is used to query, view, or update the variables. PUTVAR can be used inside other AutoLISP programs to update a variable. It stores the variable as a linetype definition. RETVAR retrieves the variable from the linetype definition. PVCHK inserts or verifies that the personal variables block is defined. GETPVAL is used to get a new variable value from the user. This system works like a set of personal system variables.

Symbol Tables

AutoCAD and AutoLISP use symbol tables to store drawing information which is not tied to any specific entity. Symbol table names include: BLOCK for named *things* like block definitions (not insert entities); VIEW, UCS, and VPORT for named *places* like views, UCSs, and viewports; and LAYER, LTYPE, and STYLE for named layer, linetype, and text style *properties*. You won't find information about specific entities in symbol tables, although the BLOCK table's definitions hold entity-type data. You will find the data that defines these named things, places, and properties. Unlike entity access, AutoLISP's table access functions only let you retrieve this data. AutoLISP cannot modify the tables in the database; only AutoCAD commands can do that.

AutoLISP has only two functions that deal with symbol tables. They are TBLSEARCH and TBLNEXT. TBLSEARCH scans the specified table and returns the data for the specific symbol name you supply. You commonly use TBLSEARCH to search for a specific block definition, layer, or style name. For example, the ATEXT2.LSP program on the IL DISK accesses the style data to determine if a text style is fixed or variable in height.

tblsearch

> *Returns a data description list for the table name specified by tname and the symbol name. If flag is T, a subsequent TBLNEXT function will return the table data of the next entry.*
> **(tblsearch** *tname* **symbol** *flag***)**

The TBLNEXT function is your tool for stepping through and looking at each symbol in a table. You don't need to know the specific name of a symbol to use TBLNEXT. For example, this chapter's WLAYER command scans the names of all layers defined in a drawing so it can selectively erase layers or WBLOCK their contents to separate drawings.

tblnext

> *Returns a data description list for the table name specified by tname. If the optional rewind flag is T, the first table data is returned, otherwise TBLNEXT steps through tname and returns the next table entry each time the function is used.*
> **(tblnext** *tname* **flag)**

The first time TBLNEXT is called in a drawing session, it returns the first item of the specified table. Each additional call returns a subsequent item. The function automatically advances itself to the next item. You can force TBLNEXT to restart at the first item of the table by including an optional (non-nil) rewind argument like T.

The table functions return data in a form similar to an entity data list. Like the entity tables, the list is a sequence of association groups that use DXF codes to identify the type of information in each group. The complete set of table DXF codes follows. (The BLOCK section is a separate table, shown in the block section of this chapter.) The Table DXF Group Codes chart is also reproduced in Appendix C.

As with the entity data table, this table also shows codes broken down as they appear in the DXF file format, which is covered in Chapter 16. An important difference in the format returned by AutoLISP table access is in coordinate points. DXF files break points into three fields, such as a 10, 20, and 30 group for the X, Y, and Z coordinates. AutoLISP table access returns all three coordinate values as a single group coded by the X DXF code, such as 10.

The 70 group in the chart is a bit-coded flag. You break its value down into several component values, each being two raised to a power. A value of 69 would mean 1 (2 to the 0 power) plus 4 (2 squared) plus 64 (2 to the sixth). All tables use a 70 flag value of 64 or 0 to guide the PURGE command. If, at the end of the last drawing session, any entities exist that make reference to the flag's table, the 70 group gets a 64 component value. If not, the 70 flag is set to 0, and the PURGE command knows a table may be purged.

Additional 70 bit values are discussed in the following sections on individual tables.

TABLE DXF GROUP CODES

Code	Table Type	LTYPE	LAYER	STYLE	VIEW	UCS	VPORT
0	Table Type						
2	Symbol Name	2	2	2	2	2	2
3	Descriptive Text	3					
	Font File Name			3			
4	Bigfont File Name			4			
6	Line Name		6				
10	X of View Center Point				10		
	X of Origin Point					10	
	X of Lower Left Corner						10
11	X of View Direction				11		
	X of X Axis Direction					11	
	X of Upper Right Corner						11
12	X of Target Point				12		
	X of Y Axis Direction					12	
	X of View Center Point						12
13	X of Snap Base Point						13
14	X of Snap Spacing						14
15	X of Grid Spacing						15
16	X of View Direction						16
17	X of View Target Point						17
20	Y of View Center Point				20		
	Y of Origin Point					20	
	Y of Lower left Corner						20
21	Y of View Direction				21		
	Y of X Axis Direction					21	
	Y of Upper Right Corner						21
22	Y of Target Point				22		
	Y of Y Axis Direction					22	
	Y of View Center Point						22
23	Y of Snap Base Point						23
24	Y of Snap Spacing						24
25	Y of Grid Spacing						25
26	Y of View Direction						26
27	Y of View Target Point						27
30	Y of Origin Point					30	
31	Z of View Direction				31		
	Z of X Axis Direction					31	
32	Z of Target Point				32		
	Z of Y Axis Direction					32	
36	Z of View Direction						36
37	Z of View Target Point						37
40	View Height				40		40
	Pattern Length	40					
	Fixed Text Height			40			
41	View Width				41		
	Text Width			41			
	View Aspect Ratio						41
42	Last Height Used			42			
	Lens Length				42		42
43	Front Clipping Plane				43		43
44	Back Clipping Plane				44		44
49	Dash Length	49					
50	Obliquing Angle			50			
	Twist Angle				50		
	Snap Rotation Angle						50
51	View Twist Angle						51
62	Color		62				
70	Number of Flags	70	70	70	70	70	70
71	Text Generation Flag			71			
	View Mode				71		71
72	Alignment Codes	72					
	Circle Zoom Percent						72
73	No. of Dash Items	73					
	Fast Zoom Setting						73
74	UCS Icon Setting						74
75	Snap On or Off						75
76	Grid On or Off						76
77	Snap Style						77
78	Snap Isopair						78

Named Layers, Styles, and Views

View, layer, and text style information adds program control. Programs like ATEXT can check the STYLE table. Drawing setup or plotting routines can check to see if needed views, such as a standard view named PLOT, are already defined and prompt appropriately if not. Programs that depend on specific layers or text styles can check to see if they are already defined and if not, can assign colors and linetypes to the layer. Let's look at a few examples involving layers, styles, and views.

Looking at Layers, Styles, and Views

Begin a NEW drawing named IL07= for all default settings.

```
Command: (tblsearch "layer" "0")
Lisp returns: ((0 . "LAYER")          The type of table.
(2 . "0")                             Entry reference name.
(70 . 64)                             Flag.
(62 . 7)                              Layer's color.
(6 . "CONTINUOUS"))                   The layer's linetype.
```

```
Command: (tblnext "layer" T)          Get first layer. It's the same layer 0 data.
Lisp returns: ((0 . "LAYER") (2 . "0") (70 . 64) (62 . 7) (6 . "CONTINUOUS"))
```

```
Command: (tblnext "layer")            Step to next layer reference.
Lisp returns: nil                     No more layers, only 0 is defined.
```

```
Command: (tblsearch "style" "standard")   Look for style STANDARD.
Lisp returns: ((0 . "STYLE")          Type of table.
(2 . "STANDARD")                      Entry reference name.
(70 . 0)                              Flag value.
(40 . 0.0)                            Style fixed height.
(41 . 1.0)                            Style width factor.
(50 . 0.0)                            Obliquing angle.
(71 . 0)                              Generation flag.
(42 . 0.2)                            Last height used.
(3 . "txt")                           Regular font shape file.
(4 . ""))                             Bigfont shape file, if any.
```

```
Command: (tblsearch "style" "BOLD")   Look for BOLD style.
Lisp returns: nil                     Style is not defined.
```

```
Command: (tblnext "view" T)           Give the rewind argument.
Lisp returns: nil                     No defined views.
```

```
Command: VIEW                         Save current display as PLOT.
```

```
Command: (tblnext "view" T)          Give the rewind argument.
((0 . "VIEW")                        Type of table.
(2 . "PLOT")                         The entry reference name.
(70 . 0)                             Flag value.
(40 . 9.0)                           View height.
(10 6.49713 4.5)                     View center point.
(41 . 12.9943)                       View width.
(11 0.0 0.0 1.0)                     View direction XYZ in WCS coordinates.
(12 0.0 0.0 0.0)                     Target point in WCS coordinates.
(42 50.0)                            Lens length.
(43 0.0)                             Front clip plane distance.
(44 0.0)                             Back clip plane distance.
(50 0.0)                             Twist angle.
(71 0)                               View mode - VIEWMODE system variable.

Command: (tblnext "view")            Try again.
nil                                  There are no more views in drawing.
```

The TBLSEARCH function returns nil when the symbol name is undefined in the drawing. TBLNEXT returns nil when there are no symbols defined in the table or you have reached the table's end.

Your view center, height, and width may differ from ours because they are dependent on the X,Y aspect ratio of your display.

The LAYER table used a 70 code of 1 to flag frozen layers. A 70 code of 4 indicates a vertical style.

The STYLE table is also used to register the names of any shape files loaded in the drawing using a 70 code of 1 and a 3 code with the shape name, with all other codes irrelevant.

Use table data in your programs in the same way you use entity data. If you have the IL DISK, see ATEXT2.LSP for an application of style table access. We'll apply view table access to PVIEW in Chapter 9, along with AutoLISP (screen) device access. The PVIEW command will dynamically rotate through your defined views until you select one. Right now, let's try a program using the layer table.

How to Apply Layer Table Access

If you ever want to erase or wblock a drawing by layers, here's a simple program, called WLAYER, that does just that. The WLAYER command combines SSGET X filtering with TBLNEXT symbol table access. The WLAYER command's wblock option sends each layer to a separate file by layer name. It gives you the option of skipping layers, or erasing layers from the drawing as they are wblocked. It can also be used to simply erase layers without wblocking.

WLAYER requires Release 10 of AutoCAD. If you have the IL DISK, you will find a WLAYER9.LSP version for Release 9 as well as the WLAYER.LSP file shown below for Release 10.

```
;* C:WLAYER scans the drawing's layer list and erases, skips or wblocks each
;* layer to a drawing file name in the current directory. The file name is the
;* first 8 characters of the layer name. If file exists on disk, or the first
;* 8 characters of the name are duplicated, it skips it and prompts.
;* Otherwise, it prompts with each layer name, then erases, wblocks (and
;* optionally erases), or skips it.
;* It requires the DXF and user interface functions to be preloaded.
;*
(defun C:WLAYER( / prmpt frst bpt tbdata ents lname)
  (setvar "CMDECHO" 0)
  (setq frst t                             ;set flag to wind table to top
        bpt  (getvar "INSBASE")            ;get drawing's insertion basept
  );setq
❶
  (while (setq tbdata (tblnext "layer" frst))    ;start while loop, get each layer
    (setq ents (ssget "X" (list (cons 8 (dxf 2 tbdata))))) ;get all entities on layer
          lname (substr (dxf 2 tbdata) 1 8)          ;chop string 8 char max
          frst nil                                   ;reset rewind flag
          prmpt                                      ;make prompt
          (strcat "Erase or Wblock layer " lname "? E/W or RETURN to skip? ")
    );setq
    (if (and ents                                ;check entities
            (setq prmpt (ukword 0 "Wblock Erase" prmpt nil)) ;and choose task
      )
      (if (= prmpt "Wblock")
❷
          (if (not (findfile (strcat "./" lname ".DWG")))
            (if (= "Yes" (ukword 1 "Yes No" "Erase also? Y/N" nil))        ;then
              (command "wblock" lname "" bpt ents "")          ;wblock & erase
              (command "wblock" lname "" bpt ents "" "Oops")   ;wblock & restore
            )
            (prompt (strcat "\nLayer name " (dxf 2 tbdata) " skipped."   ;else
```

Listing continued.

Continued listing.

```
"\nThe first 8 characters duplicate a previous layer or existing drawing file."
            )          )
       );if-findfile
         (command "ERASE" ents "")              ;erases them if existing
      );if=
    );if
  );while
  (setvar "CMDECHO" 1)
  (princ)                                       ;finish cleanly
);defun
;*
```

C:WLAYER Command in WLAYER.LSP File

❶ There isn't much to the table access portion of the program. The WHILE just loops through the layer table, setting TBDATA to each layer's data list until it runs out of layers. The SSGET selects all entities of the current loop's layer, using DXF to extract the layer name. The rest of the loop is primarily a set of nested IF choices which execute WBLOCK and ERASE commands with the COMMAND function.

❷ The FINDFILE function, covered in the next chapter, is tested with an IF to see if the layer name (shortened to eight characters) conflicts with any other layer or drawing name.

Create a test drawing with several entity-containing layers. Then try the WLAYER program. Your ACAD.LSP file should load the needed DXF and UKWORD functions.

Using the WLAYER Command

Continue in the previous drawing, or begin a NEW drawing again named IL07.

Command: **LAYER   LINE   LAYER...**   Make some layers with entities on each. We used layers named PEOPLE, TREES, CHAIRS, and RAILS.

You have the C:WLAYER command in your WLAYER.LSP file.

Create the C:WLAYER command in a file named WLAYER.LSP.

Command: **(load "wlayer")**   Load the file.

```
Command: WLAYER                                                    Run the command.
Erase or Wblock layer 0? E/W or RETURN to skip? : <RETURN>        Skip it.
Erase or Wblock layer PEOPLE? E/W or RETURN to skip? : E          Erase.
Erase or Wblock layer TREES? E/W or RETURN to skip? : W           Wblock it.
Erase also? Y/N: Y                                                 And erase it.
Erase or Wblock layer CHAIRS? E/W or RETURN to skip? : W
Erase also? Y/N: N
Erase or Wblock layer RAILS? E/W or RETURN to skip? : <RETURN>

Command: DIR                    Check for new files named TREES.DWG and RAILS.DWG.
Command: DEL                    Delete them.
Command: QUIT
```

We chose to leave highlight on, so entities on the current loop's layer can be visually identified. You may want to improve the program by giving yourself a prompt which asks if the file on disk should be overwritten when it finds a conflicting file name. Or set the EXPERT system variable to skip AutoCAD's "Do you want to replace it <N>?" question. Next, let's see what can be done with blocks.

Exploring the Block Section

Blocks are strange creatures. They are not true tables, and they get their own section in the drawing database and DXF file. Although entity access gives you block insert information such as scale, location, and attributes, block table access is needed to get information about the entities that make up the block definition. A block table reference is a multiple record table with a header and any number of subsequent records, much like the complex polyline with vertexes or insert entity with attributes. The table access functions return only the block definition header. Then you use ENTNEXT and entity access techniques to step through the entities in the block definition. The end of the block's entities is marked in the DXF file by an *endblk* entity. However ENTNEXT returns nil, not an endblk entity name, when it reaches the end of the block entities.

The block's entities are not true entities; they don't appear in the drawing. They only exist in the block section of the database. When you insert a block, the insert entity refers to the block definition to see what to draw on the screen. An INSERT *name* duplicates the definition entities of the block name in the drawing as true entities.

Because the block section and the endblk entity are unique, we gave them their own table:

BLOCK SECTION		ENDBLK ENTITY	
CODE	DESCRIPTION	CODE	DESCRIPTION
0	Type: BLOCK	0	Type: ENDBLK
-2	First entity name		
2	Block name		
6	Linetype name	6	Linetype name
8	Layer name	8	Layer name
62	Color number	62	Color number
38	Elevation	38	Elevation
39	Thickness	39	Thickness
70	Block type flag		
10	X of insertion base point		
10	Y of insertion base point		
10	Z of insertion base point		

BLOCK Section and ENDBLK Entity DXF Group Codes

Use TBLSEARCH with the BLOCK table name and the name of the specific block to search for. The list returned looks like this:

```
((0 . "BLOCK") (2 . "TEST") (70 . 66) (10 0.0 0.0 0.0)
(-2 . <Entity name: 40000022>))
```

This header information includes only five groups: the 0 block type group; the 2 name group; the 70 block type flag; the 10 insertion base point (which is always 0,0,0); and the -2 group containing the entity name of the first entity in the block definition. The 70 flag is the sum of 1 for anonymous blocks, and 2 if attributes follow. The other values, such as color in the header and all the endblk values, are really irrelevant and occur only in a DXF file.

➡ *NOTE: Anonymous blocks are those blocks automatically generated by hatching or associative dimensioning. A hatch creates an insert entity and block definition with a name like "*Xnn," and an associative dimension creates a dimension entity and block definition with a name like "*Dnn," where nn is a sequential number. The hatch entity stores normal block insert data like block name, insert point, scale, and rotation. The dimension entity stores block name, three defpoints, the text middle point, and any prefix or suffix text. Any additional data, including calculated dimension text, is stored in the BLOCK section table. You can get to it by using TBLSEARCH to search for the 2 (block name) group of the entity data, and by using the block definition subentity data access techniques that are this chapter's topic.*

Let's test the process on a sample block. If you have the IL DISK, you already have the LEGEND.DWG file. If not, start a new legend drawing and create the sample blocks shown in the illustration. We'll use them again in the LEGEND.LSP program, which uses block section access to automate the generation of drawing symbol legends. (Here we *do* mean symbol in the sense of a block annotation symbol.)

To provide an identifying key for the LEGEND program's block access, each symbol block needs a special LEGEND attribute tag. Give the first entity in each symbol block to be included on the legend chart a constant attribute with the attribute tag "LEGEND." The attribute value will be the string you want to appear on the chart as legend text.

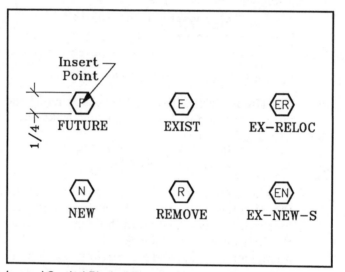

Legend Symbol Blocks Library

BLOCK NAME	ATTRIBUTE TAG	ATTRIBUTE VALUE
FUTURE	LEGEND	FUTURE
NEW	LEGEND	NEW EQUIPMENT
EXIST	LEGEND	EXISTING - NO CHANGE
REMOVE	LEGEND	EXISTING - REMOVE FROM SITE
EX-RELOC	LEGEND	EXISTING - RELOCATE
EX-NEW-S	LEGEND	EXISTING - NEW SERVICE

Legend Symbol Blocks Library

The legend symbols that you will work with are shown in the Legend Symbol Blocks Library illustration and table above. The text strings under the symbols in the illustration are their block names.

Making the LEGEND Blocks

Edit the EXISTING drawing named LEGEND, and skip the rest of this sequence.

Begin a NEW drawing named LEGEND=IL-PROTO, and make the six blocks shown.

Command: **ZOOM**   Left, corner -1,-1 with height 3.

Create three styles for the block and for testing the LEGEND program later:

Command: **STYLE**   Create STD1-8 with SIMPLEX and Height 12", default the rest.
Command: **STYLE**   Create STD1-4 with SIMPLEX and Height 24", default the rest.
Command: **STYLE**   Create STD3-32 with SIMPLEX and Height 9", default the rest.

Here's the process for the FUTURE block:

Command: **POLYGON**   6 sides, at 0,0, circumscribed with 0.125" radius.
Command: **TEXT**   Use STD3-32, middle justified at 0,0 and rotation 0:
Text: **F**   Put an F for FUTURE in the hexagon.

Command: **ATTDEF**   Change modes to Invisible and Constant:
Attribute modes -- Invisible:**Y** Constant:**Y** Verify: **N**
Attribute tag: **LEGEND**
Attribute value: **FUTURE**   Place it next to symbol.

Command: **BLOCK**
Block name (or ?): **FUTURE**
Insertion base point: **0,0**
Select objects: **L**   You must select the attdef first.
Select objects: Then select the rest.

Command: **OOPS**   Recycle it to make the others.
Command: **CHANGE**   Change Attdef tag and legend text to the next symbol.
Command: **BLOCK**   Block the next.

Repeat Oops, Change, Block for each.

Command: **SAVE**   You'll use it to test LEGEND.LSP.

➦ *NOTE: The attdef must be the first entity selected when defining the block. The LEGEND program will rely on its being first to speed up searching.*

How to Find Block Data With TBLSEARCH and ENTNEXT

Let's look at the FUTURE block definition using the TBLSEARCH and entity access functions. Since the TBLSEARCH function only returns the block definition header record and not the entities of the block, we'll use ENTNEXT to step through the entities which comprise the block and ENTGET to get their data.

Block data contains a -2 code followed by an entity name. This is not the block entity name because a block is not an entity. It is the name of the first subentity of the block definition and is the key to looking at all subentities in the block. Treat subentity names as you would any other entity names. The entity data format is same as in the previous chapter.

Stepping Through Block Definition Entities

```
Command: (setq tbdata (tblsearch "BLOCK" "FUTURE"))     Check the block table.
Lisp returns: ((0 . "BLOCK")                            The block table.
(2 . "FUTURE")                                          Block name.
(70 . 64)                                               Flag value.
(10 0.0 0.0 0.0)                                        Insertion base point.
(-2 . <Entity name: 40000018>))                         First subentity.


Command: (setq ename (cdr (assoc -2 tbdata)))           Extract the key subentity name.
Lisp returns: <Entity name: 40000018>


Command: (setq edata (entget ename))                    Get the subentity data.
Lisp returns: ((-1 . <Entity name: 40000018>) (0 . "ATTDEF") (8 . "0")
(10 0.203125 -0.046875) (40 . 0.09375) (1 . "FUTURE") (3 . "")
(2 . "LEGEND") (70 . 3) (73 . 0) (50 . 0.0) (41 . 1.0)
(51 . 0.0) (7 . "STD3-32") (71 . 0) (72 . 0) (11 0.0 0.0))


Command: (entget (entnext (cdr (assoc -1 edata))))      Next entity in the block def.
Lisp returns: ((-1 . <Entity name: 4000004c>) (0 . "TEXT") (8 . "0") (10 -0.029018 -
0.046875) (40 . 0.09375) (1 . "F") (50 . 0.0) (41 . 1.0) (51 . 0.0) (7 . "STD3-32")
(71 . 0) (72 . 4) (11 0.0 0.0))
```

The attdef subentity data list begins with the same entity name as the -2 group (ours is 40000018), but now it has a normal -1 code and normal entity groups. Refer to the Entity DXF Group Codes table in the previous chapter to decode the values.

ENTGET found your special LEGEND attdef first because you selected it first when you created the block. Since you specified a fixed order during object selection, you can depend on the LEGEND attribute's being first in the block definition. Our LEGEND program will need to search a drawing's entire block section to find all possible legend symbols. Making the key attdef the first subentity in the block definition eliminates the need to ENTNEXT through each block's entire block definition to determine if it's a legend symbol. This efficiency is not always possible in block data searches. If you don't have complete control over the original block definitions, don't plan on any specific order of entities within blocks.

Applying Block Table Access to LEGEND

In the next few exercises, we'll show you how to pick your way through the table data, build and use a list of this data, and place it in the drawing to form a drawing symbol legend. This is a routine task at some point in most drafting projects, so why not automate it?

LEGEND.LSP is a group of three functions that automate table searching, get needed data, prompt for the location, and build the legend using the global drawing scale and default text.

The first function, called LEGEND, retrieves the legend symbol names and attribute text, and stores them in a list. Then the LEGEND program calls two other functions, OUTLEDG and LEDSWAP, to output and format the list. We'll show you those in a moment. First, here is the LEGEND program.

```
;* LEGEND.LSP scans the BLOCKs table and extracts all specially marked symbol
;* blocks, then builds a legend in the drawing listing all such blocks.
;* Mark symbol blocks with a constant invisible attdef-tagged LEGEND with
;* the symbol's description as its value.
;* The attdef MUST be the first selected entity when making the block.
;* The LEGEND.LSP functions consist of C:LEGEND, OUTLEDG and LEDSWAP.
;* Legend must have the DXF and user interface functions loaded, and expects a
;* global dwg scale variable named #DWGSC to be set to plot scale.
;*
(defun C:LEGEND ( / frst tbdata elist edata llist)
   (prompt "\nBuilding legend list...\n")        ;tell user what is going on
   (setq frst t)                                 ;flag to rewind to first block
❶
   (while (setq tbdata (tblnext "BLOCK" frst))    ;loop thru all Blocks, retrieve head data
     (setq edata (entget (dxf -2 tbdata)))       ;get 1st subentity's data.
     (if (and (= (dxf 0 edata) "ATTDEF")         ;if it is a legend symbol
          (= (dxf 2 edata) "LEGEND")
       )
```

Listing continued.

Continued listing.

```
❷
      (setq llist                                     ;then append
            (append llist (list (list (dxf 2 tbdata)   ;block name
                                (dxf 1 edata)      ;and legend descr,
              )                )      )
        );setq
    );if and =
    (setq frst nil)                                ;resets flag to disable rewind
  );while
❸
  (outledg llist)                                  ;outputs legend, using the list LLIST
  (ledswap)                                        ;allows user to swap entries
  (princ)                                          ;end cleanly
);defun C:LEGEND
;*
```

LEGEND Function in LEGEND.LSP File

❶ The function begins by searching through the block table. It looks for the attdef tag of LEGEND, ignoring all blocks that were not created with the LEGEND attdef as the first subentity.

❷ Each time it finds a legend entry, it uses the APPEND function to build a list of lists, with each sublist being the block name and attribute value. When TBLNEXT reaches the end of the BLOCKS table, it returns nil and LEGEND stops looping.

❸ You can test C:LEGEND without the OUTLEDG and LEDSWAP subroutine calls by disabling them with a leading comment, like ; **. If you don't have the IL DISK and you run LEGEND without disabling these functions, it will crash because they are not yet defined.

Let's disable these functions and test LEGEND.

Creating the Data List With C:LEGEND

Continue in the previous drawing, or edit an EXISTING drawing named LEGEND.
Make sure the DXF and UPOINT functions were loaded, and #DWGSC was set to 96 by ACAD.LSP.

You have C:LEGEND in the LEGEND.LSP file. Make the changes below and try it.

Create C:LEGEND as shown above, in a file named LEGEND.LSP. Make the changes below and try it.

Even if you have the IL DISK, change the end of C:LEGEND to read:

```
;** (outledg llist)              ;disabled - outputs legend, using the list llist
;** (ledswap)                    ;disabled - allows user to swap entries
   (princ llist)                 ;print results - end cleanly

Command: (load "legend")     Load the file.
Command: LEGEND              Test it.
Building legend list...
Lisp returns: (("FUTURE" "FUTURE") ("NEW" "NEW EQUIPMENT") ("EXIST" "EXISTING – NO
CHANGE") ("REMOVE" "REMOVE FROM SITE") ("EX-RELOC" "EXISTING – RELOCATED") ("EX-NEW-
S" "EXISTING – NEW SERVICE"))
```

If you got the list shown, you're ready to try the OUTLEDG function. It automatically draws legend entries using predefined text styles, and scales the symbols with the #dwgsc global scale factor.

```
;* OUTLEDG is used by LEGEND to draw the legend. It uses STD1-8 and STD1-4
;* text height styles which must be defined.
;*
(defun outledg (llist / pt1 txtht txdist step)
  (setq ortho (getvar "ORTHOMODE"))                ;save
  (setvar "ORTHOMODE" 1)                           ;turn ortho on
❶
  (prompt                                          ;number of entries
    (strcat "\nThere are " (itoa (length llist)) " entries for the legend."))
  );prompt
  (setq pt1 (upoint 1 "" "Starting point of first legend symbol" nil nil))
  (command "insert" (caar llist) pt1 #dwgsc "" "")     ;temp. inserts 1st symbol
  (setq txtht (dxf 40 (tblsearch "STYLE" "STD1-8"))   ;gets ht of text style
        txdist (udist 1 "" "Distance to first legend text" txdist pt1) ;horiz space
        step (udist 1 "" "Distance to next legend symbol" step pt1)    ;vert space
  );setq                                              ;get relative positions
```

Listing continued.

Continued listing.

```
❷
  (command "erase" "l" ""                                 ;erase temp insert
          "text" "S" "STD1-4"                             ;switch text styles
          (polar pt1 (* 0.5 pi) (- step txtht))           ;enter LEGEND title above
          0.0 "%%uLEGEND%%u"                              ;pt1, %%u underscores
          "text" "s" "STD1-8" nil                         ;resets the style
  );command
  (foreach item llist                                     ;insert ea symbol & descr
    (command "insert" (car item) pt1 #dwgsc "" "")        ;inserts symbol
    (setq bpt (polar pt1 (* pi 1.5) (/ txtht 2.0)))       ;calc vert base pt of text
    (command "text" (polar bpt 0 txdist) 0.0 (cadr item)) ;puts in text
    (setq pt1 (polar pt1 (* 1.5 pi) step))                ;steps to next line
  );foreach
  (setvar "ORTHOMODE" ortho)                              ;restores
);defun OUTLEDG
;*
```

OUTLEDG Function in LEGEND.LSP File

❶ First, the function figures the number of legend entries to guide you in positioning the legend. OUTLEDG prompts you with the number of symbols in the legend and temporarily inserts the first block to give you visual help in selecting the text position and vertical spacing. You pick the insertion point for the first legend symbol, the horizontal offset of the descriptive text, and the vertical step down to the next symbol. This process lets you adjust the format for any symbols-to-text proportion.

❷ Then the block is erased and the "LEGEND" title is placed. FOREACH steps through each sublist of legend entries, inserting each symbol block (car item) and its descriptive text (cadr item). STEP is the variable that contains the insertion point for the text height. Text is offset by the horizontal distance, TXDIST. After stepping down a vertical step, the process repeats until all the symbols are placed.

Add the OUTLEDG function to the LEGEND.LSP file if you don't have the IL DISK. Be sure to enable the OUTLEDG function call and remove the LLIST variable from the PRINC statement before trying OUTLEDG.

Outputting the Legend

Continue in the previous drawing, or edit an EXISTING drawing named LEGEND.

 You have OUTLEDG in the LEGEND.LSP file. Make the changes below and try it.

Add OUTLEDG as shown above to your LEGEND.LSP file. Make the changes below and try it.

Even if you have the IL DISK, change the end of C:LEGEND to read:

```
(outledg llist)        ;outputs legend, using the list LLIST
;** (ledswap)          ;disabled - allows user to swap entries
(princ)                ;end cleanly
```

Command: **ZOOM**   Window from 3',0 to 88',60'.

Command: **(load "legend")**   Reload the file.

Command: **LEGEND**
Building legend list...   Tells you what's happening.
There are 6 entries for the legend.
Starting point of first legend symbol: Pick a point.
Distance to first legend text: Pick about 24 inches.
Distance to next legend symbol: Pick about 36 inches and it draws the legend.

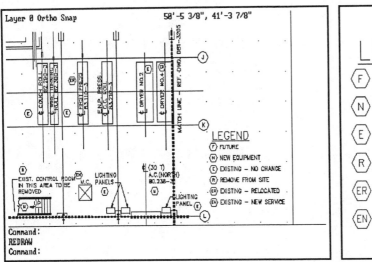

The Output Legend

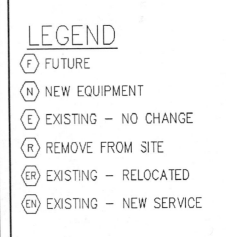

Detail of Legend

Since the legend may not be built in the order you would have chosen, you may wish to automate swapping its parts around.

How to Swap Entities With LEDSWAP

The LEDSWAP tool, shown next, is a simple entity access tool that lets you pick a pair of legend symbols and swap their positions. It automatically finds the associated descriptive text string and swaps them also.

Certain commands, like EXPLODE, will rearrange entities. Since LEDSWAP is called by the LEGEND command immediately after OUTLEDG, the order of the legend entities is predictable, and LEDSWAP can use ENTNEXT to find the text entity following the block insert.

```
;* LEDSWAP is called by LEGEND to rearrange the entries.
(defun LEDSWAP ( / redrw s1name s2name t1name t2name bp1 bp2 )
❶
(while (setq s1name (entsel "\nSelect first symbol to swap or RETURN to exit: "))
   (if  (setq s2name (entsel "\nSelect second symbol or RETURN to skip: "))
     (progn
       (setq t1name (entnext (car s1name))       ;get 1st descr. ename
             t2name (entnext (car s2name))       ;get 2nd descr. ename
             bp1 (osnap (cadr s1name) "INS")     ;get 1st INSert pt.
             bp2 (osnap (cadr s2name) "INS")     ;get 2nd INSert pt.
       )
❷
       (command "MOVE" s1name t1name "" bp1 bp2   ;move 1st to 2nd
                "MOVE" s2name t2name "" bp2 bp1   ;move 2nd to 1st
       )
       (entupd (car s1name))                      ;"redraw" 1st
       (entupd t1name)
     );progn
   );if s2name
);while s1name
 (princ)                                          ;finish cleanly
);defun LEDSWAP
(princ)
;*
;* end of LEGEND.LSP
```

LEDSWAP Function in LEGEND.LSP File

❶ The LEDSWAP function buffers its action with a WHILE and an IF in case you want to exit or change your mind by striking a <RETURN> or <SPACE> key. ENTSEL is used to get the symbol block names, then

ENTNEXT is used to get the text entity names which immediately follow the block entity names. (If the block had variable attributes, ENTNEXT would have to step through them first to reach the text.) Then, OSNAP uses the points CADR extracted from the ENTSEL lists to set the BP1 and BP2 points for the move.

❷ The MOVE commands issued by LEDSWAP accept either ENTSEL style lists like S1NAME (the symbol block) or bare entity names like T1NAME (the text). However, the ENTUPD function that redraws the first pair must use bare entity names like T1NAME to avoid a bad argument type error.

Let's test it.

Testing LEGEND With the LEDSWAP Function

Continue in the previous drawing, or edit an EXISTING drawing named LEGEND.

You have LEDSWAP in the LEGEND.LSP file. Make the changes below and try it.

Add LEDSWAP as shown above to your LEGEND.LSP file. Make the changes below and try it.

Even if you have the IL DISK, change the end of C:LEGEND to read:

`(outledg llist)`	;outputs legend, using the list LLIST
`(ledswap)`	;disabled - allows user to swap entries
`(princ)`	;end cleanly

Command: **(load "legend")**	Reload the file.
Command: **ERASE**	Erase any legends already in the drawing to test it all.
Command: **LEGEND**	The LEGEND appears, with the same questions as before.

```
Building legend list...
There are 6 entries for the legend.
Starting point of first legend symbol:          Pick point.
Distance to first legend text:                  Show it.
Distance to next legend symbol:                 Show it.
Select first symbol to swap or RETURN to exit:  This is new. Pick the FUTURE symbol.
Select second symbol or RETURN to skip:         Pick the NEW symbol.
Select first symbol or RETURN to exit:          Keep swapping if you like.
```

OUTLEDG and LEDSWAP were made as separate subroutines to make testing easier, and to make it easier to use them individually in other applications.

The LTYPE table is essentially similar to the LAYER, VIEW, and STYLE tables. However, the LTYPE table's flexibility offers some interesting customization possibilities.

Named Properties: Linetypes and More

AutoCAD makes it easy to create linetypes with the LINETYPE command. You can also create linetypes by writing their definitions in an ASCII file with a .LIN extension. The default AutoCAD linetypes are in the ACAD.LIN file. For a complete review of linetype use and creation, see CUSTOMIZING AutoCAD and INSIDE AutoCAD, both from New Riders Publishing.

Linetype table access offers the usual advantages of check and control, so programs that depend on the existence of specific linetypes can check and load them if not present. Unlike other table data, linetypes apply to all entities in a drawing. This makes them useful for tagging entities. It's like being able to attach a global attribute to any entity. As a linetype application, we'll create TAKOFF.LSP, a program that uses this feature to extract material take-off data. The PVAR.LSP program on the New Riders AutoLISP Utilities Disk 1 uses the linetype table to store user-defined variables between drawing sessions.

Let's take a quick look at linetype definition, file format, and table format. First, use the LINETYPE command to see how AutoCAD lists the description and contents of a linetype from its ACAD.LIN file. Then, create your own linetypes. Call them MATL-WT01 and MATL-WT02 and store them in IL-MATL.LIN. You'll need these linetypes later in the TAKOFF program.

Creating and Examining Linetypes

```
Enter NAME of drawing: 1      Begin a NEW drawing named ILTYPE.

Command: ZOOM                 Zoom Left with height 5.
```

You already have the IL-MATL.LIN linetype file, so you can just read the rest of this sequence.

Perform this sequence to create the IL-MATL.LIN file.

```
Command: LINETYPE                          First check an existing one.
?/Create/Load/Set: C
Name of linetype to create: DASHDOT
```

```
File for storage of linetype <ACAD>: <RETURN>
Wait, checking if linetype already defined...
DASHDOT already exists in this file. Current definition is:
   *DASHDOT,__ . __ . __ . __ . __ . __ . __ . __ . __
   A,0.5,-0.25,0,-0.25
```
Overwrite? <N> **N**   No to not change it.
?/Create/Load/Set: **C**   Create your own.
```
Name of linetype to create: MATL-WT01
```
File for storage of linetype <ACAD>: **IL-MATL**   Keep the ACAD.LIN file clean.
```
Creating new file
```
Descriptive text: **5/8 gyp ea. side 3-1/2 stl studs no insul**
```
Enter pattern (on next line):
```
A,**1.25,-0.25,0.25,-0.25**
```
New definition written to file.
```
?/Create/Load/Set: **<RETURN>**

Command: **SHELL**   Use your text editor to edit the IL-MATL.LIN file.
                                              You will see:

```
*MATL-WT01,5/8 gyp ea. side 3-1/2 stl studs no insul
A,1.25,-0.25,0.25,-0.25
```

Copy and edit the first to create MATL-WT02:

```
*MATL-WT01,5/8 gyp ea. side 3-1/2 stl studs no insul
A,1.25,-0.25,0.25,-0.25
```
*MATL-WT02,5/8 gyp ea. side 3-1/2 stl studs 2-1/2 insul
A,1.25,-0.25,0.25,-0.25

                                              Be sure to <RETURN> after the last line.

Save the file and exit to AutoCAD.

Command: **SAVE**   Save the drawing for TAKOFF.LSP.

Notice how we use the C (create) option to see the definition of an existing linetype, such as DASHDOT. Now we have two linetypes, one created by AutoCAD and one by your text editor. As you can see, the descriptive text can be any text string you desire, up to 47 characters. If longer, it will be truncated.

The pattern field is a little trickier. The dash-dot pattern is defined by a series of numbers separated by commas. The A is the alignment code (only A is currently supported). A zero is a dot, a negative number is a pen-up space, and a positive number is a pen-down dash. The first number following the A code must be zero or greater. Each linetype must have a minimum of two values with at least one non-zero pen-up or pen-down. Zero dot values must be separated by non-zero values. The entire field is applied as a loop. So for example, a dotted line is A,0,-.25, not A,0,-.25,0. If you entered A,0,-.25,0 it would become 0,-.25,0,0,-.25,**0,0**,-.25,0... when applied, resulting in two zeros in a row. The maximum number of dash-dot values is limited by line length. They must all fit on a single 80-character line.

➡ *NOTE: AutoCAD filters your input when you use the LINETYPE command to create a linetype. But it isn't so forgiving when loading a linetype file created by your text editor. If the file contains an error, some versions of AutoCAD will crash. Creating linetypes with the LINETYPE command is safest.*

➡ *TIP: A,9999999,9999999 acts like a continuous linetype, and A,0,-9999999 is a sort of invisible linetype, with a dot at each end and one big space between them.*

Like any other linetype, AutoCAD requires you to load MATL-WT01 and set it current before using it. Load it, set it current, and draw a line with it. It should look like a center line, because we copied its dash-dot pattern from the CENTER linetype in ACAD.LIN. Then use TBLSEARCH to see how AutoCAD stores information in the LTYPE symbol table. List DASHDOT for comparison, then get the table data for MATL-WT01.

Looking at Linetype Tables

Continue in the previous drawing.

```
Command: LINETYPE          Continue or restart the command.
?/Create/Load/Set: L
Name of linetype to load: *  Wildcard to load all.
File to search <IL-MATL>: <RETURN>
Linetype MATL-WT01 loaded.
Linetype MATL-WT02 loaded.
?/Create/Load/Set: L       Load Linetype DASHDOT from the ACAD.LIN file.

?/Create/Load/Set: S       And set MATL-WT01 current to use it.
New entity linetype (or ?) <BYLAYER>: MATL-WT01
?/Create/Load/Set: <RETURN>

Command: LINE              Draw one. It looks like a center line.
```

```
Command: (tblsearch "LTYPE" "DASHDOT")        Check it out.
Lisp returns: ((0 . "LTYPE")                  The linetype table name.
(2 . "DASHDOT")                               Linetype name.
(70 . 64)                                     Flag.
                                              The visual description:
(3 . "__ . __ . __ . __ . __ . __ . __")
(72 . 65)                                     Alignment code, ASCII value for "A," the only allowed code.
(73 . 4)                                      Number of dash length items.
(40 . 1.0)                                    Absolute total of dash pattern.
(49 . 0.5)                                    First dash length.
(49 . -0.25)                                  Pen up dash length.
(49 . 0.0)                                    Dot.
(49 . -0.25))                                 Pen up dash length.

Command: (tblsearch "LTYPE" "MATL-WT01")   Your first linetype.

Lisp returns: ((0 . "LTYPE") (2 . "MATL-WT01") (70 . 64) (3 . "5/8 gyp ea. side 3-1/2
stl studs no insul") (72 . 65) (73 . 4) (40 . 2.0) (49 . 1.25) (49 . -0.25) (49 .
0.25) (49 . -0.25))
```

The 2 group linetype name can be any string value you like, up to 47 characters. The 3 group description is also any string up to 47 characters. The 73 value tells how many 49 groups will follow. The 49 groups are the actual linetype pattern values: zero denotes a dot; positive values are pen-down segment lengths; and negative values are pen-up (space) lengths. These 49 values are simply real numbers, but the leading one must be zero or greater to satisfy AutoCAD's alignment and, as we said before, there must be at least two. The 40 group is the unit pattern length, the sum of the absolute values of all 49 group segments.

Linetypes are stored internally, like block definitions. The values, once they are loaded in the drawing, are independent of the .LIN file containing their original definitions. They travel with the drawing whether or not they are in any current .LIN file.

As you might have surmised from the description of our MATL-WT01 linetype, we intend to use it to represent a wall.

How to Apply Linetypes to Material Takeoffs

Once you go to the effort of making an accurate CAD drawing, it would be nice if you could extract data for estimating materials from it. You can. Attributes are rather restricted because they can only be applied to blocks, but any entity can have a linetype attached to its data. Even entities that do not show visible linetypes, such as text, have linetype values in their entity data.

We can take advantage of this in TAKOFF.LSP, a simple program that extracts a DXF file containing only those entities with certain key linetypes, such as MATL-XXXX where *XXXX* can be any identifying text. Then you can use an external program (or write one in AutoLISP) to process and total the data.

We made MATL-WT01 and 02 center-style linetypes so they can be used as wall center lines. You can place lines drawn with them on a unique layer and turn them off when they're not needed. Ideally, you'd use a double wall drawing program that would automatically put in coded center lines such as these. Or, at estimating time, you could use them to trace over appropriate walls. In any case, once they are in the drawing, TAKOFF will find all entities drawn with MATL-XXXX linetypes and extract them. Let's look at TAKOFF.LSP.

```
;* TAKOFF checks the LTYPE table and outputs all entities of linetype MATL-*
;* (where * is any string) to a DXF file for lineal material take-offs.
;* It returns nil if none are found, or a list of the linetype names if OK.
;* It requires the DXF function.
;*
❶
(setq expert (getvar "EXPERT")) (setvar "EXPERT" 3)
(command "LINETYPE" "L" "MATL*" "IL-MATL" "")              ;loads IL-MATL.LIN defs
(setvar "EXPERT" expert) (setq expert nil)

(defun takoff ( / lt ltlist flag next)
  (tblnext "LTYPE" T)                        ;rewind, ignore 1st continuous Ltype
❷
  (while (setq next (tblnext "LTYPE"))               ;check ea Ltype in table
    (if (= "MATL-" (substr (setq lt (dxf 2 next)) 1 5))  ;if it begins "MATL-"
        (setq ltlist (cons lt ltlist))                ;then add it to list
    );if
  );while
  (if ltlist                                   ;if matl Ltypes exist
    (progn                                     ;then
      (setq hilite (getvar "HIGHLIGHT"))       ;save and turn off
      (setvar "HIGHLIGHT" 0)
      (command "DXFOUT" "TAKOFF" "E")          ;start DXFOUT command
```

Listing continued.

Continued listing.

❸
```
    (foreach lt ltlist                                  ;each defined matl Ltype
      (if (princ (setq next (ssget "X" (list (cons 6 lt))))))   ;get and test next ss
        (progn (command next) (setq flag T))            ;select, and set flag
      )
    )
```
❹
```
    (if flag                                            ;if any ss were found
      (command "" 6)                                    ;complete command
      (command nil)                                     ;cancel command
    );if
    (setvar "HIGHLIGHT" hilite)                          ;restore
 ) );if&progn
 (if flag
   ltlist                                               ;return list
   (prompt "\nMaterial linetypes not defined or not in use. ")   ;return nil
 );if
);defun
```

The TAKOFF Function in TAKOFF.LSP File

❶ First, when TAKOFF.LSP loads the IL-MATL linetype file, it has to toggle the EXPERT system variable to avoid conflict with linetypes already loaded.

❷ TAKOFF uses TBLNEXT to step through the LTYPE table and uses CONS to add the names of all linetypes beginning with the string "MATL-" to the LTLIST list. DXF extracts the linetype name and SUBSTR gets its first five characters to test. TAKOFF doesn't bother to actually check the first linetype because it will always be "continuous."

❸ The COMMAND function starts the DXFOUT command with the entities option. FOREACH loops through each name in the LTLIST list and uses SSGET "X" to send a selection set to the DXFOUT command.

❹ The FLAG variable is set in the FOREACH if any entities are output. It then properly ends the DXFOUT command with a precision of six and a <RETURN> if entities are output, or cancels it with a nil if not.

We made TAKOFF a subroutine instead of a command function because it likely will only be used once or twice per drawing. As a subroutine, it can easily be called as part of a more elaborate program that does the area takoffs.

Now let's see TAKOFF in action. You'll need the IL-MATL.LIN file from the IL DISK or from earlier in this section.

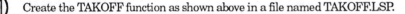

Extracting Linetype Data With TAKOFF

Enter selection: **1**   Begin a NEW drawing again named ILTYPE.

You have the TAKOFF function in your TAKOFF.LSP file.

Create the TAKOFF function as shown above in a file named TAKOFF.LSP.

```
Command: (load"takoff")
LINETYPE                              First it loads the linetype file.
?/Create/Load/Set: L
Linetype(s) to load: MATL* File to search <IL-MATL>: IL-MATL
Linetype MATL-WT01 reloaded.
Linetype MATL-WT02 reloaded.
?/Create/Load/Set:
Lisp returns: TAKOFF
```

```
Command: (takoff)                     Try it.
Lisp prompts and returns: Material linetypes not defined or not in use. nil
```

Command: **PLINE LINE ARC**   Draw a few of each in a normal linetype
                                         to prove TAKOFF will ignore them.

Command: **LINETYPE**   Load MATL* from the IL-MATL.LIN file.
                                         Set MATL-WT01 current.

Command: **PLINE LINE ARC**   Draw a few of each of these entities.

Command: **LINETYPE**   Load MATL* from the IL-MATL.LIN file.
                                         Set MATL-WT02 current.

Command: **PLINE LINE ARC**   Draw a few of each in the MATL-WT02 linetype.

```
Command: (takoff)                     Execute the program.
DXFOUT File name <ILTYPE>: TAKOFF     Outputs the TAKOFF.DXF file.
Enter decimal places of accuracy (0 to 16)/Entities/Binary <6>: E
Select objects: <Selection set: 3>  1 found.
Select objects: <Selection set: 4>  3 found.
Select objects:
Enter decimal places of accuracy (0 to 16)/Binary <6>: 6
Command: ("MATL-WT02" "MATL-WT01")    Returns the LTLIST.
```

```
Command: SHELL                   Use your text editor to look at TAKOFF.DXF. It begins like:
   0
SECTION
   2
ENTITIES
   0
LINE                             A line.
   8
0
   6
MATL-WT02
  10
 2.0                             X of first point.
  20
 2.0                             Y of first point.
  30
 0.0                             Z of first point.
  11
 6.0                             X of second point.
  21
 6.0                             Y of second point.
  31
 0.0                             Z of second point.
   0
LINE                             And so on.
                                 Exit to AutoCAD.
Command: QUIT
```

A program that totals lengths needs to step through the DXF file, calculating and summing the distances between the 10-20-30 and 11-21-31 coordinates for lines and straight polylines. It should ignore text and other irrelevant entities. Calculating the lengths of arcs, circles, and curved polylines is tricky, but possible. DXF data processing will be covered in Chapter 16.

An alternate approach would be to let AutoCAD do the calculations with the Entity and Add options of the AREA command. Instead of DXFOUT, TAKOFF could wblock all its entities to a new drawing file, or copy them to a unique layer. Then, run them all through PEDIT to convert them to polylines, and through AREA Add Entity to sum their lengths. This would work for lines, polylines, and arcs. Circles are ignored by PEDIT, so they would have to be ignored or converted to arcs by BREAK. All other entities would be rejected by PEDIT and AREA.

➡ *TIP: Use linetype pattern variations or colors to help you differentiate between various MATL-XXXX linetypes. If you use LISP to total the lengths, modify TAKOFF to extract lists of entity data instead of a DXF file.*

PVAR.LSP, on the New Riders AutoLISP Utilities Disk 1, is an elaborate application of linetype table access to create and permanently store user variables in the drawing.

Using PVAR to Store Variables as Linetypes

The LTYPE table is merely a table of string and number values that AutoCAD happens to use to create linetypes. Since we can write data to it with the LINETYPE command and extract data from it with table access, we can use it for data storage. Most AutoCAD customizers wish they had access to a greater number of user variables (user-definable system variables) than the USERR1-5 and USERI1-5 that AutoCAD makes available.

They do. PVAR.LSP uses the LTYPE table to store up to 254 variables (less if other linetypes are defined). Valid data types are STRing, REAL, INTeger, POINT (actually a list), and NIL. Unlike the user system variables, these are not restricted to integers and real numbers.

The PVAR functions include: RETVAR to retrieve the value of a personal variable inside a LISP function; PUTVAR to store a value; PVCHK to check the controlling PVARS-DONOT-DELETE data block; GETPVAL to get new PVAR values from the user; and C:PVAR, which is similar to the AutoCAD SETVAR command. Sorry, PVAR is not an AutoCAD transparent command because it uses the LINETYPE command. PUTVAR and RETVAR work from within other functions if no command is pending. The flow of the PVAR program is illustrated in the PVAR.DWG file on the New Riders AutoLISP Utilities Disk 1. Additional documentation is in the PVAR.DOC file.

PVARs have many applications. Like some AutoCAD users, you may be frustrated with AutoCAD's inability to store plotting data with the drawing file. Think about building a custom plot routine that uses PVARs to make all drawing-specific plotting requirements accessible with the drawing.

Whenever your programs require a value setting that cannot be saved as a system variable, use PVAR. You can build expressions into your programs to retrieve them, or into your ACAD.LSP file to automatically initialize their values.

By now, you're familiar with the symbol table functions, TBLSEARCH and TBLNEXT. You've taken the table and block section data, and used it to find entity data and modify your drawing. As these examples show, table access is simple and straightforward, but it gives you access to information that wields great power over AutoCAD's drawing editor. Another area of increased power lies in the UCS and VPORT tables.

UCS and VPORT Tables

AutoCAD's viewports can display several views of the same drawing, even from different angles. You can have up to four simultaneous viewports in DOS machines and 16 on computers with 32-bit operating systems. Each set of viewports can be named, and you can have as many named sets as you like. The current viewport is the one where drawing entity selection and point picks take place. Different viewports can have different settings for several drawing environment controls. These include snap, grid, 3D viewpoint, zoom extents, VIEWRES, the fast zoom and circle resolution command, UCSICON, and several DVIEW settings.

The VPORT symbol table stores viewport settings and allows you to access the data with the AutoLISP table functions. Your programs can use this data to determine whether multiple viewports are present, which is the current active viewport, or to select a particular viewport for the program's action. For example, a program might use one of a set of multiple viewports to display graphic prompt data through a slide file. Checking the VPORT table data allows a program to determine which of the current viewports has sufficient size and an appropriate aspect ratio for the display.

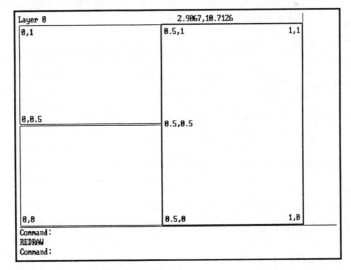

Typical Viewport Configuration

UCSs (User Coordinate Systems) are the keys to AutoCAD's implementation of 3D. You can move, twist, and rotate your current UCS anywhere in space. Once established, any entity created is placed in relation to the X,Y plane of the current UCS, not the original default coordinate system, called the WCS (World Coordinate System).

The typical table access example of checking for the viewports and UCSs that your programs need, and defining them if they don't exist, also applies to these two tables.

Viewports trigger undesirable side effects in commands that cause redraws. UCS changes cause redraws if settings such as grid or UCSICON are present. The redraw time is compounded if several viewports are set up. Viewport table access makes it possible to manage these settings so redraws in programs (and user actions) that change UCSs or otherwise cause redraws can be avoided. We'll apply this in Chapter 14.

Two AutoCAD commands deserve passing mention in our viewports discussion: REDRAWALL (or 'REDRAWALL) and REGENALL. Use them from the COMMAND function if you want your program to redraw or regenerate all visible viewports.

Both the UCS and viewport features are important to 3D. They will be applied in greater depth in Chapter 14, our 3D chapter. For a complete review of the *use* of UCSs and viewports, see INSIDE AutoCAD, also from New Riders Publishing.

Now, let's take a look at VPORTs, UCSs, and their table data.

Looking at VPORTS and UCSs

```
Enter selection: 1            Begin a NEW drawing again named IL07.

Command: VPORTS                                    Make a set of viewports.
Save/Restore/Delete/Join/SIngle/?/2/<3>/4: <RETURN>    The default 3.
Horizontal/Vertical/Above/Below/Left/<Right>: <RETURN>  The default Right.
Command: VPORTS
Save/Restore/Delete/Join/SIngle/?/2/<3>/4: S        Save it.
?/Name for new viewport configuration: STANDARD    Call it STANDARD.

Command: UCS                                        Change your UCS.
Origin/ZAxis/3point/Entity/View/X/Y/Z/Prev/Restore/Save/Del/?/<World>: X
Rotation angle about X axis <0.0>: 25
Command: UCS
Origin/ZAxis/3point/Entity/View/X/Y/Z/Prev/Restore/Save/Del/?/<World>: S Save it.
?/Name of UCS: X25                                  Give it the name X25.
```

Command: **(TBLNEXT "VPORT" T)** Get the first viewport listing.

Lisp returns:

((0 . "VPORT")	Type of listing.
(2 . "STANDARD")	Name of VPORT.
(70 . 0)	Flags.
(10 0.5 0.0)	Lower left corner of unit screen.
(11 1.0 1.0)	Upper right corner of unit screen.
(12 5.86807 8.53728)	View center of unit screen.
(13 0.0 0.0)	Snap base point on unit screen.
(14 0.1 0.1)	Unit snap spacing.
(15 1.0 1.0)	Unit grid spacing.
(16 0.0 0.0 1.0)	View direction from target.
(17 0.0 0.0 0.0)	View target point.
(40 . 17.0746)	View height (real units).
(41 . 0.687347)	Viewport aspect ratio.
(42 . 50.0)	Lens length.
(43 . 0.0)	Front clip plane distance.
(44 . 0.0)	Back clip plane distance.
(50 . 0.0)	Snap rotation angle.
(51 . 0.0)	Twist angle.
(71 . 0)	View mode from VIEWMODE setvar.
(72 . 100)	Circle resolution zoom percent.
(73 . 1)	Fast zoom setting.
(74 . 1)	UCSICON setting.
(75 . 1)	Snap ON/OFF setting.
(76 . 1)	Grid ON/OFF setting.
(77 . 0)	Snap style setting.
(78 . 0))	Snap ISO pair setting.

Command: **(TBLNEXT "VPORT")**   Get the next viewport listing.
Lisp returns: ((0 . "VPORT") (2 . "STANDARD") (70 . 0) (10 0.0 0.5) (11 0.5 1.0) (12 5.90001 4.25) (13 0.0 0.0) (14 0.1 0.1) (15 1.0 1.0)...etc.

Command: **(TBLNEXT "VPORT")**   Get the third viewport listing.
Lisp returns: ((0 . "VPORT") (2 . "STANDARD") (70 . 0) (10 0.0 0.0) (11 0.5 0.5) (12 5.90001 4.25) (13 0.0...etc.

Command: **(TBLNEXT "UCS" T)**

Lisp returns: ((0 . "UCS")	Type of listing.
(2 . "X45")	Name of UCS entry.
(70 . 0)	Flags.
(10 0.0 0.0 0.0)	Origin point in WCS.
(11 1.0 0.0 0.0)	X axis direction in WCS.
(12 0.0 0.707107 0.707107))	Y axis direction in WCS.

Get the first UCS listing.

The UCS table is as simple as it seems, just a WCS base point and a couple of WCS vector coordinates (from the base point to points on the X and the Y axes). But the viewports warrant further study. The 12 group is the center point in the WCS coordinates, but the 10 and 11 corner point groups are in the screen's *display coordinate system*. The lower left corner of the full-screen drawing area is 0,0 and the upper right corner is 1,1.

The second and third ENTNEXT returned viewports with the same name as the first. (They differed only in the 10, 11, and 12 corner and center codes, since we changed no storable settings.) Any one *group* of viewports (called a viewport configuration) receives a *single* name when saved by the VPORTS command. How can you reliably access table data if three or more viewports duplicate one name? You use the setnext option of the TBLSEARCH function: `(tblsearch "vport" name T)`.

If the setnext argument is non-nil, it resets TBLNEXT to return the next viewport of the named configuration. Then you keep doing TBLNEXT until it returns null or a different viewport name.

How can you tell which viewport is current? And how can AutoLISP transparently change the current viewport? Try the VPORTS function and the CVPORT (Current ViewPORT) system variable. The VPORTS function returns an association list keyed by its viewport ID number. It lists each corner of the viewports currently dividing the screen area.

vports | *Returns a list of the current viewport settings. The list contains sublists with the viewport numbers and display coordinate corner points for each port. The active viewport is first on the list.*
`(vports)`

The CVPORT system variable stores the ID number of the current viewport. If the CVPORT variable is changed, even if changed transparently by AutoLISP, the current viewport is reset. Let's take a closer look at VPORTS and CVPORT.

How to Identify and Change Viewports

Continue in the previous drawing.

```
Command: VPORTS                                         Check them.
Save/Restore/Delete/Join/SIngle/?/2/<3>/4: ?           Inquire.
Current configuration:
id# 1
   corners: 0.5000,0.0000 1.0000,1.0000
id# 3
   corners: 0.0000,0.5000 0.5000,1.0000
```

```
id# 6
   corners: 0.0000,0.0000 0.5000,0.5000
```

Configuration STANDARD: Appears only if a named configuration.
    0.5000,0.0000 1.0000,1.0000
    0.0000,0.5000 0.5000,1.0000
    0.0000,0.0000 0.5000,0.5000

Command: **(getvar "CVPORT")**   Check the current number.
Lisp returns: 1

Command: **(vports)**   Get the current VPORT configuration.
Lisp returns: ((1 (0.5 0.0) (1.0 1.0))   First vport corners.
(3 (0.0 0.5) (0.5 1.0))   Second vport corners.
(6 (0.0 0.0) (0.5 0.5)))   Third vport corners.

Command: **(setvar "CVPORT" 3)**   Sets it current, just like clicking on the upper left.

When several viewports divide your screen, you control which port is active by clicking on it with the pick button of the mouse or puck. In AutoLISP, (setvar "CVPORT" *n*), where *n* is the ID number, accomplishes the same thing. But don't depend on ID numbers being constant or predictable. They are assigned rather unpredictably. Notice the numbers 1, 3, and 6 above. If a user resaves an identical configuration to the same name, the ID numbers will change.

The following program uses AutoLISP's VPORTS function to change active ports by display coordinates instead of depending on ID numbers.

Applying VPORTS to Changing Viewports

It's easier for your program to know what geographic viewport it wants to use than to know the VPORT number assigned to that area. If you have a setup routine that rescales and sets up the drawing, it needs to reset settings such as snap and grid in *each* viewport. It needs a function to make specific viewports current so it can make these settings.

The SETVP function uses a viewport's lower left display coordinate instead of its ID number to find it and make it active. SETVP compares the screen location you provide to the current configuration returned by the VPORTS function. The function arrives at the correct viewport number and uses SETVAR to change the active port by resetting CVPORT.

```
;* SETVP.LSP uses the VPORT function and CVPORT system variable to set a viewport
;* current. The viewport is specified by the X and Y display coordinates of its
;* lower left corner. In display coordinates, the lower left of the entire
;* display screen is 0,0 and the upper right is 1,1.
;*
(defun setvp (x y / var alist count)
  (setq count -1  var (vports))                    ;get current viewport config
  (while (and var (setq alist (nth (setq count (1+ count)) var)))) ;step thru data
    (and (equal x (caadr  alist) 0.01)             ;if the x coord
         (equal y (cadadr alist) 0.01)             ;and the y coord match,
         (setvar "CVPORT" (car alist))             ;then set it current
         (setq var nil)                            ;and set nil to kick out of while
  ) )
  (princ)
);defun
;*
```

SETVP Function in SETVP.LSP File

The function looks at the current viewport configuration and tests to determine which viewport area matches the coordinates supplied as arguments to the function. A fuzz factor of 0.01 is applied to the match in the EQUAL command. Let's see how it works.

Testing SETVP for AutoLISP Port Selection

Enter selection: **1**   Begin a NEW drawing again named IL07.

Command: **VPORTS**   Make a set of viewports.
Save/Restore/Delete/Join/SIngle/?/2/<3>/4: **<RETURN>**   The default 3.
Horizontal/Vertical/Above/Below/Left/<Right>: **<RETURN>** The default Right.

Command: **(load "setvp")**   Load the file.

Command: **(setvp 0 0.5)**   The upper left port is activated.

Call SETVP whenever your programs or setup routines need to set a viewport current.

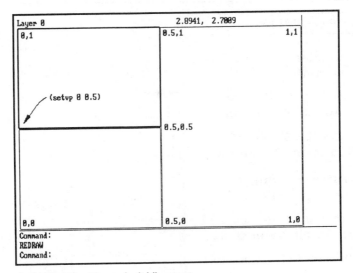

Activating the Upper Left Viewport

Getting Blocks Without Loading Drawings

XINSERT.LSP, on the New Riders AutoLISP Utilities Disk 1, uses block table access to get a block that you *know* is in another drawing, but isn't wblocked to disk. It lists all the other drawing's block names and extracts the selected block without leaving the current drawing. Except for the extracted block, it leaves no part of the other drawing in the current drawing's database.

Summary

Symbol table access complements entity access to extend your control over AutoCAD. Don't let the DXF codes intimidate you. Remember, you don't have to know it all — just where to find it.

Use AutoLISP's TBLNEXT and TBLSEARCH functions to read the LAYER, LTYPE, VIEW, STYLE, BLOCK, UCS, and VPORT reference tables. But only AutoCAD commands can update table data. Table access is the key to definitions of all the named things, places, and properties in your drawings. Use this access in your programs to control drawing choices and prevent user errors.

Think about ways to extend your knowledge in applications like our TAKOFF. Table access opens up all of AutoCAD's internal data to your programs. Now it's time to open up AutoLISP to the rest of the system with input and output, our next chapter.

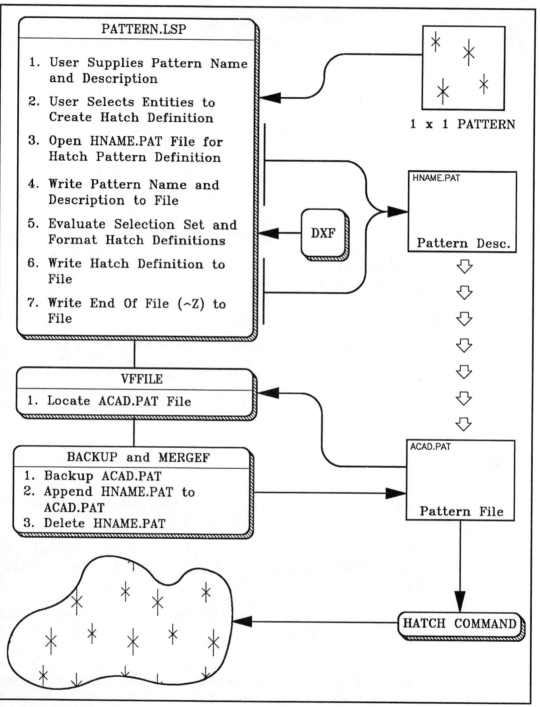

Automatic Hatch Generator

CHAPTER 8

AutoLISP Input/Output

READING AND WRITING DATA

Entity and table access increase your control over AutoCAD files, but you don't just use AutoCAD to create information that gets written to disk and forgotten. Your AutoCAD drawings transfer dynamic information for building, constructing, communicating, and keeping track of real world things.

AutoLISP I/O (Input/Output) is a key to the efficient creation and transfer of information. It's your primary AutoCAD link to the outside world. AutoLISP I/O lets you import external data that might be used to form drawing schedules or draw parts parametrically. It lets you export data from your drawing that can be used for bills of materials. It allows your programs to directly deal and manage disk files. And it adds to your bag of AutoLISP communication tools. You can read and write files with AutoLISP, and manage them using a combination of DOS and AutoLISP controls. This chapter's exercises integrate file I/O in two applications: an automatic hatch generator program called PATTERN, and REFDWG, a program that generates a drawing reference schedule and inserts the schedule in your drawing.

There are two main benefits to using AutoLISP I/O in your customized applications. The first is data access. Powerful programs, such as parametric parts generators, need data that is best kept in external text files. With AutoLISP, you can process large amounts of data and centralize your data efficiently. If you store much data internally in AutoCAD, such as in attributes, your drawing files can get enormous. Using external files gives you more efficient data storage, easier maintenance, and better control over your data. The second major benefit is improved file management. Well-managed files make efficient systems, and file management from AutoLISP allows robust, controlled programs.

This chapter will show you how to write data to your screen, files, and programs, how to control text screen appearance with ANSI codes, and how to choose the most efficient file format for your programs. We will also demonstrate how to manage, back up and merge files with AutoCAD, AutoLISP, and DOS (or UNIX), how to find and verify files and directories from within your programs, how to verify the execution of

SHELL commands, and how to execute multiple DOS commands or programs with a single SHELL command.

AutoLISP Tools and Programs

AutoLISP Tools

FILELIB.LSP defines AutoLISP utilities for file management:

CPATH retrieves the current DOS directory path.

PSLASH formats path names with back or forward slashes as needed by DOS or UNIX. Your programs need to control slashes to deal with the differing syntaxes of DOS and UNIX.

FFNAME formats a file name with a path.

VFFILE and **VPATH** verify a file's or path's existence.

BACKUP makes a backup up file with the extension .BAK.

MERGEF merges two files, without verification.

ANSILIB.LSP is a library of functions for formatting text screens with ANSI escape calls. These functions clear the text screen, position the cursor, and permit special effects like text coloration and blinking.

ETOS is a data conversion function that returns any value or expression as a string.

SHELL.LSP, on the New Riders AutoLISP Utilities Disk 1, contains a subroutine that uses techniques developed in the FILELIB FFNAME function to execute and verify multiple DOS commands with a single SHELL execution.

MERGEV is also in FILELIB.LSP on the New Riders AutoLISP Utilities Disk 1. It adds verification to MERGEF.

Programs

C:PATTERN is an automatic hatch generator. This program generates hatch patterns from selected entities within a 1 x 1 unit pattern definition drawn in AutoCAD. It can append the pattern to the ACAD.PAT file.

C:REFDWG is a drawing reference schedule program. It generates a drawing schedule and inserts it in your drawing. C:REFDWG displays a list of project reference drawings on the text screen. Then, using ANSI library functions, you can mark the reference drawings to list. After the selections are made, the program lists them as text on a schedule in the current drawing.

Reading and Writing Data

AutoLISP provides several ways to read and write data to and from a screen, file, or other device. In addition to the PROMPT, PRIN1, PRINC, and PRINT functions covered in Chapter 5, AutoLISP has several other input and output functions. The functions are WRITE-LINE, WRITE-CHAR, READ-LINE, and READ-CHAR. All eight of these functions are important to this chapter.

The WRITE- functions are used to output information from your LISP programs to the screen or to files for storage. Outputting data is critical to data reporting programs such as our drawing revision tracking system in Chapter 11. AutoLISP provides two WRITE- functions, one which outputs a string of data, and another which writes individual ASCII characters.

write-line

> *Writes a string to the screen or to a file specified by the optional file-desc.*
> (**write-line** *string* file-desc)

write-char

> *Writes a character specified by the ASCII character code number to the screen or to a file specified by the optional file-desc.*
> (**write-char** *number* file-desc)

Reading Lines and Characters

The similar READ- functions (not to be confused with the READ function) are used to import data into AutoLISP from external files or to get data from the keyboard. Reading data into a program is essential for accessing parametric dimensioning data and for getting other information or tables, as you will see with the REFDWG program in this chapter. Having AutoLISP access data directly saves you from re-entering it each time a program is executed. Looking up data with READ- functions also reduces errors and guarantees the integrity of the data. The READ- functions are:

read-line

> *Returns a string typed at the keyboard or read from the optional file-desc.*
> (**read-line** file-desc)

read-char
> *Returns the ASCII character code of a single character typed at the keyboard or read from the optional file-desc.*
> **(read-char** *file-desc***)**

WRITE-LINE and READ-LINE take and return strings, while WRITE-CHAR and READ-CHAR take and return the integer values of ASCII characters.

How to Read and Write to the Console

All READ- and WRITE- functions default to reading from and writing to the *console* (the CON device, generally the keyboard and video display), unless given an optional file-spec argument. The file-spec argument can be a disk file or any other device, such as COM1, COM2, LPT1, PRN, or NUL.

Let's review the four P's, PROMPT, PRINT, PRINC, and PRIN1 as we try out the READ-LINE and WRITE-LINE functions at the console.

Using the Print, READ-LINE, and WRITE-LINE Functions

Enter selection: **1**   Begin a NEW drawing named FILES.

Command: **(prompt "PROMPT only writes to the screen, without quotes. ")**
Lisp prompts and returns: PROMPT only writes to the screen, without quotes. nil

Command: **(princ "PRINC is similar, but returns a string. ")**
Lisp prints and returns: PRINC is similar, but returns a string. "PRINC is similar, but returns a string. "

Command: **(write-line "WRITE-LINE forces a <RETURN>. ")**
Lisp prints: WRITE-LINE forces a <RETURN>.
Lisp returns: "WRITE-LINE forces a <RETURN>. "

Command: **(read-line)**   Get a string from the keyboard.
READ-LINE simply returns the string it gets.   Enter this string.
Lisp returns: "READ-LINE simply returns the string it gets."

PROMPT echos the string to the screen in a neatly formatted appearance. It always returns nil. PRINC is similar to PROMPT, but returns its argument instead of nil. In the case of a string, the string is returned in quotes. WRITE-LINE is like PRINC except that it always adds a <RETURN> at the end of the string, whether you like it or not. The PROMPT and WRITE-LINE functions only accept strings as arguments, but PRINC can handle any type of data in AutoLISP.

You may have noticed our habit of putting a space at the end of the prompt string to avoid having input, or more output, run into the prompt. The PROMPT, WRITE-LINE, and print functions can also accept control characters within their strings. The most common of these codes is \n, to force a new line.

We recommend using PROMPT to present prompts because it writes the string to both text and graphics screens. On dual screen systems, PRINC doesn't print to the command prompt line, only to the second monitor's text screen.

Some other variations of I/O functions are PRINT and PRIN1. These functions work much like PRINC except for the way they add spaces, returns, and process expanded control characters, as we discussed in Chapter 5. Let's review these as we try WRITE-CHAR and READ-CHAR.

Using the Print, READ-CHAR and WRITE-CHAR Functions

Continue in the previous drawing, or begin a NEW drawing again named FILES.

Command: **(princ "While PRINC doesn't quote,\nor expand control characters,\n")**
                                        With \n's for new lines.
Lisp prints: While PRINC doesn't quote,   It executes the \n as a new line.
or expand control characters,
Lisp returns: "While PRINC doesn't quote,\nor expand control characters,\n"

Command: **(prin1 "PRIN1 quotes and expands control \ncharacters.")**
Lisp prints and returns: "PRIN1 quotes and expands control \ncharacters.""PRIN1
quotes and expands control \ncharacters."

Command: **(print "PRINT adds a leading \nnewline & trailing space. ")**
                                        A leading blank line.
Lisp prints and returns: "PRINT adds a leading \nnewline & trailing space. " "PRINT
adds a leading \nnewline & trailing space. "

Command: **(write-char "A")**   Oops, we forgot to warn you!
Lisp returns: error: bad argument type
(WRITE-CHAR "A")
Command: **(write-char 65)**   WRITE-CHAR wants an ASCII value, not a string character.
Lisp prints and returns: A65   It prints A and returns its ASCII code.

Command: **(read-char)**
AB   It doesn't prompt. Type AB<RETURN>.
Lisp returns: 65   It just returns the code for A.

Command: **(read-char)**   Try another.
Lisp returns: 66   It immediately returns the missing code for B.

Command: **(read-char)**   And another.
Lisp returns: 10   Returns the code for line feed.

Printing strings with *expanded* control characters means representing the control character in a string with two characters, like "...\n..." instead of actually issuing a new line. Note that the "\n" forced a real new line in PRINC, but remained expanded in other strings. The WRITE-CHAR function prints unquoted like PRINC, but returns the character's ASCII value, not a string.

One READ-CHAR gets and returns only one character at a time. The remaining characters on the input line, including the <RETURN>, are buffered by AutoLISP and returned by subsequent READ-CHAR calls, if any.

➤ *NOTE: AutoLISP does not differentiate between a return, a line feed, a space, or a tab. It returns an ASCII 10 for any of these characters.*

With their INITGET control and prompt strings, the GET functions are generally preferable to READ-LINE and READ-CHAR for user input. But for input from disk files, the READ- functions are the only way to go.

General File Handling

File processing is simple. You open a file and process it by reading from it or writing to it. Then you close it. AutoLISP can process only one type of file, an ASCII text file. Some programming languages have random access, which means they can jump back and forth in the file. AutoLISP does not have random access. It only reads a file in sequential order, from left to right and top to bottom.

AutoLISP provides the basic READ- and WRITE- functions to read and write data either one character at a time or a full line at a time. But before you can read and write to the file, you have to open it. Afterwards, you have to close the file to store it. It should come as no surprise that the functions to open and close files are called OPEN and CLOSE.

open

> *Opens a file specified by the filename string for the use specified by the mode. The modes are "r" for reading, "w" for writing, and "a" for appending. OPEN returns a file handle, which is supplied as the file-spec argument to the READ-, WRITE-, CLOSE, and print functions.*
> (open *filename mode*)

The OPEN function opens the file whose name is supplied as the filename argument. Later in this chapter, OPEN is used by PATTERN.LSP to provide a file handle to which WRITE-LINE writes hatch pattern definitions.

File Handles

Each time you open a file, AutoLISP returns a file handle descriptor. A file handle is the name reported by the operating system that lets AutoLISP keep track of your file. Since you can work with several files at once, each file needs a unique handle. OPEN returns the handle name. Set the handle name returned by OPEN to an AutoLISP variable so you can provide it as a file-spec argument to the READ-, WRITE-, print, and CLOSE functions. These functions cannot communicate with the operating system through a file name. They must use a file handle to refer to the file, leaving the management of the file to the operating system. The file handles change with each use, so their actual names are meaningless.

After you are done reading or writing the file, close it to release its file handle for use by other programs.

close | *Closes the file specified by the file-desc argument. The file-desc variable must be assigned to a valid file handle name.*
(close *file-desc*)

➡ *NOTE: Always close files when you finish with them, even if you wish to abandon them. The operating system has a limited number of file handles and can run out. If you close your files properly and still run out of handles under DOS, try increasing the FILES=nn statement in your CONFIG.SYS file. Unclosed files become lost clusters when you exit AutoCAD. File names are only entered on a disk directory listing after they have been closed.*

You've used AutoLISP to read input and write output to and from the default CON (console). You have to tell AutoLISP if you want to use files or other devices like a printer (such as PRN or LPT1) or a serial port (such as COM1 or COM2). Files and devices are the same to the operating system.

Files Are Devices

A *device* is a hardware or software component in your computer system. Each device has a unique name like printer, screen, or communication port. The default device is CON for console, which is the keyboard and screen. You may have copied to or from CON in DOS if you made files or printed on-the-fly. You may also be familiar with the other DOS devices. Here are a few examples of how devices are used in DOS.

```
C:>COPY CON filename        Takes input, puts it in a file.
                            Uses a Control-Z (<^Z>) to terminate.
C:>COPY filename PRN        Copies a file to a printer.
```

A file is a device that can store and retrieve the information on a disk. The console, printer ports, and disk files are all devices. If not directed to other devices, data is output to the screen and input from the keyboard. DOS reserves names for all devices except files. They are:

DEVICE NAMES	HARDWARE COMPONENTS
CON	Screen (video monitor) and keyboard.
PRN	Printer hooked to the first parallel port.
COM1	The first serial port. Can be a printer, modem etc.
COM2	Second serial port with same purposes as COM1.
LPT1	The first parallel port.
LPT2	The second parallel port.
NUL	A null device used to suppress output data.

Device Name Descriptions

You can use as many COM and LPT ports as you have installed in your computer. You need to open devices for communication, just like you open files. However, this is not recommended from AutoLISP.

➥ *NOTE: Do not use device names as file names under any circumstances. If you use them as file names in AutoLISP or with INSERT, WBLOCK, DXFOUT, PLOT, or MSLIDE, you may cause a dreaded "fatal error" or other strange results. Some versions of AutoCAD may even crash.*

Because you can both write to and read from a device, you must designate which access mode you want by passing a mode key letter to OPEN.

How to Open, Close, and Access Files

You can open a device to read, write, or append. Not all devices support all modes. For instance, you cannot open the PRN and CON devices to read. PRN and CON are write-only. Append adds to an existing file; if a file does not exist, it creates a new one.

AutoLISP communicates your access mode to the operating system at the time the file is opened. The access mode must be in lower case letters for AutoLISP to use it. Here are the device access modes:

MODE	ACCESS CONTROL MEANING
"r"	Reads the contents, only accesses existing files.
"w"	Writes to the file, creates a new file each time.
"a"	Appends data to an existing file or opens new one.

Device Access Modes

Let's process some files. Set the variable FP to store the file handle OPEN returns for the file name "TEST". Then send some data to the file with WRITE-LINE and close the file.

Using OPEN, WRITE-LINE, and CLOSE on Files

Continue in the previous drawing, or begin a NEW drawing again named FILES.

Command: **(print "Without a file handle, the data goes to the screen")**
Lisp prints and returns: "Without a file handle, the data goes to the screen."
"Without a file handle, the data goes to the screen."

Command: **(setq fp (open "TEST" "w"))**   OPEN the TEST file for writing.
Lisp returns: <File: #C136>   The file handle FP.

Command: **(write-line "It's all in the lines..." fp)**   Write data to the file handle FP.
Lisp returns: "It's all in the lines..."   But it writes to the file.

Command: **(write-line "That we write and read." fp)**   And try a PRINC.
Lisp returns: "That we write and read."

Command: **(princ (* 3 (/ 146.0 4)) fp)**   Calculates and writes the result.
Lisp returns: 109.5
Command: **(princ (chr 10) fp)**   Writes a new line.
Lisp returns: "\n"

Command: **(write-char 79 fp)**   Outputs a character, ASCII "O."
Lisp returns: 79
Command: **(write-char 75 fp)**   And a "K."
Lisp returns: 75

Command: **(close fp)**   Now close it.
Lisp returns: nil

Command: **DIR**   Check it.
File specification: **TEST**   It should list a 60-byte file named TEST.

When should you use WRITE-LINE and when should you use PRINC, PRINT, or PRIN1? WRITE-LINE only accepts a string argument, while the print functions accept any data type. PRINC and WRITE-LINE don't expand control characters, so they create files readable by READ-LINE and READ-CHAR. PRINT and PRIN1 expand control characters and put quotes around everything they write, so they create files readable by the LOAD function.

So use WRITE-LINE and PRINC for files to be read from, and PRIN1 and PRINT for files to be loaded. Use WRITE-LINE for strings and PRINC for other data types, but remember that PRINC doesn't add a line feed before or after its data.

To read a file, open it with "r" and extract data using the READ-LINE or READ-CHAR functions. Remember to supply the file handle FP variable. Don't worry about moving to the next line or character in the file, AutoLISP automatically advances with each READ-LINE or READ-CHAR. When the end of the file is reached, READ-LINE or READ-CHAR returns nil. Try reading the file you just created.

How to Read a File

Continue from the previous exercise, where you created the TEST file.

Command: **(setq fp (open "TEST" "r"))**   Open it to read this time.
Lisp returns: <File: #BF7E>

Command: **(read-line fp)**   Read the first line.
Lisp returns: "It's all in the lines..."

Command: **(read-line fp)**   And the second.
Lisp returns: "That we write and read."

Command: **(setq var (read-line fp))**   And the third, with a SETQ.
Lisp returns: "109.5"

Command: **(read var)**   Extract its value.
Lisp returns: 109.5

Command: **(read-char fp)**   Now the next character.
Lisp returns: 79   It's the ASCII code for O.

Command: **(chr (read-char fp))**   Read and convert it.
Lisp returns: "K"

```
Command: (read-line fp)
Lisp returns: nil                              There's nothing left.

Command: (close fp)                            Close it.
Lisp returns: nil
```

Note the use of the READ function to convert the string "109.5" to a number. This is an important technique in importing external data, since READ-LINE reads everything as a string.

Reading and writing to files is simple and predictable, but accessing other devices is a bit more involved.

Writing to the Printer and Other Devices

Printers and external hardware devices are almost like files. They are addressed as PRN, COMn, or LPTn, where n is the port number. But you can't read from a parallel printer, at least not through AutoLISP. Printers and other port devices can cause problems. Unlike true DOS files, printers can become "unavailable" after they are opened. If you disconnect the printer or it runs out of paper, your computer can lock up because AutoLISP has no provision for handling the error.

You can write to printers and read or write to devices like the COM ports, but it can be risky. We won't ask you to do it because we assume your digitizer or plotter is connected to your COM port(s). If you wanted to write to the PRN and COM ports, it would look like this.

Writing to Ports (Not Recommended)

```
Command: (setq fp (open "PRN" "w"))
Lisp returns: <File: #E64E>

Command: (write-line "Wake up Mr. Printer" fp)
Lisp returns: "Wake up Mr. Printer"

Command: (setq ser1 (open "COM1" "w"))
Lisp returns: <File: #D60A>

Command: (write-line "This goes to the 1st serial port" ser1)
Lisp returns: "This goes to the 1st serial port"
Command: (close fp) (close ser1) (close nowher)
```

To circumvent possible errors and avoid hanging up your system, we recommend that you write everything to a file first. Then, use the DOS

COPY command to copy the file to the printer with the PRN device name. DOS automatically handles printer errors when it performs the copying.

To apply the technique, use AutoCAD's SHELL to issue the DOS command COPY. If your printer is on the second parallel port, use LPT2 in place of PRN.

Using SHELL to Send Files to a Printer

Continue in the previous drawing with the TEST file you created.
Make sure your printer is ready.

```
Command: SHELL
Dos command: COPY TEST PRN                          The little TEST file should print.
```

One device that's always safe to write to is the NUL device. NUL means nothing, so it sends the data nowhere. Suppressed output can be useful when testing.

How to Write to Nowhere

Continue in the previous drawing, or begin a NEW drawing again named FILES.

```
Command: (setq nowher (open "NUL" "w"))
Lisp returns: <File: #D574>

Command: (write-line "This goes to nowhere..." nowher)
Lisp returns: "This goes to nowhere..."              But doesn't print it.

Command: (close nowher)
```

Those are the basics of reading and writing files. Let's apply what we've covered to create AutoLISP's missing data conversion function.

Applying File Access to String Conversion

You used all of AutoLISP's conversion functions in Chapter 5. But there was no function for converting a symbol (SYM data type) or a list to a string. With file access, you can create ETOS, a function that can convert *any* AutoLISP expression to a string.

```
;* ETOS (Expression TO String) takes any expression and converts to a string.
;* "STRings" are returned as double ""STRings"". The READ function can be used
;* to return the original value of any string returned by ETOS.
;*
(defun etos (arg / file)
  (if (= 'STR (type arg)) (setq arg (strcat "\"" arg "\"")))  ;format ""STRings""
  (setq file (open "$" "w"))                                  ;open temp file named $
  (princ arg file)                                            ;write string to file
  (close file)
  (setq file (open "$" "r"))                                  ;reopen to read
  (setq arg (read-line file))                                 ;set arg to string read from file
  (close file)
  (close (open "$" "w"))                                      ;scrunch file down to 0 bytes
  arg                                                         ;returns string read from file
);defun ETOS
;*
```

The ETOS Conversion Function in ETOS.LSP

ETOS opens a file, using PRINC (because it handles any data type) to write its argument to the file. It closes the file. It reopens it to read it. It retrieves the data with READ-LINE. It closes the file. It returns the data, now a string.

Try it out.

How to Convert Anything to a String

Continue in the previous drawing, or begin a NEW drawing again named FILES.

You have ETOS in your ETOS.LSP file.

Create the ETOS function in a new file named ETOS.LSP.

Command: **(load "ETOS")**   Load the function file.

Command: **(etos 'symbol)**   Quote the argument to suppress its evaluation.
Lisp returns: "SYMBOL"   A string.

Command: **(setq var (etos (list 1 2 3 A)))** Try it on a list.
Lisp returns: "(1 2 3 nil)"   A string. **A** was not set so it returns nil in the list.

Command: **(read var)**   Extract the original value.
Lisp returns: (1 2 3 nil)   A list again.

As with any other function, quote the argument if you don't want it evaluated before ETOS processes it. The PVAR program mentioned in the previous chapter depends on ETOS. Use it when you need to convert any symbol or list to a string.

AutoLISP only provides the basic file-handling tools. It is weak in handling printers and external devices, and lacks file management capabilities. But you can create these tools.

Programs for Testing Files and Paths

AutoLISP has only one file management function, FINDFILE. It searches AutoCAD's library path or another specified directory path to find a particular file. In a fully developed system, your file management system should be able to verify paths and current directory name, format file names, merge files, and back up files for safety before modifying them. It should also be able to interactively query you for valid, properly formatted file names and check to see if a file exists before trying to read it. To get around AutoLISP's lack of file management features, you need to integrate AutoLISP, AutoCAD, and DOS.

You can check the existence of a file by using the FINDFILE function in AutoLISP.

findfile

> *Returns the file name with the path appended if the file is found, otherwise it returns nil. It searches only the specified directory if a path is supplied as part of file name. If no path is supplied, it searches the AutoCAD library path. Wildcards are not permitted.*
> (findfile *filename*)

The FINDFILE function searches the specified path or AutoCAD library path for the supplied file name. If the file is found, the drive, path, and file name are returned. If the file is not found (or is in use by another program, device, or networked computer that supports file locking), nil is returned. The order in which the FINDFILE function searches the library path for a file is shown below.

```
Current AutoCAD directory.
Current drawing's directory.
SET ACAD=directory environment variable, if any.
ACAD*.OVL file directory.
ACAD.EXE directory.
```

➥ *NOTE: To AutoCAD, the current directory is the one that was current at the time the ACAD.EXE file was executed. We'll call it the current AutoCAD directory. You can check this with a DIR command at the start of a drawing. AutoCAD makes no provision for users switching directories via SHELL, and in fact can get quite confused. This can cause errors, like AutoCAD's not asking for permission to overwrite an existing file, or FINDFILE's searching the current AutoCAD directory, not the true current directory. You can also "lose" files, since they may not go in the directory you expect. If you need to change directories via SHELL, do it in a DOS batch or UNIX shell program that will automatically change the directory back again.*

Your AutoLISP programs should use the FINDFILE function liberally to ensure files are available prior to reading and writing to them. You don't generally need to use FINDFILE for inserts, menus, and other support files since AutoCAD automatically searches for them. Let's look closer at the FINDFILE function.

Looking at FINDFILE

Continue in the previous drawing, or begin a NEW drawing again named FILES.

```
Command: (findfile "TEMP")          Look for the file TEMP.
Lisp returns: nil
```

```
Command: (findfile "ACAD.LSP")      Look for ACAD.LSP.
Lisp returns: C:\\IL-ACAD\\ACAD.LSP   Returns path and file name of local directory file.
```

```
Command: (findfile "ACAD.EXE")      Look for ACAD.EXE.
Lisp returns: C:\\ACAD\\ACAD.EXE      File is in ACAD directory.
```

```
Command: (findfile "NUL")
Lisp returns: C:\\IL-ACAD\\NUL
```

AutoCAD's library search always explores the current AutoCAD directory first. DOS sees devices such as COM and NUL as if they exist in every directory. Therefore, (findfile "NUL") always returns the name of the current AutoCAD directory. This is unaffected by any directory changes via SHELL. RPATH, the first file library function we will create, uses this to restore the current AutoCAD directory if changed.

➥ *NOTE: UNIX paths will be returned with forward slashes and without a drive letter.*

Extending the AutoCAD Library Path With FINDFILE

Say that you have a standard parts library in the current AutoCAD directory, standard support files in the directory set by SET ACAD=*dirname*, and yet another auxiliary parts library in D:\PLIB, a directory that is not on the library path. The most flexible program would search D:\PLIB first, then the library path. It can. Just set an environment variable with SET PARTS=D:\PLIB in DOS before you start AutoCAD. Then, to return the file name supplied by the variable FILE in your menus and programs, use an expression like:

```
(findfile (if (getenv "PARTS") (strcat (getenv "PARTS") "/"
FILE) FILE))
```

We can use several utility functions to handle directories, paths, and file names. CPATH finds the true current directory and RPATH restores the current AutoCAD directory.

How to Detect and Control the Current Directory

The CPATH (Current PATH) function uses AutoCAD's SHELL command and DOS's CD (change directory) or UNIX's DIRS command to determine the true current directory path (not the current AutoCAD directory). The DOS CD, used without a directory name, and the UNIX DIRS just display the current directory name. The CPATH function redirects this display to a temporary file by using the DOS > or UNIX >! redirection symbols. Upon returning to AutoCAD, AutoLISP's READ-LINE accesses the file and returns the contents.

A DOS system can compare the path returned by CPATH to the path returned by (filefind "NUL") to see if it has changed. If so, the CD command can be issued via the SH command (a smaller and faster version of the SHELL command) to change it back. In this manner, the RPATH (Reset PATH) function lets your programs protect themselves from changes to the current AutoCAD directory.

```
;* FILELIB.LSP contains several file handling utility routines

;* CPATH returns current DOS or UNIX path: "d:\\path\\...\\" or "/path/.../".
;* WARNING: If DOS 3.3 APPEND is used results may be FALSE UNPREDICTABLY.
;* If SH (shell) fails with insufficient memory, increase its size in ACAD.PGP.
;*
(defun cpath ( / path fp slash)
```

Listing continued.

Continued listing.

```
❶                              ;creates 0 byte file, overwrite if existing...
  (close (open "$" "w"))       ;...allows READ-LINE to test SHell's success
❷
  (command "SH"                ;redirect current dir to temp file $
    (cond
      ( (getenv "COMSPEC") (setq slash "\\") "CD   >   $")          ;if DOS
      ( (getenv "USER")    (setq slash "/" ) "dirs >! $")           ;UNIX
      (T(prompt "\nUNKNOWN OPERATING SYSTEM for CPATH function. "))
  ) );command&cond
  (setq fp (open "$" "r"))
❸
  (if (setq path (read-line fp))       ;nil only if SH failed
    (setq path (strcat path slash))    ;adds trailing slash to path
                                       ;sets path to "" if SH failed
    (progn (prompt "\nSHell FAILED!") (setq path ""))
  )
  (close fp)
  path                         ;returns path, which is "" only if SHell failed
);defun CPATH
;*

;* RPATH Resets the PATH to the "current AutoCAD directory" if changed by user.
;* For DOS only. Requires CPATH function.
;*
(defun rpath ( / path)
  (if (equal                          ;if ACAD current matches true current
        (cpath)
        (setq path (findfile "nul")            ;gets "PATH/NUL"
              path (substr path 1 (- (strlen path) 3)))    ;strips last 3 char
      ) )
      nil                                                  ;then nil
      (command "SH" (strcat "CD " (substr path 1 (- (strlen path) 1)))))  ;else CD
  );if
);defun
```

CPATH and RPATH Functions in FILELIB.LSP File

❶ The CPATH function tests to make sure the shell operation of AutoCAD was successful. It does this by creating a 0-byte size scratch file.

❷ The shell operation is attempted and, if successful, writes the current path name to the same file.

❸ When AutoLISP reads the file later, it looks to see if the file is empty (still has 0 bytes). The first call to the READ-LINE function returns nil if the file is empty, which tells us that the shell failed.

CPATH uses the GETENV function to determine whether the operating system is UNIX, DOS, or something else unsupported by CPATH. GETENV was also used in the section on extending the AutoCAD library path.

getenv

Returns the string value of the operating system environment variable specified by the name argument, if found. Otherwise it returns nil. (getenv *name*)

At the DOS command prompt, for example, the environment variable MONKEY could be set to CHIMP by SET MONKEY=CHIMP. In UNIX, you would use MONKEY=CHIMP followed by export MONKEY in the Bourne shell, or setenv MONKEY CHIMP in the C shell. Every DOS system has a "COMSPEC" variable, and every UNIX system has a "USER" variable, so we use GETENV to determine which operating system is running AutoCAD.

The RPATH function uses STRCAT to truncate the "PATH/NUL" string returned by FINDFILE, and compares it to that returned by CPATH. If they don't match, it strips the trailing slash and performs a DOS CD command.

Let's try the functions.

Testing the CPATH Function

Continue in the previous drawing, or begin a NEW drawing again named FILES.

You have CPATH and RPATH in your FILELIB.LSP file. You need not reload it.

Create the CPATH and RPATH functions in a new file named FILELIB.LSP.

Command: (load "FILELIB")   Load the function file.

Command: (getenv "COMSPEC")   Try the GETENV function too.
Lisp returns: "C:\\COMMAND.COM"   Unless your boot drive isn't C: or you don't use DOS.

```
Command: (cpath)           Test it.
SH
DOS Command: CD   >  $
Lisp returns: "C:\\IL-ACAD\\"

Command: (rpath)           Test it.
Lisp returns: nil          They already matched.

Command: SH                Change directories to test RPATH.
DOS Command: CD\
Command: (rpath)           Test again.
SH
DOS Command: CD   >  $
Command: SH
DOS Command: CD C:\IL-ACAD    It changes back.
Lisp returns: nil
```

Because DOS has no provision for storing and restoring directory settings, CPATH and RPATH are invaluable tools for maintaining control and avoiding file system errors. Besides being used by RPATH, CPATH is also used in this chapter by VPATH, which verifies a path.

The format of the path returned by CPATH contains a trailing slash ("\" or "//"), like the slash returned by the AutoCAD system variables ACADPREFIX and DWGPREFIX. This is done to make the programs compatible throughout different file processing tasks. DOS can accept forward slashes in paths from AutoCAD or AutoLISP, but not through SHELL, where it must have backslashes. UNIX must have forward slashes. Well-written programs should work with either operating system, and accept either type of slash from user input. The next section develops a function to convert slashes as needed so you don't have to think about it.

Converting Slashes and Backslashes

You often need to convert forward slashes to backslashes and vice versa to work with the different DOS and UNIX operating system conventions. The PSLASH function accepts a path name, looks at each character in the name, and swaps the appropriate type of slash character for the current operating system.

```
;* PSLASH PathSLASH converts "\\"s or "/"s in path strings to whichever is
;* needed by operating system (UNIX or DOS), and forces trailing "\\" or "/".
(defun pslash (path / slash inc wpath char)
  (setq inc 1  wpath ""                         ;initialize variables
```

Listing continued.

Continued listing.

```
①
      slash (if (getenv "COMSPEC") "\\"  "/")          ;set for DOS or UNIX
  )
  (while (/= "" (setq char (substr path inc 1)))       ;test each char
    (setq wpath                                        ;append proper char back
      (strcat wpath (if (member char '("\\" "/")) slash char))
      inc (1+ inc)                                     ;increment counter
  ) );while&setq
②
  (if                                                  ;if last char isn't slash
    (and (/= wpath "") (/= (substr wpath (strlen wpath) 1) slash))
    (setq wpath (strcat wpath slash))                  ;make it a slash
  );if
  wpath
);defun PSLASH
;*
```

PSLASH Function in FILELIB.LSP File

① DOS uses backslashes to separate *path\filename* components. AutoLISP uses two backslashes, like "\\", to represent one backslash in strings, because the backslash is the string escape character. UNIX uses a forward slash like *path/filename*. The PSLASH function determines if the computer is a DOS-based system by looking for the COMSPEC environment variable with the GETENV function.

② The function checks to see if a trailing slash is included in the path string. If the slash is missing, one is added to the path name. Then the name is returned from the function.

How to Do Slash Conversions

Continue in the previous drawing, or begin a NEW drawing again named FILES.

You have PSLASH in your FILELIB.LSP file. You need not reload it.

Create the PSLASH function in your FILELIB.LSP file.

Command: **(load "FILELIB")**   Load the function file.

Command: **(pslash "\\abc/def")**   Test slash conversion.
Lisp returns: "\\abc\\def\\"   OK!

Command: **(pslash "/brg/roo")**
Lisp returns: "\\brg\\roo\\"   Or "/brg/roo/" if you have UNIX.

The PSLASH is used by several programs in this book, such as BATCHSCR, which creates batch processing scripts and LBLOCK, which manages block libraries.

The format of file names is just as important as the format of paths. The next function keeps you from worrying about file name extensions.

How to Format File Extensions

Any tool that ensures the integrity of input helps you write reliable and flexible programs. One source of errors is the input of file names. AutoCAD, like most programs, depends on specific files having specific extensions. Yet when GETSTRING gets a name, it can't control whether you enter it as "NAME", "NAME.", "NAME.EXT", or use some other (wrong) extension. The FFNAME (Format File NAME) function correctly formats a file name regardless of how you enter the extension.

```
;* FFNAME formats a filename as "filename.ext" given input FNAME with or
;* without extension, and EXT as "EXT".
(defun ffname (fname ext / inc lngth)
  (setq inc -1 lngth (strlen fname))        ;initialize, lngth is filename length
❶
  (while
    (not                                ;loops until OR is non-NIL
      (or                               ;eval 2nd AND only if 1st is NIL
        (and                            ;setq FNAME only if "." = non-NIL
          (= "." (substr fname (- lngth (setq inc (1+ inc))) 1))    ;find "."
❷
          (setq                         ;strip last char and append EXT
            fname (strcat (substr fname 1 (- lngth inc)) ext)
          )
        )
        (and                            ;setq FNAME only if...
          (or (= inc 3) (= inc lngth))     ;...if "." not found in last 3 char
          (setq fname (strcat fname "." ext)) ;then append EXT to whole fname
  ) ) ) )
  fname
);defun
;*
```

FFNAME Function in FILELIB.LSP File

FFNAME takes the easy way out, accepting the FNAME (File NAME) argument with or without an integral extension. It just replaces any extension provided in the FNAME argument with the overriding EXT extension argument.

❶ Take a moment to dissect the WHILE-NOT-OR-AND structure used as a conditional loop. Think of it as an exercise in writing a function without using deeply nested IF statements. Think of various file names and extensions, and step through the function logically to see how the AND and OR work.

❷ It checks for a period in the file name by parsing the string. Notice how the function starts looking from the end of the string and works to the beginning. This reverse parsing saves processing time.

Compare FFNAME's results to your logical step-through above.

Using FFNAME to Format File Extensions

Continue in the previous drawing, or begin a NEW drawing again named FILES.

You have FFNAME in your FILELIB.LSP file. You need not reload it.

Create the FFNAME function in your FILELIB.LSP file.

```
Command: (load "FILELIB")                    Load the function file.

Command: (ffname "new" "txt")                Append extension.
Lisp returns: "new.txt"

Command: (ffname "new.saf" "txt")            Forces correct extension.
Lisp returns: "new.txt"

Command: (ffname "new.saf" "")               Strips off extension.
Lisp returns: "new."
```

The FFNAME subroutine is used by this chapter's BACKUP function and REFDWG program. It is also used in Chapter 15's BATCHSCR and LBLOCK programs.

Now that you can ensure that the file extension is correct, what about making sure that a file or path actually exists?

Verifying File and Path Existence

When you give a nonexistent file or path name to an AutoCAD command, it politely reprompts. Your programs should do the same. You can verify a file's existence with the AutoLISP FINDFILE function. However, FINDFILE merely returns nil if not found. The VFFILE function extends FINDFILE to interactively get a verified file name, complete with path.

```
;* VFFILE verifies a file's existence. It returns fspec or NIL.
;* WARNING: DOS 3.3 APPEND may cause FALSE UNPREDICTABLE results.
;* May be called w/ fname specific path "\\path\\filename.ext", or just
;* "filename.ext", which searches ACAD library path or prompts for path.
;* Uses PSLASH to return "/"s or "\\"s for UNIX or DOS.
(defun vffile (fspec / fname fp path char prmpt)
  (setq inc -1  lngth (strlen fspec)  fname "")  ;initialize
❶
  (while (and (/= lngth (1+ inc)) (not path))   ;parse FSPEC into PATH and FNAME
      (if (member                               ;if char is a slash
            (setq char                          ;get current char, back to front
                  (substr fspec (- lngth (setq inc (1+ inc))) 1)
            )
            '("/" "\\")
          );member
          (setq path (substr fspec 1 (- lngth inc)))   ;then set path to remainder
          (setq fname (strcat char fname))             ;else
  )    )
  (if path nil (setq path ""))                  ;if no path, set "" null
  (while                                        ;while file can't be opened, reprompt
    (and
      (/= "Q" path)                             ;until Quit
      (not (setq fspec (findfile (strcat path fname)))))  ;or found
    )
    (setq prmpt                                 ;build prompt
      (strcat "\n\nFile " fname " not found in "
        (if (= "" path) "current directory," path)   ;current dir if path=""
        "\nEnter path to search, or Q to quit: "
      );strcat
      path (strcase (getstring prmpt)))
  ) );while & setq
```

Listing continued.

Continued listing.

```
  (if (= "Q" path)                                     ;returns nil or fspec
      (progn (prompt "File not found. ") nil)          ;nil
      (substr (pslash fspec) 1 (strlen fspec))         ;fspec
  )
);defun vffile
;*
```

VFFILE Function in FILELIB.LSP File

❶ VFFILE uses a backwards string parsing technique similar to that in PSLASH. It is used to divide the input filespec into its PATH and FNAME parts. Then FINDFILE uses a WHILE loop until the filespec is found.

The similar VPATH verifies that a directory (or path) exists. Although DOS and UNIX store directory names as special files, the FINDFILE function checks the existence of a directory name.

```
;* VPATH gets and verifies a PATH. On non-DOS systems, the filename "$."
;* will be left behind in the successful directory, as a 0 byte file.
;* Adding (command "FILES" "3" (strcat path "$") "" "") will delete it.
;* It calls CPATH to present a default path.
(defun vpath ( / char path fp def)
  (setq def (cpath))                                    ;default current path
  (while (not path)                                     ;loops until valid path
    (setq path                                          ;get path name
        (getstring (strcat "\nEnter path name <" def ">: ")))
    )
    (if (/= "" path)                                    ;user wants current path
      (if (getenv "COMSPEC")                            ;then, if DOS
❶
        (or (findfile (strcat path "nul"))
            (setq path (prompt "\nInvalid path, try again."))   ;path not found
        )
        (progn                                          ;not DOS
❷
          (setq path (pslash path))                     ;check for valid path syntax
          (if (setq fp (open (strcat path "$") "a"))    ;test user's path entry
            (close fp)                                  ;path found, close temp file
            (setq path (prompt "\nInvalid path, try again."))) ;path could not be accessed
          );if
        );progn
```

Listing continued.

Continued listing.

```
      );if-getenv
      (setq path def)                                      ;else set to CPATH
   );if/=
  );while
  path                                                     ;return the path
);defun VPATH
;*
```

VPATH Function in FILELIB.LSP File

❶ On DOS systems, we use the FINDFILE NUL trick. Because NUL "exists" in every directory, (findfile "*path*/nul") will return "*path*/NUL" if the directory exists.

❷ On UNIX systems, the VPATH function tests for a directory by trying to create a temporary file in the target directory. If a file can be opened in the directory, then the directory must exist. If AutoLISP returns a nil from the OPEN function, then the file could not be opened and the directory does not exist.

Test the VFFILE and VPATH functions.

Verifying Files and Paths

Continue in the previous drawing, or begin a NEW drawing again named FILES.

You have VFFILE and VPATH in your FILELIB.LSP file. You need not reload it.

Create the VFFILE and VPATH functions in your FILELIB.LSP file.

Command: **(load "FILELIB")**   Load the function file.

Command: **(vffile ".\\filelib.lsp")**   ".\\" restricts the search to the current directory.
Lisp returns: ".\\FILELIB.LSP"

Command: **(vffile "./ACAD.LIN")**
File ACAD.LIN not found in ./
Enter path to search, or Q to quit: **\ACAD**   Be sure to include a trailing slash.
Lisp returns: "\\ACAD\\ACAD.LIN"

Command: **(vpath)**   Get a path.
SH
DOS Command: CD $
Command:
Enter path name <C:\IL-ACAD\>: **<RETURN>**   Take the default.

```
Command: (vpath)                              Get a path. The SH command runs, then:
Enter path name <C:\IL-ACAD\>: JUNK          Try a bad name.
Invalid path, try again.
Enter path name <C:\IL-ACAD\>: \ACAD\         Be sure to include a trailing slash.
Lisp returns: "\\ACAD\\"
```

VFFILE is used by this chapter's MERGEF and PATTERN.LSP functions. VPATH will be used by the LBLOCK program in Chapter 15.

Now that you have formatted paths and files, and verified their existence, you need a way to merge and back up your files.

How to Back Up and Merge Files

Before AutoCAD saves a drawing, it makes a backup file from the original. Most programs do the same with their files. There is no reason your AutoLISP programs can't back up the files they write. AutoLISP can merge files by opening one for reading and one for appending, and by appending the contents of the one to the other, one READ-LINE at a time. This is slow for large files. The following file merge function provides you with two file handling functions called BACKUP and MERGEF (MERGE Files). These backup and merge utilities use the AutoCAD FILE and SH (shell) commands to copy and manage files more efficiently.

```
;* BACKUP copies file FSPEC to its path\name.BAK, using
;* the FFNAME function to format the filename.
(defun backup (fspec)
  (command "FILES" "5" fspec      ;copy filespec.EXT to
    (ffname fspec "BAK")          ;filespec w/ EXT stripped & repl w/ BAK
    "" "" nil                     ;nil cancels error if file didn't exist.
  ) ;command
) ;defun
;*
```

BACKUP Function in FILELIB.LSP File

➡ *NOTE: BACKUP will overwrite any existing path\name.BAK file sharing the same path and name.*

If you need to verify that a backup file has been created, have your programs test for a *filename*.BAK after running BACKUP.

The MERGEF function merges two files using the DOS COPY command with a plus symbol. In DOS, a plus symbol placed between successive file names causes it to combine the files using the last file name. MERGEF writes everything to the first file name, and deletes the second file.

```
;* MERGEF appends file2 to file1, strips file1's ^Z if present, deletes file2
;* If SH (shell) fails w/ insufficient memory, increase size in ACAD.PGP
;* It uses the VFFILE function to verify the filenames' existence. Returns T.
(defun mergef (file1 file2)
  (setq file1 (vffile file1)  file2 (vffile file2))        ;verifies files
  (cond
    ( (getenv "COMSPEC")                                    ;if DOS
      (command "SH" (strcat "COPY " file1 " + "  file2  " " file1) nil) ;copy
      (command "SH" (strcat "DEL " file2) nil)              ;delete 2nd file
    )
    ( (getenv "USER")                                       ;if UNIX
      (command "SH" (strcat "cat " file1 file2 " >! $"      ;use cat command
                    " ; mv $ " file1 " ; rm " file2         ;delete 2nd file
      ) nil           );command&strcat                      ;nil cancels if SH fails
    )
    (T(prompt "\nUNKNOWN OPERATING SYSTEM for MERGEF function. "))
  );cond
  T                                          ;returns T
);defun
;*
```

MERGEF Function in FILELIB.LSP File

If you like, you can add code to ask if a backup file should be created and call the BACKUP function to do so.

➡ *NOTE: Control-Z end-of-file characters are another reason you need MERGEF. Many text files end with a <^Z> to tell programs to stop reading them. If you use the "a" append mode of OPEN to write additions to a file, the <^Z> remains in the file above your additions. AutoLISP and most other programs will stop reading at the <^Z> and never reach your appended additions. The easy solution is to use DOS's COPY with a plus character. It strips the first file's <^Z>, if any, and ends the newly merged file with a single <^Z>. MERGEF automates this process.*

Let's test the BACKUP and MERGEF functions now.

Using AutoLISP to Back Up and Merge Files

Continue in the previous drawing, or begin a NEW drawing again named FILES.

You have BACKUP and MERGEF in your FILELIB.LSP file. You need not reload it.

Create the BACKUP and MERGEF functions in your FILELIB.LSP file.

Command: **(load "FILELIB")**   Load the function file.

Command: **SHELL**   With your text editor, create a small test file named TEST.

Command: **(backup "TEST")**   Back up a file.

Flips through the FILES menu and creates TEST.BAK.

Command: **DIR**   Enter TEST.* to see if it worked. Note the sizes.

```
Command: (mergef "TEST" "TEST.BAK")
SH
DOS Command: COPY C:\IL-ACAD\TEST + C:\IL-ACAD\TEST.BAK C:\IL-
ACAD\TEST C:\IL-ACAD\TEST.BAK
1 File(s) copied
Command: SH
DOS Command: DEL TEST.BAK
Lisp returns: nil
```

Command: **DIR**   Enter TEST.* If OK, its size doubled and TEST.BAK is gone.

Command: **DEL**   Delete TEST.

You can try these functions on other files to see how they handle errors. The MERGEF subroutine is used later in this chapter by the PATTERN program. MERGEF returns T for compatibility with the New Riders AutoLISP Utilities Disk 1 function, MERGEV.

MERGEV and SHELL on the New Riders AutoLISP Utilities Disk

If you want verified file merging, try MERGEV, a function in the FILELIB.LSP file on the New Riders AutoLISP Utilities Disk 1. It combines two files and verifies the copy procedure. MERGEV uses an interesting technique of creating a small batch file using AutoLISP. It runs the batch file through AutoCAD's SHELL facility. The last statement of the batch file causes the batch file to delete itself. If the batch file has not been deleted, it means that the COPY was never completed or the

SHELL command failed. Then, MERGEV checks to see if the batch file exists after the combine process. If it is not there, the function returns nil. It deletes the second file.

The SHELL function, also in FILELIB.LSP on the New Riders AutoLISP Utilities Disk 1, makes a general utility of combining several DOS commands in a batch file. It saves AutoCAD from having to execute multiple shells to run multiple DOS commands. It's particularly useful where you have multiple commands that require a large shell memory.

Now it's time to put these file handling functions to use in a hatch generation program named C: PATTERN.

Applying File Handling to a Hatch Pattern Generator

Custom hatch patterns add pizzazz to drawings and help CAD approach the creative flair of manual drafting. But we hate calculating hatch patterns. Regardless of the pattern, it's a time-consuming, repetitive process — obviously a job for AutoLISP. PATTERN works by examining the entities of a sample pattern created in a 1 x 1 box. The sample pattern operates under the following conventions:

- Dots are drawn using the POINT entity.

- Line segments are drawn using the LINE entity.

- Line angles must be in increments of 45 degrees (0, 45, 90, 135, 225, etc.).

If you aren't familiar with the hatch pattern file format, refer to Appendix B in the AutoCAD Reference Manual, or pick up a copy of CUSTOMIZING AutoCAD and read the chapter on linetypes and hatches.

The PATTERN function starts by gathering input from you. It gets the name of the pattern, the pattern description, and the entities of the sample pattern. It opens a temporary file and writes the name and description to the file, then loops through the selected entities and writes their line definitions to the file.

```
;* C:PATTERN writes a hatch pattern from selection set of LINES and/or POINTS.
;* LINES must be at 0 or angular multiples of 45 degrees. Other angles are NOT
;* filtered out and will become irregular in alignment. The selection set
;* should be created relative to a 1-unit square box for correct alignment.
;* Calls DXF, MERGEF, BACKUP and VFFILE (FILELIB.LSP) functions.
;*
```

❶

```
(if mergef nil (load (findfile "filelib.lsp")))  ;ensure load of support functions


(defun C:PATTERN ( / hname hdes ss1 fp count en ed et pt1 pt2 ang dlen
                     deltax deltay skip olin fspec)
                                                 ;begin input section of program
  (setq  hname ""   hdes "" )                    ;init for input
  (while (not (and                               ;force a hatch name < 9 char
               (/= "" (setq hname (getstring "\nName of pattern: "))
               (< 9 (strlen hname))
  )      )    )    )
  (while (= "" (setq hdes  (getstring "\nDescription: " T))))  ;for ACAD.PAT file
  (prompt "\nSelect unit pattern entities...")
  (while (not (setq ss1 (ssget))))               ;get entities
  (setq fp (open (strcat hname ".pat") "w"))      ;open temp pattern file
  (textscr)
                                                 ;this section writes the header
  (princ (strcat "*" hname) fp)                   ;mark start of entry with *
  (write-line (strcat "," hdes) fp)               ;write ,description to file
```

❷

```
                                                 ;calculate & write body of pattern
  (setq count 0   emax (sslength ss1))           ;EMAX=number of entities selected
  (while (< count emax)                          ;examine ea entity selected
    (setq en (ssname ss1 count)                  ;entity name
          ed (entget en)                         ;entity data
          et (dxf 0 ed)                          ;entity type
          count (1+ count)
    )
    (cond
      ((= et "POINT")                            ;cond-1 - If it's a POINT...
       (setq olin                                ;...calc & format the hatch "line"
          (strcat "0," (rtos (car  (dxf 10 ed)) 2 6) ","
                       (rtos (cadr (dxf 10 ed)) 2 6) ",0,1,0,-1"
```

Listing continued.

Continued listing.

```
      ) )
      (prompt (strcat "\n" olin))            ;display "line" for amusement
      (write-line olin fp)                   ;write it to file
   );cond-1
   ((= et "LINE")                            ;cond-2 - If it's a LINE...
     (setq pt1 (dxf 10 ed)                   ;endpt 1
           pt2 (dxf 11 ed)                   ;endpt 2
           ang (angle pt1 pt2)               ;angle
           dlen (distance pt1 pt2)           ;length
     );setq
     (if (= "1.00"                           ;test whether 90 deg multiple
            (rtos                              ;if so, abs of sin or cos...
              (+ (setq deltax (abs (cos ang)))  ;...will be 1 and other 0
                 (setq deltay (abs (sin ang)))
              ) 2 2
        ) );=
        (setq deltax 0.0                     ;then set offset along line &
              deltay 1.0                     ;offset to parallel line &
              skip (- dlen deltay)           ;dash length
        )
                     ;else assume to be 45 deg family & use offsets set in IF test above
        (setq skip (- dlen (* deltay 2.0)))  ;& set dash length
     );if
     (setq olin                              ;format LINE hatch "line"
       (strcat (angtos ang 0 6)      "," (rtos (car pt1) 2 6)
          "," (rtos (cadr pt1) 2 6) "," (rtos deltax 2 6)
          "," (rtos deltay 2 6)      "," (rtos dlen 2 6)
          "," (rtos skip 2 6)
     ) );setq&strcat
     (prompt (strcat "\n" olin))
     (write-line olin fp)
   );cond-2
   (T  (prompt                               ;cond-3 - not LINE or POINT
        (strcat "\nInvalid entity " et " skipped.")
     )  )
  );cond
);while
```

Listing continued.

Continued listing.

```
❸
                                    ;this section closes file & appends for use
  (write-char 26 fp)                           ;write ^Z EOF char
  (close fp)                                    ;close temp ACADPAT.$ file
  (setq fspec (vffile "ACAD.PAT"))             ;verify path of ACAD.PAT
  (initget "Yes No")
  (if
    (and                    ;test - do you want to merge and did it work?
      (/= "" fspec)                             ;did VFFILE find ACAD.PAT
      (/= "No"                                  ;do you want to append
        (getkword
          (strcat
            "\n" hname ".pat file may be appended to ACAD.PAT for general use."
            "\nDo you want to append to " fspec
              " and delete " hname ".pat? Yes/No/<Y>: "
      ) ) )
❹
      (not (backup fspec))                      ;backup ACAD.PAT
      (mergef fspec (strcat hname ".pat"))      ;then merge & del HNAME.pat
    )
    nil                                         ;then, if above OK
    (prompt (strcat "\n" hname ".pat file left in current directory. ")) ;else
  );if
  (graphscr)
  (princ)
);defun PATTERN
(princ)
;*
```

PATTERN Function in PATTERN.LSP File

❶ We use FINDFILE to make sure the required support functions for the program are loaded. Do this for any set of functions that are not assumed to be in the ACAD.LSP file. Several alternative methods of file loading will be covered in Chapter 17.

❷ The sticky part is calculating the geometry. Fortunately, it's already done for you. PATTERN retrieves the entity name, data, and type from the AutoCAD database. It tests the type using a COND structure and calculates the hatch entry for the entity. Then it sets it to OLIN, a variable which is written to the file. If the entity is a point, the calculation is simple. If it's a line, the function tests the line's angle and makes the pattern calculations based on that angle. If you have a valid entity, the function writes the hatch entry to the file and to the screen. The screen output reassures you that it's working.

❸ The final part of PATTERN manages the files. It looks for the ACAD.PAT file using our VFFILE function. Once ACAD.PAT has been found, the program asks if it should merge the temporary file with ACAD.PAT.

❹ If merging is chosen, PATTERN uses our BACKUP and MERGEF functions to back up ACAD.PAT and merge the pattern. If not, it leaves the individual pattern file in the current directory.

Let's give PATTERN a try. Draw a sample unit pattern similar to that shown in the Initial Hatch Pattern illustration, then test the PATTERN command.

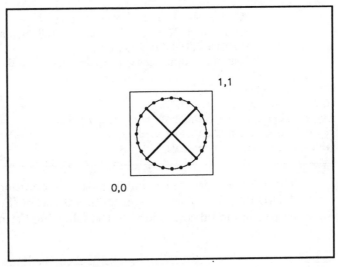

The Initial Hatch Pattern

Creating Hatch Patterns With PATTERN

Enter selection: **1**   Begin a NEW drawing named HATCH.

 You have C:PATTERN in your PATTERN.LSP file.

 Create the C:PATTERN command in a new file named PATTERN.LSP.

Command: **SH**   Make a working copy of ACAD.PAT.
DOS command: **COPY \ACAD\ACAD.PAT \IL-ACAD*.***
Command: **ZOOM**   Left -.5,-.5 with Height 3.

```
Command: GRID                 Set to 0.2.

                              Draw the hatch definition entities, using the above illustration as a guide.

Command: PLINE                Draw a 1 x 1 box at 0,0.
Command: CIRCLE               Pick center point of square.
Diameter/<Radius>:            Pick polar point @0.4243<45.
Command: DIVIDE               Divide the circle into 24 segments to create 24 points.
Command: LINE                 Draw two lines at 45 deg., using the coords display.

Command: (load "FILELIB")     Load the file for PATTERN's use.
Command: (load "PATTERN")     Load the file.
```

Try PATTERN on the X and circle of dots you just made:

```
Command: PATTERN
Name of pattern: XDOTS
Description: Dots in a circle pattern with a large X
Select unit pattern entities...
Select objects:               Window the X and points you drew.
Select objects:               Return and 27 lines of numbers scroll by, ending with:
                              0,0.910935,0.605510,0,1,0,-1
                              Your numbers may vary, depending on entity order.
0,0.924264,0.500000,0,1,0,-1
Invalid entity CIRCLE skipped.
Invalid entity POLYLINE skipped.
XDOTS.pat file may be appended to ACAD.PAT for general use.
Do you want to append to C:\ACAD\ACAD.PAT and delete XDOTS.pat? Yes/No/<Y>: N      No.
XDOTS.pat file left in current directory.
```

The program created a hatch pattern definition and added it to the ACAD.PAT file. Check the contents of the XDOTS.PAT file with your text editor. It should correspond to the following listing, although line order may vary.

```
*XDOTS,Dots in a circle pattern with large X
135.000000,0.800000,0.200000,0.707107,0.707107,0.848528,-0.565685
225.000000,0.800000,0.800000,0.707107,0.707107,0.848528,-0.565685
0,0.909808,0.390192,0,1,0,-1
0,0.867423,0.287868,0,1,0,-1
0,0.800000,0.200000,0,1,0,-1
0,0.712132,0.132577,0,1,0,-1
0,0.609808,0.090192,0,1,0,-1
0,0.500000,0.075736,0,1,0,-1
0,0.390192,0.090192,0,1,0,-1
```

Listing continued.

Continued listing.

```
0,0.287868,0.132577,0,1,0,-1
0,0.200000,0.200000,0,1,0,-1
0,0.132577,0.287868,0,1,0,-1
0,0.090192,0.390192,0,1,0,-1
0,0.075736,0.500000,0,1,0,-1
0,0.090192,0.609808,0,1,0,-1
0,0.132577,0.712132,0,1,0,-1
0,0.200000,0.800000,0,1,0,-1
0,0.287868,0.867423,0,1,0,-1
0,0.390192,0.909808,0,1,0,-1
0,0.500000,0.924264,0,1,0,-1
0,0.609808,0.909808,0,1,0,-1
0,0.712132,0.867423,0,1,0,-1
0,0.800000,0.800000,0,1,0,-1
0,0.867423,0.712132,0,1,0,-1
0,0.909808,0.609808,0,1,0,-1
0,0.924264,0.500000,0,1,0,-1
```

XDOTS Pattern in ACAD.PAT File

Go ahead and use the hatch pattern for a project. Here's a sample of what it will look like.

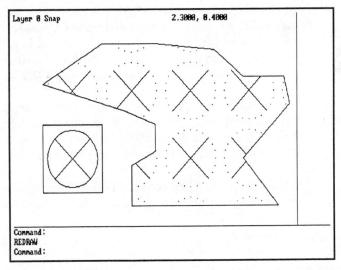

The Final Hatch Pattern

Using the XDOTS Pattern

```
Command: <F7>                    Toggle grid off.
Command: PLINE                   Make a hatch boundary of irregular shape.
Command: HATCH                   Enter XDOTS and try it on the Pline.
```

➡ *NOTE: If you use PEDIT to fit the polyline, AutoCAD will take longer to hatch the area because the pattern must conform to PEDIT's curve fitting. This is typical of the HATCH command and not the pattern.*

Try using PATTERN a few more times, and try giving it wrong input. You are at the point where you have developed enough tools to write robust and forgiving programs.

We've mastered and applied file access and control. Let's see what we can do with the text screen.

➡ *NOTE: The following section applies to DOS only.*

The ANSI Formatting Codes

ANSI.SYS is a system level device driver. Like the AutoCAD tablet, printer, and plotter drivers, it contains a set of instructions that control device operations. The ANSI system device driver is not part of the AutoCAD program. It comes with your DOS operating system. The device driver's standard name, ANSI.SYS, is used in all DOS versions. As you may recall from Chapter 1, the ANSI driver automatically loads when the system is booted if it is in your system's CONFIG.SYS file.

The rest of our programs and exercises require the ANSI driver. If the screen formatting effects are not working, your driver may not be loaded. Check Chapter 1 for instructions on how to load this device driver. Remember to reboot your computer after editing the CONFIG.SYS file.

Let's look at the ANSI codes. The IL DISK includes a help screen showing common ANSI formatting codes, together with their screen effects.

Sample Text Screen Formatting

Continue in the previous drawing, or begin a NEW drawing named ANSI.

```
Command: TYPE                    Only if you have the IL DISK.
File to list: ANSI.HLP           It displays a screen of ANSI formatting effects.
```

```
┌─────────────────────────────────────────────────────────────────┐
│         AutoLISP code to generate ANSI.SYS display control        │
│  ┌──────────────────────────────────────────────────────────────┐│
│  │ Lisp string              Description                          ││
│  │                                                              ││
│  │ "\e[2J"              Clear screen                            ││
│  │ "\e[K"               Erase from cursor position to the end of line││
│  │ "\e[<ROW>A"          Moves cursor up the number of rows      ││
│  │ "\e[<ROW>B"          Moves cursor down the number of rows    ││
│  │ "\e[<COL>C"          Moves cursor right the number of columns ││
│  │ "\e[<COL>D"          Moves cursor left the number of columns ││
│  │ "\e[<ROW>;<COL>H"    Moves cursor to row and col position    ││
│  │ "\e[s"               Saves cursor position                   ││
│  │ "\e[u"               Restores cursor position                ││
│  │ "\e[<values>m"       Controls effects and color              ││
│  │ Format: "\e[<EFFECT>;<FOREGROUND>;<BACKGROUND>m              ││
│  │   Exp: "\e[0;30;43m Black on yellow"     [Black on yellow]   ││
│  │        "\e[5;31;47m Blink red on white"  [Blink red on white]││
│  │        "\e[0;30;42m Black on green"      [Black on green]    ││
│  │        "\e[1m High intensity - bold"     High intensity - bold││
│  │        "\e[m Normal"                     [Normal]            ││
│  └──────────────────────────────────────────────────────────────┘│
│     NOTE: \e is the lisp notation for the ESC character (ASCII code 27)│
│                                                                   │
│Command:                                                           │
└─────────────────────────────────────────────────────────────────┘
```

ANSI Formatting Effects

Your screen should look like the illustration, in color if your screen supports color. Colors may vary with some video devices.

AutoLISP can give you this same screen formatting control through the escape and control codes. You've used the \n new line character in strings. The backslash character acts like an escape character in AutoLISP to send a formatting sequence to the screen. ANSI codes depend on a similar escape mechanism.

How to Use ANSI Format Codes in AutoCAD

The ANSI device driver works with an ASCII 27 <ESC> escape character. The escape character must precede any instruction to the ANSI driver device. The escape character is written as "\e" in an AutoLISP string. It must be lower case. The escape character is only a code to invoke a formatting instruction; it does not cause any formatting effect itself. The additional format codes are shown in the illustration. A typical ANSI formatting code in AutoLISP looks like "\e[2J".

➡ *NOTE: Upper case and lower case codes are not equivalent. Please input them carefully.*

The ANSI formatting codes are dependent on the text screen controller and not on the graphics screen. Entering code is simple and carefree if you have a dual screen system. If you have a single screen system, apply the codes according to the following rules:

- Only apply the codes to the *text* screen. Flip to the text screen first.

- Do not flip to the graphics screen while formatting.

- Always return the screen to the original mode.

Let's try a little interactive formatting with AutoLISP. Refer to the previous illustration for formatting codes.

Using ANSI Formatting With AutoLISP

Continue in the previous drawing.

```
Command:  <F1>                                 First, flip to the text screen.

Command:  (progn (prompt "\e[2J") (princ))     Clears the screen.

Command:  (prompt "\e[1m")                     Sets the screen to bold.

Command:  (prompt "\e[m")                      Resets the screen.
```

You can also save and restore the text cursor position, and make the cursor move to an exact place on the text screen. Cursor positioning is determined according to a row and column map. The typical screen has 25 rows and 80 columns. Use a screen position chart like the 25 x 80 chart shown below to help you design programs to format a screen of text.

Plan the screen by filling in the chart with the information you want to present. We'll do this with our next program. If you have the IL DISK, the chart shown is the SCR-MAP.DWG file.

PROGRAM NAME: _____
SCREEN DESCRIPTION: _____

25 x 80 Screen Position Chart

You tell ANSI where to put the cursor by supplying the desired row and column. Let's try it.

How to Position the Text Cursor

Continue in the previous drawing.

Command: **(prompt "\e[s")**	This saves the current screen cursor position.
Command: **(prompt "\e[10;40H")**	Go near the screen center.
Lisp returns: nil	Nil is returned to line 10, col. 40.
Command: **(prompt "\e[u")**	Restores the position saved before.
Lisp returns: nil	Nil and the cursor jumps near the top of the screen.
Command: **<F1><F1>**	Flip twice to return the normal text screen.

You can use these codes to highlight data screens, to blink instructions to the user, or just to spiffen up text displays. But it's a nuisance to remember the codes.

Making a Library of ANSI Screen Functions

An easy-to-use AutoLISP library will help us remember the ANSI code functions. Most of the functions are simple one-line PROMPT commands. Use PRINC to suppress nil and keep the functions clean.

```
;*;WARNING: ANSILIB.LSP uses ; semicolons in strings - Do Not run LSPSTRIP/S
;* ANSILIB.LSP library of screen formatting functions, for DOS only.
;* It consists of the most common tasks required for screen formatting,
;* using the ANSI escape calls.
;* It requires DEVICE=ANSI.SYS in the config.sys file.
;*
;*CLS clears the text screen.
(defun cls ()
    (prompt "\e[2J")                    ;issues ansi code
    (princ)
);defun


;*BOLD sets high intensity character mode on.
(defun bold ()
    (prompt "\e[1m")                    ;issues ansi code
    (princ)
);defun


;* NORMAL resets character mode to normal intensity.
(defun normal ()
    (prompt "\e[m")
    (princ)
);defun


;* CENTER takes a string as an argument and centers it on the text screen.
(defun center (str / hleng)
    (prompt "\e[;1A")          ;omit row number causes cursor to move in left col
    (setq hleng (/ (- 80 (strlen str)) 2))     ;gets half the string length
    (prompt (strcat "\e[" (itoa hleng) "C"))   ;move half distance of cols
    (prompt str)                               ;prints the string
    (princ)
);defun
```

Listing continued.

Continued listing.

```
;* GOTO moves cursor to a position on the screen.
(defun goto (row col)
   (prompt (strcat "\e[" (itoa row) ";" (itoa col) "H"))
   (princ)
);defun

;* DOWNROW moves cursor down a number of rows.
(defun downrow (numb)
   (prompt (strcat "\e[" (itoa numb) "B"))        ;issues ansi code
   (princ)
);defun

;*SAVEROW saves the current position of the cursor.
(defun savepos ()
   (prompt "\e[s")
   (princ)
);defun

;* RESTPOS restores previously saved cursor position.
(defun restpos ()
   (prompt "\e[u")                               ;issues ansi code
   (princ)
);defun
;*
(princ)
;*End of ANSILIB.LSP
```

ANSI Function Library in ANSILIB.LSP File

The library provides two ANSI formats we haven't tried yet. CENTER takes a string of text and calculates the text indent to achieve a centered look. DOWNROW moves the cursor down a specified number of rows.

Try these functions.

Using the ANSI Library

Continue in the previous drawing, or begin a NEW drawing, again named ANSI.

 You have these functions in your ANSILIB.LSP file.

 Create all of the above functions in a new file named ANSILIB.LSP.

```
Command: (load "ansilib")                      Load the library.
Command: <F1>                                  Flip to the text screen.
Command: (cls)                                 Clears the screen.
Command: (bold)                                Sets to bold.
Command: (normal)                              Makes them normal.
Command: (center "HELLO")                      Centers the string.
Command: (goto 10 20) (prompt "HERE! ")        Puts HERE! nil at the 10 20 screen position.
Command: (savepos)                             Saves the position.
Command: (downrow 5)                           Moves down five rows.
Command: (restpos)                             Restores the position.
Command: QUIT
```

We'll use these subroutines to format a text screen of drawing names in REFDWG, a program that generates a drawing reference schedule and inserts the schedule in your drawing.

REFDWG gets its drawing list from an external file, so let's investigate data storage formats for disk files.

Formatting Files for External Data Handling

Files can have many formats. The important part of creating and reading external files is deciding what format is efficient for the type and quantity of your data. Plan data file formats with your entire system in mind. If possible, standardize one or two formats and write standard functions to process those formats.

The simplest format is a series of entries formatted as they are to appear on the screen. These files are read and processed one full line at a time. A typical series of lines might look like:

```
REFERENCE DRAWINGS - PAPER PLANT
D78-1042 SECONDARY FIBER SYSTEM PIPING
D81-3003 NO.3 PAPER MACHINE - WET END PROCESS FLOW DIAGRAM
D81-3888 SHT.6 MAIN CONTROL PANEL-BACK PANEL & BILL OF MAT'L
```

The advantage of this format is simplicity; the disadvantage is inflexibility.

To format several pieces of information on a single line, use a file record delimiter to separate the data. A common delimiter is the comma. The following example uses the *CDF* (Comma Delimited File) format:

```
PIPE-1,12.5,3000,1800,0,134.0
PIPE-2,14.5,2400,1200,0,122.0
```

READ-LINE will return such a data line as a string. AutoLISP processes comma-delimited files by parsing the string and searching for the commas. Not only is this format flexible, but other programs that handle CDF can write and share the data. The disadvantage is that AutoLISP is slow and poor at parsing strings. To step through the string in AutoLISP, you use an expression like:

```
(while (/= "," testchar)
  ... get the next character ...
);while
```

You also can use a space as a delimiter, but only for files where spaces have no significance. AutoLISP can process the file and look for space delimiters exactly like it looks for commas.

Space delimiting enables you to arrange your data in a column format, separating entries by one or several spaces. This is the *SDF* (Standard Data File) format, the old Fortran language standard for data files. Each entry is expected to start in one column and end in a specific later column. A column format file with fields that start at specific column locations looks like:

```
PIPE-1     12.5      3000 1800 0   134.0
PIPE-2     14.5      2400 1200 0   122.0
```

The file is processed by parsing the string at predetermined columns, like tab settings. Put this in a FOREACH loop with a list of all the column positions. Each time through the loop, you can chop the string by SUBSTR. Think of it as making the string eat itself.

Try parsing a string of tabular data in this exercise at the command line.

Extracting Data From an SDF Format

```
Enter selection: 1
```
                        Begin a NEW drawing again named FILES.
                        Use it throughout this section.

Type a string for variables substituting a <SPACE> for each • shown:

```
Command: (setq str "PIPE-1•••••12.5••••••3000•1800•0••134.0")
Lisp returns: "PIPE-1     12.5      3000 1800 0   134.0"
```

```
Command: (foreach tab '(11 10 5 5 3 5) (princ (read (substr str 1 tab))) (terpri)
1> (setq str (substr str (1+ tab)))
1> (prompt str) (terpri))
PIPE-1                                    Use TERPRI to line feed.
                                          PROMPTs the first parsed value, a symbol.
12.5         3000 1800 0  134.0           The remaining string.
12.5                                      Second value, a real.
3000 1800 0  134.0                        Remaining string.
3000                                      Third value... etc.
1800 0  134.0
1800
0   134.0
0
134.0                                     The string.
134.0                                     And the last value.
Lisp returns: nil                         Returned from FOREACH.
```

The advantage of this format is speed. SUBSTR can quickly parse the data in predetermined chunks. Also, other programs that handle SDF can write and share the data. The disadvantage is that the spacing format must be predefined. The READ function strips trailing spaces, converting the data to symbols and numbers. To include strings in the data, each string must be individually set in quotation marks, like:

```
"PIPE-1•••••\"A string\"•••••12.5"
```

Other data format variations include using an asterisk as the first character on a line to mark the data entry. An asterisk combined with a comma-delimited entry would appear in the data file as:

```
*PIPE-1
12.5,3000,1800,0,134.0
```

You have a choice between putting all the data on the line following the key or on the same line. If you put the data on two lines, AutoLISP will process it faster. You may recognize this format as the ACAD.PAT and ACAD.LIN file formats.

This format quickly retrieves multiple lines of data grouped by a key word. You can READ-LINE through the file, checking only the first character of each line with SUBSTR. If the first character is an asterisk, test the rest of the line to see if it is the desired key word. If it is, READ-LINE and process until you hit the next asterisk.

Structuring your data as a list inside the string to be read from a file is a format uniquely suited to AutoLISP. Since the READ function reads the first atom or expression in a string, you can use it to convert the string to a list, and then get its data directly with FOREACH. This is fast because it avoids parsing the individual string characters. It's simple because it avoids the need to count columns. And it's flexible because the lists can be any length up to the AutoLISP 100-character string limit.

To try it, make a string as if you had read it from a file, then READ it and extract the data.

Structuring Data in a List Format

```
Command: (setq lst "(PIPE-1 12.5 3000 1800 0 134.0)")
Lisp returns: "(PIPE-1 12.5 3000 1800 0 134.0)"
Command: (setq lst (read lst))                          Convert to a list.
Lisp returns: (PIPE-1 12.5 3000 1800 0 134.0)

Command: (foreach s lst (princ s) (terpri))             Extract the data:
PIPE-1
12.5
3000
1800
0
134.0
Lisp returns: nil
```

This format can be used like an *array* data structure in other languages. You can use (repeat *n* (read-line ...)) to get the row, and NTH (starting at 0) to get the column. With the above example list and the SET function, you can set symbols like PIPE-1 to values in the list.

Accessing Arrayed Data Lists

```
Command: (set (car lst) (nth 1 lst))      Set PIPE-1 to 12.5.
Lisp returns: 12.5
Command: !pipe-1                           Check it.
Lisp returns: 12.5
```

A similar method, unconstrained by string lengths, is to format the data in a file that can be read by the AutoLISP LOAD function. For example, a file named TEST.DAT in this format might look like:

```
'((PIPE-1 12.5 3000 1800 0 134.0)
  (PIPE-2 14.5 4000 2400 0 186.0)
)
```

Try accessing the fourth column in the second row, using LOAD and NTH.

Accessing LOADed Data Formats

```
Command: SHELL                        Use your text editor to create TEST.DAT, containing the above data.

Command: (setq data (load "test.dat"))    Import the data file
((PIPE-1 12.5 3000 1800 0 134.0) (PIPE-2 14.5 4000 2400 0 186.0))
Command: (nth 3 (nth 1 data))             Access the data.
Lisp returns: 2400                        The fourth column in the second row.
```

This format avoids the need to open and close files, and should be the fastest when you need to import the entire data file. The data list size is limited only by available memory. However, there is one drawback. The entire data list must be loaded at once, instead of line by line. Large amounts of data can use up all your AutoLISP memory.

Applying Data File Access to REFDWG

REFDWG uses a simple, pre-formatted data file. One piece of information in the file is especially significant. The project name must occupy the second line of the file. The first line is left blank to conform to database output restrictions of dBASE III. The first drawing name starts on the third line of the file. Subsequent drawing names follow on successive lines, one per line. The example REFDWG.TXT file looks like this:

```
(Leave the first line blank, start on the second line.)
REFERENCE DRAWINGS - PAPER PLANT
D78-1042   SECONDARY FIBER SYSTEM PIPING
D78-1060   SECONDARY FIBER SYSTEM - SECTIONS
D81-3003   NO.3 PAPER MACHINE - WET END PROCESS FLOW DIAGRAM
D81-3204   NO.3 PAPER MACHINE - GENERAL ARRANGEMENT
D81-3211   NO.3 PAPER MACHINE - PROFILE VIEW
D81-3862   MOTOR AND CONTROL CONDUIT LAYOUT
D81-3862   NO.3 PAPER MACHINE MOTOR AND CONTROL CONDUIT LAYOUT
D81-3887   MAIN CONTROL PANEL STEEL LAYOUT & CUTOUTS
D81-3888 SHT. 1   MAIN CONTROL PANEL PUSHBUTTON WIRING
D81-3888 SHT. 2   MAIN CONTROL PANEL PUSHBUTTON WIRING cont.
D81-3888 SHT. 3   MAIN CONTROL PANEL I/O LAYOUT RACK #MC1
D81-3888 SHT. 4   MAIN CONTROL PANEL I/O LAYOUT RACK #MC2
D81-3888 SHT. 5   MAIN CONTROL PANEL FACE LAYOUT
D81-3888 SHT. 6   MAIN CONTROL PANEL-BACK PANEL LAYOUT & BILL OF MAT'L
```

REFDWG.TXT File

You can generate this type of file easily with common database programs. In Chapter 13, covering Lotus and dBASE file processing, we will show you a powerful project drawing manager written in dBASE that generates a reference drawing text file.

The REFDWG Program

In this section, we'll create functions to read a file of reference drawings, list the drawings on the text screen, ask which drawings to select, then place those names on a reference drawing schedule in the current AutoCAD drawing.

The main function is REFDWG. Using ANSI formatting, it displays the drawing names to the screen and then calls two other functions: REFSEL to select the drawing names and REFOUT to put the names as text in the AutoCAD drawing. We'll show the REFDWG function first.

```
;* C:REFDWG is a command which displays a file of project reference drawings,
;* permits the user to make any number of selections from the drawing list
;* and then formats and enters the drawings as text in AutoCAD. There is a max.
;* limit of 15 drawings per input file. It requires a fixed height text style.
;* The FILELIB.LSP and ANSILIB.LSP files, and user GET functions must be loaded.
;*
❶
(if mergef nil (load (findfile "filelib.lsp")))   ;ensure support function load
(if bold   nil (load (findfile "ansilib.lsp")))   ;ensure support function load

(defun C:REFDWG ( / fp label row col count item itlist)
  (setq file (ustr 0 "Reference drawing file name" nil nil) ;get the input file
        file (ffname file "TXT")        ;deletes extension, adds TXT
  );setq
❷
  (if (setq fp (open file "r"))          ;if the file exists, get the file handle
    (progn                               ;then do it
      (textscr)                          ;flip to the text screen
      (cls)                              ;clear it - cursor's at upper left cell
❸
      (read-line fp)                     ;skip first blank line
      (setq label (read-line fp))        ;read the first line of file
      (bold)                             ;turn on high intensity characters
      (center label)                     ;center and print project label to screen
      (normal)                           ;reset character attribute to normal
```

Listing continued.

Continued listing.

```
    (setq row 3                         ;initialize cursor positioning variables
          col 2
          count 65                      ;and the first letter for entry ids
    );setq
❹
    (while (setq item (read-line fp)) ;start a loop, read each line of file
      (goto row col)                    ;move to screen position
      (prompt (strcat (chr count) ". " (substr item 1 75))) ;print letter and entry
      (setq itlist (append itlist (list item))  ;make a list of all entries
            row (1+ row)                          ;increment row and column
            count (1+ count)
      );setq
    );while
    (close fp)                          ;close the input file
    (bold)
    (savepos)
    (goto 24 1)
    (center "DO NOT FLIP THE SCREEN!")          ;add warning
    (restpos)
    (normal)
    (goto (+ row 1) 2)                  ;move down 1 row
    (savepos)                           ;save the current cursor position
    (setq slist (refsel itlist))        ;call REFSEL function to select entries
    (refout slist label)                ;send to REFOUT output function
  );progn-then
  (prompt "\nFile not found.")          ;else
  );if
  (princ)                               ;finish cleanly
);defun C:REFDWG
;*
```

The REFDWG Command in REFDWG.LSP File

❶ The ANSI and file handling support function libraries are automatically loaded, if not already loaded, when the REFDWG function loads.

❷ REFDWG begins by asking for the reference drawing list file name. Then it enters an IF PROGN structure if the file exists and can be opened for reading. It flips to the text screen with TEXTSCR and clears it with ANSILIB's CLS function.

❸ It reads and discards the first blank line in the input file. The second line is your label header for the screen. REFDWG clears the screen with CLS, leaving the cursor at the top left screen position. It turns on BOLD mode, and centers the label on the first line. REFDWG initializes the start row, column, and count (65 is the letter A). Then it resets the screen to normal and starts writing the reference names in a WHILE loop.

❹ The program loops with WHILE until it reads the last line of the file. As each item is read, it is displayed and appended to ITLIST, the master list of drawings. A letter is placed before each name on the screen so you can pick the drawing names. The function uses STRCAT with CHR to convert a number to its letter equivalent. The function starts at 65 to get an upper case "A." Each time through, the "row" and "count" variables are incremented. When it is done reading the file, REFDWG closes the file, moves the cursor down two rows, and stores the current position.

To test C:REFDWG, temporarily disable the two lines that call the REFSEL and REFOUT subroutines.

Testing the REFDWG Function

```
Enter selection: 1
```
Begin a NEW drawing named REFDWG=IL-PROTO.

You have the C:REFDWG command function in your REFDWG.LSP file.

Create C:REFDWG in a new file named REFDWG.LSP.

```
Command: SHELL
```
Even if you have the IL DISK, change the subroutine calls, adding ";** disabled" with your text editor, like:

```
;** disabled   (setq slist (refsel itlist))   ;call REFSEL function to select entries
;** disabled   (refout slist label)           ;send to REFOUT output function
```

```
Command: (load "refdwg")
```
Load the file.

```
Command: ZOOM
```
Left 0,0 with height 6.

```
Command: REFDWG
```
Test it.
```
Reference drawing file name: REFDWG
```
Enter the file name.

A bold title and an alphabetically coded list appear.

REFSEL, the next part of the program, loops while waiting for you to identify each drawing you need. When you enter a letter, REFSEL marks the line with a bold asterisk.

```
;*REFSEL is called by C:REFDWG to get the drawing names
;*
(defun refsel (itlist /  ltr ltrs elemno mnulist pt txtst)
  (if itlist                              ;if test for list of entries
    (progn                                ;then
      (bold)                              ;set high intensity on
❶
      (while                              ;test for null input from user
        (/= 0 (setq ltr (ascii (strcase  ;converts to uppercase, then to integer
              (getstring "\e[u\e[KEnter letter or RETURN: "))) ;restore cursor & prompt
        )       );/=setq
        (if (and (> ltr 64) (< ltr count))    ;check range of letter from user
            (progn
              (setq elemno (- ltr 65))        ;find which one they selected
              (goto (+ elemno 3) 1)           ;goto that element line
❷
              (prompt "*")                     ;mark it with asterisk
              (setq addelem (nth elemno itlist)) ;extract marked element from list
              (if (not (member addelem mnulist)) ;check for duplicates
                  (setq mnulist (append mnulist (list addelem))) ;add it to selected list
              );if
            );progn
❸
            (getstring "\e[u\e[KInvalid selection. RETURN to continue. ") ;out of range
        );if
      );while
      (normal)                           ;reset character attributes
      (cls)                              ;clear screen
    );progn-then
  );if-itlist
  mnulist                               ;return selected list of entries
);defun REFSEL
;*
```

The REFSEL Subroutine in REFDWG.LSP File

❶ REFSEL loops in a WHILE, getting characters that identify the desired drawings. When it receives a likely character, REFSEL converts the letter to an integer and tests it. If it is within the range of "A" through the last item, it sets the cursor to the matching line with GOTO.

❷ If the input is valid, the program puts a bold asterisk in the first column to the left of the item. The program checks to see if there is a duplicate entry. If not, the name is put on the selected list. After each selection, the prompt is reissued. The prompt first restores the cursor to its previous place, saved in the REFDWG function, and deletes to the end of the line with \e[K.

❸ If the input is invalid, the program gives a warning message. It uses GETSTRING to pause for input and clear the error. The \e[K clears the line before the prompt. After all drawings are marked, the program sets the screen to NORMAL and clears it with CLS.

Re-enable the REFSEL subroutine call that you disabled in the previous exercise. Try the REFDWG command with the support of the REFSEL function.

Testing the REFSEL Selection Function

Continue in the previous drawing.

 You have the REFSEL function in your REFDWG.LSP file.

Add REFSEL to your REFDWG.LSP file.

```
Command: SHELL
```
Even if you have the IL DISK, change the REFSEL subroutine call with your text editor to look like this:

```
        (setq slist (refsel itlist))    ;call REFSEL function to select entries
;** disabled    (refout slist label)    ;send to REFOUT output function
```

```
Command: (load "refdwg")
```
Reload the file.

```
Command: REFDWG
Reference drawing file name: REFDWG     It displays as before.
Enter letter or RETURN: A                Enter several letters.
```

Your screen should look like the Marked Reference Drawing illustration.

```
        REFERENCE DRAWINGS - PAPER PLANT

  A. D78-1042  SECONDARY FIBER SYSTEM PIPING
 *B. D78-1060  SECONDARY FIBER SYSTEM - SECTIONS
  C. D81-3003  NO.3 PAPER MACHINE - WET END PROCESS FLOW DIAGRAM
  D. D81-3204  NO.3 PAPER MACHINE - GENERAL ARRANGEMENT
 *E. D81-3211  NO.3 PAPER MACHINE - PROFILE VIEW
 *F. D81-3862  MOTOR AND CONTROL CONDUIT LAYOUT
  G. D81-3862  NO.3 PAPER MACHINE MOTOR AND CONTROL CONDUIT LAYOUT
  H. D81-3887  MAIN CONTROL PANEL STEEL LAYOUT & CUTOUTS
  I. D81-3888 SHT. 1  MAIN CONTROL PANEL PUSHBUTTON WIRING
 *J. D81-3888 SHT. 2  MAIN CONTROL PANEL PUSHBUTTON WIRING cont.
  K. D81-3888 SHT. 3  MAIN CONTROL PANEL I/O LAYOUT RACK #MC1
 *L. D81-3888 SHT. 4  MAIN CONTROL PANEL I/O LAYOUT RACK #MC2
 *M. D81-3888 SHT. 5  MAIN CONTROL PANEL FACE LAYOUT
  N. D81-3888 SHT. 6  MAIN CONTROL PANEL-BACK PANEL LAYOUT & BILL OF MAT'L


 Enter letter or RETURN:




            DO NOT FLIP THE SCREEN!
```

Marked Reference Drawing

The final subroutine, REFOUT, places the text in the current drawing.

```
;* REFOUT is called by C:REFDWG to place the names as text.
;*
(defun refout (slist label / pt txtst $hlite)
  (if slist
    (progn
      (graphscr)                                       ;flip to graphics

      (setq pt (upoint 1 "" "Starting point" nil nil)  ;get text alignment point
            txtst (ustr 0 "\nText style" "STD" nil)     ;and the style
      );setq
      (setq $hlite (getvar "HIGHLIGHT"))               ;save setting
      (setvar "HIGHLIGHT" 0)                           ;turn off highlight
      (command "text" "s" txtst pt 0.0                 ;change text style
            (strcat "%%u" label "%%u") "text" "")       ;put on project label
      );command

      (foreach elem slist                              ;step through each entry
            (command elem "text" "")                    ;place text, restart command
      );foreach
      (command nil)                                    ;finish command - cancel
```

❶

❷

Listing continued.

Continued listing.

```
      (setvar "HIGHLIGHT" $hlite)                    ;reset highlight mode
    );progn-then
  );if
);defun REFOUT
;*
(princ)
```

The REFOUT Subroutine in REFDWG.LSP File

❶ REFOUT asks for the text starting point and the style name, using STD as the default style. The style must be a fixed height style.

❷ The function loops through each element of its argument list and puts the text on the screen.

Re-enable the REFOUT subroutine call that you disabled in the earlier exercise. Try the complete REFDWG program.

Testing the Complete Reference Drawing Program

Continue in the previous drawing.

 You have the REFOUT function in your REFDWG.LSP file.

Add REFOUT to your REFDWG.LSP file.

Command: **SHELL**   Even if you have the IL DISK, re-enable the REFOUT subroutine call with your text editor to look like this:

```
    (refout slist label) ;send to REFOUT output function
```

Command: **(load "refdwg")**   Reload the file.

Command: **REFDWG**
Reference drawing file name: **REFDWG**   It displays as before.
Enter letter or RETURN: **A**   Enter several letters.

Starting point: Pick a point.
Text style <STD>: **<RETURN>**   Stuff scrolls by, and text goes in.

Command: **QUIT**

```
Layer 0 Snap                          0.0000,0.0000




     REFERENCE DRAWINGS — PAPER PLANT
     D78—1060   SECONDARY FIBER SYSTEM — SECTIONS
     D81—3211   NO.3 PAPER MACHINE — PROFILE VIEW
     D81—3862   MOTOR AND CONTROL CONDUIT LAYOUT
     D81—3888 SHT. 2   MAIN CONTROL PANEL PUSHBUTTON WIRING cont.
     D81—3888 SHT. 4   MAIN CONTROL PANEL I/O LAYOUT RACK #MC2
     D81—3888 SHT. 5   MAIN CONTROL PANEL FACE LAYOUT




Command :
REDRAW
Command :
```

Reference Drawing as AutoCAD Text

Summary

The formula for AutoLISP file access is simply open, read or write, and close. Our ETOS expression to string conversion subroutine is a basic application of this process. Remember to close everything you open or your system will run out of file handles.

Instead of writing to printer or other port devices, we recommend writing to a file and using the DOS COPY command to copy the file to the port. This lets DOS handle printer handshaking and errors.

AutoLISP's few file-handling functions handle the essentials, but you need more tools for well-managed programs. Our FILELIB tools make it easy to manage files and to create a forgiving user interface.

Use CPATH, RPATH, and VPATH in your programs to control directories. Changing directories via SHELL and failing to restore the *current* AutoCAD directory can crash or confuse AutoCAD, or misplace files.

AutoLISP's GETENV function discerns what operating system you're running a program under and sets up directory search paths for FINDFILE.

PSLASH and FFNAME keep your programs (and you) from worrying about forward versus backslashes, or about entering file name extensions correctly.

Use VFFILE and VPATH to find, verify, and prompt for file names and paths so programs won't crash when they receive nonexistent directory or file names.

The BACKUP and MERGEF functions save backups and combine files. Because AutoLISP can't remove <^Z> end-of-file characters when appending, remember to use DOS's COPY + or MERGEF to deal with <^Z>s.

ANSI formatting is great for calling attention to text screen data and creating full-screen menus like the REFDWG selection screen. But watch out for the flip screen. It will destroy your ANSI formats. ANSI is a good tool for simple tasks, but if you can program in other languages, you can write or purchase better text screen tools for full-screen menu interfaces.

When you use ANSI for screen formatting, use the ANSILIB functions. Who can remember all the codes, anyway? ANSILIB makes programming easy. After a program is debugged, you can substitute the codes defined in ANSILIB for better efficiency, instead of calling them as subroutines.

Disk data files are AutoCAD's information link to the non-graphic world. Accessing external data is faster and more flexible that storing it in the drawing. And several drawings, or even other programs, can share the same data. Plan your file format for the type of data involved. There is no single best format for data files. Use $ to identify your temporary files so that you can find and destroy them when cleaning up your disk.

And how about that PATTERN command? We bet you never thought creating new hatches could be so easy.

By now, you've established an easy-to-control yet powerful user interface, you've accessed and modified AutoCAD drawing data and table data, and you've written, read, and managed disk data files. So what else can there be in the way of complete AutoLISP access and CAD system control? Keyboard, digitizer (or mouse), and graphics screen device access, that's what.

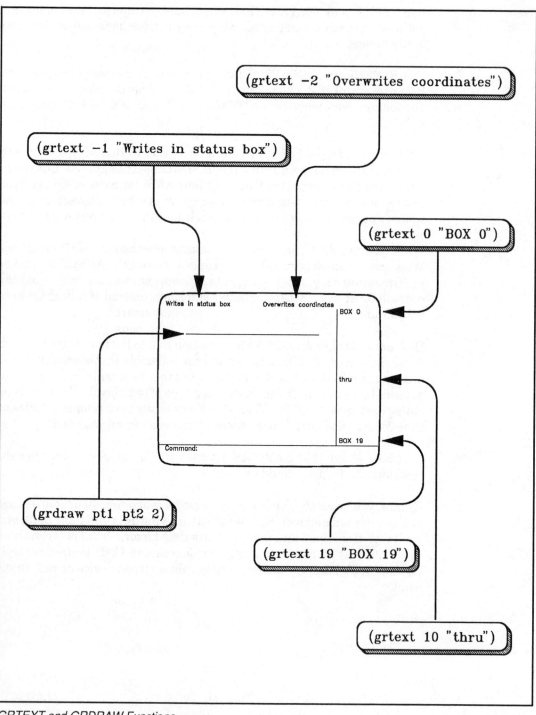

GRTEXT and GRDRAW Functions

CHAPTER 9

Working With AutoLISP Devices

GRAPHIC I/O ACCESS

You've communicated with the system and user interface on nearly every level. Right now, the only advantage AutoCAD's commands have over your programs is their access to and control of the keyboard, digitizer (or mouse), and graphics screen. AutoLISP can give you direct control over these devices too.

With AutoLISP device access, you can draw temporary lines to show graphic prompts on the screen or you can blank out existing lines. Device access provides a dynamic way for your programs to provide status information through status line and screen menu labels. Think of the flexibility and control you gain from programs smart enough to monitor and filter input from the keyboard, digitizer, or mouse.

We apply AutoLISP device access to three programs in this chapter. The PVIEW command graphically prompts for a view selection and zooms to the selected view. The ETEXT program is a single-line text editor that shows you how to integrate keyboard device access with ANSI screen formatting. The line command, DDRAW, filters digitizer input. It acts like an extension to ORTHO by locking lines to 22.5 degree increments.

In this chapter, you will learn how to use GRTEXT to put custom labels in menu and status boxes, use GRDRAW to draw temporary lines (vectors) on the screen, use GRTEXT and GRDRAW to make a window-box on the graphics screen, use GRREAD to monitor and control user input, and use GRREAD to continuously track the digitizing cursor.

Although the AutoLISP Programmer's Reference cautions that "These functions are for experienced applications developers only," the GRTEXT and GRDRAW functions are really straightforward and no harder to use than the average AutoLISP function. If you do have problems, a quick (redraw) and (grclear) will restore your screen to normal. The GRREAD function may take a little more concentration, but it will be worth the effort.

AutoLISP Tools and Programs

AutoLISP Tools

STRIP is a function that removes a specified entity association list from an entity data list. It's used for removing entity data groups to modify an entity.

Programs

C:PVIEW uses GRDRAW to display a box around each of the views defined in a drawing. It uses GRTEXT to display the view's name on the status line. Each view is displayed sequentially in a continuous loop until you select a view or quit the program.

C:ETEXT is a single-line text editor that uses GRREAD and the ANSI.SYS codes. It lets you select a single line of drawing text and edit it. You can move the cursor within the text and add or delete characters.

C:DDRAW is a drawing aid that uses GRREAD to automate drawing lines at 22.5 degree angles. It switches the snap rotation angle to the angular increment closest to a dragged line. The program displays a compass icon to assist in selecting the angle for each line.

PVIEW does for views what the Dynamic option does for zooms. It lets you quickly see where you are going, saving time and extra zoom views. Its useful graphic display makes it easy to remember what views are where so you don't have to keep track of view names. And ETEXT will save you from the frustrating job of retyping a whole line of AutoCAD text to correct a single character.

Dynamic Screen Labeling With GRTEXT

GRTEXT displays strings of text to selected boxes of the screen device. It uses the status line, coords box, and the screen menu boxes to provide information and prompts.

grtext

> *Writes a string in the text portion of the graphics screen specified by the box number. An optional non-zero mode integer highlights and zero de-highlights the box of text. A box number of -1 writes to the status line, -2 writes to the coordinate status line, and 0, 1, 2, 3 and so on write to the menu labels, with 0 representing the top label.*
> (**grtext** *box text mode*)

GRTEXT gives you access to the screen and status line boxes. It cannot access pull-down menus, icon menus, or dialogue boxes. The box codes and their characteristics are:

BOX NAME	BOX NUMBER	MAXIMUM CHARACTERS	HIGHLIGHT FEATURE
STATUS	-1	40	NO
COORDS	-2	25	NO
MENU	0 to 19+	8	YES

GRTEXT requires two arguments: the box number and the prompt string you want displayed. The maximum character widths of the status box numbers listed in the table are typical, but may vary with the type of video device you use. The maximum number of screen menu boxes also depends on the screen type. Their numbering starts at 0. The Color Graphic Adapter card (CGA standard) and many other monitors only have 20 or 21 menu boxes. Limit yourself to using 0 through 19 if you aren't sure what screen your programs will use.

How to Use GRTEXT

Using the GRTEXT function is quite simple. Call GRTEXT with two arguments: the text string to be displayed, and the box number to indicate where to display it. Try writing messages in the status, coords, and several menu boxes.

Using GRTEXT to Place Text on the Graphics Screen

```
Enter selection: 1
```
Begin a NEW drawing named IL09.

```
Command: (grtext -1 "-1 writes in status box")
Lisp returns: "-1 Writes in status box"
Command: <Ortho on><Ortho off>
```
A -1 writes to the status box.

Any toggle wipes it.

```
Command: (grtext -2 "-2 overwrites coordinates")
Lisp returns: "-2 overwrites coordinates"
```
Move the cursor to wipe it.

```
Command: (grtext 0 "Box 0")
Lisp returns: "Box 0"
```
Writes to first menu box.

```
Command: (grtext 10 "thru")
Lisp returns: "thru"
```
Writes to 11th menu box.

```
Command: (grtext 19 "Box 19")
Lisp returns: "Box 19"
```
To 20th line, the last line on a CGA screen.

Your screen should look like the AutoCAD Graphics Screen Boxes illustration.

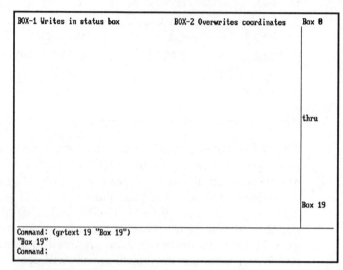

AutoCAD Graphics Screen Boxes

AutoLISP can only print one string to each screen box. AutoCAD will truncate any string that is too long to fit. You may also find that the coords box overwrites the tail of the status box.

GRTEXT is great for dynamic prompts, but the life span of a GRTEXT string is short and unstable. The text you put in the status and coords boxes is particularly transient. AutoCAD actively uses the status and coords boxes. Each time you change layers, flip a toggle, pick a point, or move the cursor, AutoCAD updates the appropriate boxes. There is no sensible way to control the status box, but you can freeze the coords box by turning AutoCAD's coordinate settings off (0) with SETVAR. We don't recommend doing this as standard practice. Just use these boxes only for short-lived information. The PVIEW program uses them for view name display.

Using the screen menu boxes 0 thru 19+ is safer for dynamic screen labeling because AutoCAD doesn't use these boxes during the drawing process. Screen menu boxes are good for showing current program settings. For example, a parametric program might display the current pipe fitting size or the current snap rotation angle.

Screen menu boxes are updated only by GRTEXT or by changing the screen page. Since screen menus are changed only by you or your programs, you have good control over the screen menu boxes. To prevent unintended page changes, your programs can use MENUCMD to put up a menu page that has no page change items.

How to Test GRTEXT's Stability

Some video devices refresh the screen boxes each time the graphics screen is redrawn. Others refresh individual boxes after they are highlighted. This causes a loss of label information. You need to be able to test your screen to see if your screen labels have changed. Test GRTEXT's stability by doing a flip screen, by doing a REDRAW, and by running the cursor along the screen menu. If the labels update, you will have to plan on using them more sparingly.

Let's test GRTEXT's stability.

Testing GRTEXT

Continue in the previous drawing, with the GRTEXT still visible.

```
Command: <F1><F1>          Flip screen twice.
Command: REDRAW
```

And move the cursor up and down the menu. Still okay?

You can easily highlight labels, or remove them and restore the original screen text.

How to Highlight and Clear GRTEXT

You can call attention to GRTEXT messages in the menu area by highlighting them. You can't highlight text sent to the status and coords boxes. Highlight labels for tutorial purposes, such as when inviting users to "follow the bouncing box."

When you highlight, include an optional argument in the GRTEXT expression. There are two modes. Zero is de-highlight, non-zero is highlight.

To highlight *real* text, such as a menu label, call GRTEXT with an empty string and a non-zero highlight argument.

To restore the entire screen to its original text, call GRTEXT with no arguments. To restore a single box, call it with an empty string. To blank a box, call it with a string of spaces.

Let's display highlighted text and restore original text with GRTEXT.

How to Highlight and Restore GRTEXT

Continue in the previous drawing, or begin a NEW drawing again named IL09.

```
Command: (grtext 0 "Brighter")        With no highlight.
Lisp returns: "Brighter"

Command: (grtext 0 "Brighter" 1)      Try it with a highlight.
Lisp returns: "Brighter"

Command: (grtext -1 "Writes in status box")
Lisp returns: "Writes in status box"
Command: (grtext -1 "")
Lisp returns: ""                       Restores status box.

Command: (grtext)                      Restores status line text to original.
Lisp returns: nil
```

The highlight effect is shown in the Highlighted and Unhighlighted Menu Boxes illustration. If a menu is loaded, (grtext) will also restore its text labels.

```
Layer 0 Snap                   0.0000,0.0000          Brighter
  .    .    .    .    .    .    .    .    .    .    .
                                                            Brighter
  .    .    .    .    .    .    .    .    .    .    .

  .    .    .    .    .    .    .    .    .    .    .

  .    .    .    .    .    .    .    .    .    .    .

  .    .    .    .    .    .    .    .    .    .    .

  .    .    .    .    .    .    .    .    .    .    .

  .    .    .    .    .    .    .    .    .    .    .

Command: (grtext 0 "Brighter" 1)
"Brighter"
Command:
         Command: (grtext 0 "Brighter")
         "Brighter"
         Command:
```

Highlighted and Unhighlighted Menu Boxes

To be sure highlighting works correctly on all video devices, you must follow a few rules. First call GRTEXT with the string unhighlighted, then call it again with the same string and a non-zero highlight argument. To de-highlight, call it again with the same string but with a zero or no highlight mode argument.

Now, let's get graphic. Graphic device access isn't limited to graphic screen text. You can draw directly on the screen with AutoLISP's GRDRAW.

Drawing Vectors With GRDRAW

AutoCAD commands draw lines representing entities. Your programs can do the same through the COMMAND function. If you don't want to create entities but just need to draw temporary guidelines as a graphic prompt, use GRDRAW.

GRDRAW puts straight lines on the screen; it doesn't create any entities. We will refer to these lines as *vectors* to differentiate them from AutoCAD's line entities. Temporary vectors can provide valuable guidance to help you make a selection or place an object. They also are helpful as temporary screen markers. GRDRAW can draw vectors between any two points on the screen in any of your monitor's supported colors. The points are in real world 2D or 3D coordinates.

grdraw

> *Draws a vector between two supplied points in the color specified by a color integer. A non-zero optional mode argument will highlight the vector.*
> (grdraw *point point color* mode)

How to Draw and Highlight Vectors

AutoCAD can highlight lines each time you make a selection set of entities. AutoCAD indicates which objects are in the selection set by dotting, dashing, or flashing them. (Selection set highlighting occurs only if the HIGHLIGHT system variable is set to 1.) Your programs can also highlight entities by using the REDRAW function with an entity name and mode argument. If you want to similarly highlight GRDRAW vectors, the GRDRAW function has an optional argument. Use a non-zero mode argument to invoke highlighting when drawing a GRDRAW temporary vector.

Let's try GRDRAW. First, get and save two points. Draw a temporary horizontal vector in yellow with GRDRAW. Then try drawing the same vector in green and with highlighting.

Using GRDRAW to Draw and Highlight Vectors

Continue in the previous drawing, or begin a NEW drawing again named IL09.

```
Command: <Ortho on>
Command: (setq pt1 (getpoint "Point: "))    Set a point.
Point:                                       Pick upper left.
Lisp returns: (2.0 6.0 0.0)

Command: (setq pt2 (getpoint "Point: " pt1))  Set another point, using base point PT1.
Point:                                        Pick horizontal at upper right.
Lisp returns: (8.0 6.0 0.0)

Command: (grdraw pt1 pt2 2)                  Give GRDRAW points and a color (2 is yellow).
Lisp returns: nil

Command: (grdraw pt1 pt2 3 1)                Draws it green and highlighted.
```

You've seen AutoCAD "reverse" the color of rubber band and window lines when they overlap other entities in the drawing. GRDRAW also can reverse colors. Color reversal occurs only if an entity or GRDRAW vector is overdrawn and if GRDRAW is given a -1 color argument. The reversed color pairs depend on your video system. Try it.

How to Reverse Colors With GRDRAW

Continue in the previous drawing, with PT1 and PT2 set.

```
Command: COLOR            Set color to BLUE.
Command: LINE             Trace over part of GRDRAW's vector.
From point: !PT1          First point.
To point:                 Pick point with ortho on.

Command: REDRAW           To clear previous GRDRAW vector.

Command: (grdraw pt1 pt2 -1)       Turns the blue line to some other color.
Lisp returns: nil
Command: (grdraw pt1 pt2 -1)       Restores the blue line and blanks itself.
Lisp returns: nil
Command: (grdraw pt1 pt2 -1 1)     Highlights itself and the blue line.
Lisp returns: nil
```

Don't try to draw complex images with GRDRAW. To draw a curve, for instance, you would have to approximate it with multiple GRDRAW calls. Later in this chapter, we'll look at some alternatives.

Now let's look at a way to clear individual vectors, blank lines, and the entire graphics screen.

How to Blank Vectors and Clear the Screen

You can seemingly "erase" and "undraw" GRDRAW vectors and real lines by drawing over them using black, color 0. When you need to clear the graphics screen entirely, use AutoLISP's GRCLEAR function.

grclear | *Temporarily clears the graphics screen in the current viewport. A redraw will refresh the screen.*
(grclear)

GRCLEAR is the simplest of AutoLISP's graphics screen functions. It clears the graphics screen like a blank slate. It doesn't take any arguments. Try a GRDRAW black vector, then try GRCLEAR.

Clearing the Screen With GRCLEAR

Command: **(grdraw pt1 pt2 0)**   Black it out.
Command: **REDRAW**   Brings the blue line back.

Command: **(grclear)**   All's clear, including the grid.
Lisp returns: nil
Command: **REDRAW**   Brings it back.

Command: **QUIT**

It's time to apply these functions to a program called PVIEW.

Making a Dynamic Preview Command

The PVIEW (PreVIEW) command is a graphic substitute for the VIEW command. It uses GRDRAW to display the bounds of each defined view and GRTEXT to display its name. It also uses TBLNEXT symbol table access to look up each view name in the drawing. It rotates dynamically through the views until you pick one or quit.

```
;* C:PVIEW draws a window box around each view in a drawing and
;* displays its name in the layer status box. It prompts for Next view,
;* Quit, or Go to the currently indicated view.
;* Requires DXF and user interface functions to be loaded.
;*
(defun C:PVIEW ( / port tbdata vname Y X CP P1 P2 P3 P4 V)
❶
  (setq $screen (getvar "SCREENSIZE")        ;screen pixel resolution
        aratio (/ (cadr $screen) (car $screen)))  ;aspect ratio based on pixels
  )
❷
  (while (and (/= V "Quit")(/= V "Go"))
    (if (setq tbdata (tblnext "VIEW" T))       ;checks to see if any view exists
      (while (/= tbdata nil)                    ;starts the loop
        (setq port (getvar "CVPORT")
          vname (dxf 2 tbdata)                  ;extracts view name
          Y (* (dxf 40 tbdata) 0.5)             ;view height
          X (* (dxf 41 tbdata) 0.5)             ;view width
        );setq
        (if (> X (* Y (/ 1 aratio)))            ;corrects for proportions of
          (setq Y (* X aratio))                 ;the screen. Either X or Y
          (setq X (* Y (/ 1.0 aratio))))        ;will determine window maximum.
        );if
❸
        (setq CP (dxf 10 tbdata)                ;center point of view
          P1 (list (- (car CP) X) (- (cadr CP) Y))  ;lower left corner
          P2 (list (- (car CP) X) (+ (cadr CP) Y))  ;upper left
          P3 (list (+ (car CP) X) (+ (cadr CP) Y))  ;upper right
          P4 (list (+ (car CP) X) (- (cadr CP) Y))  ;lower right
        );setq
        (grdraw P1 P2 7 1)                      ;draws left vertical vector
        (grdraw P2 P3 7 1)                      ;draws top horizontal
        (grdraw P3 P4 7 1)                      ;draws right vertical
        (grdraw P4 P1 7 1)                      ;draws bottom horizontal
        (grtext -1 (strcat "View name: " vname)) ;prints name in layer status box
❹
        (setq V (ukword 1 "Next Go Quit" "Display another VIEW? Quit/Go/Next" "Next"))
        (cond
          ((= "Next" V) (setq tbdata (tblnext "VIEW"))) ;gets next view from table
          ((= "Go" V)                           ;2nd cond, execute VIEW
```

Listing continued.

Continued listing.

```
          (progn
            (command "VIEW" "R" vname)          ;change view
            (setq tbdata nil)             ;nils variable causing while loop termination
        ) );progn and 2nd cond
        ((= "Quit" V) (setq tbdata nil)) ;nils variable causing while loop termination
      );cond
      (setvar "CVPORT" port)
❺
      (grdraw P1 P2 0)    ;each of these draws
      (grdraw P2 P3 0)    ;a black vector over
      (grdraw P3 P4 0)    ;the current screen
      (grdraw P4 P1 0)    ;vectors. It's the only way short of a full redraw
    );while
   );if
  );while or
  (grtext)                ;clears out the temporary screen labels
  (princ)
);defun C:PVIEW
;*
```

The C:PVIEW Command in PVIEW.LSP File

❶ The program determines the aspect ratio, ARATIO, of the screen based on the number of pixels along the X and Y directions. The SCREENSIZE system variable reports the pixel limits for the monitor. Our screen size is `(570.0 410.0)` and our aspect ratio is 410.0/570.0, or 0.719298. Your screen size and aspect ratio may differ. The program applies the aspect ratio to either the height or the width so that the GRDRAW window box is drawn in the correct proportion.

❷ The rest of the program is a WHILE loop that checks that a "Quit" or a "Go" hasn't been entered. First in each loop, PVIEW uses TBLNEXT symbol table access to look up each view defined in the drawing. It gets the view name VNAME, the height Y, and the width X. Then, it takes half the X and Y values because views are stored by their center values.

❸ The program retrieves the center point (CP) of the view and calculates the four corners (P1, P2, P3, and P4) of the box. It draws the box with white vectors and then writes the name of the view in the layer status box.

❹ PVIEW asks if you want to "Quit," see the "Next" view, or "Go" to the current choice. If you select "Go," the drawing view changes to your current choice.

❺ If another view is requested, the program overwrites the previous window box by overlaying another box drawn in black. At the end of the program, it overwrites the last window box and calls GRTEXT to clean up the status and menu box areas.

PVIEW displays the view names on the status line. You can still select them as PVIEW rotates through the names, even if the views are off-screen. We think you'll find it more intuitive and easier to use than the VIEW command. Let's try it.

Using the PVIEW Command

```
Enter selection: 1
```
Begin a NEW drawing again named IL09.

You have the C:PVIEW command in your PVIEW.LSP file.

Create C:PVIEW in a new file named PVIEW.LSP.

```
Command: CIRCLE
Command: VIEW
?/Delete/Restore/Save/Window: S
Command: VIEW
?/Delete/Restore/Save/Window: W
```
Draw a circle in the center of the screen.

Save a view named ALL.
Make three more views, with the circle in each.
Window upper right, center, and lower left.
Name them UR, CEN, and LL, windowing an appropriate area for each.

```
Command: (load "pview")
Command: PVIEW
Display another VIEW? Quit/Go/Next <Next>: <RETURN>

Display another VIEW? Quit/Go/Next <Next>:
Display another VIEW? Quit/Go/Next <Next>: G
VIEW ?/Delete/Restore/Save/Window: R
View name to restore: UR
```
Load the file.
Run the command.
Several times to look
at a few more views.
The box draws and names display.
G when it gets to UR. It restores:

Shows the view name here.

Try it a few more times.

```
Command: QUIT
```

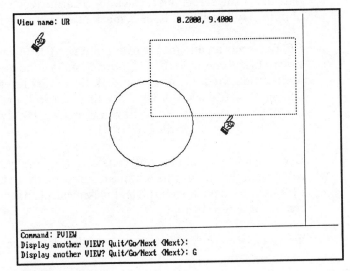

PVIEW in Progress

PVIEW can be used in any number of viewports. The active VPORT at the start of the PVIEW command becomes the port in which the GRDRAW boxes are drawn. Changing viewports during the PVIEW command has no effect on where the PVIEW boxes are drawn, but will allow you to display the view in the new viewport.

➡ *NOTE: While this version of PVIEW works well for displaying views in the WCS, it does not work in other UCSs. Chapter 14, on AutoLISP and 3D, explains how to translate coordinates and make programs like this work for any UCS.*

Alternatives for Displaying Screen Information

AutoLISP device access isn't always the most efficient solution for displaying information. Sometimes existing AutoCAD commands make good temporary tools in AutoLISP programs, particularly when showing curves and circles. Both the PLINE and POINT commands can be used to mark the progress of a custom command, such as using a temporary polyline to construct a reference frame. Polylines are good temporary markers because they are continuous and can easily be erased with ENTDEL.

Points are good entities for placing marks. You can adjust the point mode (PDMODE) and size (PDSIZE) to the style and size of the image you need. For example, a PDMODE of 3 for X and PDSIZE of -8 will size points to 8 percent of the screen size. Look for alternatives when you program. If a simple polyline shows it, or X marks the spot, use it.

GRDRAW has an advantage over points in 3D, however. Points are always drawn in the current UCS. If your screen is at an angle to the UCS, points appear flattened, or may even look like short lines. The GRPT function, on the New Riders AutoLISP Utilities Disk 1, overcomes this by using GRDRAW to emulate the point command. GRPT always draws flat to the current display, regardless of UCS.

Use blocks for complex but constant temporary objects. The DDRAW command, later in this chapter, uses such a technique. It applies ENTMOD to move a visual icon block around the screen, and ENTDEL to remove it when through.

We've covered the output side of graphic device access. Now let's look at the input side.

Getting Device Input With GRREAD

Why do you need direct device control of input when you already have a whole set of GET functions? The GET functions are limited in input flexibility. They each pause for one specific type of input (or two with INITGET key words). If you do a GETSTRING and pick a point, the digitizer pick is ignored. GET functions can accept input from menus, but they can't tell which menu box was picked. GET functions require a <RETURN> to terminate string input. If you hit a single character, a GET function has no way of telling it's been hit. And the GET functions that accept point input wait for a single pick only. They can't track the cursor continuously without requiring multiple picks. If you want the same range of input flexibility that AutoCAD commands have over your programs, you need GRREAD.

GRREAD gets around these limitations. It reads input directly from the keyboard, digitizer, or menu pick. GRREAD doesn't prompt. It accepts input from whichever device is used, so it can monitor user input. GRREAD can detect a point pick, a single key from the keyboard, or the selection of a screen, tablet, or button menu item. It can continuously track movement of the pointing device without a point pick. It returns a coded list containing the device number and the data input.

> **grread**   *Reads the input device directly. If the optional track argument is present and non-nil, it returns the current pointing device (mouse or digitizer cursor) location without a point pick.*
> **(grread** *track***)**

Let's see how this works. Enter something at the keyboard, pick a point, and select a menu item. Then, we'll look at what the device codes returned.

Using GRREAD to Monitor Device Data

```
Enter selection: 1
```
Begin a NEW drawing again named IL09.

```
Command: (setq char (grread))
Lisp returns: (2 65)
```
Enter an upper case A.
Notice that no <RETURN> was needed.

```
Command: (setq pt (grread))
Lisp returns: (3 (2.0 4.0 0.0))
```
Pick a point. Your coords may vary.

```
Command: (setq mnu (grread))
Lisp returns:(4 1)
```
Select a screen item with your pointer.

As you just saw, GRREAD always returns a list. The first element of the list is the device code number. AutoLISP programs can use this code to determine which device the input came from. The device codes and the type of data each returns are:

DEVICE	CODE	DATA RETURNED
Keyboard	2	The ASCII character number
Point pick	3	Drawing coordinate point
Screen menu pick	4	Box number
Tracked point	5	Drawing coordinate point
Button menu item	6	Button number
Tablet area 1	7	Box number
Tablet area 2	8	Box number
Tablet area 3	9	Box number
Tablet area 4	10	Box number
AUX1 menu	11	Box number
Button menu coords	12	Coord point at button pick
Menu by INS key	13	Box number

Notes: Box numbers start at box zero.
         If FLATLAND is on, 2D points are returned.

How to Extract GRREAD Data

CAR and CADR can extract the data from the list returned by GRREAD. In the above exercise, the keyboard input "A" returned the ASCII number for the character A. The digitizer point pick returned a point list of three reals and the screen menu pick returned the number of the box selected. Each list is formatted so that CAR returns the device code and CADR returns the data.

Using CAR and CADR to Return GRREAD Data

Continue in the previous drawing, with the CHAR, PT, and MNU variables set.

```
Command: (car char)
Lisp returns: 2                          The code for keyboard.

Command: (cadr pt)
Lisp returns: (2.0 4.0 0.0)              The point picked.

Command: (cadr mnu)
Lisp returns: 1                          The box number of the menu.
```

The menu item itself is not executed when GRREAD intercepts the input. Although AutoLISP can change menu pages with MENUCMD, it can't execute menu items. GRREAD is suitable for preventing menu access or for executing a program branch based on the selection of a GRTEXT menu label.

Here is a useful application of GRREAD that uses ANSI screen formatting codes. The ETEXT program is a single-line text entity editor done, of course, in AutoLISP.

Applying GRREAD to ETEXT — An AutoCAD Text Editor

ETEXT allows you to select a line of text from the AutoCAD screen and edit it. It uses entity access to get the text and update it when through, ANSI format codes to manage its interactive editing screen, and GRREAD to manage input.

```
;*;WARNING: ETEXT.LSP contains ; semicolons in strings - Do Not LSPSTRIP/S
;* ETEXT is a single line text editor allowing users to move the cursor
;* along the text and insert or delete characters as required. ANSI.SYS
;* is required for program to work. The DXF function must be loaded.
```

Listing continued.

Continued listing.

```
;* The screen cursor is moved via these keys:
;*
;* Cursor Movement Keys:     for <-- use <SHIFT TAB>      for --> use <TAB>
;* Character Insert/Delete:  Insert - just start typing   Delete - <DEL> key
;*
;* DO NOT USE THE FLIP SCREEN <F1> KEY

(defun C:ETEXT ( / entity txt txtlen curpos key)
❶
  (setq entity (entget (car (entsel "\nPick text to edit: "))))    ;get text to edit
  (if (= "TEXT" (dxf 0 entity))                    ;test if text was selected
    (progn                                         ;if text...
      (setq txt (dxf 1 entity)                     ;get text string
            txtlen (1+ (strlen txt))               ;get text length
            curpos txtlen                          ;initial cursor position = text length
      ) ;setq
      (textscr)                                    ;flip to text screen
❷
      (prompt "\e[2J")                             ;clear screen and puts header info
(prompt
"\e[7;1;37;44m                Inside AutoLISP Line Editor                         "
)
(prompt
"\e[2;1H   <SHIFT TAB> moves left, <TAB> moves right, <DEL> deletes character     "
)
      (prompt "\e[0;37;40m")                       ;sets ansi screen attributes to normal

      (prompt "\e[4;1HEdit text:")                 ;print title at line four
      (prompt "\e[1m")                             ;bold
      (prompt (strcat
        "\e[10;1H         DO NOT HIT <F1> flipscr <INS> <HOME> <END> <PG UP> <PG DN>"
        "\n                  NUMERIC KEYPAD or CURSOR KEYS!"
      )      )
      (prompt "\e[m")                              ;normal
      (prompt (strcat "\e[6;1H" txt))              ;print text at line six
❸
      (while (/= key 13)                           ;while key is not RETURN...
```

Listing continued.

Continued listing.

```
            (prompt (strcat "\e[6;" (itoa curpos) "H"))    ;position cursor
            (setq key (last (grread)))                      ;get key from keyboard
            (cond                                           ;test key
              ((= key 143)                                  ;if key was <SHIFT TAB> then
                (setq curpos (1- curpos))                   ;subtract 1 from cursor position
                (if (< curpos 1) (setq curpos txtlen))      ;if cursor <1 set cursor to text length
              );shift tab
              ((= key 9)                                    ;if key was <TAB> then
                (setq curpos (1+ curpos))                   ;add 1 to cursor position
                (if (> curpos txtlen) (setq curpos 1))      ;if cursor > text length set cursor to 1
              );tab

              ((= key 211)                                  ;if key was DEL...
                (setq txt (strcat (substr txt 1 (1- curpos)) (substr txt (1+ curpos))))
                ;create new text string less the character at the cursor position
                (setq txtlen (1+ (strlen txt)))             ;get new text length
                (prompt (strcat "\e[6;1H" txt " "))         ;display new text string
              );delete mode
              ((and (> key 31) (< key 127))                 ;if valid key...
                (setq txt (strcat (substr txt 1 (1- curpos)) (chr key) (substr txt curpos)))
                ;create new text string including the new character at the cursor position
                (setq txtlen (1+ (strlen txt)))             ;get new text length
                (setq curpos (1+ curpos))                   ;get new cursor position
                (prompt (strcat "\e[6;1H" txt " "))         ;display new text string
              );entered a text character
              (T nil)
            );cond
          );while
          (setq entity (subst (cons 1 txt) (assoc 1 entity) entity))   ;change entity list
          (entmod entity)                                   ;update entity
        );progn
        (prompt "\nEntity was not text")                    ;print bad pick message
      );if
      (prompt "\n\t\n\t\n\n\n\n\n\n\n\n\n\n\n\n\n\n\n\n\n\n\n\n\n\n\n") ;clear screen
      (princ)
    );defun C:ETEXT
  ;*
```

❹ (margin marker beside `((= key 211)` section)

ETEXT Command in ETEXT.LSP File

❶ ETEXT begins by selecting the text entity to edit. It gets the entity data and determines the number of characters in the string.

❷ The text screen is formatted using ANSI escape strings. We use in-line ANSI codes here instead of library functions from ANSILIB. This is a bit faster and more compact. ETEXT prints a headline, the cursor control key instructions, then the text string selected for editing.

❸ The editing part of the program uses WHILE to start a loop that terminates when you enter a <RETURN>. A COND test filters for the ASCII number of the key that has been pressed. For each directional key, a cursor position variable is updated and the cursor is repositioned on the screen.

❹ For the delete key, the edit string is parsed, the character removed, and the string reprinted to the screen. Insertion of any valid printable character does just the opposite. It adds characters to the string and reprints it.

The cursor keys are not intercepted by GRREAD and will cause a flip screen, so ETEXT uses the tab keys instead.

Try the program on some drawing text.

Testing the ETEXT Program

Enter selection: **1**   Begin a NEW drawing again named IL09.

You have C:ETEXT in your ETEXT.LSP file.

Create the C:ETEXT command in a new file named ETEXT.LSP.

Command: **ZOOM**	Center, height 3".
Command: **TEXT**	Type THE LAZY COW as text to test.
Command: **(load "etext")**	Load the program.
Command: **ETEXT**	
Pick text to edit:	Select the text.
	A screen shot of the ETEXT line editor is shown below.
	Use <TAB> and <SHIFT-TAB> keys as noted:
Command: **<SHIFT TAB>**	Several to get to start of COW.
Command: **BROWN**	Type BROWN — *don't* touch <INSERT> key.
Command: **<TAB>**	To delete LAZY, move cursor on each character...
Command: **<DEL>**	...and hit <DEL> key.
Command: **JUMPED OVER THE FENCE.**	To add, <TAB> to end and type.
Command: **<RETURN>**	A <RETURN> exits and updates the text in your drawing.
Command: **QUIT**	

```
                     Inside AutoLISP Line Editor
         <SHIFT TAB> moves left, <TAB> moves right, <DEL> deletes character

Edit text:

THE LAZY COW




          DO NOT HIT <F1> flipscr <INS> <HOME> <END> <PG UP> <PG DN>
                      NUMERIC KEYPAD or CURSOR KEYS!
```

The ETEXT Line Editor

As you saw in ETEXT, you can continuously fetch keyboard input by putting GRREAD in a WHILE loop. You could do the same for coordinate input and pick repeated points. But there's another way if you want to drag or continuously get points without entering them.

Continuous Coordinate Tracking With GRREAD

One unique capability of GRREAD is that it can track the motion of the digitizer or mouse pointer as you move it. It can continuously monitor the pointer's movement, similar to the SKETCH command. Let's put GRREAD in a loop and add the optional tracking argument to the function call. Then in each loop, GRREAD will return the current coordinates of the cursor without a point being picked.

Using GRREAD to Track the Pointer

Continue in the previous drawing or begin a NEW drawing again named IL09.

Command: **(grread T)**   Pick a point. Your coords may vary.
Lisp returns: (3 (2.0 4.0 0.0))   It immediately returns the point.
Command: **(while (princ (grread t)))**   And start moving the cursor.
                                                 It prints a continuous stream until cancelled.

```
(5 (3.1 2.8 0.0))(5 (3.1 2.8 0.0))(5 (3.1 2.7 0.0))(5 (3.1 1.9 0.0))(5 (3.1 1.7
0.0))(5 (3.5 1.6 0.0))(5 (4.2 1.6 0.0))(5 (4.7 1.6 0.0))(5 (5.1 2.3 0.0))(5 (5.2 3.2
0.0))(5 (5.2 4.4 0.0))(5 (5.1 5.2 0.0))(5 (4.0 5.6 0.0))(5 (3.5 5.6 0.0))(5 (2.7 5.5
0.0))(5 (2.6 5.1 0.0))(5 (2.6 4.7 0.0))(5 (2.7 3.8 0.0))(5 (2.7 3.5 0.0))(5 (2.9 3.1
0.0))(5 (3.4 3.0 0.0))
```
Lisp returns: error: console break

To use continuous tracking, you need a WHILE loop with GRREAD as the test condition and the task as part of the loop. The DDRAW program which follows applies this technique to track the digitizer coordinates and automatically rotate the snap angle to draw at preset angles.

Applying GRREAD Tracking to DDRAW

The line command, C:DDRAW, uses GRREAD to filter digitizer input to automate drawing lines at preset angles. It acts like an extension of ortho, locking lines to 22.5 degree angular offsets as an angular snap. A compass icon is displayed at each point to assist in selecting the angle for the next line. DDRAW switches the snap rotation angle based on the closest increment to the rubber-banded line.

DDRAW relies on a subroutine called STRIP, a simple support function like DXF. STRIP removes a DXF association group sublist from the entity data list and returns the modified group.

DDRAW's use of a simple block compass as a visual aid is an example of using an alternative to GRDRAW. The icon is quickly popped around the drawing by ENTMOD.

```
;* C:DDRAW automates drawing line segments at specific angles,
;* acting like a 22.5 degree ortho, or angular snap. It requires
;* DXF and the user GET functions to be loaded, and the following STRIP.
;* It requires the COMPASS.DWG block.
;*
❶
;* STRIP returns the entity data list DATA with the assoc. data group specified
;* by CODE stripped from the entity data list.
(defun strip (code data)
  (cdr                         ;remove duplicate 1st group and return rest
    (subst (car data)          ;substitute (duplicate) 1st group
           (assoc code data)   ;for group specified by CODE
           data                ;in the DATA list
  ) )
```

Listing continued.

Continued listing.

```
);defun
;*
(defun C:DDRAW ( / prmpt anginc maxd pt1 esub more inside gd ang d1 pt2)
  (setq prmpt "\nQuit, RETURN to reset angle, or enter length." ;one-time prompt
❷
        anginc 0.392699                                 ;angle increment
        maxd (* (getvar "VIEWSIZE") 0.15)               ;symbol height & max
        pt1 (upoint 1 "" "Starting point" nil nil)      ;critical distance
  );setq
  (command "insert" "compass" pt1 maxd "" 0.0 "line" pt1) ;puts in compass, starts line
❸
  (setq esub (strip 10 (entget (entlast))))           ;strips ent data list of insert point
  (setvar "ORTHOMODE" 0)                              ;turn off ortho mode
  (setq more T)
❹
  (while more                                          ;loop
    (setq inside T)                                    ;inside of compass flag
    (prompt "Drag to angle: ")
                                ;get the dynamic rotation angle...
    (while inside               ;loops until flag is nil
      (setq gd (grread t))      ;samples coordinates
      (if (= (car gd) 5)        ;if a real sampling (not a key press...)
        (if (> (distance pt1 (cadr gd)) maxd) ;if outside calc circle distance
            (setq inside nil)                 ;set flag to nil to kill while
        )
      );if=
    );while-inside
❺
                                ;set up for the new angle, calc the angle...
    (setq ang                   ;constant increment
        (* (fix (+ (/ (angle pt1 (cadr gd)) anginc) (/ anginc 2.0))) anginc)
    )
    (setvar "SNAPANG" ang)      ;change rotation angle, specific angle list
    (setvar "SNAPBASE"                                 ;reset base point
        (list (car pt1) (cadr pt1))                    ;convert to 2D point
    )
    (setvar "ORTHOMODE" 1)      ;turn on ortho mode
                                ;get line length, draw it and move compass symbol
    (if prmpt (progn (prompt prmpt) (setq prmpt nil)))  ;issue one-time prompt
```

Listing continued.

Continued listing.

```
     (setq d1 (udist 0 "Q" "Q/RETURN/<length>" nil pt1)) ;find out the length
     (cond
❻

       ((numberp d1)                                      ;cond1 see if it's nil
          (setq pt2 (polar pt1 ang d1))                   ;calc the new point
❼

          (entmod (append esub (list (cons 10 pt2))))     ;changes compass
          (entupd (entlast))                              ;redraw last line
          (command (setq pt1 pt2))                        ;pass point to line command
        );cond1
        ((= d1 "Q")                                       ;cond2 finish and quit
          (command "" "snap" "r" "0,0" "0"                ;end line, restore snap
                 "erase" (ssget "X" '((2 . "COMPASS"))) "" ;erase COMPASS
          )
          (setq more nil inside nil)                      ;set flags nil to kill whiles
        );cond2
      );cond
      (setvar "ORTHOMODE" 0)                              ;turn off the ortho
    );while-more
   (princ)
);defun
;*
```

STRIP Function and C:DDRAW Command in DDRAW.LSP File

❶ STRIP is used to remove a single DXF group and return the rest of the list. It uses SUBST to replace the specified group with a duplicate of the first DXF group in the list. Then CDR returns all but the duplicated part of the original group.

❷ The main C:DDRAW command function starts out by setting the angular resolution. In this case, it is 22.5 degrees. You could use a global variable to control it, and allow other angles. DDRAW calculates a percentage of the screen height and uses the number to scale the compass symbol. It inserts the symbol at the first point selected and waits for the crosshairs to be moved outside of the compass boundary.

❹ Two WHILE loops are set up. The MORE loop keeps the command running and the INSIDE loop allows sampling and point selection to alternate. In the INSIDE loop, the GRREAD-tracked value is compared to the center point of the compass. The loop continues until the distance has been exceeded, then the program switches the snap rotation angle and prompts for a point to be entered.

❺ The snap angle, snap base, and ortho modes are adjusted for the new direction. A length of line is requested, but you can hit a <RETURN> to reset the angle or enter Q to "Quit." No matter how you enter a length, the line is drawn in the direction of the selected rotation angle.

❻ The ENTMOD and ENTUPD functions move the compass. If you compare this technique to the MOVE command, you'll see that it's amazingly swift. It circumvents the selection set operations of AutoCAD and regenerates the entity in a different place.

❸ ❼ DDRAW uses STRIP to remove the 10 DXF code group, the insertion base point of the compass symbol. Each time a point is picked, the function APPENDs a revised insertion base point and ENTMODs it to move the compass symbol.

The compass is shown in the Drawing Compass illustration. If you have the IL DISK, you have the COMPASS drawing. Otherwise, draw a compass as illustrated and WBLOCK it, base point at center, to COMPASS.DWG.

Let's look at the DDRAW command in action. The compass icon and DDRAW's operation are illustrated in the following.

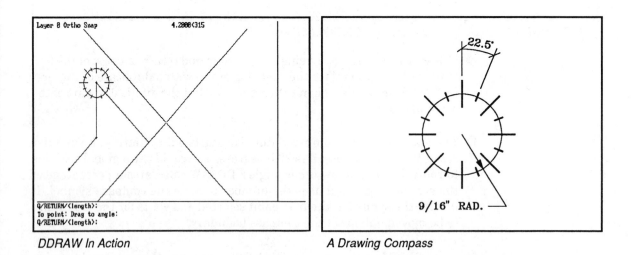

DDRAW In Action   *A Drawing Compass*

Using the DDRAW Command

Enter selection: **1**   Begin a NEW drawing again named IL09.

You have STRIP and C:DDRAW in your DDRAW.LSP file. You need not create the COMPASS block.

Create STRIP and C:DDRAW in a new file named DDRAW.LSP. Create the COMPASS block as illustrated.

Command: **CIRCLE LINE LINE ARRAY**   Draw the compass as illustrated.
Command: **WBLOCK**   Wblock it to COMPASS, insert base at center.

Command: **(load "ddraw")**   Load the file.

Command: **DDRAW**   Test it.
Starting point: Select a point.
                                    The COMPASS icon goes in at the point.
Command: line From point:
To point: Drag to angle: Drag the line in the direction desired.
                                    At a certain distance, it locks the angle.
Quit, RETURN to reset angle, or enter length.   A one-time prompt.
Q/<RETURN>/<length>:   Pick or enter a distance.
To point: Drag to angle: Drag it.
Q/<RETURN>/<length>:   Move the cursor and enter a <RETURN> to reset the angle.
To point: Drag to angle: It resets.
                                    Enter a few more points, then quit.
Q/<RETURN>/<length>: **Q**   Q to Quit, and the COMPASS erases.

Command: **QUIT**

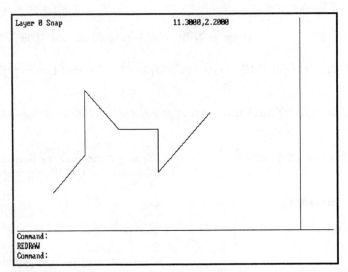

```
Layer 0 Snap                    11.3000,2.2000
```

```
Command:
REDRAW
Command:
```

DDRAW Completed

If you'd rather have DDRAW draw polylines, you can change the sixth line of the COMMAND function from "line" to "pline," or you can add code to present a "Line/Pline:" choice. You can change the preset angle increments by plugging in a different angle for ANGINC or by using a global variable. For example, a 30-degree increment is perfect for isometrics.

Using DDRAW smoothly takes practice. It's a little like walking a tightrope. Don't look down at the compass, focus on where you're going. It's a good tool for precision at fixed angles. Normally, when you try to draw even-unit lengths at non-ortho angles, the cursor snaps to even X and even Y units, leaving the angular length at an odd increment. DDRAW lets you enter a length, or use the coords readout at the current units setting, to draw even-unit lengths. It moves and rotates the snap and ortho angle relative to the last point and current angle, so snap is precise for the current line.

Summary

GRTEXT, GRDRAW, and GRREAD give you flexibility and control over the user interface of your programs. Feel free to use GRTEXT and GRDRAW to provide your programs with text prompts, status labels, and graphic screen prompts. They're easy to use. Programming with GRREAD is a little trickier. But when a program needs single character input (without a <RETURN>) or needs to continuously drag a line or object, GRREAD is the solution.

You can't use ANSI formatting codes in GRTEXT strings, but you can highlight. Just follow the rules to ensure that the highlighting in your programs will work on all systems regardless of the type of video display. Remember to control your various status line, coords system variables, and menu page change access in programs that use these areas to display GRTEXT. If you don't, user commands, toggles, and menu picks can wipe out your GRTEXT.

Use GRDRAW for simple temporary lines. It doesn't clutter up the drawing database with new entities. Use it for graphics marks like lines around a selection set or for making a temporary grid. Remember, you can obscure real lines as well as draw fake lines with GRDRAW.

GRREAD is currently the only way to get single character input. It's good for Yes/No input that doesn't need a <RETURN>. It is a good candidate for writing tutorial programs with direct access. However, for normal programs and C:commands, its use might be confusing. Users are accustomed to input requiring a <RETURN>, so single-character input could tend to cause input errors.

You can add to the ETEXT program to make a full, multi-line text editor. You have the core tools.

Remember, there are alternatives to GRDRAW for complex images. You can use ENTDEL to toggle the visibility of a block or other entity on and off. You can use entity data list modification and ENTUPD to move entities around the drawing. You can use SSGET X to delete these temporary entities before saving or plotting.

This completes our tour through the basics of AutoLISP. The next section expands upon these fundamental tools to provide a set of advanced AutoLISP applications. These advanced applications use many of the functions, subroutines, and techniques in the previous chapters. You will develop many more techniques in the following chapters. By the end of the book, we will have covered every AutoLISP function.

At this point, we're going to shift gears a little. We've covered most of the AutoLISP functions and programming concepts. The following chapters are dedicated to developing mini-applications, from which you can learn by example. We'll make explanations a bit less extensive to allow room for development of what we think are some interesting techniques and applications.

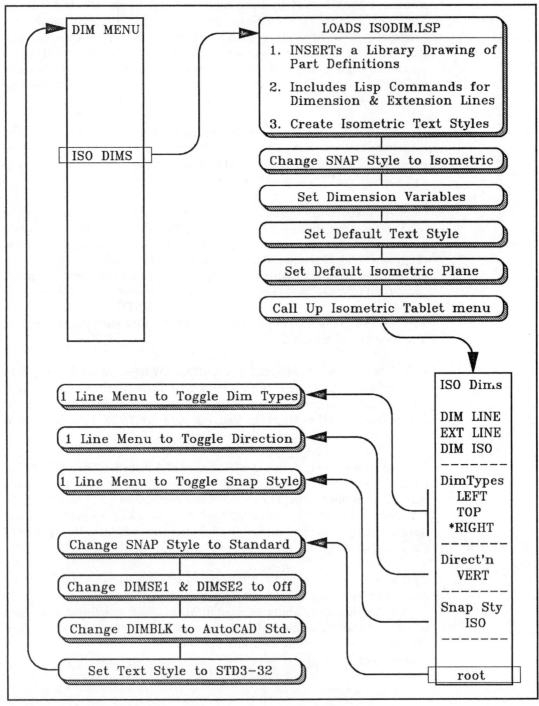

The ISO Dimensioning System

CHAPTER 10

AutoLISP and MENUS

AN ISO DIMENSIONING SYSTEM

To be effective, your AutoLISP programs and command functions have to be accessible. The C: commands are readily executed from the keyboard, if they have been loaded. But how do they get loaded when needed, and how do you easily get at the rest of your functions? Use AutoCAD's friendly, customizable menus. The topic of customizing menus is the subject of an *entire* book from New Riders, CUSTOMIZING AutoCAD. The emphasis of this chapter is on integrating AutoLISP with AutoCAD menus. We assume you already have a general understanding of menu writing, either from CUSTOMIZING AutoCAD, the customization chapters of INSIDE AutoCAD, or from practical experience. We also assume that you have a basic knowledge of AutoCAD's dimensioning commands. Many of the macros we'll develop use dimensioning system variables. These variables are listed in the AutoCAD System Variables Table in Appendix C.

Customized menu systems benefit from the brawn of AutoLISP, and AutoLISP benefits from the controlled, organized user interface of menus to channel its power. Menus provide several key advantages. Menu macros can set global AutoLISP and system variables that govern the operation of your programs. Menu labels can be used to provide instant access to program options, control input to avoid typing errors, and display current program status in a more stable manner than through the GRTEXT function.

This chapter starts with a review of menu codes and menu structure. Then we'll cover several techniques for setting variables, displaying status, controlling program environment, and accessing commands. In the second half of the chapter, we'll apply these techniques to building a complete iso dimensioning system (we'll call it *iso dim* for short) that exemplifies the integrated AutoLISP/menu interface. We'll create customized screen menus to give status information that helps you navigate your iso dim system and keeps you informed of the current command settings. The iso dim system also shows how to solve your own dimensioning problems when AutoCAD's default dimensioning system comes up short.

Even if you have no use for isometrics, you can apply the techniques developed in this system to nearly every application menu you develop.

In this chapter, you will learn how to:

■ Use AutoLISP to create intelligent macros. Through macros, build informative prompts showing defaults and current values.

■ Make isometric symbols, dimensioning blocks, text styles, and commands that work in AutoCAD's isoplanes.

■ Use point-of-menu-entry page control to set up the drawing environment for specific applications menus.

■ Use an AutoLISP file load to set up and initialize an application environment.

Menus, AutoLISP Tools, and Programs

Menus

IL10.MNU is a test menu for experimenting with menu and AutoLISP-menu techniques. It includes several status-displaying and toggling items.

ISODIM.MNU includes the following:

**ISO is the main isometric dimensioning page of the isometric menu system. Portions of it get overlaid by an integrated set of small screen menu toggle pages. The ISODIM.LSP functions are required for this menu page.

**TISO-*x* is a set of isometric TABLET1 menu sections that are included on the New Riders AutoLISP Utilities Disk 1's ISODIM.MNU menu file. Selections made from the tablet are displayed on the screen menu status labels. The ISODIM.LSP functions are required for this tablet menu.

AutoLISP Tools

C:DIMLINE is an AutoLISP command function that draws an isometric dimension line, arrows, and text.

C:EXTLINE is an AutoLISP command function that draws isometric extension lines.

Programs

ISODIM.LSP is the program file containing the two isometric dimensioning AutoLISP commands above and a set of initialization expressions. The ISODIM program integrates the isometric menu page system with the ISODIM.LSP file.

Reviewing Macros and Menus

Let's start with a quick refresher on macros and menus. A *macro* is a series of AutoCAD commands and parameters put together to perform a task. Macros are found in *menu* files. A menu file is an ASCII text file listing the macros for each box of the screen, tablet, buttons, pull-down, and icon menus. Macros use several special characters in addition to AutoCAD commands and LISP expressions. These characters help control macros, issue AutoCAD setting toggles, switch menu pages, and pause for input. The following table lists the special menu characters.

SPECIAL MENU CHARACTERS			
\	Pauses for input	;	Issues RETURN
+	Continues to next line	[]	Encloses label
*	Autorepeats, or marks page	^B	Toggles SNAP
^D	Toggles COORDS	^E	Toggles ISOPLANE
^G	Toggles GRID	^H	Issues BACKSPACE
^C	*Cancel*	^O	Toggles ORTHO
^P	Toggles MENUECHO	^Q	Toggles Printer Echo
^T	Toggles Tablet	^M	Issues RETURN
^X	*Delete* input in buffer	<SPACE>	
^Z	Suppresses automatic SPACE at end of line		

Special Menu Characters

➡ *NOTE: The <SPACE> is not actually a special character. It acts the same whether in a menu or typed at the AutoCAD command line. However, we list it above because the menu interpreter automatically adds a space at the end of each line, unless the line already ends with a space or other special character. The @ (lastpoint) is another character that is commonly used in menus because AutoCAD treats it as a command key word for the last or relative point.*

You control what is displayed on the menu items screen box by putting macro labels in [SQUARE BRACKETS]. Only eight characters display on the typical screen menu. Up to 80 characters can display on pull-down menus. Labels can include letters, numbers, and any displayable character. Labels on pull-down menus can be grayed out.

How to Define Pages of Macros

AutoCAD's menus work with *pages* of macros and commands. A menu page is simply a group of macros that follows a given page name. AutoCAD uses this name to find and activate the menu macros as a set.

You can break menus into named pages of commands and macros by labeling each page with a unique name. Distinguish this page name from other lines of the menu by two leading asterisks. The format is **name, where *name* is any name you like.

To control where they are displayed and accessed, menu pages are directed to devices. Each device has a unique name identified by the three consecutive asterisks preceding it, like ***SCREEN.

The devices available to you are: SCREEN, TABLET, BUTTONS, PULL-DOWN, ICON, and AUXiliary. By default, if the menu has no device sections defined, a menu page is displayed and accessed on the tablet, buttons, *and* screen devices. This is useful for testing, and for quick and dirty one-page menus. But normally you design and structure your menus to use specific devices for specific types of macros. You send pages to specific menu devices with the $*xx* code, where *xx* designates the device. For example, $S=*name* sends the page named *name* to the screen menu. The pull-down and icon devices must be defined to be accessed. Each device has a unique code:

CODE	ACTION
$S=	Screen menus
$P1= thru $P10=	Pull-down screen menus 1 thru 10
$B=	Buttons menu
$T1= thru $T4=	Tablet areas 1 thru 4
$I=	Icon menus
$A1=	Aux Box 1

Menu Device Codes

See INSIDE AutoCAD or CUSTOMIZING AutoCAD for a complete discussion of menu pages and devices. In this chapter, we will just consider the screen and tablet, but the AutoLISP-menu and menu toggling techniques we cover apply to all devices.

Designing Clean Menu Macros

Let's explore some macros types and evolve them into menu toggling items. A menu toggle is one or more menu items within a page that flips back and forth when selected, without changing the entire page. A typical toggle would be an on and off setting that displays [ON] when it is on and [OFF] when it is off. When the label changes, so does the menu code behind it.

The AutoCAD system variables are perfectly suited for menu toggles. There are many system variables to control in routine drawing, like the dimensioning variables, and the HIGHLIGHT and REGENAUTO variables. Yet these are not easily accessible, and can't be simply toggled on and off by a command. Bringing system variables into the menu system allows ready access and toggling. Set them up so their labels remind you of their status. Let's examine a typical macro with the dimension variable, DIMSE1, that changes the suppression of the first extension line. DIMSE1 on (1) means *suppression is on* and the extension line is not drawn. DIMSE1 on 0 (the default) means *suppression is off* so lines are drawn.

```
[DIMSE1    ]'SETVAR DIMSE1
```

This macro is nothing more than what you would type from the command line, plus a label in square brackets. But to use it, you need to know what DIMSE1 is, and what to use as settings for on and off. Its ease of use can be improved by making it into two macros, one for on and the other for off. It also helps to label each one.

```
[Draw 1st]'SETVAR DIMSE1 0
[Omit 1st]'SETVAR DIMSE1 1
```

This method is more informative, but requires two lines and does not tell you which line is currently set. It still leaves you guessing whether DIMSE1 is on or off.

How to Prompt in Menus

Let's improve on these macros by having them prompt with the current setting after a selection is made. Try this in an AutoCAD test menu. Then in the next few exercises, you'll develop it into a toggling macro that always keeps you informed and uses only one box on the screen menu.

Using a Prompt in Menus

```
Enter selection: 1              Begin a NEW drawing named IL10.

Command: SHELL                  Create a new file called TEST.MNU with your text editor.
                                Put the following text in the menu file.
```

```
***SCREEN
[Omit 1st]'SETVAR DIMSE1 1 +
(prompt "First ext line will be omitted.")
```

Save the file and return to AutoCAD.

```
Command: MENU                                   Load the TEST menu.

Select [Omit 1st]                               It executes the SETVAR command.
Command: 'SETVAR Variable name or ?: DIMSE1
New value for DIMSE1 <1>: 1
Command: (prompt "First ext line will be omitted.") First ext line will be omitted.nil
```

You can try drawing a dimension to confirm the setting.

The macro works fine. But it doesn't display the prompt very cleanly, and you don't really need to see the SETVAR command dialogue or AutoLISP PROMPT expressions. With a few tricks, we can tidy it up some more.

➡ *NOTE: Menu writing is similar to LISP file writing, except every character counts. Don't use tabs. Count all spaces and semicolons carefully. Use semicolons for multiple spaces. Don't use any trailing spaces that you can't see to count — use semicolons instead. Use a space, not a semicolon, after a page call like $S=PAGE nextcommand, not $S=PAGE;nextcommand. Watch out for spaces following plus continuation characters.*

How to Clean Up Menu Output

All we really want to see is the prompt. We need to get rid of the nil it returns, stop the display of the PROMPT expression itself, and stop the display of the SETVAR command. First, let's suppress the display of the AutoLISP expression.

One step in cleaning up menu output is to use the MENUECHO system variable. Several of its settings suppress some or all of AutoCAD's menu macro display. Macros are still executed the same, only cleaner.

```
                        MENUECHO SETTINGS
    Setting     Suppresses
      0         Nothing is suppressed. This is the default
      1         All menu item output (the characters in the menu)
      2         All system and command prompts from menu items
      4         Disables ^P toggling of suppression modes
```

These modes are not saved, so every new drawing starts with a setting of zero. The best methods for setting this control are in your ACAD.LSP file, in a LISP function load, or in a menu setup macro. The modes can be combined, for settings of 3, 5, 6, and 7. You can temporarily turn suppression modes off and on by nesting parts or all of a macro in a pair of ^P's (entered as a caret and a P). For example, if MENUECHO is 1:

```
[MACRO]this-is-suppressed^Pthis-echoes^Pthis-is-suppressed
```

If MENUECHO is set to 0, a ^P toggles it to mode 1 until another ^P is encountered. These ^P toggles are temporary, in a single menu item only. To prevent menus from using ^P toggling, you can set a mode of 4. This is often done by developers selling encrypted AutoLISP programs with compiled menus that they don't want users or competitors to decipher.

Set MENUECHO to 1 and retry the [Omit 1st] macro.

Suppressing Menu Echos

Continue in the previous drawing.

```
Command: SETVAR                        Set MENUECHO to 1.

Select [Omit 1st]
Command: Variable name or ? <MENUECHO>:
New value for DIMSE1 <1>:
Command: First ext line will be omitted.nil

Command: SETVAR                        Set MENUECHO to 3.
Select [Omit 1st]                      Only the prompt appears.
Command: First ext line will be omitted.nil
```

With mode 1, all the prompts still appear, but the menu item characters (commands, input, and expressions) are suppressed. With mode 3 (1+2), the prompts that AutoCAD returns during its normal command are suppressed. Mode 2 (or 3) can be a problem in a simple menu item like [1 Line]*^C^C^CLINE \\; where it suppresses the normal command prompts. You see only a blank command line with no indication of what to do. With a little help from AutoLISP, you can use mode 1 to solve the conflict between clean macros and simple macros.

How to Make Clean Macros With AutoLISP

You've used PROGN and PRINC to form clean displays in your programs. You can use them in macros to get rid of the nil that AutoLISP returns. Making a menu macro from a single AutoLISP expression gives you the control to suppress extra backtalk without resorting to MENUECHO mode 3. The CMDECHO system variable suppresses all COMMAND function output during the AutoLISP expression. If CMDECHO is set to 1 (the default), commands generated by a COMMAND function and their prompts are displayed normally. But if CMDECHO is set to 0, they are suppressed. Note that 0 and 1 in CMDECHO are the opposite of the similar MENUECHO.

Rewrite the [Omit 1st] macro entirely with AutoLISP. Use the COMMAND function instead of the more efficient SETVAR function to see how CMDECHO works. PROGN keeps the entire set of LISP expressions together as one program. PRINC returns a silent value at the end of the PROGN function. Try it with MENUECHO 1 and CMDECHO 0.

Using PROGN and PRINC to Suppress Nil in Macros

Continue in the previous drawing.

Command: **SHELL**   Edit the TEST.MNU file, changing the [Omit 1st] macro to:

```
***SCREEN
[Omit 1st ](progn (command "SETVAR" "DIMSE1" 1) +
(prompt "First ext line will be omitted.") (princ))
```

Save and return to AutoCAD.

Command: **MENU**   Reload the TEST menu.

Command: **SETVAR**   Make sure MENUECHO is set to 1.

Select **[Omit 1st]**
Command: 'SETVAR Variable name or ? <MENUECHO>: DIMSE1
New value for DIMSE1 <1>: 1   The commands and their prompts echo.
Command: First ext line will be omitted.   But PRINC cleaned up the nil.

Command: **SETVAR**   Set CMDECHO to 0 to suppress commands and their prompts.

Select **[Omit 1st]**
Command: First ext line will be omitted.   Perfectly clean.

Notice how cleanly the macro performs with CMDECHO 0 and MENUECHO 1. This is how your macros should look. This combination of complex but clean macros and simple macros like [1 Line] takes advantage of normal command prompts. When you want commands and their prompts suppressed, put them in a COMMAND function. When you want them displayed, just make them normal menu commands.

Now that we have clean macros, let's see how we can create informative menu labels, and use a single screen menu box toggle to perform both the [Omit 1st] and [Draw 1st] macros.

Making Menu Toggles

To create menu toggles, you create each item of a pair as a single item menu page with its own page label. Each item of the pair calls the other item to replace itself on the screen menu. Use this to create menu toggles where two macros share a single screen box and the visible label indicates the current setting. Let's edit TEST.MNU to test the principles of menu toggling. Create two menu pages as shown below and try them out in AutoCAD.

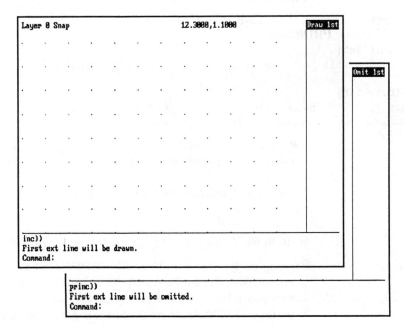

Menu toggles Change Labels

> ➡ *NOTE: Notice that we changed the sense of the [Omit 1st] label. Now each screen label shows the current setting, but the code behind it sets the opposite setting. The page name codes the current system variable value, like DIMSE1-1 for suppression on. This is confusing when writing the menu, but clear and easy to use.*

Creating Menu Toggles

Continue in the previous drawing, or begin a NEW drawing again named IL10.

Command: **SHELL**   Create or edit the TEST.MNU file to be:

```
***SCREEN
**DIMSE1-1
[Omit 1st ](progn (setvar "DIMSE1" 0) +
(prompt "First ext line will be drawn.") (princ));$S=DIMSE1-0
**DIMSE1-0
[Draw 1st](progn (setvar "DIMSE1" 1) +
(prompt "First ext line will be omitted.") (princ));$S=DIMSE1-1
```

Save and return to AutoCAD.

Command: **MENU**   Load the TEST menu.

Select **[Omit 1st]**
First ext line will be drawn.   The label changes to [Draw 1st].

Select **[Draw 1st]**
First ext line will be omitted.   And the label becomes [Omit 1st].

The technique of having one macro change a setting and than overlay itself with its opposite macro twin is the basis of menu toggling.

To use this effectively, you need to control which screen menu box will be used.

How to Build Sets of Dynamic Menu Toggles

You can assign line numbers, like **DIMSE1-1 **2**, to menu page labels in the menu file. The **2** tells AutoCAD to load the page starting at the second screen menu box rather than the first. (Note that menu lines count from 1, while GRTEXT starts at 0.) Since a page may be as short as a single item, you can load a single menu item anywhere on the screen menu. We call these *mini-pages*. For example, if **DIMSE1-1 3 was a single item page, $S=DIMSE1-ON would load it on the third screen line. The first, second, fourth, and following screen menu lines would be unchanged.

Plan your page name line numbers to control where macros are positioned on the screen menu. All pages for each option are assigned to the same menu line number. These numbers are carefully planned to overlap each other and present the options in the menu labels.

The best way to include these mini-page toggles on a menu page is to dynamically construct their screen menu page with a single menu item that loads them all. The following program listing shows a sample menu with two sets of toggles and a root menu call that loads them. Only the default (first) menu page in the ***SCREEN section will display when a menu is loaded. It will first display in screen box 1, regardless of the page line number. To control a series of mini-page toggles, you need to call them from a master menu item or from a LISP program. AutoLISP can call menu pages with the MENUCMD function.

`menucmd` — *Loads and displays the menu page specified by the string. The string must include the menu device code and the page name, like "S=NAME" for the screen device page named NAME.*
(menucmd *string*)

The following menu applies MENUCMD in a FOREACH loop in the [DIMS] macro.

```
***SCREEN
**ROOT
[]
[]
[  DIMS  ]$S=DIMS (progn (setvar "CMDECHO" 0) (setvar "MENUECHO" 1) +
(foreach page '("DIMSE1" "DIMSE2") (menucmd (strcat "S=" page "-" +
(if (numberp (setq var (getvar page))) (itoa var) var)))) (princ));
[]
[]
[]
+
**DIMS
[ExtLines]
[]
[]
[--------]
[]
[  Root  ]$S=ROOT
+
```

Listing continued.

Continued listing.

```
**DIMSE1-1 2
[Omit 1st ](progn (setvar "DIMSE1" 0) +
(prompt "First ext line will be drawn.") (princ));$S=DIMSE1-0
**DIMSE1-0 2
[Draw 1st](progn (setvar "DIMSE1" 1) +
(prompt "First ext line will be omitted.") (princ));$S=DIMSE1-1
**DIMSE2-1 3
[Omit 2nd](progn (setvar "DIMSE2" 0) +
(prompt "Second ext line will be drawn.") (princ));$S=DIMSE2-0
**DIMSE2-0 3
[Draw 2nd](progn (setvar "DIMSE2" 1) +
(prompt "Second ext line will be omitted.") (princ));$S=DIMSE2-1
```

DIMVAR Toggles in IL10DIM.MNU

For the toggle items to overlay, the [DIMS] item first loads an underlying page named **DIMS. The toggle menu page names have been carefully planned so that AutoLISP can load multiple toggle pages with one statement. Although this menu has only two sets of toggles, the FOREACH technique in [DIMS] can load any number of pages defined in its list. Each menu page name must be formatted like **sysvar-val* where *sysvar* is the system variable name and *val* is its current value. The system variable must have a string or integer value. Since each page is defined for a unique line, the toggle item falls on the underlying page at the correct line. The STRCAT function builds the page name. The name is then passed to MENUCMD, which calls the page to the screen.

The [DIMS] page call is what we call a *point of entry* into a submenu. We use such page call items for point-of-entry control. In this case, it sets MENUECHO and CMDECHO. The toggle items themselves work as before, except they now have specific line numbers following their page names. Let's see the menu in action.

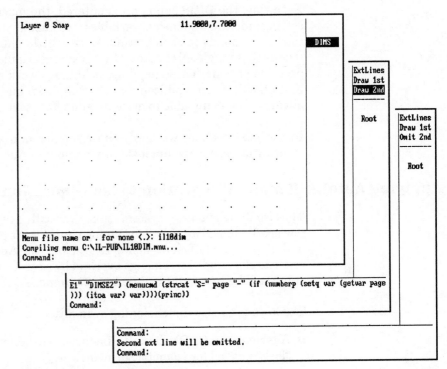

DIMS, and [Draw 2nd] Toggled

Add the [DIMS] menu-building macro and the supporting page menus.

Assembling Toggle Pages

Continue in the previous drawing, or begin a NEW drawing again named IL10.

 You have the IL10DIM.MNU file.

Create the IL10DIM.MNU file as shown above.

Command: **MENU**	Load the IL10DIM menu.
Select **[DIMS]**	See how quickly the menu builds itself.
Select **[Draw 2nd]** Second ext line will be omitted.	Label changes to [Omit 2nd].
Select **[Root]** then **[DIMS]**	Label is still [Omit 2nd].

Each time the DIMS submenu is entered, the macro checks the current settings for the dimension variables and displays the mini-page macro that corresponds to each setting. With a little planning, you can create menus that toggle all the AutoCAD system variables as well as your own program options. These toggling techniques work equally well in tablet, button, pull-down, and icon menus. Pull-down and icon menus have the advantage of being able to accommodate long text or graphic prompts.

In the next section, we apply these toggles and similar techniques to creating an isometric dimensioning menu and AutoLISP system.

Applying AutoLISP-Menu Integration to Iso Dimensioning

The iso-dimensioning system that we will develop is compact yet powerful. It uses AutoLISP to enhance AutoCAD's dimensioning features and it uses an efficient menu to control the AutoLISP functions. It consists of a single screen page overlaid by several mini-page toggles and supported by two AutoLISP-defined commands.

The keys to the iso dimensioning system are:

- Altering AutoCAD's default dimension variables settings to give the "look" needed for isometric drawings.

- Using the SNAP command to set isometric snap and grid modes.

- Creating and toggling special text styles and dimension arrow blocks to the current isoplane.

- Using AutoLISP routines to help draw extension lines, dimension lines, and text.

- Placing controls, settings, and modes on a dynamic screen menu.

The iso screen menu is a good example of how to use menu label toggling in an application. The screen menu uses several small screen pages to show you the current iso dim type, dimensioning direction, and snap mode.

How to Make Iso Dim Text Styles and Symbols

Isometric text and symbols must be skewed to the isometric planes. AutoCAD works in top, left, and right isoplanes. You need alignment symbols for these planes, however you won't need a separate style and symbol for each plane. You only need to create symbols for the left and right planes, because the top plane uses the left or the right symbol and text, depending on which side of the face you are dimensioning.

You also need two special text styles slanted left and right. You distort the text by applying an obliquing angle to the text font with the STYLE command. The styles are automatically defined with a COMMAND function in the ISODIM.LSP file. COMMAND will set them with a fixed height, adjusted to the #DWGSC, when it loads. Recall that we use #DWGSC as a global drawing-to-plot scale variable. It gets set to DIMSCALE by our ACAD.LSP file. Here are the text styles:

NAME	FONT	ANGLE	HEIGHT
DIM-R	ROMANS	-30	(* 0.125 #dwgsc)
DIM-L	ROMANS	30	(* 0.125 #dwgsc)

The following illustration shows which styles and dimension arrows are used in which isoplanes.

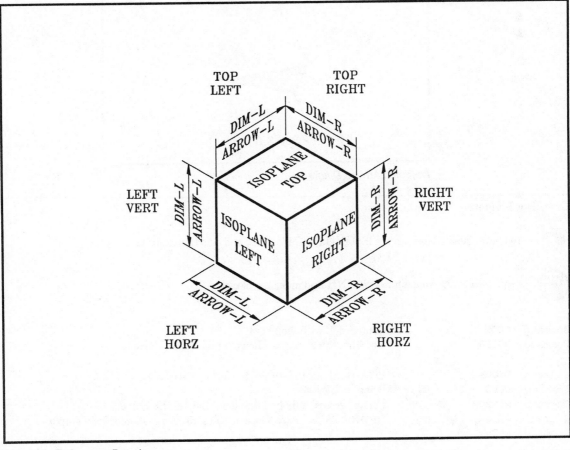

Isometric Reference Drawing

Let's take a look at the arrow dimensioning blocks we'll need.

If you have the IL DISK, you already have arrow blocks in the ISO-INIT.DWG. If not, you'll need to create them. The arrows are shown in the Isometric Arrows Diagram illustration. Use SOLID to draw an isometric arrow. WBLOCK the first arrow. OOPS it back. Then MIRROR it to make the second arrow. We'll tell AutoCAD to use the custom dimension block arrow with the DIMBLK system variable.

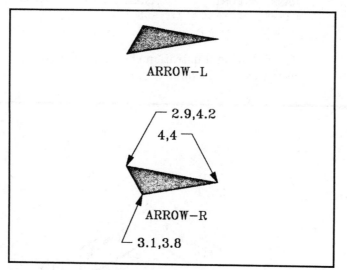

Isometric Arrows Diagram

Creating Isometric Symbols

You have the dim blocks in the ISO-INIT.DWG file. Read and skip this exercise.

Begin a NEW drawing named ISO-INIT and make the blocks.

Command: **ZOOM**	Center 4,4 with height 4.
Command: **SOLID**	Use the three points shown and <RETURN>.
Command: **BLOCK**	Base point at the tip, 4,4. Name ARROW-R.
Command: **OOPS**	Bring it back.
Command: **MIRROR**	Mirror across a horizontal line. Delete the old one.
Command: **BLOCK**	To ARROW-L. Don't Oops it. The drawing should look empty.
Command: **END**	

Now, let's examine the supporting AutoLISP iso dim functions.

Creating the Iso Dim Functions

ISODIM.LSP contains two functions: C:DIMLINE and C:EXTLINE. DIMLINE feeds the dimension points and text to the ALIGNED dimension command to generate dimension lines. DIMLINE controls alignment by restricting input to picked points. AutoCAD does not automatically align dimensions for the isometric planes. AutoCAD's dimensioning doesn't understand snap, style, or rotation. So the EXTLINE command function gets its own points and uses the LINE command to draw iso extension lines. Together, DIMLINE and EXTLINE work similarly to AutoCAD's ALIGNED dimension command.

```
;* ISODIM.LSP is a set of functions to draw isometric dimensions in coordination
;* with an isometric screen (and optional tablet) menu system.
;*
;* C:DIMLINE draws an isometric dimension line between two points.
;* It uses AutoCAD's dimensioning functions so that all DIM Variables will
;* affect the isometric dimension the same way.
(defun C:DIMLINE ( / sp ep distxt)
  (setq sp (upoint 1 "" "Pick first dim. point" nil nil)     ;get first point
        ep (upoint 1 "" "Pick second dim. point" nil sp)     ;get second point
        distxt (rtos (distance sp ep))                       ;get dist & convert to string
❶
        distxt (ustr 0 "Dimension text" distxt T)            ;verify text string
  );setq
❷
  (command "DIM1" "ALIGNED" "NON" sp "NON" ep "NON" ep distxt)  ;draw dimension
  (princ)
);defun
;*
❸
;* C:EXTLINE draws a dimension extension line similar to
;* the one AutoCAD draws using DIMEXO, DIMEXE, and DIMSCALE variables
(defun C:EXTLINE ( / sp ep)
  (setq sp (upoint 1 "" "Starting point of Ext. line" nil nil)   ;start of ext. line
        ep (upoint 1 "" "Ending point" nil sp)                   ;end extension line
  );setq
  (command "LINE"                                                ;start line command
    "NON" (polar sp (angle sp ep) (* (getvar "DIMEXO") (getvar "DIMSCALE")));line offset
    "NON" (polar ep (angle sp ep) (* (getvar "DIMEXE") (getvar "DIMSCALE")));line ext'n
```

Listing continued.

Continued listing.

```
  "")                                                     ;terminate line
  (princ)
);defun
;*
❹
;* This automatically inserts an "empty" block carrying the dimension arrow definitions.
;* The insert command is cancelled just after the definitions are added to the
;* block symbol table. An "insert" entity is not created. Text Styles are defined and
scaled.
;* The command sequence is executed upon the initial function load.
(command "INSERT" "ISO-INIT" nil
        "STYLE" "DIM-R" "ROMANS" (* 0.125 #dwgsc) "" "-30" "" "" ""
        "STYLE" "DIM-L" "ROMANS" (* 0.125 #dwgsc) "" "30" "" "" ""
)
;*
(princ)
;*end of ISODIM.LSP
;*
```

The DIMLINE Function in ISODIM.LSP File

The DIMLINE command gets two points, determines the distance between them, and uses the distance in the default prompt. After the dimension is verified, the data is passed to AutoCAD's ALIGNED dimension command to draw the line, arrows, and text.

❶ The function's distance prompt uses your USTR function, not UDIST. It lets you type a string, as in normal AutoCAD dimensioning. If you use a dim style prefix or suffix, or both, like *prefix<>suffix*, it will be passed to the dimension ALIGNED command and the calculated dimension will replace the angle brackets.

❷ The COMMAND function includes the *non* osnap filter before each point to suppress any running osnap modes. You don't want a running osnap to incorrectly snap the calculated points.

❸ The next function is the EXTLINE command. EXTLINE goes hand-in-hand with DIMLINE. Since AutoCAD's dimensioning does not recognize your iso mode, you must suppress AutoCAD's extension lines and draw extension lines with the correct orientation. The dimension variables DIMSE1 and DIMSE2 are turned on (suppressed) when you select the **ISO page from the root menu.

EXTLINE draws the extension line separately from the DIMLINE. The ISODIM menu includes a [DIM ISO] menu item that uses both commands to make isometric dimensioning seem like normal dimensioning. EXTLINE accesses several dimensioning system variables to determine the extension line length and offset defaults.

❹ You have one more COMMAND statement in the ISODIM.LSP file. It ensures that you insert the necessary block definitions in the drawing. The ISO-INIT drawing is automatically inserted by the COMMAND function during the function load. ISO-INIT has two nested arrow block definitions, but no real entities. COMMAND also sets and scales the text styles.

Let's test EXTLINE and DIMLINE.

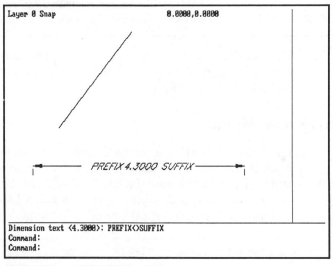

EXTLINE and DIMLINE In Action

Using EXTLINE and DIMLINE

Enter selection: **1**   Begin a NEW drawing again named IL10.

 You have the ISODIM.LSP file.

 Create the ISODIM file as shown above. You must have already created the ISO-INIT.DWG.

Command: **ZOOM**   Zoom left corner 0,0 with height 4.

```
Command: (load "ISODIM")
INSERT Block name (or ?): ISO-INIT  Insertion point:      It inserts ISO-INIT and creates
                                                          the styles.
Command: STYLE Text style name (or ?) <STD>: DIM-R       The STYLE command scrolls by.
Command: STYLE Text style name (or ?) <DIM-R>: DIM-L     And again for the left style.
DIM-L is now the current text style.

Command: EXTLINE
Starting point of Ext. line:                Pick a point.
Ending point:                               Pick a point above the first.
LINE From point: NON                        It uses the LINE command.

Command: DIMLINE
Pick first dim. point:                      Pick a point.
Pick second dim. point:                     Pick a point horizontally.
Dimension text <4.3000>: PREFIX<>SUFFIX     Our program prompt. Try a prefix and suffix.
DIM1                                        It dimensions with Dim ALIGNED.
Dimension text <4.3000>: PREFIX<>SUFFIX     The text becomes PREFIX 4.3000 SUFFIX.
```

The extension line is nothing fancy and the dimension line is probably strangely aligned, with oddly skewed text and arrows. We need the iso menu to control it all.

Making an Iso Screen Menu

The ISODIM.MNU sets up the dimension variables and snap style for iso dims. It also provides a page of toggle settings to switch between top, left, and right, and to execute the ISODIM.LSP functions. The following chart of the isoplanes, text styles, and dimension blocks for each of the six *dimtypes* (dimension types) should help simplify the screen menu.

DimType-Direction	DIMBLK	Text Style	AutoCAD Isoplane
RIGHT-VERT	ARROW-R	DIM-R	RIGHT
RIGHT-HORIZ	ARROW-R	DIM-R	TOP
LEFT-VERT	ARROW-L	DIM-L	LEFT
LEFT-HORIZ	ARROW-L	DIM-L	TOP
TOP-LEFT	ARROW-L	DIM-L	RIGHT
TOP-RIGHT	ARROW-R	DIM-R	LEFT

Iso Dimensioning Types

Our exercise's Dimtype right/left/top does not correspond to AutoCAD's standard isoplanes. Dimtype-Direction is our convention for relating the six types of iso dimensions to their positions on a standard cube. Following the DIMBLK dimension variable and the text-setting styles is easier if you remember that all dimtype-directions with *left* get ARROW-L and DIM-L, and all the *rights* get -R's. You saw this earlier in the Isometric Reference Drawing.

The menu has only one full page, **ISO, which is called by [ISO DIMS] on the root screen menu. [ISO DIMS] establishes the dimensioning environment as it calls the **ISO page. The ISODIM menu formats the drawing screen for isometric dimensioning, creates a set of toggle menus to switch isoplanes, and changes text styles and dim blocks for the six dimtypes. [ROOT] resets the normal environment when you switch back to the root menu.

```
***SCREEN
**ROOT
[ISO MENU]
[]
[]
[]
[]
[]
[]
[]
❶[ISO DIMS]^C^C^C(if C:DIMLINE (princ) (load "/IL-ACAD/ISODIM"));+
(if C:DIMLINE ;+
  (progn (command "SNAP" "S" "I" "" "ORTHO" "ON" "DIM" "DIMSE1" "ON" ;+
          "DIMTIH" "OFF" "DIMTOH" "OFF" "DIMSE2" "ON" "DIMBLK" "ARROW-R" ;+
          "STYLE" "DIM-R" "EXIT" "ISOPLANE" "RIGHT" ;+
        ) ;+
        (menucmd "S=ISO") ;+
        (foreach mnu '("TISO-A" "TISO-B" "TISO-C" "TISO-D" "TISO-E" "TISO-F");+
          (menucmd (strcat "T1=" mnu)) ;+
        ) ;+
        (princ) ;+
  ) ;+
  (progn (prompt "ISODIM.LSP not found. ISO DIM menu disabled. ") (princ)) ;+
);
[]
[]
[]
[]
[]
[]
[]
```

Listing continued.

Continued listing.

```
[]
[]
[]
[]
+
❷**ISO
[ISO Dims - The master ISODIM screen page upon which toggle pages overlay.]
[]
[DIM LINE]^C^C^CDIMLINE
[EXT LINE]^C^C^CEXTLINE
[DIM ISO ]^C^C^CEXTLINE \\EXTLINE \\DIMLINE
[--------]
[DimTypes]
[  LEFT  ]^C^C^CISOPLANE LEFT DIM DIMBLK ARROW-L STYLE DIM-L EXIT +
$S=DIM-LEFT $S=VERT-L
[  TOP   ]^C^C^CISOPLANE LEFT DIM DIMBLK ARROW-R STYLE DIM-R EXIT +
$S=DIM-TOP $S=TOP-R
[ *RIGHT ]^C^C^CISOPLANE RIGHT DIM DIMBLK ARROW-R STYLE DIM-R EXIT +
$S=DIM-RIGHT $S=VERT-R
[--------]
[Direct'n]
[  VERT  ]^C^C^CISOPLANE TOP DIM DIMBLK ARROW-R STYLE DIM-R EXIT $S=HORZ-R
[--------]
[Snap Sty]
[  ISO   ]^C^CSNAP S S;;$S=SNAPS
[--------]
[]
[]
[  root  ]^C^C^CSNAP S S;;DIM DIMSE1 OFF DIMSE2 OFF DIMBLK . STYLE STD EXIT;+
$S=SCREEN $T1=TABLET1
+
❸**DOCUMENTATION
[The following are the DimTypes LEFT RIGHT TOP page toggles.]
**DIM-LEFT 8
[ *LEFT  ]^C^C^CISOPLANE LEFT DIM DIMBLK ARROW-L STYLE DIM-L EXIT +
$S=DIM-LEFT $S=VERT-L
[  TOP   ]^C^C^CISOPLANE LEFT DIM DIMBLK ARROW-R STYLE DIM-R EXIT +
$S=DIM-TOP $S=TOP-R
[  RIGHT ]^C^C^CISOPLANE RIGHT DIM DIMBLK ARROW-R STYLE DIM-R EXIT +
$S=DIM-RIGHT $S=VERT-R
```

Listing continued.

Continued listing.

```
**DIM-TOP 8
[ LEFT  ]^C^C^CISOPLANE LEFT DIM DIMBLK ARROW-L STYLE DIM-L EXIT +
$S=DIM-LEFT $S=VERT-L
[ *TOP  ]^C^C^CISOPLANE LEFT DIM DIMBLK ARROW-R STYLE DIM-R EXIT +
$S=DIM-TOP $S=TOP-R
[ RIGHT ]^C^C^CISOPLANE RIGHT DIM DIMBLK ARROW-R STYLE DIM-R EXIT +
$S=DIM-RIGHT $S=VERT-R
**DIM-RIGHT 8
[ LEFT  ]^C^C^CISOPLANE LEFT DIM DIMBLK ARROW-L STYLE DIM-L EXIT +
$S=DIM-LEFT $S=VERT-L
[ TOP   ]^C^C^CISOPLANE LEFT DIM DIMBLK ARROW-R STYLE DIM-R EXIT +
$S=DIM-TOP $S=TOP-R
[ *RIGHT ]^C^C^CISOPLANE RIGHT DIM DIMBLK ARROW-R STYLE DIM-R EXIT +
$S=DIM-RIGHT $S=VERT-R
+
❹**DOCUMENTATION
[The following are the Direct'n VERT HORZ RIGHT LEFT page toggles.]
**VERT-L 13
[ VERT  ]^C^C^CISOPLANE TOP DIM DIMBLK ARROW-L STYLE DIM-L EXIT $S=HORZ-L
**HORZ-L 13
[ HORZ  ]^C^C^CISOPLANE LEFT DIM DIMBLK ARROW-L STYLE DIM-L EXIT $S=VERT-L
**VERT-R 13
[ VERT  ]^C^C^CISOPLANE TOP DIM DIMBLK ARROW-R STYLE DIM-R EXIT $S=HORZ-R
**HORZ-R 13
[ HORZ  ]^C^C^CISOPLANE RIGHT DIM DIMBLK ARROW-R STYLE DIM-R EXIT $S=VERT-R
**TOP-R 13
[ RIGHT ]^C^C^CISOPLANE RIGHT DIM DIMBLK ARROW-L STYLE DIM-L EXIT $S=TOP-L
**TOP-L 13
[ LEFT  ]^C^C^CISOPLANE LEFT DIM DIMBLK ARROW-R STYLE DIM-R EXIT $S=TOP-R
+
❺**DOCUMENTATION
[The following are the Snap Style page toggles.]
**SNAPS 16
[STANDARD]^C^C^CSNAP S I;;$S=SNAPI
**SNAPI 16
[ ISO  ]^C^C^CSNAP S S;;$S=SNAPS
```

The Isometric Dimensioning Menu ISODIM.MNU

❶ [ISO DIMS] is a good example of point-of-entry page change menu control. It loads ISODIM.LSP, but only if C:DIMLINE has no value. If it has a value, then ISODIM.LSP must already be loaded, so the IF returns PRINC to avoid a visible nil. The rest of [ISO DIMS] sets up the isometric environment and makes page changes. It is all in one big IF, so nothing will happen if LOAD fails. Several dimension variables must be set for the iso dim system to work. You can find their meanings in the system variables table in Appendix C. Then, (menucmd "S=ISO") loads the **ISO menu page. The following FOREACH loads six ***TABLET1 mini-pages. The IL DISK ISODIM.MNU includes tablet isometric macros. If you don't have the IL DISK, the FOREACH does nothing. The individual screen menu mini-page toggle items are not loaded by [ISO DIMS]. [ISO DIMS] always forces each setting to an initial default instead of loading a toggle page to indicate a current setting. Finally, [ISO DIMS] ends with a PROMPT and a PRINC that execute to tell you if the load fails.

Notice that the format of the big IF expression is much like an .LSP file format. White space *inside* a LISP expression doesn't matter, even in a menu item. So, we can format it for readability. Just be sure to end each intermediate line with a plus sign to continue to the next menu line.

❷ **ISO is the screen page of the isometric menu. It is called by the [ISO DIMS] item on the root screen menu. The [DIM LINE], [EXT LINE], and [DIM ISO] simply call the ISODIM.LSP AutoLISP commands to draw the isometric dimensions. The design of the rest of the **ISO page is coordinated with the following mini-page toggles to ensure that the toggles overlay their **ISO page counterparts. Make sure the [LEFT] label is item 8, the [VERT] label 13, and the [ISO] label 16. The menu system will use these locations in menu toggles.

Look at the [DimTypes] part of the **ISO screen menu. [DimTypes] is a blank header for the three dimtype macros which follow. Each menu macro uses the AutoCAD ISOPLANE command to set the correct plane. Then the DIM command is called to set the DIMBLK block name and text style. Each macro's last task is to place a three line mini-page to overlay these three [DimTypes] boxes.

❸ The three mini-pages called by the dimtypes are **DIM-LEFT 8, **DIM-TOP 8, and **DIM-RIGHT 8 for left, top, and right dimtypes. Each mini-page contains the same [LEFT], [TOP], and [RIGHT] macros as the **ISO page. The only difference between each of these three pages is the location of the asterisk in one of the labels. Each time a new dimtype is selected, it loads the appropriate mini-page, putting an asterisk in the label to mark the current dimtype, like [*LEFT].

❹ The [VERT] macro following the [Direct'n] label is a normal single-item mini-page, loading at line 13. The important thing to remember here is that if your current dimtype is left or right, then the dimension's direction is VERTical or HORIZontal. If the dimtype is top, then dimensions are drawn on either the left or right side. Each time a left or right dimtype is chosen, you must make the direction vertical. Vertical is the initial default. If top is selected, you need to make the direction right (the default) or left. Each time the line is selected, it changes the settings and loads the opposite macro, labeling it with the new current setting.

❺ For convenience, [Snap Sty] offers a [STANDARD] and [ISO] toggle on the screen menu. It is often necessary to switch back and forth between snap styles to reach points based on the non-rotated grid. It works like the [Direct'n] mini-pages, but assigns its single-line pages to box 16. The SNAP pages complete the screen menu.

Note the **DOCUMENTATION pages in the menu. They are never called by a macro, but act as dummy pages that allow you to store documentation in the harmless macro labels that follow.

The menu is diagrammed in the Isometric Screen Menu illustration.

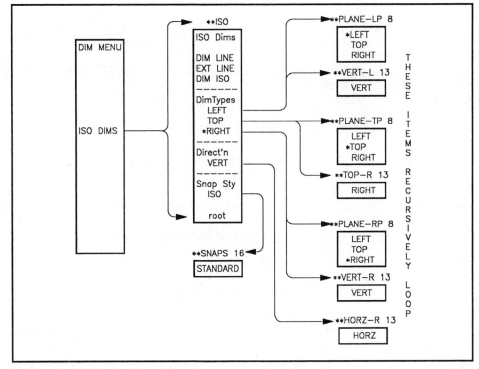

The Isometric Screen Menu

Now it's time to try it out.

How to Use the ISODIM Menu

First, test the toggles, then draw an isometric cube and dimension it as shown in the Iso Cube and Toggle Sequence illustration.

Testing the ISODIM Menu

Enter selection: **1**   Begin a NEW drawing again named IL10.

You have the ISODIM.MNU file.

Create the ISODIM.MNU file as shown above. You must have already created ISO-INIT.DWG and ISODIM.LSP.

Command: **ZOOM**   Zoom Left corner 0,0 with height 6.

Command: **MENU**   Load the ISODIM menu.

Select **[ISO DIMS]**   It scrolls through the setup described in ❶ above, ending:
Current Isometric plane is: Right   [*Right] displays and Direct'n shows [VERT].

Select DimTypes **[TOP]**   Shows [*TOP] and Direct'n [RIGHT]. Try the [Direct'n] toggles:
Select Direct'n **[RIGHT]**   It toggles to Direct'n [LEFT].
Select Direct'n **[LEFT]**   It toggles to Direct'n [RIGHT].
Select DimTypes **[LEFT]**   [*LEFT] displays.
Select Direct'n **[VERT]**   Toggles to [HORZ].

Select **[ISO]**   Toggle Snap Style [STANDARD] and [ISO].
                Watch the grid/axis flip normal/iso.

Select **[root]**   Resets normal settings and loads the root screen menu.

                If the page toggles worked, test the whole system.

Select **[ISO DIMS]**   Back to iso.

Command: **LINE**   Draw the iso cube shown in the illustration.

When drawing the cube, use the ISO menu to toggle isoplanes. But remember, the dimtypes are not the same as isoplanes. Use a horizontal direction to get the top isoplane. The illustrations will help you keep dimtypes, isoplanes, and directions straight.

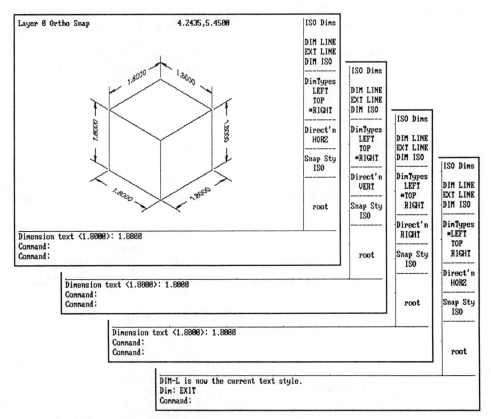

Iso Cube and Toggle Sequence

Now, dimension the cube.

Using Iso Dimensioning

Continue in the previous drawing, with the above settings.

Select **[LEFT]** and **[VERT]**	[*LEFT] [HORZ] shows.
Select **[EXT LINE]**	Draw extension line at lower left corner.
Starting point of Ext. line:	Pick corner.
Ending point:	Pick point to lower left.
Select **[EXT LINE]**	Repeat for right ext. line at lower center corner.

```
Select [DIM LINE]                           Place between extension lines.
Pick first dim. point:                      Pick the left arrow point.
Pick second dim. point:                     Pick the right.
Dimension text <1.8000>:                    <RETURN> for default.
DIM1                                        Uses AutoCAD's ALIGNED dim, draws the line,
Dimension text <1.8000>: 1.8000             arrows, and puts in the text.

Select [TOP]                                Keep testing.
```

Try [DIM ISO] and all six dimtype-direction combinations as illustrated.

Your finished test should match the above Iso Cube and Toggle Sequence illustration. The order of the DIMLINE picks controlled the text orientation.

➡ *TIP: To coax AutoCAD into fitting more text between dimension points, use an "oversize" block, like a 12-inch DIMBLK. Set DIMASZ to a correspondingly small value, say 0.78125 or 5/64ths.*

➡ *TIP: Drawing and switching isoplanes works easier if you use SNAP to reset your snap base point to a relevant osnapped object point.*

Remember the current style applies to both text and dimensioning. Use the [root] item or DIM1 STYLE to reset your text style for standard text.

You probably noticed that the command line was pretty busy, since we didn't turn MENUECHO and CMDECHO off.

Cleaning Up the ISODIM Menu

We purposely left MENUECHO and CMDECHO alone until now. It's easier to design, write, and debug menus and programs if you can see all of the output. Now that the iso dimensioning system is complete, you can suppress the unnecessary command line output. We recommend designing all of your menus with MENUECHO set to 1 and CMDECHO set to 0. After debugging, set MENUECHO and CMDECHO in your ACAD.LSP file, and you will find the menu and program operation much cleaner. For simplicity in writing the menu, the toggle pages of ISODIM.MNU were written as a series of AutoCAD commands. For the cleanest interface after debugging, convert the settings to AutoLISP COMMAND or SETVAR functions. Then CMDECHO can suppress them. For example, look at [VERT] before and after conversion to a COMMAND function form.

```
[  VERT  ]^C^C^CISOPLANE TOP DIM DIMBLK ARROW-R STYLE DIM-R EXIT $S=HORZ-R

[  VERT  ]^C^C^C(command "ISOPLANE" "TOP" "DIM" "DIMBLK" "ARROW-R" "STYLE" +
"DIM-R" "EXIT") $S=HORZ-R
```

For convenience and ease of use, you can put the iso macros on the tablet or icon menu. If you have the New Riders AutoLISP Utilities Disk 1, you have them on the ***TABLET1 menu device.

Putting Iso Dims on Your Tablet

The ISODIM.MNU file on the New Riders AutoLISP Utilities Disk 1 includes a TABLET1 iso dim menu. The various iso dimtypes, and their relationships to AutoCAD's isoplanes, are often confusing to first-time or infrequent isometric users. Putting iso dimtypes on your tablet menu provides helpful visual cues. We suggest an iso tablet menu consisting of six rows (A to F) and six columns (1 to 6). These are shown in the illustrated Isometric TABLET1 Template.

Each row is divided into three double boxes, so each of the iso screen menu toggles gets repeated in the tablet menu twice. The [ISO DIMS] root screen item goes in the center pair of boxes, [D-3] and [D-4], on the fourth row. When the tablet menu first loads, only the [D-3] and [D-4] items are active. This ensures that the [ISO DIMS] setup occurs before the other items are accessed. When [D-3], [D-4], or [ISO DIMS] is selected, the setup occurs and the other tablet items are toggled into place by:

```
(foreach mnu '("TISO-A" "TISO-B" "TISO-C" "TISO-D" "TISO-E" "TISO-F");+
(menucmd (strcat "T1=" mnu))) (princ))
```

You can photocopy the template illustration and tape it to the upper left corner of your tablet area 1. If you have the New Riders AutoLISP Utilities Disk 1, you already have this template as ISO-TAB.DWG.

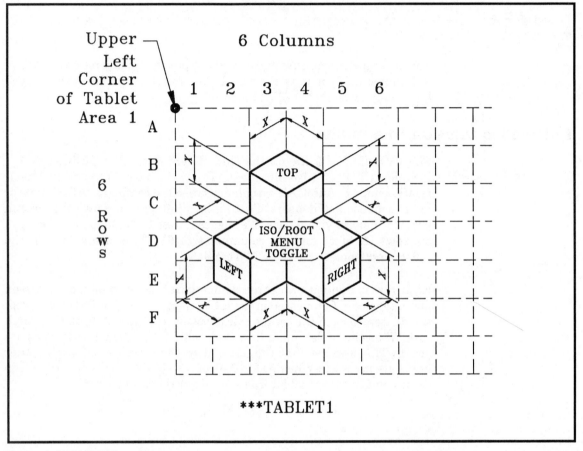

Isometric TABLET1 Template

Using Associative Dimensioning With Iso Dimensioning

If DIMASO is on, ISODIM allows associative dimensioning. But use associative dimensioning with caution. The STRETCH command and the associative dimensioning UPDATE command will update any selected dimensions to use the current dimension variable settings. Since iso dims depend on flipping the DIMBLK and STYLE around, updating will mess them up badly. To restore, select the appropriate dimtype-direction settings, and select the dimensions with the DIM UPDATE command. To prevent the problem, set DIM DIMASO off.

For safest use of associative dimensioning with iso dim, redefine (or disable) STRETCH and take care in the use of UPDATE. See Chapter 17 for command redefinition techniques. You can't redefine DIM UPDATE without redefining the entire DIM and DIM1 commands.

Summary

The isometric dimensioning system is a useful tool if you use isometrics. If you want to extend the system, try developing an iso-leader routine, or other routines to dimension isometric angles.

The real substance of this chapter, however, was the development of clean, integrated AutoLISP-menu systems. You can use the techniques in the iso dimensioning system to help you develop other applications. The greatest benefit of the extra work that writing such a menu takes is the resulting ease of use. Here are some general techniques used in this chapter that we recommend using in your applications.

Use screen menu status to help you keep track of program settings and progress. Plan box numbers for your screens. Use toggling screen pages liberally. The extra up-front effort is worth it.

Use icon menus for graphic page labels, and use pull-down menus for long text labels. Remember, you can use mini-page toggles with any menu device.

Use LOADing of your .LSP files to initialize your environment, such as the insertion of library .DWG files to carry your application block definitions, styles, and layers.

Use point-of-entry screen page environment controls in your application. For example, reset text and dimension arrows when changing isometric modes. Overkill is better than nothing in point-of-entry controls. It keeps the unexpected from happening.

You need good planning when doing mini-page toggle overlays. Plan ahead to keep them aligned. Name your pages for efficient loading, like the *sysvar-value* technique with FOREACH that we used in the IL01DIM.MNU.

The next chapter, Automating With Attributes, expands on the technique of mixing AutoLISP and menus to simplify attribute handling.

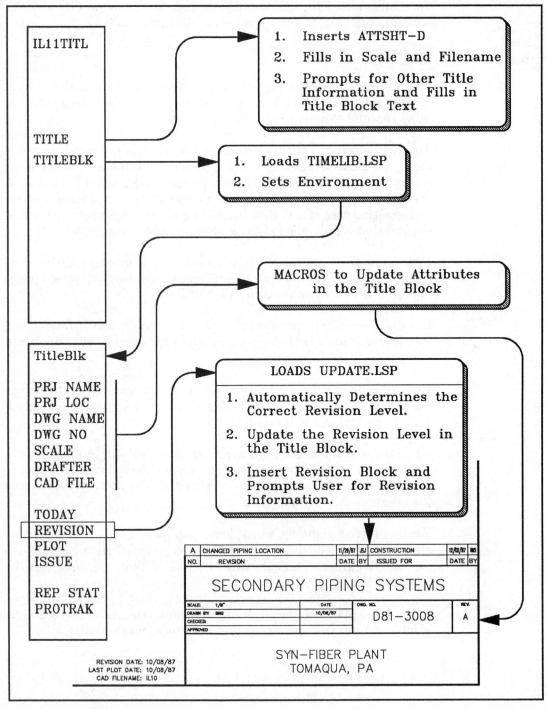

A Custom Title Block Program

CHAPTER 11

Automating With Attributes

ATTRIBUTES AS DATA TOOLS

Whether you employ AutoCAD *attributes* or not, you are probably familiar with their typical uses. Attributes are text strings, attached to AutoCAD blocks, which can be exported to ASCII text files. The external text files can then be used to prepare bills of materials or other reports, usually by processing through programs such as Lotus 123 or dBASE. Other uses include tagging and counting drawing parts for things like inventory or space planning.

But this chapter isn't about generating reports through other programs. We'll cover that in Chapter 13. This chapter is about other, often overlooked, ways to use attributes. Although we will create and insert attributes in this chapter, our emphasis will be on using AutoLISP and macros to manipulate them. We will examine the entity and block symbol table data formats of attributes and look at how this data can be interactively used by macros and AutoLISP programs in your drawings. We call this using attributes as *data tools*.

Using attributes as data tools in your application provides several benefits. With attributes, you can default the content of text in a drawing, and control and preset text size, style, and placement. You can automate text updating and manipulation by arranging information, such as a drawing schedule, in a block. This permits you to move and manipulate an attribute-based schedule as a single entity, or update a number of its attribute text strings in one operation. And you can use attributes to store data in a block. That data can then be input to a program that controls the insertion or manipulation of the block or associated entities.

This chapter uses attributes as data tools in three applications. The first application is a title block system. This system intelligently inserts border sheets with information like last plot date, AutoCAD drawing name, and plan scale already in the title block. The associated IL11TITL.MNU menu helps manage and update this information.

The second application is a drawing revision system, which builds upon the title block system. The system uses attributes to automatically record and update drawing revision histories, like time- and date-stamping.

The third application makes use of autobreaking blocks. Autobreaking blocks have special scalar attributes that automate their insertion and enable them to break the lines upon which they are inserted.

In this chapter, you will learn how to:

■ Use the ATTDEF options to define attributes.

■ Control the block insertion attribute prompt order. The prompt order is determined by the order in which the attributes were selected in the block definition.

■ Control attribute input with menu macros, and create macros that automatically insert, update, and edit attributes.

■ Use the TEXTEVAL system variable to tell AutoCAD to let AutoLISP evaluate expressions or variables input to attribute prompts. The returned values are then entered as string input to the attribute prompts.

■ Extract the system clock time, and format calendar date, time, and year, to be fed to attribute input.

Macros, AutoLISP Tools, and Programs

Macros

IL11TITL.MNU is the title block system menu. It includes:

[TITLE], a macro that inserts the ATTSHT-D title block, fills out some attribute text automatically, and prompts for the rest.

[TITLEBLK] loads TIMELIB.LSP, sets up the environment, and calls the **TITLEBLK menu page.

**TITLEBLK, a page of macros, automates the updating of title block information such as last plot date, CAD drawing name, plan scale, and more. This menu page includes macros to insert and update drawing revision blocks.

AutoLISP Tools

TIMELIB.LSP is a time and date library of functions. This file contains:

TODAY, which returns the current date as mm/dd/yy.

TIME, which returns the current time as hh:mm:ss.

YEAR, which returns the current year.

GETBK and **LINEBLK** are subroutines used by the autobreaking block commands C:BBLOCK and C:BLINE.

Programs

UPDATE.LSP is a program that finds and increments drawing revision levels. It adds a revision bar and prompts for revision notes and drawing reissue data. It includes:

C:UPDATE, the update command function. It uses the following subroutines:

REVALL handles the attribute entity data access for C:UPDATE.

REVTIME handles the revision time updating.

UPD handles the attribute entity data modification for REVALL.

AUTOBLK.LSP provides functions for creating lines with blocks interrupting them. It includes:

GETBLK, the subroutine that gets the name of a specially designed autobreaking block, searches for and verifies the block, and extracts the attribute data that stores the information for calculating the break points.

LINEBLK, the subroutine that inserts the autobreaking block and breaks the line or polyline.

C:BLINE draws a line, inserts an autobreaking block at the midpoint of the line, and breaks the line based on data stored in the block's attribute. It uses GETBLK and LINEBLK.

C:BBLOCK inserts an autobreaking block on an existing line or polyline, breaking the line for the block. It also uses GETBLK and LINEBLK.

AutoCAD's Attribute Data Treatment

Attributes are intelligent text with controlled style, alignment, size, position, and default values. You can use attributes to store AutoLISP variables or data and use the stored values to control drawing actions. Attributes are defined and grouped in blocks. While the *attdef* (attribute definition) data is defined in the block symbol table definition, the *attrib* (attribute entity) is in the blocks insert. Your attdefs determine how AutoCAD stores and manages an attribute. You can define attributes as visible or invisible, and as constant, variable, or preset. You can individually or globally update all but constant values.

AutoCAD stores all constant attribute data, including values and prompts, in the block definition. They can only be changed through block redefinition.

Variable or preset attribute values vary, so they are stored with each insert entity, not in the block definition. However, their default values and prompts are stored in the block definition as well as in the insert entity. Variable attributes prompt for values unless the ATTREQ system variable is set to 0.

During insertion, you can make variable attributes act like presets with the ATTREQ system variable. Setting ATTREQ to 0 causes variable attributes to take on the default values defined in their attdef. If ATTREQ is set to 1 (the default), variables prompt for values during insertion. Unlike constant attributes, variables and presets can be changed after insertion by the ATTEDIT command.

Let's look more closely at attributes and inserts. AutoCAD attributes have been used for many purposes, from automating title blocks to creating a graphic database of beer inventories on supermarket shelves (a real application, believe it or not). We might as well use them to keep track of players in a golf tournament. Create a block with several attributes and different types of definitions. Then we'll insert it and examine its data.

How to Create Blocks With Attributes

```
Enter selection: 1            Start a NEW drawing called IL11.
Command: ZOOM                 Zoom Left corner 0,0, height 4.

Command: ATTDEF
Attribute modes  --  Invisible:N  Constant:N  Verify:N  Preset:N
Enter (ICVP) to change, RETURN when done: C          Make it constant.
Attribute modes  --  Invisible:N  Constant:Y  Verify:N  Preset:N
Enter (ICVP) to change, RETURN when done: <RETURN>
Attribute tag: SPORT-CON                      The -CON reminds us it's constant.
Attribute value: GOLF                         Enter the sport, a constant value.
Start point or Align/Center/Fit/Middle/Right/Style:    Pick a point, say 2,2.
Rotation angle <0>: <RETURN>        There is no height prompt. Style has preset height.

Command: ATTDEF
Attribute modes  --  Invisible:N  Constant:Y  Verify:N  Preset:N
Enter (ICVP) to change, RETURN when done: C          Turn constant off to make variable.
Attribute modes  --  Invisible:N  Constant:N  Verify:N  Preset:N
Enter (ICVP) to change, RETURN when done: <RETURN>
Attribute tag: GOLFER-VAR
                                              The -VAR reminds us it's variable.
```

```
Attribute prompt: Enter contestant's name
Default attribute value: None
Start point or Align/Center/Fit/Middle/Right/Style: <RETURN>
```
                                                                    Defaults to place under previous.


```
Command: ATTDEF
Attribute modes  --  Invisible:N  Constant:N  Verify:N  Preset:N
Enter (ICVP) to change, RETURN when done: P                    Make it preset.
Attribute modes  --  Invisible:N  Constant:N  Verify:N  Preset:Y
Enter (ICVP) to change, RETURN when done: <RETURN>
Attribute tag: HCAP-PRE
Attribute prompt: Enter handicap
Default attribute value: 6
Start point or Align/Center/Fit/Middle/Right/Style: <RETURN>
```

```
Command: BLOCK                          Now make a block and then insert it.
Block name (or ?): GOLFER               Name it GOLFER.
Insertion base point: @                 @ for lastpoint.
Select objects:                         Select them in order of creation.

Command: INSERT                         Insert GOLFER on the screen.
Enter contestant's name <None>: WESSON  The constant and preset go in automatically.
```

All attdefs must have tags, which are used to identify them. Only presets and variables get prompts and default values. If you enter a <RETURN> at the attdef attribute prompt, it defaults to use the tag name as a prompt during insertion. If you enter a <RETURN> at the default attribute value prompt, it enters nothing as a default during insertion. The order of selection in the BLOCK command controls the prompt order in the INSERT command. First selected is first prompted. This is important for blocks with multiple variable attributes.

➡ *TIP: To "erase" an attribute from a block, simply change it to an empty value.*

How Attribute Data is Stored

AutoCAD groups attributes within the insert entities of a drawing. The inserted *attribs* are subentities of the insert. In Chapter 6, we said that subentities are entities that belong to another main entity. Use the ENTNEXT function to access subentities. ENTNEXT steps from the main entity to the first subentity, steps through each subentity to the *seqend* entity, and then to the next main entity. Let's look at the insert entity and attribute data for the GOLFER block.

How to Access Attribute Data

Continue in the previous drawing, with the attributes inserted.

Command: **<F1>**   Flip to the text screen.

Command: **(setq en (entget (entlast)))**   Get the head entity.
Lisp returns: ((-1 . <Entity name: 600000c0>) (0 . "INSERT") (8 . "0") (66 . 1) (2 .
"GOLFER") (10 2.0 2.0 0.0) (41 . 1.0) (42 . 1.0) (50 . 0.0) (43 . 1.0) (70 . 0) (71 .
0) (44 . 0.0) (45 . 0.0) (210 0.0 0.0 1.0))

Command: **(setq en (entget (entnext (dxf -1 en))))**   Give ENTNEXT the entity name
                                                             of the head (the -1 group).
                                                             ENTNEXT gets the first subentity.
Lisp returns: ((-1 . <Entity name: 600000d8>) (0 . "ATTRIB") (8 . "0") (10 2.0
1.79762 0.0) (40 . 0.125) (1 . "WESSON") (2 . "GOLFER-VAR") (70 . 0) (73 . 0) (50 .
0.0) (41 . 1.0) (51 . 0.0) (7 . "STD") (71 . 0) (72 . 0) (11 0.0 0.0 0.0) (210 0.0
0.0 1.0))

The variable entity is the first subentity because the constant attribute is not stored in the insert.

Command: **(setq en (entget (entnext (dxf -1 en))))**   Get the next subentity, the preset.
Lisp returns: ((-1 . <Entity name: 600000f0>) (0 . "ATTRIB") (8 . "0") (10 2.0
1.59524 0.0) (40 . 0.125) (1 . "6") (2 . "HCAP-PRE") (70 . 8) (73 . 0) (50 . 0.0) (41
. 1.0) (51 . 0.0) (7 . "STD") (71 . 0) (72 . 0) (11 0.0 0.0 0.0) (210 0.0 0.0 1.0))

Command: **(setq en (entget (entnext (dxf -1 en))))**
Lisp returns: ((-1 . <Entity name: 60000108>) (0 . "SEQEND") (8 . "0") (-2 . <Entity
name: 600000c0>))

The attrib entity stores the data of variable attributes in the drawing data immediately following the block insert entity. A DXF group 66 code of 1 in the insert entity data indicates that the insert has attributes. You can only access attribs by getting the insert's entity name, then following the trail with ENTNEXT. When stepping through insert entities, step through the attribs in a WHILE loop. Test each 0 entity type group until you find the seqend (sequence end), then you know you are at the end of the attributes. Notice that the seqend has two entity names. The -1 group is the seqend's entity name. The -2 group is the entity name of the head entity, the insert. Given the name of any subentity, you can find an insert entity by stepping to the seqend and extracting its -2 group.

The attrib includes the same DXF groups as text entities, plus the following:

DXF CODE	ATTRIB MEANING
1	The attribute value
2	The TAG name
70	Flags
73	Field length

The 70 group flags are the sum of 1 for invisible, 2 for constant, 4 for verification required upon insertion, and 8 for preset.

The rest of the data you defined in the attdef is stored in the block symbol table, not the insert entity data.

How Attribute Definitions Are Stored

The values of constant attributes, variable defaults, and preset attributes and their prompt strings are stored only in the attdef, which is part of the block definition. The attdef entity is accessible only through the BLOCK table. We covered block definition access in Chapter 7. Let's look at the BLOCK table for the GOLFER definition.

How to Access Attribute Definitions

Continue in the previous drawing, with the attributes inserted.

Command: **<F1>**   Flip to the text screen.

Command: **(setq tbdata (tblsearch "BLOCK" "GOLFER"))**   Get the symbol entry.
Lisp returns: ((0 . "BLOCK") (2 . "GOLFER") (70 . 66) (10 0.0 0.0 0.0) (-2 . <Entity name: 40000018>))

Command: **(setq tbdata (entget (dxf -2 tbdata)))**   First, the constant attdef's data.
Lisp returns: ((-1 . <Entity name: 40000018>) (0 . "ATTDEF") (8 . "0") (10 0.0 0.0 0.0) (40 . 0.125) (1 . "GOLF") (3 . "") (2 . "SPORT-CON") (70 . 2) (73 . 0) (50 . 0.0) (41 . 1.0) (51 . 0.0) (7 . "STD") (71 . 0) (72 . 0) (11 0.0 0.0 0.0) (210 0.0 0.0 1.0))

Command: **(setq tbdata (entget (entnext (dxf -1 tbdata))))**   The variable one is next.
Lisp returns: ((-1 . <Entity name: 4000004d>) (0 . "ATTDEF") (8 . "0") (10 0.0 – 0.202381 0.0) (40 . 0.125) (1 . "None") (3 . "Enter contestant's name") (2 . "GOLFER-VAR") (70 . 0) (73 . 0) (50 . 0.0) (41 . 1.0) (51 . 0.0) (7 . "STD") (71 . 0) (72 . 0) (11 0.0 0.0 0.0) (210 0.0 0.0 1.0))

Command: **(setq tbdata (entget (entnext (dxf -1 tbdata))))**   The preset is last.
Lisp returns: ((-1 . <Entity name: 4000009a>) (0 . "ATTDEF") (8 . "0") (10 0.0 -
0.404762 0.0) (40 . 0.125) (1 . "6") (3 . "Enter handicap") (2 . "HCAP-PRE") (70 . 8)
(73 . 0) (50 . 0.0) (41 . 1.0) (51 . 0.0) (7 . "STD") (71 . 0) (72 . 0) (11 0.0 0.0
0.0) (210 0.0 0.0 1.0))

Command: **(entnext (dxf -1 tbdata))**   After the last subentity,
Lisp returns: nil   ENTNEXT returns nil.

The 2 value of the DXF group 70 in the GOLFER block head indicates the block contains attdefs. From the head, you extract the -2 group, which is the name of the first subentity. You feed it to ENTNEXT to start stepping through the data. Subentities may be any type of entity, so you have to test them when processing block definitions. You can't just assume the attdefs will appear in a particular order among the block def entities unless you control the creation of the block. The SPORT-CON attribute is first in the block definition only because you selected it first while blocking. When searching a block, test the 0 DXF group to see if it is an attdef.

You'll notice that many of the entity data fields are the same for both the attdef in the block definition and the attrib in the inserted entity. At first glance it appears wasteful, but it lets you use the ATTEDIT command to edit attributes after their insertion.

There is no seqend to tell you when you have gone through all the attdefs. Any seqends you encounter in a block definition belong to polylines or nested inserts with their own attribs. ENTNEXT returns each of the entities in the block definition until it eventually reaches the end of the block's entities and returns nil. When searching a block, test what ENTNEXT returns. When it returns nil, you've reached the end.

Besides the usual text entity groups, other DXF group codes you will encounter in the attdef are:

DXF CODE	ATTDEF MEANING
1	The DEFAULT value
2	The TAG name
3	The PROMPT string
70	Flags
73	Field length

The 70 group flags are the sum of 1 for invisible, 2 for constant, 4 for verification required upon insertion, and 8 for preset.

You can use the usual entity update techniques covered in Chapter 6 to modify inserted attribs, but attdefs are part of the block definition and can only be changed by redefining the block with the BLOCK command.

That's the end of this chapter. Well, except for some applications. We've covered almost all there is to know about attrib and attdef data, but what you do with this data is the valuable lesson. There are some techniques to be learned from the three applications that follow. Let's start by using attributes for a title block system.

Controlling Text With Attributes

One problem in drafting, even in CAD, is keeping text entries consistent. In a title block, for example, you need particular bits of information in specific spots, with several standard text sizes. Trying to pick the right spots and set the right styles or heights for each string gets tedious.

This section shows you how to make a border sheet with intelligent attribute definitions that carry the name of a drawing, date of issue, and revision history. We recommend using attributes instead of text for title blocks and other standard text entries because attributes control text height, style, and position. Our title block system defines attributes, manages them with menu macros, updates them with ATTEDIT, and automates the updating with menus.

➥ *TIP: Code visible attributes with a different color than the drawing's text to distinguish between permanent text and values that are entered or updated. Use a dark color for attributes like DWG NO., DRAWN BY:, or LAST PLOT DATE:. Use a lighter color for attributes that are input.*

The Title Block System

If you have the IL DISK, you already have the title block, called ATTSHT-D.DWG, and do not need to draw it. If you don't have the disk, you need to create a simple title block and add the attributes. The title block is shown in the Border With Title Block illustration.

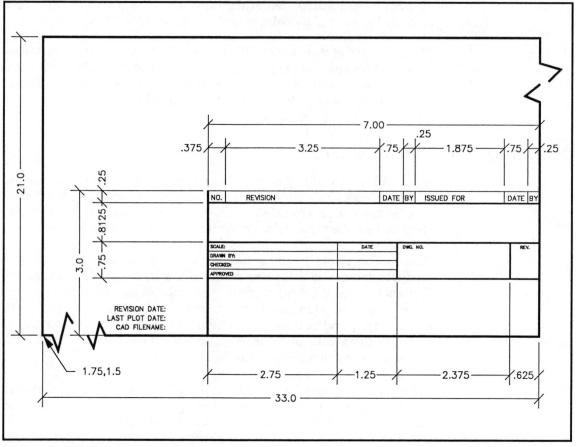

Border With Title Block

Creating a Title Block With Attributes

  You have the ATTSHT-D.DWG. Just read this exercise.

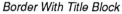 Create the title block with permanent text.

Enter selection: **1**	Begin a NEW drawing named IL11.
Command: **LIMITS**	Set from 0,0 to 36,24.

Command: **STYLE**   Make these styles, defaulting the settings not shown:

STYLE NAME	FONT	HEIGHT
STD1-16	ROMANS	0.0625
STD3-32	ROMANS	0.09375
STD1-8	ROMANS	0.125
STD3-16	ROMANS	0.1875
STD1-4	ROMANS	0.25

Draw the title block as illustrated above.

Command: **PLINE**   Draw the 33 x 21 border at 1.75,1.5 with width .03.
Command: **ZOOM**   In on the title block area.
Command: **PLINE**   Draw the 7 x 3 title block perimeter with width .02.

Command: **LAYER**   Make a new BDR00BDR layer and leave it current.

Command: **PLINE**   Draw the title block's wide lines with width .015.
Command: **LINE**   Draw the narrow lines shown.
Command: **DTEXT**   Enter the text shown, using styles STD1-16 and STD3-32.

Now you need to define the attributes. Define them as variable attributes so you can change them when you insert them. Their order is important for controlling their insert prompt order. The attributes that you want are:

ORDER	TAG	PROMPT	DEFAULT	STYLE	JUSTIFICATION
1.	PRJ-NAME	Project name	None	STD3-16	Center
2.	PRJ-LOC	Project location	None	STD3-16	Center
3.	DWG-NAME	Drawing name	None	STD1-4	Center
4.	DWG-NO	Drawing number	0	STD3-16	Center
5.	DWG-SCALE	Drawing scale	None	STD1-16	Left
6.	DWG-FILE	CAD file name	None	STD3-32	Left
7.	DWG-REV	Revision number		STD1-8	Center
8.	DATE-REV	Revision date	None	STD3-32	Left
9.	DATE-PLOT	Last plot date	None	STD3-32	Left
10.	DATE-ISSUE	Issue date	None	STD1-16	Center
11.	DRAFTER	Enter your initials	None	STD1-16	Left

None in the defaults above means to type "None" as the default, not to omit any default.

The following Title Block With Attributes illustration numbers each attribute to show where it goes in the title block.

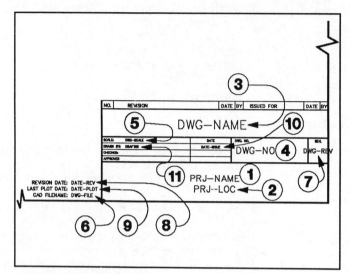

Title Block With Attributes

The next exercise sequence shows the ATTDEF command for the first two and the last attribute. You need to define all the attdefs shown above, unless you have the IL DISK.

When you are finished, WBLOCK the attributes and border sheet to the ATTSHT-D file. Select the entities for WBLOCKing in the exact order shown in the table. Do *not* window them. If you window, they will reverse their creation order. After selecting the attributes, you can Window or use Crossing to select the rest of the border sheet. Duplicate entities are ignored when reselected and will not shuffle your order.

Adding Attributes to the Title Block

You have the ATTSHT-D.DWG. Just read this exercise.

Continue in the previous drawing. Add the attributes to the title block and wblock it to ATTSHT-D.

Command: **SNAP**	Set to 1/16.
Command: **ATTDEF**	Create the eleven attdefs in the order shown in the table above. Make them all Invisible:N Constant:N Verify:N Preset:N. Use the tags, prompts, defaults, text styles and justification shown above for each.

```
Command: ZOOM                    All.
Command: WBLOCK
File name: ATTSHT-D
Block name: <RETURN>
Insertion base point: 0,0
Select objects:                  Remember to select everything in the numbered order shown.

Command: INSERT                  Insert ATTSHT-D to test the attributes.
                                 Enter appropriate values for each prompt.

Command: QUIT                    The WBLOCK saved it.
```

You could use the title block like it is now, manually inputting the attributes with each insertion. That's better than using TEXT for the information. But would we stop here? Not when we can automate it with a menu.

Controlling Attribute Data Entry With Macros

Although the title block's attributes control its text placement, we can create a menu macro to insert the title block and automate much of the text entry in response to the attribute prompts. Some of the input data, like the scale and AutoCAD drawing file name, can be filled in automatically. Other information, like the project name, requires user input. And some areas need to be left blank, for filling in at a later stage in the drawing's development. We'll create a [TITLE] menu macro that pauses with backslashes for the first four entries, fills in scale and file name by itself, defaults entries seven through ten, and then lets you finish by entering your initials as the drafter. The other item on the **ROOT page of our IL11TITL.MNU is [TITLEBLK]. It is a point-of-entry control macro that sets up the environment for the rest of the title block menu system. After loading and setting, it changes to the **TITLEBLK page. The **TITLEBLK page is already in your menu if you have the IL-DISK, otherwise you will create it soon.

```
***SCREEN
**ROOT
[IL11ATT ]
[]
[]
[]
[]
[]
```

Listing continued.

Continued listing.

```
[]
[]
[]
[]
[ TITLE  ]^C^C^C+
LAYER M BORDER C CYAN ;;SETVAR TEXTEVAL 1 INSERT ATTSHT-D 0,0 !#DWGSC;;;\\\\+
❶(cond ;+
  ( (= (setq lu (getvar "LUNITS")) 4) ;+
    (strcat (rtos (/ 12.0 #dwgsc) lu 8) "=" "1'-0" (chr 34)) ;+
  ) ;+
  ( (= lu 3) (strcat "1" (chr 34) "=" (rtos #dwgsc lu 8))) ;+
  (T(strcat "1=" (rtos #dwgsc lu 2))) ;+
);+
❷(getvar "DWGNAME");;;;;\LAYER S 0 ;SETVAR TEXTEVAL 0
[]
[TITLEBLK]^C^C^C(if today (princ) (load "/IL-ACAD/TIMELIB"));+
(if today ;+
(progn (command "SETVAR" "HIGHLIGHT" 0 "SETVAR" "TEXTEVAL" 1 "LAYER" "M" "BORDER" ""));+
(menucmd "S=TITLEBLK") (princ) ) ;+
(progn (prompt "TIMELIB.LSP not found. TITLEBLK menu disabled. ") (princ)) );
[]
[]
[]
[]
[]
[]
[]
+
```

The **ROOT Page of the IL11TITL.MNU

The [TITLE] macro defines a border layer and turns on the TEXTEVAL system variable to evaluate AutoLISP expressions. Then INSERT is used to put ATTSHT-D in the drawing on the BORDER layer. It is assigned the #DWGSC drawing scale established with the ACAD.LSP file. Four backslash pauses at the end of the first line wait for you to enter the first four attributes of title block data.

❶ The COND expression calculates the drawing plot scale from the LUNITS (linear units setting) system variable and our #DWGSC global scale variable. If LU is 4 (architectural), divide scale by 12 to convert to an n"=n'-n" format. If LU is 3 (engineering), it is formatted n"=n'. Otherwise, it is formatted n=n. All unit types are converted to strings by

RTOS with the appropriate precision. If architectural is not forced to more than four places of precision, 3/32-inch will be rounded off to display as 1/8-inch. The (chr 34) puts inch marks in the menu without using a \ ", which would pause the macro. The semicolon ending the COND is required to terminate the text value returned from AutoLISP. A space would be seen as more text, and AutoCAD would then include the following part of the macro as part of the input text string. The DWG-SCALE attribute receives the returned value from the COND.

❷ GETVAR enters the AutoCAD system variable DWGNAME value as a text string, followed by a semicolon to terminate the text entry. The remaining four semicolons skip the assignment of the remaining values, defaulting them to nothing. Since this is a new drawing, you don't want to assign any values to the revision number, revision date, last plot date or issue date categories. The final \ pauses the macro for the drafter's name. Then the layer is reset to 0 and TEXTEVAL is turned off to avoid trouble should you enter something like (El. 145'-6) at a Text: prompt.

Let's test the [TITLE] macro and create the SYNPLANT.DWG file for the following exercises in this chapter. We'll test [TITLEBLK] in the next section after we create the **TITLEBLK page and TIMELIB.LSP files.

Using a Macro to Insert Attributes

Enter selection: **1**   Begin a NEW drawing named IL11.DWG=IL-PROTO.

You have the IL11TITL.MNU file.

Create the IL11TITL.MNU as shown above. You also need ATTSHT-D.DWG from earlier in this chapter.

Command: **MENU**   Load the IL11TITL menu.
Command: **ZOOM**   Window from 25,1 to 35,6.

Select **[TITLE]**   Executes settings and inserts attribute-laden ATTSHT-D block.
Project name <None>: **SYN-FIBER PLANT**   Enter all input as shown for later use.
Project location <None>: **TOMAQUA, PA**
Drawing name <None>: **SECONDARY PIPING SYSTEM**
Drawing number <0>: **D81-3008**
Drawing scale <None>:   The COND scrolls by, and enters the scale.
CAD file name <None>: (getvar "DWGNAME")   Enters the file name.
Revision number: Defaults.
Revision date <None>:   Defaults.
Last plot date <None>:   Defaults.
Issue date <None>:   Defaults.
Enter your initials <BRG>: **JSJ**   Give your initials.

If you have the IL DISK, you can quit. You already have SYNPLANT.DWG.

Command: **SAVE**   Save this as SYNPLANT for later use.

To use [TITLE] with other scales, you need to reset limits, snap, grid, #DWGSC, and all the STDn-nn fixed height text styles. A nuisance like that deserves automation. You will find that the CA-SETUP.MNU menu in our book, CUSTOMIZING AutoCAD, performs these adjustments for you. You could easily combine [TITLE] with the CA-SETUP.MNU menu's [INITIATE] macro.

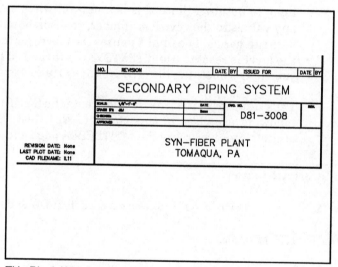

Title Block With Intelligent Data

After testing, your title block should look like the Title Block With Intelligent Data illustration. Several of the attribs are blank or say "None," because you wouldn't normally have the information they need at the beginning of a project. The second part of our title block system updates the title block attributes.

Updating Attributes

You routinely update attribute values using AutoCAD's ATTEDIT command. But in a controlled environment like the title block system, why not use menus and AutoLISP to perform the routine? First, let's review how AutoCAD's ATTEDIT command updates attributes. Then, we'll write a group of title block maintenance macros that use ATTEDIT. To look at the ATTEDIT command, try the following at the keyboard:

Updating Attributes With ATTEDIT

Continue in the previous drawing, or edit an EXISTING drawing named SYNPLANT.

```
Command: ATTEDIT
Edit attributes one at a time? <Y> <RETURN>        Default to one at a time.
Block name specification <*>: <RETURN>             Default to all with *.
Attribute tag specification <*>: DATE-PLOT
Attribute value specification <*>: <RETURN>        Default to any value with *.
Select Attributes: C
First corner:                                      Select the entire title block.
1 attributes selected.                             An X highlights LAST PLOT DATE.
Value/Position/Height/Angle/Style/Layer/Color/Next <N>: V

Change or Replace? <R>:                            You will replace the value.
New attribute value: 5/12/89                       Enter new date.
Value/Position/Height/Angle/Style/Layer/Color/Next <N>: <RETURN>   Return to finish.
```

The ATTEDIT command offers considerable flexibility in editing specific attributes, and it offers power in editing globally. But it can get tedious. Here's a novel thought; why don't we automate it?

Automating Attribute Editing

The ATTEDIT command lets you explicitly search for a specific attribute tag to edit. You can easily automate ATTEDIT with a macro that updates a project name, for example. The title block menu is a combination of macros and functions to update individual attributes.

The [TITLEBLK] macro changes to the **TITLEBLK menu page, the title block management screen menu. It includes macros to change attributes in the border sheet and fill in items left blank when the border was inserted.

```
**TITLEBLK
[TitleBlk]
[]
[PRJ NAME]^C^C^CATTEDIT Y *;PRJ-NAME *;C (getvar "EXTMIN") +
(getvar "EXTMAX") V R \N
[PRJ LOC ]^C^C^CATTEDIT Y *;PRJ-LOC *;C (getvar "EXTMIN") +
(getvar "EXTMAX") V R \N
[DWG NAME]^C^C^CATTEDIT Y *;DWG-NAME *;C (getvar "EXTMIN") +
(getvar "EXTMAX") V R \N
[DWG NO  ]^C^C^CATTEDIT Y *;DWG-NO *;C (getvar "EXTMIN") +
(getvar "EXTMAX") V R \N
[SCALE   ]^C^C^CATTEDIT Y *;DWG-SCALE *;C (getvar "EXTMIN") +
(getvar "EXTMAX") V R (cond ((= (setq lu (getvar "LUNITS")) 4)+
(strcat (rtos (/ 12.0 #dwgsc) lu 8) "=" "1'-0" (chr 34)))+
((= lu 3) (strcat "1" (chr 34) "=" (rtos #dwgsc lu 8)))+
(T (strcat "1=" (rtos #dwgsc lu 2))));N
[DRAFTER ]^C^C^CATTEDIT Y *;DRAFTER *;C (getvar "EXTMIN") +
(getvar "EXTMAX") V R \N
[CAD FILE]^C^C^CATTEDIT Y *;DWG-FILE *;C (getvar "EXTMIN") +
(getvar "EXTMAX") V R (getvar "DWGNAME");N
[]
[TODAY   ] (today);
[REVISION]^C^C^C(if C:UPDATE (princ) (load "/IL-ACAD/UPDATE"));+
(if C:UPDATE (C:UPDATE) (progn (prompt "UPDATE.LSP not found. ") (princ)));
[PLOT    ]^C^C^CATTEDIT Y *;DATE-PLOT *;C (getvar "EXTMIN") +
(getvar "EXTMAX") V R (ustr 0 "Enter plot date" (today) nil);\N
[ISSUE   ]^C^C^CATTEDIT Y *;DATE-ISSUE *;C (getvar "EXTMIN") +
(getvar "EXTMAX") V R (ustr 0 "Enter issue date" (today) nil);\N
[]
[]
[]
[]
[]
[  root  ]$S=SCREEN LAYER S 0 ;SNAP ON GRID ON ORTHO ON;+
SETVAR TEXTEVAL 0 ;HIGHLIGHT 1
```

The **TITLEBLK Page in IL11TITL.MNU File

[PRJ NAME] is a typical maintenance macro. It ensures finding the attribute by using the system variables EXTMIN and EXTMAX to window the drawing extents. It then specifies the PRJ-NAME attribute by its tag.

The [SCALE] and [CAD NAME] macros automatically update the current drawing scale and drawing name, employing the same techniques as the TITLE macro on the root page.

Since an attribute value string can have spaces within it, macros can't respond to the attribute <*>: prompt with <SPACE> or *<SPACE>. You need a semicolon to force a <RETURN>. We recommend always using "*;" when accepting the default <*> in ATTEDIT macros.

The **ROOT menu [TITLEBLK] page change macro turns on TEXTEVAL so the update macros can use AutoLISP to provide attribute strings. It also turns HIGHLIGHT off to speed up selections. The [root] macro resets several settings, including TEXTEVAL and HIGHLIGHT, when returning to the root page.

[TODAY], [REVISION], [PLOT], and [ISSUE] don't work yet unless you have the IL DISK. If not, you'll create the AutoLISP files that they use in the next section.

Let's test the macros that don't need AutoLISP support. The [TITLEBLK] page change on the root menu checks to see if the TODAY symbol has a value and refuses to do anything if not. TODAY normally is defined in the TIMELIB.LSP file that we haven't created yet, but we can fool [TITLEBLK] with a SETQ.

Using the Attribute Edit Macros

Continue in the previous drawing, or edit an EXISTING drawing named SYNPLANT.

You have the **TITLEBLK menu page in your IL11TITL.MNU file.

Add the **TITLEBLK menu page shown above to your IL11TITL.MNU file.

Command: **(setq today T)**

Command: **MENU**	Reload IL11TITL.MNU.
Select **[TITLEBLK]**	It skips the (load "TIMELIB") and changes pages.
Select **[PRJ NAME]**	It "X" highlights the PRJ-NAME.
New attribute value:	Enter a new value.
Command: **(setq #dwgsc 96.0)**	Change it to test.
Lisp returns: 96.0	
Select **[TITLEBLK]**	
Select **[SCALE]**	Did the scale change to 1/8"=1'-0"?
Select **[CAD NAME]**	You'll see it blink and update, but it is the same name.
Select **[PLOT]**	Enter the date 2/01/89.

Try the other macros, except [TODAY], [REVISION], [PLOT] and [ISSUE].

Command: **QUIT**

That's the title block system. The next section extends this to provide an attribute-based system of tracking and logging drawing revisions, and to provide tools for time- and date-stamping drawings.

AutoLISP Timekeeping

Keeping track of revisions is important in any drawing management scheme. Our drawing revision system uses attribute-laden revision blocks to record and update drawing revision histories, including time- and date-stamping. Time and date generation tools are also handy items to put on macros. We'll create the TIMELIB functions that enter the time and date for you.

First, you need to see how AutoLISP can retrieve and format the system clock and calendar. Then we'll make a revision block containing several attributes to store time and date text in alignment with the previous title block. Finally, you'll write a function to update time and date attributes in the title block. It will also insert REVBLOCK (a revision block) and provide it with current attribute data.

The AutoCAD CDATE system variable returns the date in the form of YYYYMMDD.hhmmss:

```
YYYY =   Year
MM   =   Month
DD   =   Day
hh   =   Hour
mm   =   Minutes
ss   =   Seconds
```

It's a simple task to use AutoLISP's SUBSTR to extract the date and time. You parse the date string and STRCAT it back together in the form that you need. Take a look at date and time with CDATE.

How to Extract Time and Date

Edit any new or existing drawing.

```
Command: (setq dt (rtos (getvar "CDATE") 2 6))        Convert to a string.
Lisp returns: "19890417.142902"                       Yours will vary.

Command: (setq yr (substr dt 3 2))                    What year is it?
Lisp returns: "89"
```

Let's create a small library of date and time subroutines. The first, TODAY, is used by the [TODAY], [REVISION], [PLOT], and [ISSUE] macros in the **TITLEBLK menu. It is also used to update revision dates in the UPDATE.LSP functions which follow.

```
;* TIMELIB.LSP contains commonly used date and time conversions based on
;* the Julian calendar and clock format.

;* TODAY returns the current date as mm/day/yr
(defun today ( / d yr mo day)
  (setq d (rtos (getvar "CDATE") 2 6)      ;gets the Julian date
        yr (substr d 3 2)                  ;parses out year as '89
        mo (substr d 5 2)                  ;takes the month number
        day (substr d 7 2)                 ;and the day number
  );setq
  (strcat mo "/" day "/" yr)               ;shuffles order and puts it together
);defun

;* TIME returns current time as hh:mm:ss
(defun time ( / d yr m s)
  (setq d (rtos (getvar "CDATE") 2 6)      ;gets Julian date
        hr (substr d 10 2)                 ;hours
        m  (substr d 12 2)                 ;minutes
        s  (substr d 14 2)                 ;seconds
  );setq
  (strcat hr ":" m ":" s)                  ;mends together
);defun

;* YEAR returns year in form 1989
(defun year ()                             ;full year, as in 1989 is returned
  (substr (rtos (getvar "CDATE") 2 6) 1 4)
);defun
(princ)
;* end of TIMELIB.LSP file
;*
```

TIMELIB.LSP File

Putting the technique into three little defuns makes these subroutines just as simple as the previous exercise. Let's try them, and test the previous [TODAY], [PLOT], and [ISSUE] macros.

Testing the Time Library

Enter selection: **2**   Edit an EXISTING drawing named SYNPLANT.
Command: **MENU**   Load IL11TITL.

```
Select [TITLEBLK]              It loads TIMELIB, sets up and changes pages.

Command: (time)               Returns:  "15:05:40."
Command: (year)               Returns:  "1989."

Select [TODAY]                It calls (today) and returns:  "04/17/89."

Select [PLOT]                 It finds and updates the DATE-PLOT attribute.
                             It scrolls through ATTEDIT, and uses USTR and TODAY.
New attribute value: (ustr 0 "Enter plot date" (today) nil)
Enter plot date <04/17/89>: <RETURN>       Defaults to today.
Value/Position/Height/Angle/Style/Layer/Color/Next <N>: N
```

Try [ISSUE]. It works the same way.

```
Command: QUIT
```

The [PLOT] and [ISSUE] macros differ from the earlier title block macros only in their use of the user GET function, USTR, to prompt for and provide a new default value. USTR calls the TODAY subroutine to get the default.

The next section uses these TIMELIB functions to automate the task of tracking drawing revisions.

Creating a Drawing Revision System

The drawing revision system works much like the title block system. It uses REVBLOCK, an attribute-laden revision block. REVBLOCK is designed to align in a stack, with each insertion going in above the previous one. The initial insertion goes in above the title block.

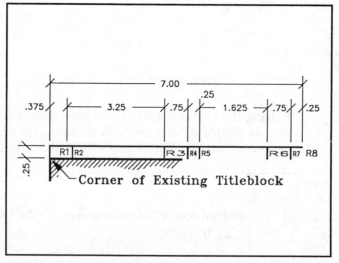

Revision Block With Attributes

If you have the IL DISK, you already have the REVBLOCK.DWG and can skip making it. If you don't have the disk, you must make it before you can add it to the title block drawing. The revision block, with its attributes, is shown in the above illustration. After you make the drawing, add the eight attribute definitions in the table below, using the exact order shown. Be sure to make the revision time attribute invisible.

ORDER	TAG	PROMPT	DEFAULT	STYLE	ALIGNMENT
1.	R1	Revision number:	(blank)	STD3-32	Center
2.	R2	Description:	(blank)	STD3-32	Start
3.	R3	Revision date:	(blank)	STD3-32	Fit
4.	R4	Revised by:	(blank)	STD3-32	Fit
5.	R5	Issued for:	(blank)	STD3-32	Start
6.	R6	Revised issue date:	(blank)	STD3-32	Fit
7.	R7	Issued approved by:	(blank)	STD3-32	Fit
8.	R8	Revision time:	(blank)	STD3-32	Start
		(R8 is invisible)			

The REVBLOCK insertion is keyed to the title block. The title block inserts at 0,0 so you define REVBLOCK to use the 0,0 base point. When you block it to the REVBLOCK.DWG file, select the attributes in the order shown.

Making a Revision Box With Attributes

You have the REVBLOCK.DWG. Just read this exercise.

Make REVBLOCK.DWG as shown.

Enter selection: **1**	Begin a NEW drawing named IL11=ATTSHT-D.
Command: **ZOOM**	In on the title block area.
Command: **LAYER**	Set BORDER current.
Command: **LINE**	Draw the revision block lines, aligned to the title block.
Command: **ATTDEF**	Create all eight attributes in the order shown above. Use the tags, prompts and justification shown. All get blank defaults and use style STD3-32.
Command: **WBLOCK**	Give the name REVBLOCK. Use 0,0 as insertion base point.
Select objects:	Select the attributes in the order shown.
Select objects:	Select the lines of the revision block.
Command: **QUIT**	WBLOCK saved REVBLOCK.

The [REVISION] macro in the IL11TITL.MNU inserts the REVBLOCK and fills out its attributes by loading and calling the UPDATE.LSP program. Let's create the UPDATE.LSP program and try it out.

Automating REVBLOCK Insertion With UPDATE.LSP

The revision updating program consists of several functions in the file UPDATE.LSP. Together, they find the previous drawing revision data, increment the revision number, insert REVBLOCK, and prompt for revision notes and drawing reissue data. C:UPDATE is the master update command function. It automatically updates all related dates. C:UPDATE uses several subroutines: REVALL to get the attribute entity data; REVTIME to do the revision time updating; and UPD to modify the attribute entity data for REVALL.

Several completed revision update blocks are shown in the Drawing Revision Blocks illustration.

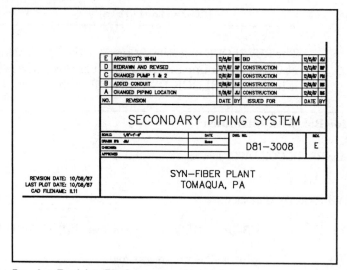

Drawing Revision Blocks

C:UPDATE is a good function to call when ending a drawing. You can ensure that this is done and that revision information is automatically updated by redefining the END command. See the AutoCAD Command Redefinition section of Chapter 17 in this book.

```
;* UPDATE.LSP revises information in drawing titleblock "ATTSHTxx"
;* It changes dates, records revision information and insert a block containing
;* the revision data. It uses DXF and UKWORD, and the TIMELIB.LSP functions.

;* C:UPDATE is the main revision function. It calls the REVALL subroutine.
(defun C:UPDATE ( / ss1 count emax en ed blkn found $txtev)
  (if (= "Y" (ukword 1 "Y N" "Is this a revision" "Y"))     ;permission to update
    (progn                                  ;then run
❶
      (setq ss1 (ssget "X" '((0 . "INSERT")   ;gather all inserts
                            (8 . "BORDER")    ;on border layer
                            (66 . 1)))        ;with attributes following
      );setq ssgetx
      (if ss1                                 ;if found possibles
        (progn
          (setq count 0                       ;initialize count
                emax (sslength ss1)           ;max entities in SS1
          );setq
          (setq $txtev (getvar "TEXTEVAL"))
          (setvar "TEXTEVAL" 1)               ;force eval on
❷
          (while (< count emax)
            (setq en (ssname ss1 count)       ;entity name
                  ed (entget en)              ;entity data
                  blkn (dxf 2 ed)             ;block name
            );setq
            (if (= "ATTSHT" (substr blkn 1 6)) ;test insert's block name substring
              (setq count emax found T)        ;it's the border sheet - set flag T
              (setq count (1+ count))          ;it's some other block - keep looking
          ) );while&if                         ;last "en" value is our border
❸
          (if found                            ;if we have the title block
            (progn
;* (princ en) ;prints block insert ename for testing
              (revall en)                      ;call revision function
              (entupd en)                      ;update the title block
            );progn
            (prompt "\nError: No border sheet found")   ;else tell them
          );if found
          (setvar "TEXTEVAL" $txtev)           ;restore text evaluation
      ) );if-ss1&progn
```

Listing continued.

Continued listing.

```
   ) );if&progn then run
   (princ)
);defun C:UPDATE
;*
```

UPDATE Function in UPDATE.LSP File

❶ UPDATE first asks if the session is a drawing revision. If so, it uses SSGET X to get the title sheet data by looking for all insert entities on layer BORDER with attribute flags of 1 (true). Remember, insert entities reside on their layer of insertion, not their layer of definition. The [TITLE] macro inserts the ATTSHT-D title block on the BORDER layer, so we know where to find it.

❷ UPDATE searches the SS1 selection set in the WHILE loop, using SSNAME and ENTGET to find an entity with an "ATTSHT" substring. (We don't test for the full ATTSHT-D name, so you can add other title blocks to the system, like ATTSHT-C.)

❸ If a block insert starting with "ATTSHT" is found, UPDATE feeds its entity name to the REVALL function. REVALL modifies the title block attribute entity data lists with ENTMOD, then UPDATE uses ENTUPD to update them in the drawing. The ;* (princ en) facilitates testing C:UPDATE alone, without REVALL and the rest of the program.

Testing the C:UPDATE Function

Enter selection: **1**   Begin a NEW drawing named IL11=SYNPLANT.

You have the C:UPDATE command function in your UPDATE.LSP file.

Create the C:UPDATE function in a new file named UPDATE.LSP.

Command: **SHELL**   Even if you have the IL DISK, edit the UPDATE.LSP file. Remove the ";*" from (princ en) and add a leading ";*" to (revall en) and (entupd en) to disable them for testing:

```
  (princ en)    ;prints block insert ename for testing
;*              (revall en)              ;call revision function
;*              (entupd en)              ;update the title block
```

Save and exit to AutoCAD.

```
Command: (load "UPDATE")        Load the file.

Command: UPDATE                 Test it.
Is this a revision <Y>:         Answer Y for yes.
Lisp returns: <Entity name: 400006A2>     A returned entity name shows it found the block.

Command: SHELL                  Edit the UPDATE.LSP file.
```

Delete the entire (princ en) line and remove the disabling leading ";*" from
the (revall en) and (entupd en) lines to re-enable them for use:

```
        (revall en)                  ;call revision function
        (entupd en)                  ;update the title block
```

Save and exit to AutoCAD.

UPDATE feeds its entity name to the REVALL function. REVALL gets the
attribute entity data lists and uses UPD to modify them and REVTIME to
do the revision time updating. Let's examine the rest of these
UPDATE.LSP functions.

```
;* REVALL is called by C:UPDATE to search and update attributes.
;* It calls the REVTIME and UPD subroutines, and TODAY from TIMELIB.LSP.
❶
(defun revall (en / date ed ctime etime atag lstrev ipt) ;en is attribute border block
  (setq date (today)                    ;save the date
        en (entnext en)                 ;get the first subentity of title block
        ed (entget en)
        ctime (getvar "DATE")           ;get the current Julian time
  );setq
❷
  (while (/= "SEQEND" (dxf 0 ed))       ;while not at the end of insert entity
    (if (= "ATTRIB" (dxf 0 ed))         ;if it's an attribute
        (progn
          (setq atag (dxf 2 ed))        ;then get the tag id
          (cond                         ;test id in a cond loop
            ((= atag "DATE-REV")        ;it's a revision date
❸
              (upd ed en date)          ;call the updater function
            );last revision date
            ((= atag "DATE-PLOT")       ;it's the plot date
              (if (= "Y" (ukword 1 "Y N" "Update last plot date?" "Y")) ;ask them
                  (upd ed en date)      ;if ok - call the updater
```

Listing continued.

Continued listing.

```
              );if
          );last plot date
          ((= atag "DATE-ISSUE")            ;it's the drawing issue date
              (if (= "" (dxf 1 ed))         ;if it's not filled in
                (if (= "Y" (ukword 1 "Y N" "Issue the drawing?" "N"))   ;ask them
                    (upd ed en date)         ;and if they say yes - update it
              ) );if&if
          );issue date
```
❹
```
          ((= atag "DWG-REV")               ;it's the revision level letter
              (if (= "" (dxf 1 ed))         ;if it's not filled in
                  (progn
                    (upd ed en (setq lstrev "A")) ;make it the A rev
                    (setvar "USERR1" ctime)       ;save the original creation time
                  );progn
                  (upd ed en                 ;increment the letter
                      (setq lstrev (chr (1+ (ascii (dxf 1 ed)))))))
              );if                           ;that is in there
          );revision level
        );cond - the rest of attributes can be skipped
      );progn
    );if = ATTRIB
    (setq en (entnext en)
          ed (entget en)
    );setq
  );while /= SEQEND
```
❺
```
;Now that the main title block is updated, insert a new rev block
;at an insert point based on the revision level letter - A is at 0,0
;but B is at 0,0.25 (adjusted for the dwg scale) and so on...
  (setq ipt (polar '(0 0) (* pi 0.5) (* 0.25 #dwgsc (- (ascii lstrev) 65)))))
  (command "insert" "revblock" ipt #dwgsc #dwgsc 0.0        ;insert a revblock
          lstrev pause (today) pause pause pause pause   ;pause for entry from user
          (revtime ctime)                                ;time stamp for revision period
  );command
);defun REVALL
;*
```
❻
```
;* REVTIME stores revision time logs in the AutoLISP USER variables.
;* USERR1 is the time period of original creation for the drawing.
```

Listing continued.

Continued listing.

```
;* USERR2 is the time period from last update.
(defun revtime (ctime / period)
  (setq period (- ctime (getvar "USERR2")))      ;rev period = current time - last rev time
  (setvar "USERR2" ctime)                         ;update rev time to start next rev period
  (rtos (* period 1440) 2 0)                      ;time in minutes as a string, no places
);defun
❼
;* UPD is a simple ENTMOD function called by REVALL to reduce repetitive code.
(defun upd (ed en nval / el)
  (setq el (subst (cons 1 nval) (assoc 1 ed) ed)) ;swaps the entity data
  (entmod el)                                      ;sends updated list to AutoCAD
);defun
;*

(princ)
;*end of UPDATE.LSP
;*
```

REVALL, REVTIME, and UPD Functions in UPDATE.LSP File

❶ REVALL receives the EN border sheet entity name as an argument from C:UPDATE. It uses the DATE function from our TIMELIB.LSP file to get the current date string, and the DATE system variable to get a numeric date to store in the revision for future comparisons.

❷ REVALL searches all attributes of the title block insert using typical entity access techniques. It loops through a WHILE and COND until the seqend entity indicates that there are no more subentities. The COND sorts out what kind of data needs to be updated in each of the supported attribute tags, like DATE-REV and DATE-PLOT.

❸ ❼ Then the attribute entity name and its new value are passed to UPD. UPD is a small function that performs the entity modifications. This saves having to repeat the ENTMOD code in each condition's expression.

❹ DWG-REV is the attribute for the current drawing revision level. It is initially blank in the title block. The first time it is run, REVALL assigns a revision level of "A." Then it finds the DWG-REV attribute value and automatically increments it each time it is run. The ASCII and CHR functions are used to increment the level. The new revision level is stored in the LSTREV variable for the REVBLOCK's later insertion.

❺ The REVBLOCK's revision bar block insertion point is calculated relative to 0,0 and offset by 0.25 *times* #DWGSC *times* the number of revision levels in the drawing. During insertion, attributes are requested and either filled in automatically, or the COMMAND function's PAUSEs stop for you to enter them. The TODAY function is used inside the command function for the revision date.

❻ The REVTIME function calculates the amount of time used by the current revision. It stores the current time and date at the moment the revision command is started. It employs the *user* system variables, USERR1 and USERR2, to store the original creation and most recent revision times. (The *user* variables USERR1 through USERR5 store real numbers; USERI1 through USERI5 store integers.) The function returns the time difference between the current date/time and the last revision date/time to the COMMAND function that inserts the REVBLOCK.

☞ Even if you have the IL DISK, you need to update and save your SYNPLANT.DWG. You will use this updated file in Chapter 13 for drawing tracking and time log reporting in dBASE.

Using REVBLOCKs to Update SYNPLANT.DWG

Enter selection: **1**   Begin a NEW drawing named IL11=SYNPLANT.

 You have the REVALL, REVTIME, and UPD functions in your UPDATE.LSP file.

Add the REVALL, REVTIME, and UPD functions to your UPDATE.LSP file.

Command: **MENU**   Load the IL11TITL menu.

Select **[TITLBLK]** then **[REVISION]**   It loads and executes C:UPDATE.
Command: UPDATE
Is this a revision <Y>: **<RETURN>**   Take default Yes.
Update last plot date? <Y>: **<RETURN>** Yes. It inserts REVBLOCK, then:
Enter attribute values
Revision number: Revision number filled itself in.
A Description: Enter a description.
Revision date: 11/28/87   Revision date filled itself in.
Revised by: **PMH**   Enter your initials.
Issue the drawing? <N>: **Y**   Enter Y for Yes. This only prompts if blank.
Issued for <CONSTRUCTION>: **<RETURN>**
Issue date: **4/17/88**   Enter the date.
Issued by: **PMH**   Enter initials.
Revision time: **120**   Enter the number of minutes to timelog for the revision.

Select **[REVISION]**	Make a few more revisions using UPDATE. Enter the information shown in the previous Drawing Revision Blocks illustration.
Command: **SAVE**	Save as SYNPLANT, to replace the previous drawing for use in a later chapter.
Command: **QUIT**	

You should now have an updated title block with several filled-out drawing revision blocks stacked above it.

Now that we've used AutoLISP to control attributes, let's try using attributes to control AutoLISP. It's only fair.

Using Attributes to Store Parametric Data

An often overlooked use of attributes is to store parametric data in blocks. The concept is simple. Blocks can store information as constant attributes within the block definitions. A function that controls the insertion gets the attribute value from the block definition table, processes it, and does something with it. What you do with it can range from very simple to extremely complex, even extending to controlling entire parametric drawings. The example that we use to show parametric attribute use is an "autobreaking block."

AutoBreaking Blocks

The autobreaking block breaks out a line segment as it inserts. This allows you to put annotation bubbles in lines, such as those used to mark utilities. The way the block is defined is important. To avoid extensive subentity searches in our program, your attribute must be tagged BREAKDIM and it must be the first entity in the block definition. Otherwise, the program would have to be written to search every entity in the block definition. That would be slow in complex blocks.

If you have the IL DISK, you have an example block in VALVE-B.DWG. Otherwise you need to make and wblock a valve as shown in the Autobreaking VALVE-B Block illustration. The valve is designed so the breakout distance is a horizontal dimension centered on the insertion base point. Any block that meets that criteria and includes the BREAKDIM attribute as its first entity is usable by our program.

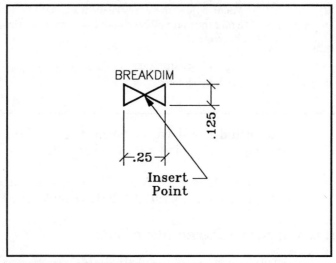

Autobreaking VALVE-B Block

Making an Autobreaking Block

You have the VALVE-B block. Just read this sequence.

Create the block in this sequence.

Enter selection: **1**	Begin a **NEW** drawing again named IL11.
Command: **ZOOM**	Center with 4" height.
Command: **SNAP**	Set to 1/16.
Command: **LINE**	Draw the valve as dimensioned.
Command: **ATTDEF**	Define the attribute as Invisible and Constant.
Attribute tag: **BREAKDIM**	The special tag name.
Attribute value: **0.25**	Break out distance.
	The attribute can be any text style, alignment, or location you wish.
Command: **WBLOCK**	To file name VALVE-B, with insertion base point at the center.
Select objects:	You must select the attribute first, then the lines.

Now we need a program to insert autobreaking blocks and break lines, or to draw lines while inserting autobreaking blocks. The system is modular, using subroutines so that you can insert individual blocks, break existing lines and polylines, or draw new lines. Let's look at the core routine that gets the block's break information.

The GETBK subroutine prompts you for a block name, looks up the break data, and returns the block name and the break distance as a list.

```
;* AUTOBLK.LSP contains routines that allow the placement of a BLOCK on a
;* PLINE or LINE and automatically break the line out of the Block area.
;* The block must be built with its first entity a constant invisible attribute
;* tagged BREAKDIM, containing a value equal to the length of break required.
;* The insertion point must be in the center of the horizontal BREAKDIM location.
;* The DXF, NO-PATH and USTR functions, and the global #DWGSC scale factor are
;* required.

;* GETBK prompts for block name, searches & returns block name & breakdim data.
;* If BLNAME argument is non-nil it serves as the prompt default.
;* It must be supplied a valid BKDIST argument if supplied a name as BLNAME.
(defun getbk (blname bkdist / ok tbdata bldata tmp)
  (setq expert (getvar "EXPERT")) (setvar "EXPERT" 2)
  (while (not ok)
❶
    (while (not (setq tmp (ustr 0 "Block name" blname nil))))   ;get BLOCK name
    (if (/= tmp blname)                        ;if new block name given
      (progn                                   ;then
        (while
          (not
            (if
❷
                (and (= tmp (no-path tmp))                 ;no path supplied and
                     (setq tbdata (tblsearch "BLOCK" tmp)) ;search table for BLOCK name
                )
                (setq bldata (entget (dxf -2 tbdata)))     ;then get first subentity
                (progn
                  (command "INSERT" tmp nil)   ;else insert BLOCK in database, & loop
                  (setq tmp (no-path tmp))      ;strip path if any from block name
                  nil                          ;return NIL to cause loop
                )
    ) ) );while not if
    (setq attag (dxf 2 bldata))
    (if                       ;if it's an attribute and has the proper format
      (and (= (dxf 0 bldata) "ATTDEF") (= (dxf 2 bldata) "BREAKDIM"))
      (setq bkdist (atof (dxf 1 bldata))   ;then get breakdim data
            blname tmp                     ;and save blname
            ok T                           ;exit flag
```

Listing continued.

Continued listing.

```
            )
            (prompt "\nError: Block must have BREAKDIM attribute as 1st entity.")
          );if an attrib...
        );progn then
        (setq ok T)                         ;else used same block name
      );if new
    );while
    (list blname bkdist)                    ;return block name and break dist.
);defun GETBK
;*
❸
;*NO-PATH strips path from a fully qualified file or block name.
;*
(defun no-path (fname / lngth str char)
    (setq lngth (1+ (strlen fname))  str "")  ;initialize, lngth is filename length
    (while                                  ;loops until AND is non-NIL
      (and
        (/= 1 lngth)                        ;exit to avoid invalid substr
        (setq lngth (1- lngth)  char (substr fname lngth 1))   ;get next char in reverse
        (/= "/" char)                       ;find "/" and exit
        (/= "\\" char)                      ;find "\" and exit
        (setq str (strcat char str))        ;otherwise add last char to str
    ) )
    str
);defun NO-PATH
;*
```

GETBK and NO-PATH Subroutines in AUTOBLK.LSP File

❶ The GETBK routine takes a block name and break dimension as arguments. The arguments may be nil. This allows its use in a loop, where the values returned by GETBK become its arguments in the next loop. If the arguments are non-nil, the block name is used as a default prompt. If the default is accepted, it skips the table access because it already has the BKDIST dimension from the previous pass.

❷ If a new block name is entered, it uses table access to find it, and entity access to extract the break attribute data. The NO-PATH strips a path from the entered name. If the block isn't already in the drawing or if a path is supplied, COMMAND inserts it and the WHILE loops again to get its data from the table. GETBK returns the name and distance as a list. A block with a supplied path will redefine its current definition in the drawing. If no path is supplied and the default is taken, the GETBK arguments are returned without change or table checking. This allows GETBK to be used in a loop, with defaults, by the calling program.

❸ NO-PATH is used by GETBK to avoid problems if the block file name is supplied with a path. If so, NO-PATH strips the path so the block name can be used to search the block table. You may wish to add NO-PATH to your FILELIB.LSP functions.

Before we create the functions that insert and draw lines, let's see how GETBK works.

Testing the GETBK Function

Continue in the previous drawing, or begin a NEW drawing again named IL11.

  You have the GETBK and NO-PATH functions in your AUTOBLK.LSP file.

  Create the above GETBK and NO-PATH functions in a new file named AUTOBLK.LSP. You must have previously created the VALVE-B block.

```
Command: (load "autoblk")               Load the function.

Command: (getbk nil nil)
Block name: \IL-ACAD\VALVE-B            If given nil, it prompts without default.
INSERT Block name (or ?): \IL-ACAD\VALVE-B  Insertion point:   It inserts and
                                            cancels if not already in dwg database.
Lisp returns: ("VALVE-B" 0.25)

Command: (getbk "VALVE-B" 0.25)         Give it defaults.
Block name <VALVE-B>: <RETURN>          Take the default.
Lisp returns: ("VALVE-B" 0.25)          It returns it without table searching.
```

GETBK is only the engine to get the data. The C:BLINE command function calls the GETBK function, gets the points from the user, and draws the line. C:BLINE then calls another function, LINEBLK, to break the line and insert the block.

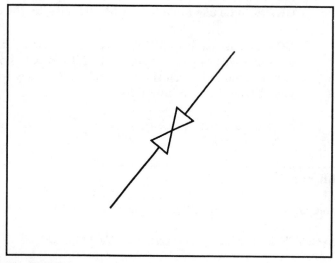

The BLINE Command

```
;* C:BLINE gets a block name, gets its data, draws a line and calls LINEBLK to
;* insert the block and break the line.
(defun C:BLINE ( / linent blkprmt spt ept)        ;bbname and bbdata float for defaults
  (setq bkdata (getbk bbname bbdist))             ;get block name and break data
❶
        bbname (car bkdata)
        bbdist (cadr bkdata)
  )
  (setq spt (getpoint "\nStart point of line: "))        ;get first point of line
  (if spt
    (while (setq ept (getpoint "\nPick end point of line: " spt)) ;get 2nd point of line
      (command "LINE" spt ept "")                 ;draw LINE
      (setq linent (entlast))                     ;get insert point
      (setq pt1 (osnap ept "MIDP,QUI"))           ;determine midpoint of LINE
❷
      (lineblk bbname bbdist pt1 linent)          ;perform Block insert routine
      (setq spt ept)                              ;establish a new start point
      );while
  );if
  (setvar "LASTPOINT" spt)                        ;resets properly to end of line
  (princ)
);defun C:BLINE
;*
```

Listing continued.

Continued listing.

❸
```
;* LINEBLK inserts the autobreaking block and breaks the line or pline
;* To force to 0 degrees or a range -15 to 105 deg, replace the (command "INSERT"...)
;* line with one of the following (the second one requires the ROTANG function,
;* to force block to read from horizontal or right side).
; (command "INSERT" blname pt1 #dwgsc "" 0)                ;alt. to force angle to 0 degrees
; (command "INSERT" blname pt1 #dwgsc "" (angtos (rotang ang nil))) ;restrict angle
;* Or revise programs to use a second attribute in block to control insertion angle.
;
(defun lineblk (blname bkdist pt1 linent / blname brkdim
                blkname blkent validatt atttag ang)
  (setq pt2 (osnap pt1 "ENDP,QUI"))                        ;get end point for rotation
  (setq ang (angle pt1 pt2))                               ;get angle of line
  (command "INSERT" blname pt1 #dwgsc "" pt2)              ;insert BLOCK
  (setq pt1 (polar pt1 ang (* (/ bkdist 2) #dwgsc)))       ;calculate 1st break point
  (setq pt2 (polar pt1 (+ ang pi) (* bkdist #dwgsc)))      ;calculate 2nd break point
  (command "BREAK" linent pt1 pt2)                         ;break LINE or PLINE
);defun LINEBLK
;*
```
❹
```
;* ROTANG converts ANG argument in radians to -15 to 105 degree range, in radians.
;* If align FLAG is True, angles from 105 to 285 are flipped 180 degrees.
;* Note: this is in radians but comments are in degrees for ease of reading.
;*
(defun rotang (ang flag)
  (while (>= ang 6.28318531) (setq ang (- ang 6.28318531)))  ;adj to 0 to 2pi 360 range
  (while (<= ang 0) (setq ang (+ ang 6.28318531)))
  (cond
    ((and (>= ang 3.92699081) (<= ang 6.02138591))          ;225-345
      (cond
        ((not flag) (setq ang 0))                           ;to 0
        ((< ang 4.974188368) (setq ang (- ang pi)))         ;225-285 flip 180 deg
        (ang)
      ) )
    ((and (>= ang 1.83259571) (< ang 3.92699081))           ;105-225
      (if flag
        (setq ang (- ang pi))                               ;flip 180
```

Listing continued.

Continued listing.

```
      (setq ang 1.570796327)                                    ;to 90
    )
  )
    (ang)
  )
);defun ROTANG
;*
```

BLINE, LINEBLK, and ROTANG Functions in AUTOBLK.LSP File

❶ C:BLINE calls GETBK to get the block name and break distance. It saves the name and distance as the global variables BBNAME and BBDIST for use as defaults in repeated uses.

❷ After drawing the line and saving it with ENTLAST, it calls the LINEBLK subroutine to break the line.

❸ LINEBLK determines the angle, inserts the block, and breaks out a piece of the line. Notice the suggested modifications that allow you to control the angle.

❹ ROTANG is used to force angles horizontal, or to the more appropriate of a horizontal or vertical choice. It isn't used unless you modify LINEBLK as suggested. You may want to put it in a separate file for general use by other programs.

Using BLINE

Continue in the previous drawing, or begin a NEW drawing again named IL11.

    You have the C:BLINE, LINEBLK, and ROTANG functions in your AUTOBLK.LSP file.

    Add the above C:BLINE, LINEBLK, and ROTANG functions to your AUTOBLK.LSP file.

```
Command: (load "autoblk")                Reload the file.
Command: ZOOM                            Left corner 0,0 with height 3.
```

Command: **BLINE**	Test it.
Block name: **VALVE-B**	Your special block.
Start point of line:	Pick.
Pick end point of line:	Pick.
Command: LINE	It draws the line,
Command: INSERT Block name (or ?) <VALVE-B>: VALVE-B	inserts the valve,
Command: BREAK Select object:	breaks the line, and
Pick end point of line:	prompts for the next point. Return when through.

The last function, BBLOCK is similar to C:BLINE. It uses the previous routines to break an *existing* entity, then places the autobreak block at the selected point.

```
;* C:BBLOCK uses GETBK and LINEBLK to insert an autobreaking block on existing entities.
(defun C:BBLOCK ( / linent bkdata)            ;bbname and bbdata float for defaults
  (setq linent (entsel "\nPick BLOCK insert point: ")) ;get entity and point
  (if linent
    (progn
      (setq bkdata (getbk bbname bbdist)        ;get the block data
            bbname (car bkdata)                 ;store the block name
            bbdist (cadr bkdata)                ;and its break distance
      )
      (setq pt1 (osnap (cadr linent) "NEA"))    ;get nearest point on line
      (lineblk bbname bbdist pt1 (car linent));perform BLOCK insert & break
    );progn
    (prompt "\nMust select Line or Pline. ")
  );if
  (princ)
);defun C:BBLOCK
;*


(princ)
;* end of AUTOBLK.LSP
;*
```

BBLOCK Function in AUTOBLK.LSP File

C:BBLOCK is essentially the same as C:BLINE, except it doesn't draw a line. Try it on an existing line.

Using the BBLOCK Function

Continue in the previous drawing, or begin a NEW drawing again named IL11.

 You have the C:BBLOCK function in your AUTOBLK.LSP file.

 Add the above C:BBLOCK function to your AUTOBLK.LSP file.

```
Command: (load "autoblk")          Reload the file.
Command: ZOOM                      Left corner 0,0 with height 3.

Command: BBLOCK                     Try it:
Pick BLOCK insert point:           Pick point on a line.
Block name <VALVE-B>: VALVE-B      It breaks it.
                                   The default shows if you're still in the previous drawing.

Command: QUIT
```

AUTOBLK is a versatile program, easily adapted to your needs. You can change the angle handling as suggested above. You can add a command or modify BLINE to divide or measure a polyline, and then break it at each division or measurement point. If the BREAKDIM attribute is the only entity in the block, this would create continuous polyline linestyles.

➥ *TIP: You can use attributes to invisibly store user variables retrieved in a similar manner to this autobreaking block program and the earlier title block example.*

A Word about Block Redefinition and Lost Attributes

When blocks are redefined, several attribute data management compromises occur. Constant block attributes are lost or changed because constant attributes always reflect the current definition of the block. Old variables and preset attributes remain with their block inserts, but new insertions observe the new definitions of block attributes. It's possible to have two identically named block inserts, but with different variable tag attributes defined because the block has been redefined.

This is a management problem, but if good habits don't solve it, there is a customization solution. You can use AutoCAD command redefinition and redefine the BLOCK command to filter names and warn you if the block being redefined contains attributes which already exist in current inserts. See Chapter 17 on command redefinition.

Summary

You saw a kind of daisy chain of attributes in this chapter. You used attributes to control text in the drawing. You used AutoLISP and menus to relieve the tedium and eliminate errors in updating those attributes. And you used attributes to control AutoLISP's insertion of blocks.

The first few pages of this chapter covered all of the ins and outs of attribute and attribute definition data, but the important lesson here is that you can use attributes as drawing tools and not just little slots to store data for reports.

ATTEDIT is flexible, but a nuisance to use manually. Write menu macros to update commonly changed attributes. If you need to do editing that ATTEDIT doesn't allow, or if you want faster processing speed, use entity access and modification like we did in our drawing revision system.

When you mix attributes and text in a drawing, it's hard to tell the difference. This complicates text editing. However, from what you've learned in this chapter, you could write a function that edits all text in the same way regardless of whether it is in an attribute or text entity.

The title block and revblock systems are strong, but dull, drawing management tools, and we'll extract and use the data stored by them for project tracking in Chapter 13. Compared to the title block and revblock systems, autobreaking blocks are downright sexy. And they're just the tip of the parametrics iceberg. Let's see what else you can do with parametrics in the next chapter.

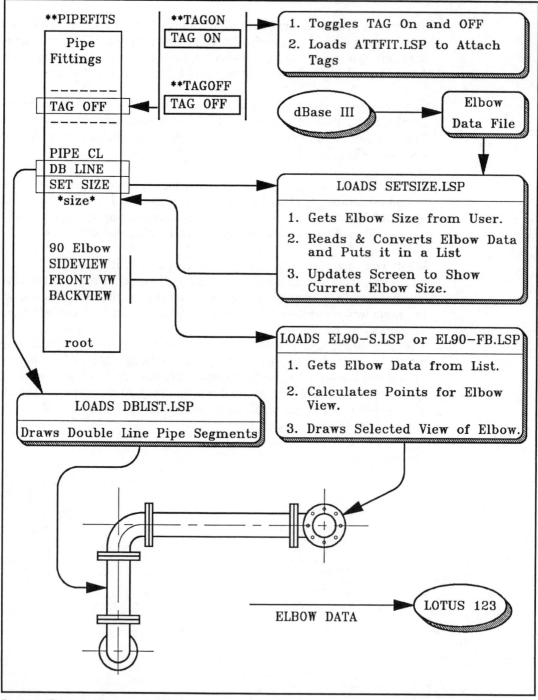

Program Flow of a Parametric System

CHAPTER 12

Using AutoLISP to Create Parts

PARAMETRICS AND MATERIAL TAGGING

AutoCAD parametric programs are AutoCAD and AutoLISP-based programs that get parameters from you or from external files, and then generate an image in an AutoCAD drawing. One program can draw many different sizes and shapes of a common component. You've seen simple parametrics in last chapter's autobreaking blocks. The AutoCAD INSERT command is parametrics at its simplest. But you can only scale blocks in their entirety. For example, you can't use blocks to change the number and pitch of teeth on a gear, or generate windows of varying sizes while holding the mullions constant.

With parametrics, you can draw any set of complex objects that share common geometric relationships. Where scale is the only variation, blocks are the best solution. But where variations would otherwise require a large library of similar blocks, parametrics offer flexibility, reduce errors, and yield greater efficiency.

While this chapter's example parametrics program draws pipe fittings and tags materials, the basic ideas and many of the routines are applicable to any parametrics system.

We will show you how to plan and design a parametric system. You'll learn to take advantage of geometric similarities in the parametric image, efficiently handle large numbers of variables, and parse component input data into a list of characteristics, like size and design properties. This chapter's parametric system includes parts tagging to provide data for next chapter's bill of materials reporting.

Macros, AutoLISP Tools, and Programs

Macros

IL12PARA.MNU is the parametrics screen menu. The main page is ****PIPEFITS**, which includes:

[TAG ON] and [TAG OFF] to toggle component material tagging on and off.

[DB LINE] to draw double line pipes and flanges between fittings with dimensions based on current pipe data.

[SET SIZE] to load the requested pipe data.

[SIDEVIEW], [FRONT VW], and [BACKVIEW] to draw the parametric pipe fittings.

AutoLISP Tools

GETSIZE searches a data file, retrieves the requested data, and parses the data string into a list of values.

ATTFIT and ATTLINE are tools that automatically attach material tags to the elbows and pipe segments.

EL90SUBR.LSP includes ELDATA and FLANGE, two subroutines used by all three of our parametric drawing programs.

Programs

SETSIZE.LSP is the program that manages the data retrieval process. The main function, SETSIZE, is the user interface function for the parametric drawing programs. It gets the part name, opens the data file, and uses GETSIZE to return the component data.

EL90-S.LSP is a parametric program that makes a 90-degree pipe elbow in side view.

DBLINE.LSP draws double line pipes between pipe fittings.

The EL90-FB.LSP program draws elbows in front and back views.

ATTFITS.LSP is the program file containing the ATTFIT and ATTLINE tools.

What Can Parametrics Do?

A parametric program can generate different parts, views, or sizes from a single set of dimension and geometric data. The data can be compiled from sources outside AutoCAD, such as parts lists and engineering references. You can use Lotus 123, dBASE, and other application programs to make files suitable for parametric processing. The data files may also be accessed by external programs to do engineering calculations. AutoLISP-based parametrics can make intelligent decisions, alert you to potential component problems, and suggest alternative solutions. Like blocks and their attributes, parametric programs can automatically tag components with materials data. And parametric programs reduce the chances of error by reducing the need for user input.

The Elements of a Parametric System

The parts of a more elaborate parametric component system vary with the system design, but they are likely to include:

■ External (non-AutoCAD) files containing the component data and design properties.

■ A user interface function that prompts and informs.

■ An AutoLISP subroutine that reads the data files.

■ Functions to calculate and draw images.

■ A menu interface to the programs and functions.

■ A help support screen with a list of components.

■ Material tags.

This may seem like a lot of system parts. Why not just write one big C:command that does it all? By designing the system in modules, you can use many of the modular parts to expand the system or to be used in other parametric applications.

We'll start by making the screen menu interface of the parametric system. Then, we'll add the AutoLISP programs, menus, and text data files to support the menu. The program flow for the parametric system is shown in the illustration at the beginning of the chapter.

Designing the Parametric System and Screen Menu

To construct the IL12PARA.MNU screen menu, we need to lay out the basic skeleton of the system and the macro labels we will use. We will have four components to draw: [SIDEVIEW], [FRONT VW] (front view), and [BACKVIEW] of an elbow, and [DB LINE], the pipe connecting them. The drawing procedure will first use [PIPE CL] to draw a center line, then put in the elbows, and, lastly, connect the pipes.

We'll store the data in an external file. Instead of accessing the file for each use of each parametric drawing command, we'll use a global variable, #ARGLIST, to minimize file access. This variable will be set by the [SET SIZE] macro using the SETSIZE.LSP program. It allows each drawing function to have immediate access to the data. The current size will be displayed by GRTEXT on the screen menu.

The system will have optional materials tagging, which will be set on or off by the value of the global #TAG flag variable. The current state of the #TAG flag will be displayed and reset by a [TAG ON] and [TAG OFF] mini-page toggle pair of macros.

The menu macro labels mentioned above make up the entire **PIPEFITS menu page. The **PIPEFITS page is accessed from the root menu by [PIPEFITS], a typical point-of-entry control macro. Here's the screen menu.

```
***SCREEN
**ROOT
[IL12PARA]
[]
[]
[PIPEFITS]^C^C^CLAYER M CEN31 C 2 ;LTYPE CENTER ;M OBJ01 ;+
(if setsize nil (load "SETSIZE")) (if flange nil (load "EL90SUBR"));+
(if (and setsize flange (or #arglist (findfile "PIPEFIT.DAT")));+
  (progn (menucmd "S=PIPEFITS") (grtext 4 (if #tag "TAG ON" "TAG OFF"));+
    (if #size (grtext 10 (strcat "* " #size)) (princ));+
  );+
  (progn (prompt ;+
        "SETSIZE.LSP, EL90SUBR.LSP or PIPEFIT.DAT not found. PIPEFITS disabled";+
        ) (princ);+
) );
[]
[]
```

❶   And 12 more lines, blank except for [], for a total of 20 [labels] in the **ROOT page.

```
[]
[]
+
**PIPEFITS
[ Pipe  ]
[Fittings]
[]
[--------]
[  TAG   ]^C^C^C(if attfit nil (load "ATTFITS"));+
(if attfit (progn (if #tag (menucmd "S=TAGOFF") (menucmd "S=TAGON")) (princ));+
(progn (prompt "ATTFITS.LSP not found. Tagging disabled. ") (princ)));
[--------]
[]
[PIPE CL ]^C^C^CLAYER S CEN31 ;LINE
```

Listing continued.

Continued listing.

```
[DB LINE ]^C^C^CLAYER S OBJ01 ;(if dbline nil (load "DBLINE"));+
(if dbline (dbline #tag #arglist) (progn (prompt "DBLINE.LSP not found. ") (princ)));
[SET SIZE]^C^C^C(setq #arglist (setsize (findfile "PIPEFIT.DAT") ;+
"Nominal pipe size (or ?)" ));
[* size *]
[]
[]
[90 Elbow]
[SIDEVIEW]^C^C^CLAYER S OBJ01 ;(if el90-s nil (load "EL90-S"));+
(if el90-s (el90-s #tag #arglist) (progn (prompt "EL90-S.LSP not found. ") (princ)));
[FRONT VW]^C^C^CLAYER S OBJ01 ;(if el90-fb nil (load "EL90-FB"));+
(if el90-fb (el90-fb #tag #arglist T) (progn (prompt "EL90-FB.LSP not found. ") ;+
(princ)));
[BACKVIEW]^C^C^CLAYER S OBJ01 ;(if el90-fb nil (load "EL90-FB"));+
(if el90-fb (el90-fb #tag #arglist nil) (progn (prompt "EL90-FB.LSP not found. ") ;+
(princ)));
[]
[]
[  root  ]$S=SCREEN LAYER S 0 ;
**TAGOFF 5
[TAG OFF ](setq #tag T) $S=TAGON
**TAGON 5
[TAG ON  ](setq #tag nil) $S=TAGOFF
```

The IL12PARA.MNU File

❶ The **ROOT and **PIPEFITS pages are each 20 square-bracket labels long, so they overlay each other.

[PIPEFITS] makes the two needed layers, leaving OBJ01 current. Its first IF loads SETSIZE.LSP, if not already loaded. The second IF checks to see that SETSIZE was found and loaded, and that either #ARGLIST has been set, or the PIPEFIT.DAT data file can be found. If not, it displays the PIPEFITS disabled prompt. If okay, it continues the setup. We could just check PIPEFIT.DAT, but it's quicker to check #ARGLIST after it has been initialized. The setup uses MENUCMD to change to the **PIPEFITS screen menu, then it uses GRTEXT to display the #TAG flag and size on the screen menu.

The **PIPEFITS screen page controls the parametric sizes and options, and displays current settings. [Pipe], [Fittings], and [90 Elbow] are just labels, not macros. **PIPEFITS has two status features. First, [TAG] uses the **TAGON and **TAGOFF mini-page menu label toggles to display whether the material tagging feature is on or off. [TAG] also loads

ATTFITS.LSP if not already loaded, and if okay, checks the current #TAG value to decide which tag mini-page to display. Second, [SET SIZE] uses the SETSIZE function to set #ARGLIST. SETSIZE also uses GRTEXT to dynamically display the pipe size over the [* size *] label. If you expand the system to include fittings other than 90-degree elbows, have it use GRTEXT or mini-page toggles to display the current types.

[PIPE CL] is a simple LINE command preceded by a layer setting. The rest of the macros, [DB LINE], [SIDEVIEW], [FRONT VW], and [BACKVIEW], call the drawing functions. They are virtually identical, loading their LISP files if not already loaded, and executing them if they are okay. Each feeds the #ARGLIST value and #TAG flag to its drawing function. The only difference between the [FRONT VW] and [BACKVIEW] is that [FRONT VW] feeds EL90-FB a **T** argument and [BACKVIEW] feeds it a nil argument. This tells the EL90-FB function whether to draw a front or back view.

If you don't have the IL DISK, you'll have to trick IL12PARA.MNU into letting you test it. We haven't created the supporting AutoLISP files yet, and the macros will just display disabled prompts if they don't find their functions. A couple of SETQs should do the trick.

Testing the PIPEFITS Menu

Enter selection: **1**	Begin a NEW drawing named IL12.
Command: **MENU**	Load the menu IL12PARA.

Command: **(setq #arglist T setsize T #size "1-1/2" attfit T)**

Select **[PIPEFITS]**	The settings occur and the page changes. GRTEXT displays [TAG OFF] and [* 1-1/2].
Select **[TAG OFF]**	Its (setq #tag T) returns T and toggles the label to [TAG ON].
Select **[TAG ON]**	It toggles it off and returns nil.
Select **[PIPE CL]**	It changes layers and issues LINE.
Command: LINE From point:	Pick 2 points and <RETURN>. It draws a yellow center line.
Select **[DB LINE]**	If you don't have the IL DISK, it prompts.
DBLINE.LSP not found.	If you have the IL DISK, it crashes, because #ARGLIST isn't properly set.
Select **[root]**	It resets the layer to 0 and changes pages.

Like [DB LINE], the [SIDEVIEW], [FRONT VW], [SET SIZE], and [BACKVIEW] macros will refuse to run or crash until you write some AutoLISP functions and create the PIPEFIT.DAT data file. Let's take a look at file formats for the parametric data.

Planning External File Formats for Parametrics

You can create data files with any ASCII text editor. When you write parametric systems, standardize your data file formats with your entire system in mind. Decide which of the file formats discussed in Chapter 8 works best for your type of data and application. Then write one or two types of functions to process the standard formats. Balance your data file size. Don't make one giant file or a million tiny files.

Small, single-component data files are faster than any string-parsing method when your application requires frequent changes of component data in memory. These are files where each set of component or size data is stored in a separate file, and each line of the file is a list that can be set directly to one or more variables without string parsing.

If you have to use one large file that's over 10K in size, consider writing an external program in BASIC, FORTRAN, C, or some other language. It can extract the data via SHELL, and output it to a temporary file to be read by an AutoLISP program.

Use medium-sized component library files if the data will be used for several drawing operations per access. Group components in families, where the family shares something like size or type.

How to Do Data Files

Our parametric system is of the medium-sized style, although it actually only uses one component, one type of 90-degree elbow, to keep the example simple. If it incorporated different 90-degree elbow components, the file could be divided into sections by coded key word header lines. Our example uses a comma-delimited format with an asterisk tag keying the start of each record. The first line of each record is the material ID, like *size, and the second line is the data for that size.

```
*1
1.0,3.5,4.25,0.41375,4.0,0.5
*1-1/4
1.25,3.75,4.625,0.5,4.0,0.5
*1-1/2
1.5,4.0,5.0,0.5625,4.0,0.5
*2
2.0,4.5,6.0,0.625,4.0,0.625
*2-1/2
2.5,5.0,7.0,0.6875,4.0,0.625
*6
6.0,8.0,11.0,1.0,8.0,0.75
```

Pipe Data in PIPEFIT.DAT File

In this example, *1-1/2 is the key for a 1-1/2 inch nominal diameter fitting, followed by a data line describing the pipe-turning radius, bend diameters, and flange dimensions. The dimensions in the data file are real numbers, not integers, because our program needs real numbers for calculations. This data describes the elbow illustrated in the Parametric Elbow Fittings illustration below.

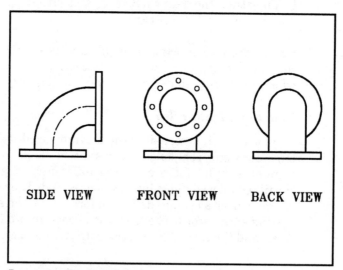

SIDE VIEW   FRONT VIEW   BACK VIEW

Parametric Elbow Fittings

If you have the IL DISK, the file PIPEFIT.DAT already has the parametric data. Otherwise, you need to make a new file and enter the data.

Creating the PIPEFIT.DAT File

 You already have the PIPEFIT.DAT file.

 Create the PIPEFIT.DAT file as shown above.

Once the sizes are in the file, you need a way to remember which sizes and types are available. One way to do this is to use AutoCAD's help facility.

Providing Help Support

The AutoCAD HELP command looks up and displays information stored in a file called ACAD.HLP. The help file is an ASCII text file, divided into pages by backslash-prefixed key words. You can modify ACAD.HLP to add documentation for your own programs, menus, and C:commands. Here's our PIPEFIT.HLP screen.

```
\PIPEFIT
\PIPEFITS
        Available pipe diameter fitting sizes

Nominal     Center  Flange  Flange      No.     Diam.
Pipe size   to End  Diam    Thickness   Bolts   Bolts
PDIAM       CE      FDIAM   FTHK        NB      DB
 1          3.5     4.25    0.41375     4       0.5
  1-1/4     3.75    4.625   0.5         4       0.5
  1-1/2     4       5       0.5625      4       0.5
 2          4.5     6       0.625       4       0.625
  2-1/2     5       7       0.6875      4       0.625
 6          8       11      1           8       0.75


Example of use:

Select [SET SIZE] from screen menu.

Nominal pipe size (or ?): 1-1/4       Enter as 1-1/4 (not 1.25 or 1-1/4").

Select [SIDEVIEW]                     Or another component draw command.
Select two lines...
First pipe center line:
Second pipe center line:
```

Help Screen in PIPEFIT.HLP File

Using the AutoCAD HELP command to display a parametrics help screen is a natural application. Less efficient alternatives might be to have your program read in your entire parametric data file, format it, and display the data, or to use the DOS TYPE command via SHELL to display a help screen.

\PIPEFIT is the name AutoCAD will use to find the help screen. ACAD.HLP uses the backslash to identify each help screen name. If the help topic needs more than one screen, you divide it into pages by inserting *blank* lines containing only a leading backslash. A page can have multiple labels, like the \PIPEFIT and \PIPEFITS labels shown above. But to use the help page, it must be part of a file named ACAD.HLP.

The standard ACAD.HLP file should be in your ACAD program directory. We'll copy \ACAD\ACAD.HLP to our IL-ACAD directory, merging it with PIPEFIT.HLP. (If your ACAD files are in a different directory, substitute your own directory name for \ACAD.) For fast help access, AutoCAD uses a file called ACAD.HDX (Help inDeX). If it can't find the .HDX file, AutoCAD creates a new index. It uses the normal AutoCAD library path (see Chapter 8) to look for the ACAD.HDX file, and uses the ACAD.HLP file in that index file's directory. When remaking the HDX file, AutoCAD has a preference for seeing the ACAD.HLP file in *its* program directory. To make AutoCAD use our help file, you need to force it to look in the current drawing directory. To do so, delete the ACAD.HDX and temporarily rename the ACAD.HLP file in the ACAD directory to another name, such as ACAD.HHH. Then AutoCAD will find our merged ACAD.HLP file and create an ACAD.HDX for it. This will only affect our IL-ACAD configuration, because our IL.BAT file does a SET ACAD=\IL-ACAD when we start up AutoCAD. Your other configuration(s) will be unchanged. When you rename ACAD.HHH back to ACAD.HLP and run your normal AutoCAD configuration, the ACAD directory's ACAD.HDX file will be remade, allowing both HDX files to co-exist.

Generating a Help Index File

Continue in the previous drawing, or begin a NEW drawing named IL12.

 You already have the PIPEFIT.HLP file. Just do COPY, DEL, and REN and try it out.

 Create the PIPEFIT.HLP file as shown above. Then do COPY, DEL, and REN and try it out.

```
Command: SHELL                  And <RETURN> to shell out to the DOS prompt.
C:\IL-ACAD>> COPY \ACAD\ACAD.HLP + PIPEFIT.HLP  ACAD.HLP
                                Merges the 2 files in a new ACAD.HLP, in the current directory.
C:\IL-ACAD>> REN \ACAD\ACAD.HLP *.HHH          Temporarily rename it.
C:\IL-ACAD>> DEL \ACAD\ACAD.HDX                 Delete the index.
C:\IL-ACAD>> EXIT                               Exit back to AutoCAD.

Command: ?                                      Test the new help.
"C:\IL-ACAD\ACAD.hdx":  Can't open file
HELP index being created.
Command name (RETURN for list): PIPEFIT        And the help screen shown above displays.

Command: SHELL
DOS Command: REN \ACAD\ACAD.HHH *.HLP          Rename it back.
```

To complete our system, all we need now are the AutoLISP files to get the data, process it, and draw the elbows. The first step is to get the data from the PIPEFIT.DAT file.

Retrieving External Parametric Data

To keep our system flexible and modular, data retrieval is handled by two functions. The [SET SIZE] macro calls SETSIZE to handle user input and prompting. SETSIZE gets the part name, opens the data file, and uses the GETSIZE subroutine to search the data file and parse the data string into a list of values. The data is returned as a list which is set to the global #ARGLIST variable by the [SET SIZE] macro.

Both functions are in the SETSIZE.LSP file. Let's look at SETSIZE first.

```
;* SETSIZE.LSP prompts for and retrieves request of parametric data files.
;* Data retrieval uses two functions. SETSIZE handles input and prompting.
;* GETSIZE gets the data, which is returned as a LIST.
;*

;* SETSIZE is for the PIPEFIT parametric system. Support for the AutoCAD Help
;* facility is added to the prompting sequence of the program.
;* The user get functions are required. It requires filespec and prompt string
;* args and returns NIL or a data list. #SIZE is global for defaulting.
;*
(defun setsize (datfile prmpt / fp size found arglist)
  (if (setq fp (open datfile "r"))              ;test for file
    (progn
      (setq size #size)                         ;store default
```

Listing continued.

Continued listing.

```
❶
        (while (not found)    ;flag to terminate loop, local "found" initially nil
          (while (or
                     (not (setq #size (ustr 0 prmpt #size nil)))  ;get the pipe size
                     (= #size "?")                   ;allow a ? to list'em
                 );or
                 (if (= #size "?")                   ;use the acad.hlp to display pipe sizes
                     (command "'?" "PIPEFIT")        ;call acad for help
                 );if
          );while or
❷
          (if (setq arglist (getsize fp (strcat "*" #size))) ;gets size, puts * in front of name
             (setq found T)                       ;stop size prompting
             (progn
               (prompt "\nSorry, that size not found! ") ;prompt for size again
               (close fp)                          ;close the file
               (setq fp (open datfile "r")         ;reopen to rewind to top
                     #size size                    ;restore default
             ) );setq&progn
          );if
        );while not found
        (close fp)                                 ;close the file
❸
        (grtext 10 (strcat "* " #size))            ;print size on screen label
      );progn
   );if
   arglist                                         ;return data list
);defun SETSIZE
;*
```

SETSIZE Function in SETSIZE.LSP File

The data file name and a prompt are passed into the SETSIZE function as the DATFILE and PRMPT arguments. The SETSIZE function determines that the data file exists by opening it. If it exists, the rest of the program runs in a big PROGN.

❶ The major portion of the program is in a WHILE that loops until the FOUND flag indicates that valid data has been found. A nested WHILE-OR-NOT expression uses USTR to prompt for the size to draw, or for a question mark. If it gets a "?," it uses (command "?" "PIPEFIT") to display the help file, and the WHILE reloops the USTR to get the size.

❷ GETSIZE is called to search the file for the component data, which is set to ARGLIST. The IF tests whether the component was found. If so, the FOUND flag is set to T to kill the WHILE and exit the program. If not, the PROGN prompts, closes the file, and reopens it to try again.

❸ The SETSIZE function uses GRTEXT to print the current #SIZE on the screen menu page. The final ARGLIST returns the value to the calling [SET SIZE] macro, which sets it to the global #ARGLIST variable.

Now let's examine the core data retrieval subroutine, GETSIZE.

```
;* GETSIZE is a general purpose data search and retrieval function for
;* asterisk tagged "*name" comma delimited data format. Its FP arg is the file
;* handle. SIZE is the key "*name" to find the data. It returns NIL or a data list.
(defun getsize (fp size / item data dline dlist maxs count chrct numb)
  (setq item (read-line fp))              ;first line is a label for file
❶
  (while item                            ;process each line of file
    (if (= item size)
      (setq data (read-line fp)          ;read a line
            item nil                      ;stop searching for item
      );setq
      (setq item (read-line fp))          ;keep searching for item
    );if
  );while
  (if data                               ;if the size has been found
    (progn
      (setq maxs (strlen data)            ;establish length of input
            count 1    chrct 1            ;initialize count and char position
      );setq
❷
      (while (< count maxs)               ;process string one chr at a time
        (if (/= "," (substr data count 1))   ;look for the commas
          (setq chrct (1+ chrct))          ;increment to next pos
          (setq numb (atof (substr data (1+ (- count chrct)) chrct))   ;convert to real
                dlist (append dlist (list numb))    ;add it to the list
                chrct 1                    ;resets field ct
          );setq
        );if
        (setq count (1+ count))           ;increment the counter
      );while
      (setq numb (atof (substr data (1+ (- count chrct)))))  ;convert to real
```

Listing continued.

Continued listing.

```
          dlist (append dlist (list numb))        ;add it to the list
     );setq
   );progn
  );if data
  dlist                                      ;may be nil or a list of reals
);defun GETSIZE
;*

(princ)
;* end of SETSIZE.LSP
;*
```

GETSIZE Function in SETSIZE.LSP File

❶ GETSIZE loops in a WHILE to read through an asterisk-tagged comma-delimited file looking for *keyword*, in this case, the size. When it finds the key word, it reads the next line, the desired data string.

❷ The second WHILE loops through each character of the string looking for commas. Each group of characters between commas is extracted by SUBSTR, converted to a real number by ATOF, and added to the DLIST list by APPEND. DLIST returns the data list, or nil, at the end of the process.

Now we have enough supporting functions in place that we don't have to trick the [PIPEFITS] macro in order to test it.

Testing the SETSIZE.LSP Data Retrieval Program

```
Enter selection: 1            Begin a NEW drawing again named IL12.
```

You have SETSIZE and GETSIZE in your SETSIZE.LSP file.

Create the SETSIZE and GETSIZE functions in a new file named SETSIZE.LSP.

```
Command: MENU              Load the IL12PARA menu.
Select [PIPEFITS] [SET SIZE]               Test it with the screen menu.
Nominal pipe size (or ?): 6                Enter 6, and the data is returned.
Lisp returns: (6.0 8.0 11.0 1.0 8.0 0.75)  It's now set to #ARGLIST.
                                           The [* size *] menu label is replaced by [* 6].
```

With the data in AutoCAD, we're ready to generate parametric images.

Generating Parametric Images

You've calculated object points, selected appropriate AutoCAD commands, and drawn groups of similar parts many, many times. That's all that parametrics does, except it automates it. But to write a parametrics program, you need to do a little planning. You should sketch out each component view on paper, labeling the variables, relationships, and critical points on the image. Show linetypes and identify common graphic constructions. For instance, elbow fittings all have a least one flange drawn as a rectangle. That's one routine you can centralize. Make a mini tool box of subroutines that can generate images piece by piece. Standardize the common routines and create specific parametric commands to use them.

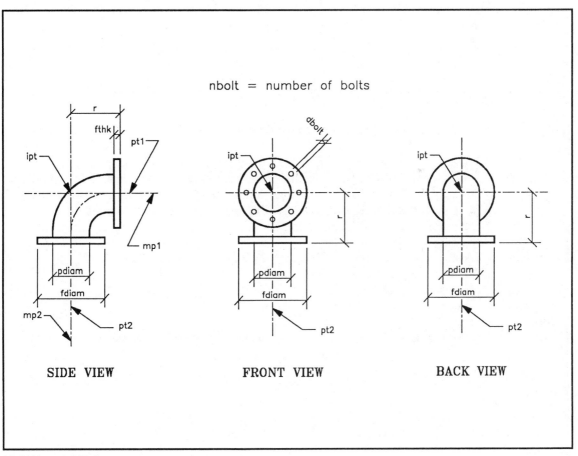

Variables and Fittings

Figure out which points you will need to select, and which you will need to calculate in your program. Label the points you'll pass back to AutoCAD when drawing the image. The variables and points for our elbow are shown in the Variables and Fittings illustration.

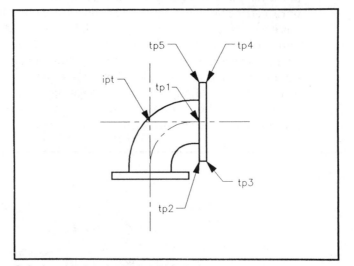

Calculated Points for Fitting Sideview

Once you have decided all the points, variables, commands, and subroutines you'll use to draw the image, you can create the programs. We'll have three main functions, EL90-S, EL90-FB and DBLINE, that call the FLANGE, ELDATA, ATTFIT, and ATTLINE subroutines.

```
;* EL90SUBR.LSP contains two subroutines common to both EL90-S.LSP and EL90-FB.LSP.
;* Variables are not declared, as they are used by the calling functions.
;* The calling function should declare them local.
;*
;* FLANGE calculates and draws a flange at angle ANG.
(defun flange (ang)
  (setq tp1 (polar ipt ang r-fthk)           ;calculate the temporary points
        tp2 (polar tp1 (+ ang #pi270) h-fdiam)
        tp3 (polar tp2 ang fthk)
        tp4 (polar tp3 (+ ang #pi90) fdiam)
        tp5 (polar tp4 (+ ang pi) fthk)
  );setq
  (command "pline" tp2 tp3 tp4 tp5 "c")       ;draw the flange
);defun FLANGE
;*
```

Listing continued.

Continued listing.

```
;* ELDATA initialized PI constants and sets the #ARGLIST variables
(defun eldata ()
  (mapcar 'set '(pdiam r fdiam fthk nbolt dbolt) arglist) ;sets all local vars
  (setq #pi90 (/ pi 2)  #pi270 (* pi 1.5)      ;set constants
        h-fdiam (/ fdiam 2.0)                  ;half the flange diameter
        h-pdiam (/ pdiam 2.0)                  ;half the pipe diameter
        r-fthk (- r fthk)                      ;radius minus the flange thickness
  )
);defun ELDATA
;*
(princ)
;* End of EL90SUBR.LSP
```

ELDATA and FLANGE Subroutines in EL90SUBR.LSP File

EL90SUBR.LSP contains a couple of functions common to our three main parametrics drawing functions. First, it gets loaded by the [PIPEFITS] macro. Second, it uses FLANGE to draw the flanges found in all our elbows and pipes. It takes the orientation angle of the flange and calculates the corner points, which are fed to PLINE. It's a good idea to use polylines instead of lines and arcs to draw parametrics. Polylines keep the number of separate entities to a minimum, making later edits easier. Because the variables used in FLANGE are also used by the calling functions, they are not declared local.

ELDATA is fed the #ARGLIST data via the calling function. ELDATA sets variables to each element of the argument list, then sets several other variables common to all three calling programs. The variables are declared local in the calling programs, not in ELDATA. ELDATA employs an extremely efficient MAPCAR technique for setting a list of data to a list of variable names.

mapcar | *Sequentially executes a lisp function on each set of elements in one or more argument lists.*
(mapcar *function list* ...)

MAPCAR maps the arguments supplied by its argument list(s) to the function specified. The function argument must be quoted. It's kind of a multiple FOREACH, dealing with all first elements of each list, then all second elements, and so on. A slower alternative would be to have six program statements, one for each variable. The following lines compare both ways, assuming ARGLIST is a list of six data values:

(setq pdiam (nth 0 arglist))   The slow way takes 6 of these.

(mapcar ′set ′(pdiam r fdiam fthk nbolt dbolt) arglist)   Fast.

The program maps the SET function to each element of the first list and its corresponding element in the second list. SET is used instead of SETQ to evaluate each element of the quoted first list. With the currently set #ARGLIST, it sets PDIAM to 6.0, R to 8.0, FDIAM to 11.0, and so on.

The first calling program, EL90-S, draws the side view of the elbow.

Drawing a Side View of a 90-Degree Elbow

The [SIDEVIEW] macro calls the EL90-S function. It takes two arguments, the #TAG flag to toggle component tagging and the #ARGLIST list of pipe fitting data. It prompts you to select two orthogonally intersecting center lines (lines or polylines), and the fitting is drawn around the intersection of the center lines. The INTERS function finds the intersection.

inters

> *Returns a point value of the intersection of a line between the first two points and a line between the second two points. If the optional flag is not nil, the lines are infinitely projected to calculate the intersection.*
> (inters *point point point point* flag)

The IL90-S function uses osnaps to find points. In programs, you must carefully control osnap and object selection to avoid getting wrong points and entities that could crash the drawing, especially when zoomed way in or out. There are two ways to use osnap in a program. You can use SETVAR to reset the running osnap. This is safest for use with GET functions, because it won't crash if it doesn't find the point. Running osnaps also allows you to override them by typing an osnap in before selection. This program sets NEA (512) for object selection. But be sure to set osnap back to NON (0) before proceeding, to avoid interfering with the program's COMMAND functions. The IL90-S function also uses the OSNAP *function* to find points.

osnap

> *Returns a point value specified by the osnap mode string on the supplied point value. The mode argument is a string, like "END,INT".*
> (osnap *point mode*)

The IL90-S selection points are OSNAPed END with a small aperture to get the other two points, enabling INTERS to obtain the intersection point.

```
;* EL90-S.LSP generates parametric 90 degree elbow fittings in side view.
;* It requires selecting two intersecting orthogonal center lines about
;* which the fitting is drawn at the preselected fitting size.
;* Its TAG arg is an attrib tagging flag T or NIL. ARGLIST is the pipe data,
;* generally global variable #ARGLIST.
;* The user get functions and EL90SUBR.LSP are required.

(defun el90-s (tag arglist / $op $ap pt1 pt2 ep1 ep2 ipt pdiam r fdiam fthk nbolt dbolt
                        alist h-fdiam r-fthk tp1 tp2 tp3 tp4 tp5 ent)
   (if arglist                                  ;if user selected a size
     (progn
```

❶
```
       (setq aperture (getvar "APERTURE")  osmode (getvar "OSMODE"))
       (setvar "OSMODE" 512) (setvar "APERTURE" 5)
       (prompt "\nSelect two lines...")           ;info prompt
                                                   ;get 2 points, be sure entity is selected
       (setq pt1 (upoint 1 "" "First pipe center line" nil nil))
            pt2 (upoint 1 "" "Second pipe center line" nil nil))
       )
       (setvar "APERTURE" 1)                       ;set a smaller aperture
       (setvar "OSMODE" 0)                         ;NONe
       (setq ep1 (osnap pt1 "end")                 ;get the endpoint of first entity
            ep2 (osnap pt2 "end")                  ;end of second entity
            ipt (inters ep1 pt1 ep2 pt2 nil)       ;intersection of the points
       );setq
```

❷
```
       (if ipt                                     ;if an intersection exists
         (progn
           (eldata)                                ;set variables
           (setq e1ang (angle ipt pt1)             ;angle of first entity
                e2ang (angle ipt pt2)              ;angle along second entity
           );setq
```

❸
```
           (flange e1ang)                          ;draw first flange
           (flange e2ang)                          ;draw second flange
```

❹
```
                                                   ;* add the arcs
           (command "pline" (polar ipt e1ang r-fthk) ipt ;pline arc along center of fitting
              (polar ipt e2ang r-fthk) ""
              "fillet" "r" pdiam "fillet" "p" "l"  ;fillet polyarc with fitting diameter
              "offset" (/ pdiam 2.0)               ;offset center arc to each side
```

Listing continued.

Continued listing.

```
          (setq ent (list (entlast) tp1)) tp5 ent tp2 ""     ;using ENTSEL style list
            "change" tp1 "" "p" "la" "cen31" ""                ;change center arc to a center line
          );command
❺
          (if tag (attfit "ELBOW" arglist ipt))               ;insert material tag if [TAG ON]
          (setvar "APERTURE" aperture) (setvar "OSMODE" osmode)   ;restore
        );progn
        (prompt "\nError: No intersection point found. ")   ;abort if no intersection found
      );if
    );progn
    (prompt "\nSelect a size first. ")                      ;abort if no size selected
  );if
  (princ)
);defun EL90-S
;*
(princ)
;*end of EL90-S.LSP
;*
```

EL90-S Function in EL90-S.LSP File

❶ The first part of EL90-S flip-flops the osnaps, gets the input points with UPOINT, and calculates the EP1, EP2, and IPT points with OSNAP and INTERS.

❷ The IF tests that an intersection point, IPT, is found. If not, EL90-S aborts. If found, it executes the rest of the program with PROGN. The inconspicuous ELDATA subroutine sets most of the variables needed to draw.

❸ The FLANGE function is called twice, once for each angle of the center line.

❹ Now the hard part, drawing the curves! Let's let AutoCAD calculate those. Draw the center line of the fitting as straight polyline segments, then use FILLET to create the curve and OFFSET to make the inner and outer pipe curves. The center of the pipe curve line is given a CENTER linetype.

OFFSET requires entities to be selected by a point. If you are zoomed way out, the pick box may find the wrong entity. So we control point selection by building an ENTSEL style list with ENTLAST and TP1, and using it to select the entity to offset.

❺ If the tag flag is set, the ATTFIT function is called to insert material tagging. We'll leave #TAG off until we create the ATTFITS.LSP file in the last part of the chapter.

That's it. The function closes by restoring the system variables and adding error prompts as the *else* of the two IF tests. Let's try it.

Using the EL90-S Function

```
Enter selection: 1
```
Begin a NEW drawing named IL12=IL-PROTO.

    You have EL90-S in your EL90-S.LSP file.

    Create the EL90-S function in a new file named EL90-S.LSP.

```
Command: MENU
Command: SNAP
Command: GRID
Command: ZOOM
Command: LIMITS
```
Load the IL12PARA.MNU.
Set to 2.
Set to 6.
Zoom Left corner 0,0 with height 6'-0".
From 0,0 to 12',8'.

```
Select [PIPEFITS] [SET SIZE]
Select [PIPE CL]
```
            Enter 6 as a size.
Draw a few lines as illustrated below.

```
Command: SAVE
```
Save as IL12A, for use in later exercises.

```
Select [SIDEVIEW]
Select two lines...
First pipe center line:
Second pipe center line:
```
Try it.

Pick first line.
Pick second. It draws the fitting and filleted center line.

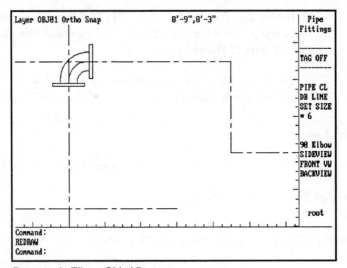

Parametric Elbow Side View

Now that one is drawn, creating the others will be easy.

Creating Multiple Parts — the Beauty of Parametrics

Drawing with parametrics gives you more objects with less overhead! You can make a front and back view of the same elbow with mostly the same code and data.

How to Do Front and Back Views in One

The next function, EL90-FB, draws front and back views. You tell it which to draw by the FRONT flag in the argument list. This flag is set by the [FRONT VW] and [BACKVIEW] macros that both call EL90-FB. In creating EL90-FB, you can copy portions of code from EL90-S.LSP.

```
;* EL90-FB.LSP parametrically draws a Front/Back view 90 degree elbow fitting.
;* The fitting is drawn at the preselected fitting size.
;* Its TAG arg is an attrib tagging flag T or NIL. ARGLIST is the pipe data,
;* generally global variable #ARGLIST. If the FRONT arg is T, it draws the
;* front, otherwise the back is drawn.
;* The user get functions and EL90SUBR.LSP are required.

(defun el90-fb (tag arglist front / e1 e2 $op pt2 ipt pdiam h-pdiam
                r fdiam fthk nbolt dbolt elang h-fdiam r-fthk h-inca
                tp1 tp2 tp3 tp4 tp5 tp6 tp7 tp8 tp9)
```

Listing continued.

Continued listing.

```
(if arglist                              ;if user selected a fitting size
  (progn
    (setq aperture (getvar "APERTURE") osmode (getvar "OSMODE"))
    (setvar "APERTURE" 5) (setvar "OSMODE" 1)                ;endpoint
    (setq ipt (upoint 1 "" "Centerpoint of 1st flange" nil nil))
    (setvar "OSMODE" 512)                                    ;nearest
    (setq pt2 (upoint 1 "" "2nd Flange direction" nil ipt))
    (setvar "OSMODE" 0)
    (eldata)                             ;set variables, material tag
    (setq nbolt (fix nbolt)              ;convert from a real for ARRAY command
          elang (angle ipt pt2)          ;angle of selected line

          h-inca (/ (incang pdiam h-fdiam) 2.0)    ;half the included angle
    );setq
    (flange elang)                       ;draw flange, calc tp1 - 5

    (setq tp6 (polar tp1 (+ elang #pi90) h-pdiam)  ;calc other temp points
          tp7 (polar tp6 (- elang #pi90) pdiam)
          tp8 (polar ipt (+ elang h-inca) h-fdiam)
          tp9 (polar tp8 (- elang #pi90) pdiam)
          tp10 (polar ipt (+ elang #pi90) h-pdiam)
          tp11 (polar ipt (- elang #pi90) h-pdiam)
    );setq

    (if front                                ;check which view
      (command  "circle" ipt "d" pdiam       ;draw the front view
                "circle" ipt "d" fdiam
                "line" tp6 tp8 "" "line" tp7 tp9 ""
                "circle" (polar ipt elang (+ h-pdiam (/ (- fdiam pdiam) 4.0)))
                "d" dbolt "array" "l" "" "p" ipt nbolt 360 "n"    ;array the bolt holes
      );command
      (command  "line" tp6 tp10 "" "line" tp7 tp11 ""  ;else draw back view
                "arc" "C" ipt tp10 tp11
                "arc" "C" ipt tp8 tp9
      );command
    );if direction
    (if tag (attfit "ELBOW" arglist ipt))         ;insert material tag if [TAG ON]
    (setvar "OSMODE" osmode) (setvar "APERTURE" aperture)  ;restore
  );progn
  (prompt "\nSelect a size first. ")              ;no size was set
```

Listing continued.

Continued listing.

```
  );if data
  (princ)
);defun EL90-FB
;*

❹
;* We took a copy of INCANG from il-3d.lsp.
;* INCANG calculates the included angle given a chord distance and radius
(defun incang (chord radius)
  (* 2.0 (atan                                    ;twice the arc tangent
    (/ chord 2.0                                  ;of opposite over adjacent
      (sqrt (- (expt radius 2) (expt (/ chord 2.0) 2))))  ;calcs adjacent leg of triangle
    ));divide & atan
  );
);defun INCANG
;*
(princ)
;*end of EL90-FB.LSP
;*
```

EL90-FB Function in EL90-FB.LSP File

The EL90-FB function begins very much like EL90-S, with osnap controls and UPOINT functions to get the input points.

❶ ❹ The H-INCA (half angle) is calculated with the help of INCANG, one of our tools from Chapter 14's IL-3D.LSP file. It's included in the EL90-FB.LSP file for convenience.

❷ After the FLANGE subroutine is called, we calculate several more TPxx temporary points, like the points on the lines that intersect the curved surfaces of the pipe diameter. The calculated points are shown in the Front and Back Views illustration.

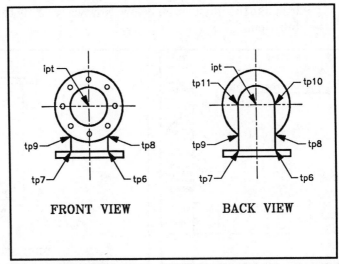

Front and Back Views

❸ Here is where you add the difference in views. The FRONT flag is tested in an IF to tell the program which set of drawing instructions to use. If FRONT is true, the front view is drawn, with CIRCLE and ARRAYed bolt holes shown in the view. Otherwise, a back view is constructed using ARC commands.

Using EL90-FB for Front and Back Views

Continue in the previous drawing, or edit the EXISTING drawing named IL12=IL-PROTO from the earlier "Using the EL90-S Function" exercise.

 You have EL90-S in your EL90-S.LSP file.

Create the EL90-S function in a new file named EL90-S.LSP.

Select **[PIPEFITS] [SET SIZE]**   Enter 6 as a size.

Select **[FRONT VW]**   Draw one.
Centerpoint of 1st flange: Pick point.
2nd Flange direction: Pick, and it scrolls and draws.

Select **[BACKVIEW]**   Test this one also.

If all went well, and if your drawing still has the side view elbow, it should look like the illustration below. Now we're ready to do the connecting pipe function.

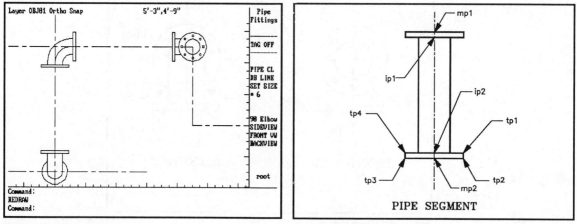

Fittings in Three Views   Double Line Pipe Points

Drawing Linear Parts — DBLINE

To finish the drafting task for this application, you need a command to connect all these fittings. The DBLINE function creates double pipe lines and draws the flanges at each end. It uses the flange subroutine. DBLINE assumes the ends will abut an existing flange, so it osnaps its two input points with MID, unless overridden.

```
;* DBLINE constructs double line pipes at the preselected fitting size by
;* selecting points on two flanges. Its TAG arg is an attrib tagging flag T or
;* NIL, controlling the option of calculation and recording of pipe segment
;* lengths and parametric properties. The ARGLIST argument is the pipe data,
;* generally global variable #ARGLIST.
;* The user get functions and EL90SUBR.LSP are required.

(defun dbline (tag arglist / pdiam r fdiam fthk nbolt dbolt h-fdiam h-pdiam
                     r-fthk mp1 mp2 ang ipt ip1 ip2 tp1 tp2 tp3 tp4)
  (if arglist                            ;if the size data exists
    (progn                               ;then run
      (eldata)                           ;set variables
      (setq osmode (getvar "OSMODE") aperture (getvar "APERTURE"))
      (setvar "APERTURE" 5) (setvar "OSMODE" 2)    ;turn on MIDP Osnap mode
```

Listing continued.

Continued listing.

```
     (while (setq mp1 (getpoint "\nFrom point: ")) ;start WHILE loop, get the first point
       (setq mp2 (upoint 1 "" "To point" nil mp1)) ;second point
       (setvar "OSMODE" 0)                        ;turn Osnap off
       (setq ang (angle mp1 mp2)                  ;calc the angle
             ip1 (polar mp1 ang fthk)        ;point on first flange
             ip2 (polar mp2 (+ ang pi) fthk) ;point on second flange


             ipt (polar mp1 (+ ang pi) r-fthk) ;compensate for tp1 offset of FLANGE
       );setq
       (flange ang)                              ;draw pipe flange
       (setq ipt (polar mp2 ang r-fthk))         ;compensate for tp1 offset of FLANGE
       (flange (+ ang pi))                       ;draw pipe flange


       (command "line" (polar ip1 (+ ang #pi90) h-pdiam)  ;draw parallel lines
                (polar ip2 (+ ang #pi90) h-pdiam) ""       ;for the double line
                "line" (polar ip1 (+ ang #pi270) h-pdiam)  ;pipe
                (polar ip2 (+ ang #pi270) h-pdiam) ""
       );command
       (if tag (attpipe arglist ip1 ip2))  ;if material tagging ON, insert attribute block
       (setvar "OSMODE" 2)                 ;turn on MIDP again for next pipe segment
     );while
     (setvar "OSMODE" osmode) (setvar "APERTURE" aperture)  ;restore
   );progn
   (prompt "\nSelect a size first. ")                       ;no size selected
 );if
 (princ)
);defun DBLINE
;*
(princ)
;* end of DBLINE.LSP
;*
```

DBLINE Function in DBLINE.LSP File

DBLINE's beginning is like the elbow functions, osnapping and getting points. Again, the ELDATA subroutine sets most of the variables and FLANGE draws the flanges.

❶ To accommodate the elbows, the FLANGE routine offsets its IPT start point by the flange radius minus the flange thickness. For DBLINE, we compensate by offsetting its IPT the same distance in the opposite direction. After drawing the first flange, IPT is reset for the opposite end and the second FLANGE call uses the opposite angle. PI radians is 180 degrees, so any angle plus PI yields the opposite angle.

❷ The pipe is easy. It's just four lines, using POLAR to offset the points. When completed, the entire DBLINE function loops back around for more points to draw another pipe.

Let's try it out between the elbows we drew.

Testing the Double Line Pipe Function

Continue in the previous drawing, or edit the EXISTING drawing named IL12=IL-PROTO, from the earlier "Using the EL90-S Function exercise."

 You have DBLINE in your DBLINE.LSP file.

Create the DBLINE function in a new file named DBLINE.LSP.

Select **[PIPEFITS] [SET SIZE]** Enter 6 as a size.

Draw some elbows if they aren't already in the drawing.

Select **[DBLINE]**	Draw between two opposite flanges.
From point:	Pick point on one flange.
To point:	Pick on other flange. It draws pipe and flanges.

And the finished drawing should look like the illustration below.

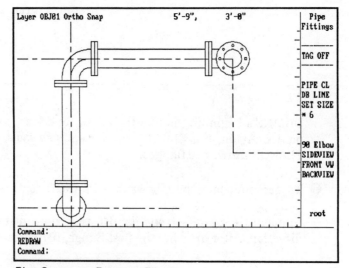

Pipe Segments Between Flanges

Since you already have all the data, why not tag the elbows and pipe with attributes that can be extracted for a materials report?

Adding Material Tags

One great advantage of CAD over a manual drawing is that the CAD drawing carries an electronic database with it. Blocks with attached attributes make it very easy to extract a listing of materials represented in a drawing. You can do the same thing with parametrically generated parts. A program can insert sets of invisible attributes along with each part it draws. Then AutoLISP or ATTEXT can extract the information to generate reports of materials.

How to Tag Parametric Parts

We'll use two pipe material blocks, ATTFIT and ATTPIPE, to tag our pipe and elbows. Each block contains nothing but invisible, variable attributes. Note that the ATTFIT tags are in the same order as the #ARGLIST data.

```
Block: Order:  Tag:              Block:   Order:  Tag:
ATTFIT  1.     F_TYPE            ATTPIPE  1.      P_DIAMETER
        2.     F_DIAMETER                 2.      P_LENGTH
        3.     F_RADIUS                   3.      P_FLANGE_DIAM
        4.     F_FLANGE_DIAM              4.      P_FLANGE_THICK
        5.     F_FLANGE_THICK             5.      P_NUMBER_BOLTS
        6.     F_NUMBER_BOLTS             6.      P_BOLT_DIAM
        7.     F_BOLT_DIAM
Note: All are invisible and variable with blank prompts
and defaults.
```

You don't need default prompts or values because they will be filled in automatically. Here's the sequence for creating the blocks.

Material Tagging

Continue in the previous drawing, or begin a NEW drawing again named IL12.

 You have the ATTPIPE.DWG and ATTFIT.DWG. You can skip this sequence.

 Do the following to create the attribute blocks.

```
Command: ZOOM                                  To a clear area, with height 8.
Command: LAYER                                 Set 0 current.

Command: ATTDEF                                Define the ATTFIT, set first.
Enter (ICVP) to change, RETURN when done: I    Set Invisible: Y  Constant: N
Attribute tag: F_TYPE                          The first tag.
Attribute prompt: <RETURN>                     None.
Default attribute value: <RETURN>              None.
Start point or Align/Center/Fit/Middle/Right/Style:   Pick, then default rotation.

Command: ATTDEF          Repeat for each of the rest of the ATTFIT set.

Command: WBLOCK
File name: ATTFIT
Block name (or ?): <RETURN> Return to select entities.
Select objects:          Select in the exact order of the table above.

Command: ATTDEF          Repeat for the ATTPIPE set.
Command: WBLOCK          Wblock them to name ATTPIPE.

Command: INSERT          Test them. Default scale and rotation.
Block name (or ?): ATTFIT
Enter attribute values   Default the values to nothing.
F_TYPE: <RETURN>
F_DIAMETER: <RETURN>
F_RADIUS: <RETURN>
F_FLANGE_DIAM: <RETURN>
F_FLANGE_THICK: <RETURN>
F_NUMBER_BOLTS: <RETURN>
F_BOLT_DIAM: <RETURN>    And you see nothing. It's invisible!

Command: QUIT
```

Since the material data for an elbow is different from a length of pipe, you need two functions to insert the attribute blocks.

How to Tag Parts

The ATTFIT function will place the fitting attributes, and ATTPIPE will record the pipe length and flange data of a pipe section. These are called automatically from the parametric elbow and DBLINE functions when the global #TAG variable is on (non-nil). They load when you toggle material tagging on from the **PIPEFITS menu.

```
;* ATTFITS.LSP inserts attribute data with the elbows and pipes drawn by
;* the EL90-S, EL90-FB and DBLINE functions.

;* ATTFIT assigns fitting data to an attribute block and inserts it
;* at the fitting intersection
(defun attfit (elbow arglist pt)
  (if (and elbow arglist pt)                      ;tests if all defined
    (progn
      (command "insert" "attfit" pt 1 1 0 elbow)  ;inserts attribute data tag
      (foreach item arglist                       ;send each one to attribute prompts
        (command (rtos item 2 6))                 ;rounds output to 6 places
      );foreach
    );progn
  );if
);defun ATTFIT
;*


;* ATTPIPE inserts the attribute block for pipe lengths.
(defun attpipe (arglist pt1 pt2 / leng pdiam r fdiam fthk nbolt dbolt mpt)
  (if (and arglist pt1 pt2)                            ;if everything is defined
    (progn
      (mapcar 'set '(pdiam r fdiam fthk nbolt dbolt) arglist) ;sets all local vars
      (setq leng (- (distance pt1 pt2) fthk fthk)      ;compute the pipe length
            mpt (polar pt1 (angle pt1 pt2) (* leng 0.5))) ;calc the midpoint
      );setq
      (command "insert" "attpipe" mpt 1 1 0)           ;insert the attribute block
      (foreach item (list pdiam leng fdiam fthk nbolt dbolt) ;builds a new list for output
        (command (rtos item 2 6))                      ;convert to decimal string
      );foreach
    );progn
  );if
);defun ATTPIPE
;*
(princ)
;* end of ATTFITS.LSP
;*
```

ATTFIT and ATTPIPE Functions in ATTFITS.LSP File

ATTFIT takes three arguments, the fitting description, the fitting data, and the point at which the attribute block gets inserted. The first COMMAND function inserts the ATTFIT attribute and enters the ELBOW argument as the first attribute value. Then it simply steps through ARGLIST with a FOREACH, entering each piece of data as another attribute value.

ATTPIPE is a little more complex. It needs the pipe length, not the fitting radius, as the second attribute. To calculate length, we need FTHK, the flange thickness. So we use MAPCAR to set the variables. Then we calculate LENG, the length of pipe. The FOREACH enters the attributes by stepping through the rebuilt list, which includes the LENG value.

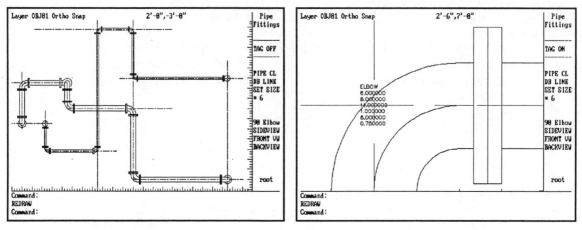

Populated Drawing   Elbow with Tag

Reporting the component tag information is covered in the next chapter. You need to generate a set of tagged materials for reporting. Draw twelve fittings and pipe lengths. Your drawing should look like our Populated Drawing illustration. Use [SET SIZE] to change sizes. Make sure you keep the [TAG ON].

Making Some Tagged Fittings

Enter selection: **1**   Begin a NEW drawing again named IL12=IL-PROTO.

You have ATTFIT and ATTPIPE in your ATTFITS.LSP file.

Create the ATTFIT and ATTPIPE functions in a new file named ATTFITS.LSP.

Command: **MENU**	Load the IL12PARA.MNU.
Command: **SNAP**	Set to 6.
Command: **GRID**	Set to 12.
Command: **ZOOM**	Zoom Left corner 0,0 with height 16'-0".
Command: **LIMITS**	From 0,0 to 24',16'.

Select **[PIPEFITS] [SET SIZE]**
Nominal pipe size (or ?): **2-1/2**
Lisp returns: (2.5 5.0 7.0 0.6875 4.0 0.625)

Select **[TAG OFF]**   Toggle TAG ON.

Select **[PIPE CL]**   Draw some center lines.
Select **[SIDEVIEW]**   Draw one, see how it puts in data.
Enter attribute values
Fitting type: ELBOW Pipe diameter: 2.5 Fitting curve radius: 5.0 Flange diameter: 7.0
Flange Thickness: 0.6875 Number of bolts: 4.0 Bolt diameter: 0.625
                          And the ATTFIT block attribute values appear.

Command: **ATTDISP**	Set ON so you can see the invisible attributes.
Command: **REGEN**	To see the attributes.
Command: **ZOOM**	Zoom in to see a close-up, as illustrated above.
Command: **ZOOM**	Zoom Previous.

Select **[FRONT VW]**   Try it too.
Select **[BACKVIEW]**   Try it. And some more.
Select DBLINE   Draw some pipe lengths.

You already have PIPEMATL.DWG. Skip the SAVE.

Command: **SAVE**   To name **PIPEMATL**. It's used in the next chapter.

Command: **QUIT**

Now you have a complete set of parametric tools for creating and tagging pipe fittings. The same techniques explored in our piping example can be applied to nearly any other parametric drawing application, from cabinetry to dress patterns to ski design to custom windows.

One strength of parametrics is that, unlike one-piece blocks, the objects can be edited. However, this is also a disadvantage. When you copy or move a block, it all moves together, with attributes. But our elbows each consist of five or more entities, plus attributes. Great care is required in editing, even to just erase. It's often hard to select the entire set of objects, particularly the invisible attributes.

There is a solution — GROUPS.

Grouping Entities for One-Pick Selection

It would be great if you could select any single entity from a parametric part, and have AutoCAD select the entire set. We have a program that does precisely that. It even selects frozen entities.

There is a GROUP.LSP program on the New Riders AutoLISP Utilities Disk 1. It includes the BEGGRP and ENDGRP subroutines, the C:SETGRP command, and the GETGRP function.

The BEGGRP starts a group. ENDGRP ends a group. All entities created, copied, exploded, or inserted between the execution of the BEGGRP and the ENDGRP functions will become a group. The C:SETGRP command also creates groups, prompting with normal object selection.

Unlike blocks, individual members of a group may be edited, moved to another location, or even deleted. The group will remain intact in spite of such editing. To select an existing group, you can use the GETGRP function, even in the middle of an editing command. GETGRP can be called as a subroutine by your programs. It prompts for an object selection and returns the selection set of the entire group associated with that member.

GROUP.LSP makes parametric programs truly practical, and helps to generally manage any type of drawing by allowing you to control groups of entities.

Summary

Once you've done a complete parametric system (and you just did), you can do any parametric system. The differences between systems are the specific points, variables, data files, menu macros, subroutines, help tools, drawing functions, attributes, AutoLISP functions, and AutoCAD commands you use. But the concepts and techniques are the same for almost any application.

Your computer's speed influences how complex you can make your parametric system. If a program seems slow, you'll have bored users, even if it draws ten times faster than they can. When you design a parametric program, try to intersperse any noticeable delays in processing or drawing with user input.

Don't stop with just drawing the parametric image. Use the component data to drive any other command that might supplement the system. Use the data file for external engineering calculations. Make programs that automatically tag materials with attributes or draw other parts of a system. And extract the data for materials reports, the topic of the next chapter.

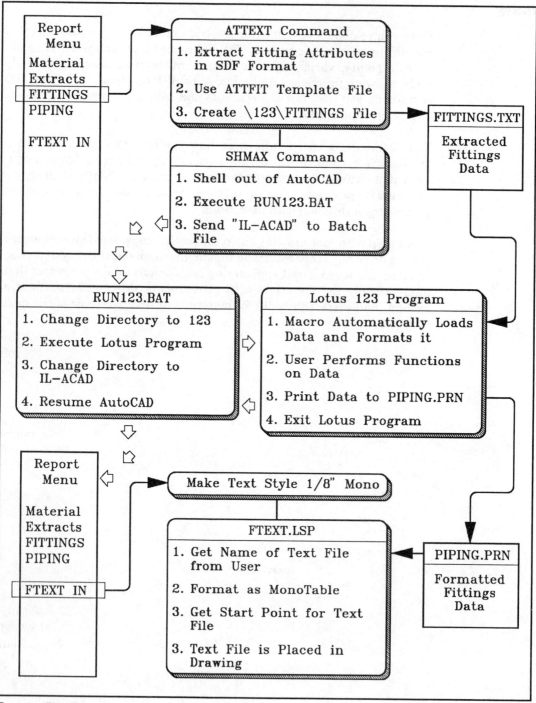

Program Flow Diagram Passing Data to Lotus 123

CHAPTER 13

Lotus and dBASE

REPORTING AutoCAD INFORMATION

You can make your system extract design information from AutoCAD drawings with very little effort. This chapter shows you how to enable your system to do two types of reporting: material estimating reporting, and project drawing schedule reporting. We'll generate the material reports using the attribute blocks that were attached to pipe segments and fittings in Chapter 12. Although our example involves piping, the same techniques can be adapted to any application. The project drawing schedule is a summary reporting operation for the title block management system from Chapter 11.

This chapter provides a simple, yet seamless transition between AutoCAD and Lotus 123, and between AutoCAD and dBASE III or IV. If you wish to run the Lotus 123 exercise, we'll assume that you have the Lotus 123 program set up and running in a directory called C:\123. If you have the IL DISK, the dBASE program is not required. The IL DISK contains an executable file of Clipper-compiled dBASE code.

Interfacing with Lotus and dBASE is useful for generating almost any type of report from AutoCAD drawing information. Architects might develop door and finish schedules, cost projections, and occupancy and lease management information. Civil engineers may consider applying these techniques to manage highway construction schedules, output elevation coordinates, or calculate retention pond requirements. Steel fabricators can generate bills of material, including steel pieces, delivery schedules, and bolt counts. Power and lighting applications might measure cable length needs, amperage requirements, and light intensity levels.

External programs like Lotus 123 and dBASE have different advantages. You must decide which is best for your particular application. Generally, determine if you are simply mixing, sorting, and outputting information from your AutoCAD drawing or if you are doing intensive calculations (more common in engineering applications). Lotus 123 is better suited to intensive calculations while dBASE is a good program for sorting and searching your AutoCAD data.

In this chapter, we will show you how to track your drawing revisions using dBASE. We will use Lotus to calculate a materials report from attributes exported from an AutoCAD drawing.

Using AutoCAD to report data provides several key benefits. It launches your CAD system into another dimension of material reporting, providing up-to-date part counts and component descriptions. You can determine how much material the design requires and you can calculate costs. Tracking your project drawings keeps you informed on the latest revisions and drafting time for a project. Project schedules and estimates will help your office coordinate CAD drawings and prepare financial billing records.

In this chapter, you will learn how to::

- Make template files that control drawing data extraction, the output data format, and field spacing.

- Extract component data from an AutoCAD drawing.

- Integrate the Lotus 123 spreadsheet program with AutoCAD.

- Set up a Lotus 123 spreadsheet to accept data from AutoCAD, import, format, and tally the data in Lotus 123.

- Write a Lotus macro to automate the data importing process.

- Send the spreadsheet file back to AutoCAD and use AutoLISP to import it into the drawing.

- Write AutoCAD macros to automate the entire report process.

- Report the drawing status to a master project status file.

- Output reference drawing data to a dBASE III program, process the data in dBASE, and report and print the data to a reference drawing schedule file.

Macros and Programs

Macros

**REPORT is a menu page added to the Chapter 12 IL12PARA.MNU. The following macros are on it.

[PIPING] and [FITTINGS] are macros that extract pipe length and fitting attributes from a drawing and call the Lotus 123 program.

[FTEXT IN] imports ASCII print file output from Lotus using the FTEXT AutoLISP program we will develop in Chapter 15.

TITLEBLK is a page of Chapter 11's IL11TITL.MNU. To it, you will add these macros.

[REP STAT] and [PROTRAK] call the REPSTAT.LSP and PRO_TRAK.EXE programs.

AutoLISP Programs

REPSTAT.LSP generates a project-tracking record for the current drawing and adds to the master PROJECT.DAT file.

External Programs

PRO_TRAK.EXE is a Clipper-compiled dBASE III program that tracks drawing information like project name and location, drawing number and revision level, dates of issue, plotting, last revision, and other project management details.

Making an Attribute Extract Template File

Let's start with the Lotus interface and report the pipe data generated earlier. The program flow is shown in the Program Flow Diagram at the beginning of the chapter. Use the AutoCAD ATTEXT command to extract attributes and write their data to an ASCII text file.

A special ASCII template file tells ATTEXT which materials to report and how to format the report during the attribute extraction process. The template file controls which attributes will be included in the report. It directs numeric and character data, and the width of each output field. The template also can include data about block insert scaling, coordinates, and nesting levels.

The purpose of the template file is to match attribute *tag* names in the file with those in the drawing and to extract the attribute value attached to each block insert. Attribute tags not listed in the template file are ignored. Tags listed in the template but not found in the drawing report as blank.

How to Format the Template File

Attribute extract files must have a .TXT file extension. You need a unique attribute tag for each component type. There must be at least one attribute tag in a template file. You should have at least one space between the attribute tag name and the format string.

Format strings, like C010000 and N009006, control the form of the output data. A "C" or "N" indicates character or numeric output. The first three digits tell AutoCAD the total output field character width (010 allots a ten character wide field). The last three digits specify the number of decimal places to output (always 000 for character fields).

The string, N009006, has six digits following the decimal point (which counts as a character). This leaves two leading digits for the whole part of the number (9-6-1=2). It outputs in the form: 12.123456. Integers may be output by using 000 decimal precision. The distinction between character and numeric is strictly for formatting. The data is written as ASCII characters in the output file.

Several problems may arise from incorrect field length numbers. AutoCAD issues a "field overflow" warning and truncates the output if the extracted attribute values don't fit in the template's specified field width. The output record may run together as one string, making processing of the output in Lotus difficult. AutoCAD does not report this run-on as an error, but it will cause errors in Lotus. To avoid a run-on string, increase the field width by one character. AutoCAD fills in any extra spaces. For example:

```
ELBOW   6.0000008.00000011.0000001.00000080.750000     Wrong!
ELBOW   6.000000 8.000000 11.000000 1.000000 8 0.750000  OK!
```

You can include block insert information in the template, without defining attributes, by using these standardized keys:

KEY NAME	FORMAT	DESCRIPTION
BL:LEVEL	Nwww000	(block nesting level)
BL:NAME	Cwww000	(block name)
BL:X	Nwwwddd	(X coordinate of insertion point)
BL:Y	Nwwwddd	(Y coordinate of insertion point)
BL:Z	Nwwwddd	(Z elevation of insertion point)
BL:LAYER	Cwww000	(layer name inserted on)
BL:ORIENT	Nwwwddd	(insert rotation angle)
BL:XSCALE	Nwwwddd	(X scale factor)
BL:YSCALE	Nwwwddd	(Y scale factor)
BL:ZSCALE	Nwwwddd	(Z scale factor)

AutoCAD outputs attribute fields in the same order listed in the template file. There is no automatic control for the order of records in the output file. AutoCAD outputs the records in the entity order. To control order, you have to select entities using ATTEXT's Entity Select option. In most applications, record order does not matter.

Let's look at the format of the two template files. One file will be for pipe fittings and other for pipe length segments.

If you don't have the IL DISK, you'll need to create the files as shown below. Do not use tabs or trailing spaces and be sure to <RETURN> after the last line.

The ATTFIT.TXT template file has seven fields for each fitting record. The first is character and the rest are numeric.

```
F_TYPE            C010000
F_DIAMETER        N009006
F_RADIUS          N009006
F_FLANGE_DIAM     N010006
F_FLANGE_THICK    N009006
F_NUMBER_BOLTS    N003000
F_BOLT_DIAM       N009006
```

ATTFIT.TXT Template File

The ATTPIPE.TXT template reports the length of each pipe segment in a drawing. It contains six numeric fields.

```
P_DIAMETER        N009006
P_LENGTH          N012006
P_FLANGE_DIAM     N010006
P_FLANGE_THICK    N009006
P_NUMBER_BOLTS    N003000
P_BOLT_DIAM       N009006
```

ATTPIPE.TXT Template File

➡ *TIP: Keep backup copies of your template files. The *.TXT extension makes it easy to accidentally delete these files.*

How to Extract Attributes With ATTEXT

Try making a standard data format (SDF) output file using the attribute extract command, ATTEXT.

Extracting Attributes With Template Files

You have the ATTFIT.TXT, ATTPIPE, and PIPEMATL.DWG files.

Create the ATTFIT.TXT and ATTPIPE files shown above. You also must have the PIPEMATL.DWG file from Chapter 12.

```
Enter selection: 2              Edit an EXISTING drawing named PIPEMATL.
Command: ATTEXT
CDF, SDF or DXF Attribute extract (or Entities)? <C>: S
Template file: ATTFIT
Extract file name <PIPEMATL>: \123\FITTINGS
15 records in extract file.        Yours may vary.

Command: TYPE                   Look at the output.
File to list: \123\FITTINGS.TXT

ELBOW      6.000000 8.000000 11.000000 1.000000  8 0.750000
ELBOW      6.000000 8.000000 11.000000 1.000000  8 0.750000
ELBOW      6.000000 8.000000 11.000000 1.000000  8 0.750000
ELBOW      6.000000 8.000000 11.000000 1.000000  8 0.750000
ELBOW      6.000000 8.000000 11.000000 1.000000  8 0.750000
ELBOW      6.000000 8.000000 11.000000 1.000000  8 0.750000
ELBOW      6.000000 8.000000 11.000000 1.000000  8 0.750000
ELBOW      6.000000 8.000000 11.000000 1.000000  8 0.750000
ELBOW      2.500000 5.000000  7.000000 0.687500  4 0.625000
ELBOW      2.500000 5.000000  7.000000 0.687500  4 0.625000
ELBOW      2.500000 5.000000  7.000000 0.687500  4 0.625000
ELBOW      2.500000 5.000000  7.000000 0.687500  4 0.625000
ELBOW      2.500000 5.000000  7.000000 0.687500  4 0.625000
ELBOW      2.500000 5.000000  7.000000 0.687500  4 0.625000
ELBOW      2.500000 5.000000  7.000000 0.687500  4 0.625000
```

➨ *TIP: Use the SDF file format for ATTEXT output to Lotus-type programs. Use CDF for dBASE and other general program imports.*

The default output file name is the current file name with a .TXT file extension. It's unfortunate that the output file and template file both use a .TXT extension. Many unwary users have overwritten their template file. Don't use the same name for both template and output files.

Next, let's see how to use the data with Lotus 123.

Importing Data Into Lotus

Our example shows just a few features of Lotus 123. Lotus is a popular program for making engineering and financial calculations with AutoCAD-imported data. Even if you don't have Lotus, we encourage you to read along to gain some understanding of integrating a spreadsheet with AutoCAD. The exercise can help you decide if a spreadsheet program might be a worthwhile extension to your AutoCAD application.

To start, we'll show you how to get the data into Lotus and automate some of the transfer steps. The most convenient way to use Lotus is from inside AutoCAD, using a shell.

How to Run Lotus From a Shell

To use a shell, you need to define a command in your ACAD.PGP file. The default ACAD.PGP file should be in your AutoCAD program directory, which we assume is C:\ACAD (if not, substitute your directory name in the following exercise). ACAD.PGP defines access and memory allocations for commands that can execute DOS commands and external programs from AutoCAD. Because Lotus needs more memory than the SHELL command provides, you need to add a new SHMAX command to a copy of your ACAD.PGP file so you can access Lotus.

Even if you have the IL DISK, copy and modify ACAD.PGP and create a new spreadsheet in Lotus.

Shelling Out to Manually Import to Lotus

```
Command: SHELL
DOS command: COPY \ACAD\ACAD.PGP \IL-ACAD\*.*
Command: SHELL
```

Use your text editor to add the following line to the copied ACAD.PGP file:
SHMAX,,480000,*DOS Command: ,0

Save the file, quit AutoCAD to the Main Menu, and again begin a NEW drawing named IL13 to force AutoCAD to reload the new PGP file.

Command: **SHMAX**	Use new PGP command.
	See the NOTE below if it fails.
DOS Command: **<RETURN>**	<RETURN> to shell out to DOS.
C:\IL-ACAD>>**CD \123**	Change to Lotus 123 directory.
C:\123>>**123**	Start 123. You'll be in a new file.

➡ *NOTE: The 480000 in the SHMAX line allocates memory. If the SHMAX command fails, you need to reduce the number by trial and error, to the largest size that works for your system. If Lotus fails in that memory size, you will have to quit AutoCAD and run Lotus directly from DOS.*

In the following exercises, Lotus commands are depicted much like we show AutoCAD commands, like `Choose` **WORKSHEET**. The WORKSHEET command choice is illustrated below.

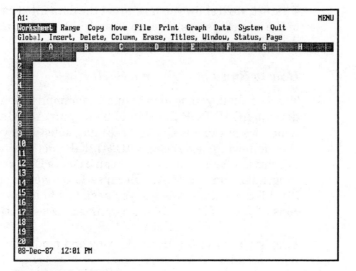

The Worksheet Display

Use Lotus commands to bring AutoCAD data into Lotus. First, position the cursor at the top left cell of the section where you want the data to be placed. Bring up the command menu with the slash character "/." This is Lotus's activate key. Enter a file name, and tell Lotus to interpret the file as text information.

Importing Data in Lotus 123

`Enter` **/**	To activate the Lotus menu.
`Choose` **FILE**	This gives the file utility menu.
`Choose` **IMPORT**	You want to import data.
`Choose` **TEXT**	Choose the text form.

Hit <ESC> twice to clear out the default name given by Lotus.

Then enter the name of the attribute extract file. It's in the 123 directory:

`Enter name of file to import:` **\123\FITTINGS.TXT**

The screen sequence is shown below.

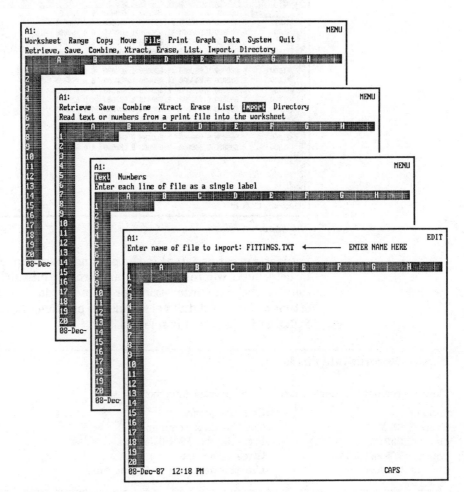

Importing Procedure

Lotus makes a long, single-cell entry for each line of the imported file. The numeric values are still ASCII text characters. They are not yet numbers in Lotus. Converting the lines of text into individual numeric fields is a two-part process using the PARSE command from the Lotus' DATA menu.

The Imported File

Lotus is a great assistant in the parsing operation. Parsing requires you to determine where text lines are broken into fields, and whether to convert the data into string or numeric data. Lotus makes its best estimate for the data types and the positions for each field when the FORMAT-LINE option is selected.

Parsing Records Into Fields

Move the cursor to the upper left cell of the imported data, then:

Choose **/**	Call the menu.
Choose **DATA**	Get the data commands.
Choose **PARSE**	Presents the PARSE menu.
Choose **FORMAT-LINE**	Gives some options.
Choose **CREATE**	Use this to make a format line.

The FORMAT-LINE command looks at the spaces and decimal points in the text line and guesses at a format. The format line is placed above the imported data. It uses special characters to reveal its guess to you:

CHAR	DESCRIPTION
L	Beginning of a text label.
V	Starts a numeric value.
*	Places holder for future characters of preceding cell.
>	Occupied character positions in the cell.

Format-Line Characters

The parsing screen sequence is shown in the Parsing Input Data illustration.

Parsing Input Data

INPUT-COLUMN tells Lotus which rows of text strings to convert. Select the command and highlight the range of cells occupied by the imported data. Notice that only the first column is marked. Each line is still a single text string. You can see the entire entry in the cell edit buffer at the top of the screen.

Selecting the Input Columns

➡ *TIP: Make sure you have adequate space between each field in the Lotus import file. The Lotus parser needs at least one empty cell between each field.*

Choose **INPUT-COLUMN**
Choose **A1..A16**   For the columns. Yours may differ.

You can place converted data in any cell range of the spreadsheet, but you have to tell Lotus where to put the data. To keep from jumping around the spreadsheet, make Lotus overwrite the imported text strings. Use the OUTPUT-RANGE command to highlight all the data lines including blank, but apparently filled, cells. Do *not* include the format string in the output range. When both ranges are set, select the GO command. GO performs the actual parsing.

The Output Range

Choose **OUTPUT-RANGE**	
Choose **A2..G16**	For the book's data. Yours may differ.
Choose **GO**	Start the parser.

Raw Labels and Numeric Data in Lotus

Lotus converts the data to labels for the "ELBOW" column, and to numbers for the fitting dimensions and components. Trailing 0's and decimal points are omitted and the cells are formatted to the maximum precision of the original number. This is shown in the Raw Labels and Numeric Data illustration. The translation process is complete.

You can add additional information, headers, and totals as shown in the illustration below to embellish the spreadsheet file.

The Pipe Fitting Material Spreadsheet

Although the book does not require it, you may want to save the spreadsheet for your own purposes. Now let's return to AutoCAD.

```
Choose /
Choose FILE
Choose SAVE
Enter save file name: \123\FITTINGS          It writes FITTINGS.WK1.
Choose /
Choose QUIT
Choose YES

C:\123>>CD \IL-ACAD                            Go back to your directory.
C:\IL-ACAD>>EXIT                               Exit Shell to AutoCAD.
```

How to Automate the Link to Lotus

You can automate the link between AutoCAD and Lotus with several menu macros. We will add these to a copy of the Chapter 12 menu, renamed IL13PARA.MNU. [FITTINGS] extracts the fittings, and [PIPING] extracts the pipe lengths. Both call Lotus. [FTEXT IN] imports the printed Lotus file back into AutoCAD.

```
***SCREEN
**ROOT
[IL13PARA]
[]
[]
[PIPEFITS]                    The [PIPEFITS] item is unchanged
[]
[REPORT ]$S=REPORT
[]
❶                 The rest of the **ROOT page and the **PIPEFITS are unchanged
                                 Add a new **REPORT page
**REPORT
[ Report ]
[  Menu  ]
[]
[Material]
[Extracts]
[FITTINGS]^C^C^CATTEXT S /IL-ACAD/ATTFIT /123/FITTINGS SHMAX RUN123 IL-ACAD;
[PIPING  ]^C^C^CATTEXT S /IL-ACAD/ATTPIPE /123/PIPING SHMAX RUN123 IL-ACAD;
[]
```

Listing continued.

Continued listing.

```
[FTEXT IN]^C^C^CSTYLE MONO1-8 MONOTXT (* 0.125 #dwgsc) ;;;;+
(caload "/IL-ACAD/" "FTEXT") FTEXT \MT
[]
[FITTINGS]^C^C^CATTEXT S /IL-ACAD/ATTFIT /123/FITTINGS SHMAX RUN123 IL-ACAD;
[PIPING  ]^C^C^CATTEXT S /IL-ACAD/ATTPIPE /123/PIPING SHMAX RUN123 IL-ACAD;
[]
[FTEXT IN]^C^C^C(if (tblsearch "STYLE" "MONO1-8") (princ) ;+
(command "STYLE" "MONO1-8" "MONOTXT" (* 0.125 #dwgsc) "" "" "" "" ""));+
(if C:FTEXT (princ) (load "FTEXT"));FTEXT \MT
[]
[]
[]
[]
[]
[]
[]
[]
[]
[]
[  root  ]$S=SCREEN LAYER S 0 ;
```

*[REPORT] and **REPORT in IL13PARA.MNU File*

❶ The changes to the root page of the IL12PARA.MNU are shown in bold. The entire **REPORT page is new, at the end of the menu.

The new macros execute the ATTEXT command, writing an SDF file of the attribute extract data to the Lotus 123 directory. They call a batch file that automates the DOS directory changes.

```
CD \123
123
CD \%1
```

RUN123.BAT File

The "%1" in the RUN123.BAT batch file is replaced by "IL-ACAD" from the end of the [FITTINGS] and [PIPING] macros. This restores the directory when the macros are run, preventing the AutoCAD errors that can occur if you return to ACAD from a different directory.

➥ *NOTE: Change the \123 to your Lotus directory name, if it isn't \123.*

➡ *TIP: Use a batch file to control execution of your external programs and directory changes. Use replaceable parameters, like %1, in your .BAT file to substitute the current AutoCAD working directory.*

Now, try the batch file and menu in AutoCAD.

Using the RUN123.BAT File and Reports Menu

 You have the IL13PARA.MNU and RUN123.BAT files.

Copy the IL12PARA.MNU to IL13PARA.MNU and make the above changes. Create the RUN123.BAT File.

Command: **MENU**	Load the IL13PARA menu.
Select **[PIPING]**	Report the pipe segment lengths. [PIPING] makes the output file PIPING.TXT, and RUN123.BAT takes you right into Lotus 123.

An annoying limitation of the Lotus 123 program is that Lotus cannot go right into the worksheet file of your choice. You have to load the spreadsheet manually by typing or highlighting its name.

How to Import Data Using Lotus Macros

Lotus does have macro capability. It can import and convert the data without instructions from you. Here are the rules for the automation game:

■ Macro definitions are stored within the worksheet cells and executed in a row-by-row fashion. Commands in one row are immediately followed by commands in the next row.

■ Macros can call subroutines, like one LISP function calls another.

■ Macro names are two characters long. All names begin with a backslash and then a single letter, A through Z. A special macro called \0 automatically executes each time a worksheet file is retrieved.

■ Macros are executed with <ALT> keys. Holding down <ALT> and hitting I (that's <ALT-I>) would execute \I.

If you are unfamiliar with Lotus' macro programming tools, here is a partial list:

MACRO COMMAND	FUNCTION
{GOTO}	Moves cursor to a cell position.
{NAME}	Used to call a range name in macros.
{ESC}	The <ESC> key.
{END}	Jumps to the end of a filled range.
{UP n}	Moves cursor up *n* positions.
{DOWN n}	Moves cursor down *n* cells.
{LEFT n}	Moves cursor left.
{RIGHT n}	Moves cursor right.

Develop a simple macro to import data and parse it. Document and organize your macros to the side or top of your calculation area.

Since there is no telling how many text lines will be imported from the attribute output file, they might overwrite your macro space. To prevent this, put the macro above the actual calculation area. Plan your sheet to accommodate the six fields of output as six Lotus columns.

Go to an open area of the spread sheet, like cell A1. The macro to import and parse the data is shown in the Import Macro illustration.

The Import Macro

In the Lotus macro, we will use two range names, UL-DATA and \I, to hold the data and the macro's positions inside the worksheet.

The macro \I finds the last line of text brought in from the import command. It positions the cursor at the range location UL-DATA and imports the file. A parse format string is created. The input and output ranges are identified and the data is parsed.

Define the ranges and try the macro. Use the <ALT> key and the macro letter to call the macro, and Lotus will begin the operation.

➥ *TIP: You can make your Lotus macros autoexecute by naming the special 0 (zero) macro in Lotus. Have the macro prompt immediately for a new file name so the spreadsheet file with the imported data is reassigned and the initial Lotus spreadsheet file is saved intact.*

Defining a Lotus Macro

 Copy the PIPING.WK1 file from the \IL-ACAD directory to \123 and examine the macro.

Create the macro as shown below.

Go to cell A1 and type in the macro, including comments, as shown in the screen shot. Then define the macro range.

```
Choose /
Choose RANGE
Choose NAME
Choose CREATE
Enter name: \I
Enter range: B5          The top cell of the macro.
```

Next define the data range. It should be located at the first cell of the imported data.

```
Choose /
Choose RANGE
Choose NAME
Choose CREATE
Enter name: UL-DATA
Enter range: A19         In the book's spreadsheet.

                         Reposition the cursor to cell A1, then save:
Choose /
Choose FILE
Choose SAVE              Save to \123\PIPING only if you do not have the IL DISK.

<ALT-I>                  Hold down <ALT> and hit I to call the macro.
```

If you defined the ranges and entered the macro correctly, the data will automatically be imported, parsed, and formatted. The format line is erased at the end of the operation.

```
A19: 6                                                               READY


        A         B        C        D       E        F       G       H
14 ═══════════════════════════════════════════════════════════════════
15
16             PIPE SEGMENT AND COMPONENT ESTIMATE
17    Pipe      Pipe    Flange   Flange  # Bolts   Bolt
18 Diameter   Length  Diameter   Thick   Flange  Diameter
19      6         28       11        1       8      0.75
20      6         34       11        1       8      0.75
21      6         10       11        1       8      0.75
22      6         58       11        1       8      0.75
23      6         64       11        1       8      0.75
24      6         94       11        1       8      0.75
25    2.5   19.8052        7   0.6875       4     0.625
26    2.5   49.35278       7   0.6875       4     0.625
27    2.5   130.8052       7   0.6875       4     0.625
28    2.5     29.25        7   0.6875       4     0.625
29    2.5   44.87469       7   0.6875       4     0.625
30      3       101        7        1       4         1
31
32
33
08-Dec-87  01:23 PM
```

Data After Importing

Next, add some descriptive labels and total the fields as shown in the Tally of Pipe Length and Bolt Numbers illustration. Then create a range to print the spreadsheet.

```
A32: (F4) 'TOTALS                                                    READY


        A         B        C        D       E        F       G       H
14 ═══════════════════════════════════════════════════════════════════
15
16             PIPE SEGMENT AND COMPONENT ESTIMATE
17    Pipe      Pipe    Flange   Flange  # Bolts   Bolt
18 Diameter   Length  Diameter   Thick   Flange  Diameter
19   6.000    28.000   11.000   1.0000       8     0.750
20   6.000    34.000   11.000   1.0000       8     0.750
21   6.000    10.000   11.000   1.0000       8     0.750
22   6.000    58.000   11.000   1.0000       8     0.750
23   6.000    64.000   11.000   1.0000       8     0.750
24   6.000    94.000   11.000   1.0000       8     0.750
25   2.500    19.805    7.000   0.6875       4     0.625
26   2.500    49.353    7.000   0.6875       4     0.625
27   2.500   130.805    7.000   0.6875       4     0.625
28   2.500    29.250    7.000   0.6875       4     0.625
29   2.500    44.875    7.000   0.6875       4     0.625
30   2.500   101.250    7.000   0.6875       4     0.625
31               ═══════                     ════
32 TOTALS   663.3379                          72
33
08-Dec-87  01:28 PM
```

Tally of Pipe Length and Bolt Numbers

Printing the Spreadsheet

Choose **/**	Call the menu.
Choose **PRINT**	Make a print file of your work.
Choose **FILE**	Later, it is brought back into AutoCAD.
Enter print file name: **\IL-ACAD\PIPING**	Hit <ESC> twice to clear name.
Choose **RANGE**	To establish the print range.
Choose **A16..F32**	Give this range. It is the book's spreadsheet.
Choose **GO**	Starts the printing to PIPING.PRN file.
Choose **QUIT**	The print menu.
Choose **/QUIT**	It was saved in the master form.

Return to AutoCAD.

```
F32: (F3)                                                    POINT
Enter Print range: A16..F32

       A       B       C       D       E       F       G    H
14 ==============================================================
15
16         PIPE SEGMENT AND COMPONENT ESTIMATE
17     Pipe    Pipe   Flange  Flange  N Bolts  Bolt
18   Diameter Length Diameter Thick   Flange  Diameter
19     6.000   28.000  11.000  1.0000     8    0.750
20     6.000   34.000  11.000  1.0000     8    0.750
21     6.000   10.000  11.000  1.0000     8    0.750
22     6.000   58.000  11.000  1.0000     8    0.750
23     6.000   64.000  11.000  1.0000     8    0.750
24     6.000   94.000  11.000  1.0000     8    0.750
25     2.500   19.805   7.000  0.6875     4    0.625
26     2.500   49.353   7.000  0.6875     4    0.625
27     2.500  130.805   7.000  0.6875     4    0.625
28     2.500   29.250   7.000  0.6875     4    0.625
29     2.500   44.875   7.000  0.6875     4    0.625
30     2.500  101.250   7.000  0.6875     4    0.625
31             =======                   ====
32 TOTALS 663.3379                        72
33
08-Dec-87  01:30 PM
```

Print Out Range

In reality, you would extract and process a good deal more data than this. You would have your spreadsheet program produce and print a summary report, then you would import the report to AutoCAD as a BOM (Bill Of Materials).

Bringing Data Back to AutoCAD

In the next exercise, we'll import the Lotus-reformatted data. Regardless of your application, the import process is the same. The FTEXT command just reads a text file.

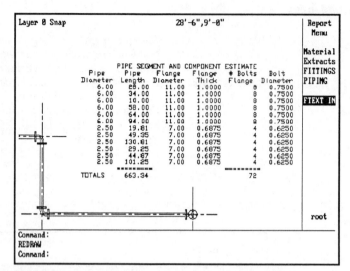

Imported Text in Drawing

There is no direct way to import Lotus spreadsheets to AutoCAD drawings. However, with a little help from our C:FTEXT function (from Chapter 15 on batch programming), you can import data as text. The **REPORT page of our IL13PARA screen menu includes an [FTEXT] macro. The macro uses FTEXT in its monospaced table mode. When you select [FTEXT], it runs the STYLE command and sets it to MONO1-8, then loads and executes FTEXT.

Try importing the Lotus output, PIPING.PRN:

Importing the .PRN File Into AutoCAD

    You have the C:FTEXT command in your FTEXT.LSP file.

See Chapter 15 to create the FTEXT.LSP file.

```
Select [REPORT] [FTEXT IN]
Command: STYLE Text style name (or ?) <MONO1-8>: MONO1-8
MONO1-8 is now the current text style.
Command: FTEXT
Enter text source filename.ext: \IL-ACAD\PIPING.PRN
MonoTable or Word Wrap? MT/WW <WW>: MT
Start point:            Pick, and it puts tabular text in. Zoom to see it all.

Command: END             You are finished with the drawing.
```

Although the pipe length example here imports a schedule back into AutoCAD, other types of applications use similar techniques. You can, for example, apply Lotus to generating data files for parametric input. You can make Lotus output a file in a particular format and have one of your LISP programs read the data and generate parts or drawings parametrically. This output can be controlled with the printer options of the 123 menus.

Let's review the basic steps you need to take in working with Lotus. You need to create an attribute template file, extract the attribute values of your drawing with ATTEXT, bring the file into Lotus, and use its parsing tools to break the data into cells. After you use the data in your spreadsheet, you can optionally use it with AutoCAD by printing it to a file.

While Lotus is good with numbers, dBASE is good with names, alphanumeric listing, and sorting.

Using dBASE With AutoCAD

dBASE III and many other database programs can process data from an AutoCAD extract file. The program outlined here tracks AutoCAD project drawings. Many of the steps shown in the exercise are common to data transfer between AutoCAD and most database programs. Extrapolate the steps you need for your own application.

Let's start with a look at the drawing attributes that will go into the reporting system. Our attribute chapter (Chapter 11) developed title block and drawing revision routines that create the data you will use here. You need two more attribute template files for project tracking. The TITLEBLK.TXT file should contain:

```
PRJ-NAME     C031000
DWG-NAME     C031000
DWG-NO       C010000
DWG-FILE     C031000
DRAFTER      C003000
DWG-REV      C001000
DATE-REV     C008000
DATE-ISSUE   C008000
```

TITLEBLK.TXT Template File

The REVBLOCK.TXT file should contain:

R1	C001000
R2	C031000
R3	C008000
R4	C003000
R5	C016000
R6	C008000
R7	C003000
R8	C010000

REVBLOCK.TXT Template File

You will need to use the SYNPLANT drawing and IL11TITL.MNU from the IL DISK or from Chapter 11 for the macros and programs in this section. Load the drawing with its title block and revisions. Run the ATTEXT command to extract the attributes.

Testing the Attribute Files

You already have the TITLEBLK.TXT, REVBLOCK.TXT, SYNPLANT.DWG, and IL11TITL.MNU files.

Make the TITLEBLK.TXT and REVBLOCK.TXT template files as shown above. You also need the IL11TITL.MNU and SYNPLANT.DWG from Chapter 11.

```
Enter selection: 1                          Begin a NEW drawing named IL13=SYNPLANT
Command: MENU                               Load IL11TITL.MNU from Chapter 11.
Select [TITLEBLK] [CAD FILE]                To update the DWG-FILE attribute.

Command: ATTEXT                             This time, use the default CDF extract.
CDF, SDF or DXF Attribute extract (or Entities)? <C>: <RETURN>
Template file: TITLEBLK                     Do the title block information first.
Extract file name <IL13>: $PRJ             Give it a temporary name.
1 records in extract file.                  Should only be one.

Command: TYPE                               Look at it.
File to list: $PRJ.TXT                      It should be similar to:

'SYN-FIBER PLANT','SECONDARY PIPING SYSTEM','D81-
3008','CA22','JSJ','E','12/15/87','None'

Command: ATTEXT
CDF, SDF or DXF Attribute extract (or Entities)? <C>: <RETURN>
Template file <TITLEBLK>: REVBLOCK          Do the revision blocks.
Extract file name <IL13>: $REV             Use another temporary name.
```

```
Command: TYPE                          Look at the revision file.
File to list: $REV.TXT                 It should be similar to:
```

```
'A','CHANGED PIPING LOCATION','11/29/87','JSJ','CONSTRUCTION','12/02/87','RMS','42870'
'B','ADDED CONDUIT','12/06/87','PJS','CONSTRUCTION','12/06/87','DBS','1441'
'C','CHANGED PUMPS 1 & 2','12/07/87','TBB','CONSTRUCTION','12/09/87','PTM','751'
'D','REDRAWN AND REVISED','12/11/87','CMP','CONSTRUCTION','12/13/87','MMP','6063'
'E','ARCHITECTURAL ADJUSTMENTS','12/15/87','RBG','BID','12/15/87','JSJ','6090'
```

The generated records of the $REV.TXT file include all data concerning revision history, including revision time. Yours may be different. Now let's make the master project data file.

Preparing the Input Record

Normally, you would like to do just one attribute extraction, but the ATTEXT command cannot provide the data in the order you want. A little file manipulation is required. You can open three files at one time, read data from the temporary file $PRJ.TXT, splice it together with each record of the $REV.TXT file, and append the combined record to PROJECT.DAT, the master project file. The REPSTAT routine that does this is short and sweet.

```
;* The C:REPSTAT command extracts the title sheet and drawing revision information
;* from the current drawing and records the information in the master project
;* file called PROJECT.DAT, which is processed by the PRO_TREK data base program.
                                                 ;make the attrib extract files
(defun C:REPSTAT ( / pf p$ r$ prdat rvdat)
   (command "ATTEXT" "C" "TITLEBLK" "$PRJ")      ;extract title block data
   (command "ATTEXT" "C" "REVBLOCK" "$REV")      ;extract revision block data
                                                 ;open the external files
   (setq pf (open "PROJECT.DAT" "a")   ;open master project data file to append
         p$ (open "$PRJ.TXT" "r")      ;open title block data file to read
         r$ (open "$REV.TXT" "r")      ;open revision block data file to read
   );setq
❶
                                                 ;build and output title block record
   (if (and p$ (setq prdat (read-line p$)))      ;check for file, read title block data
     (progn
```

Listing continued.

Continued listing.

```
        (close p$)                                      ;close the file, we're done
        (if (= 0.0 (getvar "USERR1"))                   ;no revisions have been made yet
          (setq dwgtime (rtos (* 1440 (getvar "TDINDWG")) 2 0)) ;user ACAD sys var time
          (setq dwgtime (rtos (getvar "USERR1") 2 0))   ;use our original dwg creation time
        );if
        (write-line (strcat prdat                       ;merge title block record with
                         ",'','','','','','','','"       ;dummy revision record (7 fields)
                            dwgtime "'") pf              ;add in 8th field, original creation time
        );write-line

                                                        ;process the revision file
        (if r$                                          ;if a revision file exists.
          (progn
            (while (setq rvdat (read-line r$))          ;loop and read each revision entry
              (write-line (strcat prdat "," rvdat) pf)  ;put together & write to master file
            );while
            (close r$)                                  ;close the file, we're done
          );progn
        );if
      );progn
      (prompt "\nNo title block information extracted from drawing.")
    );if
    (close pf)                                          ;close the project file
    (princ)
);defun
```

❷

REPSTAT Function in REPSTAT.LSP File

❶ This splices together the original drawing creation time with a dummy revision record. This will hold the correct number of fields for importing later to dBASE. The original creation time is placed in the same field as the time of a revision record. In effect, original creation time is treated the same way as any revision. If no revision level has been assigned, the value of USERR1 will be 0.0 and the programs will use the AutoCAD system variable TDINDWG. The program truncates the time to minutes precision.

❷ The revision records are processed, added to the project title block data, and a record is output to the master project data file.

Next, generate the revision records.

Generating Revision Records

 You have the REPSTAT.LSP file.

Create the C:REPSTAT command in a new file named REPSTAT.LSP.

```
Command: (load "repstat")     Load the file.
Command: REPSTAT              This starts the revision status program.
```

Check the contents of the PROJECT.DAT file with the PGP command TYPE.

```
Command: TYPE
File name to type: PROJECT.DAT          The master file will be similar to:
```

```
'SYN-FIBER PLANT','SECONDARY PIPING SYSTEM','D81-
3008','CA22','JSJ','E','12/15/87','None','','','','','','','','2447130'
'SYN-FIBER PLANT','SECONDARY PIPING SYSTEM','D81-
3008','CA22','JSJ','E','12/15/87','None','A','CHANGED PIPING
LOCATION','11/29/87','JSJ','CONSTRUCTION','12/02/87','RMS','42870'
'SYN-FIBER PLANT','SECONDARY PIPING SYSTEM','D81-
3008','CA22','JSJ','E','12/15/87','None','B','ADDED
CONDUIT','12/06/87','PJS','CONSTRUCTION','12/06/87','DBS','1441'
'SYN-FIBER PLANT','SECONDARY PIPING SYSTEM','D81-
3008','CA22','JSJ','E','12/15/87','None','C','CHANGED PUMPS 1 &
2','12/07/87','TBB','CONSTRUCTION','12/09/87','PTM','751'
'SYN-FIBER PLANT','SECONDARY PIPING SYSTEM','D81-
3008','CA22','JSJ','E','12/15/87','None','D','REDRAWN AND
REVISED','12/11/87','CMP','CONSTRUCTION','12/13/87','MMP','6063'
'SYN-FIBER PLANT','SECONDARY PIPING SYSTEM','D81-
3008','CA22','JSJ','E','12/15/87','None','E','ARCHITECTURAL
ADJUSTMENTS','12/15/87','RBG','BID','12/15/87','JSJ','6090'
```

Generate some additional records by changing the project name,
the drawing number, dates, and locations.

```
Select [DWG NO]              Then run REPSTAT again.
New attribute value: D81-4000
```

```
Command: REPSTAT
```

```
Select [PRJ NAME]           Enter a new value.
```

```
Command: REPSTAT            Run it again.
```

Generate several records in this manner.

The rest of the process is done in the database program. But first, let's add [REP STAT] and [PROTRAK] to the **TITLEBLK screen page of the IL11TITL.MNU we developed in Chapter 11.

Updating the IL11.MNU File

Command: **SHELL**   Whether you have the IL DISK or not, edit the IL11TITL.MNU.

Add the following [REP STAT] and [PROTRAK] items to the **TITLEBLK page, just above [root]:

```
[REP STAT]^C^C^C(caload "/IL-ACAD/" "REPSTAT") REPSTAT
[PROTRAK ]^C^C^CSHMAX PRO_TRAK;
[]
[  root  ]
```

Save, exit and reload AutoCAD.
Command: **MENU**   Reload IL11TITL.MNU and try the [REP STAT] macro.

Tracking CAD Drawings

The PRO_TRAK database program has been kept simple, but is still too long to print here. PRO_TRAK.EXE is a Clipper-compiled version of the dBASE III program. The source code is in the PRO_TRAK subdirectory on the IL DISK.

This section shows you how the program was developed, why certain reporting options are used, and gives an outline of the program's steps. PRO_TRAK.EXE is on the IL DISK.

The dBASE III program helps you create database structures. Virtually anyone can effectively use dBASE in an application. Clipper creates easy-to-use, fast-running compiled database programs with the added advantage of protecting the source code.

The PRO_TRAK program starts with a main menu, giving you several database reporting choices. One menu choice exits the program. Another reads the master project data file and transcribes the records found there into the dBASE environment. The options available are shown in the PRO_TRAK Main Menu illustration.

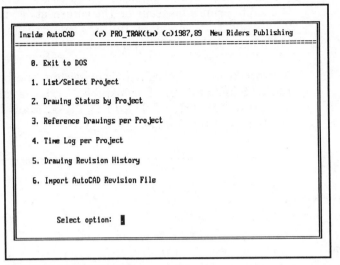

The PRO_TRAK Main Menu

Like AutoLISP's ability to create named subroutines through DEFUN, dBASE has a subroutine-like feature called a procedure. Procedures define most of the program's tasks. They are then combined to form the main program. Using these subroutines lets you concentrate on one small task at any given moment. Procedures keep the program from becoming overwhelmingly complex and permit easy maintenance. In addition to the program's procedures, two database structures, CATEMP.DBF and CADATA.DBF, are defined. These also are included on the IL DISK.

➥ TIP: Plan your dBASE structure first. Next create your dBASE program to manage the data files. Test it with a dummy data file. Then write your AutoLISP routine to extract the data from AutoCAD in the form you need.

A procedure can be as simple as the header for the program's menu. Take a look at the TITLE procedure.

```
PROCEDURE TITLE
    CLEAR
    @  2,  3  SAY "Inside AutoLISP(r) PRO_TRAK(tm)        (c)1987,89 New Riders Publishing"
    @  3,  2  SAY
"==========================================================================="
RETURN
```

The TITLE Procedure in PRO_TRAK Program

First, the procedure clears the screen with a CLEAR command, then SAY is used to print a message on the screen at "@" row and column location 2, 3. A RETURN command finishes the procedure to make the program jump back to the calling procedure.

A procedure can be called from within another procedure, just like DEFUNS in AutoLISP. For instance, TITLE is called by the MAINMENU procedure "DO TITLE." The PRO_TRAK Main Menu is defined in the MAINMENU procedure as:

```
PROCEDURE MAINTITLE
   DO TITLE
   @ 5,  6  SAY "0. Exit to DOS"
   @ 7,  6  SAY "1. List/Select Project"
   @09,  6  SAY "2. Drawing Status by Project"
   @11,  6  SAY "3. Reference Drawings per Project"
   @13,  6  SAY "4. Time Log per Project"
   @15,  6  SAY "5. Drawing Revision History"
   @17,  6  SAY "6. Import AutoCAD Revision File"
   @21,  9  SAY "   Select option: " GET OPTION PICTURE "!"
   @ 1,  1  TO 23, 78    DOUBLE
   READ
RETURN
```

The MAINTITLE Procedure in PRO_TRAK Program

Prompting on the screen is as simple as SAYing something. Two other parts of the program are the database structure, and a program that will manipulate the data into the form needed.

The PRO_TRAK Database Structure

The database structures for the program were defined using the dBASE program menu CREATE command and the DATABASE file option. A database structure is like a template that formats the database. dBASE presents a screen to help create the files. CADATA.DBF is the file name for the database structure. The following illustration shows how CADATA is created.

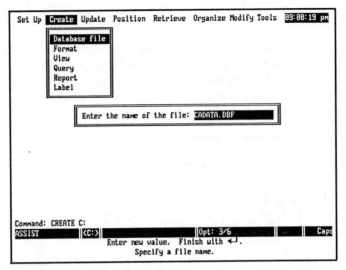

Creating a Database Structure

The program itself is one giant WHILE loop, similar to that used in DDRAW.LSP. The DDRAW.LSP function monitored your key strokes and cursor movements. The dBASE WHILE loop waits for you to select an option from the program Main Menu. If the option is one of the supported numbers, the CASE program command filters the input and determines the desired task. The CASE program command functions like AutoLISP's COND.

Each CASE option is specific to a task. Let's look at CASE 6, the most challenging CASE in the program.

Importing Project Data

CASE 6 is the project data file import option. It prints the screen headers, tells you which options are available, and waits for a selection. Then the program opens two data files for project reporting, CATEMP.DBF and CADATA.DBF. Since this task is performed by a call to a procedure, you don't actually see the file names in the example. The call to open a data file is simple: USE CATEMP.

dBASE can open many data files for use at one time. The SELECT command tells dBASE which open file is being addressed. This is similar to file pointers in AutoLISP, but with a friendlier touch. The data files are assigned the SELECT file slot number current at the time the files are first opened. In the program, SELECT 1 is the master data file CADATA.

SELECT 2 is the temporary data file CATEMP. The temporary data file is used only while the PROJECT.DAT file is being transferred to dBASE.

CASE 6 flips between the two file slots, 1 and 2, and compares the recently read project name and drawing number with entries found in the master database. If an existing matching record is found in the master database, the record is updated. Revisions are added to the record. A maximum of five revisions may be recorded for each drawing number.

```
Inside AutoCAD     (r) PRO_TRAK(tm) (c)1987,89  New Riders Publishing
===================================================================

PRJ_NAME  : SYN-FIBER PLANT
DWG_NAME  : SECONDARY PIPING SYSTEM        DWG_NO  : D81-3008
DWG_FILE  : CAZZ                           DRAFTER : JSJ
START DATE: None                           LAST REV: 12/15/87    REV:  E

Level  Revised   Issued   Description                  Issued for
-----  -------   ------   -----------                  ------ ---




Adding...
```

Importing Project Records

The routine branches at this point, one direction to update an existing record, the other direction to add the new record. If the record is being updated, the transfer of data is made from the temporary data file CATEMP to the master data file CADATA. The transfer is done by the TRANSFER procedure. It looks like:

```
PROCEDURE TRANSFER
   SELECT 1
   REPLACE CADATA->PRJ_NAME    WITH CATEMP->PRJ_NAME
   REPLACE CADATA->DWG_NO      WITH CATEMP->DWG_NO
   REPLACE CADATA->DWG_NAME    WITH CATEMP->DWG_NAME
   REPLACE CADATA->DWG_FILE    WITH CATEMP->DWG_FILE
   REPLACE CADATA->DRAFTER     WITH CATEMP->DRAFTER
   REPLACE CADATA->L_DWG_REV   WITH CATEMP->L_DWG_REV
   REPLACE CADATA->L_DATE_REV WITH CTOD(CATEMP->L_DATE_REV)
```

Listing continued.

Continued listing.

```
    REPLACE CADATA->START_DATE WITH CTOD(CATEMP->START_DATE)
    REPLACE CADATA->REV_LTR    WITH CATEMP->REV_LTR
    REPLACE CADATA->DESC       WITH CATEMP->DESC
    REPLACE CADATA->DATE_REV   WITH CTOD(CATEMP->DATE_REV)
    REPLACE CADATA->WHO_REV    WITH CATEMP->WHO_REV
    REPLACE CADATA->RES_ISU    WITH CATEMP->RES_ISU
    REPLACE CADATA->DATE_CHK   WITH CTOD(CATEMP->DATE_CHK)
    REPLACE CADATA->WHO_CHK    WITH CATEMP->WHO_CHK
    REPLACE CADATA->REV_TIME   WITH VAL(CATEMP->REV_TIME)
RETURN
```

The TRANSFER Procedure in PRO_TRAK Program

The procedure behaves the way it looks, slipping and sliding data from one file to the other with the dBASE REPLACE command. It replaces the named data field of one file with the named data field of another file. Field names like PRJ_NAME don't have to match across the replacement, but the data types do. Strings that are too long to transfer to another field are simply truncated.

New project entries also are transferred, but a blank database record is added to CADATA prior to the transfer. In effect, the program transfers the data into a new record.

At the file's import option ends, the program indexes the CADATA file, using the project name, PRJ_NAME, as the key name. After indexing, it zaps the temporary file with a procedure. ZAP clears the data records from the .DBF file, but leaves the data structure intact for the next file import.

➡ *NOTE: The PROJECT.DAT file is deleted each time the IMPORT DATA command is given. If you want to save the file, copy it to another name prior to running PRO_TRAK.*

Reporting Project Data

The PRO_TRAK Main Menu allows you to select a report type. You can select from a variety of data reporting formats, depending on your application. You may even want to take the dBASE source code and design reports for yourself. The example selection discussed here is for tracking drawing revisions.

```
Inside AutoCAD    (r) PRO_TRAK(tm) (c)1987,89  New Riders Publishing
===================================================================

PRJ_NAME  : SYN-FIBER PLANT
DWG_NAME  : SECONDARY PIPING SYSTEM      DWG_NO  : D81-3008
DWG_FILE  : CA22                         DRAFTER : JSJ
START DATE:  / /                         LAST REV: 12/15/87    REV:  E

Level  Revised   Issued   Description             Issued for


          / /     / /

  A    11/29/87  12/02/87  CHANGED PIPING LOCATION    CONSTRUCTION

  B    12/06/87  12/06/87  ADDED CONDUIT              CONSTRUCTION

  C    12/07/87  12/09/87  CHANGED PUMPS 1 & 2        CONSTRUCTION

  D    12/11/87  12/13/87  REDRAWN AND REVISED        CONSTRUCTION

  E    12/15/87  12/15/87  ARCHITECTURAL ADJUSTMENTS  BID

Hit [RETURN] when ready.
```

Revision History of Drawing D81-3008

The CASE 5 drawing revision option presents information about individual drawing revision levels, a description of the revisions, date of revision, who did it, purpose of issue, date of reissue and the person who checked the revision. It represents a fair sampling of the type of data recorded for drawing revisions.

```
CASE OPTION = "5"
@15,  3 SAY "Please enter Drawing Number" GET MDWG_NO PICTURE "!!!!!!!!!!"
READ
DO O_FILES
SELECT 1
SET INDEX TO DWG_NO
SEEK MDWG_NO
IF .NOT. EOF()
  DO TITLE_TOP
  DO &TITLE
  DO SET_VAR1
  DO WHILE DWG_NO = MDWG_NO
    DO TITLE_REV
    SKIP
  ENDDO
```

Listing continued.

Continued listing.

```
ELSE
   ? CHR(7)
   @15,  3 SAY "I'm sorry " + TRIM(MDWG_NO) + " NOT  FOUND!!"+SPACE(47)

ENDIF
DO PAUSE
CLOSE DATA
```

CASE 5 of the PRO_TRAK Program

CASE 5 begins by opening the project data files and setting the INDEX search name to the drawing number. It looks for the database record of the named drawing using dBASE's SEEK procedure. It formats the screen with the standard menu. The program sets the drawing record entries to temporary variables. It then loops through the database, comparing subsequent drawing numbers with original drawing numbers.

How does this work? The program is designed to order the database by drawing number. There may be several entries in the database with the same drawing number, but different revision levels. Each subsequent entry with the same drawing number is considered a revision level. The WHILE loop continues displaying the revision data until all revisions are found.

Time Log Reports

You can write a simple routine that totals drawing creation and revision time. If you have the IL DISK, look at CASE 4 in the PRO_1.PRG program file in the PRO_TRAK subdirectory. It examines the time field in each revision record and produces a report similar to the one shown in the Project Log Time illustration.

```
Inside AutoCAD     (r) PRO_TRAK(tm) (c)1987,89  New Riders Publishing
===========================================================================

Time Log for Project: LOST MOUNTAIN SKI RESORT

R Dwg#    Drawing Name                    Drafter      Hours
- ----    ------- ----                    -------      -----
    S-21  LIFT STRUCTURE                     JSJ     40785.50
A  S-21   LIFT STRUCTURE                     JSJ       714.50
B  S-21   LIFT STRUCTURE                     JSJ        24.02
C  S-21   LIFT STRUCTURE                     JSJ        12.52
D  S-21   LIFT STRUCTURE                     JSJ       101.05
E  S-21   LIFT STRUCTURE                     JSJ       101.50
                                          ------- -----  -------
                                          Project Time:  41739.08


Hit [RETURN] when ready.
```

Project Log Time

Running PRO_TRAK

Start the program with the PRO_TRAK command from the DOS prompt. It's a single-directory program, meaning that all support, project, and data files are expected in the local directory. Run it from the DOS prompt in the C:\IL-ACAD directory by typing PRO_TRAK, or run it from AutoCAD using the [PROTRAK] menu macro.

Using PRO_TRAK

You need the PROJECT.DAT file you created earlier in this chapter during the Generating Revision Records exercise.

Select **[PROTRAK]**	Starts it.
Select **6**	To import the project information.
Select **1**	Get a listing of the projects.
Select **2**	List the drawing status for a project.
Select **3**	Look at a list of reference drawings.
Select **4**	Get the time for a project using this option.
Select **5**	Look up the revision history for a drawing.
Select **0**	Exit to AutoCAD
Command: **QUIT**	And exit to DOS.

Your screen should show the PRO_TRAK Main Menu screen illustrated at the beginning of this section when you make your report choices.

Summary

The interaction between AutoCAD and external programs like Lotus and dBASE can be made transparent. Developing macros and batch files can automate this link. Creating PGP commands for the shell operations helps ensure that an adequate amount of DOS memory is available for the external program to run beside AutoCAD.

To use external programs, you need to prepare your AutoCAD data using either AutoLISP, attributes, or both. Then create a file in a form that the external program can read. Load the external program, read in the prepared file, and perform your application. If you want, you can output the information to a file, come back into AutoCAD, and use the data again.

Entity handles, unique names for each entity of a drawing, can be transferred to the external programs. By knowing the names of entities from your database, you can develop LISP routines to copy, edit, move, and even erase items in the drawing.

dBASE does most of the work for you when importing data from AutoCAD. Lotus requires a little more of your assistance to parse the data. However, Lotus' macro definition capability lets you automate the parsing of data into separate cells.

As of this printing, no spreadsheet or database software package can directly read the AutoCAD drawing and provide free-form multi-purpose reporting features. The real meat in an AutoCAD drawing is uncovered through the DXF file. Writing a program in a language such as BASIC or C is a minor undertaking if you are familiar with these languages. You simply need to read the DXF file and convert the drawing into the correct format for database and spreadsheet programs. We recommend processing DXF files only with compiled programs like BASIC and C.

We'll cover the DXF file format and demonstrate examples later in Chapter 16, DXF and External Processing.

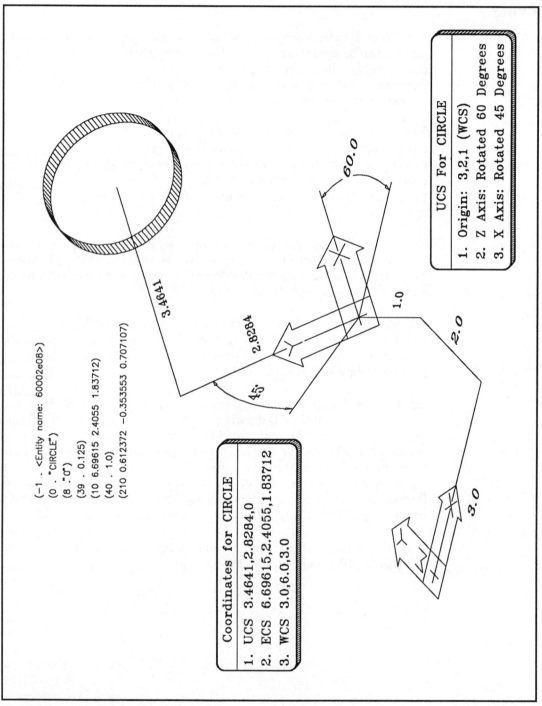

Coordinates for the Center of a Circle

CHAPTER 14

AutoLISP and 3D Space

THE CONCEPTS AND THE TOOLS

The ability to depict a 3D image on a micro-computer is a significant breakthrough in software technology. AutoCAD Release 10 brings full 3D to low cost CAD, offering a wide range of efficient ways to create, view, and edit objects in 3D. However, AutoLISP has only one function specifically designed for 3D. The TRANS function translates points to and from the various coordinate systems. Otherwise, there is nothing unique about using AutoLISP in 3D applications. Everything you've learned in this book can be applied to 3D (and much of this chapter applies to 2D). The difficulty of programming for 3D lies in understanding how AutoCAD deals with entities in 3D space.

AutoCAD actually has only five full 3D entities. A full 3D entity is one for which any point accepts a Z coordinate. AutoCAD's full 3D commands (and the entities they create) are POINT, LINE, 3DPOLY (3D polyline), 3DFACE, and 3DMESH. The RULESURF, TABSURF, REVSURF, and EDGESURF commands also create a polyline mesh. The rest of AutoCAD's 3D abilities come from using UCSs (User Coordinate Systems) to place AutoCAD's 2D entities anywhere in space. To learn to use these commands, we suggest INSIDE AutoCAD. It has more 3D information packed into three chapters than most 3D manuals have in their entire books.

Developing programs to do your 3D work can relieve you from some of the difficulty and tedium associated with working in 3D. It may take more *mental* effort to develop 3D programs than to simply draw in 3D, but it will pay off. Drawing in 3D is error-prone. Once a 3D drawing program has been debugged, it reduces the likelihood of user errors. Creating a set of 3D subroutines increases your efficiency as you develop more and more 3D programs.

Your AutoCAD program comes with a good set of AutoLISP 3D entity creation and editing tools. We suggest that you look to them for source material, techniques, and subroutines. The AutoCAD 3D.LSP file includes several tools that use AutoCAD's 3D entities to create shapes. These include a cone, box, dome, pyramid, wedge, torus, and sphere. It also includes tools to create 3D arrays, toggle the visibility of 3Dface edges, rotate entities about any axis, move vertices of 3Dfaces, plot a function in two variables to generate a 3D mesh, draw a slot or hole with 3D faces, and project a 3D drawing onto the current UCS. These are all described in Appendix A of your AutoLISP Programmer's Reference. You will also find a set of menu-based 3D utility commands and 3D constructions in our other book, CUSTOMIZING AutoCAD.

So what can you get from this chapter? You may be interested in the concept of how AutoCAD draws entities in 3D space and how data is stored and modified. Or you may like the subroutines we'll develop that make programming and understanding 3D easier. This chapter will give you the knowledge, and some useful tools, for creating your own 3D applications like 3D parametrics, 3D piping, 3D mechanical design, or 3D building models. You will learn how to deal with 3D points and various UCSs, to decipher and modify the AutoCAD 3D point and orientation storage format, to control UCS-induced redraws, to calculate points, angles, distances, arcs, and altitudes in 3D space, and to convert entities and views between 2D and 3D.

Macros, AutoLISP Tools, and Programs

AutoLISP Tools

SHOW3D.LSP contains C:SHOW3D, a visualization tool to help you study entities in 3D space.

IL-3D.LSP is a collection of functions for determining and manipulating points, lines, and curves in 3D space. Many of its subroutines are also useful for 2D. At least one or two of these are likely to be useful to any 3D program that you write. The subroutines include:

BANGLE, a 3D angle of inclination function.

3DPOLAR, which provides the 3D equivalent to the AutoLISP POLAR function.

3DP, a transparent user interface for the 3DPOLAR function.

RADIUS, which calculates the radius of an arc from its chord and altitude.

ARCLEN, which calculates an arc length given a radius and included angle.

INCANG, which calculates the included angle given the chord and radius.

ALTITD, which calculates altitude from the radius and included angle.

MID3D, an extra function on the IL DISK, which returns the midpoint of any 3D point.

VPOFF, which turns off all display controls that cause redraws. Otherwise, many editing operations in 3D cause tedious and unnecessary redraws of all viewports.

ZAXIS, which calculates an ECS extrusion vector from two points.

NEWECS, which translates planar entities from one coordinate system to another.

STK-PIPE.LSP contains the C:STK-PIPE command. It converts line entities into extruded circles, to represent piping. It uses the ZAXIS and NEWECS subroutines.

ROUNDOFF.LSP is a file on the New Riders AutoLISP Utilities Disk 1 that contains functions for rounding off real numbers, points, and lists of real numbers to any precision between one and 14 significant digits. Round-off errors can be a problem in 3D point translations. These functions provide a means of dealing with precision.

GRPT.LSP, also on the New Riders AutoLISP Utilities Disk 1, contains GRPT, a function that draws GRDRAW temporary points with any PDSIZE or PDMODE system variable setting. The points are drawn parallel to the plane of the display regardless of UCS. Otherwise, points that are skewed or edge-on in 3D will be difficult to see.

2D Versus 3D Points

The most basic element of AutoCAD's 3D database is the 3D point. In AutoLISP, points can be returned in either 2D or 3D. A 2D AutoLISP point has both X and Y coordinates, like this:

```
(1.0 2.0)
```

A 3D point has X, Y, and Z coordinates, like this:

```
(1.0 2.0 3.0)
```

You can control whether AutoCAD and AutoLISP deal in 2D or 3D with FLATLAND.

How FLATLAND Works

AutoCAD uses the FLATLAND system variable as a compatibility bridge between Releases 9 and 10. Setting Release 10's FLATLAND to 1 (on) makes the world flat so AutoCAD and AutoLISP act as much as possible like they did in Release 9. With FLATLAND on, most commands accept only 2D points, AutoLISP returns 2D points, and osnaps work as they always have. Turning FLATLAND off (to 0, the default) allows most commands to accept 3D points, AutoLISP to return 3D points, and enhanced osnaps for 3D. If you edit a drawing created in an earlier AutoCAD release, FLATLAND is automatically turned on and the world is flat.

➥ *NOTE: AutoCAD is dropping FLATLAND in Release 11, so develop your programs to support full 3D points now.*

Let's take a look at 2D and 3D points and the effects of the FLATLAND variable.

Looking at 2D and 3D Points

Enter selection: **1**	Begin a NEW drawing named IL14.
Command: **SETVAR**	Set FLATLAND to 1 (on).
Command: **LINE**	
From point: **1,2,3**	Try to enter a 3D point.
Invalid 2D point.	AutoCAD is working in 2D.
From point: **<^C>**	Cancel it.
Command: **(getpoint "Point: ")**	Test AutoLISP.
Point: **1,2,3**	It also is working in 2D.
Invalid 2D point.	
Try again: **1,2**	2D points are acceptable.
Lisp returns: (1.0 2.0)	
Command: **SETVAR**	Set FLATLAND back to 0 (off).
Command: **LINE**	Try a 3D line.
From point: **1,2,3**	This is acceptable to AutoCAD.
To point: **<^C>**	Cancel it.
Command: **(getpoint "Point: ")**	Try AutoLISP.
Point: **1,2,3**	AutoLISP also agrees.
Lisp returns: (1.0 2.0 3.0)	
Command: **(getpoint "Point: ")**	Try it again.
Point: **1,2**	Give only a 2D point.
Lisp returns: (1.0 2.0 0.0)	The Z is filled in with the current elevation, 0.

As a rule, AutoLISP returns only 2D points if the FLATLAND variable is on. However, you can specifically request a 3D point through the INITGET function. INITGET has a bit code (16) that instructs the GET functions to return 3D points even when FLATLAND is on.

When entering 3D points with FLATLAND off, Z coordinates are returned whether you supply them or not. If not provided, the Z coordinate is automatically filled, based on the current *construction plane*. With FLATLAND on, 3D-initialized INITGET functions fill in Z coordinates in the same manner. The construction plane is determined by a combination of UCS and elevation.

What Makes AutoCAD Full 3D

The User Coordinate System is the key to AutoCAD's ability to draw in 3D. To understand the UCS concept, you need to understand the World Coordinate System (WCS). You've worked in the WCS since your very first day using AutoCAD. The WCS is the normal XYZ Cartesian coordinate system that AutoCAD was restricted to prior to Release 10. It is still the default coordinate system. Most entities are created parallel to the XY plane, either at the default zero Z, or at some Z distance above or below the default plane if the ELEVATION system variable is set. The ELEVATION determines the current construction plane. In Release 9 (or with FLATLAND on) the base of most entities is determined by the current construction plane when they are created. In Release 10, entities default to the current construction plane, but you can also override it by specifying a Z coordinate. You can supply a Z coordinate for the initial or base point of 2D entities, or for any point of 3D entities.

3D versus 2D Entities

While Release 10 has five 3D entities, most entities are still 2D.

3D Entities	2D Entities	
LINE	CIRCLE	TRACE
3DFACE	ARC	ATTDEF
3D POLYLINE	TEXT	INSERT
3D MESH	SHAPE	SOLID
POINT	ATTRIB	DIMENSION
		2D POLYLINE

3D Versus 2D Entities

Two-dimensional entities accept a Z coordinate only for the single point that determines their base point in space, and they must lie in or parallel to the current construction plane. You can extrude 2D entities (and points and lines) perpendicular to their construction plane. But this is really just two and a half dimensions. How does AutoCAD get full 3D out of this? With the UCS.

What Is a UCS?

A UCS is a coordinate system just like the default WCS. You can define a UCS anywhere in space. You can offset its local 0,0,0 from the WCS 0,0,0 by any distance at any angle, and you can rotate its XYZ axis system to any angle in space. A UCS has a current construction plane, just like the WCS. But, because the UCS can be anywhere at any angle, you can create a current construction plane anywhere in space. Since 2D entities are created on or parallel to the current construction plane, this allows you to create 2D entities anywhere in space, for full 3D AutoCAD. AutoCAD's full 3D entities also get their points relative to the current UCS.

➥ *NOTE: The combination of an ELEVATION setting and a UCS can get confusing. We (and Autodesk) recommend always leaving the ELEVATION system variable set to 0, and using only UCSs to set your desired construction planes. The ELEVATION setting will be dropped in the future, so you should not use it in your programs. The ELEV command will also be dropped, so use SETVAR, not ELEV, to change the THICKNESS system variable.*

How to Work in the UCS

Our initial experiment in 3D will be to create some circles and examine how AutoCAD stores them as 3D entities. We'll draw one circle parallel to the WCS and another in a rotated UCS. Circles are good test entities because they're easy-to-see planar entities, with only one point.

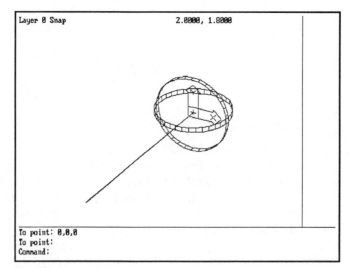

Two Circles in 3D Space

Examining Circles in 3D

Continue in the previous drawing, or begin a NEW drawing again named IL14.

Command: **UCSICON**	Set ON.
Command: **UCSICON**	Set to ORigin.
Command: **VPOINT**	Set to .4,-.8,.5
Command: **ZOOM**	Left corner -1,-2, with a height of 5.
Command: **SETVAR**	Set THICKNESS to 0.125.
Command: **SAVE**	This setup is used in several exercises.

```
Command: CIRCLE
3P/2P/TTR/<Center point>: 2,2,2
Diameter/<Radius>: 1
```

Command: **(setq en1 (entlast))**   Store the entity name.

```
Command: UCS                          Set Origin to 2,2,2.
Origin/ZAxis/3point/Entity/View/X/Y/Z/Prev/Restore/Save/Del/?/<World>: OR
Origin point <0,0,0>: 2,2,2
Command: UCS                          Rotate the X axis 90 degrees.
Origin/ZAxis/3point/Entity/View/X/Y/Z/Prev/Restore/Save/Del/?/<World>: X
Rotation angle about X axis <0.0>: 90
```

```
Command: CIRCLE
3P/2P/TTR/<Center point>: 0,0,0       Same world center point as the first circle.
Diameter/<Radius>: 1
```

Command: **(setq en2 (entlast))**   Store the entity name.

Command: **LINE**   Draw a reference line from *0,0,0 to 0,0,0.
The * overrides the UCS and enters the point as a WCS point.

➡ *TIP: VPOINT always performs a zoom extents, which may not be the view you want. To get around zoom extents, you can make a DVIEW-based replacement to control magnification, you can make a command or macro to restore a named view, or you can do a zoom center to 0.75X after each viewpoint.*

You might wonder how AutoCAD knows to put the circle in a different plane. Cleverly, AutoCAD uses the direction of the Z axis to determine how to orient the entity. In the WCS, this Z axis is always straight up, and plan view always looks straight down the Z vector. With the UCS command, you can change this Z vector to any direction in space.

Entity Extrusion Vectors

The direction of the current Z axis at the time an entity is created is stored with the entity data. This vector is called the *extrusion vector*. Think of an extrusion vector as the direction in which a 2D entity extrudes along its thickness. Extrusion vectors determine the orientation of an entity relative to the world construction plane. It is the 210 DXF group of the entity's data.

Examining Entity Data in 3D

The entity data lists for 3D are just the same as for 2D, but we must start paying attention to the Z coordinates and 210 groups which we have ignored until now.

How Extrusion Vectors Are Stored

The 210 group is a list containing the 210 code followed by the X component, the Y component, and the Z component of the direction vector. This 3D point value is stored as a WCS value. A typical extrusion vector would be:

```
(210 0.3433 0.898 0.5)
```

The extrusion vector of an entity created in the world coordinate system (WCS) is always:

```
(210 0.0 0.0 1.0)
```

A simple method for understanding how to interpret the 210 code is to imagine drawing a line from the WCS point of origin (0,0,0) to the point defined by the 210 code. The line will always be parallel to the positive Z extrusion direction of the entity. The illustration below shows this for the extrusion vector (210 0.75 0.5 0.375).

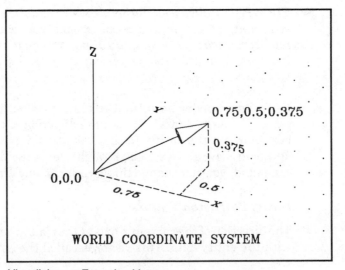

Visualizing an Extrusion Vector

Only 2D entities have meaningful extrusion vectors. The five full 3D entities can have differing Z coordinates for each point, so they have no overall orientation.

ECS — the Entity Coordinate System

The extrusion direction alone is not enough to define where an entity is in space. The displacement of the WCS to the UCS must be accounted for. AutoCAD does this automatically by storing the entity's point values and elevation relative to the WCS. The UCS is *not* stored with the entity. Instead, the combination of an entity's base point relative to the WCS and its extrusion vector determines its *ECS* (Entity Coordinate System). Its ECS can be used to recreate the position and orientation of any entity in 3D space. The UCS command Entity option uses this to match a new coordinate system to that of an existing entity.

Let's use the ENTGET function to take a closer look at the entity data for the circles.

Looking at Extrusion Codes

Continue in the previous drawing.

```
Command: (setq e1 (entget en1))
Lisp returns: ((-1 . <Entity name: 60000210>) (0 . "CIRCLE") (8 . "0") (39 . 0.125)
(10 2.0 2.0 2.0) (40 . 1.0) (210 0.0 0.0 1.0))

Command: (setq e2 (entget en2))
Lisp returns: ((-1 . <Entity name: 60000228>) (0 . "CIRCLE") (8 . "0") (39 . 0.125)
(10 2.0 2.0 -2.0) (40 . 1.0) (210 0.0 -1.0 -1.83772e-16))
```

➡ *NOTE: The 210 code (210 0.0 -1.0 -1.83772e-16) of the second circle is, for all practical purposes, (210 0.0 -1.0 -0.0). The Z value shown is scientific notation for -0.000000000000000183772, a very small number. We recommend ROUNDOFF.LSP to correct values such as this prior to comparing 3D points in your programs.*

The first circle should be easy to understand. The 10 code is exactly the same as the center point you provided. The 210 code shows that the extrusion direction is straight up the Z axis of the WCS. The second circle is a little different and requires some examination.

The second circle was constructed with the UCS point of origin at 2,2,2 of the WCS and the X axis rotated 90 degrees. Its positive Z axis points in the direction of the WCS negative Y. Its 10 code of (10 2.0 2.0 -2.0) doesn't show the 0,0,0 which was entered to construct the circle, or the WCS point of origin for the UCS (2,2,2). The 10 code of each entity is the XYZ vector (or offset) from the WCS origin relative to the entity's 210 code extrusion vector. In other words, its ECS.

If you examine the second circle's 210 code, rounded to (210 0.0 -1.0 0.0), you will see that its extrusion vector is in the negative Y direction of the WCS. The ECS point of origin is always located at the WCS point of origin, with the Z axis matching the extrusion direction, so you can use the 10 code (and the stored elevation, if any) to find the center of the circle. Use the diagrams below to see how the two circles are stored.

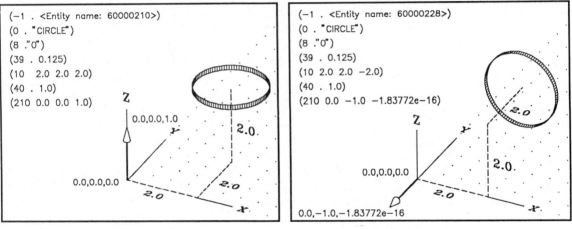

3D Diagram of First Circle   3D Diagram of Second Circle

➥ NOTE: The UCS created by selecting an entity with the UCS command's Entity option is parallel to, but not at, the ECS. The ECS origin is the WCS origin.

The X and Y orientation of an ECS depends on the type of entity. To see how AutoCAD determines the orientation, see the entity table under the UCS command and the Appendix C entity coordinate system section, both in your AutoCAD Reference Manual.

While the ECS is how AutoCAD makes 2D entities act like 3D, it is irrelevant to the full 3D entities because they have all points stored as WCS points.

➡ *NOTE: If FLATLAND is on, WCS entities return a 2D 10 group and a 38 elevation group, but non-WCS entities return entity data as shown above. To avoid programming around this, your 3D programs should assume, or ensure, that FLATLAND is off and ELEVATION is set to 0.*

Try another exercise. This time, the circle will be drawn in a UCS that is a little more complex.

Examining a Skewed Circle

Continue in the previous drawing, or edit an EXISTING drawing named IL14, with the saved settings from the "Examining Circles in 3D" exercise.

Command: **ERASE**	Erase the two circles and the line, if you continued.
Command: **UCS**	Set UCS back to world.
Command: **UCS**	Create a new UCS with the origin at 2,2,2, the Z axis rotated -30 degrees, and the Y axis rotated 30 degrees. Make the UCS settings in this order.

Command: **CIRCLE**   Draw circle at 0,0,0 with a radius of 1.
Command: **(setq e3 (entget (entlast)))**
Lisp returns: ((−1 . <Entity name: 600026a0>) (0 . "CIRCLE") (8 . "0") (39 . 0.125)
(10 2.73205 0.366025 2.09808) (40 . 1.0) (210 0.433013 −0.25 0.866025))
Command: **SAVE**   Save it as IL14A, for later use.

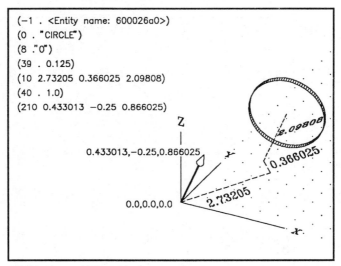

(−1 . <Entity name: 600026a0>)
(0 . "CIRCLE")
(8 ."0")
(39 . 0.125)
(10 2.73205 0.366025 2.09808)
(40 . 1.0)
(210 0.433013 −0.25 0.866025)

3D Diagram of Third Circle

Examining the diagram above doesn't show the construction as clearly as the previous examples. To help you see what's happening, let's look at an exercise that shows how the 10 and 210 codes determine the ECS. We'll draw X, Y, and Z lines from the WCS point of origin to the center of the circle using the values in the 10 and 210 code. First, use the 210 code to orient the UCS at the ECS. Then, draw the lines from the point of origin to the 10 code of the circle.

Using the 10 and 210 Codes to Locate the Circle

Continue in the previous "Examining a Skewed Circle" exercise drawing.

```
Command: SETVAR                          Set THICKNESS back to 0.

Command: UCS                             Set to World.
Command: UCS
Origin/ZAxis/3point/Entity/View/X/Y/Z/Prev/Restore/Save/Del/?/<World>: ZA
Origin point <0,0,0>: <RETURN>          World coordinate origin.
Point on positive portion of Z-axis <0.0000,0.0000,1.0000>: (dxf 210 e3)
                                        The 210 group is the extrusion vector.

Command: LINE From point: 0,0,0          Start the line at WCS origin.
To point: @2.73025,0,0                   Draw a line for the X value of the 10 code.
To point: @0,.366035,0                   Draw a line for the Y value of the 10 code.
To point: @0,0,2.09808                   The Z value of the 10 code, to the circle's center.
To point: <RETURN>
```

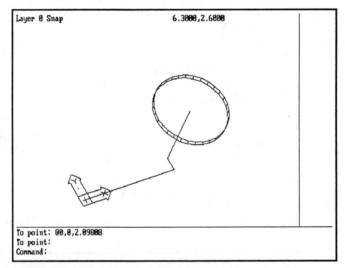

Line Drawn With 10 Code

The line should end at the center of the circle. The ZA option of the UCS command uses the same process to orient the axis as AutoCAD uses to establish an ECS for any given entity. You could write an alternate function to the UCS Entity option to use the 210 code to position the UCS at the ECS, at the WCS origin point instead of on the entity.

You might ask why we have to torture our minds with WCS, UCS, and ECS. Well, the WCS is the real thing, the UCS makes it easy to draw 3D, and the ECS makes storing 3D's extra data extremely compact. The only additional data value needed for full 3D was the 210 group, Autodesk's brilliant solution to 3D. Since AutoCAD stores 2D planar entities in the ECS format, you need a way to translate these coordinates to other systems to deal with 2D entities in your 3D programs.

Translating 3D Points

When a 2D planar entity is drawn in a UCS, the ECS coordinates that are stored with the entity won't match the UCS or WCS coordinates. The circles proved this because the 10 codes were different, even though the circles were drawn at the same WCS point in space.

```
(10 2.0 2.0 2.0)                    First circle center point in WCS.
(10 2.0 2.0 -2.0)                   Second circle in ECS terms.
(10 0.732051 3.36603 0.366025)      Third circle in ECS terms.
```

The points returned are always in the terms of the coordinate system at the time the entity was created. AutoLISP provides the TRANS function to translate coordinates to and from any coordinate system.

trans

> *Returns a translated point of the supplied point from the first coordinate code to the second coordinate code. The code values are: 0 for World Coordinate System, 1 for User Coordinate System, and 2 for Display Coordinate System (screen). If the flag is not omitted or is nil, the point value is treated as a 3D displacement. An entity name or 3D extrusion vector may be used in place of the code(s).*
> (**trans** *point code code* flag)

For full 3D non-planar entities whose points are all WCS points, translation between ECS and WCS is meaningless but harmless. However, specifying an ECS by supplying an extrusion vector in lieu of one of the codes does not work for such entities. It's safer to specify an ECS by supplying an entity name. When supplied the entity name of a full 3D non-planar entity, TRANS will ignore the ECS-WCS translation and return the point unchanged.

When asked to translate a 2D point, TRANS uses zero for the Z for all displacements, and for points coming from the WCS or ECS. For points coming from the DCS or a UCS, the Z is projected to the current construction plane. The DCS (Display Coordinate System) is the screen's coordinate system.

AutoLISP and all user interaction defaults occur in the current UCS. So, when you are providing the user with points obtained from entity data, the points should be translated from their ECS to the UCS. When you are modifying entity data with new point input, it needs to be translated to the ECS for compatibility with the entity's existing points. When you compare or operate upon points from multiple entities, translate them to either the UCS or WCS so that all points are in equal terms. You may want to use our New Riders AutoLISP Utilities Disk 1 ROUNDOFF.LSP program to compensate for the round-off error in translating 3D points.

Try using the TRANS function to convert the third circle's center point to the WCS.

Using TRANS to Translate Points

Continue in the previous "Examining a Skewed Circle" exercise drawing, with the E3 variable set.

```
Command: (setq lpt (dxf 10 e3))          The original ECS center point.
Lisp returns: (2.73205 0.366025 2.09808)
Command: (setq ev (dxf 210 e3))          The extrusion vector.
Lisp returns: (0.433013 -0.25 0.866025)
Command: (trans lpt ev 0)                Point LPT translated to WCS.
Lisp returns: (2.0 2.0 2.0)
```

The TRANS function converted the local point (LPT) from the entity's coordinate system (specified by EV, its extrusion vector) to the WCS (coded by the 0). You can also use the entity name to specify a coordinate system.

Using Entity Names With TRANS

```
Command: (trans '(2 2 2) 0 (dxf -1 e3))   DXF extracts the entity name from E3.
Lisp returns: (2.73205 0.366025 2.09808)  The original ECS center point.
```

Applying the TRANS function comes down to knowing which coordinate system you are in and to which system you want to go. You can use the DCS along with TRANS to display graphics parallel to the plane of the screen, regardless of the current UCS.

DCS — the Display Coordinate System

The DCS is the screen's coordinate system. You can use it to *visually* compare points and entities in the current view, like a line-of-sight comparison. Its origin is at the current viewpoint target point, the WCS 0,0,0. Its X and Y axes are parallel to the screen's edges, and its Z is irrelevant.

How to Prompt With GRDRAW, TRANS, and the DCS

You can use DCS translation to display graphic prompts or icons. Let's display an X.

Graphics in the DCS

Continue in the previous drawing, or edit the EXISTING drawing named IL14A from the
"Examining a Skewed Circle" exercise.
Make sure your UCS is skewed to the display.

```
Command: (grdraw (trans '(0 0) 2 1) (trans '(2 2) 2 1) 2)
Lisp returns: nil
Command: (grdraw (trans '(0 2) 2 1) (trans '(2 0) 2 1) 2)
Lisp returns: nil
```

That should have drawn an X from 0,0 to 2,2 of the DCS. The lower left corner of the X is also at 0,0,0 of the WCS. The points were translated from the DCS (code 2) to the current UCS (code 1). You might think that since we're drawing in the DCS, we should translate *to* the DCS. But, AutoCAD draws in the current UCS, so we take the DCS points that we want to *appear* on the screen and translate them by line-of-sight to UCS points in the current construction plane. If you get unexpected results using TRANS, you probably just have the *to* and *from* codes flipped.

The New Riders AutoLISP Utilities Disk 1 contains GRPT, a program that applies TRANS and GRDRAW to the DCS. Point entities, with the PDMODE and PDSIZE system variables set to display a combination of circles, squares, points, X's, or crosses, are useful visual prompts for AutoLISP-controlled drawing programs and parametrics. But in a skewed UCS, you get a skewed "point" which is often unintelligible. GRPT is a function that draws GRDRAW temporary points with any PDSIZE or PDMODE system variable setting and draws them parallel to the plane of the display, regardless of UCS.

You could also use TRANS to improve Chapter 9's PVIEW (Preview VIEW) program, which was restricted to the WCS. Let's make a program that uses TRANS and GRDRAW as a tool to quickly see an entity's orientation to the WCS.

How to Visualize Orientation With TRANS

A simple, but helpful, application of the TRANS function is to use it to display lines on the screen showing the Z axis extrusion vector direction and the XY axes of an entity's ECS. The SHOW3D program uses TRANS to convert the entity's base point and X, Y, and Z offsets to the current UCS for GRDRAW. It's useful for studying entities in 3D when you are planning construction techniques and debugging your programs.

```
;* SHOW3D.LSP
;* C:SHOW3D displays an entity's Z-extrusion vector and XY components with GRDRAW.
;* Z-Extr=green, X=red, Y=yellow. It require the DXF support function.
;*
(defun C:SHOW3D ( / exs en ed bpt zpt xpt ypt)
  (while (setq en (entsel "\nSelect entity: "))

❶
    (setq exs (* 0.33 (getvar "VIEWSIZE"))        ;screen size factor
          en (car en)                             ;entity name
          ed (entget en)                          ;entity data
          bpt (dxf 10 ed)                         ;entity base point in ECS

❷
          xpt (trans (mapcar '+ bpt (list exs 0 0)) en 1)   ;trans X to UCS
          ypt (trans (mapcar '+ bpt (list 0 exs 0)) en 1)   ;trans Y to UCS
          zpt (trans (mapcar '+ bpt (list 0 0 exs)) en 1)   ;trans Z to UCS
          bpt (trans bpt en 1)                    ;entity base point in UCS
    );setq

❸
    (grdraw bpt xpt 1)                            ;draw vectors
    (grdraw bpt ypt 2)
    (grdraw bpt zpt 3)
  );while
  (princ)
);defun SHOW3D
;*
```

C:SHOW3D Command in SHOW3D.LSP File

❶ EXS is set to a proportion of the current VIEWSIZE to establish a length for the temporary direction vectors. Then the entity name and data list are set to EN and ED and the base point, BPT, is extracted by DXF.

❷ The points XPT, YPT, and ZPT are each converted by TRANS from the ECS (supplied as the entity name EN) to the UCS (code 1). But first, MAPCAR adds EXS to the X, Y, or Z component of BPT, using lists like (list exs 0 0) to supply zero for the other components. MAPCAR is the standard way to do addition, subtraction, multiplication, and division of 3D points. BPT is also translated to the UCS.

❸ Each vector is drawn with GRDRAW, from BPT to XPT, YPT, or ZPT, using colors 1, 2, and 3.

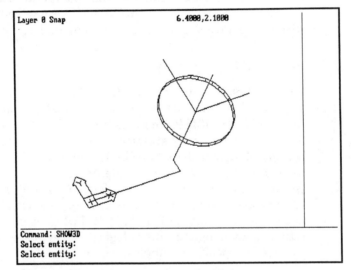

Z Axis Extrusion and XY Vectors of a Circle

Try SHOW3D on the last circle you drew.

Displaying Z Axis Extrusion and X,Y Orientation

Continue in the previous drawing, or edit the EXISTING drawing named IL14A with the skewed circle.

You have C:SHOW3D in your SHOW3D.LSP file.

Create the C:SHOW3D command in a new file named SHOW3D.LSP.

```
Command: (load "show3d")
Command: SHOW3D
Select entity:                    Select the circle.
Select entity: <RETURN>
```

Command: **UCS**	Set it to the entity.
Command: **PLAN**	Set to current UCS.
Command: **SHOW3D**	Select the circle again. Return to exit.
Command: **QUIT**	

Looking at the circle in plan view, you can only see a dot for the Z axis extrusion direction because it's in line with your current view.

A thorough understanding of the various coordinate systems and how to relate and translate entities and points in space is essential for programming 3D. It also helps to have a set of core subroutines to deal with things such as arcs, distances, and angles.

Programming Tools for 3D

We've collected a number of useful tools to make 3D programming easier. Tools for handling 3D angles are needed in many 3D programs. In Release 10, AutoLISP functions that deal with points and distances are fully 3D, but angles are still tied to the current construction plane. You've become accustomed to AutoCAD's polar coordinates in 2D. AutoCAD commands accept a polar coordinate in the form DISTANCE<ANGLE. However, 3D has no current equivalent. The POLAR, GETANGLE, and ANGLE functions project their points onto and consider their angles to be in the current construction plane. (If POLAR is given a 3D point, the Z is returned unchanged.) This is logical, since to specify an angle in space, you need to specify two angles.

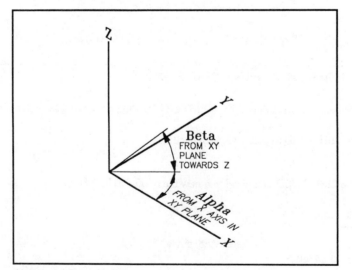

Alpha and Beta Angles

Polar notation in a 3D coordinate system requires two angles. The first angle is the familiar angle from the X axis in the XY plane, usually requested with a `Rotation angle <90>:` prompt. In 3D polar calculations, you also need to determine the angle from the XY plane toward the Z axis. This is the same as the VPOINT Rotate option angle specification. We will call the XY plane *rotation* angle *alpha*, and the *inclination* angle toward the Z axis will be *beta*.

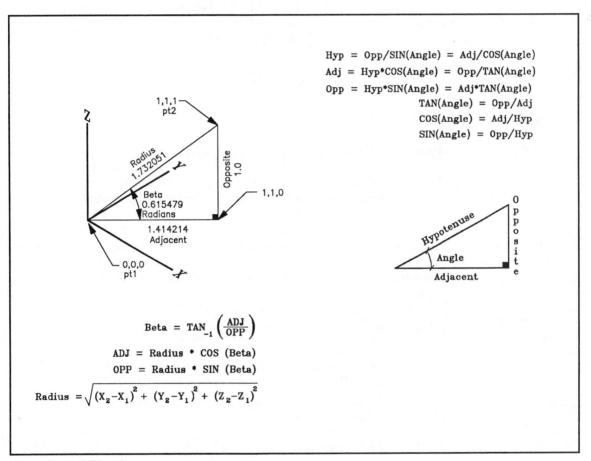

Formulas and Triangles

Let's write a function called BANGLE (Beta ANGLE) that calculates the beta angle. In 3D polar functions, the distance along the XY plane will be the ADJacent distance, and the OPPosite leg will be the rise in Z elevation. The equation is TAN(angle)=OPP/ADJ where OPPosite is Z1 - Z2 (the vertical Z difference), and ADJacent is the base distance from PT1 to PT2 in the XY plane.

```
;* BANGLE calculates the inclined angle from the XY plane between two points.
(defun bangle (pt1 pt2 / dist)
  (setq dist                                ;projected dist in xy plane
        (distance (list (car pt1) (cadr pt1) 0) (list (car pt2) (cadr pt2) 0))
  )
  (if (zerop dist)                          ;if dist is 0, angle is 90 or all Z
    1.57079633                              ;half of pi, 90 degrees
    (atan (/ (- (caddr pt2) (caddr pt1))    ;divides the rise - delta Zs
            dist                            ;by the run - length in XY plane
    )       );atan&/
  );if
);defun BANGLE
;*
```

BANGLE Function in IL-3D.LSP File

Because DISTANCE returns a 3D distance in Release 10, the DIST variable is set to the projected distance in the XY plane. This allows ZEROP to test for a zero projected angle, avoiding a division-by-zero error in the ATAN function. BANGLE uses the AutoLISP arctangent function, ATAN, to determine the angle.

atan *Returns the arctangent of number1, from -pi to pi. If number2 is provided, the arctangent of the number1/number2 is returned. If number2 is 0, either -pi/2 or +pi/2 radians (-90 or +90 degrees) is returned, depending on the sign of number1.*
(**atan** *number1* number2**)**

Try the ATAN function at the keyboard, using equal numbers for the OPPosite and ADJacent distances. Then test BANGLE.

Using ATAN and the 3D Polar Function BANGLE

Enter selection: **1**   Begin a NEW drawing again named IL14.

You have the BANGLE subroutine in your IL-3D.LSP file.

Create the BANGLE subroutine in a new file named IL-3D.LSP.

Command: **(atan 1 1)**	Test an equal leg triangle.
Lisp returns: 0.785398	That's pi/4 radians, or 45 degrees.
Command: **(load "IL-3D")**	Load the file.
Command: **(bangle '(0 0 0) '(1 1 1))**	Test it.
Lisp returns: 0.61548	Equals 35.2643 degrees.

BANGLE finds the beta angle of existing points. If you want to use that angle (or any beta angle) to specify a new point in space, you need a 3DPOLAR function.

How to Specify Polar Locations in Space

3DPOLAR is useful for calculating a new point at the same angle as an existing point or entity from a base point. 3DPOLAR works much like POLAR, but takes a beta angle in addition to the alpha angle and point arguments of POLAR. It returns a 3Dpoint that is not tied to the construction plane.

```
;* 3DPOLAR calculates a point in 3D space given rotation from X axis in XY plane,
;* rotation from XY plane toward Z, base point, and offset distance.
(defun 3dpolar (pt alpha beta dist / dx dy dz)
    (setq dx (* dist (cos alpha) (cos beta)) ;shortened by X and Z projection
          dy (* dist (sin alpha) (cos beta)) ;shortened by Y and Z projection
          dz (* dist (sin beta))             ;only Z projection causes shortening
    );setq
    (mapcar '+ (list dx dy dz) pt)           ;adds delta values to base point
);defun 3DPOLAR
;*


;* 3DP is a friendlier interface for the above 3DPOLAR.
;* To use transparently, enter (3dp) in menu macros or commands.
(defun 3dp ( / bpt)
  (3dpolar
    (setq bpt (getvar "LASTPOINT"))
    (uangle 1 "" "Angle from X axis in XY plane" nil bpt)
    (uangle 1 "" "Angle from XY plane toward Z" nil bpt)
    (udist 1 "" "Distance" nil nil)
  )
);defun 3DP
;*
```

3DPOLAR and C:3DPOLAR Functions in IL-3D.LSP File

3DPOLAR calculates the projection of the 3D point on the XY plane, then takes the Z difference (the rise) between the two points. The X and Y components are shortened by the beta angle, using the SIN and COS trig functions. Again, MAPCAR adds the point components to the base point.

The 3DP function is merely a user interface for 3DPOLAR, allowing it to be used transparently in the middle of any point entry command. It uses the LASTPOINT system variable for its base point.

Say you need to calculate a line of sight to place a camera, either a real surveillance camera or an AutoShade camera. You know the angles for clearance, and you know the maximum distance for image clarity. 3DPOLAR can find the point.

Testing the 3DPOLAR Functions

Continue in the previous drawing, or begin a NEW drawing again named IL14.

You have the 3DPOLAR and 3DP functions in your IL-3D.LSP file.

Add the 3DPOLAR and 3DP functions to your IL-3D.LSP file.

```
Command: (load "IL-3D")              Reload the file.
Command: ID                          Reset the lastpoint, enter 0,0,0.

Command: (3dp)                       Tests both functions at once.
Angle from X axis in XY plane: 45
Angle from XY plane toward Z: 30
Distance: 240
Lisp returns: (146.969 146.969 120.0)
```

In addition to angles, other useful calculation tools for 3D are subroutines for arcs, circles, and spheres.

Other Helpful Polar and Curve Formulas

You will find the following subroutines helpful when you work with curved surfaces, arcs, and circles in both 2D and 3D. All functions use the basic curve formulas shown in the diagram.

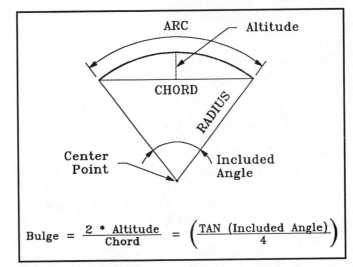

$$\text{Bulge} = \frac{2 * \text{Altitude}}{\text{Chord}} = \left(\frac{\text{TAN (Included Angle)}}{4} \right)$$

Trigonometry of a Curve

Given an angle and the radius, the formula for a circle calculates a point on its circumference:

```
Coord = Radius*COS(angle),Radius*SIN(angle)
```

In AutoLISP you write it:

```
(list (* rad (cos ang)) (* rad (sin ang)))
```

This formula or derivations of it appear in most of the following functions.

---

cos   *Returns the cosine of a radian angle.*
(cos angle)

---

sin   *Returns the sin of a radian angle.*
(sin angle)

```
;* RADIUS calculates the radius of an arc given the chord distance and
;* altitude dimensions.
(defun radius (chord altitude)
   (/ (+ (expt (/ chord 2.0) 2.0) (* altitude altitude)) (* 2.0 altitude))
);defun
;*


;* ARCLEN calculates the arc length given the radius and included angle.
(defun arclen (radius ang)
   (while (> ang #pi360)
     (setq ang (- ang #pi360))      ;assures angle is less than full circle
   )
   (* radius ang)                   ;multiplies radius by included angle
);defun
;*


;* INCANG calculates the included angle given a chord distance and radius.
(defun incang (chord radius)
  (* 2.0 (atan                      ;twice the arc tangent
         (/ chord 2.0               ;of opposite over adjacent
           (sqrt (- (expt radius 2) ;calcs adjacent leg of triangle
                 (expt (/ chord 2.0) 2)
  )      ) ) )      )
);defun INCANG
;*


;* ALTITD calculates the altitude of an arc given the radius and included angle.
(defun altitd (radius angle)
   (- radius (* radius (cos (/ angle 2.0)))) ;radius minus the adjacent leg of
);defun                             ;the triangle
;*
```

Arc Functions in IL-3D.LSP File

These arc functions treat angles in the same manner that AutoCAD draws arcs; north is 90 degrees and positive is counterclockwise. The function code is a straightforward application of the AutoLISP trig functions illustrated earlier.

Testing the Arc Functions

Continue in the previous drawing, or begin a NEW drawing again named IL14.

You have the ARCLEN, RADIUS, and INCANG functions in your IL-3D.LSP file.

Add the ARCLEN, RADIUS, and INCANG functions to your IL-3D.LSP file.

```
Command: (load "IL-3D")          Reload the file.
Command: PLAN                    Go to WCS plan view.

Command: ARC                     Center 0,0, Start 1,0 and End 0,1.
Command: LINE                    Draw a line between two endpoints of the arc.

Command: LIST                    Both the line and arc.
                                 LINE reports:   Length = 1.4142, Angle in X, Y Plane = 135
                                 ARC reports:    center point X=0.0000 Y=0.0000 Z=0.0000
                                                 radius 1.0000  start angle 0  end angle 90

Command: (setq dst (sqrt 2))     Returns: 1.414214 — equal to line's length.

Command: (setq ia (incang dst 1))   Returns: 1.570796, 90 degrees.
                                    IA saves included angle.

Command: (setq alt (altitd 1 ia))   Returns 0.292893, the altitude distance.
Command: DIST                       Compare ALTITD to the distance reported by
                                    osnapping MID line to MID arc. It reports: Distance = 0.2929

Command: (arclen 1 ia)           Returns: 1.570796, the arc length.
                                 Compare it to a polyline:

Command: PEDIT                   Select the arc. It changes to a pline arc.
Command: LIST                    It reports:  Length = 1.5708

Command: (radius dst alt)        Returns: 1.0
```

If you looked at Chapter 12's parametric subroutine, you will recognize the INCANG subroutine. We don't doubt that you will invent other subroutines for this useful programming tool. Let's add a few drawing tools to the 3D toolkit.

Drawing Tools for 3D

In this section, we'll look at a few 3D drawing tools from our collection. They include functions and macros to automate multiple views of objects, suppress UCS-viewport redraws, and convert drawings from single-line to full 3D. Along the way, we'll add a few more subroutines to our IL-3D.LSP tool kit.

How to Generate Multiple Views Via the UCS

One common application of multiple viewports is to create alternate views of a drawing, such as front, top, and side. This can be automated by a menu macro called [Const 2D]. This macro uses the UCS command to establish front and side views and uses blocks to manipulate the entities. You'll notice that AutoLISP is not required.

```
[Const2D]^C^C^CBLOCK;PLAN;\BOX;\\;UCS;O;@;INSERT;PLAN;@;;;;+
UCS;X;90;BLOCK;FRONT;@;L;;OOPS;UCS;Y;90;BLOCK;SIDE;@;L;;UCS;W;+
INSERT;*PLAN;\;;INSERT;FRONT;\;;;INSERT;SIDE;\;;;
```

The [Const 2D] Macro in the IL14-3D.MNU File

[Const 2D] makes a block of the plan view, changes the UCS, and inserts the block in the correct orientation for each view. The macro requires you to select the insertion base point of the block and to select the object(s) to include in the block definition with a box window. Then you can pick a drawing location for each of the distinct views.

Draw a simple part as illustrated in the plan view, and try the [Const 2D] macro.

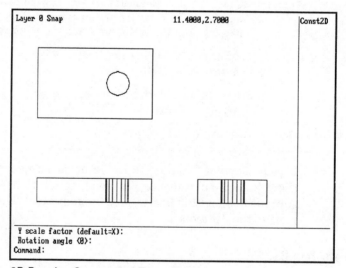

2D Drawing Constructed From 3D Part

Testing the [Const 2D] Macro

Enter selection: **1**   Begin a NEW drawing again named IL14.

You have the [Const 2D] macro in your IL14-3D.MNU file.

Create the [Const 2D] macro in a new file named IL14-3D.MNU.

Command: **PLINE**   Draw the shape.
From point: **1,4.5**   To points **1,7.5   6,7.5   6,4.5** and **C** to close.
Command: **CIRCLE**   Draw at 4.5,6 with radius 0.5.
Command: **CHPROP**   Change both to thickness of 1.

Command: **MENU**   Load the IL14-3D.MNU.
Select **[Const 2D]**
Insertion base point: **1,4.5**   Pick lower left corner of polyline.
First corner: Pick first corner of window.
Second corner: Pick second corner.
Insertion point: Pick absolute point 1,4.5.
Insertion point: Pick absolute point 1,1.
Insertion point: Pick absolute point 8,1.

The macro creates a block named PLAN. It inserts the block, modifies the UCS, and creates new blocks named FRONT and SIDE. The front and side blocks are nested blocks containing the PLAN block. After the blocks are created, the INSERT command places each block at the points you enter. Because the PLAN block is nested in the others, you can update all the views by editing the entities in the plan view (which were inserted exploded) and by redefining the PLAN block.

The construction macro involves no AutoLISP, which keeps it simple. But it does have some shortcomings. Don't use it twice in an editing session or it will crash and you'll have to UNDO. Turning MENUECHO off or making the macro into an AutoLISP function, adding prompts in either case, would improve its usefulness and clarify the construction process.

➡ *TIP: To combine perspectives with 2D plan drawings, or to mix hidden line-removed views with normal views, you can plot to a DXB file and use DXBIN to import the plotted image into another drawing. AutoCAD can plot any view in a drawing, even DVIEW perspectives, to a DXB file. To do so, you reconfigure AutoCAD to an ADI plotter for an AutoCAD DXB file, get your desired viewpoint, and plot it. Then you use DXBIN to import the file. It comes in as a 2D drawing of a 3D view composed completely of line entities. Circle, arcs, and curves are composed of small line segments. You can control accuracy and resolution by the plot scale and plotter step size setting in ADI DXB configuration. See INSIDE AutoCAD from New Riders Publishing for more explanation and an example.*

The [Const 2D] macro requires several UCS changes, each of which causes a redraw. In complex drawings with multiple viewports, redraws from UCS changes are particularly tedious.

Working With Viewports and the UCS

The combination of 3D entities, UCSs, and multiple viewports can make redraws extremely slow. If certain settings are present, every UCS change causes a redraw. To make working in viewports more practical, you can suppress UCS-triggered redraws by turning these four system variables off: AXISMODE, GRIDMODE, UCSICON, and UCSFOLLOW.

Multiple viewports disable the AXIS command and do not display axis ticks. However, if AXIS is on when you bring up multiple viewports, UCS will still cause a redraw even though the ticks are not displayed. Turning AXISMODE off works for all viewports, but the other three system variables must be turned off individually in each viewport. The C:VPOFF function is a quick method to disable UCS redraws in multiple viewports.

```
;* C:VPOFF turns off all display controls that cause redraws.
;* It can be called transparently or from another function as (c:vpoff).
(defun C:VPOFF ()
  (setvar "AXISMODE" 0)                    ;turn axismode off
  (foreach item (vports)                   ;cycle through each viewport
    (setvar "CVPORT" (car item))           ;make a viewport current
    (setvar "UCSICON" 0)                    ;turn ucsicon off
    (setvar "UCSFOLLOW" 0)                  ;turn ucsfollow off
    (setvar "GRIDMODE" 0)                   ;turn gridmode off
  );foreach
```

Listing continued.

Continued listing.

```
  (princ)                                  ;clean exit
);defun C:VPOFF
;*

(princ)
;* end of 3DTOOLS.LSP
;*
```

C:VPOFF Command in IL-3D.LSP File

The function above is simple, with no variables. The AXISMODE is turned off first. Then FOREACH cycles through the list of viewports provided by the VPORTS function and turns each system variable off.

A similar function could turn all the system variables back on, assuming that all the settings *should* be on. An even more sophisticated method could store the status of each variable in each viewport before turning it off. A new function could then read the stored variable values and return each viewport to its original state.

Test the VPOFF function with multiple viewports and different grids.

Continue in the previous drawing, or edit an EXISTING drawing again named IL14.

 You have the C:VPOFF command in your IL-3D.LSP file.

Add the C:VPOFF functions to your IL-3D.LSP file.

```
Command: VPORTS          Turn them on.
Save/Restore/Delete/Join/SIngle/?/2/<3>/4: <RETURN>
Horizontal/Vertical/Above/Below/Left/<Right>: <RETURN>
Regenerating drawing.

Command: (load "IL-3D")  Reload the file.
Command: VPOFF           It quietly does its work.
Command: UCS             Rotate X 90 to test it. It doesn't redraw.
```

Notice that the grid remains even after it has been turned off. Except for the snap variables related to isometrics, all axis, grid, and snap system variables can be modified without the display redrawing, as long as AutoLISP is used to make the settings.

The drawback to VPOFF is that you no longer have the UCS icon to guide you. But you can define a modified UCS command to fix that. Use table access to check the current UCS after it changes, and use entity access to modify an inserted block that looks like the UCS icon (or your own symbol). Check the limits and screen system variables to determine placement and scale, check the UCS table to determine orientation, and use ENTMOD to regenerate the icon block only. With command redefinition, discussed in Chapter 17, you can replace the real UCS icon with your own version.

Another alternative to UCS-caused redraws is to just avoid changing the UCS when you don't *have* to.

Alternatives to Changing UCS Planes

Sometimes it's faster to draw an entity in the current UCS and then change its orientation to the desired plane, particularly when the entity is created by an AutoLISP function anyway. To do so, modify the entity after creation with ENTMOD, supplying new point values and a new 210 code for the extrusion direction. In other words, redefine its ECS.

Our example of this is the C:STK-PIPE command. It represents piping by converting line entities into extruded circles. It requires two subroutines which you can apply to ECS redefinition in general. The ZAXIS function calculates the new 210 code (Z axis extrusion vector) for an entity, and NEWECS translates and updates the entity based on the ZAXIS vector. We'll add both functions to the IL-3D.LSP file.

How to Calculate Extrusion Vectors

An extrusion vector is a one-unit length vector in the extrusion direction of the entity, specified by a 210 group point list relative to 0,0,0. The ENTMOD function will accept a 210 point specifying any length vector, which it will convert to unit length. However, a vector supplied to the TRANS function must have a one-unit length. The ZAXIS function calculates the distance between two points provided as arguments and returns the vector point.

```
;* IL-3D.LSP is a set of subroutines and tools for 3D programming.

;* ZAXIS calculates a 1-unit extrusion vector from two 3D points.
(defun zaxis (pt1 pt2 / delta sqrpt sum unitm unitv)
   (setq delta (mapcar '- pt2 pt1)           ;take difference of points
         sqrpt (mapcar '* delta delta)        ;square them
         sum (apply '+ sqrpt)                  ;add them together
         unitm (sqrt sum)                      ;get unit length
         unitv (mapcar '/ delta                ;divide by unit magnitude
                 (list unitm unitm unitm)
               )
   );setq
);defun ZAXIS
;*
```

ZAXIS Function in IL-3D.LSP File

MAPCAR subtracts PT1 from PT2, which is set to DELTA. The new DELTA point specifies a vector from 0,0,0 that is equivalent to the PT1-PT2 vector. To specify a vector with a single point, as required for the 210 code, it must be relative to a standard base point such as 0,0,0. This DELTA point is then converted to a one-unit length by MAPCAR *, APPLY +, and SQRT. The APPLY function provides a method for executing a function based on values supplied by a variable. It's the most efficient way to sum the contents of a list without extracting individual elements.

apply | *Applies a function to the arguments supplied by list. Generally, function and list are quoted so their contents will be supplied unevaluated.* **(apply *function list*)**

The other function that we need for ECS redefinition will automate the process of updating the entity data to the new ECS.

How to Update Entity 210 Codes

To modify an ECS, both the entity's extrusion vector and all point values associated with the entity have to be updated. For simplicity, NEWECS only deals with the 10 group, so it can just be used for single point-type entities like circles, arcs, inserts, and points. You can extend its usefulness by adding code to deal with other point groups, testing each entity type, and ensuring each point is appropriately updated. In our example, we apply it to circles.

```
;* NEWECS reorients a circle, arc, insert or point entity to the UCS plane
;* of the specified Z-axis. It requires the DXF function.
(defun newecs (zaxis ename / ed bpt)
  (setq ed (entget ename)                         ;get entity data
        bpt (trans (dxf 10 ed) ename zaxis)
        ed (subst (cons 10 bpt) (assoc 10 ed) ed)      ;substitute new 10 point
        ed (subst (cons 210 zaxis) (assoc 210 ed) ed)  ;update alternate zaxis
  );setq
  (entmod ed)                                     ;update the entity data
);defun NEWECS
;*
```

NEWECS Function in IL-3D.LSP File

The entity name is passed in as an argument to get the entity data ED. Next, the 10 DXF point is translated to the new Z axis. The base point, BPT, is translated from the ECS specified by ENAME to the new ECS specified by the ZAXIS argument. SUBST replaces new 10 and 210 DXF groups for the old groups. ENTMOD updates the entity.

Let's apply the NEWECS and ZAXIS functions to a real example, converting single-line pipe diagrams to full 3D images.

Applying ECS Redefinition to Piping

The STK-PIPE program takes lines in a single-line piping diagram and converts them to 3D pipes. The function takes each line endpoint and draws a circle at the first end. Then it draws the circle in the current UCS, converts it to the new ECS, and updates the circle to extrude in the direction of the line.

STK-PIPE starts by getting a line entity from you. The input is nested within a WHILE loop, so the program automatically repeats. The function tests to ensure that you selected a line entity, then proceeds to get the data for the line. It asks for the diameter of the pipe section to draw.

Both endpoints are stored in variables (wpt1 and wpt2) and the length of the line is calculated. This length will later be used as the extrusion length.

```
;* STK-PIPE.LSP
;* C:STK-PIPE converts a line entity into an extruded circle to represent
;* a pipe in 3D. It requires the DXF, NEWECS and ZAXIS subroutines.

(defun C:STK-PIPE ( / dia ep en ed wpt1 wpt2 lpt az)
   (while (setq ep (entsel "\nSelect line to convert to pipe: "))
     (setq en (car ep)  ed (entget en)) ;ename and entity data
     (if (= "LINE" (dxf 0 ed))              ;if it's a line
       (progn                               ;then
         (setq dia (udist 1 "" "Pipe diameter" dia nil)
               wpt1 (dxf 10 ed)             ;get the world start point
               wpt2 (dxf 11 ed)             ;get the world end point
               tk (distance wpt1 wpt2)      ;calc the thickness for circle
               lpt (trans wpt1 en 1)        ;trans start point to local
               az (zaxis wpt1 wpt2)         ;get new extrusion direction
         );setq
         (command "CIRCLE" lpt dia)         ;draw circle
         (newecs az (entlast))              ;update pipe orientation
         (command "CHPROP" (entlast) "" "T" tk "")   ;extrude pipe
       );progn
       (prompt "\nSorry, STK-PIPE only works for line entities. ") ;else
     );if a line entity
   );while
   (princ)
);defun C:STK-PIPE
;*
```

STK-PIPE Function in IL-3D.LSP File

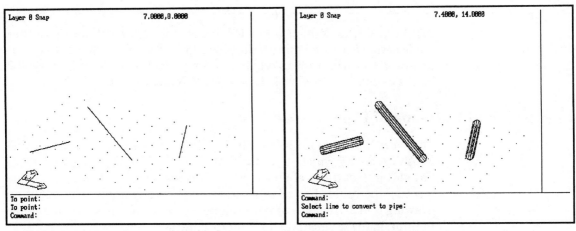

Lines Before Conversion   *Circles After Conversion*

Now test the new function. First draw some lines in 3D space, like the Lines Before Conversion illustration.

Testing the STK-PIPE Command

Continue in the previous drawing, or begin a NEW drawing again named IL14.

 You have C:STK-PIPE in your STK-PIPE.LSP file. ZAXIS and NEWECS are in your IL-3D.LSP file.

Create C:STK-PIPE in a new file named STK-PIPE.LSP, and add ZAXIS and NEWECS to your IL-3D.LSP file.

```
Command: VPOINT                             Set to .4,-.8,.5.
Command: ZOOM                               Left corner 2,-4 with height 10.
Command: LINE                               Draw lines in 3D as illustrated.

Command: (load "il-3d")
Command: (load "stk-pipe")

Command: (zaxis '(1 1 1) '(2 2 2))          Test ZAXIS.
Lisp returns: (0.57735 0.57735 0.57735)     Compare it to a 1-unit vector at the same angle,
                                            using the 3DPOLAR and BANGLE functions.
Command: (setq pt (3dpolar '(0 0 0) (/ pi 4) (bangle '(0 0 0) '(1 1 1)) 1))
Lisp returns: (0.57735 0.57735 0.57735)     The same point.

Command: STK-PIPE
Select line to convert to pipe:             Select a line.
Pipe diameter: .5                           Try other diameters and lines.
Command: QUIT
```

STK-PIPE works without any UCS changes for 3D creation. It's rather crude because it doesn't finish the pipe bends. To make STK-PIPE a useful program, you will want to create a mesh to enclose the bend, or use 3D blocks as shown in the book, CUSTOMIZING AutoCAD.

Creating Flat Patterns of Pipes

The New Riders AutoLISP Utilities Disk 1 contains a program called **FLATPAT.LSP** which, in contrast to STK-PIPE's 3D piping, generates flat pattern drawings of pipe ends. It draws a template for any size pipe meeting the center line of another size pipe at any angle. The resulting drawing is in 2D, but the program demonstrates that you sometimes have to think in 3D to calculate a 2D representation.

Summary

You now have the basic knowledge and tools that you need to work and program efficiently in 3D. You can control UCS changes and redraws. You can deal with the UCS, ECS, WCS, and DCS, calculate 3D points, angles, distances, arcs, and altitudes, and convert entities and views between 2D and 3D.

We're sure you'll create many more tools and 3D drawing programs. But developing a good 3D program is more involved than developing the average 2D program. Because we have to deal with 3D on a 2D screen, it's easy to get lost. When drawing in 3D, you need all the help you can get. Points and objects may appear to be where and what they are not. Circles, text, solids, and lines all look the same when viewed edge-on. Object selection is difficult when the object you want is behind others. Round-off errors occur easily in 3D and can fool your programs when comparing and aligning points. Many 3D editing operations cause unnecessary redraws of all viewports.

A good 3D drawing program makes 3D drawing easier and reduces errors. Your programs should take liberal advantage of prompts, menu page toggles, GRDRAW, and GRTEXT to keep you informed as you draw. Don't forget non-standard applications of 3D, such as DCS point translation combined with GRDRAW to put graphic prompts or icons on the screen. Use colors, temporary entities, temporary entity removal with ENTDEL, automated DVIEW views, and highlighting to see what you're doing and to aid object selection.

Try not to put the overhead of calculating 3D points, distances, and angles on yourself. Make your programs do it with a library of subroutines. You do the conceptual work, but make AutoLISP do what it does well — calculate. You don't need to reinvent the 3D wheel. Take advantage of our programs and the 3D entity creation and editing tools that came with your AutoCAD program as sources for techniques and code in your 3D drawing programs. Remember, entity modification and ECS redefinition are efficient methods of creating 3D objects, as shown in our STK-PIPE program. Whether you work with parametrics, piping, mechanical designs, building models, or heart valves (as one of our readers does), you'll find that a few reliable 3D programs will be among your most valuable tools.

By now, you may have noticed that hidden line removal and plotting of complex 3D images can take a very long time. These are ideal applications for unattended processing with batch programming, our next topic.

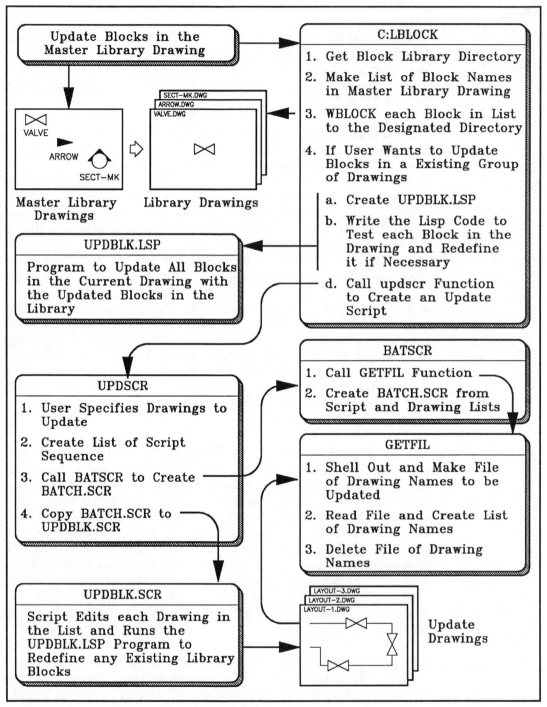

LBLOCK, a Custom Block Library Update Program

CHAPTER 15

Batch Programming

AutoLISP AND SCRIPTS

AutoCAD's flexibility means there are usually several ways to accomplish most tasks, including batch processing. Basically, batch processing applies a set of commands to a list of drawings or files. In the AutoCAD world, batch processing is most often done with a script file. AutoCAD scripts can drive any part of AutoCAD, from plotting to configuring. Alternative batch methods include DXF files, DOS *filename*.BAT or UNIX script files, external programs, and AutoLISP programs.

For repetitive operations on multiple files, batch processing is more efficient than processing the files one by one. Often, a combination of AutoLISP, menus, scripts, and external programs turns out to be the most efficient method. This chapter will discuss the strengths and weaknesses of batch processing with AutoLISP, scripts, and other methods. We'll give you some guidelines and hands-on examples to help you choose the best techniques for your application. We'll develop a script batch builder — an AutoLISP-based program to easily create script files. Any type of script can be created with the batch builder. It can even create DOS batch (.BAT) files to do batch processing of files that are totally unrelated to AutoCAD.

The major benefit of using scripts is that they operate throughout the entire AutoCAD environment, from configuration to drawing to Main Menu to plot and back. Meanwhile, AutoLISP and menus are confined to the drawing editor. Writing scripts is tedious and prone to errors. However, using AutoLISP to automate building repetitive scripts can make it easy and reduce script errors. You can use automated scripts to do unattended plotting of multiple files, make and show a series of slides, create a series of AutoShade and AutoFlix movie image files, extract attribute information from multiple files, update block libraries, and even redefine blocks in a series of drawings. These are mostly tasks that don't apply to any particular application, but are useful to many.

In this chapter, we'll also compare the relative merits of reading external data through scripts, DXF files, and AutoLISP programs. We'll create scripts that work around their inability to pause. We'll automate script building and automate the creation of the input slide list file for

AutoCAD's SLIDELIB program. We'll use an AutoLISP function to create an AutoLISP file that can itself be executed. And we'll develop a block library program that maintains a master block library in a single file, automatically updates a library directory of block (.DWG) files, and updates a group of drawing files with a group of redefined blocks.

AutoLISP Tools and Programs

AutoLISP Tools

GETFIL is an AutoLISP routine that builds a list of file names from a wildcard search of the directories you specify.

GETSCR builds a list of AutoCAD commands in a script file format. It has special symbols that are replaced by file names from the GETFIL directory listing.

BATSCR builds scripts from directory listings. It's used by several functions.

Programs

FTEXT.LSP contains C:FTEXT, which reads an external text file, formats the text to your specifications, and places it in the drawing.

BATCHSCR.LSP is the script batch builder. It contains the GETFIL, GETSCR, and BATSCR subroutines. It also contains C:MSCRIPT, a user interface which handles the input and formatting for BATSCR.

SLIDE.LSP contains C:CSLIDE and C:SSLIDE, two useful examples of specialized script building programs. C:CSLIDE uses BATSCR to make a script that produces slide files from a directory listing. C:SSLIDE, for ShowSLIDEs, makes a script to display each slide in a directory.

LBLOCK.LSP contains C:LBLOCK, which automatically updates a library directory of wblocked "block" files from a single block library file. Also included is UPDSCR, which optionally creates UPDBLK.LSP and UPDBLK.SCR to update a group of drawing files with a directory of redefined blocks.

The script batch builder is a powerful tool for automating those tasks that span across multiple drawings. It's a complex program, but it makes scripts easy to create and is very flexible. LBLOCK can be a life saver when you suddenly have to replace hundreds of block insertions in a whole project of drawings. And SLIDE.LSP makes slide shows, or sets of slide files, for dazzling AutoFlix shows. What's more, all of these programs can do their work while you're out to lunch or home sleeping.

Comparing Batch Processing Methods

Let's take a look at reading external data through scripts, DXF files, and AutoLISP programs. We'll compare how each method imports a group of text notes and we'll look at the differences, advantages, and disadvantages of each. We'll be using the following example text in various formats throughout the chapter.

```
A SCRIPT CAN READ IN EXTERNAL TEXT BUT IT
MUST BE FULLY PREFORMATTED.


EXTERNAL PROGRAMS CAN PREFORMAT TEXT AND
IMPORT IT AS A .DXF FILE OR A SCRIPT.


MENUS CAN INCLUDE STANDARD TEXT NOTES IN
PREFORMATTED FORM, BUT ARE INFLEXIBLE.


AUTOLISP OFFERS FLEXIBILITY AND DYNAMIC
FORMATTING, BUT REQUIRES MORE PROGRAMMING.
```

Sample Text File

Say that you need to put some standard notes or specifications into your drawings. The text may also need reformatting to fit in some of the drawings, so blocks are out. You could edit each drawing and fit the text to each, but that doesn't offer an automated solution. We're looking for a lazy way out. Let's see what scripts can do.

AutoCAD Scripts

A script is an ASCII text file containing a list of AutoCAD commands. Script files look like long menu macros with some minor differences. A script is an ASCII file of characters that control AutoCAD exactly as if you were typing in commands from the command line. One major difference between macros and scripts is that scripts can't pause for input from the user (without our work-around technique). But the advantage of scripts is that they can skip in and out of the AutoCAD drawing editor while menu macros are confined to a single drawing session. Since scripts can control AutoCAD from anywhere, a script can drive AutoCAD to start new drawings from the Main Menu, edit existing drawings, plot, print, or configure AutoCAD.

To import text with a script, you have to format the text file in a form that
AutoCAD can enter with the TEXT command. The first several lines of
our example text are shown in script format below. Our commentary,
shown to the right of the commands, is not part of the file.

`1`	Begin a NEW drawing
`IL-NOTES`	Give it a name
`TEXT`	Start the TEXT command
`S`	Set the style
`STANDARD`	We'll use STANDARD, not a fixed height
`2,3`	Enter location point
`0.25`	Then the height
	Blank line defaults rotation angle
`A SCRIPT CAN READ IN EXTERNAL TEXT`	This is the first line of text
	<RETURN> to recall TEXT command
	Default location point
`BUT IT MUST BE FULLY PREFORMATTED.`	Next line of text
	<RETURN> to recall TEXT command
	Default location point
`EXTERNAL PROGRAMS CAN PREFORMAT TEXT AND`	Third line of text
	<RETURN> to recall TEXT command
	Default location point
`IMPORT IT AS A .DXF FILE OR A SCRIPT.`	Fourth line of text

Sample Text Script IL-NOTES.SCR

Script files do not need the **+** continuation character at the end of a line.
AutoCAD automatically includes a <RETURN> at the end of each script
line. Script files must have a name with an .SCR extension. You can
generate scripts manually with a text editor, or automatically using
another program such as Lotus, dBASE, or one you write. We will write
scripts with AutoLISP later in this chapter.

Scripts can be started either from the DOS command prompt or by using
the SCRIPT command from within a drawing file. When started from
DOS, you need to supply a default drawing name and the name of the
script file. Let's test the script file, using our IL.BAT batch command to
start it.

Running Scripts From DOS

    You have the IL-NOTES.SCR file.

Create the IL-NOTES.SCR file as shown above.

Run the script from the DOS command line with our IL.BAT file.

`C:\IL-ACAD>`**`IL IL-NOTES IL-NOTES`**   The 1st IL-NOTES is the drawing, the 2nd is the script.

AutoCAD begins the new drawing, starts the TEXT command and places the four lines of text.

Scripts aren't flexible; they can't stop gracefully for input. You must either preset or hard-code the text characters line by line. The style, height, rotation, and start point must also be preset or hard-coded.

To edit an existing drawing, the script shown above would begin with a 2, not a 1. To apply a script like this to multiple drawings, add an END at the end of the script and repeat the sequence for each drawing name. Each new drawing name would replace the IL-NOTES line.

Menus versus Scripts

Since you can run a script from within a drawing, you can use a macro to improve script flexibility. A macro can help set the script's defaults. Such a script would not have the "1 and IL-NOTES" lines because it would be executed from within a drawing. A blank line in the script could default past the point, height, and style options of the TEXT command, which are set by the menu. The macro could preset the start point with the ID command so that the script could default to start the text at the last point with an @. It could set the TEXTSIZE system variable to the text height and use the DIM1 STYLE command sequence to establish the text style. A macro to control the entire setup might be like this:

`[IN-TEXT ]^C^C^CID \SETVAR TEXTSIZE 0.25 DIM1 STYLE STD SCRIPT`

We believe it's a misuse of menus to make them do batch processes such as drawing setup. In general, it's better to use scripts, prototype drawing settings, or AutoLISP to handle processes involving numerous settings and commands. Menu items offer flexibility for settings, but for our example text importation, a macro alone requires you to know the text and exact line length, and requires a separate macro for each set of notes. You would have to edit such a menu when you wanted to change the text or line length. Avoid long, multi-line menus. We recommend restricting menus to invoking and handling input and settings for scripts and AutoLISP batch processes.

How to Import DXF Files

A DXF file is an ASCII file that describes an entire drawing's data base in a readable, documented form. AutoCAD can create and import DXF files, the standard for micro-CAD transfer between differing CAD systems. DXF files are also used by many AutoCAD third party programs which typically get drawing data via DXF, process it with a C language program, and feed it back to AutoCAD through DXFIN. AutoWORD, a popular text formatting utility for AutoCAD, uses DXF. AutoCAD can also create and import partial DXF files containing only entities but no table or system variable header information.

Chapter 16 covers DXF files extensively. But here we will try a ready-to-load DXF file to compare DXF to our other batch methods. The following file contains a single text entity.

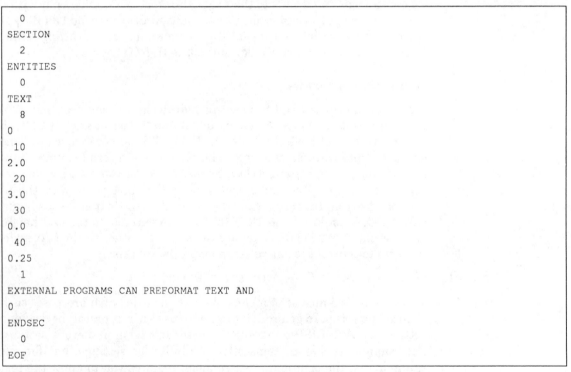

```
   0
SECTION
   2
ENTITIES
   0
TEXT
   8
0
  10
2.0
  20
3.0
  30
0.0
  40
0.25
   1
EXTERNAL PROGRAMS CAN PREFORMAT TEXT AND
   0
ENDSEC
   0
EOF
```

IL-NOTES.DXF File Form

➡ *NOTE: Be sure to <RETURN> after the end of file (EOF) marker.*

Importing a DXF Text File

Continue in the previous drawing and erase the old text, or begin a NEW drawing named IL-NOTES.

 You have the IL-NOTES.DXF file.

Create the IL-NOTES.DXF file as shown above.

```
Command: DXFIN                              Import the text.
File name <IL-NOTES>: <RETURN>              And it imports the text line.
Not a new drawing — only ENTITIES section will be input.
```

Using the DXF file to import a text file has several drawbacks besides being hard to read and edit. It is inflexible, requiring that you hard-code the layer, color, start point, height, rotation, and line length. Style can be hard-coded or, if omitted from the DXF file, it will assume the current setting. DXF offers the simultaneous advantage and disadvantage of absolute control in spite of the current drawing's environment.

How to Read Data With AutoLISP

The most flexible approach is to format your data in an external file and let AutoLISP import it by running AutoCAD commands.

The following example ASCII text file, IL-NOTES.TXT, consists of four one-line paragraphs separated by blank lines. The example text file can be created by any program or word processor that creates plain ASCII format.

```
A SCRIPT CAN READ IN EXTERNAL TEXT BUT IT MUST BE FULLY PREFORMATTED.

EXTERNAL PROGRAMS CAN PREFORMAT TEXT AND IMPORT IT AS A .DXF FILE OR A SCRIPT.

MENUS CAN INCLUDE STANDARD TEXT NOTES IN PREFORMATTED FORM, BUT ARE INFLEXIBLE.

AUTOLISP OFFERS FLEXIBILITY AND DYNAMIC FORMATTING, BUT REQUIRES MORE PROGRAMMING.
```

IL-NOTES.TXT File for AutoLISP Reading

You can use AutoLISP, which can provide as much flexibility as you wish, to read this file into AutoCAD. As is, FTEXT uses the defaults for style and height (height must be fixed), but lets you specify rotation, start point, and line length. It optionally does monotext tables, which require the default style to use a monotext font. If you often import text, or wish to preset defaults, use a menu macro like the one you used in Chapter 13 to set defaults and import Lotus output with FTEXT.

FTEXT will work with any ASCII input text file with single or multiple line paragraphs, separated by blank lines. Long lines are most efficient because that minimizes the number of lines to be read.

```
;* C:FTEXT imports an ASCII file into AutoCAD as text. It uses the default
;* style which must be fixed height. The WW option wordwraps, or the MT
;* option imports unformatted as a table. MT is designed to use a default
;* MONOTXT.SHX font style. If WW, it prompts for the maximum characters per
;* line. Variables MAXC and ROT float for defaults.
;*
(defun C:FTEXT ( / mtable file pt lftovr instr str len pos c)
  (if (setq file (open (getstring "\nEnter text source filename.ext: ") "r"))
    (progn                                        ;then do it
      (setq mtable (ukword 1 "MT WW" "MonoTable or Word Wrap? MT/WW" "WW")
            pt (upoint 1 "" "Start point" nil nil)    ;text start point
            lftovr ""                              ;initialize leftover string
      );setq
```
❶
```
      (if (= mtable "MT")                          ;if mono table
        (progn                                     ;then warn and
          (prompt
          "\nLines over 132 chars will truncate. Current font should be MONOTXT.\n"
          )
          (setq rot 0)                             ;hardcode rotation
        )
```
❷
```
        (progn                                     ;else
          (setq mtable nil                         ;nil flag and get format
                maxc (uint 1 "" "Maximum characters per line" maxc)
                rot (uangle 1 "" "Rotation angle" rot pt)
      ) ) );setq, progn & if mono table
      (command "TEXT" pt (angtos rot))             ;start Text command
```
❸
```
                                                   ;while loops for each line of text
      (while (setq instr (read-line file))         ;loop for each line of file
        (cond                                      ;filter for conditions
          (mtable (command instr "TEXT" "" ))      ;enter txt & start new line
          ((and (= lftovr "") (= instr ""))        ;nothing left, and blank line
            (command "" "TEXT" "")                 ;start a new paragraph
          )
```

Listing continued.

Continued listing.

❹
```lisp
            ((and (/= lftovr "") (= instr ""))            ;something left, but new line
              (command lftovr "TEXT" "" "" "TEXT" "")     ;finish string, then new paragraph
              (setq lftovr "")                            ;reset leftover to nothing
            )
            (T                                            ;all other cases
              (if (= lftovr "")                           ;if nothing left
                (setq str instr)                          ;only the input string
                (setq str (strcat lftovr " " instr))      ;else add leftover to new input
              );if
              (setq len (strlen str))                     ;determine string length
              (while (> len maxc)                         ;loop while string is too long
                (setq pos maxc)                           ;set or reset position
                (while (not (member
                    (setq c (substr str pos 1)) '("" "-" " "))) ;loop in search of characters
                  (setq pos (1- pos))                     ;decrement position
                );while
                (command (substr str 1                    ;pass to waiting Text command
                    (if (= c "-") pos (1- pos))) "TEXT" "" ;then restart Text command
                );command
                (setq str (substr str (1+ pos))           ;chop old part of string
                      len (strlen str)                    ;get length of (remaining) string
                );setq
              );while > len
              (setq lftovr str)                           ;save remaining as leftover
            );T
          );cond
        );while setq instr
        (command lftovr)                                  ;finish Text, might be a leftover
        (close file)                                      ;close file
      );progn
      (prompt "\nSource text file not found.\n")          ;file was never found
  );if
  (princ)
);defun FTEXT
;*
(princ)
;*end of FTEXT.LSP
;*
```

FTEXT Function in FTEXT.LSP File

❶ ❷ The MTABLE flag tells FTEXT whether to divide the text into formatted lines or leave lines uncut exactly as in the source text file. If not "MT," then it sets the MTABLE flag to nil and prompts for the word-wrap length and rotation angle.

❸ The COMMAND function starts the TEXT command, then WHILE loops through each line of the file and the big COND function. If the MTABLE flag is set, the simple first condition just enters the line and restarts the text command. Otherwise, one of the two AND conditions, or the T condition, is evaluated, depending on whether LFTOVR contains leftover text from the last line and whether INSTR contains text from a new line. If both are empty, it enters a blank line and starts a new paragraph.

❹ If only LFTOVR has text, it enters it and starts a new paragraph. Otherwise, the T condition STRCATs any new text to the leftovers, then loops through a WHILE. This inner WHILE chops off and enters lengths of text with SUBSTR until it ends up with only a leftover. Then the next line is read by the outer WHILE. Let's see it work.

AutoLISP Text Importation

Continue in the previous drawing and erase the old text, or begin a NEW drawing named IL15.

You have the IL-NOTES.TXT file, and C:FTEXT in your FTEXT.LSP file.

Create the IL-NOTES.TXT file, and the C:FTEXT command in a new file named **FTEXT.LSP.**

Command: **(load "ftext")**	Load the file.
Command: **DIM1** DIM: **STYLE**	The quickest way to set style. Set to STD. FTEXT requires fixed height.
Command: **FTEXT** Enter text source filename.ext: **IL-NOTES.TXT** MonoTable or Word Wrap? MT/WW <WW>: **<RETURN>** Start point: Maximum characters per line: **30** Rotation angle: **0** Command: **ZOOM**	 <RETURN> for word-wrap. Pick it. If you repeat FTEXT, it'll default. The next time it'll show a default. Zoom in to see it, then quit.

Your screen should look like the Text Formatted by FTEXT.LSP illustration, with the text word-wrapped into paragraphs with 30 or less characters per line. If you have to import text into multiple drawings, control FTEXT with a script.

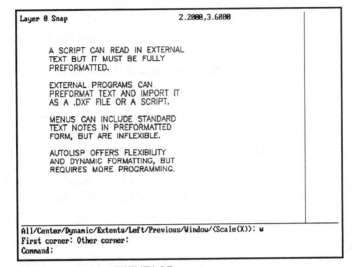

```
Layer 0 Snap                              2.2000,3.6000


        A SCRIPT CAN READ IN EXTERNAL
        TEXT BUT IT MUST BE FULLY
        PREFORMATTED.

        EXTERNAL PROGRAMS CAN
        PREFORMAT TEXT AND IMPORT IT
        AS A .DXF FILE OR A SCRIPT.

        MENUS CAN INCLUDE STANDARD
        TEXT NOTES IN PREFORMATTED
        FORM, BUT ARE INFLEXIBLE.

        AUTOLISP OFFERS FLEXIBILITY
        AND DYNAMIC FORMATTING, BUT
        REQUIRES MORE PROGRAMMING.




All/Center/Dynamic/Extents/Left/Previous/Window/<Scale(X)>: w
First corner: Other corner:
Command:
```

Text Formatted by FTEXT.LSP

What, When, and Where for Scripts, AutoLISP, and DXF

Now that we've compared menus, AutoLISP, scripts, and DXF processes, when does each make sense?

Generally, AutoLISP is your best bet. Often, when scripts or DXF transfers *do* make sense, AutoLISP is still involved in controlling the process and handling input and options.

We recommend DXF mainly for data transfer between AutoCAD and other CAD programs, and for things that can't be accessed from AutoLISP, like block definitions and symbol table data. DXF is a comprehensive standard for drawing data, intended for intensive applications. Most DXF applications involve importing complex graphic data generated by external programs. In Chapter 16, we'll show you how to use it to globally update drawing data that is difficult to get at with AutoLISP. We'll also use it to make an AutoCAD spelling checker.

Use scripts for repetitive batch processes where you need to transcend the AutoCAD drawing editor. Scripts can automate the Main Menu, Configuration Menu, and Plot Menu. You might want to use scripts for batch plotting, making a series of slides, showing slides, extracting attribute information, loading multiple .LSP files, updating block libraries, or even updating redefined blocks in a series of drawings.

How to Pause Scripts for Input

One of the limitations of scripts is that they supposedly cannot stop for input. If you try to use a GET function for user input in a script, it won't work. The next word or line in the script file will be used as the input, probably causing an error and stopping the script.

There is a way to work around this. If a script is stopped by an error, a RESUME command will restart it. You can have a script call an AutoLISP function. The first action of the function is a COMMAND function that intentionally causes an error to stop the script. Then the function is free to do whatever you want, using GET and COMMAND pauses as needed. The last action of the function is a RESUME command. (You can't do a *transparent* 'RESUME from AutoLISP.) Such a script looks like this:

```
CIRCLE 2,2 1
(command "stop" "line" '(1 1) pause '(4 4) "" "resume")
CIRCLE 3,3 1
```

Use the AutoLISP COMMAND function in the same manner to protect your scripts from errors in execution, when the script may encounter unpredictable conditions. It also pays to have a script load an AutoLISP file or call an AutoLISP function to do most of its work when running a lengthy standard sequence on multiple drawing files. It saves repeating the standard sequence in the script for every drawing name processed.

When you *do* need to use scripts, with or without AutoLISP, they are a pain to create. Their syntax must be exact, character by character. That is why the rest of this chapter is dedicated to BATCHSCR, a program that automates the creation of scripts, and to example applications of BATCHSCR.

Creating a Script Batch Builder

The two major components of a script that performs a batch process are a list of file names and the commands or functions to be performed on each of the files. Our BATCHSCR.LSP program will automate the creation of the file name list, create another list of the commands and functions to perform, and then combine the two into a script file.

The GETFIL function builds a list of files to be processed from the filespec you give it. Your file name specification can include the wildcard characters, **?** and *****.

GETSCR takes your input and builds a list of script commands. To tell it where to put a file name for each iteration of the script, you enter the key word FNAME. It temporarily substitutes a variable as a place marker in the command list for each of the files on GETFIL's file list.

Then BATSCR combines the file list with the script command list to make the final script file. The BATCHSCR.LSP program also includes C:MSCRIPT, an interface function that makes the program easier to use.

How to Create a File List

Use the GETFIL routine to generate a list of files from the directory path and file specifications supplied as arguments. Because it uses a temporary file to hold the file names before creating the list, we programmed in an option to allow it to stop at that point instead of creating the file name list. This is useful for creating DOS batch programs, UNIX command scripts, or file name lists for the AutoCAD SLIDELIB program. SLIDELIB groups multiple AutoCAD slide files in a single library file.

➡ *NOTE: The file created has trailing blanks on each line, which you must remove before using with SLIDELIB.*

```
;* BATCHSCR.LSP contains 4 Script building functions. FILELIB.LSP is required.

;* GETFIL builds the listing of specified files used by the batch builder.
;* GETSCR gets the script commands from the user and returns them in a list.
;* BATSCR builds a script from a GETFIL directory and a script command listing.
;* C:MSCRIPT is an easy user interface for BATSCR.
❶
(if pslash nil (load "filelib"))        ;ensure needed files are loaded


;* GETFIL returns a listing of files matching the path and file spec provided
;* by its arguments. Wildcards are optional for FSPEC filename part but not
;* allowed for the extension (the FSPEC "CA*.DWG" is OK, but *.* is illegal).
;* PATH format "/path/" or "\\path\\" -- use / or \\ as req'd for DOS or UNIX.
;* Trailing \\ or / req'd, (& ..\\ dots illegal). Nil or "" means current dir.
;* It may fail with insufficient string or node space on large file listings.
;* If FNAME is supplied the list is written to that file, and FNAME is returned.
;* If FNAME is nil, a list is returned.
;*
(defun getfil (fspec path fname / flag files fp)
❷
  (if fname (setq flag T) (setq fname "DIR.$"))
```

Listing continued.

Continued listing.

```
   (if (setq path (pslash path))            ;test nil (current) path, convert slashes
     (setq fspec (strcat path fspec))       ;string together path/file
   );if
❸
   (close (open fname "w"))                 ;ensure empty file
   (command "SH"                            ;make filename file
     (cond
       ( (getenv "COMSPEC")                 ;check if DOS
         (setq funct '(list (substr fspec 1 (1- (strlen fspec)))))
         (strcat "for %f in (" fspec ") do echo %f >> " fname)
       )
       ( (getenv "USER")                    ;if UNIX
         (setq funct '(list fspec))
         (strcat "ls -1 " fspec " >> " fname)
       )
       (T (prompt "\nUNKNOWN OPERATING SYSTEM for GETFIL function. ")
         (setq flag T fname nil)            ;exit with error
   ) ) )
❹
   (if flag fname                           ;if FNAME, return it and quit
     (progn                                 ;else
       (setq fp (open fname "r"))           ;open temp file to read filenames
       (if (setq fspec (read-line fp))      ;if there are files in dir
         (progn
           (setq files nil)
           (prompt "\nMaking file listing.")
❺
           (while (and fspec (/= "" fspec)) ;loop for each file name
             (prompt ".")
             (setq files (append files (eval funct))) ;put file name on list
             (setq fspec (read-line fp))    ;get next filename
           );while
           (close fp)                       ;close temp dir file
           (command "FILES" "3" fname "" "") ;delete temp dir file
         );progn
         (prompt (strcat "\nNo " files " found\n")) ;no files were found
       );if
       files
   ) );if&progn
);defun GETFIL
```

GETFIL Function in BATCHSCR.LSP File

❶ First, we make sure the FILELIB.LSP functions are loaded.

❷ ❹ If a file name is supplied to the FNAME argument, then FLAG is set, the file list is written to FNAME, and the list building part of the GETFIL function is skipped. If no FNAME is supplied, the temporary file DIR.$ is used and the file list is returned as a list.

❸ The CLOSE OPEN technique creates an empty, 0-byte file to ensure that our file list is written to a clean file. Then the SH shell command is used to access the operating system. In DOS it uses the FOR batch command, which works like a FOREACH function. The name of each file meeting the filespec is echoed and appended to the file name set to FNAME by the >> redirection symbol. The UNIX condition works similarly, using the LS command. GETENV is used to check environment variables certain to exist on DOS or UNIX systems. You can easily add conditions to support other operating systems. If it's an unknown system, the FLAG is set to T and FNAME is set to nil to exit without further execution.

❹ If the FLAG is not set, PROGN evaluates the temporary file. If it is set, the file name is returned and GETFIL exits.

❺ WHILE loops through READ-LINE and APPEND for each file name, adding each to the FILES list, which is returned at the end. The prompt, ".", reassures you that something is happening.

Let's try it on the IL-ACAD directory's TXT files.

Getting a File List With GETFIL

`Enter selection:` **1**   Begin a NEW drawing again named IL15.

You have the GETFIL subroutine in your BATCHSCR.LSP file.

Create the GETFIL subroutine in a new file named BATCHSCR.LSP.

`Command:` **(load "batchscr")**   Load the file.

`Command:` **(getfil "*.TXT" "\\IL-ACAD\\" nil)**   Test our IL-ACAD directory.
                                                          Your listing may differ from ours.
`Making file listing.........`   The FILES menu scrolls by, then:
Lisp returns: ("\\IL-ACAD\\XINSERT.TXT" "\\IL-ACAD\\ATTPIPE.TXT" "\\IL-
ACAD\\REFDWG.TXT" "\\IL-ACAD\\TITLEBLK.TXT" "\\IL-ACAD\\ATTFIT.TXT" "\\IL-ACAD\\IL-
NOTES.TXT" "\\IL-ACAD\\REVBLOCK.TXT")

If you try GETFIL again, with a file name like TEXTFILE.LST in place of the nil argument, it won't return a list but will create a file named TEXTFILE.LST with the above file names. This type of file is the type SLIDELIB needs.

The second step of creating a script-building system is creating the list of commands the script will perform.

How to Create a Script Command List

The GETSCR subroutine creates the script command listing. The script runs one loop for each file name, executing this command list each time. It allows you to indicate where the file name goes in the command sequence when the script is executed.

```
;* GETSCR assists the user in building a list of commands for the script.
;* It prompts for command input and returns a list in the form:
;*    ("string1" "str2" FNAME "srt3" "str4" ...)  where each string becomes
;* 1 script line, & FNAME is a symbol to be replaced by each file name in sequence.
;*
(defun getscr ( / script input item)
  (setq script '()                                 ;initialize script list
        input T                                    ;set a flag for input control
  );setq
  (while input                                     ;get script input
    (setq item (ustr 0 "Enter commands, FNAME or . to exit" nil T))
    (if (= item ".")                               ;exit code
      (setq input nil)                             ;set flag to nil
      (if (= (strcase item) "FNAME")               ;test for file name
        (setq script (append script (list 'FNAME)))   ;append atom to list
        (setq script (append script (list item)))     ;otherwise, append command string
      );if
    );if
  );while
  script
);defun GETSCR
;*
```

GETSCR Function in BATCHSCR.LSP File

Each string you enter at the USTR prompt is added to the script list. If the key FNAME is input, the quoted symbol FNAME is added to the command list. When BATSCR merges the command list with the file list, each occurrence of FNAME is replaced in each iteration by each file name in turn. A period exits the program.

Getting the Script's Commands With GETSCR

Continue in the previous drawing, or begin a NEW drawing again named IL15.

  You have the GETSCR subroutine in your BATCHSCR.LSP file.

Create GETSCR in your BATCHSCR.LSP file.

```
Command: (load "batchscr")              Reload the file.

Command: (getscr)                       Test the program.
Enter commands, FNAME or . to exit: 2
Enter commands, FNAME or . to exit: FNAME
Enter commands, FNAME or . to exit: ZOOM ALL MSLIDE
Enter commands, FNAME or . to exit: FNAME
Enter commands, FNAME or . to exit: END
Enter commands, FNAME or . to exit: .
Lisp returns: ("2" FNAME "ZOOM ALL MSLIDE" FNAME "END")  This is the command list.
```

Now that you have functions for getting file names and commands, you need one for merging the names and commands into a script file.

How to Create a Script With AutoLISP

BATSCR is the master function that creates a script file to process commands and filespecs. It creates the script file by merging a file list like the one GETFIL creates with a command list like the one GETSCR returns. It writes the combined string out to a file, line by line. BATSCR writes a script file named BATCH.SCR, which can be executed like any other script.

BATSCR writes one loop of the script for each filespec. Each loop consists of the full list of commands, with each occurrence of the FNAME symbol replaced by each filespec in sequence. The script file is terminated by a stop character string. Stopping with RSCRIPT reruns the script, 0 exits to DOS from the Main Menu, and STOP stops it cold by forcing an intentional error.

```
;* BATSCR processes a GETFIL list & script command list into a script file named
;* BATCH.SCR, which can be executed in the normal manner for scripts.
;* Its SCRIPT arg is the command list, if nil it calls GETSCR.
;* Its file/path args are same as GETFIL's. STOP is the script termination char.
;* Each string becomes 1 script line. If STOP is nil, BATSCR prompts for it.
;* It uses the FILELIB.LSP FFNAME function to strip file extensions.
;*
(defun batscr (fspec path script stop / files fp bfp item)
  (setq files (getfil fspec path nil))
  (if files
    (progn

❶
      (if (not script) (setq script (getscr)))        ;if no script, call subr to get it
      (setq bfp (open "BATCH.SCR" "w"))               ;open output script file
      (prompt "\nCreating script file.")

❷
      (foreach name files                             ;process each file name
        (prompt ".")
        (setq name (ffname name "")
              FNAME (substr name 1 (1- (strlen name)))) ;strips .EXT & assigns
        )                                             value to FNAME atom
        (foreach item script                          ;process each script list
          (write-line (eval item) bfp)                ;eval & output script commands
        );foreach
      );foreach

❸
      (if (not stop)
        (progn
          (prompt "\nR=rerun script, 0=exit to DOS, S=Stop")
          (setq stop (ukword 1 "0 Rscript Stop" "Script terminator" "R"))
        );progn
      );if
      (write-line stop bfp)                           ;write script terminator
      (close bfp)                                      ;close script file
    );progn
  );if
  (if bfp T nil)                                      ;return T if script file was opened
);defun BATSCR
;*
```

BATSCR Function in BATCHSCR.LSP File

❶ ❸ BATSCR is a flexible function. If the SCRIPT command list is supplied as nil, then the function uses GETSCR to obtain it. If the STOP argument is supplied as nil, then the function prompts for it. It uses GETFIL to get the file list.

❷ The core of the function is the section with the two nested FOREACH functions. The outer one loops the inner one for each file name in the files list. The inner one writes a script line for each item in the SCRIPT command list. When it encounters the FNAME symbol in the list, it is evaluated as the current file name of the files list.

Let's write a script that zooms all and makes a slide for a directory of drawing files.

Writing a Script With BATSCR

Continue in the previous drawing, or begin a NEW drawing again named IL15.

You have the GETSCR subroutine in your BATCHSCR.LSP file.

Create GETSCR in your BATCHSCR.LSP file.

Command: **(load "batchscr")**   Reload the file.

Command: **(batscr "*.DWG" "\\ACAD\\" nil nil)**   The nil nil tells it to use GETFIL
                                                        and to prompt for the stop character.

Making file listing.......
                                                        Following is the GETSCR subroutine.
Enter commands, FNAME or . to exit: **2**   Enter 2 to edit an existing drawing.
Enter commands, FNAME or . to exit: **FNAME**   Place-keeper symbol for file name.
Enter commands, FNAME or . to exit: **ZOOM A MSLIDE**   As many commands as needed.
Enter commands, FNAME or . to exit: **FNAME**
Enter commands, FNAME or . to exit: **END**   End each drawing.
Enter commands, FNAME or . to exit: **.**   That's all.
Creating script file..........
R=rerun script, 0=exit to DOS, S=Stop
Script terminator <R>: **0**   The exit to DOS character.
Lisp returns: T   And it writes a script file named BATCH.SCR.

Check the contents of the BATCH.SCR script file you just created. A portion of the batch file from the exercise above looks like this:

```
2
\ACAD\ACAD
ZOOM A MSLIDE
\ACAD\ACAD
END
2
\ACAD\BORDER
ZOOM A MSLIDE
\ACAD\BORDER
                                          and  so  on.
END
0
```

Test BATCH.SCR File Contents

You also can feed BATSCR the STOP string and a script command list as arguments. This is useful if you have standard script commands that you use on a variety of different file lists. A pre-defined list avoids errors that you might make when inputting to GETSCR. We can make BATSCR easier to use with a user interface.

MSCRIPT, the BATCHSCR User Interface

It's a nuisance to call BATSCR from the command line. The C:MSCRIPT command function makes it act like an AutoCAD command. The command function gets the input to feed BATSCR and GETFIL. The program flow for C:MSCRIPT is shown in the following diagram.

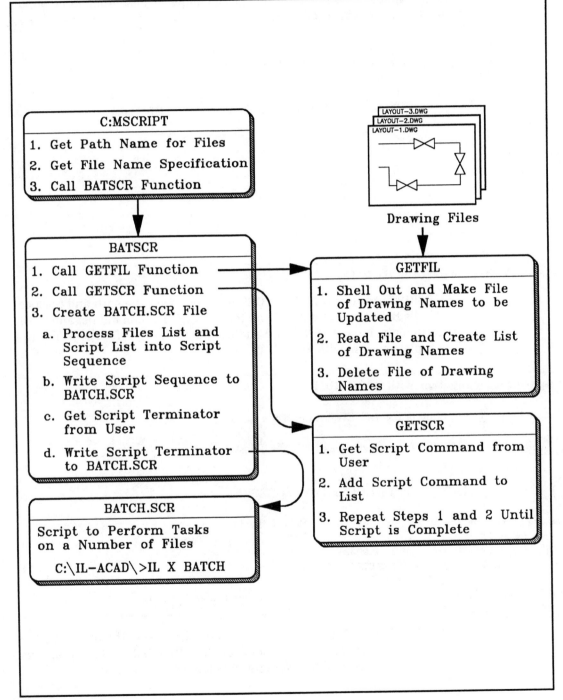

C:MSCRIPT

1. Get Path Name for Files
2. Get File Name Specification
3. Call BATSCR Function

LAYOUT–3.DWG
LAYOUT–2.DWG
LAYOUT–1.DWG

Drawing Files

BATSCR

1. Call GETFIL Function
2. Call GETSCR Function
3. Create BATCH.SCR File
   a. Process Files List and Script List into Script Sequence
   b. Write Script Sequence to BATCH.SCR
   c. Get Script Terminator from User
   d. Write Script Terminator to BATCH.SCR

GETFIL

1. Shell Out and Make File of Drawing Names to be Updated
2. Read File and Create List of Drawing Names
3. Delete File of Drawing Names

GETSCR

1. Get Script Command from User
2. Add Script Command to List
3. Repeat Steps 1 and 2 Until Script is Complete

BATCH.SCR

Script to Perform Tasks on a Number of Files

C:\IL–ACAD\>IL X BATCH

Diagram of C:MSCRIPT

The C:MSCRIPT command function is simple. It just prompts for input and calls the BATSCR function.

```
;* C:MSCRIPT is an easy user interface command for the above BATSCR.
(defun C:MSCRIPT ( / script path fspec)
  (setq path (ustr 0 "Path name (or RETURN for none)" nil nil)  ;get path name
        fspec (ustr 0 "Enter files to list" "*.DWG" nil)         ;get file spec
  );setq
  (if (not path) (setq path ""))
  (batscr fspec path nil nil)                     ;call batscr, no script or terminator
  (princ)
);defun
;*
(princ)
;*end of BATCHSCR.LSP
;*
```

C:MSCRIPT Command in BATCHSCR.LSP File

MSCRIPT uses our USTR user GET function to get the path and filespec. It calls BATSCR with a double nil for its SCRIPT command list and STOP arguments, because BATSCR handles obtaining input for them. Try the complete system with MSCRIPT.

Putting the Pieces Together With C:MSCRIPT

Continue in the previous drawing, or begin a NEW drawing again named IL15.

 You have the C:MSCRIPT command in your BATCHSCR.LSP file.

Create the C:MSCRIPT command in your BATCHSCR.LSP file.

```
Command: (load "batchscr")          Reload the file.
Command: MSCRIPT                     Test it.
Path name (or RETURN for none): \ACAD\
Enter files to list <*.DWG>: <RETURN>   Take the default.
```

Enter commands, FNAME, and a terminator as in the previous exercise. It works the same.

The BATCH.SCR file it creates should be identical to the file created in the previous exercise. This completes our BATCHSCR.LSP program. Let's use it to automate making scripts for specific purposes.

Making Specialized Script Builders

Scripts make unattended batch plotting, slide creation and showing, and AutoFlix movies an easy process. If you use scripts often, you probably will need similar but not identical scripts. If so, it makes sense to have a specialized script builder. Such programs are similar to the C:MSCRIPT command, except they hard-code the script command list. All you have to input is the filespec and path. The following program, for example, makes slides. We will also develop specialized interfaces to the BATCHSCR program to show slides and to update block libraries and blocks in drawings.

Creating Slides With Scripts

The C:CSLIDE command function creates a group of slides. C:SSLIDE makes a script and shows any set of slides, not necessarily the same set created by CSLIDE.

```
;* SLIDE.LSP
;* C:CSLIDE uses BATSCR to make a Script to produce slides of a dir's dwgs.
;* C:SSLIDE - ShowSLIDEs makes a script to display each slide in a dir.
;* The BATCHSCR.LSP file must be loaded.

(if batscr nil (load "BATCHSCR"))                  ;ensures needed files are loaded


;* C:CSLIDE - CreateSLIDEs uses BATSCR to make a Script to produce .SLD slides
;* of the current display view of all drawings in a given directory.
(defun C:CSLIDE ( / script path)
❶
  (setq script '("2" FNAME "ZOOM" "A" "MSLIDE " "QUIT Y")  ;make script string
        path (vpath)                                ;get path to search
  )setq
  (if (not path) (setq path ""))
  (if (batscr "*.DWG" path script "0")             ;if script builds OK
❷
                                                   ;then copy script
    (progn
      (command "FILES" "5" "BATCH.SCR" (strcat path "CSLIDE.SCR")
        "" "" "FILES" "3" "BATCH.SCR" "" "" "GRAPHSCR"   ;delete original file
      );command
      (prompt (strcat "\nTo make slides, QUIT or END and restart ACAD with: \n"
              (pslash "\\path\\") "ACAD X " path "CSLIDE")
      );prompt
```

Listing continued.

Continued listing.

```
    );progn
   );if
   (princ)
);defun
;*
```

C:CSLIDE Function in SLIDE.LSP File

❶ CSLIDE sets SCRIPT to the command list and uses the VPATH function from FILELIB.LSP to get the path. Then it calls BATSCR to do the work.

❷ The FILES command copies BATCH.SCR to CSLIDE.SCR and then deletes BATCH.SCR.

Let's try creating a script that will make slides of all drawings in our IL-ACAD directory.

Creating Slides With the CSLIDE Command

Continue in the previous drawing, or begin a NEW drawing again named IL15.

You have the C:CSLIDE command in your SLIDE.LSP file.

Create the C:CSLIDE command in a new file named SLIDE.LSP.

```
Command: (load "slide")                    Load the file.

Command: CSLIDE                            Test it.
Enter path name <C:\IL-ACAD\>: <RETURN>    It only needs a path name.
SH
DOS Command: DIR *.DWG  DIR.$
Making file listing...                     And the FILES menu scrolls by, then:

To make slides, QUIT or END and restart ACAD with:
\path\ACAD X CSLIDE                        Or you can use your IL.BAT file.

Command: QUIT                              Exit to DOS.
C:\>IL X CSLIDE                            Starts ACAD with IL.BAT. Runs the script and makes the slides.
```

The "X" in the \ACAD X CSLIDE prompt is a place-keeper for the default file name. It could be any word, since it is ignored. The \path\ACAD prompt is a reminder to start AutoCAD in your normal manner, adding the command line arguments X CSLIDE.

Use the slides you just created to test SSLIDE.

Scripts That Replay Slides

The C:SSLIDE command makes a script which displays a directory full of slides when it is run. SSLIDE is virtually identical to CSLIDE.

```
;* C:SSLIDE - ShowSLIDEs makes a script and displays each .SLD slide in a given
;* directory with a specified delay between each.
(defun C:SSLIDE ( / script path delay)
  (setq delay (* 1000 (uint 1 "" "Delay between slides in seconds" 5))  ;get delay time
        script (list "VSLIDE" 'FNAME "DELAY" (itoa delay)) ;script list
        path (vpath)                                       ;get path
  );setq
  (if (not path) (setq path ""))
  (if (batscr "*.SLD" path script "RSCRIPT")               ;if script OK
    (command                                               ;then
      "FILES" "5" "BATCH.SCR" (strcat path "SSLIDE.SCR") "" ""  ;copy script file
      "FILES" "3" "BATCH.SCR" "" "" "GRAPHSCR"             ;delete original
      "SCRIPT" (strcat path "SSLIDE")                      ;start show
    );command
  );if
  (princ)
);defun
;*
(princ)
;*end of SLIDE.LSP
;*
```

C:SSLIDE Function in SLIDE.LSP File

The only real differences between C:CSLIDE and C:SSLIDE are the delay, which prompts with UINT, and of course, the SCRIPT command list. SSLIDE also automatically executes the VSLIDE command to show the slides it creates.

Replaying a Slide Show

Continue in the previous drawing, or begin a NEW drawing again named IL15.

 You have the C:SSLIDE command in your SLIDE.LSP file.

 Create the C:SSLIDE command in your SLIDE.LSP file.

```
Command: (load "slide")    Reload the file.

Command: SSLIDE
Delay between slides in seconds <5>: 3
Enter path name <C:\IL-ACAD\>: <RETURN>
SH
DOS Command: DIR *.SLD  DIR.$
Command:
Making file listing....    And FILES scrolls, then the slide show starts.
```

Hit <^C> to stop it.
Stay in the current drawing.

How to Do Unattended Plotting

Plotting is one batch process where you can take advantage of a script's unique ability to control all parts of AutoCAD. Batch pen plotting requires a roll or automatic sheet feed plotter and reliable pens. Laser, dot matrix, and other raster output devices really benefit from batch plotting. You can use the BATSCR program to create plot or prplot batch scripts.

You can create a specialized plot script builder, much like the C:CSLIDE command. You also can create one-shot plot scripts to handle the plot menu input in a friendlier manner, so that you only have to respond to the settings in your application that vary . To do so, prompt for input in an AutoLISP routine which calls the script to run the plotter, as we discussed earlier in the section on stopping and resuming scripts.

The greatest power of scripts comes from combining scripts with AutoLISP.

Coordinating Scripts and AutoLISP

Let AutoLISP do what it does best. Use it for tasks that require variable input, and for tasks that are identical in each drawing. Use scripts to change drawings, change configurations, and plot. Have the scripts call AutoLISP and have AutoLISP resume or call the scripts.

The following C:LBLOCK program is a powerful example of coordinating scripts and AutoLISP.

How to Create a Block Update Program

C:LBLOCK updates a library of blocks. It's executed from within a master *block library* drawing. LBLOCK wblocks out all defined blocks to update a designated block library drawing file directory.

The C:LBLOCK program also has an option to create coordinated UPDBLK.LSP and UPDBLK.SCR files, which combine to perform a batch insertion of all blocks into a designated list of drawing files. UPDBLK.LSP and UPDBLK.SCR are saved in the block library directory, along with the wblocked drawings. Defined blocks within each drawing file are updated. However, no additional library "blocks" are added to any drawing where they do not exist. Block names can't exceed eight characters, so it's a good practice to limit all names to eight characters in case they might need to be wblocked.

```
;* C:LBLOCK updates a Library of BLOCKS. It is executed from within
;* a master "block library" drawing. It Wblocks out all defined Blocks
;* to a designated directory. It optionally creates an UPDBLK.LSP file and
;* UPDBLK.SCR file which combine to perform a batch insertion of all
;* blocks into a designated list of drawing files. If so, defined blocks within
;* each drawing file are updated. However, no additional library "blocks"
;* are added to a drawing where they were not previously defined.
;*
;* UPDBLK.LSP and UPDBLK.SCR are saved in the block library directory,
;* along with the Wblocked drawings.
;*
;* Required CA LISP functions are DXF, the user GET functions, FILELIB.LSP
;* and BATCHSCR.LSP.
;*
(if getfil nil (load "batchscr"))   ;ensure loaded, batchscr also loads filelib


(defun C:LBLOCK ( / flag blkdef blist path wpath expert cmd file fun)
❶
   (if (setq blkdef (tblnext "BLOCK" T))          ;test for blocks in drawing
     (progn
       (textscr)                                  ;flip to text screen
       (prompt "\e[2J")                           ;clears the screen if ANSI.SYS
       (prompt (strcat "\n** NOTE: Existing .DWG files in designated directory **"
                 "\n  ** will be overwritten if Blocknames match. **\n")
```

Listing continued.

Continued listing.

```
);prompt
(prompt "\nSpecify block library directory...")  ;instruct directory type
(setq path (vpath)                               ;assign verified path name
      blist (list (dxf 2 blkdef)))               ;start block list
)
```

❷

```
(while (setq blkdef (tblnext "BLOCK"))           ;loop and make list of block defs
  (setq blist (cons (dxf 2 blkdef) blist))       ;append to block list
);while
(setq expert (getvar "EXPERT")                   ;store current setting
      cmd (getvar "CMDECHO"))                    ;save echo state
);setq
(setvar "CMDECHO" 0)                             ;turn off echo
(setvar "EXPERT" 3)                              ;suppress file overwrite by expert mode
```

❸

```
(foreach blknam blist
  (if (or (> (strlen blknam) 8)(= "*" (substr blknam 1 1)))) ;omit hatch and dim blocks
    (prompt                                      ;then
      (strcat "\nBlock " blknam " exceeds 8 characters or is a dim or hatch. ")
    )
    (progn                                       ;else
      (command "WBLOCK" (strcat path blknam) blknam) ;wblock each out
      (prompt (strcat "\nWblocking " blknam))    ;prompt which block
) ) );if,progn&foreach
```

❹

```
;* If you don't have a need for updating of existing blocks within a group
;* of drawings, you can omit or delete the entire following IF expression:
    (if (= "Y" (ukword 1 "Y N" (strcat
          "\nYou may create a program to update blocks in other drawings."
          "\nDo you want to do so?") "Y"))
      (progn                                     ;yes create an UPDBLK.LSP file
        (setq file (open (strcat path "updblk.lsp") "w")
              wpath (pslash path)                ;back or forward slash
        )
        (write-line "(setq blist '("  file)       ;write list of blocks
        (foreach blkdef blist                    ;loop for each block name
          (print blkdef file)                    ;print each, quoted 1 per line
        );foreach
        (write-line (strcat ") path \"" wpath "\" )" ) file)  ;write out path name
        (setq fun '((setq regen (getvar "REGENMODE"))    ;make list for our output file
```

Listing continued.

Continued listing.

```
                       (setvar "REGENMODE" 0)              ;set regen auto off
                       (foreach blkdef blist              ;loop through each block
                         (if (tblsearch "BLOCK" blkdef)   ;check in block table
                           (command "INSERT" (strcat blkdef "=" path blkdef) ;insert file
                             (not (setq flag T))          ;set save flag to true
                           );command
                           (setq flag nil)                ;block not in drawing -- set flag
                         );if
                       );foreach
                       (setvar "REGENMODE" regen)         ;reset regenauto
                       (if flag (command "SAVE" ""))      ;if flag T save drawing
                       (command "RESUME")                 ;resume the script
                     )                                    ;end list of expressions to write out
            );setq
            (foreach expr fun                             ;write ea above expr to file
              (print expr file)
            );foreach
            (close file)                                  ;done writing updblk.lsp

❺
            (updscr wpath)                                ;make the update script UPDBLK.SCR
            (setvar "EXPERT" expert)                      ;reset expert mode
            (setvar "CMDECHO" cmd)                        ;reset echo
          );progn
        );if create program -- end of optional omit/delete
      );progn
      (prompt "\nNo Blocks found in current drawing.\n")      ;the else of the if blist
    );if blocks
    (princ)
);defun C:LBLOCK
;*
```

C:LBLOCK Command in LBLOCK.LSP File

❶ You can't do anything to blocks if they don't exist, so the entire program is in an IF test to see if the block table has any contents. LBLOCK has two major parts. The first part wblocks all blocks except associative dimensions, hatches, and those exceeding the DOS eight-character file name limit. The second part writes a program to update all occurrences of these blocks in all drawings in a directory.

❷ ❸ At LBLOCK's core are the WHILE and FOREACH functions. WHILE loops through the block table and adds each block name to the BLIST list. FOREACH tests and excludes dims, hatches, and long names, and wblocks all other names in BLIST to the directory specified for PATH. CMDECHO is set to 1 (off) to keep the screen clean, and EXPERT is set to 0 (on) to suppress the "already exists" prompt. (If you crash LBLOCK during testing, be sure to reset the CMDECHO and EXPERT system variables.)

❹ ❺ The most interesting part of LBLOCK is its option to create an updated script and program. The major portion of this option creates a quoted AutoLISP function, set to FUN. This function is a big FOREACH that does an INSERT= on each name in the BLIST list. But the function isn't executed now. Instead, it is written to a UPDBLK.LSP file so it can be called later by each iteration of the update script. The UPDBLK.SCR script is created by the following UPDSCR function.

```
;* If you omitted or deleted the above IF to update existing blocks within
;* a group of drawings, you can omit or delete the entire following function:

;* UPDSCR generates a list of files to update using the block library.
;* It gets a path and drawing spec from the user and creates a batch script
;* using the BATCH.LSP program. The BATCH.SCR file is copied to UPDBLK.SCR.
(defun updscr (wpath / fspec dpath)
  (prompt "\nSpecify drawings to update...")         ;tell user type of file spec
  (setq dpath (vpath)                                 ;get the verified path
        fspec (ffname (ustr 0 "Drawing names" "*" nil) "DWG") ;get filespec w/ extension
        scrlst (list "2" 'FNAME                       ;the script line, enter drawing
                 (strcat "(load \"" wpath "UPDBLK\")") ;load "updblk.lsp" function
                 "QUIT" "Y"                            ;quit - UPDBLK Saves if updated
               );list
  );setq
  (batscr fspec dpath scrlst "0")                     ;call the batch builder
  (command "FILES" "5" (strcat wpath "BATCH.SCR")     ;copy the file
                       (strcat dpath "UPDBLK.SCR") "" "")
  );command
  (prompt (strcat "\nStart AutoCAD from DOS by"       ;instruct on use
                  "\n" (pslash "\\path\\") "ACAD X " dpath "UPDBLK")
  );prompt
  (princ)
);defun UPDSCR
;*
(princ)
;* end of LBLOCK.LSP
;*
```

UPDSCR in LBLOCK.LSP File

The optional UPDSCR generates a list of files to update from the block library. It uses BATSCR, in the same manner as earlier programs in this chapter, to get a path and drawing specification and to create a batch script. The resulting BATCH.SCR file is copied to the name UPDBLK.SCR. The SCRLIST command list loads the UPDBLK.LSP file created by C:LBLOCK for each drawing file in the named directory.

Testing the LBLOCK Functions

Continue in the previous drawing, or begin a NEW drawing again named IL15.

You have the C:LBLOCK and UPDSCR functions in your LBLOCK.LSP file.

Create the C:LBLOCK and UPDSCR functions in a new file named LBLOCK.LSP.

```
Command: (load "lblock")      Load the file. It loads batchscr, which loads FILELIB.
Command: (setq inc 0)                   This and the next two lines will make six test
Command: (repeat 6 (setq inc (1+ inc))    blocks named T1, T2, T3, T4, T5 and T6.
1> (command "CIRCLE" "@" inc "BLOCK" (strcat "T" (itoa inc)) "@" "L" ""))

Command: BLOCK              Type a ? to check that you have the defined blocks:
                            T1, T2, T3, T4, T5 and T6.

Command: SAVE               Save to name TX.

Command: LBLOCK            It prints on text screen:
** NOTE: Existing .DWG files in designated directory **
** will be overwritten if Blocknames match. **

Specify block library directory...
Enter path name <C:\IL-ACAD\>: \IL-ACAD\   Or return.
Wblocking T5              Block names print here.

You may create a program to update blocks in other drawings.
Do you want to do so? <Y>: <RETURN>      Yes if you wrote and kept UPDSCR.

Specify drawings to update...
Enter path name <C:\IL-ACAD\>: <RETURN>
Drawing names <*>: T?
Making file listing......
Start AutoCAD from DOS by        This is the final message.
\path\ACAD X \IL-ACAD\UPDBLK
```

Before you run the UPDBLK combo, check the UPDBLK.LSP and UPDBLK.SCR files.

```
Command: TYPE              Check the UPDBLK.LSP file.
File to list: UPDBLK.LSP   It should be:

(setq blist '(
"T6"
"T5"
"T4"
"T3"
"T2"
"T1"
) path "/IL-ACAD/" )
(SETQ REGEN (GETVAR "REGENMODE"))
(SETVAR "REGENMODE" 0)
(FOREACH BLKDEF BLIST (IF (TBLSEARCH "BLOCK" BLKDEF) (COMMAND "INSERT" (STRCAT BLKDEF
"=" PATH BLKDEF) (NOT (SETQ FLAG T))) (SETQ FLAG nil)))
(SETVAR "REGENMODE" REGEN)
(IF FLAG (COMMAND "SAVE" ""))
(COMMAND "RESUME")
```

```
Command: TYPE
File to list: UPDBLK.SCR   Check UPDBLK.SCR. The last part should be:

2
\il\il-acad\T2
(load "/il-acad/UPDBLK")
QUIT Y
2
\il\il-acad\T1
(load "/il-acad/UPDBLK")
QUIT Y                     Or UPDBLK saves the drawing, if it updates any blocks.
0
```

```
Command: QUIT              To test the UPDBLK combo. Quit your drawing to DOS.
C:\>IL X UPDBLK            Start AutoCAD with IL.BAT. Run the script from the
                           DOS command line. It loads TX.DWG, and
Command: (load "UPDBLK")   starts the update program.
INSERT Block name (or ?): T6=T6 Block T6 redefined
Insertion point:          This repeats for T5 thru T1, then:
Command: INSERT Block name (or ?): ATTSHT-D=ATTSHT-D Block ATTSHT-D redefined
Insertion point:
Command: SAVE File name <TX>:
Command: RESUME
Command: QUIT Y
```

UPDBLK cycles through the rest of the T1–T6 drawings, but doesn't change them since they have no defined blocks within them. It leaves you in DOS.

➡ *Batch scripts processing multiple drawing files like these still have to wait for ACAD.LSP to load with each drawing file. You can make a small alternate ACAD.LSP that includes only the functions, if any, that the script needs. Be sure to carefully save your regular ACAD.LSP.*

Summary

Look for alternatives before you resort to a script process, but when you need one, the BATCHSCR method is the way to go. If you can, use a combination of AutoLISP, menus, scripts, and external programs, asking each to do what it does most efficiently. Coordinate AutoLISP and scripts to work around the scripts' inability to pause, so your scripts can run AutoLISP across multiple drawings and be protected from unexpected but controllable errors.

LBLOCK's ability to use an AutoLISP function to create an AutoLISP file that can itself be executed in each iteration of a script is a particularly powerful technique. Study LBLOCK.LSP carefully. It is well-documented and is about as complex a batch builder as you will ever need. You can borrow from it to create programs of your own.

GETFIL is a useful subroutine for any application requiring lists of file names. FTEXT will handle almost any text importation task, with a little enhancement to add variable heights. To do so, use table access to check the current style and add height options to the program.

AutoShade and AutoFlix movies are becoming popular presentation tools. The SLIDE.LSP functions can be adapted to help automate production of the files these programs need.

LBLOCK can quickly replace hundreds of block insertions at a time. The XINSERT program saves a lot of time when you need a block that you *know* is in another drawing, but isn't wblocked to disk. And SLIDE.LSP makes slide shows, or sets of slide files for dazzling AutoFlix shows. What's more, all of these programs can do their work while you're doing other things.

The techniques developed in this chapter apply to nearly any application. We are certain you will develop programs from them, whether you use them for unattended plotting, making and showing slides, creating a series of AutoShade files and AutoFlix movie image files, extracting attribute information from multiple files, or something else interesting that you can tell us about.

The next chapter continues batch processes with DXF file processing.

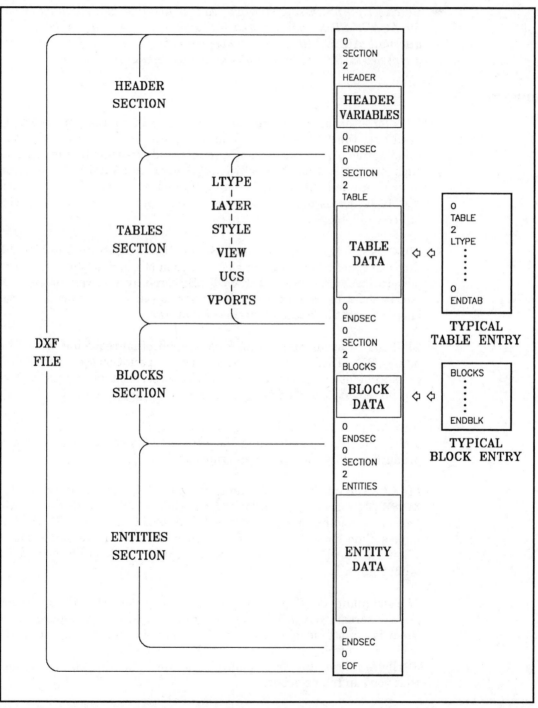

The DXF File Structure Revealed

CHAPTER 16

DXF Files and External Processing

MORE POWER, MORE SPEED!

In the previous chapter, you saw AutoCAD's flexibility with batch processing. You made script files, constructed AutoLISP programs to automate script building, and touched upon the DXF file. This chapter discusses the strengths and weaknesses of processing DXF files, and presents guidelines and hands-on examples to help you decide where DXF processing might fit into your application.

The DXF file is designed primarily to allow drawing data transfer between AutoCAD and other CAD programs. Most DXF applications involve importing complex graphic data from other programs. A typical DXF application might generate drawing data that is then converted or merged into an AutoCAD drawing, or it might modify a DXF file exported by AutoCAD and then re-import it to change the AutoCAD drawing.

While the DXF file is intended for intensive applications, we will show you how to use it for a very simple task that applies to every drawing you do. We will use DXF to spell-check the text in a drawing. The DXF file format can also globally update drawing data that is difficult or impossible to modify with AutoLISP. We will use DXF to change the color of all associative dimension text, so you can plot it with a wider pen. We'll use a relatively easy BASIC program to read and rewrite the DXF file to accomplish this otherwise impossible task. Even if you don't know BASIC, you will be able to follow the comments in the program code.

The two major benefits of processing DXF files are speed and control of the drawing database. When making global or major changes to complex data, you can update the drawing faster through DXF processing than through the drawing editor. DXF's speed comes from using BASIC, C, or other compiled language programs to do the work. Our associative dimension text modification program could be written in AutoLISP, but it would be slow. Because the DXF file fully describes the drawing, a DXF processing program has more control over the drawing than AutoLISP. AutoLISP cannot directly modify table data or block definitions. The only rule for DXF processing is that the resulting DXF file must not contain any invalid data. This speed and control makes DXF the method of choice for most AutoCAD third-party applications packages.

DXF file processing allows you to create utility programs that add otherwise unavailable features to the AutoCAD program. You can convert drawings back to earlier versions of AutoCAD. With some limitations, you can translate drawings from other CAD programs into AutoCAD's format. You can, for example, export a single-line piping diagram to an engineering program that creates a fully detailed DXF file, then bring the file back to AutoCAD to create a dimensionally accurate 3D drawing. You can write programs to read the DXF file and use the information for tasks like material reporting and design analysis. And you can pass the DXF file to other DXF-compatible programs, like Ventura Publisher, to merge drawings with text documents.

This chapter will show you how to export, modify, and import a DXF file, and how to use DXF to add new features to AutoCAD. We'll also evaluate the merits of CAD drawing transfers to and from other CAD software programs via DXF files.

Macros, AutoLISP Tools, and Programs

Macros

[SPELL] is a macro that exports text entities to a DXF file, shells out to your word processor so you can run its spell checker, and then imports the corrected text.

Programs

FIX-TEXT.EXE is a simple utility program written in the BASIC language. By changing the color of associative dimension text, it gives you control over the plotted pen width of text.

If you don't have time to worry about your spelling, [SPELL] may be the most useful tool in this book. And if your boss or clients complain that the dimension text gets lost in complex AutoCAD drawings, FIX-TEXT will make it stand out.

The Drawing eXchange Format

You use AutoCAD's main file format constantly. The DWG file stores the drawing compactly and is rapidly accessed by AutoCAD. But it's in an undocumented binary format that requires an expert programmer to read, and it's subject to change without notice. AutoCAD provides another file format, in ASCII text, that is just as complete. This DXF

(Drawing eXchange Format) file is more readable than the DWG file. Changes to it are documented as they occur and it's guaranteed to be upwardly compatible with future versions of AutoCAD.

The ASCII DXF file is designed for general drawing data transfers. It has become the micro-CAD industry standard for exchange between various CAD programs, and it's used in most professionally written third-party AutoCAD programs that process or import large amounts of drawing data.

But you don't have to be a professional programmer to benefit from using DXF files. Working with the DXF file is not complicated, just tedious. DXF programs have a reputation for being complicated only because they are often used for sophisticated applications, like engineering design and analysis.

Our two DXF examples are not complex. Before we get to them, however, let's examine the DXF format. To look at the DXF format, we need a DXF file. We can make AutoCAD create one with the DXFOUT command. Let's make it simple:

Making a DXF File

```
Enter selection: 1            Begin a NEW drawing named DXFTEST.
Command: LINE                 From 0,0 to 5,5,5.
Command: BLOCK                Name it ABC, base at 0,0 and select the line.

Command: OOPS                 Bring it back as a line too.

Command: LAYER                Make layer PARTS, color 1 (red), leave it current.
Command: INSERT               Insert block ABC at 2,2 and default the scale and rotation.

Command: DXFOUT               Default name to DXFTEXT, six places.
File name <DXFTEST>: <RETURN>
Enter decimal places of accuracy (0 to 16)/Entities/Binary <6>: <RETURN>

Command: SHELL                Use your text editor to examine DXFTEST.DXF.
```

Inspect this DXFTEST.DXF file as you read the next several sections and try finding each item as it is described. At first glance, the DXF file looks like a long column of unintelligible numbers and a few words. A study of the DXF codes will sort it out.

Understanding DXF Group Codes and Data Elements

The DXF file codes are similar to the entity and table data DXF groups from Chapters 6 and 7. Put a bookmark at the Entity DXF Group Codes and Table DXF Group Codes in Chapters 6 and 7 or in Appendix C; you may want to refer to them occasionally as we proceed.

The entire DXF file consists of code-data groups, much like the group code association lists returned by AutoLISP entity and table access. But the code and data in the DXF file are presented in two-line groups. The first line, the group code, identifies the second line. Every second line is the data value of the group. Always think in terms of DXF groups — a DXF code followed by the data. A portion of a typical DXF file might look like this:

```
    0              DXF  group  code
LINE               data  element
    8              DXF  group  code
WALLS              data  element
   10              DXF  group  code
22.5               data  element
```

DXF processing programs use the group code to interpret how to read the data that follows it. The major types of data and their DXF group codes are:

Code Values	Data Type	Major Uses
0-9	Strings	Entity type, named objects, text values, handles.
10-37	Reals	Coordinates.
38, 39	Reals	Elevation, thickness.
40-59	Reals	Scale factors, angles.
60-79	Integers	Colors, flags, counts, modes.
80-209	Unused	
210, 220, 230	Reals	X, Y, Z extrusion direction.
999	Strings	Comments (string)

DXF Group Codes and Data Types

There are several differences between the DXF file group codes and AutoLISP's entity or table access group codes. First, point values in AutoLISP are returned as a single group, like (10 22.5 30.0 0.0). In the DXF file, a point requires an individual group for each of the X, Y, and Z coordinates, like:

```
 10
 22.5         X value
 20
 30.0         Y value
 30
 0.0          Z value
```

The 0 and 2 group codes in AutoLISP entity and table data are used for entity type (0), shape, block, or tag name (2), table type (0), and symbol name (2). In the DXF file, the 0 is used to mark the beginnings and endings of tables and sections, and the 2 is used to identify section names. The -1 and -2 groups are not used in the DXF file because they only exist during a drawing session.

Since you access entity and table data through AutoLISP, order matters very little. But DXF files are read line by line. Their order is flexible, but organized in several sections. Let's take a look at these now.

How DXF File Sections Are Organized

A DXF file is organized into four categories of information about a drawing. Like AutoLISP's entity and table data, the DXF file has a symbol table section, a block table section, and an entities section. The DXF file also has a header section which contains its system variable settings. Each section is given a unique name.

SECTION	DRAWING INFORMATION
HEADER	Lists the drawing variable settings.
TABLES	Lists reference symbols: LAYER, LTYPE, VIEW, STYLE, VPORT, and UCS. A DWGMGR table is included, but is reserved for future use.
BLOCKS	Lists all BLOCK definitions.
ENTITIES	Lists the entities.

DXF Section Names

➤ *NOTE: Much smaller, partial DXF files, containing only the entities section of the file, can be made with the E (select entities) option of the DXFOUT command. A full DXF file can only be imported into a new drawing file. In an existing drawing, DXFIN (the DXF import command) will ignore the header, tables, and blocks sections and only import the entities section. So if entities are all you are interested in, it's most efficient to just deal with partial instead of full DXF files.*

In addition to these section names, AutoCAD uses key words to help guide a program through the DXF file. The key words typically indicate the beginning and ending of sections, table and block definitions, complex entities, and the end of the file. Each key word is preceded by a 0 code in the file. AutoCAD uses the following key words:

KEY WORD	USED TO INDICATE
SECTION	Marks the beginning of a section.
ENDSEC	Marks the end of a section.
TABLE	Marks the start of a table entry.
ENDTAB	Ends a table entry.
BLOCK	Starts a block definition.
ENDBLK	Ends the block definition.
SEQEND	Ends an entry for complex entities (inserts with attributes and polylines).
EOF	End of file marker.

DXF Key Words

Following each 0 section marker is data from one of the four sections, each preceded by a 2 code. In a full AutoCAD-generated DXF file, the first section is header, then tables, blocks, and finally entities. However, your programs and future versions of AutoCAD may rearrange this order. The DXF format's section order is independent for easy transportability to future AutoCAD releases, so don't depend on its staying in the same order.

The beginning of our DXFTEST file shows these key words and section names:

0	String follows, start of a new record.
SECTION	Identifies this as the start of a section.
2	String value follows, section name follows.
HEADER	This marks the start of the header information.

Section and Header Groups

Following this group is the drawing's header data.

How to Read the DXF Header

The header contains facts about a drawing's setup, like the current menu name, the snap rotation angle, and the current drawing view. Each header variable is preceded by a 9 group code. The header variable data in the DXF file includes the AutoCAD system variables, but some names differ. Most names are similar and all are prefixed by a $ symbol. The header section includes the following types of information.

NAME	SAMPLE INFORMATION	PURPOSE
$MENU	ACAD	Current menu file.
$INSBASE	0.0,0.0,0.0	X,Y,Z insert base point.
$SPLFRAME	0	Show spline curve frame.
$TDCREATE	2447143.9502840280	Time and date of creation.

These appear in the DXF file format like this:

9	String value follows, next item is system setting.
$ACADVER	AutoCAD version system setting.
1	Next value is a string.
AC1006	The version number of DXF format file.
9	String value follows, start of next header record.
$INSBASE	Insertion base system variable.
10	X coordinate follows.
0.0	The data value 0.0.
20	Real value follows, Y coordinate.
0.0	The Y data value 0.0.
30	Z coordinate follows.
0.0	The Z data value 0.0.
9	Next header variable name, etc. . . .

DXF Header Information (partial listing)

➡ *The leading space indenting each DXF group code in the file is not required. AutoCAD just puts it there to make it easier to tell codes from data values.*

At the end of each section, the DXF file contains an *end of section* group. This *endsec* tells AutoCAD and DXF processing programs that there is no more data for that particular section. The group appears as:

0	A key word follows.
ENDSEC	Section is ended.
0	If there is more,
SECTION	another section is started.

End of Section/Start of Section Groups

Generally, the tables section follows the header.

How to Read the Tables Section

AutoCAD uses tables to store lists of layers, linetypes, views, viewports, styles, and UCSs. The DXF file groups each under the same table name used by AutoLISP table access. (The blocks section is separate from the tables section.) The tables section's table names are:

```
LAYER  LTYPE  STYLE  VIEW  UCS  VPORT and DWGMGR (future use)
```

The tables section begins with the following record.

0	Start of a record.
SECTION	New section.
2	Section name follows.
TABLES	Tables section.

Tables Section Record

Within the tables section, each of the tables begins with a table record, followed by the number of entries for that table. Somewhere in the tables section is a linetype table:

0	Start of new record.
TABLE	A table entry.
2	Table name.
LTYPE	This is the beginning of a linetype.
70	Flag, number of table entries.
1	Only one linetype in our drawing.
0	Start of a record.
LTYPE	Linetype record.
2	Linetype name follows.
CONTINUOUS	Specific linetype name.
70	Flags.
64	Do not purge flag.
3	String follows.
Solid line	Verbal description of linetype.
72	Alignment code.
65	A type alignment.
73	Number of dash dot entries.
0	None.
40	Real value follows.
0.0	Pattern length.
0	New record.
ENDTAB	End of table.

DXF of Linetype Table

Except for the linetype table, each table can have an apparently unlimited number of entries. AutoCAD can only store 254 linetypes per drawing.

➡ *NOTE: The 70 flag for number of table entries follows each table name. The actual number of entries will not exceed the value following the 70 code, but may be less. Don't confuse the table length use of the 70 code in the table section records with other 70 code flags in the individual table and entity data.*

The other table listings are like the linetype's. At the end of each table is the *endtab* key word, and at the end of the entire tables section is the *endsec* marker. The blocks section usually comes next.

How to Read the Blocks Section

Although AutoLISP table access treats block definitions in the same manner as table entries, the DXF file keeps blocks in a separate section. This section defines each block by its block name, insertion base point, layer of creation, properties, and the included entities of the block. The blocks section starts with these identifying records:

0	Again, the start of a record.
SECTION	The record is a new section.
2	Section name.
BLOCKS	Block reference section.

Blocks Section Record

Each block definition contains some specific base information as well as a list of entities that form the block. Each block entry starts with a group of records similar to the following.

0	Start of new record.
BLOCK	Record type is a block definition.
8	Layer of creation.
0	Layer name of 0.
2	Block reference name.
ABC	Our name.
70	Information flag.
64	Purge flag (64 means do not purge).
10	X coordinate follows.
0.0	X value of insertion base point.
20	Y coordinate follows.
0.0	Y value of insertion base point.
30	Z coordinate follows.
0.0	Z value of insertion base point.

Block Head Definition Data

Following the block's header are the entities of its definition:

0	Start of new record.
LINE	First entity is a line.
8	Line's layer.
0	Layer 0.
10	X start point coordinate.
0.0	
20	Y start point coordinate.
0.0	
30	Z start point coordinate.
0.0	
11	X end point coordinate.
5.0	
21	Y end point coordinate.
5.0	
31	Z end point coordinate.
5.0	

Block Containing a Line Entity

The block's list of entities continues until the end of the block definition. If attributes are defined in the block, an additional DXF 66 flag code will be included in the block header and the attribute definitions will be included. An *endblk* marks the end of the block definition.

```
   0
ENDBLK          End of block definition marker.
   8            Layer for ENDBLK marker.
0               Layer name of 0.
   0            Section identifier.
ENDSEC          End of section.
```

End of Block Definition Section

➡ *NOTE: The endblk key word is an entity, with an assigned layer name. For compatibility with the entity data structure, some key words, like endblk and seqend, have properties as if they were entities. Ignoring this can cause an error in your DXF program.*

The last section of the DXF file is usually the entities section.

How to Read the Entities Section

The entities section contains all primitive entities in the drawing file, including line, arc, text, and inserts. It is usually the largest section of the file. The entities section is the *only* section if you are dealing with a partial DXF file. AutoCAD Release 10 supports 14 types of entities, two of which are subentities of the complex insert and polyline entities:

ENTITY NAMES IN DXF FILES

```
ARC                 INSERT              SOLID
ATTDEF              LINE                TEXT
ATTRIB (subentity)  POINT               TRACE
CIRCLE              POLYLINE (& meshes) VERTEX (subentity)
DIMENSION           SHAPE               3DFACE
```

Each entity type has different data requirements. There are five properties common to all entities: layer, linetype, color, elevation, and thickness. Some properties are not relevant for some entities. For example, elevation and thickness are not relevant to a 3Dface. All properties, with the exception of layer, are optional. Optional properties are only output to the DXF file if they are assigned non-default values. The default settings are: linetype BYLAYER, color BYLAYER, elevation 0, and thickness 0.

Look at the entry of a typical line:

```
    0
SECTION
    2
ENTITIES              Starts entity section of DXF file.
    0                 Start of a record.
LINE                  Record is a line entity.
    8                 Layer name code.
0                     Name of layer.
   10                 X coordinate, first point.
0.0                   X value.
   20                 Y coordinate, first point.
0.0                   Y value.
   30                 Z coordinate, first point.
0.0                   Z value.
   11                 X coordinate, second point.
5.0                   X value.
   21                 Y coordinate, second point.
5.0                   Y value.
   31                 Z coordinate, second point.
5.0                   Z value.
    0                 End of entity.
```

DXF Entity (Line) Entry

This line has only default properties. If all properties were assigned, you would also find optional properties like this:

```
    6                 Linetype group code.
DASHED                Linetype.
   62                 Color group code.
3                     Color green.
   38                 Elevation group code.
12.000000             1'-0" elevation.
   39                 Thickness.
144.000000            12'-0" thickness value.
```

Optional Entity Properties

As AutoCAD has evolved, so have its data file formats. The DWG drawing file format often undergoes incompatible changes from version to version. That's why you can't load a Release 10 drawing in Release 9. However, the documented DXF file format is designed to be upwardly compatible. A DXF file can also be edited or processed by a conversion program for reasonably good downward compatibility. The few DXF file changes that have been made in new releases of AutoCAD are usually additions due to new entity types and drawing environment variables.

The preceding part of this chapter should give you enough information to follow our two DXF processing examples and to evaluate how DXF fits your applications. If you want more information on the DXF file format, consult Appendix C of the AutoCAD Reference Manual.

It's time to see DXF at work. First, in review, is a repeat of the text import exercise from Chapter 15.

Importing DXF Files

An external program can modify or generate drawing data in the form of a DXF file, ready to import into AutoCAD. The following DXF file contains a single text entity.

```
  0
SECTION
  2
ENTITIES
  0
TEXT
  8
0
 10
2.0
 20
3.0
 30
0.0
 40
0.25
  1
EXTERNAL PROGRAMS CAN PREFORMAT TEXT AND
  0
ENDSEC
  0
EOF
```

IL-NOTES.DXF File Contents

Be sure to use a <RETURN> after the end of file (EOF) line. Now, try importing the file.

Importing a DXF Text File

Enter selection: Begin a NEW drawing named IL16.

You have the IL-NOTES.DXF file.

If you don't have the IL-NOTES.DXF file from Chapter 15, create it now.

Command: **DXFIN**   Import the text.
File name <IL16>: **IL-NOTES**   It inserts the text.
Not a new drawing -- only ENTITIES section will be input.

DXFIN created the text with the specified location and height, assuming the current default text style. However, DXFIN has a number of limitations.

How to Work Within DXFIN's Limitations

Only the entities section of a DXF file can be imported to an existing AutoCAD drawing. If you try to import a full DXF into an existing drawing, AutoCAD will ignore all but the entities section. Whether you import an entities only or full DXF file into an existing drawing, the tables and blocks information needed by its entities must already exist in the current drawing. For example, all styles, linetypes, views, UCSs, viewports, and blocks which are referenced by the imported entities must already exist. If they don't, DXFIN will fail. Luckily, layers are flexible. Undefined layers referenced by entities are created without a warning by DXFIN. They assume the defaults of white and continuous for color and linetype.

To import a *full* DXF file, you need to start a NEW drawing with the factory default ACAD.DWG prototype, or use an equal sign like *NAME=* to set the new drawing equal to nothing. This forces AutoCAD to start an empty drawing. Only when a drawing is completely empty can AutoCAD import the header variables or table definitions without potential conflict with existing entities.

➡ *TIP: The most frequent cause of error in importing data from a full DXF file (except for just plain bad data) is trying to import to an existing drawing that doesn't have table or block definitions to support its entities. If it fails for you, import the DXF file to a new NAME= file, END, reload your existing drawing, and then use the INSERT command to merge the new drawing with the existing one.*

DXFIN can handle several types of errors without failure. If the header section contains unknown but properly formatted variables, you will get an "unknown variable ignored" message, but the DXFIN will work. Likewise, doing a DXFIN of properly formatted but unknown entities or tables generates "entity ignored" or "table ignored messages," but does not fail.

```
Unknown header variable $GARBAGE ignored on line 10.
Unknown table HORSEFEATHERS ignored on line 686.
Unknown entity type DOGBONE ignored on line 738.
```

This flexibility allows Release 10 to more easily accept a DXF file from future AutoCAD releases, or accept data valid to other CAD programs but not supported by AutoCAD. Earlier AutoCAD versions had more limitations and required manual editing of DXF files to remove unknown data.

Let's apply DXF to a really useful utility.

How to Make a DXF Drawing Spell-Checker

Because of its data order completeness and flexibility, the DXF file can be used for some powerful applications. It can also be applied to some simple tasks that would otherwise be difficult or impossible in AutoCAD. One of the simplest is to spell-check the text in your drawings. Here's the idea:

- Export an entities DXFOUT file, using SSGET "X" to select all text in the drawing.

- Use the AutoCAD shell feature to run the resulting DXF file through your spell-checker or your word processor's spell-checker.

- Save the file in your word processor's plain, unformatted ASCII text file mode, and exit back to AutoCAD.

- Erase the previously selected text with the P option.

- DXFIN the spell-checked DXF file.

This can all be done by a menu macro. The following macro uses a larger shell than the SHELL command provides. We use the SHMAX shell command, defined in the Lotus section of the ACAD.PGP file in Chapter 13. See Chapter 13 for instructions on defining SHMAX if it's not already in your ACAD.PGP file. The macro uses the FILES command to delete the $PELL.DXF file when through. The $ indicates that we consider it a temporary file.

➥ *NOTE: In the following exercise's menu, you need to substitute your word processor command where we show* WORDPROCESSOR*. The macro shows* WORDPROCESSOR $PELL.DXF *where $PELL.DXF is the file name to load in your word processor from the DOS (or other operating system) command line. If your word processor cannot automatically load a file from the command line, omit $PELL.DXF and load it manually once the word processor is running.*

If you have a word processor with a spell-checker that can save to an ASCII format, try [SPELL].

Using DXF to Check Spelling

Continue in the previous drawing, or begin a NEW drawing again named IL16.

Command: **SHELL**   Use your text editor to create the following [SPELL] macro in a menu named IL-SPELL.MNU. Modify the *WORDPROCESSOR $PELL.DXF* portion as required by the above note.

```
***SCREEN
[SPELL]^C^C^C(setq hilite (getvar "HIGHLIGHT")) DXFOUT $PELL;+
(ssget "X" '((0 . "TEXT"))) ;;SHMAX WORDPROCESSOR $PELL.DXF;+
ERASE P ;DXFIN $PELL (setvar "HIGHLIGHT" hilite) FILES 3 $PELL.DXF ;;
```

Be sure you have the SHMAX command defined in your ACAD.PGP file.

Command: **TEXT**   Enter the following test text.
Text: **This text has varoius mispelled words to proccess.**

Command: **MENU**   Load IL-SPELL.
Select: **[SPELL]**   Test it. It exports $PELL.DXF and starts your word processor.

Run its spell command on the $PELL.DXF file and correct "varoius," "mispelled," and "proccess."

Use your spell add option to add the DXF key words ENDSEC and EOF to its dictionary.

Then save the file in ASCII format and exit back to AutoCAD.

The macro's DXFIN imports the corrected text back to its original position.

Don't underestimate the advantage of running your drawings through a spell-checker. It only takes a minute to ensure your drawings are correct. If we didn't have a good spell-checker for this book, our editors would pull their hair out.

➥ *WARNING: Make sure you edit the file in an ASCII text, unformatted, or non-document mode.*

➧ *TIP: Besides the key words endsec and EOF, add byblock and your standard abbreviations, terms, and layer names to your spell-checker's dictionary. Because the $PELL.DXF file contains only text entities, it has very few key words.*

In Chapter 11 on attributes, we demonstrated and recommended using attributes as controlled text. If you use attributes often, make an AutoLISP program to export any block that has an "attributes follow" flag, and use the same process to spell check.

Other simple DXF utilities can also improve your drawings. They aren't too hard to write if you know another programming language. We'll use BASIC on a full DXF file to modify the color of associative dimension text.

Writing BASIC Utilities for DXF

Learning your first foreign language can be intimidating. But as anyone who speaks several languages knows, learning a second foreign language isn't as hard as the first. Understanding programming languages like BASIC and C are easier after you've conquered AutoLISP. BASIC and C provide greater power and speed than AutoLISP, and like AutoLISP, each language has a syntax that must be followed and a set of commands or functions that control its programs. You'll find that most of the function names in BASIC and C are identical to those in AutoLISP, so you'll have a certain amount of familiarity with these languages right from the start. In this section, we'll focus on BASIC. Even if BASIC is unfamiliar to you, follow along by reading the comments in the program code for a general overview.

FIX-TEXT, our example BASIC program, is written for Microsoft's Quick Basic. If you have the IL DISK, you can simply run the compiled version, FIX-TEXT.EXE. Otherwise, you can create and compile the FIX-TEXT.BAS source code file with Quick Basic. If you are familiar with another dialect of BASIC, you can use it, although you will probably need to make some minor changes to the source code.

The BASIC Language

BASIC has always been a favorite of the casual programmer. Many of us started with BASIC to solve calculation problems relating to engineering or accounting. Recently, compiled BASIC dialects have displaced the slower interpreted BASICs, adding power and speed to this easy language. With library functions available to handle the more complex chores like text screen menus and mouse access, you can write professional quality programs with surprisingly little effort.

The BASIC language has a syntax similar to AutoLISP, but without the parentheses. Expressions are written in a more *algebraic* manner. For example, to set a variable in AutoLISP, you commonly write:

```
(setq blk 0)
```

In BASIC, you write:

```
blk = 0
```

Each programming language has its own structural differences. AutoLISP only allows one *then* and one *else* in an IF expression. In recent versions of BASIC, you can have as many *then* and *else* statements as you wish. However, you need to show BASIC the end of the IF expression with an END IF. Let's compare the IF structures of AutoLISP and BASIC.

AutoLISP	BASIC
```(if (= blk 0)```	```IF BLK = 0 THEN```
``` (prompt "True")```	``` PRINT "True"```
``` (progn```	
``` (prompt "False")```	```ELSE```
``` (setq BLK 0)```	``` BLK = 0```
```)```	``` PRINT "False"```
```)```	```END IF```

To use two *else* statements in AutoLISP, you have to use a PROGN. In BASIC, you just use additional statements as desired. You don't really need to use the END IF function if the IF contains only one statement. BASIC always expects at least one expression, which allows you to simplify IF statements to a single line like:

```
IF BLK = 0 THEN PRINT "True"
```

Other BASIC end functions are WEND, for ending a WHILE structure, and just plain END to finish a program.

How to Use BASIC With DXF

Let's explore our FIX-TEXT BASIC program. Many drafting standards dictate that the dimension text should be heavier than the dimension lines. However, AutoCAD generates dimensions as a single associative dimension block, with a single layer and color. The FIX-TEXT program changes the color of associative dimension text without affecting the other components of the associative dimension. Since AutoCAD assigns plotter pens by color, this lets you control the boldness of associative dimension text.

You can't accomplish this by entity or table access. And if you explode the dimensions, you lose the advantages of having associative dimensions.

We'll explain the FIX-TEXT.BAS after the following source code file listing. In BASIC, comments are preceded by an apostrophe instead of the semicolon used in AutoLISP.

```
'    New Riders FIX-TEXT - Utility to change dimension text color
'    Copyright (C) 1989 New Riders Publishing.

'FIX-TEXT.BAS is a program to change the color of dimension text.
❶
  ON ERROR GOTO Quit                          'If there is an error, quit the program.
  CmdLine$ = COMMAND$                         'Get file name and color number.


'Test if Command Line Exist.
  IF CmdLine$ = "" THEN                        'If file name and color number is not...
    PRINT "Bad command or file name"          'provided, print error message and...
    PRINT                                      'command line example then exit program.
    PRINT "  Example: FIX-TEXT file name/Color number"
    SYSTEM
  END IF
❷
'Format File Names
    ColorNumb$ = MID$(CmdLine$, INSTR(CmdLine$, "/") + 1)    'Get color number.
    CmdLine$ = LEFT$(CmdLine$, INSTR(CmdLine$, "/") - 1)     'Get file name.
    Period = INSTR(CmdLine$, ".")                            'Test for period in file name.
    IF Period <> 0 THEN CmdLine$ = LEFT$(CmdLine$, Period - 1) 'Strip ext. if period exists.
    Inputfile$ = CmdLine$ + ".DXF"            'Add extension to input file.
    Outputfile$ = CmdLine$ + ".TMP"           'Add extension to output file.
❸
'Clear Screen and Display Message
    CLS
    PRINT "Changing dimension text color in file: "; Inputfile$
❹
'Open Files for Processing
    OPEN Inputfile$ FOR INPUT AS 1
    OPEN Outputfile$ FOR OUTPUT AS 2
❺
'Initialize Flags
    BlocksFlag = 0                            'Flag for Block Table.
    DimBlkFlag = 0                            'Flag for dimension block.
    DimTxtFlag = 0                            'Flag for dimension block text.
    DimColFlag = 0                            'Flag for dimension block text color.
```

Listing continued.

Continued listing.

❻
```
'Process DXF File
   WHILE NOT EOF(1)                              'Loop process until end of file.
      LINE INPUT #1, Text$                       'Read a line of text from the file.
```
❼
```
      IF Text$ = "BLOCKS" THEN BlocksFlag = 1    'Set flag when blocks table is found.
      IF Text$ = "ENDSEC" THEN BlocksFlag = 0    'Reset flag when blocks table is exited.
      IF BlocksFlag = 1 AND LEFT$(Text$, 2) = "*D" THEN DimBlkFlag = 1
                                                 'Set flag when dimension block is found.
      IF DimBlkFlag = 1 AND Text$ = "TEXT" THEN DimTxtFlag = 1
                                                 'Set flag when dimension text is found.
      IF DimTxtFlag = 1 AND Text$ = " 62" THEN DimColFlag = 1
```
❽
```
                                                 'Set flag when dimension text color code is found.
      IF DimColFlag = 1 THEN
         LINE INPUT #1, Text$                    'Read the next line of text from the file.
         Text$ = "       " + ColorNumb$          'Change text color.
         DimBlkFlag = 0                          'Reset flag for dimension block.
         DimTxtFlag = 0                          'Reset flag for dimension block text.
         DimColFlag = 0                          'Reset flag for dimension block text color.
      END IF
      PRINT #2, Text$                            'Write line of text to output file.
   WEND                                          'Loop for next line of text.
```
❾
```
'Close and Switch the File Names
   CLOSE #1                                      'Close the input file.
   CLOSE #2                                      'Close the output file.
   NAME Inputfile$ AS "DXF.$"                    'Name the input file to a temporary file.
   NAME Outputfile$ AS Inputfile$                'Name the output file to the input file.
   NAME "DXF.$" AS Outputfile$                   'Name the temporary file to the output file.

'Print Closing Message
   PRINT
   PRINT "Color change was successful"

'End the Program
   END
```

Listing continued.

Continued listing.

```
❿
'Quit Routine for an Error Condition
Quit:
  PRINT "Bad file name or option"          'Print error message.
  KILL Outputfile$                          'Kill temporary output file.
  SYSTEM                                     'Return to system.
  RESUME
```

FIX-TEXT Source Code in the FIX-TEXT.BAS File

❶ Like AutoLISP's *ERROR* function, BASIC allows you to specify what to do when an error occurs. The ON ERROR statements instruct the program to *call*, or GOTO, the quit function if an error occurs. The quit function is defined at the end of this program at the ❿ marker. You can define you own quit function, as we will do for AutoLISP's *ERROR* function in the next chapter.

The CmdLine$ = COMMAND$ sets the string variable CmdLine$ to the COMMAND$ command line arguments. Command line arguments are file names, switches, flags, and other pieces of data that follow the command name of a program entered at the DOS (or other operating system) command line. You've seen these when running scripts in Chapter 15, like:

```
C:\IL-ACAD>IL IL-NOTES IL-NOTES
```

The IL-NOTES were the drawing name and script name, passed to the IL batch command as data.

COMMAND$ is a BASIC system variable that contains the string of arguments entered at the DOS prompt when the program is executed. We make a copy of the string by setting it equal to our CmdLine$ variable.

➥ *NOTE: In BASIC, all string variable types are indicated by a $ at the end of the variable name. This is part of the syntax BASIC uses to recognize data.*

The IF CmdLine$ tests to see if command line arguments were entered with the program name. If no arguments exist, an instruction message is printed and the program is terminated by returning control back to the calling system with the SYSTEM function.

❷ The program then parses the CmdLine$ argument string to get the color number and file name to process. It uses the INSTR function to find the position of the / character in the string. It then assigns the character just following the / character to the ColorNumb$ variable. The MID$ function returns the right-side portion of the string. Notice that we treat the color as a string, not a number. The CmdLine$ variable is reassigned to the LEFT$ side of the / character. Then the file extension is stripped from the file name and new file names are reconstructed. Instead of AutoLISP's STRCAT, BASIC uses a + function to merge strings.

❸ Since the program has all the input data it needs, it prints a message telling you that the file is being changed.

❹ The InputFile$ DXF file is opened for reading input and a temporary OutputFile$ TMP file is opened for writing output. The OPEN function name is identical to AutoLISP, but its syntax is different. In BASIC, you can control the name of the file stream or pointer. Remember that when you open a file in AutoLISP, the OPEN function returns a file descriptor like <File #3A83> which you assign to a variable. Here, BASIC lets you assign the file descriptor to a number, in this case 1 and 2. The words, INPUT and OUTPUT, correspond to the "r" and "w" read and write flags in AutoLISP.

❺ Here we set four flags for the four items in the DXF file that are of interest to FIX-TEXT.

❻ The program starts by reading and comparing each line of the DXF file in sequence to find the dimension block text. It acts like a sort of sieve, filtering until the appropriate data is found. At this point, we're filtering for the associative dimension text. The WHILE loop continues reading lines until it reaches the end of file EOF(1). Each loop reads a line of the DXF file and sets it to the Text$ variable.

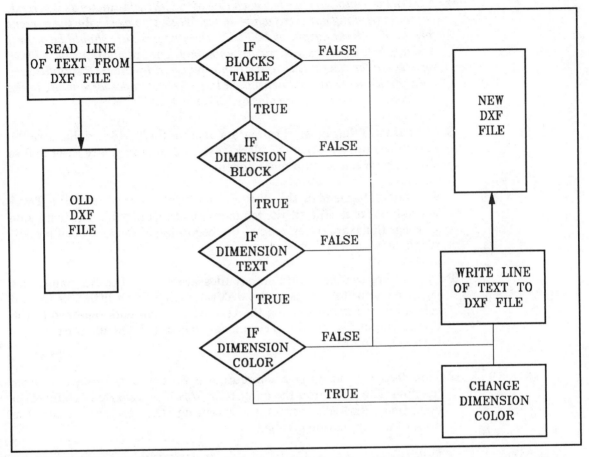

The FIX-TEXT Program Flow

❼ The processing during the WHILE loop is done by a series of IF tests, testing for "BLOCKS", "ENDSEC", "*D", "TEXT," and the " 62" DXF color code. First, the program has to reach the blocks table of the DXF file. When the blocks table is found, the BlocksFlag is set to 1. Once in the blocks table, the program must find a dimension block. The program looks for a substring of "*D", the first two characters of any dimension block name. If this is found, the DimBlkFlag is set to 1 and the program loops to read the next line of the DXF file. If the line is text, the DimTxtFlag is set. Finally, the program looks for the DXF code 62, the entity color group code. If found, it sets the DimColFlag.

➤ *NOTE: For simplicity, we test each line of the DXF file exactly as it is read, without stripping out extra white space. While this works for the current format of DXF file output by DXFOUT, the strings really should be parsed and any leading spaces discarded for safety. The indentations in the DXF format are for readability and are not required by the DXF standard, so your program should not depend on it. If these changes were made to the program, it would test for color by "62", not " 62."*

❽ If the DimColFlag is set, the program updates the Text$ variable with the new color number. Then the block, text, and color flags are reset to 0 so the program can loop for more dimension blocks.

The last statement of the WHILE loop prints the value of the Text$ variable out to the file #2, the temporary OutputFile$ file. The text value is either the exact string read at the beginning of the loop or, if a color, it's the new color string.

❾ To tidy up, the input and output files are closed. The file names are swapped with three calls to the NAME function. It's a little like the old coin and shell game, leaving the OutputFile$ contents renamed to the original input file. Finally, a closing message is printed and the program is ended with END.

❿ This section is actually a subroutine definition for our Quit: error function. The colon after the name tells BASIC to treat this as a function definition. RESUME continues executing the program after the error-trapping routine is called.

Let's try out the program. If you have the IL DISK, you can just run the compiled FIX-TEXT.EXE program provided on the disk. If not, you need to create the source code file listed above and compile the program with QUICK BASIC, from Microsoft, or another BASIC.

Using FIX-TEXT to Alter Associative Dimension Text Color

You have the FIX-TEXT.EXE program.

Write the FIX-TEXT.BAS source code file shown above, then compile it to create the FIX-TEXT.EXE program.

```
Enter selection: 1          Begin a NEW drawing again named IL16.
Command: SETVAR             Make sure DIMASO is ON.

Command: DIM                Draw a few dimensions.
```

```
Command: DXFOUT              Make a full DXF file.
File name <IL16>: <RETURN>
Enter decimal places of accuracy (0 to 16)/Entities/Binary <6>: 16      Full accuracy.

Command: SHELL               Run the program.
DOS Command: FIX-TEXT IL16/3      Make the text green (color 3).
Changing dimension text color in file: IL16.DXF
Color change was successful

Command: QUIT                You have to import it into a new drawing.

Enter selection: 1           Begin a NEW drawing named IL16=, replacing the old one.

Command: DXFIN               Import the modified file.
File name <IL16>: <RETURN>
Regenerating drawing.        The text is now green.
```

You can automate the transition between FIX-TEXT and drawings with an AutoLISP function to prompt for a new color, shell out, and run the FIX-TEXT program. You can have it create and run an AutoCAD script that quits, restarts the drawing from the AutoCAD Main Menu, and does the DXFIN.

➡ *TIP: An alternative to changing the text color is to use a multi-stroke font for associative text. Before creating any associative dimension, set the text style to one which uses a bolder stroke font file, such as ROMAND or ROMANT. Although using a bold font achieves a similar appearance, it also slows down plots, redraws, and regens.*

The FIX-TEXT program demonstrates how to search the DXF file for a specific type of data (dimension block text). Translating data between various CAD programs and between various AutoCAD versions often requires similar techniques.

Translating Between Versions and Other CAD Programs

Although the Release 10 DXFIN is forgiving of unknown data, you may not want the data simply ignored. Versions prior to Release 10 were not so forgiving. Other CAD programs can read and write DXF files, but they may be a version behind AutoCAD or may not support some types of AutoCAD DXF data. All of these problem can be helped by DXF file editing to remove or modify unknown data. The only practical way to do this is with a program that works much like our FIX-TEXT program. Ideally, it should convert unknown data into the closest possible valid AutoCAD data type.

Besides DXF, there are alternative formats. One is the binary DXF. The DXF we have been discussing is the ASCII version. AutoCAD also supports a binary form of DXF that is 25 percent smaller than the ASCII version. The main advantage of the binary DXF is speed. It is harder to write a program to process it, but such a program should perform five times faster than an ASCII DXF process. The DXFOUT command has an option to create either version and DXFIN automatically distinguishes which. For safety, your DXF processing programs should check for version and report an error message if they receive the wrong version. See Appendix C of the AutoCAD Reference Manual for more information.

Another alternative is IGES, using AutoCAD's IGESIN and IGESOUT commands. IGES is an attempt at a comprehensive universal standard for CAD transfer. In the fast changing CAD world, perfection in such a standard is just about impossible so test any IGES product carefully.

AutoCAD DXB file format is another binary format that supports most AutoCAD entities. The DXBIN command imports a DXB file, in the current UCS only. AutoCAD can generate DXB files by configuring for the DXB option as an ADI plotter, but such files represent everything in vector form as straight line segments. AutoCAD can also plot a Postscript file, but it is generally useful only to desktop publishing programs.

AutoCAD has two other vector formats which can be imported by various desktop publishing packages and other programs. These are not true CAD databases, but graphically describe the drawing with straight lines. You can plot to a PLT file in any plot configuration, and you can create a SLD slide file. These vector formats are used for limited translations by several third-party products. PLOTMANAGER and SLIDEMANAGER are both low cost shareware products available from the Autodesk forum on CompuServe. They use SLD and HPGL (Hewlett Packard) PLT files to rapidly display drawings without loading AutoCAD. They can also translate to and from various pixel-based drawing and desktop publishing programs.

There are commercial AutoCAD to AutoCAD version translators available. Many other CAD programs also output a DXF file and advertise AutoCAD compatibility. Effective CAD translations are possible, but you should check them carefully before investing your drawing database. The key to successful translation is testing the effects of placing one drawing database in the environment of another. The only dependable translation is one which has been tested. Develop a test drawing that includes all entity types, text formatting options, attributes, layers and other requirements of your application. Test the translation and make provisions to accommodate problems.

The most common areas of translation problems occur in text formatting, block definitions, polyline entity widths, and 3D entities. You can isolate the problem areas by testing the conversion. Convert problem entities to an acceptable entity by writing a DXF processing program. You can handle others, like DIMENSION entities, inside AutoCAD by exploding dimensions before DXFing to programs that can't handle them. If you're investing in translation software, make sure the translation is bidirectional and can provide the drawing data features your application requires.

Summary

Look for alternatives before you resort to DXF processing. If the problem can be solved effectively with AutoLISP, then don't use an external program.

When do you use DXF? Here are some factors to consider:

- Does the application require you to scan the entire drawing file?

- Will the program depend on any design or analysis data?

- Do you have to determine relationships between components within the drawing?

- Do you need to make global changes, like table data changes, to the drawing that AutoLISP can't accomplish?

- Do you need to import complex graphic data generated by an external program?

- Do you need to convert drawings to an older AutoCAD version, or between AutoCAD and another program?

These are all potential reasons to use a DXF process. Simple utility applications like those in this chapter can be easy and fun, but most DXF applications are more extensive. Typical DXF file processing applications include structural analysis, piping flow design, air circulation requirements, square footage, and 2D to 3D conversions. These are not casual applications. You might consider purchasing a third-party solution. But if you have to do it yourself, you can.

In the BASIC program we mentioned *ERROR* function control. That, and a number of other aspects of controlling your customized system, are the topics of our next and final chapter.

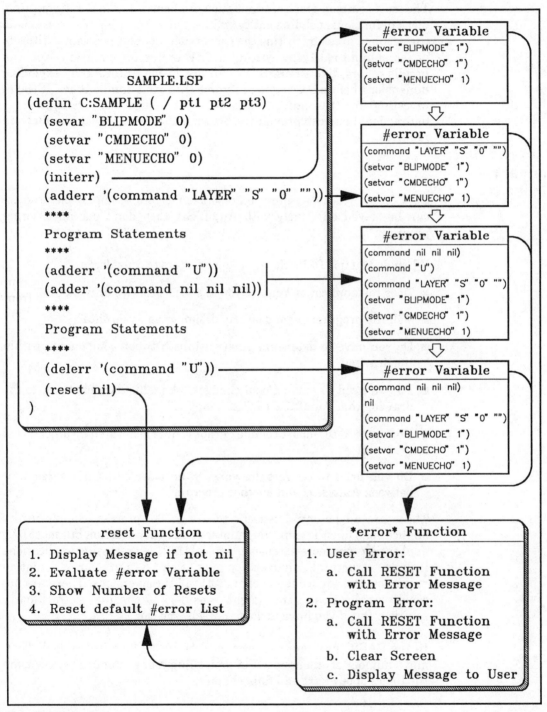

Error Recovery System

CHAPTER 17

Controlling Your System

MANAGEMENT, CONTROL, DOCUMENTATION

A recent trend in successful CAD installations has been to employ a system manager who customizes and maintains systems for several users. Centralized customization and management has several advantages. It is standardized, so drawings have a distinctive company "look" to them. It is efficient, with fewer errors and redos, less time lost, and less duplication of effort. Not everyone has to be a CAD expert. On a properly organized system, many average drafters can quickly reach a speed several times that of manual methods. Left to individual effort, most would never reach the level of productivity that a good system manager can bring about. And if several AutoCAD users benefit from your programming efforts, you can afford to invest more time programming. This additional programming time can give you better, faster programs that further support your users. We call this the AutoCAD circle of productivity.

So when we say "you," think about how improving your system controls and documentation can help other users, and when we say "users," think about what the CAD operator needs to see or know as he or she works.

This chapter resurrects the ACAD.LSP file and treats it as the central manager of your system. The automatic loading feature of the ACAD.LSP file makes it an ideal control, and you can use it to nest other function loads.

There are many benefits to good system management. Developing a common set of subroutines simplifies your AutoLISP programming and provides a consistent user interface. Memory management lets you do large drawings faster and run larger programs. Using the ACAD.LSP file as the central AutoLISP function and setup management tool ensures that error handling and system management tools are loaded in all drawings. A consistent system enhances productivity, is easy to add to and maintain, and is easy to learn. System documentation and on-line program help also make a system easy to maintain and quick to learn.

The best balance of benefits is gained by providing the information and tools to draw efficiently, but restricting the potential for alterations to your system standards.

Security is also an important management issue. A customized system is valuable property to your company, and trained CAD drafters are valuable investments. Simple security measures can help you keep your investments from benefiting your competitors.

In this chapter, you will learn how to:

- Make your menus and programs independent of directory path names.

- Organize your ACAD.LSP file and use it to control setup.

- Define an autoexecuting startup function that runs each time a drawing is loaded.

- Redefine AutoCAD commands to control and enforce procedures.

- Create keyboard macros using only DOS and ANSI.SYS.

- Build an error-trapping system, and use it in your AutoLISP programs.

- Regulate efficient function loading to avoid "out of memory" errors.

- Manage AutoLISP memory to avoid errors and improve performance.

- Improve your system security.

- Document your applications and provide on-line help using AutoCAD's HELP command, slides, external text files, and our LSPSTRIP program.

System Tools and Programs

External Tools and Programs

Our ANSI.SYS keyboard macro facility consists of:

ACAD.KEY, an external text file using ANSI.SYS to create macro keys for use with AutoCAD.

TOGGLE.KEY to toggle ANSI.SYS key definitions back off.

KILL.KEY to clear ANSI.SYS key definitions.

LSPSTRIP.EXE reduces an AutoLISP file's size by stripping comments and white space. It also provides a help display for AutoLISP programming.

Menu and AutoLISP tools available from Autodesk, Inc., are:

MNUCRYPT.EXE to encrypt menus.

PROTECT.EXE to encrypt AutoLISP files.

KELV.EXE, also called the Kelvinator, to strip white space and comments, and turn AutoLISP files into executable semi-gibberish.

AutoLISP Tools and Programs

GPATH.LSP sets aliases for directory paths and loads the GPATH subroutine, which formats path and file name.

MLAYER makes sure a layer is defined.

ERROR.LSP is our error control and recovery program. It includes:

ERROR to evaluate errors, display an error message, and perform a list of error recovery tasks when an error occurs.

INITERR to initialize a default environment.

ADDERR to build a list of error recovery tasks.

DELERR to remove tasks from the list.

RESET, a function that uses the error list to restore the drawing environment after normal program completion.

LEADTEXT.LSP is a multiple segment straight line leader program used to demonstrate our error handling. It includes:

C:S-LEAD to draw the polyline leader with the arrow head incorporated as part of the polyline.

L-TEXT to determine text placement and justification, and initiate a DTEXT command to place the text.

C:MFLY, an on-the-fly macro program to save and repeat a series of commands.

ILLOAD, a subroutine to manage file loading.

SELFLOAD.LSP, a tool to make self-loading commands and functions that conserve memory by not loading themselves until needed.

Error control is perhaps the most critical of these topics, but they all are important. Let's start at the beginning, with the setup controls that you do before you even start up AutoCAD.

Managing Your System

Most companies have always had manual drafting standards which include lineweights, linetypes, notes, and dimensions. With CAD, your standards must also include disk directory organization, file names, layers, colors, blocks, attributes, and other items important to drawing consistency. Although CAD presents more things to control, a well-managed system makes the job easier to enforce than manual methods. Approaches range from wishful expectation to very rigid, limited systems. How much you want to control is a matter of individual choice. This chapter adds some techniques to supplement system controls already covered in the book. Many of these suggestions assume that your systems will be supervised by a system manager, probably you.

If you are implementing a management system, all routines, macros, and symbol block drawings should pass through the system manager *before* they are added to the system. That gives you the means to control what directories are used for which files.

Directory and File Control

For simplicity's sake, we've kept all our the programs, drawings, configuration, and support files in the IL-ACAD directory. However, we recommend organizing your system into several directories, such as block library, AutoLISP library, support, and project drawing directories.

If your application is complex or varied, you may have more than one directory of the same type. For example, you may have a set of directories for schematics and another set for production drawings, or a different directory for each project's drawings. You may also run on various drives other than the ubiquitous C:. In either case, you need to direct AutoLISP, menu, and drawing paths to appropriate directories.

The basic technique is to refer to an alias for specific directories in your menus and programs. We will show you several ways to establish aliases. Even if your setup is simple, without duplicity of directories or drives, programming aliases is still beneficial. For example, you may later add drives, a network (which has additional logical drives), or change your directory structure. Using aliases instead of hard-coded drive and directory names means changes only have to be made in one place instead of throughout all programs and menus.

AutoCAD's set environment variables make establishing aliases easy.

How to Use Set Environment Variables

AutoLISP lets you use operating system environment variables to establish its library search path for program and support files. You've seen AutoCAD use several environment variables, set prior to entering AutoCAD, to direct its file locations and memory usage. In your IL.BAT file you used:

```
SET ACAD=\ACAD
SET ACADCFG=\IL-ACAD
SET ACADFREERAM=20
SET LISPHEAP=25000
SET LISPSTACK=10000
```

You can also create your own environment variables to set file paths. We discussed this in the section explaining the FINDFILE and GETENV functions in Chapter 8. The GETENV function returns a string containing its environment variable argument. For example, given the above IL.BAT settings, (getenv "ACAD") will return "\ACAD". If ACAD isn't set, it will return nil.

➡ *NOTE: In UNIX, you can use the EXPORT or SETENV commands to set the environment variables. UNIX versions of AutoCAD also have a SETENV command that can set or change environment variables from within AutoCAD.*

Environment variable access is a flexible way to control your program and menu settings. It allows you to use aliases in place of path or drive names. For example, if you set the alias variable #ACAD to (getenv "ACAD"), then you can use #ACAD in place of "\\ACAD," like INSERT (strcat #ACAD "PART1") to insert the block PART1. The advantage of this is that if you load the future Release 11 in a directory named ACAD11 or decide to store your support file blocks in a directory named PARTS, you can adapt to the change without changing your menus and programs. All you have to do is a SET ACAD=ACAD11 or a SET ACAD=PARTS before running AutoCAD, and it's done.

Here, we'll use environment variables to control paths sytematically.

How to Control Paths

Establishing a different path alias for each file type or purpose is the most flexible type of system. To make it easy to accomplish, we use a program called GPATH. The GPATH.LSP file contains two parts. The first part is the GPATH function, which is used to format *path/file names*. The second part initializes any number of path aliases as global variables.

```
;* GPATH.LSP
;* GPATH takes a path name and a file name. It returns the joined filespec.
;* If the PATH argument is nil or "", it returns the file name unaltered. You
;* can feed it one of the #NAME path variables defined below, or an explicit
;* path name in the form "/name/".
;*
(defun gpath (path file)
  (if path                ;if the path is not nil
    (strcat path file)    ;combine with the file name
    file                  ;else just return the file name
  );if
);defun


;* Initialize #NAME path variables.
(setq #dwg "/IL-ACAD/")    ;hard-codes the drawing path variable


;* LAMBDA is used to initialize a set of paths. The function below sets
;* each #NAME path to the value returned by GETENV for NAME. Use SET #NAME=\path
;* to set environment variables. If GETENV returns nil, the #NAME is set to the
;* corresponding DEF default. It appends an / to return the format "/name/".
;*
(mapcar '(lambda (path def)            ;map lambda to each set of path and def args
           (set (read path)           ;convert path arg to symbol and set to if...
             (if (setq path (getenv path))   ;if env. var. path set
               (strcat path "/")             ;then use it, adding /
               def                           ;else use default
             ) )
         );lambda
         '("#lsp"      "#blk"      "#mnu"      "#shx"    )    ;PATH arguments
         '("/IL-ACAD/" "/IL-ACAD/" "/IL-ACAD/" "/ACAD/" )    ;DEF arguments
);mapcar
;*end of GPATH.LSP
```

GPATH Function and Global Path Variables in GPATH.LSP

Two methods of initializing path aliases are shown in GPATH.LSP. The (setq #dwg "/IL-ACAD/") is simple and inflexible. The MAPCAR LAMBDA expression uses GETENV to retrieve the path set as an environment variable. The LAMBDA has two lists of argument pairs for its PATH and DEF arguments. The MAPCAR runs the LAMBDA once on each argument pair.

<table>
<tr><td>lambda</td><td>Defines an in-line function supplying argument(s) to expression(s) for evaluation.
(lambda argument expression . . .)</td></tr>
</table>

LAMBDA is also used in the SETUP.LSP file called by the ACAD.MNU [Setup] macro. It sets all variables to nil after SETUP.LSP has finished loading.

Let's see GPATH.LSP in action.

Using LAMBDA and GETENV to Set Aliases

 You have the GPATH.LSP file.

 Create the GPATH.LSP file as shown above.

Execute a SET command from the DOS prompt (not through SHELL).

```
C:\> SET SHX=\FONTS          You don't need a trailing slash.

Enter selection: 1           Begin a NEW drawing named IL17.
Command: (load "gpath")      It sets the aliases as it loads.
Lisp returns: ("/IL-ACAD/" "/IL-ACAD/" "/IL-ACAD/" "\\FONTS/")   MAPCAR returns a list.
Command: !#SHX               Check its value.
Lisp returns: "\\FONTS/"
```

The #SHX alias variable assumes the environment setting, but the others have no environment setting, so they assume the GPATH.LSP defaults. Now that our aliases are set, we can use the GPATH function to format them.

Using GPATH for Path Management

Continue in the previous drawing.

```
Command: (gpath #shx "STUFF")        Test it.
Lisp returns: "\\FONTS/STUFF"
Command: (gpath #parts "STUFF")      #PARTS was not set.
Lisp returns: "STUFF"                So it returns STUFF without a path.
```

You can use GPATH in menu macros like this:

```
[1hpMOTOR]^C^C^CINSERT (gpath #blk "MOTOR1") \1.0 ;\
```

Your calling programs or macros can also use FINDFILE in conjunction with GPATH to search the AutoCAD library path if the file isn't found. See FINDFILE in Chapter 8.

To keep our programs and macros simple, we haven't used GPATH throughout the book, but we recommend that *you* use this approach to control directory access. If you do, and if you incorporate our programs and menus in your system, change the /IL-ACAD/ path names to aliases like #LSP or #MNU. An alternative method for controlling paths is available to you in DOS 3.2 (or later DOS versions).

DOS SUBST Directory Path Control

The DOS SUBST command lets you substitute an alias *logical* drive name for any *drive\path* combination. For example, if drive P: doesn't exist, you can define it at the DOS command prompt as if it did, like:

```
C:\> SUBST P: C:\PARTS
```

Then if you preface a file name with D:, the system will find the file in the directory and drive substituted. This works in DOS and other programs as well as AutoCAD:

```
[1hpMOTOR]^C^C^CINSERT P:MOTOR1 \1.0 ;\
```

When it sees the P:, AutoCAD looks in the substituted \PARTS directory of drive C:. You can establish logical drives for any of your support directories, like:

DRIVE	USED FOR
D:	for project drawings.
P:	for parts to insert.
L:	for AutoLISP programs.
M:	for menus.

If you use logical drives, your menus and AutoLISP programs only need to use the logical drive letters, instead of paths. You can create these substituted drives in a startup batch file, like our IL.BAT, for each application or project. You may need to include a LASTDRIVE=*X*: in your CONFIG.SYS file, where *X* is the highest letter used. See your DOS manual or a DOS reference book for more detail.

➡ *NOTE: The DOS command APPEND may also look like a good alternative. It allows you to tell the system to treat any directory as if it were the local directory. This works fine for reading files, such as block inserts, text fonts, and AutoLISP programs. However, it's dangerous for writing files because it does not affect them. For example, if you load a drawing that is in an appended directory, AutoCAD will find it. However, when you save or end it, AutoCAD will write it to the current directory. If you use APPEND, do so with caution.*

Once you have your directories under control and are ready to start drawing, you need to control setup.

Controlling the Initial Drawing Setup

The most direct way to control drawing setup is to use prototype drawings, like those we set up in Chapter 1. Prototype drawings can pre-set layers, colors, linetypes, and views, and they can pre-set system variable defaults such as REGENAUTO and MIRRTEXT

We recommend prototype drawings for constant, non-scale related settings. They also work for scale-related settings, such as snap, grid, text height, or style *if* you have a limited number of standard drawing types and plot scales. All you need is one prototype drawing for each type and scale combination. But prototypes for more that a few combinations are confusing. Setup menus, or using the ACAD.LSP file, are better alternatives.

Setup Menus Versus ACAD.LSP

You can use menus, like the CA-SETUP.MNU in our CUSTOMIZING AutoCAD book, to further enforce and adjust your standard settings. A setup menu makes the drawing startup process easy, nearly automatic, and consistent. Setup menus work great for new drawings.

Existing drawings load with their normal working menu. When you edit an existing drawing, your setup system needs to be able to reset a portion of the drawing's environment, or skip some settings to avoid interfering with the drawing.

Existing drawing settings that you might want modified through a setup program could be to:

- Reset global variables like #DWGSC, the drawing scale variable.

- Set the current layer, snap, and grid to correspond to the initial screen menu and current view.

- Reset system variables like MENUECHO and CMDECHO that are not saved with the drawing or AutoCAD's configuration file.

Another drawback of setup menus is that they depend on a user to activate them. ACAD.LSP provides a more automatic way of enforcing these and other wake-up default settings.

The ACAD.LSP File

ACAD.LSP is an AutoLISP file that AutoCAD automatically loads each time it starts a new or existing drawing. AutoLISP evaluates each item of the ACAD.LSP file, defining functions and making settings. The ACAD.LSP file can ensure that your drawing environment's initial settings are established correctly for your programs and menus. The duties of the ACAD.LSP file commonly include:

- Defining or loading custom functions.

- Ensuring that frequently used subroutines are loaded.

- Setting global variables, constants and AutoCAD system variables, like:

```
(setvar "aperture" 6)     ;Reset aperture size
(setvar "skpoly" 1)       ;Sketch with polylines
(setvar "regenmode" 0)    ;Turn auto-regens off
```

- Loading menus that depend on the video device supporting the AUI (Advanced User Interface) pull-downs, like:

```
(if (= (getvar "POPUPS") 1) (menucmd "P1=OSNAPS"))
```

- Initializing error routines.

- Immediately executing certain AutoLISP expressions.

- Determining and displaying drawing status messages.

- Undefining commands, like STYLE, to prevent changes to standard styles.

- Installing keyboard macro definitions (later in this chapter).

How to Set Up With ACAD.LSP

Using AutoLISP routine setup is similar to using a setup menu, but AutoLISP routines are more automatic and more transparent. ACAD.LSP's advantage is that it enforces setup on existing drawings, regardless of the menu loaded.

When you consider using a prototype drawing vs. ACAD.LSP vs. a setup menu, you need to consider transparency (whether the user sees or needs to see the settings), how automatic you want the setup to be, and whether your setup requires input choices that can easily be provided and controlled by a menu.

You've been using an ACAD.LSP file throughout this book to set #DWGSC and to load a few core subroutines like the DXF and user GET functions. Let's re-examine the file and add a little organization to it. We'll add some comments to structure the file, and some standard subroutines and variable settings.

It's a good idea to keep the ACAD.LSP file relatively compact. You *could* add all of your standard functions, like GPATH, to the ACAD.LSP file. However, it's cleaner to keep functions in separate files and just put a LOAD function in ACAD.LSP to load them. Then, you can change or update any subroutine function without altering the ACAD.LSP file. You can also turn off the loading of any subroutine by just putting a semicolon in front of its ACAD.LSP load line. Consider ACAD.LSP as the master controller that does nested loading of any number of other LSP files.

➡ *NOTE: This nested loading was not supported prior to Release 10, although you could do it and ignore the generally harmless "invalid character" error message that resulted. Also, if you do this using earlier releases, the nested loads do not get evaluated until after the ACAD.LSP load has completed.*

The following shows your ACAD.LSP file from the IL-ACAD directory, with new additions shown in bold.

```
;* ACAD.LSP for Inside AutoLISP
;*
(prompt "\nLoading INSIDE AutoLISP Tools...")
❶
;****************** Initialize Global and System Variables *****************
(setq #dwgsc (getvar "DIMSCALE"))
(setvar "aperture" 6)    (prompt "\nAperture is 6. ")
(setvar "skpoly" 1)      (prompt "\nSketch uses polylines. ")
(setvar "regenmode" 0)  (prompt "\nAuto-regens are off. ")
(setvar "snapunit" (list (/ #dwgsc 8) (/ #dwgsc 8)))
(prompt (strcat "\nSnap is " (rtos (/ dwgsc 8))))
❷
;********************** Load Standard Function Files **********************
(load "gpath" "\nGPATH.LSP not found. ")                ;Set and control paths
(load (gpath #lsp "etos") "\nGPATH.LSP not found. ")     ;expr to string
(load (gpath #lsp "mlayer") "\nMLAYER.LSP not found. ") ;layer control function
;*
;*********************** Load In-Line Functions ***********************
;* DTOR converts any decimal degree angle to radians
(defun dtor (deg) (* deg 0.017453292519943))            ;deg times PI/180
;*

;* ANGTOC is an angle formatting function that takes an angle
;* argument in radians and returns it with 6 decimal places
;* in a form universally acceptable to AutoCAD command input.
;*
(defun angtoc (ang)
   (setq ang

❸    ...THE REST OF ANGTOC AND THE USER GET FUNCTIONS ARE HERE...

;* DXF takes an integer dxf code and an entity data list.
;* It returns the data element of the association pair.
;*
(defun dxf(code elist)
   (cdr (assoc code elist))    ;finds the association pair, strips 1st element
);defun
;*

(prompt "\nDone. ")
(princ)
```

Reorganized ACAD.LSP File

There are many other settings and functions that could be included, but the above file is just a representative sample, not an all-inclusive ACAD.LSP. You don't actually need to change your file. We won't do anything in the rest of the book that requires it.

There are several kinds of expressions in the file. Prompts, like those in the second and second-to-last lines, keep you informed as the ACAD.LSP file is being loaded. The drawing scale is retrieved from the DIMSCALE setting to use in other settings and in our other programs.

❶ Settings like aperture and skpoly can include prompts to give current information.

❷ Once the GPATH file is loaded, its GPATH functions and path aliases can be used to load other functions, like ETOS. Notice the *on-failure* string arguments in the LOAD expressions. They act like error prompts, and are returned only if the load fails. DTOR is short, so we define it in-line in the ACAD.LSP file. But, it's best to keep ACAD.LSP clean, so other standard subroutines like ETOS are best loaded as nested loads.

❸ DXF is also short enough to be an in-line ACAD.LSP function. However, we recommend that you put functions like ANGTOC and all of the user GET functions in separate files and load them from ACAD.LSP with GPATH expressions.

We haven't yet seen the MLAYER function loaded by the above ACAD.LSP file. It's a layer management function.

How to Control Layers

AutoCAD is heavily dependent on layers for organizing objects and controlling plotting. You can code layer changes into your programs and macros, assuming the layers exist. But if the layer doesn't exist, the macro or program will crash. Rather than have each macro or program test for the layer's existence, it's easier to make a standard layer control function.

MLAYER automates creation and setting of layers. It checks the layer symbol table to see if the layer exists. If so, MLAYER makes it current. Otherwise, MLAYER creates a new layer and assigns the specified color and linetype to it.

```
;* MLAYER.LSP defines MLAYER, which checks to see if NAME layer is defined.
;* It makes it if not and sets it current. If it exists it just makes it current.
(defun mlayer (name color ltype)
  (if (tblsearch "LAYER" name)              ;if exists
    (command "layer" "s" name "")           ;then set
    (progn                                  ;else
      (setq regen (getvar "REGENMODE")) (setvar "REGENMODE" 0)
      (command "layer" "m" name)            ;make it
      (if color (command "c"  color name))  ;set color if specified
      (if ltype (command "lt" ltype name))  ;set ltype if specified
      (command "")                          ;end layer command
      (setvar "REGENMODE" regen)
    );progn
  );if
  (princ)
);defun
;*
```

MLAYER Function in MLAYER.LSP File

MLAYER checks color and linetype. If you give it a nil argument for either, it uses the white and continuous defaults. It suppresses automatic regenerations, because a linetype change will otherwise cause one. Previously defined layers in the drawing will override the settings passed to MLAYER by your menu macros or functions. Give MLAYER a try.

Creating Layers With MLAYER

Continue in the previous drawing, or begin a NEW drawing again named IL17.

You have the MLAYER function in your MLAYER.LSP file.

Create the MLAYER function in a new file named MLAYER.LSP.

Command: **(load "mlayer")**   Reload the ACAD.LSP file.

Command: **(mlayer "OBJ01" "RED" "HIDDEN")**
                         Command scrolls, OBJ01 is created as red, hidden, and set current.

Command: **(mlayer "OBJ02" "BLUE" nil)**
                         Command scrolls, OBJ02 is created as blue and set current.

Command: **(mlayer "OBJ01" "YELLOW" nil)**
                         Test on existing layer. It only sets it current.

MLAYER can easily be used in your menu macros, for example:

```
[DTEXT]^C^C^C(mlayer "TXT01" "GREEN" nil) DTEXT
```

You may encounter other settings besides layers when editing existing drawings. You may have an ACAD.LSP setup routine that makes settings for snap, grid, axis, limits, drawing plot scale, views, viewports, text or style heights, and linetype scale. You don't want these settings changed on existing drawings, but how can a program tell if the drawing is new or existing?

New or Existing Drawing?

To detect a new drawing, you can process a system variable in your ACAD.LSP. The sequence is:

■ Set a system variable like AXIS as a new drawing flag in your prototype drawing(s). Set it to an unrealistic value like 99.99.

■ Test the system variable's setting in your ACAD.LSP. If it's 99.99, then the drawing is new.

■ Have your ACAD.LSP do whatever it should for the new or existing drawing.

■ Reset the flag system variable axis to a proper value.

➡ *NOTE: The TDCREATE and TDUPDAT time system variables are identical in new drawings. Comparing them may seem like a good alternative to the method above, but it's not safe. An existing drawing created by WBLOCK also shows identical dates for both settings!*

While you can set system and AutoLISP variables in the ACAD.LSP file, you can't execute AutoCAD commands because the AutoCAD command processor doesn't load until after ACAD.LSP.

S::STARTUP — the Automatic Start-Up Function

You may want to insert title blocks or do other actions that require AutoCAD commands during setup. Previously, this required a setup menu and user interaction. AutoCAD ignores any COMMAND functions in the ACAD.LSP file, and may give an error message. However, in Release 10 there is a work-around function, S::STARTUP.

The S::STARTUP function, a specially named function, is like an autoexec function that is executed immediately after the command processor is loaded. The S::STARTUP function is defined like a C:*command* function,

with no arguments. You can even call it as a function, like
(S::STARTUP). It's often used to automatically run AutoCAD commands
upon entering a drawing.

Possibly the most important use of the S::STARTUP function is in
redefining AutoCAD commands.

Controlling Command Access

Your prototypes, setup functions, and menus can organize your system
and set standards like fixed height text styles, linetype scale, or layer
color standards. However, since a user has access to any AutoCAD
command from the keyboard, the potential for chaos from users who don't
follow the standards is always present. Your most effective control over
this is to UNDEFINE troublesome commands, like STYLE, LAYER, or
LTSCALE.

How to Undefine and Redefine Commands

The UNDEFINE command makes a standard AutoCAD command
unrecognizable. If you define a C:*command* function with another name
or string, it is executed instead. To use the original command from a
menu, the keyboard, or a COMMAND function, preface it with a period,
like .STYLE or (command ".STYLE"). The REDEFINE command restores
the standard AutoCAD command. This is simple to do. Try it for yourself.

Using the UNDEFINE and REDEFINE Commands

```
Command: UNDEFINE                        Undefine a command.
Command name: STYLE
```

```
Command: STYLE                           Now try to use STYLE, and you get:
Unknown command.  Type ? for list of commands.
```

Use DEFUN to create a prettier message:

```
Command: (defun undef () (prompt"\nCommand reserved for System Manager!"(princ)))
```

```
Command: (defun C:STYLE () (undef))      Define a substitute command for STYLE.
```

```
Command: STYLE                           Try to use it again and you get:
Command reserved for System Manager!
```

```
Command: .STYLE                          Try it with a period to override.
Text style name (or ?) <STD>:            The standard command.
```

Defining a prompt function like UNDEF makes it easy for all your undefined commands to issue a standard message. It reduces the overhead of a prompt in each substitute C:*command* function.

Use the S::STARTUP function to automatically redefine commands before system control passes to the user. As a system manager, it's best to set the CMDECHO system variable to suppress the screen display to keep these techniques from being observed.

We'll apply S::STARTUP to defining a substitute END command.

Controlled Landings With a Redefined END

A custom END command can eliminate doing an accidental END when you meant to just use an ENDpoint osnap. It can also ensure that drawings are ended in a consistent manner, zoomed all, with all layers visible and settings like QTEXT, ATTDISP, and FILL set normally. Another nice feature is an option to make a record slide, for quick review of drawing status.

If you have a number of undefined and substitute commands, it's a good idea to keep them in one file under a name like REFEFS.LSP (although we only have a single function for now). Then they can be loaded by a single line in the S::STARTUP function of your ACAD.LSP file.

```
;* REDEFS.LSP is a master file of all undefined and substitute commands.
;*
(command "UNDEFINE" "END")


;* C:END replaces the AutoCAD END command with a customized version that
;* resets the environment, and optionally makes a slide of the drawing.
;* It requires the UKWORD function.
(defun C:END ()
 (if (= "Y" (ukword 1 "Y N" "Are you sure? (Y/N)" "Y"))          ;safety option
    (progn
      (command "SETVAR" "EXPERT" "3" "LAYER" "ON" "*" ""         ;std settings
              "FILL" "ON" "QTEXT" "OFF" "ATTDISP" "N" "ZOOM"     ;start zoom
      );command
      (if (= "Y" (ukword 1 "Y N" "Make a record slide? (Y/N)" "N")) ;if slide option
        (command "ALL" "MSLIDE" "" ".END")     ;then finish zoom, make slide, do end
        (progn                                 ;else abort the regen and end
          (prompt "\nDON'T wait for the regen! Hit  ^C  for immediate END...\n")
          (command "ALL" ".END")               ;finish zoom, and end
```

Listing continued.

Continued listing.

```
   ) ) );progn,if&progn
   (princ)
 );if="Y"
);defun C:END
;*
;*End of REDEFS.LSP
```

Undefined END and C:END Substitute in REDEFS.LSP File

> You can adapt this substitute END command to standardize your routine and enforce your defaults. The best way to load it is from the S::STARTUP function in the ACAD.LSP file. Let's see it and S::STARTUP at work.

Testing Command Redefinition With S::STARTUP

You have the REDEFS.LSP file.

Create a new file named REDEFS.LSP.

Command: **SHELL**   Edit your ACAD.LSP file. Add S::STARTUP at the end:

```
;******************** Autoexec S::STARTUP Function*********************
(defun S::STARTUP ()
   (prompt "\nRunning STARTUP function...\n")
   (load "REDEFS" "\nREDEFS.LSP not found. ")
);defun S::STARTUP
```

Command: **QUIT**   Exit to see ACAD.LSP reload.
Enter selection: **1**   Begin a NEW drawing again named IL17.

```
Loading acad.lsp...
Loading INSIDE AutoLISP Tools...
Done. loaded.                           ACAD.LSP is done.
Command:                                The command processor is loaded.
Running STARTUP function...
UNDEFINE Command name: END
Command: C:END
```

Command: **END**   Try our command now.
Are you sure? (Y/N) <Y>: **<RETURN>**   Take default. It makes settings and starts a zoom.
Make a record slide? (Y/N) <N>: **<RETURN>** Skip the slide and it zooms.
DON'T wait for the regen! Hit ^C for immediate END... Stop the zoom with a <^C>,
Command: .END   and it ENDs.

Enter selection: **2**   Edit an EXISTING drawing named IL17.

```
Command: SHELL                    Edit your ACAD.LSP file. Disable the (load "REDEFS" line with a
                                  semicolon so it doesn't interfere with the rest of this chapter.

;  (load "REDEFS" "\nREDEFS.LSP not found. ")
Command: QUIT
```

Moments after you re-entered the drawing, AutoCAD executed the S::STARTUP function. S::STARTUP loaded REDEFS.LSP, which undefined the normal END command and defined a C:END replacement. AutoCAD used C:END when you entered the END command.

Another way to control access to commands, or to make the most-used commands easier to execute, is to control the keyboard.

Controlling the Keyboard

Some system managers actually forbid the typed entry of commands to force users to work within the bounds of the menu system. Rather than forbid keyboard entry, we recommend making menus attractive enough to be preferred over keyboards. Or, you can control and extend the keyboard by redefining keys with ANSI.SYS, or with macro programs such as Prokey, Keyworks, and Superkey, or with abbreviation programs like PRD+. These programs provide quick command entry with predefined keystrokes. After only a little practice, such programs can easily beat menus for quick access to your standard commands and functions.

Memory-resident abbreviation programs let you assign any sequence of keystrokes to a two- to eight-character abbreviation. When you hit a punctuation key, space, or <RETURN>, the program looks back at the preceding characters. If they match a definition, it replaces them with the keystroke sequence. For example, if you define CI to be CIRCLE, when you type CI<RETURN> the program enters it as CIRCLE.

Memory-resident macro programs let you redefine <CTRL> or <ALT> key combinations, as well as function keys. If you define <ALT-C> to be CIRCLE<RETURN>, then whenever you hit <ALT-C> the program enters it as CIRCLE<RETURN>.

You can also make your own abbreviations for AutoCAD commands using DEFUN. Just define a set of functions like C:CI for CIRCLE, like:

```
(defun C:CI () (command "CIRCLE"))
```

A limited alternative to commercial keyboard macro programs is redefining keys using DOS and the ANSI.SYS driver.

ANSI.SYS Key Redefinition

The advantage of using ANSI.SYS over memory-resident programs is that ANSI.SYS does not use memory otherwise available to AutoCAD. You can define any key to be any other key or string. You can change key definitions through AutoCAD or DOS. We'll use DOS to create files of ANSI redefinition sequences and direct them to the display screen. To take effect, DOS has to *see* the redefinitions.

The disadvantages of using ANSI.SYS are that you can redefine relatively few keys and that ANSI.SYS can be difficult to work with.

Let's define some example <ALT> key combinations for commonly used AutoCAD commands. We'll use three files, one to define the keys, one to clear the definitions, and one to toggle them on and off. These definitions use ASCII characters and *extended* ASCII character codes. See a good DOS book for details. Here are the codes and the commands we'll define.

KEY	CODE	AutoCAD COMMAND
<ALT-T>	0;20	TYPE UNDEF.KEY (toggles defs Off)
<ALT-S>	0;31	SAVE to default name
<ALT-K>	0;37	TYPE KILL.KEY (kills key defs)
<ALT-L>	0;38	LINE
<ALT-Z>	0;44	ZOOM W
<ALT-C>	0;46	COPY Auto

➥ *NOTE: The ^[at the start of each line represents the single ASCII character <ESCAPE>. DOS recognizes what follows as an ANSI sequence by the second [after the ^[. Text editors differ in their procedures for entering <ESCAPE>. Do whatever your text editor requires.*

The ACAD.KEY file redefines the <ALT> keys.

```
        *** THIS REDEFINES several ALT KEYS to AutoCAD COMMANDS ***
^[[0;20;0;20p
^[[0;20;3;3;3;"TYPE TOGGLE.KEY";13p
^[[0;31;3;3;3;"SAVE ";13p
^[[0;37;3;3;3;"TYPE KILL.KEY";13p
^[[0;38;3;3;3;"LINE";13p
^[[0;44;3;3;3;"ZOOM W";13p
^[[0;46;3;3;3;"COPY Auto";13p
        ***    HIT  <ALT-T>  TO TOGGLE DEFINITIONS ON/OFF    ***
        ***        HIT  <ALT-K>  TO KILL DEFINITIONS         ***
```

ACAD.KEY Definition File

Semicolons are used to separate the code numbers. The 0 indicates that the following code is an extended ASCII code, above ASCII 127. For example, in the "ZOOM W" definition, 0;44 is the extended code for <ALT-Z>. The numeral 3 is the ASCII code for <^C>. The example uses three 3's for three <^C>s. Strings are put in quotes, like "Zoom W." The numeral 13 is the ASCII code for <RETURN>. The closing **p** identifies the sequence as an ANSI *key* sequence.

The KILL.KEY file clears the definitions and resets the original key definitions.

```
        ***        THIS UNDEFINES AutoCAD COMMAND ALT KEYS       ***
^[[0;20;0;20p
^[[0;31;0;31p
^[[0;37;0;37p
^[[0;38;0;38p
^[[0;44;0;44p
^[[0;46;0;46p
 *** Enter:  TYPE ACAD.KEY     to Redefine ALT KEYS  to AutoCAD COMMANDS ***
```

KILL.KEY Restoration File

The KILL.KEY file redefines each key code to the default DOS definitions. The TOGGLE.KEY file toggles the definitions on and off with <ALT-T>.

```
        ***       THIS TOGGLES AutoCAD ALT KEY DEFINITIONS OFF     ***
^[[0;20;0;20p
^[[0;20;"TYPE ACAD.KEY";13p
^[[0;31;0;31p
^[[0;37;0;37p
^[[0;38;0;38p
^[[0;44;0;44p
^[[0;46;0;46p
        ***       HIT  <ALT-T>  TO TOGGLE DEFINITIONS ON      ***
```

TOGGLE.KEY redefinition file.

The TOGGLE.KEY file is the same as the KILL.KEY file, but resets <ALT-T> to reload ACAD.KEY. In ACAD.KEY, <ALT-T> is defined to load TOGGLE.KEY, so <ALT-T> toggles on and off. The ^[[0;20;0;20p line above each <ALT-T> line in ACAD.KEY clears the definition before redefining it. If a toggle isn't first cleared, you may get garbage when toggling.

Let's test the key definitions.

Using ANSI.SYS Key Redefinition

Enter selection: **1**   Begin a NEW drawing again named IL17.

You have the ACAD.KEY, TOGGLE.KEY, and KILL.KEY files.

Create the new files named ACAD.KEY, TOGGLE.KEY, and KILL.KEY.

Command: **TYPE**
File to list: **ACAD.KEY**   You should see only:

```
    *** THIS REDEFINES several ALT KEYS to AutoCAD COMMANDS ***

    ***     HIT  ALT-T  TO TOGGLE DEFINITIONS ON/OFF     ***
    ***           HIT  ALT-K  TO KILL DEFINITIONS        ***
```

If you see anything else, like the ANSI sequence codes, it didn't work.

Command: **<ALT-Z>**   Hit <ALT-Z> and you get:
Command: Zoom
All/Center/Dynamic/Extents/Left/Previous/Window/<Scale(X)>: W

Try each of the others, saving <ALT-T> and <ALT-K> for last.

Command: **<ALT-T>**   Types TOGGLE.KEY which gives you:

```
    ***    THIS TOGGLES AutoCAD ALT KEY DEFINITIONS OFF    ***

    ***        HIT  ALT-T  TO TOGGLE DEFINITIONS ON        ***
```

Command: **<ALT-T>**   Again, it types ACAD.KEY to toggle them on.
Command: **<ALT-K>**   Types KILL.KEY which gives you:

```
    ***    THIS UNDEFINES AutoCAD COMMAND ALT KEYS    ***
```

```
*** Enter: TYPE ACAD.KEY  to Redefine ALT KEYS  to AutoCAD COMMANDS ***
```

Command: **<ALT-T>**   Check to make sure they're gone.

If you saw anything else, like part of the ANSI sequence codes themselves, it didn't work correctly. The *screen* must see them, but you shouldn't. If you have problems with the definitions at the end of your file, you've exceeded the available ANSI storage space and you need to reduce the definitions. Use a memory-resident macro program if you need a lot of key definitions.

One limitation of ANSI key redefinition is that it will affect anything you do when you SHELL out. For example, it conflicts with Norton's Editor, which uses ALT keys extensively. To avoid conflict, you can add a "^C^C^CTYPE TOGGLE.KEY" to the start of menu macros that shell out to other programs. Then, add a "^C^C^CTYPE ACAD.KEY" to the end of the macros to reinstall the definitions.

You can make a setup batch file, like IL.BAT, to load the key definitions before AutoCAD, and restore the keys when leaving AutoCAD. Place the TYPE commands just before and after the line that calls AutoCAD.

You also can define the ANSI.SYS keys in your ACAD.LSP file. We like to redefine the <ESCAPE> key to a <^C> followed by an <ESCAPE>. To do this, we use the following lines in our ACAD.LSP file.

```
(textscr)
(write-line (strcat (chr 27) "[27;3;27p"))
```

This <^C> is harmless to virtually all programs, and doesn't bother you at the DOS command line. But you should test it to see if you can use it with your other programs.

You can create another form of macro in AutoLISP.

Creating Macros On-The-Fly

The MFLY.LSP program makes it so easy to create simple macros that even AutoLISP-intimidated users can use it. The macros created with it may give you ideas for routines worth adding to your system(s). MFLY creates a repeating macro command on-the-fly. You can recall the macro any time during the drawing session with the FLY command. When MFLY is executed, it gets command input and then defuns the FLY command. The command "\" pause in AutoLISP runs the command interactively.

```
;* C:MFLY prompts for input and creates a repeatable LISP macro on the fly.
;* To run the macro it creates, type FLY. MFLY requires Release 9 or later,
;* and interactively runs commands as it makes C:FLY.
;*
(defun C:MFLY ( / input)
   (setq inlist '(command))        ;Start building an expression to evaluate later
   (prompt "\nInput one command or option per line, followed by a RETURN. ")
   (prompt "\nType \"\\\" for pause, \"EXIT\" to terminate.")
   (while (/= "EXIT"                          ;get command input
      (strcase (setq input (getstring T "\nInput, \"\\\", or \"EXIT\": ")))))
```

Listing continued.

Continued listing.

```
        (setq inlist (append inlist (list input)))  ;add to command expression
        (command input)                             ;run command interactively
   );while
❶

   (defun C:FLY () (eval inlist) (princ))           ;make command out of it to call on-the-fly
   (princ)
 );defun
 ;*
```

MFLY.LSP File

❶ The key to MFLY is the C:FLY function that it defines with a defun in a defun. C:FLY does nothing more than evaluate the INLIST list, which is a list containing a COMMAND function. The command expression is built in the WHILE loop, each loop appending one item of input. If the item is a backslash, it causes C:FLY to pause when executed. The `(command input)` expression also executes each item of input interactively as the C:FLY function is being created.

Testing MFLY, the Macro-On-The-Fly Command

Continue in the previous drawing, or begin a NEW drawing again named IL17.

You have the C:MFLY command in your MFLY.LSP file.

Create the C:MFLY command in a new file named MFLY.LSP.

```
Command: (load "mfly")                        Load the file.
Command: MFLY                                 Test it.
Input one command or option per line, followed by a RETURN.
Type "\" for pause, "EXIT" to terminate.
Input, "\", or "EXIT": CIRCLE
CIRCLE 3P/2P/TTR/<Center point>:
Input, "\", or "EXIT": \                       Tell it to pause for center point.
                                               It pauses. Pick point.
Diameter/<Radius>:
Input, "\", or "EXIT": 5                        Enter a radius.
5                                               It passes radius to command.
Command:
Input, "\", or "EXIT": EXIT

Command: FLY                                    Test it.
CIRCLE 3P/2P/TTR/<Center point>:                Pick a point.
Diameter/<Radius>: 5                            It draws another circle.
```

That was a rather simple example of MFLY's use. It can handle complicated sequences, including errors with UNDO commands, so it's quite flexible. It's a useful function to have handy in your ACAD.LSP file for temporary macros.

Thus far we've paid little attention to handling errors and resetting the environment when functions fail. We've just left you and the UNDO command to clean things up. There is a better way.

Controlling Errors

All programs experience errors, whether they are caused internally by the program or by the user. It's important to control a program and restore the drawing editor environment with a few simple steps after an error occurs.

AutoLISP has an error-trapping function called *ERROR*. Yes, the name includes the asterisks. AutoLISP executes this function each time it detects an error.

error

> *A redefinable error function. The string receives a message from AutoLISP describing the error. You can redefine *error* with your own additional functions.*
> **(*error* string)**

You've seen *ERROR*'s standard response many times. It prints the cause and the guilty code from inside out in increasingly deep nests, then returns the function name.

Not only does AutoLISP have automatic error handling, it lets you redefine the steps that it performs in an error. To do this, you redefine the *ERROR* routine with DEFUN.

➡ *NOTE: This is the ONLY standard AutoLISP function that we recommend redefining. *ERROR* is intended to be redefined and is not required for the general execution of AutoLISP programs.*

*How to Use the *ERROR* Function*

ERROR has only one argument, an error message string. Normally, *you* don't call the *ERROR* function or pass it an argument. AutoLISP calls the function and passes the argument. It's up to you to decide what to do with the message and what to make the *ERROR* function do. Let's look at a simple hands-on example.

Redefining Error Handling

Continue in the previous drawing, or begin a NEW drawing again named IL17.

```
Command: (defun *error* (msg)          A new error function.
1> (prompt (strcat "Error: " msg))
1> (prompt "\nDon't do that!\n"))
Lisp returns: *ERROR*                  The function name.

Command: (defun test ()                Make a test function.
1> (while (getreal "Cancel this. "))
Lisp returns: TEST

Command: (test)                        Test it.
Cancel this. <^C>                      Hit a <^C> to cancel it.
Error: console break                   The error prompt with MSG.
Don't do that!                         The second error function prompt.
Lisp returns: nil                      Unless you change it, *ERROR* returns nil.
```

The MSG argument "console break" was supplied by AutoLISP. You can add any number of AutoLISP expressions to the error routine.

Creating an Error-Trapping System

At the least, the *ERROR* function cleanly exits from a cancelled or flawed program. However, you can make it do much more to protect the drawing editor's environment and avoid scrambled settings and system variables. The error recovery system can and should do the following:

- Reset SETVAR system setting variables.

- Reset the previous current layer.

- Undo any entities or task sequences left incomplete.

- Report the error to the user.

- Print messages to an external error file, like STDERR.TXT.

Since the state of the drawing changes throughout the execution of a program, the tasks required to restore the system also change. You can't just depend on UNDO, because some of the settings AutoLISP changes aren't restored by UNDO. Programs need a way to update and alter the settings to execute when an error occurs. Our error system keeps track of the state of the program and updates a list of error recovery tasks as a global #ERROR list. ADDERR adds tasks to, and DELERR removes individual tasks from, the master #ERROR list.

Later, the main *ERROR* function will process the #ERROR list by evaluating each expression of the list. The error list initialization routine, INITERR, establishes the starting contents of this error list. A RESET routine will reset the settings back to these *ERROR values after a program is completed.

Let's look at the functions to initialize, add, and delete error tasks from the #ERROR global error variable list.

```
;* ERROR.LSP
;* The *ERROR* function is designed to maintain the system's integrity. The main
;* function executes each item on the #error list. The list must be a valid LISP
;* expression. The error list can be modified throughout the course of a
;* program using ADDERR and DELERR. INITERR resets the #error list to your
;* standard settings. RESET resets the environment. It can be called at the end
;* of a program.
;*

;* INITERR sets default #ERROR list for resetting environment and/or error recovery
(defun initerr ()
  (setq #error (append
    '((setvar "BLIPMODE" 1))         ;blipmode should be on
    '((setvar "CMDECHO" 1))          ;command echo on
    '((setvar "MENUECHO" 1))         ;menu echo on
  ));setq
);defun

;* ADDERR adds one item to the #ERROR list. ITEM must be quoted expression,
;* or in form: (list 'FUNCTION arg arg arg...) where arguments are quoted or
;* not depending on whether you pass current value or use them literally.
(defun adderr (item)
    (if (not (member item #error))    ;if it's not a duplicate item
      (setq #error (cons item #error)) ;add it to the list
    );if
);defun
;*

;* DELERR deletes one item from the #ERROR list.  ITEM is same format as ADDERR.
(defun delerr (item)
    (setq #error (subst '() item #error))  ;replace item with a null list
);defun
;*
```

INITERR, ADDERR, and DELERR Functions in ERROR.LSP File

These three single-minded functions build #ERROR as a list of lists. Each sublist is a single expression that, when later evaluated, accomplishes one task. INITERR creates the initial error list with whatever you wish to define in the INITERR defun. These tasks are intended to be whatever settings you want for *your* standard environment. ADDERR just adds a task to the list. When you use this error system in a program, the program tells ADDERR what tasks to include. DELERR removes tasks from the list by substituting null lists. It is called by your programs when a task is no longer necessary because the program has completed something successfully.

Let's load the ERROR.LSP file and try these functions.

Building and Testing Error Lists

Enter selection: **1**   Begin a NEW drawing again named IL17.

You have the INITERR, ADDERR, and DELERR functions in your ERROR.LSP file.

Create the INITERR, ADDERR, and DELERR functions in a new file named ERROR.LSP.

Command: **(load "error")**

Command: **!#ERROR**   Check the global list.
Lisp returns: nil   It's empty.

Command: **(initerr)**   Creates our default global #ERROR list:
Lisp returns: ((SETVAR "BLIPMODE" 1) (SETVAR "CMDECHO" 1) (SETVAR "MENUECHO" 1))

Command: **!#ERROR**   Check again, now it returns task list:
Lisp returns: ((SETVAR "BLIPMODE" 1) (SETVAR "CMDECHO" 1) (SETVAR "MENUECHO" 1))

Command: **(adderr ' (command "ERASE" "Last" ""))**   Adds task to #ERROR list.
Lisp returns: ((COMMAND "ERASE" "Last" "") (SETVAR "BLIPMODE" 1) (SETVAR "CMDECHO" 1)
(SETVAR "MENUECHO" 1))

Command: **(adderr ' (do stuff))**   Adds task to #ERROR list.
Lisp returns: ((DO STUFF) (COMMAND "ERASE" "Last" "") (SETVAR "BLIPMODE" 1)
(SETVAR "CMDECHO" 1) (SETVAR "MENUECHO" 1))

Command: **(delerr ' (do stuff))**   Deletes task from #ERROR list.
Lisp returns: (nil (COMMAND "ERASE" "Last" "") (SETVAR "BLIPMODE" 1)
(SETVAR "CMDECHO" 1) (SETVAR "MENUECHO" 1))

Our *ERROR* function redefines the standard AutoCAD *ERROR* function to make it do what we want. In our example, we examine the error message AutoLISP provides and then either print a message or call the RESET function. *ERROR* relies on the RESET function to process the #ERROR list of tasks.

```
;* #ERR stores the original standard error function, before it gets redefined.
❶
(if #err nil (setq #err *error*))

;* *ERROR* redefines the standard error function.
(defun *error* (msg)
❷
  (command nil nil nil)              ;cancels any pending command
  (reset msg)                        ;processes #ERROR list, restoring environment
  (grtext)                           ;clear the graphics text boxes
                   ;Check the type of error. If user did not cancel program,
❸                  ;use standard message. Otherwise, it's a program bug.
  (if (and (/= msg "console break") (/= msg "Function cancelled")) ;compare messages
     (progn                          ;then program bug
        (grclear)                    ;clear the graphics screen
        (grtext -1 "Program ERROR!") ;prompt the user in status box
     );progn
  );if
  (princ)
);defun *ERROR*
;*

;* RESET function resets the standard environment. You can call it at the end
;* of a function to put the settings back in order, including any tasks you
;* ADDERR but do not DELERR. If you call it from a function for normal
;* termination, pass it a NIL argument.
(defun reset (msg / x)
❹
  (if msg
    (prompt (strcat "Error: " msg "\n"))   ;print out error message
    (prompt "\nResetting environment... ")
  )
  (setq x 1)                              ;sets the counter x
❺
  (foreach func #error                    ;loops through error items
    (eval func)                           ;evaluates each one
    (grtext -2 (strcat "Reset " (itoa x))) ;Shows user a running count of
```

Listing continued.

Continued listing.

```
   (setq x (1+ x))                              ;the number of items reset
 );foreach
 (initerr)                                      ;resets default #ERROR list
 (princ)
);defun RESET
;*
❻
;* C:*ERROR* restores the standard AutoLISP *ERROR* function for testing,
;* using the #ERR variable which stored *ERROR* at the top of ERROR.LSP.
(defun C:*ERROR* () (setq *error* #err))


(princ)
;* End of ERROR.LSP
;*
```

ERROR and RESET Functions in ERROR.LSP File

❶ ❻ The first expression saves the standard AutoLISP *ERROR* function so you can restore it without reloading your drawing when you are testing programs. The C:*ERROR* function defines a command that restores the original error function. Type *ERROR* at the AutoCAD command prompt to restore the original error function when you want to test unfinished programs. Then, to return to our custom error function, just reload ERROR.LSP.

❷ *ERROR* cancels any pending commands with three Control-Cs, generated by nils in the COMMAND function. GRTEXT restores all text boxes on the screen in case the errant program has written to any of them. Then *ERROR* calls RESET to restore the environment by performing the tasks on the #ERROR list.

❸ A Control-C in AutoCAD generates one of these two AutoLISP error messages, so we test for them. If the error was not caused by a Control-C, then we display a further "Program error!" message on the status line. GRCLEAR blanks the graphics screen to get your attention.

❹ RESET prints out a prompt including the MSG error message it receives. If MSG is nil, it prints a standard "Resetting environment . . ." message. This allows it to be called as a system reset function, independent of *ERROR*.

❺ The core of RESET is the EVAL in the FOREACH function. FOREACH loops through each task expression of the #ERROR list and the EVAL evaluates the expression to perform the task. GRTEXT displays an incremented counter to assure you something is happening during long resets.

Now let's test the full error system.

Testing the Error-Trapping System

Continue in the previous drawing, or begin a NEW drawing again named IL17.

You have the *ERROR* and RESET functions in your ERROR.LSP file.

Add the *ERROR* and RESET functions to your ERROR.LSP file.

```
Command: (load "error")        Reload it.
```

```
Command: (initerr)             Reset the default #ERROR list.
Command: (adderr ' (command "ERASE" "Last" ""))   Add a task to the #ERROR list.
Lisp returns: ((COMMAND "ERASE" "Last" "") (SETVAR "BLIPMODE" 1) (SETVAR "CMDECHO" 1)
(SETVAR "MENUECHO" 1))
```

```
Command: LINE                  Draw two lines for the test.
Command: SETVAR                Set BLIPMODE from <1> to 0 for testing.
```

```
Command: (getpoint a b c)      Oh oh, an error:
Error: bad argument type
ERASE                          *ERROR* erased Last and evaluated each #ERROR list
Select objects: L 1 found.     expression. It blanked the screen to call attention to
Command:                       the status line message: "Program ERROR"
```

```
Command: REDRAW                Yes, the last line is gone.
```

```
Command: !#ERROR               Check again, it's back to your defaults:
Lisp returns: ((SETVAR "BLIPMODE" 1) (SETVAR "CMDECHO" 1) (SETVAR "MENUECHO" 1))
```

```
Command: SETVAR                Check BLIPMODE again. It's reset back to 1.
```

The RESET function is designed so you can call it by itself to restore the system to the standard default settings of the initial #ERROR list created by INITERR.

Reset Controls

To use RESET, just enter (reset nil). You can make a reset command like:

```
(defun C:RESET () (reset nil) (command "UNDO"))
```

A good root menu item would be:

```
[*RESET*]^C^C^C(reset nil) UNDO;
```

Use RESET and UNDO to restore your standard environment whenever the unknown or unexpected occurs in menu macros, programs, or AutoCAD commands. Edit the INITERR function to include *your* standard settings.

Because error control is integral to a good drawing system, we suggest that you load ERROR.LSP from your ACAD.LSP file and use it in all your finished programs. When testing unfinished programs, disable it with the *ERROR* command we created in ERROR.LSP.

Integrating Error Control in Programs

Now, let's see how error recovery works by using it in a program called LEADTEXT, which also demonstrates RESET and MLAYER layer setting.

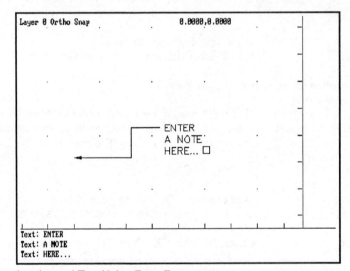

Leader and Text Using Error Recovery

The LEADTEXT.LSP program has two parts. S-LEAD is a command function that draws a leader line with any number of segments. It then calls L-TEXT. L-TEXT is a function that determines text orientation and uses DTEXT to place text at the end of the leader line. As is often the case in finished programs, half of LEADTEXT is error control code.

```
;* LEADTEXT.LSP is an example of error control. S-LEAD draws leaders.
;* L-TEXT adds text to leaders. It requires ERROR.LSP and the user GET functions.

;* C: S-LEAD (Straight LEADer) draws a pline leader using as many line segments
;* as desired. The start point is the arrow head. L-TEXT is called to provide
;* correctly justified DTEXT.
;*
(defun C:S-LEAD ( / pt1 pt2 pt3)
  (setvar "BLIPMODE" 0)                              ;turn blipmode off
  (setvar "CMDECHO" 0)                               ;turn command echo off
  (setvar "MENUECHO" 0)                              ;turn menu echo off
❶
  (initerr)                                          ;initialize error list
  (adderr                          ;adds command function to reset layer name
    (list 'command "LAYER" "S" (getvar "CLAYER") "")     ;getvar current layer
  )                                                    ;name in #ERROR list
  (mlayer "ANN01" "G" "")                              ;creates/sets annotation layer
  (setq pt1 (upoint 1 "" "Pick arrow head point" nil nil) ;get start point of arrow head
       pt2 (upoint 1 "" "To point" nil pt1)             ;get point for 1st line segment
       pt3 (polar pt1 (angle pt1 pt2) (* 0.125 #dwgsc))  ;calc arrow head size
  );setq
❷
  (adderr '(command "U"))                            ;add undo to error list
  (adderr '(command nil nil nil))                    ;add cancel to error list
  (command "PLINE" pt1 "W" "0" (* 0.0625 #dwgsc) pt3 "W" "0" "0" pt2) ;draw arrow head
                                                     ;and 1st line segment
  (while (setq pt2 (getpoint "\nTo point: " pt2))    ;loop for additional line segments.
    (command pt2)                                    ;until ENTER is pressed
  );end while
  (command "")                                       ;end pline
❸
  (delerr '(command "U"))                            ;the pline can stay now if user cancels
  (l-text)                                           ;call l-text function
❹
  (reset nil)                                        ;resets environment and #ERROR list
);end defun

;* L-TEXT (Leader TEXT) starts a DTEXT command following any leader. The text
;* justification (Left or Right) is determined by the last point and mid point
;* of the last line or arc of the leader.
```

Listing continued.

Continued listing.

```
;*
(defun l-text ( / pt1 pt2)
    (setq pt1 (getvar "LASTPOINT")              ;get last point of leader
          pt2 (osnap pt1 "quick,midp")          ;get midpoint using pt1, use quick
          txtht (dxf 40 (tblsearch "STYLE" (getvar "TEXTSTYLE")))) ;current height
    );setq
    (prompt "\nEnter text: ")
    (if (> (car pt1) (car pt2))                 ;determine X point position
        (progn                                  ;if X of pt1 is greater, Left text
          (setq pt1 (polar pt1 5.759 txtht))    ;based on text size
          (command "DTEXT" pt1 0)               ;start DTEXT command - leave user there
        );end progn
        (progn                                  ;if X of pt2 is greater use Right text
          (setq pt1 (polar pt1 3.665 txtht))    ;based on text size
          (command "DTEXT" "R" pt1 0)           ;start DTEXT command - leave user there
        );end progn
    );end if
);defun L-TEXT
;*
(princ)
;*end of LEADTEXT.LSP
```

S-LEAD and L-TEXT Functions in LEADTEXT.LSP File

Because we're discussing error control, and the LEADTEXT program is well-documented, we'll concentrate only on LEADTEXT's error recovery sections.

❶ Along with the SETVAR settings, we invoke INITERR to start the #ERROR list with our standard settings. Then ADDERR adds a COMMAND function list to the #ERROR list to restore the original layer in case of error. COMMAND is quoted to suppress its evaluation until later evaluation by RESET if an error occurs.

❷ As the LEADTEXT program proceeds, we have more potential tasks to undo, so ADDERR adds an undo and triple nil command (for three Control-C's).

❸ We've passed the point where the undo is needed, so DELERR removes it from the #ERROR list, then the L-TEXT subroutine is called to do the text.

❹ All's well and we're finished, so we call RESET with a nil argument to restore our settings to the INITERR standard.

Let's see LEADTEXT work, then force an error.

Testing the Leader Program Error Recovery

```
Enter selection: 1          Begin a NEW drawing again named IL17.
```

You have the LEADTEXT.LSP file.

Create the C:S-LEAD command and L-TEXT function in a new file named LEADTEXT.LSP.

```
Command: (load "error")     Unless you added an ERROR load to ACAD.LSP.
Command: (load "mlayer")    Unless you added an MLAYER load to ACAD.LSP.

Command: (load "leadtext")
Command: ZOOM                         Center, height of 6.

Command: S-LEAD                       Run the command. It makes a new layer.
Pick arrow head point:                Pick it.
To point:                             Pick a couple of points.
To point: <RETURN>                    Return when finished picking.
Enter text: TESTING LEADTEXT          Enter some text.
Text: <RETURN>                        Return when done.
Resetting environment...              RESET restores the old layer.

Command: S-LEAD                       Try again, but cancel after two points.
Pick arrow head point:                Pick one point.
To point:                             Pick one more point.
To point: <^C>                        Now CANCEL.
Error: Function cancelled             Our *ERROR* undoes the line and restores settings.
Command: QUIT
```

The leader line was erased because the program knew that the entire leader was not complete. It didn't blank the screen because it was a cancel, not a program error. If you were to cancel after the text prompt, the leader would remain.

➥ *NOTE: If you added an ERROR.LSP load to your ACAD.LSP, disable it with a leading semicolon for the remainder of the book so it doesn't interfere with our program testing.*

Two causes of program errors are not having all necessary subroutines loaded, and running out of node or string memory space because you have too many unnecessary functions loaded. You can control these problems.

Controlling Function Loading

Control of function loading involves three major concerns. First, you don't want to wait for a load when the function is already loaded. Our ILLOAD function or the self-loading function technique in this chapter will handle this. Second, you want functions and subroutines to automatically load when needed. We'll show you how to add an IF test to your LSP files to do this. The self-loading function technique will also automatically load command functions the first time they are used. Third, you don't want to run out of memory for your functions. The managing memory section of this chapter will give you some memory management ideas. The STACK.LSP program on the New Riders AutoLISP Utilities Disk 1 also provides a function manager. It loads functions when needed, and purges the least used functions when you need memory for others.

We'll present several alternatives, so you can choose the methods that best fit your system. Let's first look at eliminating unnecessary loads.

How to Control Program Loads With ILLOAD

ILLOAD manages function file loading by keeping a global list of files that have been loaded. If the specified function is on the list, the load operation is ignored. Otherwise, the file is loaded. If a file is not found, ILLOAD informs the user and issues a cancel.

```
;* ILLOAD.LSP
;* ILLOAD manages file loading by using a global #ILFUNS list. When loaded,
;* each file name is placed on the list. If a requested load is on the list,
;* it skips the load, otherwise it loads it. If it can't find it, it cancels
;* and prompts. It assumes and adds an .LSP extension for file checking.
(defun ilload (subdir fname / fn fspec)
  (if (not (member (strcase fname) #ilfuns))          ;if not prev loaded
❶
    (progn                                            ;then load it
      (setq fspec (strcat subdir fname ".LSP"))       ;assumes .LSP
      (if (setq fn (open fspec "r"))                  ;if exists
❷
        (progn
          (prompt "\nInitial load.  Please wait...")  ;give a message
          (setq #ilfuns (cons (strcase fname) #ilfuns)) ;then put it on list &
          (close fn)                                  ;close test "r" file name &
          (load fspec)                                ;load it
        )
```

Listing continued.

Continued listing.

```
      (command nil nil          ;else ^Cs cancel command or macro which needed file
        (prompt (strcat "\n" fspec " not found. "))    ;prompt=NIL=^C
      )                                              ;returns nil on failure
    );if
  );progn then
  fname                                    ;else already loaded, return name
 );if
);defun ILLOAD
;*
;* End of ILLOAD.LSP
```

ILLOAD Function in ILLOAD.LSP File

❶ If the function is not a MEMBER of the #ILFUNS list, then PROGN is evaluated to load and add it to the list. A file extension is needed with the OPEN test, so STRCAT combines FSPEC with ".LSP."

❷ If the file can be opened, it exists. If it exists, then ILLOAD closes it, loads it, and adds its name to the #ILFUNS list with CONS. Otherwise, a COMMAND issues three nils to cancel, using the nil returned by the prompt as the third one.

If the load succeeds, it returns the file name or the last expression from the file. If it fails, it returns nil so you can test the load. Let's test the function on the MLAYER.LSP file. If you didn't create MLAYER, substitute another LSP file name.

Testing Function Loading

Enter selection: **1**   Begin a NEW drawing again named IL17.

 You have the ILLOAD.LSP file.

 Create ILLOAD in the ILLOAD.LSP file as shown above.

Command: **(load "ilload")**

Command: **(ilload "\\IL-ACAD\\" "MLAYER")**   Test it.
Initial load. Please wait...   This is its first time loaded by ILLOAD.
Lisp returns: MLAYER

```
Command: LINE                              Try it transparently.
To point: (ilload "" "MLAYER")             Try to load it again.
Lisp returns: "MLAYER"                     It's already loaded.
To point:

To point: (ilload "\\WHERE\\" "WHAT")      And if it can't load it:
\WHERE\WHAT.LSP not found.
Lisp returns: nil                          Nil signifies failure.
Command:                                   And LINE is cancelled.
```

You can use the ILLOAD function in menu macros to load a function, then run it if the load is okay. A typical example is:

```
[ATEXT  ]^C^C^C(if (ilload "/IL-ACAD/" "ATEXT") (C:ATEXT));
```

Now let's look at making needed functions load automatically.

How to Load Subroutines Automatically

In many LSP files, we've used a technique similar to the IF test in the [ATEXT] macro shown above to ensure that needed functions are loaded. For example, we use the following entry in the BATCHSCR.LSP file:

```
(if pslash nil (load "filelib"))
```

This is a simple technique that will load a subroutine file like FILELIB.LSP if it can be found. However, it won't stop erroneous attempts to use the functions in the calling program, like BATCHSCR. There are two safer methods. The first is to use ILLOAD and the undocumented AutoLISP QUIT function. The QUIT function immediately aborts a program and calls the error function. This method aborts the loading of both files. Our example assumes ILLOAD has been loaded, along with our redefined *ERROR* function to suppress the normal error display, and GPATH.LSP to set #LSP to a path name. If so, you can replace the (if pslash...) line in BATCHSCR.LSP with:

```
(if (ilload #lsp "filelib") nil (quit))
```

Then, if FILELIB.LSP can't be found when BATCHSCR.LSP is found, you'll get the following messages:

```
/IL-ACAD/filelib.LSP not found.    From ILLOAD.
Command: Error: quit / exit abort   From the error function.
```

➥ *TIP: An alternative method is to place the entire first file's contents in a giant IF function that tests for the success of the nested load of the subroutine file. Then let IF evaluate the first file if the load succeeds, or give an error prompt if it fails.*

Besides loading subroutines when needed, it would be nice to have major functions and C:*commands* automatically load if and when needed. There is a way to define them as self-loading commands.

How to Write Self-Loading Commands

Self-loading functions are most useful with C:*command* functions. The self-loading technique makes putting functions in menus easier. It eliminates the need for menu macros to test and load functions and commands before executing them. The technique is simple. You just define all self-loading functions as little functions that do nothing but load their real function files. Put them all in a separate file, like our SELFLOAD.LSP. Then you add a line to execute the command or main function of each file that you want loaded in this manner.

Here is an example SELFLOAD.LSP file, which assumes ILLOAD is loaded and #LSP is set to a path (or GPATH is loaded).

```
;* SELFLOAD.LSP uses a technique suggested by Phil Kreiker of Looking Glass
;* Microcomputer Products. ILLOAD and the #LSP path variable must be defined.
;* Define all desired self-loading functions like the MFLY example.
;* Put a call to execute the function at the end of its file like:  (C:MFLY)
;* The function or command will then execute whether or not already loaded.

(defun C:MFLY () (ilload #LSP "MFLY") (princ))

;* End of SELFLOAD.LSP
```

The Self-Loading C:MFLY in SELFLOAD.LSP

There isn't much to this — just a good idea that's easy to do. When you load SELFLOAD, it defines C:MFLY as a function that loads MFLY.LSP. This means that the first time such a function or command is used, it loads itself. And, if you add a (C:MFLY) to the end of MFLY.LSP, the load executes itself. Subsequent uses are normal, since it's then already loaded. Let's try it.

Using Self-Loading Functions

```
Enter selection: 1
```
                        Begin a NEW drawing again named IL17.

You have the self-loading C:MFLY in you SELFLOAD.LSP file.

Create the self-loading C:MFLY in a new file named SELFLOAD.LSP.

```
Command: (load "SELFLOAD")
Command: (load "ILLOAD")
Command: (setq #lsp "/IL-ACAD/")
```

Command: **SHELL**   Edit your MFLY.LSP file. Add the following as its last line:

(C:MFLY)   ;executes command when self-loaded

Save MFLY.LSP and exit to AutoCAD.

Command: **MFLY**   Test it.

```
Initial load.  Please wait...          And it loads MFLY.LSP, then executes:
Input one command or option per line, followed by a RETURN.
Type "\" for pause, "EXIT" to terminate.
Input, "\", or "EXIT": EXIT
```

If you use this technique, put a line in your ACAD.LSP file to load SELFLOAD.LSP. We recommend this technique for C:*commands* and functions executed by menus. It's easy, automatic, transparent, and doesn't load functions until they're needed. This keeps AutoLISP memory available for the functions that are actually being used.

But what about large functions and commands that you use and then don't need for a while? Once loaded, they take up valuable memory that you may need for other functions. We have a tool you can use to juggle them.

How to Juggle Functions in Limited Memory

STACK.LSP is a function-managing program on the New Riders AutoLISP Utilities Disk 1. It's called in the same manner as ILLOAD, and keeps track of the functions in much the same manner. However, it's limited to six functions at a time. When you tell it to load another function, it replaces the least frequently used of the current six. This minimizes memory conflicts when using several moderate to large AutoLISP functions at once by treating them as a rotating stack.

Even with these function management techniques, you still may run out of AutoLISP memory.

Managing Memory

As you create more functions and larger programs, the demand on AutoLISP memory becomes ever more intense. Programmers are always hungry for bigger, faster, better computers. AutoLISP, a tiny but significant companion to AutoCAD, occupies only 128K of memory, about 83K for the program itself and 45K for your personal programs and data. Forty-five thousand bytes of data doesn't go very far. At some point, you begin to see the dreaded messages:

```
error: insufficient node space
error: insufficient string space
```

When you get insufficient memory messages, it's time to manage your AutoLISP memory.

There is also the broader and related topic of AutoCAD memory management. We provide some information on this in Appendix B, but for complete and current information, check your AutoCAD Installation and Performance Guide, and read AutoCAD's README.DOC file for information that supercedes the guide.

Unless you use DOS for AutoCAD, you can ignore memory management. Other operating systems have nearly unlimited AutoLISP memory. However, you should still observe the following good programming practices.

How to Write Efficient Programs

No matter what memory management route you take, good habits will make your programs more efficient. Good practices include:

- Keeping your variables local whenever possible.

- Standardizing your variable names and reusing them throughout all your programs.

- Resetting variables to nil when you don't need them.

- Limiting variable and function names to six characters or less.

- Making one-shot routines as LSP files that execute as they load and resetting their variables to nil at the end of the file. You can use LAMBDA for this. See the AutoCAD SETUP.LSP file for an example.

- Using LAMBDA for recursive operations, minimizing the demands on stack space (arguments and temporary data) that recursion otherwise uses.

- Using our STACK.LSP or SELFLOAD.LSP techniques to load large functions only when you use them.

- Defining all your very large functions with the same function name, such as ROUTINE. Keep each in a separate file, loading and executing it from a menu that presents a more appropriate name to the user. Since the functions share the same name, each will replace the previous one in memory when loaded.

If you reuse function names, like ROUTINE, AutoLISP must have enough memory to hold both the old and new definitions for a short time. To avoid this, set ROUTINE to nil at the top of each file before the file defines the new function, again named ROUTINE.

You can also avoid needing double data space for large variables. When setting a new value to an existing variable that holds a large data list or string, set the variable to nil first, then set the new value.

If you use a *real* operating system that doesn't have the memory constraints of DOS, such as UNIX, these practices will put you in good shape. But if you run DOS, all these practices still won't be enough. You'll need to manage your memory.

How to Control AutoLISP Memory

There are two ways to manage AutoLISP memory. The first is the easiest. Just turn on VMON, the AutoCAD memory swapping function. The second is to use ExtLISP (Extended AutoLISP, which we'll cover soon). ExtLISP requires extended memory and cannot tolerate conflicts with other programs that use or manage it.

Let's look at VMON first. The VMON function tells AutoCAD to swap AutoLISP functions in and out of memory any time it needs to.

vmon | *Turns on AutoLISP's virtual paging of functions. It makes function definitions eligible to be swapped to disk or in and out of RAM, to allow for the loading of more programs.*
(vmon)

Since the very early days of AutoCAD, the program has *paged* drawing data out of memory to the disk when it needs more memory. The hard disk has served as *virtual memory,* so AutoCAD drawings have never been limited by the amount of the computer's RAM. This paging consumes a good percent of AutoCAD's time, which is one reason non-DOS systems are usually faster. You can speed AutoCAD up by using a RAMdisk for your drawings. With the advent of expanded and extended RAM memory, AutoCAD extended its paging to use RAM for faster paging.

The VMON (Virtual Memory ON) function invokes this same paging for AutoLISP-defined functions. This allows you to develop larger programs than could previously fit in the 45K space allotted by AutoCAD. To turn VMON, you just type (vmon), or better yet, put it at the top of your ACAD.LSP file.

Turning VMON On

Continue in the previous drawing, or begin a NEW drawing again named IL17.

Command: **(vmon)**   Turns paging on.

Command: **SHELL**   Edit your ACAD.LSP file and add a (vmon) line at the top.

Putting a VMON line in ACAD.LSP ensures that it will always be on. Once VMON is turned on during a drawing session, it can't be turned off. The only disadvantage to having virtual memory on is that when a function has been paged out, it takes time to retrieve it before it can execute.

➡ *TIP: You can prevent a function from being paged out. For example, use (setq mlayer (cdr mlayer)) to keep the MLAYER function in real memory.*

Unfortunately, good memory management is not as simplistic as just turning VMON on and forgetting it. One problem is that VMON won't help with memory used by variables and strings. Variable values and strings are data, not programs, and are not paged. VMON paging is for user-defined function definitions only, not their data.

Let's examine AutoLISP's division of memory.

Understanding AutoLISP Memory

AutoLISP memory is divided into two major areas: heap and stack. Large complex functions put more load on heap, and recursive functions impact stack. Heap and stack are allocated in the following manner:

AutoLISP HEAP	AutoLISP STACK
Default 40000 bytes	Default 3000 bytes
AutoLISP functions	Function arguments
Symbols (variable names)	Partial results
User function definitions	Temporary data during function
String space	AutoLISP pointers
Node space	Program counters
Data	
VMON relieves	VMON doesn't help

AutoLISP Memory Usage

The only thing that VMON relieves is user-defined function memory demands, but this relief indirectly helps free memory for other uses. It will directly relieve "out of node space" errors, although nodes are also used by more than just function definitions. A *node* is the basic unit of AutoLISP data storage, 10 bytes on DOS and 12 bytes with ExtLISP or non-DOS operating systems. Nodes are grouped and allocated in segments, with a default size of 512 nodes.

The division of memory between heap and stack is controlled by the LISPHEAP and LISPSTACK environment variables, which we set in our IL.BAT file in Chapter 1. You can use these environment variables to set any division of heap and stack up to a combined total of 45000 bytes. However, if your other AutoCAD memory settings leave less than 45000 bytes for AutoLISP, you may not get as much as you ask for. You almost never will get the LISPSTACK overflow error message, but if you do, increase the LISPSTACK setting. You should usually keep stack smaller than the rather large 10000 bytes set in our IL.BAT file. A smaller stack leaves more room for heap.

You can see what memory is actually allocated to AutoLISP by AutoCAD with the MEM function, one of the other memory management functions in AutoLISP. These functions and their purposes are:

MEM	Reports the usage of AutoLISP memory.
ALLOC	Controls size of groups of nodes called segments.
EXPAND	Assigns more of the heap to node space.
GC	Collects any "garbage," unused portions of memory.

AutoLISP uses these functions to manage memory. They are not recommended for our use, although MEM can give us a harmless peek at memory usage and help determine how to adjust heap and stack. GC is slow and is used automatically by AutoLISP when needed, so trying to use it yourself will probably only slow your programs down.

Let's try MEM to see our memory allocation. Your allocation will probably differ from ours.

A Look at MEM

```
Enter selection:                Begin a NEW drawing named IL17.

Command: (mem)
Nodes:       2560               ExtLISP increases this.
Free nodes:  145                Current available.
Segments:    5                  5 x 512 nodes = 2560.
Allocate:    512                Segment size.
Collections: 24                 Count of GC's performed.
Free heap:   17480              Heap not assigned to nodes.
Swap-ins:    0                  Functions paged out.
Page file:   504               Page file size.
Lisp returns: nil
```

You can, and professional AutoLISP programmers do, manipulate AutoLISP's memory with ALLOC and EXPAND, but it can be dangerous. It's easy to rob strings to pay nodes, causing errors rather than improving things in the process. AutoLISP memory management is well-documented in the AutoLISP Programmer's Reference if you wish to attempt it.

Short of scrapping DOS, the best thing you can do to relieve memory congestion is to use ExtLISP.

Using Extended AutoLISP

There is nothing difficult about using ExtLISP — you just use it and instantly have virtually unlimited heap space. Stack space is still restricted, but you'll never run out since the heap no longer comes from the 45000 bytes that stack shares with regular LISP. In addition to heap, most of the AutoLISP code is relocated into extended memory. This frees up about 80K of memory for AutoCAD's other uses, making your drawings more efficient all around. Due to hardware restrictions, ExtLISP may not be faster on the 80286 processor chip, but you should see performance as well as memory improvement if you use it on an 80386.

To use ExtLISP, you must have an 80286 (AT class) or 80386 DOS-based computer with at least one megabyte of extended (not expanded) memory in addition to the standard DOS 640K base. Some other programs and memory managers that create emulated expanded memory from real extended memory are incompatible with ExtLISP.

Install ExtLISP by running the EXTLISP.EXE program before loading AutoCAD. You must tell AutoCAD to use extended LISP by making a setting in the operating parameters submenu of the configuration menu.

If your computer uses extended memory for *anything* else, you'll have to use the SET LISPXMEM environment variable before loading ExtLISP. This avoids memory conflicts. If you have problems, make sure you have the latest version of ExtLISP, check your AutoCAD Installation and Performance Guide, and read the EXTLISP.DOC file for information that supercedes the guide.

Some programmers use a technique called CLEAN as an alternative to VMON.

The CLEAN Alternative

The CLEAN technique involves manipulating the ATOMLIST. CLEAN is a user-defined function that resets the ATOMLIST to a subset of itself. All function and variable names not included in the reset ATOMLIST are discarded, releasing memory. Typically, systems using CLEAN will call the function to clean the ATOMLIST before loading a new program. This means that the next time you want to use a function that CLEAN has wiped from the ATOMLIST, you have to wait for it to reload. You also must be careful to not clean out your standard subroutine functions and global variables. An example using a CLEAN function is shown in the Memory Management section of the AutoLISP Programmer's Reference.

CLEAN is incompatible with VMON because access to the ATOMLIST is blocked when paging occurs. We have seen attempted techniques recommended for working around this, but they are dangerous and can cause errors.

Give AutoCAD the task of managing your memory by using VMON and ExtLISP.

Now that you have your system fully under control, you may want to protect it. Unlimited memory won't help your profits if you have a security problem.

Encryption and Security

File security and control are ongoing management issues. We'll offer a few recommendations for your applications. There are DOS and other file management utilities that you can use to make your files "read-only," to hide and unhide files, and to keep files in hidden directories. You can control these utilities with your BAT files, making them transparent to your user if ECHO is off. Look at the DOS ATTRIB command or the Norton Utilities FA (File Attribute) if you want to hide files or make them read-only.

You can control where files are stored by SUBSTituting drives for paths, or coding path variables in your functions and macros. Eliminating user input from paths reduces errors and files that are misplaced or overwritten. Users can deposit user-defined wblocked symbols, DWG files and on-the-fly menu macros in assigned user directories for the system manager to examine and consider for inclusion in the system.

Encrypting LISP and Menus

You don't want your customization effort to walk out the door and into your competitors' offices. In the days of manual drafting, it was easy to tell one person's work from another's. On disk, everybody's work looks the same. It helps to take precautions to protect your menu and AutoLISP files.

Menus are easy to protect. Keep MNU files under lock and key, and distribute only MNX files.

You can encrypt AutoLISP by using a utility program called PROTECT.EXE, available through your local AutoCAD dealer. If you use it, be sure to rename your master source LSP files to an extension such as LSC (for LISP Source Code) before encryption. There is no way to decrypt files once they are encrypted.

Unfortunately, software hackers have found a way to break the encryption codes. Another Autodesk utility called the Kelvinator strips extra white space from the code and systematically substitutes random nonsense names for variables. Although not true encryption, it turns still-workable code into gibberish. Kelvination followed by encryption offers the best security. Kelvinating the ATEXT.LSP file looks like:

```
C:\>REN ATEXT.LSP ATEXT.LSC        Back it up to .LSC first.
C:\>KELV ATEXT.LSC > ATEXT.LSP
The Kelvinator (July 27th, 1988)
Release 2b:  The Kelvinator Strikes Back
(C) Copyright 1986, 1987, 1988 Autodesk, Inc.
```

The file it produces looks like:

```
(DEFUN C:ATEXT(/ Qj Q@ QQ Q1 Q& Q1 Q# Q0 Q$ QO Q| Q% Q?j Qjj)(SETQ
Q@j(GETVAR"CMDECHO"))(SETVAR"CMDECHO"0)(GRAPHSCR)(SETQ Q@(GETPOINT"\nPick radius center
point: ")Qj(GETPOINT"\nPick middle point of text: "Q@)Q#(GETDIST(STRCAT"\nText height
"(RTOS(SETQ QQ(GETVAR"TEXTSIZE")))":  "))Q#(IF Q# Q# QQ)QQ(GETSTRING"\nText:
"T)Q1(DISTANCE Q@ Qj)Q&(STRLEN QQ)Q|(STRCASE(GETSTRING"\nIs base of text towards radius
point Y: ")))(IF(OR(= Q|"")(= Q|"Y"))(SETQ Q1(- Q1(/ Q# 2)))(SETQ Q1(+ Q1(/ Q#
2))))(SETQ Q0(* Q& Q#)Q1(/ Q0 Q&)Q$(/ Q0 Q1)QO(-(+(ANGLE Q@ Qj)(/ Q$ 2))(/ Q1 Q1 2))QQj
1)(REPEAT Q&(IF(OR(= Q|"")(= Q|"Y"))(SETQ Q%(Q1j(- QO(/ PI 2)))Q&j QQj)(SETQ Q%(ANGTOS(-
QO(* PI 1.5))0)Q&j(-(1+ Q&)QQj)))(SETQ Q?j(POLAR Q@ QO Q1)Qjj(SUBSTR QQ Q&j
1))(COMMAND"TEXT""C"Q?j Q# Q% Qjj)(SETQ QQj(1+ QQj)QO(- QO(/ Q1
Q1))))(SETVAR"CMDECHO"Q@j)(PRINC))
```

Encrypted ATEXT.LSP File

A bit confusing? You might figure it out by the prompts in the program, but anyone not familiar with your code will have a difficult time. And if it's also encrypted, it's even harder.

Kelvination has a beneficial side effect. It reduces AutoLISP file size, resulting in faster loading, smaller functions. We have a program to clean out comments and white space, if that's all you want to do.

Compacting LISP Files With LSPSTRIP

Our LSPSTRIP.EXE program, on the IL-DISK, takes out all comments and white space from files. It does not encrypt the files. LSPSTRIP is written in BASIC. The source code is also on the IL DISK. LSPSTRIP can provide most of the efficiency advantages of the Kelvinator without the problems associated with cryptic variable and function names. You can call LSPSTRIP from the DOS command line or through SHELL.

Stripped of comments and white space, GPATH reduces from 1500 bytes to a mere 307, and looks like this.

```
(defun gpath (path file)
(if path
(strcat path file)
file
)
)
(setq #dwg "/IL-ACAD/")
(mapcar '(lambda (path def)
(set (read path)
(if (setq path (getenv path))
(strcat path "/")
def
) )
)
'("#lsp"      "#blk"       "#mnu"       "#shx"   )
'("/IL-ACAD/" "/IL-ACAD/" "/IL-ACAD/" "/ACAD/" )
)
```

Stripped GPATH.LSP

Try LSPSTRIP on the GPATH.LSP file.

Using LSPSTRIP.EXE

```
Command: SHELL
DOS Command: <RETURN>
C:\IL-ACAD>> COPY GPATH.LSP TEST.LSP          Or use another LSP file.

C:\IL-ACAD>>LSPSTRIP TEST.LSP /S              The /S option strips the file.

C:\IL-ACAD>>TYPE TEST.LSP                     Views the resulting file as shown above.
```

LSPSTRIP creates a backup file with an LLS extension to protect your original source code. If you try to strip the same file twice and LSPSTRIP finds an existing LLS file, it displays "File has been stripped," and refuses to strip it to avoid overwriting the source code in the LLS file.

LSPSTRIP also has a help feature that will display specially noted comments of an AutoLISP file. Throughout the book, we've used a leading ;* to code header comments and other key comments in LSP files. If you use LSPSTRIP without the /S option, it displays all comment lines starting with the ;* code.

Displaying Comments With LSPSTRIP

```
C:\IL-ACAD>>LSPSTRIP ANSILIB.LSP            Display the following.

;WARNING: ANSILIB.LSP uses semicolons in strings - Do Not run LSPSTRIP/S
 ANSILIB.LSP library of screen formatting functions, for DOS only.
 It consists of the most common tasks required for screen formatting,
 using the ANSI escape calls.          And the rest of the ;* comment lines.

C:\IL-ACAD>> EXIT                           Return to AutoCAD.
```

There is one thing LSPSTRIP can't handle. It can't strip LSP files with semicolons imbedded in strings, like the ANSILIB.LSP file. LSPSTRIP can't distinguish between these semicolons and comments. To prevent accidental stripping of such files, LSPSTRIP looks at the top line of the LSP file. If you begin the first line with ;*; instead of ;* then LSPSTRIP will refuse to strip the file. It will display the top line, which should identify the file and give a warning. The top line of ANSILIB is:

```
;*;WARNING: ANSILIB.LSP contains ; semicolons in strings. Do Not LSPSTRIP/S
```

Our last topic is the first thing you do when you get a program working in its rough form. You should document it.

Documenting and Presenting an Application

You can always enhance your program's effectiveness by providing easily accessible and clear documentation. We've been showing documentation-by-example throughout the book. There are two main reasons for documentation. One is to make it easier for you or others to decipher and modify a program in the future. The other is to make the program's use clear to the user with how-to documents and well-commented code.

Commenting LISP Programs

The time saved in maintenance pays for the time it takes to document your programs. Good comments don't have to be long. However, they should remind you of how a program works and the critical assumptions you've embedded within the program. Two types of documentation are procedural descriptions and in-line comments.

Procedural descriptions tell what the program is and how to use it. These are the several lines of text, preceded by our ;* codes, that you have seen throughout the book. The in-line comments that we have used at the right-hand side of the programs to explain the code and action are equally important. These comments identify variables, explain loops, explain nested and complex logic, and generally help decipher the program. They will be just as valuable to you as to others reading your programs when you try to decipher a program that you wrote two years ago!

You can also comment your menu files to make their purpose and logic clearer.

How to Comment Menu Files

We also recommend commenting your menus, as we did in the ISODIM.MNU file from Chapter 10. Here is a piece of it.

```
**DOCUMENTATION
[The following are the Direct'n VERT HORZ RIGHT LEFT page toggles.]
**VERT-L 13
[  VERT  ]^C^C^CISOPLANE TOP DIM DIMBLK ARROW-L STYLE DIM-L EXIT $S=HORZ-L
```

Sample Comments From the ISODIM.MNU Menu

**DOCUMENTATION is not a *real* menu page. It's never called by a menu page change call. It's used only to store some comments about the **VERT-L and other toggle pages following it. The comments are stored in [brackets]. AutoCAD ignores all but the first eight characters when it compiles the menu. They increase the MNX menu size by 8 bytes per comment line. A small price to pay for documentation. Although the screen displays only the first eight characters of a menu label, you can make the actual labels much longer. (We've tested up to 256 characters). The [VERT] could have been:

```
[  VERT  - Toggles to vertical left dim-type.]
```

Of course, you can't do this in pull-down menus because they display their entire labels.

The second type of documentation tells users about your menus and programs.

How to Write "How-To" Documents

We've learned several helpful program documentation techniques. One is to use a memory resident cut and paste utility program to cut text screens from AutoCAD and dump them into a word processor. All of our exercises were done this way with a freeware program called CTRLALT (Control Alt). Refer to the section on Freeware in Appendix D to learn how to obtain the program. It saved us from the laborious task of retyping all the AutoCAD prompts, options, and commands into our documents.

There are several styles of educational documents. They include:

■ Quick reference instruction sheets or books listing commands in alphabetical order.

■ Tutorials giving step-by-step instructions.

■ User manuals giving general information on CAD management, how layers are set up, file naming conventions, and any other information a user may need to run your system.

■ Screen Menu Maps illustrating the layout of commands within the program.

Beyond documentation, the interface that your programs present affects their usability.

Program Presentation

The first rule of good program presentation is not to confuse your users with misleading or hard to remember command names. AutoCAD is much better than most CAD programs in using clear names for command functions. Try to use familiar terms in your customization. Make the program as much like your design and drafting application as you can, taking terms from familiar templates, operations, and tools.

The second rule is to keep your users informed. Let them know what's happening through clear and concise prompts, menu labels, help screens, and external help files. Display program status using GRTEXT and menu label toggles.

The third rule is to make your prompts consistent in appearance. Placing similar commands in similar positions on all applicable screen menus makes a system much easier and friendlier to use.

The fourth rule is to use the CMDECHO system variable in programs and MENUECHO in menus to suppress unnecessary command and option clutter. We left a lot of clutter in many of this book's programs and menus to help you learn how they worked. However, if you use the programs and menus in your daily AutoCAD work, add CMDECHO and MENUECHO control to clean up their appearance.

Help Text Screens and Slides

Help slides can be displayed using AutoCAD's VSLIDE command. Slides can visually show how a command works. Again, you can use the top menu label for this. For example, you can add the ISODIM.SLD to our

ISODIM menu to show the isoplanes, arrow and text styles, dimension, and extension lines.

Help text screens can be provided by using AutoCAD's HELP command to give quick access to ACAD.HLP. The ACAD.HLP file is an ASCII text file that you can modify or replace with help messages about your own commands and functions. The AutoCAD HELP command can be called transparently with a leading apostrophe. If the HELP command is given a name, AutoCAD displays the text on that name's page. We added a custom page to the help file in Chapter 12's parametric system.

Let's assume you've added an ISODIM page to the ACAD.HLP file (similar to the PIPEFIT page in Chapter 12). You can provide a help screen by placing a help call macro behind one of the top labels of each screen menu.

Here's an excerpt from the ISODIM.MNU, modified to add a help screen and slide.

```
**ISO
[ISO Dims]^C^C^CVSLIDE ISODIM
[   ?    ]'HELP ISODIM
[DIM LINE]^C^C^CDIMLINE
```

If you store your help slides in a slide library *file name*.SLB file, you would use the format:

```
[ISO Dims]^C^C^CVSLIDE file name(ISODIM)
```

The help slide will look like the following illustration.

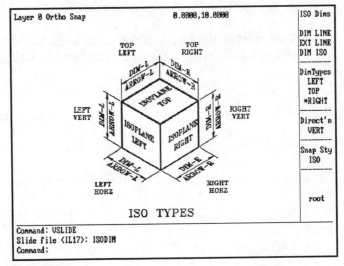

Help Slide

Good documentation will save more time than it consumes. When you plan your documentation, think about what the user needs to see.

Summary

Centralized customization and management can minimize problems, standardize drawings, increase efficiency, make less knowledgeable users productive, and reduce learning time. Remember our AutoCAD circle of productivity. It's worth the time it takes, even if you are the *entire* CAD department.

To reduce their complexity, most of our programs aren't as complete as they would be in a production environment. We've sacrificed some error-checking, resetting, subdirectory usage, and program coordination. But you now have the tools and knowledge to complete them. Modify any of these programs that might fit in with your work, adding controls and putting them in menus to make them part of your system.

Authors' Farewell

Let's see. You've set up your system, learned nearly everything about AutoLISP, created commands, written full-blown programs and menus, used subroutines to reduce repetitive effort, manipulated entities, accessed table definitions, written and read the screen and input devices, used attributes for tools as well as data reporting, created parts parametrically, coordinated AutoLISP with the system's files, devices, Lotus, dBASE, DOS batch files, and BASIC, blasted off into 3D programming, altered drawings with DXF, and gained control of the system with good management practices.

This must be the end! But don't stop here. You'll find valuable tables and information in the appendices. And good luck programming!

Menus, AutoLISP and Programs

Chapter 4

GETPTS
A subroutine that builds a list of points.

DIAM
A GET diameter function that presents the previous diameter as a default.

SLOT
SLOT draws solid slotted holes. It asks for the center of the slot, the slot diameter and the slot length, and uses a polyline to fill in the slotted area.

DRAW
DRAW constructs a list of points, processes the list, and places circles at each point.

Chapter 5

ANGTOC
A subroutine used to format AutoLISP angles for use in AutoCAD commands.

UDIST
A function that improves on the AutoLISP GETDIST function.

UANGLE
UANGLE is similar to UDIST for the GETANGLE function.

UPOINT
UPOINT improves on the GETPOINT function.

UINT
UINT formats defaults, prompts, and filters input for the GETINT function.

UREAL
UREAL uses the GETREAL function, but filters input and formats prompts and defaults.

USTR
USTR formats a string prompt and uses the GETSTRING function.

UKWORD
UKWORD implements the GETKWORD function of AutoLISP, but formats prompts and filters input.

ATEXT.LSP
A program that draws text along a curve or arc segment.

Chapter 6

DXF
A simple subroutine that retrieves the data element of an association list.

UENTSL
Another user interface GET function. It adds INITGET features and a default key word to ENTSEL, which lacks that versatility

SSTOOLS.LSP
A set of subroutines that add, subtract,

and cross-check selection sets of entities.

SSINTER builds a selection set common to two selection sets.

SSUNION adds two selection sets together.

SSDIFF creates a selection set of the difference between two sets.

CATCH.LSP

CATCH is on the New Riders AutoLISP Utilities Disk 1. It contains three functions:

C:MARK marks the drawing database.

CATCH selects the newly created entities which follow the mark.

LAST-N selects the last *n* entities in the drawing.

HEX-INT.LSP

HEX-INT is on the New Riders AutoLISP Utilities Disk 1. It is a set of hexadecimal arithmetic tools that make dealing with entity handles easier.

C:MOFFSET

A command that creates equally spaced multiple offsets of a single selected object. It eliminates the need to repeatedly select the entity during the AutoCAD OFFSET command.

C:APLATE

An area calculator that subtracts the area of holes and cutouts on any plate-like surface.

C:CSCALE

CSCALE automatically adjusts the existing drawing scale of selected annotations and symbols (text and block entities) relative to intended plot scale. It maintains existing insertion points.

C:BSCALE

A command that allows independent rescaling of X, Y, and Z factors of an existing block without reinserting the block in the drawing.

C:RCLOUD

A command program that lets you sketch a crude revision cloud that is reprocessed into a neatly reformatted cloud.

Chapter 7

SETVP

SETVP changes AutoCAD's active viewport from within AutoLISP.

TAKOFF

TAKOFF outputs a DXF file for lineal material take-offs. It reports all entity data drawn in specially named linetypes, accessing the LTYPE table to get the linetype name list for processing.

WLAYER.LSP

WLAYER is a command which scans the drawing's LAYER table. It prompts the user with each layer, asking if it should be erased, skipped, or wblocked to a drawing file named for the first eight characters of the layer's name.

LEGEND.LSP

A program that creates a symbol legend by scanning the BLOCK table and extracting all specially defined legend blocks. The program has three functions.

LEGEND collects legend blocks and formats them.

OUTLEDG draws the legend, taking a paired list of data (block and description) and putting it in the AutoCAD drawing as a list of symbols and text.

LEDSWAP lets the user easily swap or rearrange the paired items in the legend.

PVAR.LSP

A program on the New Riders AutoLISP Utilities Disk 1. It creates a personal variable system which can retain up to 254 numeric or string variable values in a drawing's LTYPE table. Unlike normal AutoLISP variables, these variables are retained when you end a drawing. The system has several functions, including:

PVAR is used to query, view, or update the variables.

PUTVAR can be used inside other AutoLISP programs to update a variable.

RETVAR retrieves the variable.

GETPVAL is used to get a new variable value from the user. This works like a set of personal system variables.

Chapter 8

FILELIB.LSP

FILELIB.LSP defines AutoLISP utilities for file management, including:

CPATH retrieves the current DOS directory path.

PSLASH formats path names with back or forward slashes as needed by DOS or UNIX. Your programs need to control slashes to deal with the differing syntaxes of DOS and UNIX.

FFNAME formats a file name with a path.

VFFILE and VPATH verify a file's or path's existence.

BACKUP makes a backup up file with the extension BAK.

MERGEF merges two files, without verification.

ANSILIB.LSP

A library of functions for formatting text screens with ANSI.SYS escape calls. These functions clear the text screen, position the cursor, and permit special effects like text coloration and blinking.

ETOS

A data conversion function that returns any value or expression as a string.

SHELL.LSP

SHELL.LSP, on the New Riders AutoLISP Utilities Disk 1, contains a subroutine that uses techniques developed in the FILELIB FFNAME function to execute and verify multiple DOS commands with a single SHELL execution.

MERGEV

MERGEV is on the New Riders AutoLISP Utilities Disk 1. It adds verification to MERGEF.

C:PATTERN

An automatic hatch generator. This program generates hatch patterns from selected entities within a 1 x 1 unit pattern definition drawn in AutoCAD.

C:REFDWG

A drawing reference schedule program. It generates a drawing schedule and inserts it in your drawing. C:REFDWG displays a list of project reference drawings on the text screen. Then, using ANSI library functions, you can mark the reference drawings to list. After the selections are made, the program puts on a schedule in the current drawing.

Chapter 9

STRIP

A function that removes a specified entity association list from an entity data list. It's used for removing entity data groups to modify an entity.

C:PVIEW

PVIEW uses GRDRAW to display a box around each of the views defined in a drawing. It uses GRTEXT to display the view's name on the status line. Each view is displayed sequentially in a continuous loop until you select a view or quit the program.

C:ETEXT

A single-line text editor that uses GRREAD and the ANSI.SYS codes. It lets you select a single line of drawing text and edit it. You can move the cursor within the text and add or delete characters.

C:DDRAW

A drawing aid that uses GRREAD to automate drawing lines at 22.5 degree angles. It switches the snap rotation angle to the angular increment closest to a dragged line. The program displays a compass icon to assist in selecting the angle for each line.

Chapter 10

ISODIM.MNU

ISODIM.MNU includes the following:
**ISO is the main isometric dimensioning page of the isometric menu system. Portions of it get overlaid by an integrated set of small screen menu toggle pages. The ISODIM.LSP functions are required for this menu page.
**TISO-*x* is a set of isometric TABLET1 menu sections that are included on the New Riders AutoLISP Utilities Disk 1's ISODIM.MNU menu file. Selections made from the tablet are displayed on the screen menu status labels. The ISODIM.LSP functions are required for this tablet menu.

C:DIMLINE

An AutoLISP command function that draws an isometric dimension line, arrows, and text.

C:EXTLINE

An AutoLISP command function that draws isometric extension lines.

ISODIM.LSP

ISODIM.LSP is the program file containing the two isometric dimensioning AutoLISP commands above and a set of initialization expressions.

Chapter 11

IL11TITL.MNU

The title block system includes:
[TITLE] is a macro that inserts the ATTSHT-D title block, fills out some attribute text automatically, and prompts for the rest.
[TITLEBLK] loads TIMELIB.LSP, sets up the environment, and calls the **TITLEBLK menu page.
**TITLEBLK is a page of macros, automates the updating of title block information such as last plot date, CAD drawing name, plan scale, and more. This menu page includes macros to insert and update drawing revision blocks.

TIMELIB.LSP

This time and date library contains:
TODAY returns the current date as mm/dd/yy.
TIME returns the current time as hh:mm:ss.
YEAR returns the current year.

GETBK and LINEBLK

Subroutines used by the autobreaking block commands C:BBLOCK and C:BLINE.

UPDATE.LSP

A program that finds and increments drawing revision levels. It adds a revision bar and prompts for revision notes and drawing reissue data. It includes:

C:UPDATE, the update command function. It uses the following subroutines:

REVALL handles the attribute entity data access for C:UPDATE.

REVTIME handles the revision time updating.

UPD handles the attribute entity data modification for REVALL.

AUTOBLK.LSP

AUTOBLK.LSP provides functions for creating lines with blocks interrupting them. It includes:

GETBLK, the subroutine that gets the name of a specially designed autobreaking block and extracts the attribute data that stores the information for calculating the break points.

LINEBLK, the subroutine that inserts the autobreaking block and breaks the line or polyline.

C:BLINE draws a line, inserts an autobreaking block at the midpoint of the line, and breaks the line based on data stored in the block's attribute.

C:BBLOCK inserts an autobreaking block on an existing line or polyline, breaking the line for the block.

Chapter 12

IL12PARA.MNU

The parametrics screen menu. The main page is ****PIPEFITS**, which includes:

[TAG ON] and **[TAG OFF]** to toggle component material tagging on and off.

[DB LINE] to draw double line pipes and flanges between fittings with dimensions based on current pipe data.

[SET SIZE] to load the requested pipe data.

[SIDEVIEW],   **[FRONT VW]**,   and

[BACKVIEW] to draw the parametric pipe fittings.

GETSIZE

GETSIZE searches a data file, retrieves the requested data, and parses the data string into a list of values.

ATTFIT and ATTLINE

Tools that automatically attach material tags to the parametric elbows and pipe segments.

EL90SUBR.LSP

EL90SUBR.LSP includes ELDATA and FLANGE, two subroutines used by all three of our parametric drawing programs.

SETSIZE.LSP

The program that manages the data retrieval process. The main function, SETSIZE, is the user interface function for the parametric drawing programs. It gets the part name, opens the data file, and uses GETSIZE to return the component data.

EL90-S.LSP

A parametric program that makes a 90-degree pipe elbow in side view.

DBLINE.LSP

DBLINE draws double line pipes between pipe fittings.

EL90-FB.LSP

A program that draws elbows in front and back views.

ATTFITS.LSP

The program file containing the ATTFIT and ATTLINE tools.

Chapter 13

**REPORT

A menu page added to the Chapter 12 IL12PARA.MNU. The following macros are on it.

[PIPING] and [FITTINGS] are macros that extract pipe length and fitting attributes from a drawing and call the Lotus 123 program.

[FTEXT IN] imports ASCII print file output from Lotus using the FTEXT AutoLISP program.

**TITLEBLK

A page of Chapter 11's IL11TITL.MNU which includes:

[REP STAT] and [PROTRAK] to call the REPSTAT.LSP and PRO_TRAK.EXE programs.

REPSTAT.LSP

REPSTAT generates a project-tracking record for the current drawing and adds to the master PROJECT.DAT file.

PRO_TRAK.EXE

A Clipper-compiled dBASE III program that tracks drawing information like project name and location, drawing number and revision level, dates of issue, plotting, last revision, and other project management details.

Chapter 14

SHOW3D.LSP

A visualization tool to help you study entities in 3D space.

IL-3D.LSP

A collection of functions for determining and manipulating points, lines, and curves in 3D space. Many of its subroutines are also useful for 2D. The subroutines include:

BANGLE, a 3D angle of inclination function.

3DPOLAR provides a 3D equivalent to the AutoLISP POLAR function.

3DP, a transparent user interface for the 3DPOLAR function.

RADIUS calculates the radius of an arc from its chord and altitude.

ARCLEN calculates an arc length given a radius and included angle.

INCANG calculates the included angle given the chord and radius.

ALTITD calculates altitude from the radius and included angle.

MID3D, an extra function on the IL DISK, which returns the midpoint of any 3D point.

VPOFF turns off all display controls that cause redraws. Otherwise, many editing operations in 3D cause unnecessary redraws of all viewports.

ZAXIS calculates an ECS extrusion vector from two points.

NEWECS translates planar entities from one coordinate system to another.

STK-PIPE.LSP

STK-PIPE is a command that converts line entities into extruded circles, to represent piping. It uses the ZAXIS and NEWECS subroutines.

ROUNDOFF.LSP

A file on the New Riders AutoLISP Utilities Disk 1 that contains functions for rounding off real numbers, points, and lists of real numbers to any precision between one and 14 significant digits.

GRPT.LSP

GRPT.LSP, also on the New Riders AutoLISP Utilities Disk 1, contains GRPT, a function that draws GRDRAW temporary points with any PDSIZE or PDMODE system variable setting. The points are drawn parallel to the plane of the display regardless of UCS.

Otherwise, points that are skewed or edge-on in 3D will be difficult to see.

Chapter 15

FTEXT.LSP

FTEXT.LSP contains C:FTEXT, which reads an external text file, formats the text to your specifications, and places it in the drawing.

BATCHSCR.LSP

The script batch builder. It contains:
GETFIL builds a list of file names from a wildcard search of the directories you specify.
GETSCR builds a list of AutoCAD commands in a script file format. It has special symbols that are replaced by file names from the GETFIL directory listing.
BATSCR builds scripts from directory listings.
C:MSCRIPT is a user interface which handles the input and formatting for BATSCR.

SLIDE.LSP

SLIDE.LSP contains two useful examples of specialized script building programs:
C:CSLIDE uses BATSCR to make a script that produces slide files from a directory listing.
C:SSLIDE makes a script to display each slide in a directory.

LBLOCK.LSP

LBLOCK is a command which automatically updates a library directory of wblocked "block" files from a single block library file. Also included is UPDSCR, which optionally creates UPDBLK.LSP and UPDBLK.SCR to update a group of drawing files with a directory of redefined blocks.

Chapter 16

[SPELL]

A macro that exports text entities to a DXF file, shells out to your word processor so you can run its spell checker, and then imports the corrected text.

FIX-TEXT.EXE

A simple utility program written in the BASIC language. By changing the color of associative dimension text, it gives you control over the plotted pen width of text.

Chapter 17

ANSI.SYS

ANSI.SYS is used to create our keyboard macro facility, consisting of:
ACAD.KEY, an external text file using ANSI.SYS to create macro keys for use with AutoCAD.
TOGGLE.KEY to toggle ANSI.SYS key definitions back off.
KILL.KEY to clear ANSI.SYS key definitions.

LSPSTRIP.EXE

A program that reduces an AutoLISP file's size by stripping comments and white space. It also provides a help display for AutoLISP programming.

MNUCRYPT.EXE

A program to encrypt menus, is available from Autodesk, Inc.

PROTECT.EXE

A program to encrypt AutoLISP files, is available from Autodesk, Inc.

KELV.EXE

KELV.EXE, also called the Kelvinator, strips white space and comments, and turn AutoLISP files into executable semi-gibberish. It is available from Autodesk, Inc.

GPATH.LSP

GPATH.LSP sets aliases for directory paths and loads the GPATH subroutine, which formats path and file name.

MLAYER

A subroutine that makes sure a layer is defined.

ERROR.LSP

ERROR.LSP is our error control and recovery program. It includes:
ERROR to evaluate errors, display an error message, and perform a list of error recovery tasks when an error occurs.
INITERR to initialize a default environment.
ADDERR to build a list of error recovery tasks.
DELERR to remove tasks from the list.
RESET, a function that uses the error function list to restore the drawing environment after normal program completion.

LEADTEXT.LSP

A multiple segment straight line leader program used to demonstrate our error handling. It includes:
C:S-LEAD to draw the polyline leader with the arrow head incorporated as part of the polyline.
L-TEXT to determine text placement and justification, and initiate a DTEXT command to place the text.

C:MFLY

An on-the-fly macro program to save and repeat a series of commands.

ILLOAD

A subroutine to manage file loading.

SELFLOAD.LSP

A tool to make self-loading commands and functions that conserve memory by not loading themselves until needed.

Configuration and Errors

Solving Setup, Memory, and Other Problems

There are a number of problems that you may encounter when setting up AutoCAD for use with this book. And there are a number of errors you may encounter when running your programs in AutoLISP. Comprehensive coverage of all of these topics is probably enough for another book. However, in this appendix, we will help you solve common problems and get you pointed in the right direction for the rest.

The Memory Management chapter and the Error Messages appendix of your AutoLISP Programmer's Reference, as well as the entire AutoCAD Installation and Performance Guide contain detailed information on these topics.

Selecting Text Editors

Any good text editor will work. It must create pure ASCII files, including the ASCII <ESCAPE> character. It must be able to merge files. And it must allow you to turn word wrap-off. Norton's Editor, our choice, includes all this and the following additional recommended features:

■ Quick loading, compact size. Quick saving and exit. Saves to another file name. Ability to handle large files. Merges files.

■ Has line and column number counter display. Will go to line number. Has row mode.

■ Includes block copy and move. Has versatile cursor control, delete, and undelete text features.

■ Compares files for differences. Has versatile search and replace, including finding matching punctuation, like: (([ ])).

The most valuable feature for AutoLISP is punctuation matching, to find your way when you get LISPed (Lost In Stupid Parentheses).

If your text editor cannot accept file paths, make a copy of your text editor in your IL-ACAD directory and permanently configure it for non-document mode. Be sure to keep word-wrap off.

If your text editor stores any of its format settings or modes, put a copy of your editor in the IL-ACAD directory to avoid any conflicts between settings for programming (like word-wrap mode) and the settings that you use for other purposes.

If your word processor uses too much memory to run under the SHELL command, see Chapter 13 in the Lotus section for instructions on setting up an expanded shell command that we call SHMAX.

If you have doubts about your DOS editor's ability to produce ASCII files, test it with the following steps.

Text Editor Test

With your editor, create a few screens full of text. Save the file to the name TEST.TXT and exit to DOS.

```
C:\IL-ACAD> COPY TEXT.TXT CON            Test it. All the text you entered scrolls by.
C:\IL-ACAD> DEL TEXT.TXT
```

Your text editor is okay if "COPY TEXT.TXT CON" showed text identical to what you typed in your editor, with no extra ^L or åÇäÆ characters or smiling faces! If you got any garbage, particularly at the top or bottom of the copy, then your text editor is not suitable, or is not configured correctly for ASCII output.

➡ *TIP: Make development menu that includes macros for editing menu and AutoLISP files. Have the macros shell out, load your editor with a specified file, and reload the MNU or LSP file upon re-entering AutoCAD. If you have to change directories to run your editor, have the macros call a batch file that changes directories, runs the editor and changes back. Failure to restore the current AutoCAD directory will cause errors.*

The DOS Bootup Environment

When the computer starts up, it reads two important files in the root directory: CONFIG.SYS and AUTOEXEC.BAT. (These files are not used in UNIX systems.) You need a CONFIG.SYS file and an AUTOEXEC.BAT file like those shown in Chapter 1 as a minimum for using the book. Additional explanations, possible additions to, and problems with these files are shown below.

If you use any AutoCAD ADI drivers, such as for your video display, you should install them in one of these files accordint to the manufacturer's instructions.

➡️ *NOTE: The CONFIG.SYS and AUTOEXEC.BAT changes do not take effect until you reboot (restart) your computer.*

CONFIG.SYS

We recommend that your file include the following lines. If you have a CONFIG.SYS file, display your file to examine it.

CONFIG.SYS

`C:\> COPY \CONFIG.SYS CON`	Copies the file to the CONsole, the screen. The recommended minimum includes:
`BUFFERS=32`	Use a number from 20 to 48.
`FILES=24`	
`BREAK=ON`	Allows <^C> and <BREAK> whenever possible.
`SHELL=C:\COMMAND.COM /P /E:512`	/E:512 is for DOS 3.2 or 3.3. Use /E:32 for DOS 3.0 or 3.1.
`DEVICE=C:\DOS\ANSI.SYS`	Allows use of extended character set.

You can edit or create CONFIG.SYS in your root directory using your ASCII text editor. First, back up your original file, if any. Use the discussion below to help you make any modifications.

The BUFFERS line allocates more RAM to hold your recently used data. If a program frequently accesses recently used data, buffers reduce disk accesses and increase speed. Each two-buffer increment steals 1K from the DOS memory available to your programs. You may have to use a smaller number if AutoCAD runs short of memory.

The BREAK line tells DOS to recognize a <BREAK> or <^C> key whenever possible.

The FILES line allocates more RAM to keep recently used files open. This reduces directory searching and increases data access speed. FILES uses very little memory, and a large value helps with AutoCAD and AutoLISP.

The SHELL line ensures adequate space for DOS environment variables. DOS allocates a small portion of RAM to store environment variable settings and information. AutoCAD and AutoLISP use several of these. If you use DOS 2.n, you will probably get an "Out of environment space" error and need to upgrade to DOS 3.n or later. For more information, or if you get errors with DOS 3.n, see Problems With DOS Environment Space, later in this appendix.

The ANSI.SYS line is necessary for some of the routines that you will develop in the book. It provides the full 256 ANSI character set, including all characters like åÇäÆ£Ü and Ç. It enables other functions, like screen cursor control and key redefinition, to work. You need to have the DOS file ANSI.SYS in your DOS directory, or you need to change the path in the ANSI.SYS line to wherever your ANSI.SYS file is located.

Setup Problems With CONFIG.SYS

If your CONFIG.SYS settings don't run smoothly, your only indication may be that things don't work. If you get the error message:

```
Bad or missing FILENAME
```

DOS can't find the file as it is specified. Check your spelling, and provide a full path. If you get:

```
Unrecognized command in CONFIG.SYS
```

It means that you made a syntax error, or your version of DOS doesn't support the specific command. Check your spelling.

Watch closely when you boot your system. These error messages flash by very quickly. If you suspect an error, but it flashes by too quickly, temporarily rename your AUTOEXEC.BAT file so that the system stops after loading CONFIG.SYS. You also can try to send the screen messages to the printer with your <CTRL-PRINTSCREEN> key as soon as DOS starts reading the CONFIG.SYS file. Another <CTRL-PRINTSCREEN> turns the printer echo off.

AUTOEXEC.BAT

AUTOEXEC.BAT is a batch file like any other, with one important exception: it is automatically executed every time the system is turned on. Like CONFIG.SYS, it must be in the root directory. We recommend that it include the lines shown below.

AUTOEXEC.BAT

```
C:\>COPY \AUTOEXEC.BAT CON          Examine it. It should include:

PROMPT $P$G
PATH C:\;C:\DOS;
```

You can edit or create AUTOEXEC.BAT in your root directory using your ASCII text editor. First, back up your original file, if any. Include the PROMPT and PATH lines similar to those above. You should use whatever is relevant to your setup. A more extensive sample of an autoexecuting batch file is shown in Appendix D, the Authors' Appendix.

Problems With AUTOEXEC.BAT

Errors in AUTOEXEC.BAT are hard to troubleshoot. Problems may include certain combinations of programs or the order in which they are loaded. Often, the system just doesn't behave as you think it should, and you must test by trial and error. Here are some troubleshooting tips for the most common problems:

- Isolate errors by temporarily editing your AUTOEXEC.BAT. Try using a leading colon to disable a suspected problem line:

```
: NOW DOS WILL IGNORE THIS LINE!
```

- Many AUTOEXEC.BAT files have echo to the screen turned off by the command ECHO OFF or @ECHO OFF. To disable ECHO OFF and see what the AUTOEXEC.BAT file is doing, put a leading colon on the line.

- Echo to the printer. Hit <CTRL-PRINTSCREEN> while booting to see what is happening. Another <CTRL-PRINTSCREEN> turns the printer echo off.

- Make sure PROMPT, PATH, and other environment settings precede any TSR (memory resident) programs in the file.

- Check your PATH for completeness and syntax. Unsophisticated programs that require support or overlay files in addition to their EXE or COM files may not work, even if they are in the PATH. Directories do not need to be in the PATH, unless you want to execute files in them from other directories.

- APPEND (DOS 3.3 or later) works like PATH and lets programs find their support and overlay files in other directories. It uses about 5K of RAM. All files in an appended directory are recognized by programs as if they were in the current directory. If you use APPEND, *use it cautiously*. If you modify an appended file, the modified file will be written to the current directory, *not* the appended directory. Loading an AutoCAD.MNU file from an appended directory creates an MNX file in the current directory. AutoCAD searches an appended directory before completing its normal directory search pattern, so appended support files will get loaded instead of those in the current directory.

- SET environment errors are often obscure. Type SET <RETURN> to see your current environment settings. If a setting is truncated or missing, you probably are out of environment space. Fix it in your CONFIG.SYS file. Do not use extraneous spaces in a SET statement:

```
SET ACADCFG=\IL-ACAD     Okay. Sets "ACADCFG" to "\IL-ACAD"
SET ACADCFG =\IL-ACAD    Wrong. Sets "ACADCFG "
SET ACADCFG= \IL-ACAD    Wrong. Sets to " \IL-ACAD"
```

■ If your AUTOEXEC.BAT doesn't seem to complete its execution, you may have tried to execute another BAT file from your AUTOEXEC.BAT file. If you nest execution of BAT files, the second one will take over and the first will not complete. There are two ways to nest BATs. With DOS 3.0 and later, use:

```
COMMAND /C NAME
```

NAME is the name of the nested BAT file. With DOS 3.3, use:

```
CALL NAME
```

■ If you are fighting for memory, insert temporary lines in the AUTOEXEC.BAT to check your available memory. Once you determine what uses how much, you can decide what to sacrifice. Use:

```
CHKDSK
PAUSE
```

at appropriate points. Reboot to see the effect. Remove the lines when you're done. We use an alternative FREEWARE program called MEM.COM. It reports available RAM, quickly.

■ If you have unusual occurrences or lockups, and you use TSRs, suspect the TSRs as your problem source. Cause and effect may be hard to pin down. For example, there is a simple screen capture program that, if loaded, locks up our word processor — even when inactive! Disable TSRs one at a time in your AUTOEXEC file. Reboot and test.

Problems With DOS Environment Space

Running out of space to store DOS environment settings may give the error:

```
Out of environment space
```

You may see this message during a batch file. An environment space problem also may show up in unusual ways, such as a program failing to execute, AutoLISP not having room to load, or a block insertion not finding its block. This occurs because the PATH, AutoCAD settings limiting extended or expanded memory, and AutoCAD configuration, memory, and support file settings are all environment settings.

To find out how much environment space you need:

■ Type SET>TEMP.$ at the DOS prompt.

■ List the TEMP.$ file with the directory command. The file size is the number of characters. Delete the file.

■ Add the number of characters for new SET statements. Include revisions to your AUTOEXEC.BAT and startup files, like IL.BAT.

■ Add a safety margin of 10 percent.

For INSIDE AutoLISP, you need about 240 bytes (characters), plus whatever your system requires for other uses. DOS defaults environment size to 160 bytes or less, depending on the DOS version. The space expands if you type in settings, but cannot expand during execution of a BAT file, including your AUTOEXEC.BAT. Loading a TSR (memory resident) program or utility such as SIDEKICK, PROKEY, some RAM disks and print buffers, the DOS PRINT or GRAPHICS commands, and other utilities freezes the environment space to the current size.

Fortunately, DOS 3.0 or later versions can easily expand the space. Add this line to your CONFIG.SYS:

```
SHELL = C:\COMMAND.COM /P /E=nnn
```

Substitute your boot drive for "C:" if your boot drive isn't C. Do not use *nnn*; replace *nnn* with an integer value:

■ For DOS 3.0 and 3.1, *nnn* is the desired environment size divided by 16. If you want 512 bytes, use 32 since 512 divided by 16 equals 32. The maximum for *nnn* is 62.

■ For DOS 3.2 and 3.3, *nnn* is the actual size setting. For 512 bytes, use 512. The maximum for *nnn* is 32768.

If you must use DOS 2, your solution is more difficult.

Using DOS 2

We do not recommend DOS 2. If you do use it, you'll probably encounter environment space problems. In the book CUSTOMIZING AutoCAD, we describe a work-around technique to expand your DOS 2 environment space to 512 bytes. It requires making a permanent change to your COMMAND.COM file with the DOS DEBUG program.

Memory Settings and Problems

There are several DOS environment settings that deal with AutoCAD's memory usage. These settings are explained and shown in the memory usage chart in the AutoCAD Installation and Performance Guide. None of AutoCAD's settings affect other programs or tie up memory when AutoCAD is not running. The AutoCAD status command shows several memory values:

```
Free RAM:  9784 bytes        Free disk: 1409024 bytes
I/O page space: 109K bytes   Extended I/O page space: 592K
                             bytes
```

"Free RAM" is the unused portion of RAM for AutoCAD to work in. "I/O page space" is RAM used by AutoCAD to swap data in and out. An I/O page value of 60K or more is adequate for most use, and we've worked (slowly!) with values under 20K. Too little makes AutoCAD page data to disk or extended I/O page space. Too much extended I/O page space can also cause problems with regular I/O page space, as explained below.

"Extended I/O page space" uses extended or expanded memory as swap space. Extended memory is IBM AT-style memory above the 1 Mb mark. It's often used for RAM disks (VDISK), print buffers (PRINT), and a few other programs, like AutoCAD. Expanded memory is Intel Above Board style memory above the 640K mark. It is also known as LIM and EMS memory. It's used for RAM disks, print buffers, and for page swapping by many programs.

It may take some investigation to determine which type of memory you have. You often can configure Intel Above Boards and their imitators as expanded or extended memory. Expanded memory is relatively clean, with established techniques for programs to share it. Unfortunately, extended memory lacks protection. Programs wishing to use it are not always able to tell if it's already in use by another program. See the SET Environment Memory Settings section below.

Even if you don't encounter crashes, you may want to examine your memory usage. AutoCAD uses up some free RAM to enable extended I/O page space. If you have 2 Mb or more of extended or expanded memory, you may need to actually restrict AutoCAD's use of it. Each Kbyte of extended I/O page space reduces free RAM by 16 bytes.

SET Environment Memory Settings

In addition to the SET ACAD=*path* and SET ACADCFG=*path* directory settings, AutoCAD has several memory environment settings to limit, direct, and avoid problems in memory use. The complete set is:

```
SET ACADFREERAM=value    Sets size for working memory.
SET ACADXMEM=value       Limits AutoCAD's extended memory use.
SET ACADLIMEM=value      Limits AutoCAD's expanded memory use.
SET LISPHEAP=value       AutoLISP memory, see Chapter 17.
SET LISPSTACK=value      AutoLISP memory, see Chapter 17.
SET LISPXMEM=value       Limits ExtLISP's extended memory use.
```

The following discussion will get you started, but see your AutoCAD Installation and Performance Guide and README.DOC file for details, and for the values to use. Some settings may change between versions.

"SET ACADFREERAM=" reserves RAM for AutoCAD's working space, of which I/O page space is a portion. Too small a size can cause "Out of RAM" errors, slow down spline fitting, and cause problems with AutoCAD's HIDE, TRIM, and OFFSET commands. However, a large ACADFREERAM setting reduces I/O page swap space and slows down AutoCAD. The default is 14K; the maximum depends on the system, usually about 24 to 28K. A setting larger than the maximum gives you the maximum. There is no magic number, so experiment.

"SET ACADXMEM=" can be set to limit or avoid conflicts in AutoCAD's use of extended memory. If you use extended memory and get unexplained crashes or random errors, you may have a memory conflict between programs. Check to see what, if any, programs other than AutoCAD may be using your extended memory. In particular, check for DOS VDISK and PRINT. Check your CONFIG.SYS and AUTOEXEC.BAT. Figure out what addresses are in use so that you can set AutoCAD to avoid the conflict.

"SET ACADLIMEM=" configures expanded memory usage (LIM-EMS). This setting is probably not critical, since EMS avoids conflicts.

"SET ACADXMEM=" limits or avoids conflicts in ExtLISP's (EXTended AutoLISP's) use of extended memory. All of the above SET ACADXMEM comments apply to it. See your EXTLISP.DOC file for the latest information, because extended memory control has undergone recent changes. If you have problems, get the latest version of ExtLISP.

Using INSIDE AutoLISP With a RAM Disk

Running AutoCAD from a RAM disk can be more efficient than using extended/expanded memory for I/O page space. If you want to run AutoCAD from a RAM disk, there are three things to look at: AutoCAD's program files, temporary files, and the drawing itself.

AutoCAD locates its temporary files on the same drive and directory as the drawing, unless you tell it otherwise. Using the configuration menu, select Item 8 (Configure operating parameters). Then choose Item 5 (Placement of temporary files). Item 5 defaults to <DRAWING>, for the drawing's directory. You can reset this to a RAM disk and locate your temporary files there. If you use a RAM disk, we recommend allowing about two times the size of your largest drawing.

Regardless of the temporary file setting, AutoCAD still locates the temporary file (that eventually becomes the new drawing file) in the directory of the drawing file itself. This occurs because AutoCAD just closes up the files instead of copying them when the drawing is ended.

To speed drawing disk access, you can edit the drawing from your RAM disk. Make sure the finished drawing is copied back to a real drive. Use a menu macro, or redefine the END command for safety. If you have sufficient I/O page space, you won't gain much by putting the drawing on a RAM disk.

The easiest way to put the AutoCAD program on RAM disk is to copy all files to it. This may waste a little memory, but if you have plenty, it works. Make sure that you have set a real disk directory with SET ACADCFG=, ensuring any configuration changes are made on a real disk.

If you want to place AutoCAD on the RAM disk but need to conserve RAM disk space, selectively copy AutoCAD's files to it. There is little advantage to putting support files or the ACAD.EXE file on a RAM disk. Start with the OVL files. They're listed under Software Installation in your AutoCAD Installation and Performance Guide. The most important are: ACAD.OVL, ACAD0.OVL, and ACADVS.OVL. The ACAD2.OVL and ACAD3.OVL contain ADE2 and ADE3 commands, and the ACADL.OVL is AutoLISP. If you have to decide between them, refer to the AutoCAD Reference Manual's appendix on commands. Decide whether you use ADE2 or ADE3 commands the most.

Make sure that the files copied to the RAM disk are not included in the \ACAD directory of your hard disk. Put them in an \ACAD\RAM directory. Let's assume that you have the following drives and directories:

```
C:                          Hard disk.
D:                          RAM disk.
C:\ACAD                     Standard ACAD support files and
                            program files except the OVL files.
C:\ACAD\RAM                 AutoCAD OVL files to go on RAM disk.
C:\SUPFILES                 Project-specific support files.
C:\PROJECT                  Working drawing project directory.
C:\CFGFILES                 Specific configuration.
```

If D: is on your PATH, and you have copied the OVL files to D:, you start AutoCAD this way:

```
SET ACAD=SUPFILES
SET ACADCFG=CFGFILES
C:\ACAD\ACAD
```

This should work fine. AutoCAD will find its needed files. The \ACAD\ACAD explicitly tells DOS to look in the \ACAD directory for the ACAD.EXE file. AutoCAD will also look there for OVL files and remember it for support files. AutoCAD is smart, and searches the PATH to find its other needed support files. Since D: is on the PATH, it finds its OVLs, and remembers D: as a possible source of support files.

If your path is wrong, or if a file is in neither \ACAD or D:, you will get:

```
Can't find overlay file ACAD0.OVL.
Enter file name prefix (path name\ or X:) or '.' to quit=
```

See your AutoCAD Installation and Performance Guide for additional information and cautions.

Current Directory and Wrong Support File Errors

If you use SHELL to change directories (CD) from inside AutoCAD, you may get strange results. Parts of AutoCAD recognize the change and parts do not. New drawings will not default to the new current directory, yet drawings saved with SAVE will observe the directory change. Subsequent attempts to load support files, such as MNX files, can cause AutoCAD to crash. If you must change a directory on SHELL excursions, automate it with a batch file that returns to the original directory.

AutoCAD searches for support files in the following order:

```
Current AutoCAD directory.
Current drawing's directory.
SET ACAD=directory environment variable, if any.
ACAD*.OVL file directory.
ACAD.EXE directory.
```

If you get a support file from a directory other than the one you wanted, check AutoCAD's search order by typing a phony menu name at the MENU command prompt. To AutoCAD, the current directory is the one that was current at the time the ACAD.EXE file was executed.

If you keep AutoCAD's search order in mind, it will help you avoid errors in finding the wrong support files. If you have multiple AutoCAD configurations or support directory setups, a common cause of finding the wrong support files is a leftover SET ACAD=*somename* in one of your startup batch files. Make sure to SET ACAD= to clear it at the end of each batch file. Also clear your SET ACADCFG= settings.

SHELL Errors

Here are some common errors encountered when using SHELL:

```
SHELL error swapping to disk
```

This is most likely caused by insufficient disk space. Remember, AutoCAD's temporary files can easily use a megabyte of disk space.

```
SHELL error: insufficient memory for command
```

This can be caused by an ill-behaved program executed before entering AutoCAD or during a previous shell. Some ill-behaved programs leave a dirty environment behind that causes AutoCAD to erroneously believe insufficient memory exists.

```
Unable to load program: insufficient memory
Program too big to fit in memory
```

If SHELL got this far, these are correct messages. You need to modify your ACAD.PGP to allocate more memory space for program.

```
SHELL error in EXEC function (insufficient memory)
```

This can be caused by the shell memory allocation being too small to load DOS. Exactly how much memory you need to allocate depends on your versions of DOS and AutoCAD, and on what you have in your CONFIG.SYS file. DOS 3.2 and later versions must have at least 25000 bytes allocated in the ACAD.PGP. Use 30000 to give a little cushion.

Common AutoLISP Errors

The AutoLISP Programmer's Reference gives a complete listing of error messages. The following list gives a few hints of where and how to look for other causes.

```
error: invalid dotted pair
error: misplaced dot
```

Look for a missing or an extra quotation mark above the apparent error location. Look for " imbedded in a string where it should be \". Look for strings that exceed 132 characters, because they will truncate.

n>   prompts such as   **3**>

Look for the same quotation mark errors as shown in the dot errors example. Look for a missing closing parenthesis. If the error occurs while you are loading an LSP file, look in the file.

```
Unknown command
```

This may be caused by AutoLISP, if you have a COMMAND function containing a "" pair of double quotes. They try to repeat the last command *entered at the ACAD prompt*, not the last command sent to ACAD via the COMMAND function.

Miscellaneous Problems

If you run under a multi-tasking environment like CAROUSEL or DESKVIEW, you may get an error claiming a file should be in a directory it never was in. For example, you may get:

```
Can't find overlay file D:\JOB231\ACAD.OVL
Retry, Abort?
```

Don't type an "A" unless you give up. Type "R" to retry. If that doesn't work, flip partitions and copy the file to the directory listed in the error message. You may need to hit another "R" during the flip. Copy the file, flip back and try "R" again.

```
Expanded memory disabled
```

When starting ACAD from DOS, this error can be caused by a previously crashed AutoCAD. Sometimes a crashed AutoCAD, or another program, does not clear its claim on expanded memory. This causes the program to think none is available. Reboot to clear it.

Insufficient File Errors

You may encounter file error messages due to AutoCAD's inability to open a file. This may be caused by too few files requested in the FILES= statement of the CONFIG.SYS file, or by AutoLISP's OPEN function leaving too many files open. If you repeatedly crash an AutoLISP routine which opens files, you may see the following:

```
Command: (load "test")
Can't open "test.lsp" for input
error: LOAD failed
(load "test")
```

If you know the variable names set to the files, try to CLOSE them to free up files. Otherwise, you have little choice but to QUIT AutoCAD and reboot the system to clean things up. This error can also show up as:

```
Can't find overlay file C:\ACAD\ACAD.OVL
```
Or any other file.

Tracing and Curing Errors

You and your users are your best sources for error diagnosis. When problems occur, log them so you can recognize patterns. Some tips are:

- Use screen capture programs to document the text screen.

- Dump the screen to the printer.

- Write down what you did in as much detail as possible, as far back as you can remember.

- Dump a copy of AutoCAD's STATUS screen to the printer.

- Check the DOS SET command settings and current directory via SHELL.

Avoidance is the best cure.

Reference Tables

This appendix provides annotated tables of the AutoCAD system variables, entity DXF group codes, and table DXF group codes. You will also find a handy reference guide to all of the standard AutoLISP functions.

AutoCAD System Variables

Use the AutoCAD System Variables Table to decipher AutoCAD drawing environment settings. The table presents all the variable settings available through the AutoCAD SETVAR command or the AutoLISP SETVAR and GETVAR functions. The system variable name and the default ACAD prototype drawing settings are shown. A brief description is given of each variable and the meaning of flag codes. Some variables are read-only and are noted as **<RO>**. All values are saved with the drawing unless noted with **<CFG>** for ConFiGuration, or **<NS>** for Not Saved.

The AutoCAD System Variables Table starts on the next page.

AutoCAD System Variables

VARIABLE NAME	DEFAULT SETTING	DEFAULT MEANING	COMMAND NAME	VARIABLE DESCRIPTION
ACADPREFIX	"C:\ACAD\"			AutoCAD directory path **\<NS>,\<RO>**
ACADVER	"10"			AutoCAD release version **\<RO>**
AFLAGS	0		ATTDEF	Sum of: Invisible=1 Constant=2 Verify=4 Preset=8
ANGBASE	0	EAST	UNITS	Direction of angle 0
ANGDIR	0	CCW	UNITS	Clockwise=1 Counter clockwise=0
APERTURE	10	10	APERTURE	Half of aperture height in pixels **\<CFG>**
AREA	0.0000		AREA,LIST	Last computed area **\<NS>,\<RO>**
ATTDIA	0	PROMPTS		Insert uses: DDATTE dialogue box=1 Attribute prompts=0
ATTMODE	1	ON	ATTDISP	Attribute display Normal=1 ON=2 OFF=0
ATTREQ	1	PROMPTS		Insert uses: Prompts=1 Defaults=0
AUNITS	0	DEC. DEG.	UNITS	Angular units Dec=0 Deg=1 Grad=2 Rad=3 Survey=4
AUPREC	0	0	UNITS	Angular units decimal places
AXISMODE	0	OFF	AXIS	Axis ON=1 Axis OFF=0
AXISUNIT	0.0000,0.0000		AXIS	Axis X,Y Increment
BACKZ	0.0000		DVIEW	Back clipping plane offset - See VIEWMODE **\<RO>**
BLIPMODE	1	ON	BLIPMODE	Blips=1 No Blips=0
CDATE	19881202.144648898		TIME	Date.Time **\<NS>,\<RO>**
CECOLOR	"BYLAYER"		COLOR	Current entity color **\<RO>**
CELTYPE	"BYLAYER"		LINETYPE	Current entity linetype **\<RO>**
CHAMFERA	0.0000		CHAMFER	Chamfer distance for A
CHAMFERB	0.0000		CHAMFER	Chamfer distance for B
CLAYER	"0"		LAYER	Current layer **\<RO>**
CMDECHO	1	ECHO	SETVAR	Command echo in AutoLISP Echo=1 No Echo=0 **\<NS>**
COORDS	0	OFF	[^D] [F6]	Update display Picks=0 ON=1 Dist>Angle=2
CVPORT	1		VPORTS	Identification number of the current viewport
DATE	2447498.61620926		TIME	Julian time **\<NS>,\<RO>**
DIMALT	0	OFF	DIMALT	Use alternate units ON=1 OFF=0
DIMALTD	2	0.00	DIMALTD	Decimal precision of alternate units
DIMALTF	25.4000		DIMALTF	Scale factor for alternate units
DIMAPOST	""	NONE	DIMAPOST	Suffix for alternate dimensions **\<RO>**
DIMASO	1	ON	DIMASO	Associative=1 Line,Arrow,Text=0
DIMASZ	0.1800		DIMASZ	Arrow Size=Value (also controls text fit)
DIMBLK	""	NONE	DIMBLK	Block name to draw instead of arrow or tick **\<RO>**
DIMBLK1	""	NONE	DIMBLK1	Block name for 1st end, see DIMSAH **\<RO>**
DIMBLK2	""	NONE	DIMBLK2	Block name for 2nd end, see DIMSAH **\<RO>**
DIMCEN	0.0900	MARK	DIMCEN	Center mark size=Value Add center lines=Negative
DIMDLE	0.0000	NONE	DIMDLE	Dimension line extension=Value
DIMDLI	0.3800		DIMDLI	Increment between continuing dimension lines
DIMEXE	0.1800		DIMEXE	Extension distance for extension lines=Value
DIMEXO	0.0625		DIMEXO	Offset distance for extension lines=Value
DIMLFAC	1.0000	NORMAL	DIMLFAC	Overall linear distance factor=Value
DIMLIM	0	OFF	DIMLIM	Add tolerance limits ON=1 OFF=0
DIMPOST	""	NONE	DIMPOST	User defined dimension suffix (eg: "mm") **\<RO>**
DIMRND	0.0000	EXACT	DIMRND	Rounding value for linear dimensions
DIMSAH	0	OFF	DIMSAH	Allow separate DIMBLKS ON=1 OFF=0
DIMSCALE	1.0000		DIMSCALE	Overall dimensioning scale factor=Value
DIMSE1	0	OFF	DIMSE1	Suppress extension line 1 Omit=1 Draw=0
DIMSE2	0	OFF	DIMSE2	Suppress extension line 2 Omit=1 Draw=0
DIMSHO	0	OFF	DIMSHO	Show associative dimension while dragging
DIMSOXD	0	OFF	DIMSOXD	Suppress dim. lines outside extension lines Omit=1 Draw=0
DIMTAD	0	OFF	DIMTAD	Text above dim. line ON=1 OFF(in line)=0

VARIABLE NAME	DEFAULT SETTING	DEFAULT MEANING	COMMAND NAME	VARIABLE DESCRIPTION
DIMTIH	1	ON	DIMTIH	Text inside horizontal ON=1 OFF(aligned)=0
DIMTIX	0	OFF	DIMTIX	Force text inside extension lines ON=1 OFF=0
DIMTM	0.0000	NONE	DIMTM	Minus tolerance=Value
DIMTOFL	0	OFF	DIMTOFL	Draw dim. line even if text outside ext. lines
DIMTOH	1	ON	DIMTOH	Text outside horizontal ON=1 OFF(aligned)=0
DIMTOL	0	OFF	DIMTOL	Append tolerance ON=1 OFF=2
DIMTP	0.0000	NONE	DIMTP	Plus tolerance=Value
DIMTSZ	0.0000	ARROWS	DIMTSZ	Tick size=Value Draw arrows=0
DIMTVP	0.0000		DIMTVP	Text vertical position
DIMTXT	0.1800		DIMTXT	Text size=Value
DIMZIN	0		DIMZIN	Controls leading zero (see AutoCAD manual)
DISTANCE	0.0000		DIST	Last computed distance **<NS>**, **<RO>**
DRAGMODE	2	AUTO	DRAGMODE	OFF=0 Enabled=1 Auto=2
DRAGP1	10		SETVAR	Drag regen rate **<CFG>**
DRAGP2	25		SETVAR	Drag input rate **<CFG>**
DWGNAME	"TEST"			Current drawing name **<RO>**
DWGPREFIX	"C:\IA-ACAD\"			Directory path of current drawing **<NS>**, **<RO>**
ELEVATION	0.0000		ELEV	Current default elevation
EXPERT	0	NORMAL	SETVAR	Suppresses "Are you sure" prompts (See AutoCAD Reference Manual)
EXTMAX	−1.0000E+20,−1.0000E+20			Upper right drawing extents X,Y **<RO>**
EXTMIN	1.0000E+20,1.0000E+20			Lower left drawing extents X,Y **<RO>**
FILLETRAD	0.0000		FILLET	Current fillet radius
FILLMODE	1		FILL	Fill ON=1 Fill OFF=0
FLATLAND	0		SETVAR	Temporary 3D compatibility setting act like Release 9=1 R10=0
FRONTZ	0.0000		DVIEW	Front clipping plane offset - See VIEWMODE **<RO>**
GRIDMODE	0	OFF	GRID	Grid ON=1 Grid OFF=0
GRIDUNIT	0.0000,0.0000		GRID	X,Y grid increment
HANDLES	0		HANDLES	Entity handles Enabled=1 Disabled=0 **<RO>**
HIGHLIGHT	1		SETVAR	Highlight selection ON=1 OFF=0 **<NS>**
INSBASE	0.0000,0.0000		BASE	Insert base point of current drawing X,Y
LASTANGLE	0		ARC	Last angle of the last arc **<NS>**, **<RO>**
LASTPOINT	0.0000,0.0000			Last @ pickpoint X,Y **<NS>**
LASTPT3D	0.0000,0.0000,0.0000			Last @ pickpoint X,Y,Z **<NS>**
LENSLENGTH	50.0000		DVIEW	Length of lens in perspective in millimeters **<RO>**
LIMCHECK	0	OFF	LIMITS	Limits error check ON=1 OFF=0
LIMMAX	12.0000,9.0000		LIMITS	Upper right X,Y limit
LIMMIN	0.0000,0.0000		LIMITS	Lower left X,Y limit
LTSCALE	1.0000		LTSCALE	Current linetype scale
LUNITS	2	DEC.	UNITS	Linear units: Scientific=1 Dec=2 Eng=3 Arch=4 Frac=5
LUPREC	4	0.0000	UNITS	Unit precision decimal places or denominator
MENUECHO	0	NORMAL	SETVAR	Normal=0 Suppress echo of menu items=1 No prompts=2 No input or prompts=3 **<NS>**
MENUNAME	"ACAD"		MENU	Current menu name **<RO>**
MIRRTEXT	1	YES	SETVAR	Retain text direction=0 Reflect text=1
ORTHOMODE	0	OFF	[^O] [F8]	Ortho ON=1 Ortho OFF=0
OSMODE	0	NONE	OSNAP	Sum of: Endp=1 Mid=2 Cen=4 Node=8 Quad=16 Int=32 Ins=64 Perp=128 Tan=256 Near=512 Quick=1024
PDMODE	0	POINT	SETVAR	Controls style of points drawn
PDSIZE	0.0000	POINT	SETVAR	Controls size of points
PERIMETER	0.0000		AREA,LIST	Last computed perimeter **<NS>**, **<RO>**

VARIABLE NAME	DEFAULT SETTING	DEFAULT MEANING	COMMAND NAME	VARIABLE DESCRIPTION
PICKBOX	3		SETVAR	Half the pickbox size in pixels <CFG>
POPUPS	1			AUI Support=1 No Support=0 <NS>,<RO>
QTEXTMODE	0	OFF	QTEXT	Qtext ON=1 Qtext OFF=0
REGENMODE	1	ON	REGENAUTO	Regenauto ON=1 Regenauto OFF=0
SCREENSIZE	570.0000,410.0000			Size of display in X,Y pixels <NS>,<RO>
SKETCHINC	0.1000		SKETCH	Recording increment for sketch
SKPOLY	0	LINE	SETVAR	Polylines=1 Sketch with Line=0
SNAPANG	0		SNAP	Angle of SNAP/GRID rotation
SNAPBASE	0.0000,0.0000		SNAP	X,Y base point of SNAP/GRID rotation
SNAPISOPAIR	0	LEFT	SNAP [^E]	Isoplane Left=0 Top=1 Right=2
SNAPMODE	0	OFF	SNAP [^B] [F9]	Snap ON=1 Snap OFF=0
SNAPSTYL	0	STD	SNAP	Isometric=1 Snap standard=0
SNAPUNIT	1.0000,1.0000		SNAP	Snap X,Y increment
SPLFRAME	0		SETVAR	Display spline frame ON=1 OFF=0
SPLINESEGS	8		SETVAR	Number of line segments in each spline segment
SPLINETYPE	6	CUBIC	SETVAR	Pedit spline generates: Quadratic B-Spline=5 Cubic B-Spline=6
SURFTAB1	6		SETVAR	Rulesurf and tabsurf tabulations, also revsurf and edgesurf M density
SURFTAB2	6		SETVAR	Revsurf and edgesurf N density
SURFTYPE	6	CUBIC	SETVAR	Pedit smooth surface generates: Quadratic B-Spline=5 Cubic B-Spline=6 Bezier=8
SURFU	6		SETVAR	M direction surface density
SURFV	6		SETVAR	N direction surface density
TARGET	0.0000,0.0000,0.0000		DVIEW	UCS coords of current viewport target point <RO>
TDCREATE	2447498.61620031		TIME	Creation time (Julian) <RO>
TDINDWG	0.00436285		TIME	Total editing time <RO>
TDUPDATE	2447498.61620031		TIME	Time of last save or update <RO>
TDUSRTIMER	0.00436667		TIME	User set elapsed time <RO>
TEMPPREFIX	""			Directory location of AutoCAD's temporary files, defaults to drawing directory <NS>,<RO>
TEXTEVAL	0	TEXT	SETVAR	Evaluate leading "(" and "!" in text input as: Text=0 AutoLISP=1 <NS>
TEXTSIZE	0.2000		TEXT	Current text height
TEXTSTYLE	"STANDARD"		TEXT,STYLE	Current text style <RO>
THICKNESS	0.0000		ELEV	Current 3D extrusion thickness
TRACEWID	0.0500		TRACE	Current width of traces
UCSFOLLOW	0		SETVAR	Automatic plan view in new UCS=1 Off=0
UCSICON	1		UCSICON	Sum of: Off=0 On=1 Origin=2
UCSNAME	""		UCS	Name of current UCS Unnamed="" <RO>
UCSORG	0.0000,0.0000,0.0000		UCS	WCS origin of current UCS <RO>
UCSXDIR	1.0000,0.0000,0.0000		UCS	X direction of current UCS <RO>
UCSYDIR	0.0000,1.0000,0.0000		UCS	Y direction of current UCS <RO>
USERI1 - 5	0			User integer variables USERI1 to USERI5
USERR1 - 5	0.0000			User real variables USERR1 to USERR5
VIEWCTR	6.2518,4.5000		ZOOM,PAN,VIEW	X,Y center point of current view <RO>
VIEWDIR	0.0000,0.0000,1.0000		DVIEW	Camera point offset from target in WCS <RO>
VIEWMODE	0		DVIEW,UCS	Perspective and clipping settings, see AutoCAD Reference Manual <RO>
VIEWSIZE	9.0000		ZOOM,PAN,VIEW	Height of current view <RO>
VIEWTWIST	0		DVIEW	View twist angle <RO>
VPOINTX	0.0000		VPOINT	X coordinate of VPOINT <RO>
VPOINTY	0.0000		VPOINT	Y coordinate of VPOINT <RO>

VARIABLE NAME	DEFAULT SETTING	DEFAULT MEANING	COMMAND NAME	VARIABLE DESCRIPTION
VPOINTZ	1.0000		VPOINT	Z coordinate of VPOINT **<RO>**
VSMAX	12.5036,9.0000,0.0000			ZOOM,PAN,VIEW
				Upper right of virtual screen X,Y **<NS>**,**<RO>**
VSMIN	0.0000,0.0000,0.0000			ZOOM,PAN,VIEW
				Lower left of virtual screen X,Y **<NS>**,**<RO>**
WORLDUCS	1		UCS	UCS equals WCS=1 UCS not equal to WCS=0 **<RO>**
WORLDVIEW	1		DVIEW,UCS	Dview and VPoint coordinate input: WCS=1 UCS=0

<NS> Not Saved   **<CFG>** Configure File   **<RO>** Read Only

Table and Entity DXF Group Codes

Use the following tables of DXF group codes when processing AutoCAD entities and reference tables. The DXF group codes apply to both data returned by AutoLISP and DXF (Drawing eXchange Format) output files created with the DXFOUT command. A DXF "group" has two parts. The DXF code, an integer number from 0 to 74, identifies the data type. It is always followed by the data value. While identical numbers are used both with AutoLISP and DXF files, the data elements of a DXF group are not identical. See the chapters on entity access (6), table access (7) and DXF (16) for complete details.

AutoLISP returns point coordinates as one data value, such as (2.0 1.0 0.0). In AutoLISP, the 10, 20, and 30 DXF group codes of a point are combined under one 10 code. The DXF file lists each point coordinate separately, like:

```
    10
 2.000000
    20
 1.000000
    30
 0.000000
```

DXF files do not save entity names. AutoLISP uses entity names to index the entities of a drawing. Entity names are included in the returned data. They are preceded by negative DXF code numbers, like -1 or -2. These are temporary entity names that are uniquely assigned at the start of each drawing edit.

Entity properties like elevation, thickness, linetype, and color are not stored in the DXF file or returned by AutoLISP unless they are explicitly set to a value other than the default. The default values are 0 for elevation and thickness and BYLAYER for linetype and color.

ENTITY DXF GROUP CODES

LN = LINE PT = POINT CI = CIRCLE AR = ARC TR = TRACE SD = SOLID TX = TEXT 3F = 3DFACE
SH = SHAPE SQ = SEQEND IN = INSERT AD = ATTDEF AT = ATTRIB PL = POLYLINE VT = VERTEX DM = DIMENSION

ENTITIES

CODE	DESCRIPTION	LN	PT	CI	AR	TR	SD	TX	SH	IN	AD	AT	PL	VT	DM	3F	SQ
0	Entity Type																
-1	Entity Name (Primary)	-1	-1	-1	-1	-1	-1	-1	-1	-1	-1	-1	-1	-1	-1	-1	-1
-2	Entity Name (Secondary)														-1		-2
1	Primary Text Value							1			1	1			1		
2	Name: Shape, Block, Tag								2	2	2	2			2		
3	Prompt String										3						
5	Handle (Hexadecimal String)	5	5	5	5	5	5	5	5	5	5	5	5	5	5	5	5
6	Linetype Name	6	6	6	6	6	6	6	6	6	6	6	6	6	6	6	6
7	Text Style Name							7			7	7					
8	Layer Name	8	8	8	8	8	8	8	8	8	8	8	8	8	8	8	8
10	X of Start or Insert Point	10	10					10	10	10	10	10		10			
	X of Center Point			10	10												
	X of Corner Point					10	10									10	
	X of Definition Point														10		
	X of Elev. Point (2D Poly)												10				
11	X of End or Insert Point	11															
	X of Corner Point					11	11									11	
	X of Alignment Point							11			11	11					
	X of Middle Point of Dim.														11		
12	X of Corner Point					12	12									12	
	X of Insert Point														12		
13	X of Corner Point					13	13									13	
	X of Definition Point														13		
14	X of Definition Point														14		
15	X of Definition Point														15		
16	X of Definition Point														16		
20	Y of Start or Insert Point	20	20					20	20	20	20	20		20			
	Y of Center Point			20	20												
	Y of Corner Point					20	20									20	
	Y of Definition Point														20		
	Y of Elev. Point (2D Poly)												20				
21	Y of End or Insert Point	21															
	Y of Corner Point					21	21									21	
	Y of Alignment Point							21			21	21					
	Y of Middle Point of Dim.														21		
22	Y of Corner Point					22	22									22	
	Y of Insert Point														22		
23	Y of Corner Point					23	23									23	
	Y of Definition Point														23		
24	Y of Definition Point														24		
25	Y of Definition Point														25		
26	Y of Definition Point														26		
30	Z of Start or Insert Point	30	30					30	30	30	30	30		30	30		
	Z of Center Point			30	30												

Code	Description	Group code values (across entity columns)
	Z of Corner Point	30 30
	Z of Definition Point	30 30
	Z of Elev. Point (2D Poly)	31
31	Z of End Point	31 31 31
	Z of Corner Point	31 31
	Z of Alignment Point	32
32	Z of Middle Point of Dim.	32 32
	Z of Corner Point	33 33 33
33	Z of Insert Point	33
	Z of Corner Point	33
34	Z of Definition Point	33 34
35	Z of Definition Point	35
36	Z of Definition Point	36
	Z of Definition Point	36
38	Entity Elevation	38 38 38 38 38 38 38 38 38
39	Entity Thickness	39 39 39 39 39 39 39 39 39
40	Radius	40 40 40 40
	Height, Size or Width	40 40
	Leader Length	40
41	X Scale Factor or Width	41 41 41 41 41 41
42	Y Scale Factor or Bulge	42 42
43	Z Scale Factor	43
44	Column Spacing	44
45	Row Spacing	45
50	Rotation Angle	50 50 50 50 50
	Start Angle	50
	Curve Fit Tangent	50
51	End Angle	51 51 51 51
	Obliquing Angle	51
	Angle From Horizontal	51
62	Color	62 62 62 62 62 62 62 62 62 62 62 62
66	Entities Follow Flag	66 66
70	Dimension Type	70
	Vertex or Polyline Flag	70 70 70 70 70
	Attribute Flag	70
	Column Count	70
	Invisible Edges Flag	70
71	Text Generation Flag	71 71
	Row Count	71
	Mesh M Vertex Count	71 71
72	Text Justification	72 72 72 72
	Mesh N Vertex Count	72 72
73	Field Length	73
	Smooth Surface M Density	73 73
74	Smooth Surface N Density	74
74	Smooth Surface Type	75
210	X of Extrusion Point	210 210 210 210 210 210 210 210 210 210
220	Y of Extrusion Point	220 220 220 220 220 220 220 220 220 220
230	Z of Extrusion Point	230 230 230 230 230 230 230 230 230 230

TABLE DXF GROUP CODES

0	Description	LTYPE	LAYER	STYLE	VIEW	UCS	VPORT
0	Table Type	LTYPE	LAYER	STYLE	VIEW	UCS	VPORT
2	Symbol Name	2	2	2	2	2	2
3	Descriptive Text	3					
	Font File Name			3			
4	Bigfont File Name			4			
6	Line Name			6			
10	X of View Center Point				10		
	X of Origin Point					10	
	X of Lower Left Corner						10
11	X of View Direction				11		
	X of X Axis Direction					11	
	X of Upper Right Corner						11
12	X of Target Point				12		
	X of Y Axis Direction					12	
	X of View Center Point						12
13	X of Snap Base Point						13
14	X of Snap Spacing						14
15	X of Grid Spacing						15
16	X of View Direction						16
17	X of View Target Point						17
20	Y of View Center Point				20		
	Y of Origin Point					20	
	Y of Lower left Corner						20
21	Y of View Direction				21		
	Y of X Axis Direction					21	
	Y of Upper Right Corner						21
22	Y of Target Point				22		
	Y of Y Axis Direction					22	
	Y of View Center Point						22
23	Y of Snap Base Point						23
24	Y of Snap Spacing						24
25	Y of Grid Spacing						25
26	Y of View Direction						26
27	Y of View Target Point						27
30	Y of Origin Point					30	
31	Z of View Direction				31		
	Z of X Axis Direction					31	
32	Z of Target Point				32		
	Z of Y Axis Direction					32	
36	Z of View Direction						36
37	Z of View Target Point						37
40	View Height				40		40
	Pattern Length	40					
	Fixed Text Height			40			
41	View Width				41		
	Text Width			41			
	View Aspect Ratio						41
42	Last Height Used			42			
	Lens Length				42		42
43	Front Clipping Plane				43		43
44	Back Clipping Plane				44		44
49	Dash Length	49					
50	Obliquing Angle			50			
	Twist Angle				50		
	Snap Rotation Angle						50
51	View Twist Angle						51
62	Color		62				
70	Number of Flags	70	70	70	70	70	70
71	Text Generation Flag			71			
	View Mode					71	71
72	Alignment Codes	72					
	Circle Zoom Percent						72
73	No. of Dash Items	73					
	Fast Zoom Setting						73
74	UCS Icon Setting						74
75	Snap On or Off						75
76	Grid On or Off						76
77	Snap Style						77
78	Snap Isopair						78

AutoLISP Function Reference Table

Each AutoLISP function is given below with a brief description of the function's action and the results returned. The number and data type of arguments are shown.

(+ *number number* ...)

Returns the sum of all numbers, as integers or real numbers depending on the values.

(– *number number* ...)

Returns the difference of the first number subtracted from the sum of the remaining numbers. An integer or real number is returned, depending on the value.

(* *number number* ...)

Returns the product of all numbers.

(/ *number number* ...)

Returns the quotient of the first number divided by the product of the remaining numbers.

(= *atom atom* ...)

Returns T if atoms are numerically equal, otherwise returns nil. Only numbers and strings are valid.

(/= *atom atom*)

Returns T if atoms are numerically not equal, otherwise returns nil. Only numbers and strings are valid.

(< *atom atom* ...)

Returns T if each atom is numerically less than the following atom, otherwise returns nil. Only numbers and strings are valid.

(<= *atom atom* ...)

Returns T if each atom is numerically less than or equal to the following atom, otherwise returns nil. Only numbers and strings are valid.

KEY:	
...	means additional arguments may follow.
Bold italics	are required arguments.
Light italics	are optional arguments.

(> atom atom ...)

Returns T if each atom is numerically greater than the following atom, otherwise returns nil. Only numbers and strings are valid.

(>= atom atom ...)

Returns T if each atom is numerically greater than or equal to the following atom, otherwise returns nil. Only numbers and strings are valid.

(~ number)

Returns the bitwise NOT of number.

(1+ number)

Returns number incremented by 1.

(1- number)

Returns number decremented by 1.

(abs number)

Returns the absolute value of an integer or real number.

(and expression ...)

Returns T if all expressions are true, otherwise returns nil and ceases evaluation at the first nil expression encountered.

(angle point point)

Returns an angle in radians from the X axis in a counterclockwise direction to a line between the two points.

(angtos angle mode precision)

Returns a string conversion of an angle from radians to the units specified by mode. The conversion defaults to the current angular units mode and precision unless otherwise specified with the optional mode and precision arguments.

(append list ...)

Returns a single list made up of any number of lists.

(apply function list)

Applies a function to the arguments supplied by list. Generally, function and list are quoted so their contents will be supplied unevaluated.

(ascii string)

Returns the first character of the string as an ASCII integer character code.

(assoc *item list*)

>   Returns a list containing the item from a list of lists.

(atan *number* number)

>   Returns the arctangent of number1, from -pi to pi. If number2 is provided, the arctangent of the number1/number2 is returned. If number2 is 0, either -pi/2 or +pi/2 radians (-90 or +90 degrees) is returned, depending on the sign of number1.

(atof *string*)

>   Returns a real number converted from a string.

(atoi *string*)

>   Returns an integer converted from a string.

(atom *item*)

>   Returns T if item is not a list, otherwise returns nil.

(boole *function integer integer* ...)

>   Returns one of 16 possible boolean operations, based on the function value, on any number of integers.

(boundp *atom*)

>   Returns T if the atom is bound to a value, otherwise returns nil.

(cadr *list*)

>   Returns the second element in the list. Use CADR to extract the Y coordinate of a point list.

(car *list*)

>   Returns the first element in the list. Use CAR to extract the X coordinate of a point list.

(cdr *list*)

>   Returns a list minus the first element in the list.

(c????r *list*)

>   Returns an element or list defined by the combinations of *a* and *d* characters in the expression, up to four levels deep. For example, caadr, cddr, cadar, and so on.

(chr *integer*)

>   Returns a single character string converted from its ASCII integer character code.

(close *file-desc***)**

> Closes the file specified by the file-desc argument. The file-desc variable must be assigned to a valid file handle name.

(command *argument ...***)**

> Sends its arguments as input to AutoCAD. Strings and numbers are taken as literal input; other arguments send the returned value of their expressions to AutoCAD as input. The COMMAND function alone executes a return, (COMMAND nil) executes a <^C>. The symbol, PAUSE (a variable set to "\"), used as a COMMAND function argument, pauses the COMMAND function for user input.

(cond (*test expression ...***) ...)**

> Evaluates expression(s) of the first non-nil test. Any number of (test expression...) lists are scanned for the test case. The value of the last-evaluated expression is returned. COND ceases further evaluation after finding a non-nil test or after completing the list of tests.

(cons *item item***)**

> Returns a new list with the first item as the new first element of a list, if the second item is supplied as the list. If the second item is not a list, it returns a dotted pair, in the form (item . item).

(cons *item list***)**

> Adds item as a new first element of list and returns the new list, if supplied, as its second argument.

(cos *angle***)**

> Returns the cosine of a radian angle.

(defun *name (argument ...) expression ...***)**

> Creates a function with a given name. The argument list can supply variables to be passed to the function. Argument list variables following an optional slash are variables that are local to the function. The function will evaluate the program statement(s) and return the result of the last expression evaluated. Prefixing a C: to the function name will create a lisp command that acts like a standard AutoCAD command. Defining an S::STARTUP function in the ACAD.LSP file will create an automatic executing function.

(distance *point point***)**

> Returns a distance between two 3D or 2D points.

(entdel *ename***)**

> Deletes or restores the ename depending on its status in the current editing session.

(entget *ename*)

Returns a list of data describing the entity specified by the entity name.

(entlast)

Returns the last nondeleted entity name in the database.

(entmod *list*)

Updates an entity in the database with a new entity data description list. Except for complex entities (polyline vertexes and block attributes), the entities are immediately regenerated on the screen with the new data.

(entnext *ename*)

Returns the first nondeleted entity name in the database. If the optional ename is provided, the next nondeleted entity name immediately following the ename is returned.

(entsel *prompt*)

Returns a list containing the entity name and the point coordinates used to pick the entity. The optional prompt string can provide specific instructions for entity selection.

(entupd *ename*)

Allows selective updating of polyline vertexes and block attribute entity names after ENTMODs have been performed.

(eq *variable variable*)

Returns T if the first variable expression is identically bound to the second variable. Otherwise returns nil.

(equal *expression expression accuracy*)

Returns T if the first expression is equal to the second expression. Otherwise returns nil. The optional accuracy (fuzz) value determines how accurate two numbers must be to be considered equal.

(*error* *string*)

A user-definable error function. The string will contain a message describing the error.

(eval *expression*)

Returns the results of evaluating the expression.

(exp *number***)**

> Returns e raised to the power of number as a real.

(expt *base power***)**

> Returns the base number raised to the power number. The value returned is an integer or real number depending on the base and power values.

(findfile *filename***)**

> Returns the file name with the path appended if the file is found, otherwise it returns nil. It searches only the specified directory if a path is supplied as part of file name. If no path is supplied, it searches the AutoCAD library path. Wildcards are not permitted.

(fix *number***)**

> Returns an integer value of the number and drops the remainder.

(float *number***)**

> Returns a real value of the number.

(foreach *name list expression***)**

> Evaluates the expression, substituting each element in the list for a symbol for one loop of the expression(s). The symbol is an alias variable that is temporarily set to each item from the list for one loop. The expression(s) in the loop must refer to the current item of the list by its alias. The value of the symbol is local to the FOREACH.

(gcd *integer integer***)**

> Returns the greatest common denominator of two integers.

(getangle *point prompt***)**

> Returns an angle in radians. Value may be entered by a user or determined by two user-provided points. The angle is measured counterclockwise from the X axis, unless reversed by the UNITS command. An optional point value specifies the base point for a rubber-banding line. The optional prompt string can provide specific instructions for desired point values. Use GETANGLE for rotation (relative angles).

(getcorner *point prompt***)**

> Returns a point selected as the second corner of an AutoCAD window cursor. The optional prompt string can provide specific instructions for desired point selection.

(getdist *point prompt***)**

> Returns a user-entered distance or the calculated distance between two user-provided points. Value may be entered by a user or determined by two user-provided points. The optional point value specifies the base point for a

rubber-banding line. An optional prompt can provide specific instructions for desired point selection.

(getenv *name***)**

Returns the string value of the operating system environment variable specified by the name argument, if found. Otherwise it returns nil.

(getint *prompt***)**

Returns an integer provided by the user. (On DOS systems, input must be between -32768 and +32767.) The optional prompt string can provide specific instructions for input.

(getkword *prompt***)**

Returns a string matching the key word input by the user. Key words are specified in the (initget) function. The optional prompt string can provide specific instructions for input.

(getorient *point prompt***)**

Returns a radian angle as input by a user or as calculated by two user-provided points. The angle is measured in the direction, and from the 0 degree base, set by UNITS. The optional point value specifies the base point to show a rubber-banding line. An optional prompt string can provide specific instructions for desired point values. Use GETORIENT for orientation (absolute angles).

(getpoint *point prompt***)**

Returns a point. The optional point value specifies the base point of a rubber-banding line. The optional prompt can provide specific instructions for desired point selection.

(getreal *prompt***)**

Returns a real number provided by the user. The optional prompt string can provide specific instructions for input.

(getstring *flag prompt***)**

Returns a string of up to 132 characters from the user. If the optional flag argument is nil or is omitted, spaces are not allowed in the string and they act like a <RETURN> and end input. The optional prompt string can provide specific instructions for input.

(getvar *sysvar***)**

Returns the value specified by sysvar, the system variable name. Sysvar is a string value.

(graphscr)

Switches from the text screen to the graphics screen on single screen systems.

(grclear)

Temporarily clears the graphics screen in the current viewport. A redraw will refresh the screen.

(grdraw *point point color* mode**)**

Draws a vector between two supplied points in the color specified by a color integer. A non-zero optional mode argument will highlight the vector.

(grread *track***)**

Reads the input device directly. If the optional track argument is present and non-nil, it returns the current pointing device (mouse or digitizer cursor) location without a point pick.

(grtext *box text mode***)**

Writes a string in the text portion of the graphics screen specified by the box number. An optional non-zero mode integer highlights and zero de-highlights the box of text. A box number of -1 writes to the status line, -2 writes to the coordinate status line, and 0, 1, 2, 3 and so on write to the menu labels, with 0 representing the top label.

(handent *handle***)**

Returns the entity name corresponding to the permanent handle name if handles have been enabled.

(if *test expression* expression**)**

If the test is not nil, the first expression is evaluated. If the test is nil, the optional second expression is evaluated. The function returns the value of the evaluated expression.

(initget *bits string***)**

Establishes options for GETxxx functions.

```
1 Null input is not allowed.        8  Does not check limits.
2 Zero values are not allowed.     16 Returns 3D points (default).
4 Negative values are not allowed. 32 Dashed lines used for
                                      rubber-banding.
```

The optional string defines a list of key words as acceptable input to a GETxxx function.

(inters *point point point point* flag**)**

Returns a point value of the intersection of a line between the first two points and a line between the second two points. If the optional flag is not nil, the lines are infinitely projected to calculate the intersection.

(itoa *integer*)

> Returns a string conversion of an integer.

(lambda *argument expression* ...)

> Defines an in-line function supplying argument(s) to expression(s) for evaluation.

(last *list*)

> Returns the last element in a list.

(length *list*)

> Returns the number of elements in a list.

(list *expression*)

> Returns a list constructed from the supplied expression(s).

(listp *item*)

> Returns T if item is a list. Otherwise returns nil.

(load *filename* expression)

> Loads the AutoLISP file specified by the file name. The optional expression will be returned if the load function fails. The optional expression is evaluated whether or not the load fails.

(log *number*)

> Returns the natural log of the supplied number as a real.

(logand *integer integer* ...)

> Returns an integer of a logical bitwise AND of two or more integers.

(logior *integer integer* ...)

> Returns an integer of a logical bitwise OR of two or more integers.

(lsh *number numberbits*)

> Returns an integer of the logical bitwise shift of number by numberbits.

(mapcar *function list* ...)

> Sequentially executes a lisp function on each set of elements in one or more argument lists.

(max *number number* ...)

> Returns the highest value in a series of numbers.

(member *item list*)

> Returns the remainder of the list starting at the item if it is found. Otherwise returns nil.

(menucmd *string*)

> Loads and displays the menu page specified by the string. The string must include the menu device code and the page name, like "S=NAME" for the screen device page named NAME.

(min *number number ...*)

> Returns the lowest value in a series of numbers.

(minusp *number*)

> Returns T if number is negative. Otherwise returns nil.

(not *item*)

> NOT is simple. It takes a single argument and returns the opposite. NOT returns T if its argument is nil; and returns nil if its argument is non-nil.

(nth *integer list*)

> Returns the item specified by the integer position in a list. It returns nil if the integer position exceeds the list length.

(null *item*)

> Returns T if item is bound to nil. Otherwise returns nil. Typically used for lists.

(numberp *item*)

> Returns T if item is a number. Otherwise returns nil.

(open *filename mode*)

> Opens a file specified by the filename string for the use specified by the mode. The modes are "r" for reading, "w" for writing, and "a" for appending. OPEN returns a file handle, which is supplied as the file-spec argument to the READ-, WRITE-, CLOSE-, and print functions.

(or *expression ...*)

> Returns T if one of the expressions is true. Otherwise returns nil or ceases evaluation at the first true expression encountered.

(osnap *point mode*)

> Returns a point value specified by the osnap mode string on the supplied point value. The mode argument is a string, like "END,INT".

pause

The constant pause is used in the command function to wait for user input.

pi

The constant pi is set to approximately 3.1415926.

(polar *point angle dist*)

Returns a point calculated at an angle and distance from a supplied base point.

(prin1 *expression* file-desc)

Prints the expression to the screen and returns the expression. If the optional file-desc is supplied and the file is open for writing, output is redirected to file-desc. If the optional file-desc is missing or the file is closed, the expression is printed to the screen.

(princ *expression* file-desc)

Prints and returns the expression, except control characters are not evaluated. If the optional file-desc is supplied and the file is open for writing, output is redirected to file-desc. If the optional file-desc is missing or the file is closed, the expression is printed to the screen.

(print *expression* file-desc)

Prints a new line and the expression to the screen and returns a new line and expression. PRINT adds a new line before and a space after the data. If the optional file-desc is supplied and the file is open for writing, output is redirected to file-desc. If the optional file-desc is missing or the file is closed, the expression is printed to the screen.

(progn *expression* ...)

Evaluates a series of expressions, returning the value of the last expression. The arguments can be any number of valid AutoLISP expressions.

(prompt *string*)

Displays a string statement in the screen's prompt area.

(quote *expression*)

Returns the expression without evaluation, a ' does the same function.

(read *string*)

Returns a symbol of the first atom or list in a string.

(read-char *file-desc***)**

> Returns the ASCII character code of a single character typed at the keyboard or read from the optional file-desc.

(read-line *file-desc***)**

> Returns a string typed at the keyboard or read from the optional file-desc.

(redraw *ename mode***)**

> Redraws the current viewport unless ename is provided, in which case the entity represented by ename is redrawn. The mode option redraws the entity in four possible ways: 1 = standard redraw, 2 = reverse redraw (blank), 3 = highlight redraw, and 4 = de-highlight.

(rem *number number* **...)**

> Returns the remainder of the first number divided by the product of the rest of the numbers.

(repeat *number expression* **...)**

> Evaluates each expression by the number of times specified. Number must be an integer.

(reverse *list***)**

> Returns a list of items reversed from the order of the supplied list.

(rtos *number* *mode accuracy***)**

> Returns a string conversion of the supplied number in the current UNITS setting unless the optional mode and accuracy override it. The mode values are:

> | 1 | Scientific | 4 | Architectural |
> |---|------------|---|---------------|
> | 2 | Decimal | 5 | Fractional |
> | 3 | Engineering | | |

(set *symbol expression***)**

> Sets a quoted symbol with the value of the expression. An unquoted symbol can set values indirectly.

(setq *symbol expression* *symbol1 expression1***)**

> Sets symbol to the value of the matching expression.

(setvar *sysvar value***)**

> Sets an AutoCAD system variable specified by sysvar to the value supplied.

(sin *angle*)

Returns the sin of a radian angle.

(sqrt *number*)

Returns the square root of a number as a real.

(ssadd *ename selection-set*)

Creates an empty selection set when no arguments are provided. If the optional entity name is provided, a selection set is created with just that entity name. If an entity name is provided with an existing selection set, it is added to the selection set.

(ssdel *ename selection-set*)

Deletes the entity name from the selection set and returns the entity name.

(ssget *mode point point*)

Returns a selection set of entities. If SSGET fails, it returns nil. With no arguments (or a nil), SSGET uses AutoCAD's standard object selection to get a user selection. The optional mode argument specifies options to automate selection without user input. Modes are "P" for Previous, "L" for Last, "W" for Window, and "C" for Crossing. One optional point argument alone selects a single point, or two points following a mode select Window or Crossing boxes. An "X" mode returns entities matching a filtering list based on any combination in the DXF group codes table which follows.

DXF GROUP CODES

DXF	FIELD	DXF	FIELD
0	Entity type	38	Elevation (Rel. 11 will drop)
2	Block name	39	Thickness
6	Linetype name	62	Color number
7	Text style name	66	Attributes
8	Layer name	210	3D extrusion direction

(sslength *selection-set*)

Returns the number of entities in a selection set.

(ssmemb *ename selection-set*)

Returns the entity name if it is in the selection set. Otherwise returns nil.

(ssname *selection-set number*)

Returns the entity name of the number position of the selection set. The first entity is number 0.

(strcase *string* *flag*)

> Returns string converted to upper case unless the optional flag evaluates to T, which converts to lower case.

(strcat *string string ...*)

> Returns a single string by combining all the supplied strings.

(strlen *string*)

> Returns the number of characters in the string.

(subst *item item list*)

> Returns a list with the new item replacing every occurrence of the old item in the supplied list.

(substr *string start* *length*)

> Returns the portion of a string from the start position number of the supplied string to either the end of the string or to the end of the number of characters specified by the optional length value.

T

> A constant symbol T is used as the value of true.

(tblnext *tname* *flag*)

> Returns a data description list for the table name specified by tname. If the optional rewind flag is T, the first table data is returned, otherwise TBLNEXT steps through tname and returns the next table entry each time the function is used.

(tblsearch *tname symbol* *flag*)

> Returns a data description list for the table name specified by tname and the symbol name. If flag is T, a subsequent TBLNEXT function will return the table data of the next entry.

(terpri)

> Prints a new line on the screen.

(textscr)

> Switches from the graphics screen to the text screen on single screen systems.

(trace *function ...*)

> Prints the entry of the specified functions, indented by depth, and returns the value as a debugging aid.

(trans *point code code* flag)

> Returns a translated point of the supplied point from the first coordinate code to the second coordinate code. The code values are: 0 for World Coordinate System, 1 for User Coordinate System, and 2 for Display Coordinate System (screen). If the flag is not omitted or is nil, the point value is treated as a 3D displacement. An entity name or 3D extrusion vector may be used in place of the code(s).

(type *item*)

> Returns the type of the item such as real, integer, string, list, and so on.

(untrace *function* ...)

> Removes the trace function from the supplied function(s).

(ver)

> Returns a string with the current AutoLISP version.

(vmon)

> Turns on AutoLISP's virtual paging of functions. It makes function definitions eligible to be swapped to disk or in and out of RAM to allow for the loading of more programs.

(vports)

> Returns a list of the current viewport settings. The list contains sublists with the viewport numbers and display coordinate corner points for each port. The active viewport is first on the list.

(while *test expression* ...)

> Evaluates the expressions as long as the test returns T or is non-nil. Each loop of a WHILE function tests the condition and, if non-nil, evaluates each of the statements included within the closing parenthesis. WHILE returns the last evaluation of the last completed loop. If no loops are completed, it returns nil.

(write-char *number* file-desc)

> Writes a character specified by the ASCII character code number to the screen or to a file specified by the optional file-desc.

(write-line *string* file-desc)

> Writes a string to the screen or to a file specified by the optional file-desc.

(zerop *number*)

> Returns T if number equals 0 (zero). Otherwise returns nil.

The Authors' Appendix

How INSIDE AutoLISP Was Produced

We thought you might be interested in the hardware, software, and techniques that we used to produce the book. We'll tell you that, and we'll also share some of our favorite tools and sources of information for customization.

We composed our documents in Microsoft Word. Illustrations were done in AutoCAD. Screen images, both text and graphics, were captured and cleaned up with HotShot Graphics by SymSoft, Inc. Pages and illustrations were layed out and printed with Xerox Ventura Publisher, from the Xerox Corporation, on an NEC LC 890 Postscript Page (laser) Printer. The NEC was provided with the help of KETIV Technologies.

Our AUTOEXEC.BAT Files

Rusty uses both a SUN 386i and several souped up PC's. Here is Rusty's annotated AUTOEXEC.BAT file for his DOS setup. It shows a lot of his favorite tools.

Rusty's AUTOEXEC.BAT

```
set ACADFREERAM=30                    Sets AutoCAD RAM.
set LISPHEAP=39500
set LISPSTACK=5000
PROMPT $P$G                           Displays current directory at DOS prompt.
PATH d:\NORTON;d:\DOS;c:\BAT;c:\UTIL;d:\MOUSE;C:\;D:\;d:\WORD
d:\dos\FASTOPEN d:=84 c:=48           Reduces disk access with DOS 3.3.
c:\boot\SAFEPARK 15                   Parks the hard disk after 15 seconds.
ECHO ^[[1;0;59p                       An ANSI.SYS key reassignment.
c:\boot\CTRLALT                       An invaluable cut and paste utility.
c:\util\MAP > MAPMEM.$                Reads memory use map and redirects to
                                      filename MAPMEM.$.

ask "Run Carousel? ", yn              Uses Norton Utilities ASK to optionally
                                      run Carousel.
if errorlevel 2 goto SETUP            If ASK got N (No=2), go to label :SETUP.
if errorlevel 1 goto CAROUSEL         If ASK got Y (Yes=1).
```

`:SETUP`	BATCH label to optionally execute following.
`c:\util\PUSHDIR`	Saves current directory on a stack.
`CALL PUP rem POP restores path`	Calls the PUP.BAT command, and returns here.
`:CONTINUE`	
`COPY d:\acad\RAM F:`	Loads AutoCAD to RAM disk.
`D:`	
`goto end`	Skip the rest. Don't load Carousel.
`:CAROUSEL`	
`C:\CAROUSEL\CAROUSEL`	Load the invaluable Software Carousel.
`:END`	That's all!

Joe's AUTOEXEC.BAT file is a bit simpler.

Joe's AutoEXEC.BAT file.

```
path=c:\dos;c:\acad;c:\ws;c:\norton;c:\
prompt $p$g
cls
```

Directories don't need to be in the PATH, unless you want to execute files in them from other directories. Any EXE, COM, or BAT program file stored in a directory in the PATH can be executed from any other directory. For example, UTIL, DOS, and NORTON are in our PATH so we can use them.

We use several TSR (RAM resident) utilities which are always available in the background. They typically pop up when you hit some *hotkey* and disappear when retired. Ours included CTRLALT for text screen capture and copying, PUSHDIR to save and restore current directories, and HotShot Plus for AutoCAD screen captures.

Our development environment included The Software Carousel, Norton's Editor, CTRLALT, Microsoft Word, and several in-house text conversion programs developed by Pat Haessly.

A good text editor is invaluable in customizing AutoCAD. Besides creating ASCII files, it helps if your editor is comfortable, compact, quick, and easy to use. Norton's Editor was our choice as a text editor.

Our Multi-Tasking Interactive Environment

Some operating systems and operating system extensions let you load more than one program at a time. Concurrent ones, like Windows 386 and Deskview, can run programs in the background while you work. They require a 386 machine. Others, like The Software Carousel from Softlogic

Solutions, run on PC/XT/AT machines. They can flip back and forth between programs, but only one program is active at a time.

We found The Software Carousel invaluable in writing this book. It integrated our system. On the DOS systems, we set up four "partitions." Each was like a separate computer. All four co-existed in the single system, but each maintained its own settings and environment. The partitions were:

```
1    AutoCAD.
2    Microsoft Word.
3    Norton's Editor and other utilities.
4    More utilities and housekeeping.
```

CTRLALT tied the system together by extending across all partitions. CTRLALT is a memory-resident pop-up freeware program by Barry Simon and Richard Wilson. It include a pop-up ASCII table, a pop-up Hex table, a pop-up ANSI table, and a screen text cut-and-paste feature. The cut-and-paste feature made the tedious and error-prone task of documenting the book's AutoCAD and AutoLISP routines easier. We could flip into AutoCAD, hit <CTRL-ALT-RETURN>, highlight part of the text screen, and capture it. This captured the screens exactly as you see them.

Of course, none of this was required on the Sun386i workstation with its simultaneously active multiple windows.

Tools, Sources, and Support

No one knows everything there is to know about AutoCAD. Knowing where to find AutoCAD information can help you solve many application problems. Here are some tools and resources that we'd like to share.

Advanced AutoCAD Classes

Autodesk, Inc., has authorized a hundred or more AutoCAD training centers in the United States and several foreign countries. These training centers are usually affiliated with colleges and technical institutes. Many centers have specialized and advanced courses on AutoLISP. Gold Hill Computers, the makers of Golden Common Lisp, is providing AutoLISP courses through selected authorized AutoCAD training centers. You can get information about the centers from your dealer or by calling Autodesk, Inc., (800) 445-5415 or (415) 332-2344. Many AutoCAD dealers also teach courses that meet or exceed the quality of the authorized AutoCAD training centers.

The CompuServe Autodesk Forum

Autodesk's forum on CompuServe is the best source of support available today. The CompuServe Information Service, Compuserve, Inc., is available to anyone with a computer, modem, communications software, telephone, and password.

You can join CompuServe by getting a membership kit at a computer store, software store, or book store. Once you install the kit and *log on*, you just type GO ADESK to get into the Autodesk forum. There you will find message exchanges and data libraries that include:

```
ADESK File Cabinet      AEC
AutoCAD                 Wishlist
AutoLisp                3rd Party Software
AutoShade               What's New!
AutoSketch              Utilities / ADI
AutoFlix                AutoSolid
```

You can *download* many useful AutoLISP (and other) utilities from the data libraries. You can leave a message and get a reply in less than 24 hours. Some of the most knowledgeable Autodesk people contribute. And you have the benefit of the largest CAD user group anywhere. Many users have already solved the problem you've encountered and will reply to your message.

We recommend that you download the free communications package ATO from the GO IBMSW (IBM SoftWare) forum. This package is designed to automate using CompuServe forums.

We think the CompuServe forum is the best support money can buy. It averages about $6/hour of connected time and is well worth the time it takes to learn to use it. The New Riders book, CUSTOMIZING AutoCAD, has more information on the ADESK forum.

Bulletin Boards

Many other local AutoCAD bulletin boards exist. You will find a listing, maintained by New Riders Publishing, in the Autodesk Forum on CompuServe. GO ADESK and check the library for the newest upload of the list, or contact us at New Riders Publishing, Attention: Bulletin Board.

User Groups

There are numerous AutoCAD user groups. Some of the best overall support comes from these members. You may find members, or whole groups, who share a similar application to yours. New Riders also maintains a list of user groups. GO ADESK and check for the newest upload of the list, or contact us at New Riders Publishing, Attention: User Groups.

Magazines

AutoCAD has two independent magazines.

```
CADalyst                    CADalyst Publications LTD.
Subscription Manager        282-810 W. Broadway
314 E Holly, #106           Vancouver BC Canada V5Z 4C9
Bellingham, WA 98225
(604) 873-0811


CADENCE
Circulation Dept.
POB 203550
Austin, TX 78720-3550
(512) 250-1700
```

Books

After you've worked your way through INSIDE AutoLISP, you may find that you want to learn more about AutoLISP, or customizing AutoCAD. You can continue learning about AutoCAD customization with CUSTOMIZING AutoCAD, which we also wrote. It covers all the aspects of AutoCAD customization that aren't in this book. It concentrates on menu development and includes topics like text font, hatch patterns, and linetype customization.

AutoLISP is its own dialect of the LISP language. Here are three books on the general LISP language that we found useful for understanding *why* AutoLISP works the way it does.

■ The "bible" of LISP is Winston and Horn's LISP (Addison-Wesley).

■ David Touretsky's LISP A Gentle Introduction to Symbolic Computation (Harper & Row) is a good, easy introduction to LISP.

■ Tony Hasemer's Looking at LISP (Addison-Wesley) is another friendly reference.

Commercial Utilities

There are many utility programs to help you deal with DOS, the computer, and, of course, your proliferating files. The best source of information and reviews on current programs are the magazines: PC Magazine, PC World, Info World, and PC Week.

Here are a few categories of utilities, along with a few of our favorites:

Hard Disk Management and Backup

Use something more efficient than DOS BACKUP for archiving your files. We use Fastback, Fifth Generation Systems, for its speed and superb error recovery.

After you back up your hard disk, you should clean it up. Unfortunately, just deleting garbage isn't enough. DOS tends to break files into smaller and smaller chunks as time goes by. The average hard disk is probably operating at less than half its optimum speed. We do frequent cleanups with Disk Optimizer, an inexpensive utility from Softlogic Solutions. We also recommend MACE from Paul Mace Software, or the SpeedDisk utility on Norton's Utilities. These programs all rearrange files for faster access.

A unique program for problem hard disks is the Disk Technician from Prime Solutions, Inc. It diagnoses and actually repairs flaky disks by maintaining a comparative record and doing a low level format on individual problem tracks. It also includes the SAFEPARK utility which we use.

If you accidentally erase a file or even a directory, there's hope of recovery if you catch it quickly. Hope is slim if you do anything that writes to the disk before recovery. The best known utility, which we use, is the NU unerase utility of Norton's Utilities. Others are MACE (Paul Mace Software), or PC Tools (Central Point Software).

User Interface Shells

If you hate DOS, or if you are a system manager who needs to insulate users from DOS, there are numerous DOS shells that provide a point-and-shoot interface to DOS through menus. Norton Commander, PC Tools, and many others are available for almost any taste. Avoid memory-resident shells unless they use EMS. Otherwise, AutoCAD will probably be left RAM hungry.

General Utility Packages

There are dozens of little utilities that you may find useful even if you only manage a single system. Many utilities are available as shareware or freeware. There are several comprehensive utilities packages available commercially.

We use Norton Utilities from Peter Norton Computing. The programs include an easy point-and-shoot interface, and many life-saving disk restoration and cleanup tools. PC Tools from Central Point Software is another comprehensive package, which has a unique directory cut-and-past feature that can move entire directory trees intact.

Other typical features include directory and file name sorting, text searching groups of files, finding files no matter where they are on the disk, changing file attributes, directory name listing, disk testing, and almost anything else that DOS forgot and we need.

Freeware and Shareware

Some of the best things in your computer's life are free, or nearly so. Most of the AutoCAD command line and text screen sections in this book were *captured* from the AutoCAD text screen by CTRLALT. We got this freeware by downloading it from the IBMSW (IBM SoftWare) Forum on CompuServe, where many other popular utilities may be found.

There is an organization called the PC Software Interest Group (PC-SIG) which maintains and distributes a large library of public domain software, freeware, and shareware. PC-SIG publishes annual catalogues and monthly updates. PC-SIG checks its software. It charges a distribution fee of about $6 per disk. This fee is in addition to any possible shareware fees. Their entire 490+ disk, 9000 program library is available on a single CD-ROM for about $200! Here is PC-SIG's address:

```
PC-SIG
1030 E. Duane Ave., Suite D
Sunnyvale, CA 94086
(408) 730-9291
```

Authors' Last Word and Mail Box

We had a lot of fun and learned a lot doing this book. We hope that you enjoy programming AutoLISP and that you come back to the book again and again for ideas. Build on our programs. Modify and adapt the routines so that they do what you want them to do. We only ask that you give us credit for what we provide, and that you pass the credit on. If you haven't already, we hope you will continue your AutoCAD system customization with CUSTOMIZING AutoCAD.

If you want to correspond with us, we can be reached electronically on

CompuServe. Use CompuServe's EMAIL feature to send us a message. Rusty Gesner's number is: 76310,10. Please leave your name, telephone number, the version of AutoCAD that you are using, a description of the hardware, and your comments. Send us tips and new ideas that were inspired by the book.

We'll respond to you on CompuServe or by telephone as soon as possible. We try to respond within 48 hours. We scan our mail each day. Of course, you can reach us by telephone or good old-fashioned mail at the New Riders telephone number and mailing address in the back of the book.

Good luck with your customizing!

Index

!, Passing variables to AutoCAD, 3-6
character in variables, 4-22
#ARGLIST global variable, 12-13
#DWGSC drawing scale variable, 2-26
#error variable, 17-30
$ menu page codes, 10-4
% replaceable parameter, 1-14
' quote function, 5-4
* multiply function, 3-11, 4-20
*; comments, displaying, 17-49
+ add function, 3-11
- subtract function, 3-11, 4-20
/ divide function, 3-11, 4-20
/= not equal function, 4-6
/= not equal to function, 4-6
1+ increment function, 3-12, 4-15
1- decrement function, 3-13, 15-8
2D to 3D conversions, 14-27
3D
    Alpha and Beta angles, 14-20
    Angles, 14-20
    Calculating extrusion vectors, 14-31
    Construction planes, 14-5
    Controlling 2D and 3D coordinates, 3-9
    Conversion to flat plates, 14-35
    Converting from 2D, 14-27
    Converting to 2D, 14-29
    Entity types, 14-5
    Extrusion vectors, 14-8
    Formulas, 14-20
    Point, 14-3
    Polar, 14-22
3DPOLAR C:command, 14-22
3DPOLAR IL function, 14-22, 14-23
= equal function, 4-6
^[, 17-20
^M as RETURN in Lisp/Macros, 5-9
> greater than function, 4-6
>= greater than equal to function, 4-6
< less than function, 4-6
<= less than equal to function, 4-6

A

ABS function, 3-15, 8-29
Absolute values of numbers, 3-14
ACAD.CFG, 1-8
ACAD.HDX, 12-9, 12-10
ACAD.HLP, 12-9
ACAD.LSP, 17-5, 17-10, 17-11
    Automatic loading file, 2-25
    Creation of, 2-25
ACAD.PGP
    File contents for IL book, 1-11
    Shell setup, 1-9
ACADDG.OVL, 1-8
ACADDS.OVL, 1-8
ACADFREERAM
    Free RAM setting, B-9
ACADLIMEM
    Expanded memory setting, 1-14, B-9
ACADPD.OVL, 1-8
ACADPL.OVL, 1-8
ACADXMEM
    Extended memory setting, 1-14
ACADXMEM, extended memory setting, B-9
Accuracy with AutoLISP, 3-16
ADDERR IL function, 17-27
ADI
    Drivers, 1-8
ALLOC function, 17-45
ALTITD (altitude) IL function, 14-24
AND function, 4-3, 4-4, 8-22
ANGLE function, 5-19
Angles
    3D, 14-20
    Controlling, 9-21
    Included angles, 14-24
    Snapping, 9-21
    To radians, 17-13
ANGTOC IL function, 5-22
ANGTOS function, 5-20
ANSI
    Codes in AutoLISP, 8-36
    Example codes, 9-19

Format codes, 8-36
Key Redefinition, 17-20
Screen positions, 8-39
ANSI.SYS, 8-36, 17-19
Device installation, 1-6, B-4
APLATE C:command, 6-15
APPEND function, 3-25, 4-16, 7-16, 8-47, 9-21
APPEND, DOS command, B-5
Appending files, 8-9, 8-27
Applications
Documenting, 17-51
Presentation, 17-52
User interface, 17-52
APPLY function, 14-32
ARCLEN (arc length) IL function, 14-24
Arcs
Length, 14-24
Area system variable, 6-16
Arguments, 3-28
For AutoLISP functions, 2-4
Global list, 12-13
ASCII
Codes in AutoLISP, 3-20, 5-8
Extended codes, 17-20
File Format, 1-5, B-1
ASCII function, 3-20, 8-49
ASSOC function, 6-27, 6-28
Association lists
Entities, 6-27
Associative Dimensioning, 10-30
ATAN function, 14-21
ATEXT C:command, 5-24
ATOF function, 5-15, 5-22, 11-33, 12-14
ATOI function, 5-15
ATOM function, 5-5
Atomlist, 3-5, 4-19, 17-46
ATTDEF command, 11-12
ATTEDIT
Automating, 11-17
ATTEXT command, 13-5
Attributes
"Lost", 11-40
Accessing data, 11-4
Application examples, 11-1
ATTEDIT, 11-17
ATTFIT, 12-29
ATTPIPE, 12-29
Attreq, 11-4
Block redefinition, 11-40

Caution, 13-6
Defined, 11-3
DXF codes, 11-6, 11-8
Exporting to dBase, 13-24
Extract template file, 13-3
Extracting, 13-5
In macros, 11-13
Input in macros, 11-15
Invisible, 12-29
Preset, 11-4
Record order, 13-25
REVBLOCK table, 11-23
Variable, 11-4, 11-11
Autobreaking blocks, 11-31
AutoCAD
Book's version requirements, 0-9
Support files, 1-7
AutoCAD Commands
Angles from AutoLISP, 5-21
ATTDEF, 11-12
Attext, 13-5
Commands from AutoLISP, 2-9
Dimblk, 10-24
EXIT, 1-11
External, 1-9
Files, 8-27
Offset, 12-20
Osnap, 10-18
Redefining with C:commands, **17-16**
Resume, 15-12
SETVAR, 3-2
SHELL, 1-10
Sketch, 6-50
Undefine, 17-16
Vslide, 17-53
AUTOEXEC.BAT, 1-6, B-4
Echo off, B-5
AutoLISP
^C canceling, 2-10
Accuracy of numbers, 3-16
Angles and AutoCAD commands, 5-21
Arguments, 2-4, 3-28
ASCII Codes, 3-20
Atomlist defined, 3-5
Atomlist functions, 3-5
Character functions, 3-20
Classes, D-3
Conditional functions, 4-8
Conditional tests, 4-13
Creation of selection sets, 6-18

Data types, 3-3, 3-5, 5-3
Defining functions, 3-27
Defining variables, 3-4
Developing programs, 2-16
Dotted pair, 6-28
Efficient programming, 17-41
Encryption, 17-47
Entity names, 6-4
Errors, B-12
Evaluation, 2-3, 3-12
Evaluation order, 2-23
Expressions, 2-3, 3-12, 3-21
Functions, 2-3, 2-4
Getting input, 2-10, 4-16
Global variables, 4-19
Illegal characters, 3-27
Importing text, 15-7
Incrementing/decrementing numbers, 3-12
Input functions, 3-7, 3-10
Input in macros, 3-10
INTegers, 5-3
Lists, 3-21, 3-25, 4-1, 5-3
Loading programs, 2-15
Local variables, 4-19
Logical operators, 4-3
Looping functions, 4-12
Math functions, 3-11
Maximum string length, 3-17
Memory settings, 1-13
n> error, 2-4
Nesting expressions, 2-6
NIL atom, 2-10, 4-2, 4-10
Non-nil, 4-3
Parentheses matching, 2-3, 2-4
Passing variables to AutoCAD with !, 3-6
PI constants, 4-20
Points, 3-21
Precedence, 3-12
Predicates, 5-3
Program files, 2-14
Program vs. data, 4-1
PROTECT.EXE, 17-47
Quoted strings, 2-4
Reading expressions/programs, 2-23, 2-24
REALs, 5-3
Recursion of programs, 4-26
Relational functions, 4-5, 4-6
Removing extended, 1-15
Reserved characters, 3-27
Returned value, 2-3, 2-6

Rubber-banding input, 3-10
Selection sets limitations, 6-13
SET vs. SETQ, 5-24
STRings, 5-3
SYMbols, 5-3, 5-4, 15-16
Symbols, creating with SET, 5-24
System Variables, 3-2, 3-4
Table of functions, C-9
Toggle prompts, 10-12
True atom, 4-2, 4-10
Used in macros, 2-7
Using subroutines, 4-24
Variable types, 3-3
Variables and Expressions, 3-2
Version requirements, 0-9
WHILE-NOT-OR-AND, 8-22
XLISP, 4-1

AutoLISP arithmetic functions
* multiply, 3-11, 4-20
+ add, 3-11
- subtract, 3-11, 4-20
/ divide, 3-11, 4-20
1+ increment, 3-12, 4-15
1- decrement, 3-13, 15-8
EXP, 3-16
EXPT, 3-15
GCD, 3-14
LOG, 3-16
MAX, 3-13
MIN, 3-13
REM, 3-14
SQRT, 3-14

AutoLISP basic functions
' quote, 5-4
ERROR, 17-25
ATOM, 5-5
BOUNDP, 5-4
COMMAND, 2-9, 5-27
COND, 4-8, 4-10
DEFUN, 3-27
EVAL, 4-23, 5-24, 17-23
GETVAR, 2-6, 3-4
GRAPHSCR, 5-10
IF, 4-8
LAMBDA, 17-7
LISTP, 5-4, 5-5, 5-6
LOAD, 2-15, 3-29
MINUSP, 5-5, 5-6
NUMBERP, 5-6
PROGN, 4-18

QUIT, 17-38
QUOTE, 3-23, 3-24, 5-4
REDRAW, 6-7
REPEAT, 4-12
S::STARTUP, 17-18
SET, 5-24, 12-18
SETQ, 2-5, 12-18
SETVAR, 2-6, 3-4
TERPRI, 5-10
TEXTSCR, 5-10, 8-48
TYPE, 5-3
WHILE, 4-14
ZEROP, 5-6, 14-21
AutoLISP conversion functions
ABS, 3-15, 8-29
ANGTOS, 5-20
ASCII, 3-20, 8-49
ATOF, 5-15, 5-22, 11-33, 11-34, 12-14
ATOI, 5-15
CHR, 3-20, 8-49
FIX, 5-18, 9-21
FLOAT, 5-18
ITOA, 5-15
READ, 5-23
RTOS, 5-16, 5-22, 8-29
AutoLISP device access functions
GRCLEAR, 9-9
GRDRAW, 9-1, 9-7, 9-9
GRREAD, 9-14, 9-15, 9-21
GRTEXT, 9-1, 9-3, 12-6
MENUCMD, 10-11
AutoLISP entity access functions
ENTDEL, 6-8, 6-9
ENTGET, 6-26, 6-27, 7-14, 7-15
ENTLAST, 6-4, 6-6
ENTMOD, 6-41, 6-44, 9-21
ENTNEXT, 6-4, 6-7, 6-45, 6-46
ENTSEL, 6-4, 6-9, 6-15, 6-27, 6-45, 12-20
ENTUPD, 6-40, 6-47, 6-49
HANDENT, 6-53
SSADD, 6-13, 6-14
SSDEL, 6-13, 6-14
SSGET, 6-12, 6-45
SSLENGTH, 6-13, 6-14, 6-16
SSMEMB, 6-13, 6-14, 6-24
SSNAME, 6-13, 6-14
AutoLISP geometric functions
ANGLE, 5-19
ATAN, 14-21
COS, 14-22, 14-24

DISTANCE, 5-24
INTERS, 12-18
OSNAP, 12-18
POLAR, 4-20, 4-21
SIN, 14-24
TRANS, 14-13
AutoLISP I/O functions
CLOSE, 8-7, 8-16
FINDFILE, 8-14, 8-18
OPEN, 8-6, 8-7, 8-9, 8-16
PRIN1, 5-11, 5-12, 8-5
PRINC, 5-11, 8-4
PRINT, 5-11, 5-12, 8-5
PROMPT, 5-9, 5-11, 8-4
READ, 5-23
READ-CHAR, 8-4, 8-10
READ-LINE, 8-3, 8-10
WRITE-CHAR, 8-3, 8-5
WRITE-LINE, 8-3, 8-4, 8-9, 8-29
AutoLISP list functions
APPEND, 3-25, 4-16, 7-16, 8-47, 9-21
APPLY, 14-32
ASSOC, 6-27, 6-28
CADR, 3-22
CAR, 3-22, 6-27
CDR, 3-22, 6-28
CONS, 3-25, 3-26, 6-28, 6-44
FOREACH, 4-16, 8-43
LAST, 3-24
LENGTH, 3-25
LIST, 3-21, 8-47
MAPCAR, 12-17
MEMBER, 3-26, 8-49
NTH, 3-25, 8-49
REVERSE, 3-25
SUBST, 6-41, 6-42, 6-44
AutoLISP logical functions
AND, 4-3, 4-4, 8-22
NOT, 4-3
OR, 4-3, 4-4, 8-22
AutoLISP memory functions
ALLOC, 17-45
EXPAND, 17-45
GC, 17-45
VMON, 17-42
AutoLISP relational functions
/= not equal, 4-6
= equal, 4-6
> greater than, 4-6
>= greater than equal to, 4-6

< less than, 4-6
<= less than equal to, 4-6
EQ, 4-6, 4-7
EQUAL, 4-6, 4-7
AutoLISP string functions
STRCASE, 3-18, 4-11
STRCAT, 3-17, 5-24
STRLEN, 3-19
SUBSTR, 3-19, 8-43
AutoLISP symbol table functions
TBLNEXT, 7-3, 7-4, 7-15
TBLSEARCH, 5-27, 7-3, 7-11
VPORTS, 7-34
AutoLISP user input functions
GETANGLE, 3-7
GETCORNER, 2-17
GETDIST, 3-7
GETINT, 3-7, 3-8
GETKWORD, 3-7, 5-36
GETORIENT, 3-7
GETPOINT, 2-11
GETREAL, 3-7
GETSTRING, 2-12
INITGET, 5-32
Axis
Isometric, 10-16
XY orientation in UCS, 14-10

B

BACKUP IL function, 8-26
BANGLE (Inclined angle) IL function, 14-21
BANGLE IL function, 14-21
BASIC language, 16-17
BATCH file
Replaceable parameters, 1-14
Beta angles in 3D, 14-20
Bill of Materials, 13-21
BLINE C:command, 11-35
Blocks
* hidden blocks, 16-23
As temporary markers, 9-23
Autoblocking, 11-31
DXF, 16-9
Extracting, 7-37
Importing, 7-37
Parametric, 11-31
Redefinition, 11-40

Storing data in, 11-31
Symbol table, 7-3
TBLSEARCH function, 7-11
BOLD IL function, 8-40, 8-47
Books, D-5
Bootup
Starting DOS, 1-5, B-3
BOUNDP function, 5-4
BSCALE IL function, 6-42
Buffers, 1-6, B-3
Bulge
Formula, 14-23
Polyline, 6-49
Bulletin boards, CompuServe forum, D-4

C

CADR function, 3-22
CAR function, 3-22, 6-27
Case of strings, 3-18
CDF comma delimited file, 8-43, 12-7
CDR function, 3-22, 6-28
CENTER IL function, 8-40, 8-47
Character functions in AutoLISP, 3-20
Characters
Control, expanding, 8-6
Special, in macros, 10-3
CHKDSK
Memory checking, B-6
CHR function, 3-20, 8-49
CLEAN memory function, 17-46
Clipper, 13-28
CLOSE function, 8-7, 8-16
CLS IL function, 8-40, 8-47
Colors
Associative dimension fixes, 16-25
Pens, 1-18
Table, 1-18
Comma delimited files, 8-43, 12-7
Command
Redefinition, 17-16, 17-17
With scripts, 15-12
COMMAND function, 2-9, 5-27
^C canceling, 2-10
Format, 2-9
NIL, 2-10
COMMAND.COM DOS file, 1-5
Common denominators, 3-14

Complex entities, 6-45
CompuServe
  Email number, D-8
  Forum, D-4
COND function, 4-8, 4-10
Conditional tests
  AutoLISP, 4-13
CONFIG.SYS
  Files error, B-14
  Fixing problems, B-4
  Installing device drivers, 1-6
Configuration
  Environment variables, 1-13
  Files, 1-8
  Prototype drawing, 1-17
CONS function, 3-25, 3-26, 6-28, 6-44
Console device, 8-7
Control
  characters, 5-8
  Codes, 5-8
  Directories, 17-8
  Drawing environment, 17-9, 17-10
  ENDing, 17-17
  Error, 17-26
  Existing drawings, 17-15
  Files, 17-4
  Input, 9-14
  Layers, 17-13
  Osnap, 10-18
  Resetting, 17-32
  System Management, 17-4
Converting 2D to 3D, 14-27
Coordinates
  AutoLISP lists, 2-11
  Continuous tracking, 9-20
  DCS Display, 14-15
  Status display, 9-4
COS function, 14-22, 14-24
Counting with AutoLISP, 3-12
CPATH IL function, 8-16
CSCALE C:command, 6-36
Customization
  Prerequisites, 0-8

D

Data
  Attributes, 11-3

DXF codes, 16-4
  FLATLAND effects on, 14-11
  Handling external, 8-42
  Importing, 13-21
  Importing to dBase, 13-31
  Importing to Lotus, 13-7
  Parametric, 12-7
  Reporting, 13-33
  Types of, 3-5
Data files
  CDF format, 12-7
  External files, 12-7, 12-11
  Large files, 12-7
Data types
  Determining, 5-3
  Lists, 2-11
Date stamping and calculating, 11-20
dBASE
  Conditionals, 13-31
  CREATE, 13-30
  Data from AutoCAD, 13-25
  Importing data, 13-31
  Looping, 13-31
  Preparing input, 13-25
  Procedures, 13-29
  Programming, 13-29
  Prompting, 13-30
  Structure, creating, 13-30
  Transferring data, 13-32
  Using with AutoCAD, 13-23
DCS
  Display Coordinate System, 14-15
DDRAW C:command, 9-21
Decrementing numbers, 3-12
DEFUN function, 3-27
DELERR IL function, 17-27
Device access
  GRTEXT, 9-3
  Alternatives, 9-13
  GRDRAW, 9-9
  GRREAD, 9-14
Devices
  Access modes, 8-9
  Console, 8-7
  Driver installation, 1-6
  I/O, 8-8
  NUL, 8-12
  Printer, 8-11
  Table of, 8-8
Digitizer

Input control, 9-16
Tracking, 9-20
Dimblk command, 10-24
Dimensioning
Associative caution, 10-31
DXF translation of associatives, 16-18
Iso-dimensioning, 10-20
Tip on fitting, 10-28
Translation problems in DXF, 16-27
DIMLINE C:command, 10-17
DIMSCALE
Drawing scale variable, 2-26
DIMZIN and RTOS, 5-17
Directories
Control, 17-4
DOS Subst control, 17-8
Errors with AutoCAD, B-12
Unix home directory, 1-4
Disk
Management, D-6
Display coordinates, 14-15
Distance
Formatting, 5-16
DISTANCE function, 5-24
Divide / function, 4-20
Documentation, 17-51
Displaying.LSP , 17-49
Of programs, 3-30
DOS
AutoCAD environment, 1-1
Bootup, 1-5, B-3
Buffer allocation, 1-6, B-3
Directories, 1-2
Minimum version requirements, 0-8
Path, 17-5
Path command, 1-2, 1-7
Prompt, 1-7, 1-11
Redirection symbols, 8-16
Replaceable batch parameters, 1-14, 13-16
Dotted pair, 6-28
DOWNROW IL function, 8-40
Drawing
Control, 17-9
File formats, 16-3
Prototype, 17-9
Revision system, 11-20
Driver
ADI, 1-8
Device installation, 1-6
DTOR IL function, 17-13

DXB
Binary drawing exchange files, 16-26
Plotting, 14-29
DXF
-1 entity code, 6-34
-2 subentity code, 7-14
Attributes, 11-6, 11-8
BASIC programs, 16-18
Block Reference, 16-9
ENDSEC end of section, 16-7
ENDTAB file marker, 16-9
Entities section, 16-11
Extraction function, 6-34
Extrusion vectors 210, 14-8
Group codes and data, 6-29, 16-4
Header information, 16-6
Importation, 15-6, 16-13
Non-graphical entities, 16-11
Optional entity properties, 16-13
Section markers, 16-6
Spelling checker, 16-17
Tables section, 16-8
Translation of, 16-26
vs. System variables, 16-6
When to use, 15-11, 16-27
DXF entity codes
Table of, 6-32
DXF IL function, 6-34
DXFIN and DXFOUT commands, 16-14, 16-15

E

ERROR function, 17-25
Echo, in batch files, B-5
ECS
Entity Coordinate System, 14-9
Modifying 210 codes, 14-32
Editing commands
vs. ENTMOD, 9-24
EDLIN
Text editor, 1-5
EL90-S IL function, 12-18
ELEV command
Future support, 14-5
Elevation, 6-35
System variable, future support, 14-5
EMAIL number, D-8

End-of-file character, 8-27, 8-29
ENDBLK
   DXF end of block definition, 16-10
ENDSEC
   DXF end of section, 16-7
ENDTAB
   DXF end of table, 16-9
ENTDEL function, 6-8, 6-9
   vs. Erase command, 6-9
ENTGET function, 6-26, 6-27, 7-14, 7-15
Entities
   210 code modification, 14-32
   3D types, 14-5
   Accessing data, 6-25
   Appending data sublists, 9-21
   Association lists, 6-27
   Block definitions, 7-12
   Byblock, 6-35
   Complex, 6-45
   Default properties, 6-35
   DXF codes, 6-29, 16-11
   DXF extraction function, 6-34
   FLATLAND effects on data, 14-11
   Inserts, 11-4
   Modifying, 6-40
   Non-graphical DXF types, 16-11
   Optional properties in DXF, 16-13
   Planar types, 14-6
   Polyline Modification, 6-49
   Removing data sublists, 9-21
   SEQEND, non-graphical, 11-6
   Subentities, 6-45
   Thickness, 6-35
   UCS modification, 14-31
   Updating, 6-40
Entity
   Coordinate System, 14-9
   Extrusion vectors, 14-8
   Names in AutoLISP, 6-4, 6-34
   Selection by point, 12-20
   Selection Sets, 6-12
ENTLAST function, 6-4, 6-6
ENTMOD function, 6-41, 6-44, 9-21
   vs. Editing commands, 9-24
ENTNEXT function, 6-4, 6-7, 6-46
ENTSEL function, 6-4, 6-9, 12-20
   Entity selection by point, 12-20
ENTUPD function, 6-40, 6-47, 6-49
Environment
   Control drawing, 17-10

DOS setup, 1-1
   Expanding space, B-7
   Variables, B-6
EQ function, 4-6, 4-7
EQUAL function, 4-6, 4-7
ERROR.LSP file, 17-27
Errors
   n> in AutoLISP, 2-4
   AutoCAD recovery, 2-9
   AutoLISP, B-12
   Can't find overlay file ..., B-13
   Config.sys file problems, B-4
   CONFIG.SYS problems, B-4
   Controlling of, 17-26
   Expanded memory disabled, B-13
   Insufficient node space, 4-23
   Insufficient string space, 4-23
   Invalid dotted pair, B-13
   Invalid dotted pairs, 3-3
   Memory, B-8
   Misplaced dot, B-13
   Numerical rounding, 14-14
   Opening/Loading files, B-14
   Out of environment space, B-3, B-6
   Out of RAM, B-9
   Program too big to fit in memory, B-12
   SHELL error in EXEC function, B-12
   SHELL error swapping to disk, B-12
   SHELL error: insufficient memory, B-12
   Unknown command, B-13
   Unknown entity type..., 16-15
   Unknown header variable..., 16-15
   Unknown table..., 16-15
ESC escape characters, 8-37
ETOS IL function, 8-12
EVAL function, 4-23, 5-24, 17-23
Evaluation
   AutoLISP, 3-28
   Order, 2-23, 3-12
EXIT command, 1-11
EXP function, 3-16
EXPAND function, 17-45
Expanded ASCII codes, 5-8
Expanded memory, B-8, B-13
Expanding control characters, 8-6
Exponents of numbers, 3-14
EXPT function, 3-15
Extended ASCII codes, 17-20
Extended AutoLISP
   Installation, 1-14

Extended memory, B-8
External commands, 1-9
EXTLINE C:command, 10-19
Extrusion vectors, 14-8
    Calculation of, 14-31
    DXF 210 code, 14-8

F

FFNAME IL function, 8-22, 8-47
Files
    .DWG format, 16-3
    .LSB, 17-49
    .MNX, 17-47
    ACAD.CFG, 1-8
    ACAD.LSP automatic loading, 2-25
    ACAD.PGP shell command, 1-2, 1-11
    Allocation in CONFIG.SYS, 1-6, B-3
    Appending, 8-27
    AUTOEXEC.BAT system batch, 1-2
    AutoLISP program file format, 2-14
    CDF format, 12-7, 8-43
    Changing directories, 8-54
    Comma delimited, 8-43
    CONFIG.SYS, 1-2
    Configuration overlays, 1-8
    Data formats, 12-7
    Directory control, 17-4
    End-of-file character, 8-27
    Error in loading, B-14
    External, 12-7
    Formats, 8-42
    Handles, 8-7
    IL-NOTES.DXF, 16-13
    IL.BAT batch, 1-2
    Organization, 17-4
    Parametric, 12-7
    Processing, 8-7
    Reducing .LSP size, 17-48
    SDF Standard Data Format, 8-43
    Stripping .LSP files, 17-48
    Support/Driver/Configuration, 1-7
    Testing, 8-14
FILES command, 8-27
FILES=:Setting in Config.sys, B-14
FINDFILE function, 8-14, 8-18
FITTINGS.TXT, 13-5
FIX function, 5-18, 9-21

FIX-TEXT.BAS utility, 16-19
Flags, 12-18
Flat patterns, 14-35
FLATLAND
    Effect on entity data, 14-11
    System variable, 14-3
FLOAT function, 5-18
FLY C:command, 17-23
FOREACH function, 4-16, 8-43
Formats
    ANSI code, 8-36
Formulas
    3D arcs and points, 14-20
    Polyline bulges, 14-23
Freeware, software from forums, D-7
FTEXT
    C:command, 15-8
    IL function, 13-22
Function
    Arguments, 3-28
    Definition with AutoLISP, 2-4, 3-27
    Loading, 17-36
    Self-loading, 17-39

G

GC function, 17-45
GCD function, 3-14
GET functions, 3-7
GETANGLE function, 3-7
    UANGLE, 5-39
GETBLK IL function, 11-33, 11-34
GETCORNER function, 2-17
GETDIST function, 3-7, 3-9
GETINT function, 3-8
    UINT, 5-39
GETKWORD function, 5-36
    UKWORD, 5-39
GETORIENT function, 3-7
GETPOINT function, 2-11, 3-9
    UPOINT, 5-39
GETREAL function, 3-7, 3-9
    UREAL, 5-39
GETSIZE IL function, 12-14
GETSTRING function, 2-12, 3-9
    USTR, 5-39
GETVAR function, 2-6
Global variables, 4-19, 17-10

GOTO IL function, 8-40, 8-47
GPATH IL function, 17-5
GRAPHICS, DOS command, B-7
GRAPHSCR function, 5-10
GRCLEAR function, 9-9
GRDRAW function, 9-1, 9-7, 9-9
    Blanking lines, 9-9
    Highlighting lines, 9-9
    Reversing colors, 9-9
Grid
    Isometric, 10-16
GRPT IL function, 14-3
GRREAD function, 9-14, 9-15, 9-21
    Cautions, 9-19
    Devices, 9-15
    Table of codes, 9-15
GRTEXT function, 9-1, 9-2, 9-3, 12-6
    Boxes, 9-3
    Clearing, 9-5
    Highlighting, 9-5
    Updating boxes, 9-5

H

HANDENT function, 6-53
Hard disk, management, D-6
Hatches
    Automatic generation, 8-29
    Custom, 8-29
    Polyline fitting, 8-36
HEAP memory setting, 1-14
Heap space, 4-24
Help
    Displaying.LSP , 17-49
    inDeX, 12-9, 12-11
    INSIDE AutoLISP's, 12-9
    Slides as, 17-53
Highlighting
    Graphics, 9-9
    GRTEXT, 9-5

I

I/O
    Devices, 8-8
    Page space, B-8

IF function, 4-8
IGES
    Inter. Graphics Exchange Standard, 16-26
IL DISK
    Installation, 1-8
IL-NOTES.DXF, 16-13
IL.BAT start up file, 1-12
Illegal characters, 3-27
ILLOAD
    IL function, 17-36
    .LSP file, 17-36
INCANG IL function, 12-24, 14-24
Incrementing numbers, 3-12
INITERR IL function, 17-27
INITGET function, 3-9, 5-32
    Control bit table, 5-32
    Key words, 5-33
Input
    Controlling, 9-14
    Filtering, 9-14
    GRREAD control, 9-14
    With AutoLISP, 2-10
Inserts, 6-45
Inside AutoLISP Disk Files
    ACAD.KEY, 17-20
    ANSI.HLP, 8-36
    ANSILIB.LSP, 8-40
    APLATE.LSP, 6-15
    ATEXT.LSP, 5-24
    ATTFIT.DWG, 12-29
    ATTFIT.TXT, 13-5
    ATTFITS.LSP, 12-31
    ATTPIPE.DWG, 12-29
    ATTPIPE.TXT, 13-5
    ATTSHT-D.DWG, 11-13
    AUTOBLK.LSP, 11-34
    BATCHSCR.LSP, 15-13
    BSCALE.LSP, 6-42
    BUBBLE.LSP, 3-28
    CADATA.DBF, 13-29
    CATEMP.DBF, 13-29
    COMPASS.DWG, 9-21
    CSCALE.LSP, 6-36
    DBLINE.LSP, 12-26
    DDRAW.LSP, 9-23
    DRAW.LSP, 4-25
    EL90-S.LSP, 12-18
    ERROR.LSP, 17-27
    ETEXT.LSP, 9-18
    ETOS.LSP, 8-12

FILELIB.LSP, 8-16
FIX-TEXT.BAS, 16-19
GPATH.LSP, 17-5
IL-3D.LSP, 14-21
IL-ACAD.DWG decimal prototype, 1-2
IL-BLOCK.DWG, 1-9
IL-BLOCK.SCR, 1-9
IL-NOTES.DXF, 15-6
IL-NOTES.LSP, 15-8
IL-NOTES.SCR, 15-4
IL-NOTES.TXT, 15-7
IL-PROTO.DWG arch. prototype, 1-2
IL.BAT, 1-12
IL10DIM.MNU, 10-12
IL11TITL.MNU, 11-14
ILLOAD.LSP, 17-36
ISO-INIT.DWG, 10-16
ISO-TAB.DWG, 10-29
ISODIM.LSP, 10-18
ISODIM.MNU, 10-23
KILL.KEY, 17-20
LEGEND.LSP, 7-15
LSPSTRIP.EXE, 17-48
Manually Importing to 123, 13-7
MFLY.LSP, 17-23
MID3D function, 14-3
MOFFSET.LSP, 6-9
PATTERN.LSP, 8-29
PIPEFIT.DAT, 12-8
PIPEFIT.HLP, 12-9
PIPEMATL.DWG, 12-33, 13-5
PRO_TRAK.EXE, 13-28
PVIEW.LSP, 9-11
RCLOUD.LSP, 6-47
REDEFS.LSP, 17-17
REFDWG.LSP, 8-47
REFDWG.TXT, 8-46
REPSTAT.LSP, 13-25
REVBLOCK.DWG, 11-23
REVBLOCK.TXT, 13-23
SCR-MAP.DWG, 8-38
SELFLOAD.LSP, 17-39
SETVP.LSP, 7-35
SHBOX.LSP, 2-16
SHOW3D, 14-17
SLOT.LSP, 4-19
SSTOOLS..LSP, 6-21
TAKOFF.LSP, 7-26
TIMELIB.LSP, 11-21
TITLEBLK.TXT, 13-23

TOGGLE.KEY, 17-20
UDIST.LSP, 5-29
UENTSL.LSP, 6-20
UPDATE.LSP, 11-26
VALVE-B.DWG, 11-31
WLAYER.LSP, 7-8
XINSERT.LSP, 7-37
XINSERT.TXT, 7-37
Inside AutoLISP Functions
ERROR, 17-27
3DPOLAR, 14-22
ADDERR, 17-27
ALTITD (altitude), 14-24
ANGTOC, 5-22
APLATE, 6-15
ARCLEN (arc length), 14-24
ATEXT, 5-24
BACKUP, 8-26
BANGLE (Inclined angle), 14-21
BOLD, 8-40, 8-47
C:3DPOLAR, 14-22
C:BLINE, 11-35
C:BSCALE, 6-42
C:BUBBLE, 3-28
C:DDRAW, 9-21
C:DIMLINE, 10-17
C:EXTLINE, 10-19
C:FLY, 17-23
C:FTEXT, 15-8
C:LEGEND, 7-15
C:MFLY, 17-23
C:PATTERN, 8-29
C:RCLOUD, 6-47
C:REFDWG, 8-47
C:REPSTAT, 13-25
C:S-LEAD (Straight LEADer), 17-32
C:SLOT, 4-19
C:WLAYER, 7-8
C:XINSERT, 7-37
CENTER, 8-40, 8-47
CLS, 8-40, 8-47
CPATH, 8-16
CSCALE, 6-36
DELERR, 17-27
DOWNROW, 8-40
DRAW/GETPTS/DIAM, 4-25
DTOR, 17-13
DXF, 6-34
EL90-S, 12-18
ETOS.LSP, 8-12

FFNAME (Format File NAME), 8-22, 8-47
FTEXT, 13-22
GETBLK, 11-33, 11-34
GETSIZE, 12-14
GOTO, 8-40, 8-47
GPATH, 17-5
ILLOAD, 17-36
INCANG (included angle), 12-24, 14-24
INITERR, 17-27
LEDSWAP, 7-20
MERGEF, 8-27
MERGEV, 8-29
MLAYER, 17-13
MOFFSET, 6-9
NORMAL, 8-40, 8-47
OUTLEDG, 7-18
PSLASH, 8-19
RADIUS, 14-24
REFOUT, 8-52
REFSEL, 8-49
RESTPOS, 8-40, 8-47
REVTIME, 11-30
SAVEPOS, 8-40, 8-47
SETSIZE, 12-13
SETVP, 7-35
SSADD, 6-23
SSDIFF, 6-23
SSINTER, 6-23
SSUNION, 6-23
STACK.LSP, 17-40
STRIP, 9-21
TAKOFF, 7-26
TIME, 11-21
TODAY, 11-21, 11-30
UDIST, 5-29, 6-9
UENTSL, 6-20
UINT, 6-9
UKWORD, 5-36
UPD, 11-30
UPOINT, 6-9
USTR, 5-38
VFFILE.LSP, 8-23
VPATH, 8-24
YEAR, 11-21
Installation
    AUTOEXEC.BAT file check, 1-6, B-4
    CONFIG.SYS file check, 1-6
    Extended AutoLISP, 1-14
    Of IL DISK, 1-8
    Setting a prototype drawing, 1-17

Insufficient memory for command, B-12
INTEGER variables, 3-3, 5-3
Intern'l Graphics Exchange Standards,
    16-26
INTERS function, 12-18
Invalid dotted pair, 3-3, B-13
Iso-dimensioning
    Associative caution, 10-31
    Dimtypes illustrated, 10-15
    Dimtypes table, 10-20
    Symbols, 10-14
    Tablet menu, 10-29
    Text styles, 10-14
Isometric
    Axis, 10-16
    Grid, 10-16
    Snap, 10-16
Isoplanes, 10-20
ITOA function, 5-15

K

Kelvinator, 17-47
Key words
    Association list, 6-28
    INITGET, 5-33
Keyboard
    ANSI.SYS redefinition, 17-20
    Control, 17-19
    Input control, 9-16
    Macro programs, 17-19

L

Labels for macros, 10-3
LAMBDA function, 17-7
Languages
    BASIC, 16-17
LAST function, 3-24
Layers
    Filtering names, 1-18
    Management, 17-13
    Naming convention, 1-18
    Pen assignment, 1-18
    Symbol table, 7-3, 7-6
    Wildcards, 1-18

LEDSWAP IL function, 7-20
LEGEND
   Attributes, 7-15
   C:command, 7-15
LENGTH function, 3-25
Lines
   Blanking, 9-9
   Grdraw, 9-9
   Temporary, 9-9
Linetypes
   Maximum in drawings, 16-9
   Symbol table, 7-25, 7-30
   Table, 1-18
LISPHEAP, 4-24
   Memory setting, 1-13
LISPSTACK
   Memory setting, 1-13
LISPXMEM
   Memory setting, 1-14
List data types, 2-11
LIST function, 3-21, 3-22, 8-47
LIST variables, 3-3
LISTP function, 5-4, 5-5, 5-6
Lists, 4-1, 5-3
   As COMMAND input, 5-27
   Getting indexed elements, 3-24
   Length of, 3-25
   Processing, 4-16
   Reversing, Appending, 3-25
LOAD function, 2-15, 3-29
Loading
   Functions, 2-15, 17-36
   Quick loading functions, 17-48
   Self-loading programs, 17-39
Local variables, 4-19
LOG function, 3-16
Logical drives, 17-8
Logs of numbers, 3-14
Lost attributes, 11-40
Lotus
   Automating, 13-17
   Converting data, 13-11
   Importing data, 13-7
   Macros in, 13-17
   Parsing data, 13-10
LSPSTRIP caution, 17-50
LSPSTRIP.EXE, 17-48
Ltypes
   Symbol table, 7-3

M

Macros
   [labels], 10-3
   Attribute input, 11-15
   Converting to AutoLISP, 2-7
   Getting input, 3-10
   Input control, 3-10
   Keyboard, 17-19
   Long, 15-6
   Mini-page toggles, 10-10
   On-the-fly, 17-23
   Pausing and AutoLISP, 3-10
   Showing status, 10-24
   Table of special characters, 10-3
Magazines, D-5
Management
   Drawing status, 13-28
   How to manage system, 17-2
   Time, 13-35
MAPCAR function, 12-17
   Set variable lists, 12-17
Material tagging, 12-29, 13-3
Math with AutoLISP, 3-11
MAX function, 3-13
Maximum/Minimum values, finding of, 3-13
MEMBER function, 3-26, 8-49
Memory
   ACADLIMEM setting, B-9
   ACADXMEM setting, B-9
   AutoCAD free RAM, 1-13
   AutoLISP settings, 1-13
   Checking with AUTOEXEC.BAT, B-6
   Errors with AutoCAD shell, B-12
   Expanded memory disabled error, B-13
   Extended and expanded, B-8
   Fixing problems, B-8
   Management practices, 17-41
Menu
   ** page names, 10-4
   **PIPEFITS, 12-6
   **TITLEBLK, 11-17
   Box numbers, 9-3
   Defined, 10-3
   Documenting, 17-51
   Dummy pages, 17-51
   Dynamic labels, 9-3
   Long macros, 15-6
   Mini-page toggles, 10-10

Page defined, 10-4
Page switching, 10-4
Parametrics, 12-3
Reports, 13-15
Security, 17-47
Setup, 17-9
Toggle labels, 12-6
Toggling, 10-21
MENUCMD function, 10-11
MERGEF IL function, 8-27
MERGEV IL function, 8-29
MFLY C:command, 17-23
MID3D IL function, 14-3
MIN function, 3-13
Mini-page of toggling macros, 10-10
Minimum/Maximum values, finding of, 3-13
MINUSP function, 5-5, 5-6
Misplaced dot, B-13
MLAYER IL function, 17-13
MOFFSET C:command, 6-9
Move command
    vs. ENTMOD, 9-24
Multiply * function, 4-20

N

Nesting
    Evaluation order, 2-24
    Expressions, 2-6
NEWECS IL function, 14-33
NIL
    Cancelling with, 2-10
    Test conditions, 4-2
Node space in AutoLISP, 4-23
NORMAL IL function, 8-40, 8-47
NOT function, 4-3
NTH function, 3-25, 8-49
NUL device, 8-12
NULL function, 5-6
NUMBERP function, 5-6

O

Object Selection, 6-6
    Last, 6-6
Octal character codes, 3-20

Offset command, 12-20
OPEN function, 8-6, 8-7, 8-9, 8-16
OR function, 4-3, 4-4, 8-22
Organization
    Files, 17-4
Osnap, 6-6
    Control, 10-18
OSNAP command, 10-18
    Point selection cautions, 12-18
OSNAP function, 12-18
Out of environment space, B-3, B-6
OUTLEDG IL function, 7-18

P

Page
    Menu page defined, 10-4
Parametrics
    Attribute controlled, 11-31
    Autobreaking blocks, 11-31
    Calculating points, 12-24
    Calculations, 12-16
    Data retrieval, 12-14
    Drawing components, 12-16
    Menus, 12-3
    Osnap caution, 12-18
    Planning, 12-16
Parentheses matching, 2-3, 2-4
Parsing strings, 3-19, 8-43, 8-44
Path, 17-5
    DOS command, 1-7
    DOS directory searches, 1-2
    In AUTOEXEC.BAT file, B-5
    Testing, 8-14
PATTERN C:command, 8-29
Patterns
    Automatic hatches, 8-29
    Custom, 8-29
Pens
    Colors, 1-18
    Table, 1-18
PGP
    Program parameter file, 1-9
PI constant, 4-20
Pipe fitting
    Parametric, 12-1
PIPEFITS menu, 12-6
Piping cut templates, 14-35

Planes
    Construction, 14-5
Plotting
    Automation tips, 7-30
    Batch scripts, 15-26
    DXB output, 14-29
Point
    3D format, 14-3
    AutoLISP, 3-21
    Calculating, 12-24
    Coordinate lists, 2-19
    Translating coordinate systems, 14-13
    Variables, 3-3
POLAR function, 4-20, 4-21
    3D version, 14-22
Polylines, 6-45
    Bulge formula, 6-49
    Modifying, 6-49
Predicates, 5-3
    Alternatives, 5-6
Prerequisites, 0-8
    CONFIG.SYS, 1-6
    Directories, 1-2
PRIN1 function, 5-11, 5-12, 8-5
PRINC function, 5-11, 8-4
    Clean finish, 5-13
PRINT function, 5-11, 5-12, 8-5
PRINT, DOS command, B-7
Printing strings, 5-11
PRO_TRAK
    Using, 13-36
Procedures
    Dbase, 13-29
PROGN function, 4-18
Programs
    Defining, 3-27
    Developing, 2-16
    Documentating techniques, 3-30
    Evaluation order, 2-23
    Reading of, 2-23
    Recursive iteration, 4-26
    Streamlining for better performance, 2-20
    Subroutine use, 4-24
    Too big to fit in memory errors, B-12
PROJECT.DAT, 13-25, 13-33
Prompt
    Building with AutoLISP, 3-18
    DOS command, 1-7
    In DOS SHELL, 1-11
    Toggling with AutoLISP, 10-12

PROMPT function, 5-9, 5-11, 8-4
PROTECT.EXE, 17-47
Prototype
    Configuring, 1-17
    Drawings, creation of, 1-15
PSLASH IL function, 8-19

Q

QUIT function, 17-38
QUOTE function, 3-23, 3-24, 5-4

R

RADIUS IL function, 14-24
RAM
    AutoCAD's use of, B-8
RAMDISK
    AutoCAD files, B-10
    Setting up, B-9
RCLOUD C:command, 6-47
READ function, 5-23
READ-CHAR function, 8-4, 8-10
READ-LINE function, 8-3, 8-10
Reading programs, 2-23
REAL
    Converting to strings, 5-16
    Variables, 3-3, 5-3
Recursive programming, 4-26
Redefining commands, 17-16
REDEFS.LSP, 17-17
Redirection symbols
    DOS, 8-16
REDRAW function, 6-7
REFDWG C:command, 8-47
REFOUT IL function, 8-52
REFSEL IL function, 8-49
REM function, 3-14
Remainders in divisions, 3-14
REPEAT function, 4-12
Reports
    Menu, 13-15
REPSTAT C:command, 13-25
Rescaling of Blocks, 6-46
Reset controls, 17-32
RESTPOS IL function, 8-40, 8-47

RESUME command, 15-12
RETURN
    ^M in Lisp/Macros, 5-9
    ASCII codes, 5-8
REVBLOCK.DWG
    Attributes, 11-23
REVERSE function, 3-25
Revision
    A system for, 11-20
    Automating, 11-20
    Clouds, 6-50
    Level, 11-29
    Outputting status, 13-26
    Tracking, 11-22, 13-28
REVTIME IL function, 11-30
Roots of numbers, 3-14
Rotation angle, 5-20
ROUNDOFF, 14-14
    IL function, 14-3
RTOS function, 5-16, 5-22, 8-29
    0 control, 5-17
    DIMZIN, 5-17
    Formats, 5-16
Rubber-banding lines, 3-10

S

S-LEAD (Straight LEADer) C:, 17-32
S::STARTUP function, 17-18
SSADD function, 6-14
SAVEPOS IL function, 8-40, 8-47
Scale
    Of drawings, 1-17
    Setting of, 2-26
Screens
    Dynamic labeling, 9-2
    Screensize setvars, 9-11
    Size calculations, 9-11
Scripts, 15-3
    AutoLISP, 15-27
    Automate Building, 15-12
    Environment, 15-12
    Plotting, 15-26
    Resuming, 15-12
    Stopping, 15-12
SDF Standard Delimited Files, 8-43
SECTION
    Marker in DXF files, 16-6

Selection sets
    Adding, 6-21
    AutoLISP manipulation, 6-14
    Creating with AutoLISP, 6-18
    Entities, 6-12
    Intersection of, 6-21
    Subtracting, 6-21
SELFLOAD.LSP file, 17-39
SEQEND
    End of subentity marker, 11-6
SET
    ACAD= setting, 1-13
    ACADCFG= setting, 1-13
    ACADFREERAM= setting, 1-13
    ACADLIMEM= setting, 1-14
    ACADXMEM= setting, 1-14
    DOS environment command, 1-14, B-6
    LISPHEAP= setting, 1-13
    LISPSTACK= setting, 1-13
    LISPXMEM= setting, 1-14
SET function, 5-24, 12-18
    vs. SETQ, 5-24, 12-18
SETQ function, 2-5, 12-18
SETSIZE IL function, 12-13
Setup
    Drawing environment, 17-9
    Existing systems, 1-8
    Subdirectory, 1-3
SETVAR
    Command, 3-2
    FLATLAND variable, 3-9, 14-3
    Function, 2-6
    Table of, C-1
SETVP IL function, 7-35
SH
    See SHELL, 1-11
Shareware software, D-7
SHBOX.LSP file, 2-16
Shell
    AutoCAD, 1-9
    DOS environment in CONFIG.SYS, 1-6, B-3
    Error in EXEC function, B-12
    Error swapping to disk, B-12
    Error: insufficient memory..., B-12
    Exit from, 1-11
    Maximum, 16-15
    PGP and AutoLISP, 8-16
    SHELL command, 1-10
SHOW3D.LSP file, 14-17
SIN function, 14-24

SKETCH command, 6-50
  Skpoly, 6-50
SKPOLY system variable, 6-50
Slide
  Libraries, 17-53
  Starting shows from DOS, 15-25
Snap
  Isometric, 10-16
  rotated, 9-24
SPACE
  ASCII codes, 5-8
Spelling checker with DXF, 16-17
Spreadsheets, 13-7
SQRT function, 3-14
SSADD function, 6-13
SSDEL function, 6-13, 6-14
SSDIFF IL function, 6-23
SSGET function, 6-12, 6-45
SSGET"X" filtering, 7-8
SSINTER IL function, 6-23
SSLENGTH function, 6-13, 6-14, 6-16
SSMEMB function, 6-13, 6-14, 6-24
SSNAME function, 6-13, 6-14
SSUNION IL function, 6-23
STACK memory setting, 1-14
Standard Data Format
  SDF, 8-43
Status line, 9-4
STK-PIPE IL function, 14-35
STRCASE function, 3-18, 4-11
STRCAT function, 3-17, 5-24
Strings, 5-3
  Displaying, 5-11
  Flipping case, 3-18
  Formatting, 5-7
  Maximum length, 3-17
  Merging of, 3-17
  Parsing of, 3-19
  Printing, 5-11
  Space in AutoLISP, 4-23
  STRING variables, 3-3
STRIP IL function, 9-21
STRLEN function, 3-19
Styles
  Symbol table, 7-3, 7-6
Subentities, 6-45
Subentity name -2 DXF code, 7-14
Subroutines
  Definition with AutoLISP, 2-4
  Use of, 4-24

SUBST DOS command, 17-8
SUBST function, 6-41, 6-42, 6-44
SUBSTR function, 3-19, 8-43
Subtract - function, 4-20
Support files, 1-7
Symbol, 5-3, 5-4
  AutoLISP, 15-16
  Creating with SET, 5-24
  In lines, 11-31
  Iso-dimensioning, 10-14
Symbol tables, 7-3
  Block definition, 7-3
  Layers, 7-3
  Ltypes, 7-3
  Styles, 7-3
  Views, 7-3
SYNPLANT.DWG, 13-24
Syntax
  Attribute extract template, 13-4
  Layers, 1-18
System management, 17-2
System Variables, 17-10
  AutoLISP, 3-2, 3-4
  Controlling in Lisp, 5-27
  FLATLAND, 3-9
  Read only, 3-4
  SCREENSIZE, 9-11
  Table of, C-1
  TDCREATE, 17-15
  TDUPDAT, 17-15
  User, 7-30, 11-30
  vs. DXF, 16-6

T

Tables
  $ menu page codes, 10-4
  Angle formats, 5-20
  ANGTOS units, 5-20
  ASCII escape codes, 5-8
  AutoCAD System Variables, C-1, C-2
  AutoLISP Functions, C-9
  Color/Pen/Linetype, 1-18
  Device names, 8-8
  Drawing reference information, 16-8
  DXF entity codes, 6-32
  Entity properties, default, 6-35
  GRREAD codes, 9-15

INITGET control bits, 5-32
Iso-dimensioning, 10-20
Layers, 7-6
Linetype/Color/Pen, 1-18
Linetypes, 7-30
Pen/Linetype/Color, 1-18
REVBLOCK attributes, 11-23
RTOS formats, 5-16
Special characters in macros, 10-3
SSGET X Property Codes, 6-18
Styles, 7-6
Title block attributes, 11-11
Views, 7-6
Tablet
    Iso-dimensioning, 10-29
TAKOFF IL function, 7-26
TBLNEXT function, 7-3, 7-4, 7-15
TBLSEARCH function, 5-27, 7-3, 7-11
TBLSEARCH functions
    Blocks, 7-11
TDCREATE system variable, 17-15
TDUPDAT system variable, 17-15
Templates
    Attribute extract, 13-3
Temporary files, placement, B-10
TERPRI function, 5-10
Text
    Alignment codes, 6-38
    Curved, 5-24
    Editor for AutoCAD commands, 9-16
    Editors, selection of, 1-5, B-1
    Fixed height, 1-16
    Formatting with AutoLISP, 15-8
    Importing with AutoLISP, 15-7
    Importing with DXF, 15-6, 16-13
    Iso-dimensioning, 10-14
    Layering conventions, 2-8
    Line editor for AutoCAD, 9-16
    Style, 1-16
    Style tip, 10-28
    Writing to graphic screen, 9-3
TEXTSCR function, 5-10, 8-48
Thickness, 6-35
Time
    Logging and reporting, 13-35
    IL function, 11-21
    Stamping and automating, 11-20
    System variables, 17-15
Title block
    Attributes table, 11-11

ATTSHT-D, 11-13
    System, 11-9
TITLEBLK menu, 11-17
TODAY IL function, 11-21, 11-30
Toggles
    Construction of, 10-12
    Menu label, 12-6
    Menu mini-pages, 10-10
TRANS function, 14-13
    Application of, 14-16
Translating points, 14-13
Translations of DXF, 16-26
TRUE
    Test conditions, 4-2
TSR Programs, 1-6, B-4, B-7
TYPE function, 5-3

U

UCS
    Alternatives to changing, 14-31
    Axis orientation, 14-10
    Defined, 14-6
    Extrusion vectors, 14-8
    Relation to (ECS), 14-9
    User Coordinate System, 14-5
    Working with, 14-6
UDIST IL function, 5-29, 6-9
UENTSL IL function, 6-20
UINT IL function, 6-9
UKWORD IL function, 5-36
Undefine command, 17-16
Units
    Angular, 5-20
UNIX
    AutoCAD startup, 1-15
    Book compatibility, 0-8
    Home directory, 1-4
    Text editor operations, 1-12
Unknown command error, B-13
UPD IL function, 11-30
UPOINT IL function, 6-9
User Coordinate System UCS
    Defined, 14-6
User groups, D-5
User input control, 5-32
User interfaces, 17-52
User interface functions

Example, 6-9
UANGLE, 5-39
UINT, 5-39
UKWORD, 5-39
UPOINT, 5-39
UREAL, 5-39
USTR, 5-39
User macros on-the-fly, 17-23
User variables, 7-30
USTR IL function, 5-38

V

Variables
    AutoLISP, 3-2
    Defining, 3-4
    Global, 4-19, 17-10
    INTEGERs, 3-3
    LISTs, 3-3
    Local, 4-19
    Naming efficiency, 4-23
    Passing to AutoCAD with !, 3-6
    POINTs, 3-3
    REALs, 3-3
    STRINGs, 3-3
    Types, 3-3
    User, 11-30
    Valid/invalid types, 3-5
Variables and expressions in AutoLISP, 3-2
Vertexes, 6-47
VFFILE IL function, 8-23
Viewports
    Controlling redraws, 14-29
Views
    Dynamic selection, 9-11
    Symbol table, 7-3, 7-6
Virtual disk, See RAMDISK, B-9
VMON function, 17-42
VPATH IL function, 8-24
VPOFF IL function, 14-30
VPORTS function, 7-34
VSLIDE command, 17-53

W

WHILE function, 4-14

WHILE-NOT-EQUAL, 8-43
WLAYER C:command, 7-8
World Coordinate System WCS
    Axis orientation, 14-10
    Defined, 14-5
    Extrusion vectors, 14-8
    Relation to UCS, 14-6
WRITE-CHAR function, 8-3, 8-5
WRITE-LINE function, 8-3, 8-4, 8-9, 8-29
Writing
    To files, 8-9
    To printers, 8-11

X

XINSERT C:command, 7-37
XLISP, 4-1

Y

YEAR IL function, 11-21

Z

Z coordinate, 14-3
ZAXIS IL function, 14-32
ZEROP function, 5-6, 14-21

AutoCAD Software Solutions

New Riders AutoLISP Utilities

Disk 1 — Release 10
ISBN 0-934035-79-2 **$29.95**

This disk contains several valuable programs and utilities and subroutines. You will find these useful to any AutoCAD drawing application. They include:

CATCH.LSP CATCH is great for selecting the new entities created by exploding blocks, polylines, 3D meshes, and dimensions.

HEX-INT.LSP is a set of hexadecimal arithmetic tools that make dealing with entity handles easier.

SHELL.LSP contains the SHELL function that executes and verifies multiple DOS commands with a single AutoCAD SHELL command execution (DOS only).

MERGE-V.LSP contains MERGE-V, which combines two files and verifies the copy procedure (DOS only).

PVAR.LSP provides functions for creating a personal variable system which can retain up to 254 variable values in a drawing's LTYPE table.

ISODIM.MNU implements an isometric dimensioning system as a TABLET1 menu. Using a tablet menu makes iso-dimensioning more intuitive.

GROUP.LSP contains functions to create and select *groups* of entities in AutoCAD drawings.

GRPT.LSP contains GRPT, a function that draws GRDRAW temporary points with any PDSIZE or PDMODE system variable setting.

FLATPAT.LSP is a program to generate flat pattern drawings of pipe end conditions.

XINSERT.LSP contains XINSERT, an external block extraction and insertion program.

STACK.LSP is a function loading program to minimize memory conflicts in using several moderate to large AutoLISP functions at once.

These AutoLISP programs and subroutines are not encrypted and are well documented by comments in the *filename*.LSP files.

Watch for or call New Riders Publishing for information on additions to the New Riders Utilities Disk family.

New Riders Library

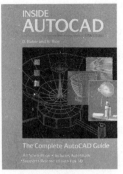

INSIDE AutoCAD

Over 250,000 sold

The Complete AutoCAD Guide
D. Raker and H. Rice
864 pages, over 400 illustrations
ISBN 0-934035-49-0 **$29.95**

Fifth Edition — Release 10

INSIDE AutoCAD, the best selling book on AutoCAD, is entirely new and rewritten for AutoCAD's 3D Release 10. This easy-to-understand book serves as both a tutorial and a lasting reference guide. Learn to use every single AutoCAD command as well as time saving drawing techniques and tips. Includes coverage of new 3D graphics features, AutoShade, and AutoLISP. This is the book that lets you keep up and stay in control with AutoCAD.

CUSTOMIZING AutoCAD

Second Edition — Release 10

A Complete Guide to AutoCAD Menus, Macros and More!
J. Smith and R. Gesner
480 Pages, 100 illustrations
ISBN 0-934035-45-8, **$27.95**

Uncover the hidden secrets of AutoCAD's 3D Release 10 in this all new edition. Discover the anatomy of an AutoCAD menu and build a custom menu from start to finish. Manipulate distance, angles, points, and hatches — ALL in 3D! Customize hatches, text fonts and dimensioning for increased productivity. Buy *CUSTOMIZING AutoCAD* today and start customizing AutoCAD tomorrow!

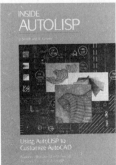

INSIDE AutoLISP

Release 10

The Complete Guide to Using AutoLISP for AutoCAD Applications
J. Smith and R. Gesner
736 pages, over 150 illustrations
ISBN: 0-934035-47-4, **$29.95**

Introducing the most comprehensive book on AutoLISP for AutoCAD Release 10. Learn AutoLISP commands and functions and write your own custom AutoLISP programs. Numerous tips and tricks for using AutoLISP for routine drawing tasks. Import and export critical drawing information to/from Lotus 1-2-3 and dBASE. Automate the creation of scripts for unattended drawing processing. *INSIDE AutoLISP* is the book that will give you the inside track to using AutoLISP.

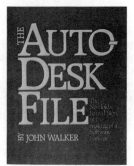

The New Riders' Library also includes products on Desktop Publishing

Style Sheets for Technical Documents

320 pages, over 100 illustrations
ISBN: 0-934035-31-8 Book/Disk Set **$39.95**

Get the maximum out of Xerox Ventura Publisher with these advanced, high-performance technical document style sheets.

Style Sheets for Newsletters

320 pages, over 100 illustrations
ISBN: 0-034035-29-6 Book\Disk Set **$39.95**

Have immediate impact with these spphisticated professionally designed one-, two-, three-, four-, and five-column layouts. Choose from two dozen attractive newsletterfor Xerox Ventura Publisher.

Style Sheets for Business Documents

320 pages, illustrations
ISBN: 0-934035-22-9 Book\Disk Set **$39.95**

Contains more than 30 top-quality business documents for Xerox Ventura Publisher. Put the power of sophisticated graphics design to work for your company.

Inside Xerox Ventura Publisher   Version 2/2nd Edition

704 pages, 330 illustrations
ISBN 0-934035-59-8 **$29.95**

The best reference guide to Xerox Ventura Publisher has been completely rewritten for Version 2.

Publishing Power With Ventura   Version 2/2nd Edition

704 pages, over 400 illustrations
ISBN 0-934035-61-X, **$27.95**

Unlock the inner secrets of Ventura Publisher Version 2. The only learning guide available with in-depth, step-by-step instructions for creating newsletters, flyers, books, and more! The optional disk makes learning even easier. Other books talk about productivity — this book delivers it!

Order from New Riders Publishing Today!

Please indicate which release of AutoCAD you are using.

❑ AutoCAD Release

Yes, please send me the productivity-boosting material I have checked below. Make check payable to New Riders Publishing.

❑ Check enclosed.

Charge to my credit card:

❑ Visa #

❑ Mastercard #

Expiration date:_____

Signature:_____

Name:_____

Company:_____

Address:_____

City:_____

State:_____ Zip:_____

Phone:_____

The easiest way to order is to pick up the phone and call (818) 991-5392 between 9:00 AM and 5:00 PM PST. Please have your credit card available and your order can be placed in a snap!

[handwritten: T 385 .S626 1989]

Quantity	Description of Item	Unit Cost	Total Cost
	Inside AutoLISP	$29.95	
	Inside AutoLISP Disk	$14.95	
	AutoLISP Utilities — Disk 1	$29.95	
	Inside AutoCAD 5th Edition	$29.95	
	Inside AutoCAD 5th Edition Disk	$14.95	
	Customizing AutoCAD 2nd Edition	$27.95	
	Customizing AutoCAD 2nd Edition Disk	$14.95	
	AutoCAD Reference Guide	$11.95	
	AutoCAD Reference Guide Disk	$14.95	
	Stepping into AutoCAD 4th Edition	$29.95	
	Stepping into AutoCAD 4th Edition Disk	$14.95	
	Inside AutoSketch	$17.95	
	Inside AutoSketch Drawing Disk	$ 7.95	
	COOKIES (Put the fun back in your computer)	$ 6.95	

Send to:

New Riders Publishing
P.O. Box 4846
Thousand Oaks, CA 91360
(818)991-5392

Shipping and Handling: see information below.		
SalesTax: California please add 6.5% sales tax.		
TOTAL:		

Shipping and Handling: $4.00 for the first book and $1.75 for each additional book. Floppy disk: [ ] pping and handling. If you have to have it NOW, we can ship product to you in 24 to 48 hours for an ad[ ] d you will receive your item overnight or in 2 days.

New Riders Publishing P.O. Box 4846 Thousand Oaks, CA 91360 ( )
FAX (818) 991-9263

[handwritten: 29.95]